amazon.com.

Greetings from Amazon.com

This item is of the best quality currently available from our distributors. Amazon.com strives to provide both quality and service; we know that sometimes getting an item in imperfect condition is better than not getting it at all, and our goal is to meet your needs.

If you are not satisfied with this item, please visit our Returns Center at www.amazon.com/returns

Thanks for shopping with us!

Amazon.com
Earth's Biggest Selection
www.amazon.com

D0876018

URBAN LIFE AND LANDSCAPE SERIES

FAITH
AND
ACTION

A HISTORY OF THE
ARCHDIOCESE OF CINCINNATI
1821–1996

Roger Fortin

THE OHIO STATE UNIVERSITY PRESS
Columbus

Library of Congress Cataloguing-in-Publication Data

Fortin, Roger A. (Roger Antonio), 1940–
    Faith and action : a history of the Catholic Archdiocese of Cincinnati, 1821–1996 /
Roger A. Fortin.
    p. cm. — (The urban life and urban landscape series)
Includes bibliographical references and index.
    ISBN 0-8142-0904-1 (alk. paper)
    1. Catholic Church. Archdiocese of Concinnati (Ohio)—History. 2. Cincinnati
Region (Ohio)—Church history. I. Title. II. Series.

BX1417.C5 F67 2002
282'.7717—dc21
                                                                    2002005665

Jacket design by Gary Gore.
Type set in Granjon by FSGraphics.
Printed by Thomson-Shore.

9 8 7 6 5 4 3 2 1

TO ANNIE,
our first grandchild

CONTENTS

PREFACE

ON SUNDAY, JUNE 16, 1996, the archdiocese of Cincinnati marked the 175th anniversary of its founding with a liturgy at St. Peter in Chains Cathedral in downtown Cincinnati. At noon, on June 19, which was the actual anniversary date, all parishes in the archdiocese rang their church bells for 175 seconds. When the diocese of Cincinnati was formed in 1821 the ten to twelve Catholic families living in Cincinnati had no idea that the diocese would take root as profoundly as it did and that the Catholic Church by 1860 would be the largest single denomination in the country.

About nine months before the celebration of the anniversary, Archbishop Daniel E. Pilarczyk decided it was time to write an up-to-date history of the Catholic archdiocese of Cincinnati. At the recommendation of Xavier University's Academic Vice President, Dr. James Bundschuh, I was asked to write it. I agreed and was given full freedom to tell the story in the manner that I saw fit. This book is not the first history of the archdiocese. Father John H. Lamott's *History of the Archdiocese of Cincinnati, 1821–1921* was published in 1921. Three years earlier Archbishop Henry Moeller had asked Lamott, then on the faculty at Cincinnati's Mount St. Mary's of the West Seminary, to write a history in commemoration of the diocese's one hundredth anniversary. I am very much indebted to Lamott's study for providing me with a detailed account of the institutional history of the archdiocese to 1921 as well as making me aware of nineteenth-century source materials on the church prelates, religious orders, and Catholic organizations.

This book is aimed at two audiences: Those readers whose main concern is local history and who are most interested in the particulars of church history in the archdiocese of Cincinnati, and those whose main interest is the history of religion or Catholicism in the United States. I have attempted to provide as much local detail as possible while placing the story of the archdiocese within the context of national and regional events.

By engaging in original archival research as well as consulting major secondary works I have also attempted to provide a portrait of the major trends and developments of the Catholic Church in the archdiocese of Cincinnati. The sources that proved most helpful in my study were the uncatalogued papers of the Cincinnati prelates and collection of parish histories at the Archives of the Archdiocese of Cincinnati and the *Catholic Telegraph,* the diocesan paper. What also proved helpful was the nineteenth-century collection of the correspondence of the church leaders at the Archives of the University of Notre Dame.

I must express a special gratitude to Archbishop Pilarczyk who, from the beginning, proved most encouraging and supportive. My thanks to Dr. James Bundschuh for his continuing interest and to Xavier University for granting me a research sabbatical and the services of a research assistant, Thomas Ward, for one year. Ward's thorough examination of the weekly issues of the *Catholic Telegraph* proved immensely helpful. I am also grateful to Mr. Don H. Buske, archivist at the Archives of the Archdiocese of Cincinnati, for his generous assistance and for sharing his knowledge of the history of the archdiocese. From the beginning he generously offered the resources of the archives without reservation. I also want to thank his secretary, Ms. Gail Cassini, for her day-to-day assistance. My gratitude also extends to the staff at the Xavier University Library (especially Mrs. Sidnie Reed), the Athenaeum of Ohio Library, and to the skillful assistance provided me at the Archives of the University of Notre Dame, Archives of the Archdiocese of Boston, and the Archives of the Diocese of Cleveland.

I am indebted to individuals who read portions of the manuscript and responded with helpful critical comments. Heading the list is Dr. Zane Miller. I will forever be indebted to him for his careful analysis and reading of the drafts of the manuscript and for his invaluable suggestions. At the risk of offending others, I must also mention Archbishop Daniel Pilarczyk, Sister Judith Metz S.C., Dr. C. Walker Gollar, Dr. John Fairfield, Dr. Brennan Hill, Rev. M. Edmund Hussey, Rev. Leo Klein, S.J., Dr. Richard Gruber, Rev. George Jacquemin, Rev. James Shappelle, and my wife, Janet. I am also thankful to my students for sharing their ideas.

INTRODUCTION

THE HISTORY OF THE ARCHDIOCESE of Cincinnati, like that of the Catholic Church in the United States, is one of almost constant change and adaptation. It has dealt with waves of immigrants, anti-Catholic sentiments, a financial crisis, parish raiding and boundary feuds, wars, economic depressions, civil and social unrest, and times of unprecedented growth and prosperity. This book deals with the growth and administration of the archdiocese of Cincinnati, the active participation of the laity in the life of the church, religious, education, social issues, and the relationship of Catholics to the larger society.

The relationship of being American and Catholic underwent several shifts between the founding of the diocese in 1821 and the celebration of its 175th anniversary in 1996. In the beginning some Catholics wanted the church, rooted in American soil, to be as little dependent on foreign jurisdiction as possible. While espousing separation of church and state and religious liberty, they wanted the church to adapt to the new American situation. From the time of its founding to the present, the way Catholics in the archdiocese have viewed their relationship with the rest of society has changed with each major change in society. They have had to respond to the challenge of adapting to the changing times. In the mid-nineteenth century the local church, a canonical term that means the diocese or archdiocese, dealt with a dominant Protestant culture and, at times, a hostile environment, whereas a century later it was much more a part of the American mainstream. Throughout most of the nineteenth and early twentieth centuries most Catholics saw themselves as outsiders. During the past fifty years, however, Catholics have felt more confident and viewed themselves as very much a part of American society. Moreover, throughout the history of the archdiocese of Cincinnati the role of the laity changed from time to time as did the amount of real authority exercised by church leaders. Whereas in the late nineteenth century the Cincinnati archbishop wrestled with ethnic groups over control of the parishes, a century later he has had to deal with the closing or merging of parishes.

Because the local church prelates were largely chosen to be the leaders of the Catholic Church in the diocese, they serve as a principal focus and their administrations provide the overall organizational framework of the book. Though this study does not provide a history of each parish or even mention every religious order and organization, it does attempt to provide a general portrait of the activities and accomplishments of the clergy, religious, lay people, parishes, and Catholic organizations. To the extent that I could find appropriate sources I have tried to incorporate those developments that figured in the growth of lay Catholicism and parish life. While writing this history, I was reminded that the historian generally finds it more difficult to measure the growth and manifestation of an active religious spirit in a diocese than assess its material growth.

The book is divided into four parts: Immigrant Catholicism (1821–1870s), Bureaucratizing Catholicism in the Archdiocese of Cincinnati (1880s–1920s), Modern Catholicism in the Archdiocese of Cincinnati (1920s–1960s), and Local Church Transformed: Of, by, and for the People (1960s–1996). The first part covers the history of the diocese of Cincinnati from its founding in 1821 to Archbishop John Baptist Purcell's resignation of his administrative duties to his newly appointed coadjutor, Bishop William Henry Elder, in 1880. It deals with the institutional development and transformation of a scattered missionary diocese into a vigorous archdiocese that largely appealed to the massive influx of immigrants and their children, especially the German and Irish Catholics. The most spectacular growth of the church occurred during this period. While attempting to integrate immigrants into its fold it saw the need to evangelize the non-Catholics and Native Americans, to convert more people to Catholicism.

The immigrants, especially the Germans, were largely alienated from the American culture. Catholics, especially those in urban settings, tended to live together in ethnic communities. They were faced with the task of promoting a culture that was different from mainstream America, while continuing to interact with that society. The immigrants sought to maintain their traditional beliefs as well as their respective ethnic heritages. The local church became to a large extent a blend of old world and American ideals and values. As it increased in size and complexity, it cared about its relationship with the rest of society. While struggling with this relationship, most archdiocesan Catholics under Purcell's leadership separated themselves from public schools and non-Catholic fraternal organizations. They developed specific structures and policies to transmit the faith. An area of significant institutional growth within the local church was education. Purcell was a champion of parochial education. One of the principal reasons for the development of parochial schools was the desire to socialize children into the Catholic community. Works of charity also assumed a major importance during this period. The parish was the center of many of these activities.

While attempting to blend Catholicism with the American ideals of separation of church and state and religious liberty generated by the American Revolution, the diocese sought to create a church that would be true to its Catholic origins, yet adaptable to the new American situation. Because there were in the beginning so few Catholic clergy the local church, especially among German Catholics, was dependent upon lay leadership. There was much active participation of the laity in the formation of parishes and in the life of the church. At the same time that the local church became more acclimated to the American context, there were Catholics who wanted more uniformity in the church. While they looked to the European Catholic tradition for some sense of order and authority, the American Catholic situation differed significantly from the European Catholic experience. Under the rule of the two Cincinnati bishops, or ordinaries, in the nineteenth century there slowly developed more uniformity and centralized rule and increasing collegiality with their episcopal colleagues in the United States. In the process, a tension between American identity and Europeanization of the church developed. While assuming more structures of the sort to be found in European Catholicism, the local church saw a gradual shift from a congregational model of the parish to a clerical model. What also contributed to more hierarchical and clerical control was the strengthening of the papacy in the nineteenth century, culminating in the definition of the doctrine of papal infallibility by the First Vatican Council in 1870. While retaining features of the American culture, the American hierarchy tended to resist Roman centralization of administration.

The second part of the book, Bureaucratizing Catholicism in the Archdiocese of Cincinnati (1880s–1920s), covers the administrations of Archbishops William Henry Elder (1883–1904) and Henry Moeller (1904–1925). Hierarchical authority grew much more during this period. Since the middle of the nineteenth century the archdiocese had sought more centralized control over church affairs. The local church became more developed administratively, as more and more power shifted from the parish to the chancery. With increasing centralization, parishes, schools, and charities were brought more directly under the archbishop's supervision. Like corporate developments in American society, centralization and efficiency became the watchwords in the archdiocese. Moreover, the leadership of Cincinnati Catholicism was primarily clerical. The growth of episcopal control and centralization of church matters facilitated clerical control. By the end of Moeller's tenure in 1925 the clergy controlled the parish, and the lay people were less involved in decision making in the government of the local church. In education, leadership was largely in the hands of the pastors and religious sisters or brothers. Within the church lay leadership was largely confined to parish groups or fraternal organizations like the Knights of Columbus. The laity took up other types of activity in social and devotional areas.

In the wake of the First Vatican Council authorities in Rome assumed more responsibility in the day-to-day affairs of the church throughout the world. The local church became doctrinally conservative and socially liberal. While attempting to live in accordance with church teaching, Cincinnati Catholics supported labor and became more involved in community social programs. Moreover, more Catholics were assimilated into American culture. The local church ordinaries thought that Catholics, especially the Germans, had to shed any appearance of foreign loyalties. Archbishops Elder and Moeller wanted Catholics to blend into American society.

The third part of the text, Modern Catholicism in the Archdiocese of Cincinnati (1920s–1960s), deals with the administrations of Archbishops John McNicholas (1925–1950) and of Karl Alter, who followed McNicholas and retired in 1969. During their years of leadership the local church attained a new level of institutional growth and saw the Catholic subculture gradually break down. There was a growing assimilation into American society. Virtually all Catholics no longer resided in ethnic neighborhoods and attended ethnic churches. Catholics moved into the middle class and beyond. While the nineteenth century was largely the era of growth for the local church, the first half of the twentieth century was largely a period of stabilization. It helped define its place in American culture more explicitly. Under McNicholas's and Alter's leadership Cincinnati Catholics took public positions on a variety of ethical, social, political, and economic issues. The church had come a long way since its founding. It no longer feared its survival in a dominant Protestant culture and assumed a higher public profile. It solidified its position in American society. During the Great Depression and World War II Catholics became more involved in the national life. While the church became more socially liberal it remained theologically conservative.

The final part of the book, Local Church Transformed: Of, by, and for the People (1960s–1996), deals with one of the most exciting periods in the American church. During the administrations of Archbishop Karl Alter and his three successors, Paul Leibold (1969–1972), Joseph Bernardin (1972–1982), and Daniel Pilarczyk (1982–), the local church responded to the challenge of adapting to the changing times. Catholics continued to blend their unique national culture and their Catholic faith. They explored new ways of being both Catholic and American. Largely influenced by the Second Vatican Council and social and cultural upheavals in American society in the 1960s, a new model of church and authority emerged as well as new forms of worship and activity. Changes in the liturgy in the American church transformed the people's experiences of worship. Catholic piety became increasingly more group-oriented. The Second Vatican Council also helped reinvigorate the role of the laity in the church. By the 1970s the tradition of clerical leadership had also begun to change and more men and women took on roles of leadership. Furthermore, the clergy, religious, and laity became more involved in public life and new directions for activism were developed. The exodus of large numbers of priests and religious brothers and sisters from formal ministry also created new kinds of problems for the local church, leading to some church and school closings and mergers. By the 1980s the local church, like the American church as a whole, began to stabilize after the great changes of the 1960s and 1970s. Efforts were made to make the new directions become more a part of the life of Catholics.

From the beginning of the diocese to the present, religious and lay people have worked hard for the betterment of the local church and the community at large. Each generation of Catholics has contributed something specific to their growth. While engaging itself in the concerns of individuals who live in a variety of changing situations, each generation has also served as social action leaders and workers for the poor. Archbishop Karl Alter of Cincinnati was quite right when he said in 1950 "that no prelate of the Church has ever stood alone when the cause of religion has made progress. . . . The unsung heroes of the army of the Church are the zealous priests, the devoted religious, and the faithful members of the laity. Without their devoted efforts and unselfish sacrifices, the Church would be poor indeed." In its own special way each generation of Catholics has sought to bring the Catholic past and teachings in line with the challenges and demands of their times. The spirit and faith of the people have been and continue to be the strength of the archdiocese. My hope is that as they continue to look with hope to their future, in some small way this book will help them remember with gratitude their past.[1]

FAITH
AND
ACTION

PART

ONE

IMMIGRANT
CATHOLICISM
1821–1870s

Introduction

From the time of its founding in 1821 to the late 1870s, the diocese of Cincinnati, under the leadership of its first two ordinaries, Edward Dominic Fenwick and John Baptist Purcell, experienced its most spectacular growth. They both traveled and preached extensively and helped increase the scattered congregation by frequent conversions. At the same time that they developed an American Catholicism congenial to the American situation, they helped bring the Catholic population into an organized and disciplined relationship with the church.

Under Bishop Fenwick's leadership the first ten years of the young diocese constituted a period of solid growth. Effectively carrying out his administrative duties, he also helped supervise the construction of diocesan buildings. At a time when the obstacles to growth were particularly demanding, by 1831 the diocese had both a college and a seminary. Fenwick also secured missionaries and teachers for Cincinnati and for the remote areas of his diocese. Fully understanding his jurisdictional responsibility and role over the Northwest, he took a special interest in ministering to the Native Americans and sent priests to work with them. Not one to try to impress others with his accomplishments, Fenwick often minimized, almost to a fault, his ability to handle the responsibilities of his office. In the end his ministry was significant not only in the founding and development of the diocese of Cincinnati but also in the American church's goals of meeting the spiritual and temporal needs of Catholics. Espousing the American system of separation of church and state, religious liberty, and the education of a native-born clergy, Fenwick, like some of his contemporaries, was sensitive to the American situation. During his administration the local church established the first parochial school in the diocese, built a cathedral, seminary, and college, and founded a newspaper, institutions that were appropriate to a well-developed see.

From the 1830s to the 1870s the American church grew at an astonishing rate to become a major force in American religious life. For nearly a half century, Purcell, as bishop and archbishop, worked incessantly and untiringly for the advancement of the church. Like his counterpart Bishop Paul Lefevere of Detroit, he headed, as a more recent historian has noted, "a missionary see." Spending most of his time building and strengthening the diocese, he proved to be one of the most pragmatic and remarkable church leaders in the American hierarchy in the nineteenth century. Purcell's brilliance of mind, energy, and administrative talent were perhaps his most notable characteristics. Because he was so well known in Europe he was able to persuade several mission societies to help support the local church as well as persuade

5

numerous religious congregations to come to his diocese. Notwithstanding the local church's financial debacle of 1878, which was a singular moment in the history of the archdiocese, Purcell left his diocese rich in tradition and institutions.[1]

The most spectacular growth of the Province of Cincinnati occurred during his administration. Through personal sacrifices and devotion, the clergy, religious, and laity helped build the many ecclesiastical institutions. The initiative taken by the immigrants, especially the Germans and Irish, in building the churches, schools, and other organizations remind us of the profound influence that ordinary folks exerted on the development of the local church. When Purcell arrived in Ohio in 1833, there were 16 churches and 14 priests. Fifty years later there were 544 churches and chapels, 480 priests, and a Catholic population of about 500,000 in the state. The majority of Catholics lived near a church with a resident priest. By 1883, there were eleven orphanages tending to 1,454 children, nine hospitals, and 238 parochial schools with an enrollment of approximately 48,446 students. The formation of the Catholic school system during Purcell's years of leadership is one of the great success stories of the local church. Commitment to transmitting the faith to the next generation and concern over the Protestant tenor of many educational and social institutions drove Catholics in the archdiocese to invest heavily in their own religious and social institutions. As they and their counterparts in other dioceses participated fully in American life, their institutions, whose development differed from place to place, helped foster the development of a unique Catholic identity.[2]

Despite the creation of the dioceses of Cleveland and Columbus out of the archdiocese, in 1883 the local church had 157 churches, thirty-two chapels, two orphanages tending to 546 children, three hospitals, and eighty-eight parochial schools with an enrollment of 20,000 students, and eighty-nine priests attending to 150,000 Catholics. There were also nine suffragan sees attached to the archiepiscopal see, whose combined area included the states of Ohio, Indiana, Kentucky, Tennessee, and the greater portion of the state of Michigan. Over a fifty-year period Purcell had helped transform the scattered missionary diocese that he inherited from Fenwick into a vigorous archdiocese of first rank and importance. In the process his strong commitment to American liberties won him many Protestant and Catholic supporters.[3]

By the time of the elevation of the diocese to the status of an archdiocese at midcentury, it had become more hierarchical. As Catholics and the American hierarchy remained committed to the republican ideas of the separation of church and state and religious liberty, U.S. bishops resisted Roman centralization of administration. As the supply of clergy, especially the foreign-born with their understanding of European Catholicism, increased, and

Purcell's ecclesiastical authority in religion, finances, and education grew, there developed more clerical control. More and more priests became involved in parish life. What also contributed to more clerical control was the loyalty and gradual strengthening of the papacy in the nineteenth century. As the traditional hierarchical view of authority in the Catholic Church was strongly reasserted by Vatican officials, there nevertheless developed a sense of episcopal autonomy and collegiality among U.S. bishops. During the course of the nineteenth century the bishops largely governed the American church by means of councils, holding thirty-four such gatherings. In the process their authority grew. In leading the local church with firmness and control, Purcell set the tone for his episcopal predecessors in the archdiocese for the next century.[4]

The Founding Bishop
Edward Dominic Fenwick

T he history of the Catholic Church in the archdiocese of Cincinnati began in the early 1800s with the pioneer efforts and contributions of lay Catholics like Michael Scott and his Irish colleagues in Cincinnati and Jacob Dittoe and the German settlers who lived near Somerset, Ohio, between Zanesville and Lancaster. The sacrifices that these early Catholics made to keep the faith alive and the burdens they carried helped lay the foundation for a viable and enduring diocese. At this time the newly formed state of Ohio, established in 1803, was under the aegis of the diocese of Baltimore, with John Carroll as the first bishop. In 1808 Pope Pius VII elevated Baltimore to the status of an archdiocese and erected four new dioceses in the United States: Boston, New York, Philadelphia, and Bardstown, Kentucky. At the head of the seat in Bardstown was Bishop Benedict Joseph Flaget, a Sulpician priest. The influence of the Society of St. Sulpice, a French society of priests, was most evident in Kentucky. The new diocese had jurisdiction over the states of Kentucky and Tennessee and the Northwest Territory, including what are now Ohio, Indiana, Illinois, Michigan, Wisconsin, and part of Minnesota.[1]

According to the Catholic tradition the Holy See, or pope, in Rome was the head of the Catholic Church. As the bishop was the supreme monarch in his own diocese, the pope was at the center of the church. It was the pope to whom important matters were referred for a final decision or approval. Generally, however, the pope left the direction of the church in the United States, as a missionary nation, to the Sacred Congregation of the Propagation of the Faith, often shortened simply to Propaganda. As the Vatican congregation in charge of all missionary lands, it served until 1907 as a common channel that was seldom bypassed. At its head stood the Cardinal Prefect. It was the exclusive prerogative of the pope, through the Propaganda, to provide for the territorial organization of the church in the United States.[2]

In 1819 Bishop Flaget and his fellow Sulpician Bishop Louis William Dubourg of Louisiana expressed concern that Catholics west of the Alleghenies would fall away from the faith because of the lack of priests. They also thought the diocese of Bardstown was too large to minister adequately to the needs of Catholics scattered throughout the diocese, which included approximately three hundred Catholic families in Ohio alone. With the consent of Archbishop Ambrose Maréchal, the third ordinary of Baltimore, Flaget and Dubourg petitioned the pope to erect a diocese in Cincinnati, Ohio, as they, like most people who moved west, sought to transplant old institutions, many from the East, to try to help civilize the West. But for the pope to establish a new diocese, there had to be hope of rapid expansion of the population in the immediate future as well as the promise of appropriate income to support a residential bishop.[3]

In March 1820 Flaget and Dubourg recommended as their first choice for the diocese of Cincinnati an American known for his theological knowledge and preaching skills, the Jesuit Benedict Joseph Fenwick of Boston. For second choice they recommended Joseph's cousin, Edward Fenwick, an American by birth and founder of the first Dominican community in the United States in 1805. Impressed by the Dominican Fenwick's ability to make converts, the bishop of Bardstown also emphasized his "great knowledge" of Ohio "and of the Catholics who are there." Edward Fenwick may have been the first Catholic priest to visit Cincinnati and was very popular among the Catholics in Ohio. But Flaget and Dubourg had reservations about his candidacy because he had, Flaget wrote, "very little learning." The bishop of Bardstown personally thought that the best candidate might very well be the Russian Demetrius Gallitzin, who was not a member of a religious order, but who knew German, the language spoken by many Catholics in Ohio. However, for Gallitzin's appointment to be effective, Flaget thought, he would have to become a member of a religious order to get support from the order for manpower. Realizing that it was highly unlikely Gallitzin would become affiliated with an order, Flaget wrote another letter to Maréchal, this time enthusiastically endorsing Edward Fenwick. "If he has not all the learning that he ought to have," he wrote, ". . . at least he has the appearance of having as much as I," and was "full of zeal and humility."[4]

Despite Flaget's and Dubourg's recommendations Maréchal proposed in April that John Baptist David, the French coadjutor bishop of Bardstown, become the first Cincinnati bishop, though Maréchal listed Edward Fenwick as an alternate. Besides thinking Kentucky did not need two bishops and that

FIG 1. Bishop Edward Fenwick, 1822–1832.

Flaget's assistant should head the proposed diocese, Maréchal thought David's experience would be good for Ohio. But by late May Flaget, Dubourg, and David made clear to the Propaganda that the Dominican Edward Fenwick was now their top choice. Flaget relied heavily on David and he did not wish to lose him. The Bardstown ordinary also thought that the sixty-year-old David was too old and too overweight to manage the frontier. The fifty-two-year-old Fenwick was better suited to handle the wilderness and ride on horseback, obvious necessities for a missionary in the West. By November Maréchal agreed that Edward Fenwick was the most suitable candidate. On June 19, 1821, Pope Pius VII issued the bull that established the diocese of Cincinnati and that appointed Edward Dominic Fenwick as bishop. Cincinnati became the second see west of the Alleghenies. In addition to the state of Ohio, parts of Michigan and the Northwest Territory, now Wisconsin, were placed temporarily in the jurisdiction of the diocese.[5]

Edward Fenwick was born on August 19, 1768, in St. Mary's County, Maryland. His parents, who became large landowners, died while he was still a boy. After an early education at home, the young Fenwick was sent to Europe for his education. He enrolled in the Dominican Holy Cross College at Bornheim in Belgium, where he was professed a Dominican in 1790 and ordained three years later at the age of twenty-five. When the French military forces in the 1790s invaded Belgium, the Dominicans fled. Fenwick was left in charge of the school. The Dominicans hoped that his American citizenship would protect him from harm. But the French took him a prisoner. After a brief imprisonment, he traveled to England where he remained with the Dominicans for almost ten years. In the summer of 1804, thirty-six-year-old Fenwick proposed that the Propaganda establish a college and Dominican community in the United States. Roman officials and Bishop Carroll of Baltimore, later consulted on the matter, liked the idea. "I should flatter myself," Fenwick wrote to Carroll, "with being able to execute in miniature the plan of Bornhem [*sic*] College and Convent." The education of youth, the training of Dominican priests, and the cause of religion were the objects of his "ardent wishes."[6]

In dire need of clerical ministry in the frontier, Carroll encouraged Fenwick to sell his family's estate in Maryland and move across the mountains to Kentucky. Jacob Dittoe, who lived near Somerset, Ohio, then in the diocese of Bardstown, had written Carroll requesting the services of a Catholic priest. At the time there were about thirty Catholics in the community. In the summer of 1806 Fenwick arrived in Springfield, Kentucky, which would serve as his base for his travels to Ohio. With all the proceeds from his inheritance from his deceased father's estate he purchased five hundred acres of land in Washington County, about two miles from the town of Springfield. In time other white-robed members of the Dominican order, including his former teacher and long-time friend, Samuel Thomas Wilson, and his nephew, Nicholas Dominick Young, soon joined him. Together they established at Springfield St. Rose Convent, the first Dominican house in North America. In October of the following year, Fenwick surrendered his authority as superior of the small group of Dominicans in order that he might be freer to engage in missionary activities. For the next thirteen years he traveled the mission circuit, attending to the needs of non-Catholics as well as Catholics in Kentucky and Ohio. He probably visited Ohio for the first time in 1808 on his way to or from the archdiocese of Baltimore. By 1818 he and his nephew were the only two missionaries at work in the state. A year later, Stephen H. Montgomery, another Dominican, assisted them in the Ohio mission.[7]

The ordinaries and priests were the only ones who could perform the rites of the Catholic Church. American Catholics subscribed to the standards of doctrine that had prevailed in Catholicism since the Council of Trent in 1545.

Catholic spirituality largely revolved around the Mass and sacraments. The sacraments of baptism, confirmation, and matrimony were received at the important occasions of birth, spiritual maturity, and marriage respectively. The sacrament of holy orders was administered to an individual upon becoming a priest. The sacrament of penance, which called for sinners to repent and to receive God's forgiveness, and that of Holy Communion, by which individuals consumed the consecrated bread and wine at Mass, were received frequently by Catholics throughout life. The sacrament of extreme unction was administered to those Catholics in grave illness or close to death. The faithful were expected to attend Mass every Sunday and on certain holy days, observe the days of fast and abstinence, and fulfill the Easter duty. The latter consisted of partaking in the sacrament of penance and receiving Holy Communion once between the first Sunday of Lent (forty days before Easter) and eight weeks after Easter. At the same time that they adhered to the teachings of the church, American Catholics benefited from the ideals of the American Revolution. As a church in a free republic, the American church exercised the civil and religious liberties afforded by the Revolution.[8]

In the spirit of republicanism, American Catholics insisted on the separation of church and state. This concept went against the traditional medieval Catholic position that envisioned a society in which church and state were united. The American Catholic hierarchy, moreover, first headed by John Carroll, promoted the idea of religious liberty. This idea, which opposed any form of coercion, also challenged the European Catholic position that stipulated false religious beliefs should not be tolerated. In addition, republicanism, along with the scattered Catholic population and the scarcity of clergy, also doubtlessly contributed to the popularity of the congregational parish. What distinguished the latter from the traditional European Catholic parish was its emphasis on a democratic model of authority, rather than a hierarchical model, and emphasis on lay and local autonomy. As a consequence, American Catholicism became increasingly centered on the parish. Moreover, the active participation of the laity in the life of the church in the United States led to the democratization of local church government through the adoption of the trustee system. Lay trustees, elected annually by those people in the parish who rented pews, presided over the government of the parish in the area of temporal affairs. Though there were precedents in Europe for the trustee system, in the new nation it emerged in many parishes and in almost every major city.[9]

Promoting its own spiritual and liturgical life, and forming and developing its own institutions, the American church developed more of an American identity. But at the same time that Catholics had interest in shaping an American Catholicism that was congenial to the new historical situation and did not want too much dependence on Rome, they nevertheless looked to models of authority in the European Catholic tradition for some sense of order and authority. The establishment of four new dioceses in 1808 had provided more ecclesiastical organization. By this time the American Catholic hierarchy depended on Rome for guidance in the establishment of dioceses and election of bishops. Even though in 1808 the five U.S. bishops had requested Roman authorities that they give the right of nomination of bishops to the archbishop of Baltimore and his suffragans, in 1819 they received a negative response. Not wanting the American hierarchy to be exclusively self-perpetuating as well as retaining the prerogative of papal appointment, Vatican officials agreed in 1822 that the United States bishops could recommend individuals to vacant sees.[10]

Before the establishment of the diocese of Cincinnati in 1821, twice a year Fenwick traversed the state in all directions, visiting the scattered Catholic families and parishes, instructing the children, and performing the rites of the church. "In the state of Ohio, which has a population of 500,000 souls," Fenwick told a friend in London in November 1818, "there is not a single priest. There are Germans and Irish who do not know any English at all, hence you can well imagine the pains I take and the efforts I make to be understood by them and to understand them, and to offer them" spiritual assistance. "It often happens," he continued, ". . . I was obliged to hitch my horse to a tree to sleep with bears on all sides." Fenwick and his Dominican brothers were frequently on horseback. In one instance a colony of thirteen families wrote him a letter, requesting his services. He traveled three hundred miles to be with them. In two years' time alone Fenwick baptized in different parts of the state 162 persons. In 1818 Fenwick established Dominican headquarters at Somerset in the southeastern section of Ohio. From there he traveled throughout the state. His annual mission journeys earned him the nickname of the "itinerant preacher."[11]

Fenwick probably celebrated the first Mass ever said in Cincinnati. It was offered in 1811 in the home of Michael Scott, a well-known Irish Catholic who had emigrated from Baltimore six years earlier. Like many Catholics in the history of the diocese, Scott was a generous supporter of Catholic activities. In his home he provided hospitality to missionaries on their visits to Cincinnati. The city occupied a significant role in the settlement of the frontier partly because of its prominent position on the Ohio River. Cincinnati, which rested on the north bank of the river, was one of the fastest growing cities in the country, eight times larger than her nearest competitors, namely, Zanesville, Steubenville, Dayton, Chillicothe, and Columbus. Fenwick continued this practice of visiting Scott's home and saying Mass for several years. Finally in 1817 Scott helped raise funds to build, as the Cincinnati *Western*

FIG 2. Christ Church in Cincinnati

Spy announced, "a Catholick [*sic*] church in the vicinity of Cincinnati." Nine men, seven women, and four children met at Scott's residence and formed the Christ Church Congregation. Scott and four of his male colleagues, Patrick Reilly, John Sherlock, Thomas Dugan, and Edward Lynch, were elected trustees. With the assistance of Flaget, who made his first episcopal visit to Cincinnati on May 19, 1818, they purchased a lot north of Liberty Street, then the corporation line of the city. In the early nineteenth century, land on the periphery of the city, which was predominantly an area characterized by poverty and poor housing, was less expensive than in the city. An architect and builder by profession, Scott laid out plans for the church building. In his journal Flaget reflected on the condition and prospects of Catholicity in Cincinnati, noting that it was "a great misfortune" that few Catholics "come to settle in the neighborhood of this splendid city. At present," he added, "there are no other Catholics in Cincinnati than laborers and clerks. Yet, I think, nothing should be neglected to establish Religion here."[12]

By the following spring a small wooden frame church was built in Cincinnati and placed under the patronage of St. Patrick. St. Patrick Church, or more commonly known as Christ Church, 55 by 30 feet in size, was the first Catholic Church in Cincinnati and the third in Ohio. It was built on an open field on Vine and Liberty Streets and stood on a plot of ground approximately 120 feet square. This was the first site of the cathedral in the diocese. The first Mass was offered in this protocathedral on Easter Sunday, April 19, 1819, with the Dominican Nicholas Young the officiating clergyman. That same year Michael Scott bought for $400 a lot adjoining the church to be used for cemetery purposes.[13]

In December 1821, a year after dioceses were established in Richmond, Virginia, and Charleston, South Carolina, Bishop Flaget received the bulls erecting the new see at Cincinnati and the appointment of Edward Fenwick as bishop. When Fenwick learned, while preaching in Ohio, of his appointment he was surprised, since he thought the bishop of Bardstown had nominated Samuel Wilson, his former Dominican teacher, for that honor. The humble Fenwick thought Wilson was more qualified. Consistent with his personality, he did not see himself as qualified for the position. He informed Flaget and Wilson that because of his lack of experience and knowledge he should not in good conscience accept the office. After strong exhortations they prevailed upon him to take it. Though Fenwick never became convinced that he had the qualifications for such an exalted position, he finally reconciled himself to the burden of the office. On Holy Name Sunday, January 13, 1822, Flaget, assisted by Fathers Wilson and John Augustine Hill, an old friend of Fenwick's from England, consecrated him at St. Rose Church. To help celebrate this special occasion, people came from great distances to see the fifty-three-year-old Dominican elevated to the American hierarchy. Shortly after his installation, Fenwick appointed Wilson vicar general, who acted as his deputy to assist him in the administration of the diocese. A few weeks later the new bishop expressed his gratitude to the pope for "this exceptional favor," even though it was bestowed, Fenwick thought, on "the least worthy of men." This low opinion of himself was a consistent part of Fenwick's character throughout his tenure.[14]

In March 1822 Fenwick and four Dominican priests—Wilson, Hill, John Baptist Vincent de Raymaecker of Belgium, and John Thomas Hynes of the Irish province—left St. Rose in Kentucky for Cincinnati. His friends and supporters supplied Fenwick with a few vestments, linens, four missals, four chalices, and a little money collected by the parish. The journey of the episcopal party to the new diocese proved to be a trying one. The caravan traveled in a "Tillbury," a two-wheeled carriage without a top, over rough and muddy roads. They swam across the Kentucky River because recent rains had made it impossible to cross with the carriage. The weary party finally reached Cincinnati on Saturday evening, March 23. Because no provisions had been prepared for them, they "were compelled," Fenwick wrote, "to send to the market for the first meal." Michael Scott meanwhile found them a large room nearby. The four rested on straw mats on the floor. Soon Catholics learned of the bishop's arrival and assembled to welcome him. Probably the morning after his arrival Fenwick celebrated Mass in Christ Church. There the papal bull erecting the new see of Cincinnati was read and Fenwick was installed, as one account put it, "with humble ceremony and silent panegyric." Christ Church was rededicated as the first Cincinnati cathedral. Many Protestants as well as Catholics rejoiced upon the installation of the new bishop. "We congratulate the Roman Catholics of this city and environs," announced the *Liberty Hall and Cincinnati Gazette*. "This circumstance interests not only the Catholics," but all those who sought to civilize society in the West, "as we understand that his intention is ultimately to open a school."[15]

A FRUITFUL EUROPEAN VISIT

From the beginning Fenwick worried about finances and the lack of personnel to satisfy the spiritual needs of his diocese. One of his first challenges was to find a home for himself and fellow Dominicans. For the sum of $200 a year he rented a small two-story brick house in a square known as Flat Iron Square in Cincinnati, bounded by Lawrence, Ludlow, and Third Streets in the east end. Though small, the building provided him with sleeping quarters on the top floor, and a room in the lower level for a chapel, parlor, and living room. Coming up with the rent money was no easy task. He explained to the head of the Dominican order in Rome that his revenue arose "from my request . . . made after mass on Sundays to the amount of 2 or 3 dollars each week. With this modest sum I am forced to manage a household . . . of 7 persons with 2 horses." Most of the Catholics in the diocese were poor, many of them arriving in America as penniless immigrants. Some of them were farmers, who struggled to keep their own land. Those who worked on canals, in mines, and in quarries were paid meager wages. As a consequence, few Catholics could make substantial contributions to the church. In January 1822 Hill noted "that in the whole church there is no bishop as poor as ours; the cross, the ring which he wears he has from charity." Some of the old garments Fenwick wore Bishop Flaget had given to him.[16]

Notwithstanding financial difficulties, in the summer of 1822 Fenwick decided to move Christ Church near the center of the city on Sycamore Street between Sixth and Seventh Streets, on a lot bought on credit for the sum of $700. The majority of his flock, which was mostly Irish, lived near the Ohio River on the southern periphery of the city. Fenwick and his clergy decided the church should be within easy walking distance. But the little wooden frame church fell apart as it was moved on rollers to its new location.

The disjointed lumber nevertheless was used to rebuild the church in the same dimensions of the former one. According to one account, while Mass was being celebrated on the first Sunday after the removal of the church, the log structure began to sway. Michael Scott jumped from his pew, crawled under the church, and steadied it until other parishioners by means of props were able to give it more secure support. By December the church was finally completed and was renamed St. Peter in Chains Cathedral, in honor of the imprisonment of St. Peter, first bishop of Rome. Fenwick and his clergy lived in four or five rooms of the basement.[17]

The removal of the church to the city led to a quarrel among the trustees. Because of the friction, Fenwick had the titles to three lots at Vine and Liberty Streets transferred to his name. Ever since the pope's appointment of John Carroll as the "Superior of the Mission in the thirteen United States" in 1784, numerous controversies arose across the country between lay trustees and clergy. This set an important precedent in the history of the diocese, whereby title to ecclesiastical property was to be legally held by the bishop. There would slowly develop in the early nineteenth century in the local church more episcopal control over church properties. Michael Scott deeded his lot for a cemetery. Because of the need for space for Catholic burials, on April 30, 1828, the diocese purchased five acres of land between Cutter and Clark Streets in the west end and founded the Catherine Street cemetery.[18]

In addition to moving the church to the city, Fenwick, in his first year as bishop, hoped to visit as many Catholic communities under his jurisdiction as possible. In late summer and fall of 1822 he made his first tour of the new diocese. Besides traveling through Ohio, he visited the Native American populations in Michigan. Fenwick hoped to send missionaries to convert these people. Like many Catholic leaders of his day, he felt especially called to evangelize the Indians. This journey made him see more strongly than ever the necessity of securing more missionaries in order to minister adequately to the needs of the large diocese. He hoped for "apostolic men," Fenwick wrote, of missionaries "who can carry the burdens of heat and cold, weariness [and] thirst, and will not find it too difficult to travel across mountains and through valleys." Yet there was little prospect of the diocese receiving more Dominicans in the near future. Fenwick learned that the Propaganda in 1822 had advised the superior of the order in Kentucky not to send any more priests to Ohio without Flaget's consent. Flaget believed that Fenwick had received more than a fair share of priests from the diocese of Bardstown. Before Fenwick had left St. Rose for Cincinnati he had appealed for additional manpower. With Flaget's approval, Father Anthony Ganilh, two of his student seminarians, and a deacon, Francis Vincent Badin, responded to the ordinary's appeal. On April 6, 1822, Fenwick ordained Francis Badin, who became the first priest ordained to the Catholic priesthood in Ohio. The following winter vicar general Wilson felt obliged to return to Bardstown to secure additional clerical assistance to Flaget. Fenwick then appointed his friend John Hill to the post.[19]

In need of money and personnel, Fenwick in 1823 made up his mind to go to Europe to seek assistance for his diocese and to make a personal appeal to the pope. He borrowed $300 without interest from a friend in Cincinnati for his trip. The poverty of the Catholic Church in Ohio, the shortage of priests, and his lack of confidence in his own ability also caused the Cincinnati ordinary to consider tendering his resignation. Fenwick appeared depressed in his letters to the archbishop of Baltimore and to officials in Rome. "My object" in going to Rome, he explained, "is to resign . . . to better hands and superior heads; if not allowed [,] to beg for means of subsistence and all necessary supplies for the mission, especially funds to build a church in Cincinnati, and to pay for the lot I have purchased." He further noted that he had no revenue "but the rent of 25 or 30 pews in the Cincinnati chapel, which produce, at most, a yearly income of 80 dollars." While on his begging tour in Europe Fenwick also hoped to secure a bishop for Detroit and a coadjutor, or assistant, for himself in case his resignation was not accepted.[20]

Fenwick arrived in Rome on September 26, 1823, shortly after the death of Pius VII and two days before the election of the new pontiff, Leo XII. Pius VII had died while the Cincinnati prelate was on his journey. On October 6, the day after the pope's coronation, Fenwick met with him and made a full statement as to the condition of his diocese. He entreated Leo to accept his resignation in order to place the diocese "in better hands." The pope, while smiling, "forbade me," Fenwick wrote, "to ever pronounce that word, exhorting me to continue the work which God had begun by me." Assuring Fenwick that he would be given all the "necessary assistance," Leo acceded to most of Fenwick's requests. The pope gave him two young priests of the Propaganda, $1,200 for traveling expenses, and church utensils, sacred vessels, ornaments, books, and linens estimated to be worth about $1,000. Fenwick felt good about his visit. "I left Rome," he later wrote, ". . . contented with and resigned to my lot."[21]

After visiting members of the Propaganda and officials of the Dominican order, Fenwick left Italy with letters of recommendation to help solicit additional support in other parts of Europe for his diocese. Father Stephen T. Badin, Francis Badin's older brother and Fenwick's contact in Europe, had extracts of the Cincinnati bishop's travels printed in the *London Catholic Miscellany,* circulated throughout Europe, in order to fan interest in potential Catholic benefactors in his mission. On the remainder of his tour Fenwick raised an additional $10,000, which included 2,000 francs from King Charles X of France. Among Fenwick's many other benefactors, the Association of the Propagation of the Faith in Lyons, France, proved to be the most generous one. Organized in 1822, partially at the initiative of Bishop Dubourg of Louisiana, this new lay organization, with the pope's approval, sought to raise and distribute funds to aid missionaries in foreign countries. It gave Fenwick 8,000 francs with the promise of annual allocations. Throughout his nearly eleven-year tenure, the Association gave the diocese of Cincinnati 128,975 francs, valued at approximately $25,367 in American dollars. During the remainder of the century it would give the Cincinnati diocese an additional $90,000.[22]

Fenwick had gone to Rome seeking not only relief from poverty but more personnel. Fenwick was naturally anxious to recruit priests for his underdeveloped diocese. The number of Catholics under his jurisdiction was steadily increasing. When he established residence in Cincinnati, there were six Catholic communities in the diocese "[N]ow there are 23," he wrote two years later, "at least I have visited that many." Shortly before he left for Europe, Fenwick estimated that Ohio had "no less than eight thousand Catholics" and ten churches, and about ten to twelve thousand Catholics in Michigan. In Ohio alone there were about two thousand Indians who had to go to Canada "to have their children baptized and their marriages celebrated by a Catholic priest." Fenwick hoped to have two additional "missionaries travelling continually from place to place, especially devoting their labors and services to the Indians." Though Fathers John Hill and Stephen Montgomery took care of the western congregations as far as Vevay, Indiana, and Chillicothe in Ohio, and three other Dominicans conducted missionary duties to the east, as far as Marietta, St. Clauville, and New Lisbon, Fenwick still needed more helpers.[23]

In Europe the bishop's goal was met. He secured the services of Frederic Rese, a young German-speaking priest who had just completed his studies at the Urban College of the Propaganda in Rome and had volunteered for pastoral work among the Germans in the new see. Founded in 1627, the Urban College was established to educate young men to be missionary priests. As a poor French orphan, Rese had walked to Rome in order to enter a seminary. His self-reliance and shrewdness would prove helpful in the development of the new diocese. He served as secretary to Fenwick and then as vicar general. Together with three recruits, Sister St. Paul, a French Sister of Mercy, and two other priests, Jean Bellamy and Peter Dejean, provided by the pope, Rese arrived in Cincinnati in September 1824. Sister St. Paul became the first woman religious to minister in Cincinnati. For the first time, moreover, diocesan clergy—who were not members of a religious order—assisted in the ministerial work of the new see. The bishop was their immediate superior.[24]

While in Rome Fenwick also actively promoted the creation of a diocese for Detroit. Not only did he think a new see was necessary to help enhance the growth of the Catholic Church in the West, he also thought that a new see would help lighten his work load. But the Propaganda postponed the decision pending further consultation with the archbishop of Baltimore. The Propaganda wanted more financial and legal information on the territory. It was also customary for church leaders in Rome to expect a residential bishop to have adequate income. Fenwick's request for a coadjutor to assist him in his new diocese, the first of several such requests he would make during his term, also was denied. Authorities in Rome were not convinced of the necessity for one.[25]

After a fourteen-month stay in Europe, Fenwick sailed for the United States in October 1824. His tour not only had consoled him spiritually but also proved to be a success financially for his diocese. He did not, however, receive everything that he requested. He certainly was disappointed that he was denied a coadjutor and that there was yet no Detroit diocese. But he was pleased both with the generosity of so many European Catholics with funds and ecclesiastical articles and the arrival of four priests and a religious sister to work in his diocese.[26]

A SCHOOL AND A NEW CATHEDRAL

Catholic and many non-Catholic admirers rejoiced upon the return of the bishop to the episcopal city. Fenwick also received an uplifting letter from Bishop Flaget, who shared his early difficulties in building up his own diocese, hoping that this would help console Fenwick. In general Flaget was pleased with the progress in Cincinnati. A number of developments had taken place in the diocese while Fenwick was in Europe. His vicar general, John Hill, who had become an eloquent and popular lecturer, attracted non-Catholics and Catholics alike to the cathedral. Out of curiosity large numbers of Protestants, including ministers, came to Cincinnati to hear his lectures. He usually spoke on Catholic doctrine. There was often standing room only, some people sitting on the windowsills. Writing to Fenwick in Europe in the spring of 1824, Hill informed him that the "lectures are crowded at an early hour by the chief people in the town; all the ministers" of the community, except one, "have attended." Hill was especially successful in making converts. A convert himself, it was very satisfying to him that several lawyers and doctors had become persuaded by his arguments. As the crowds had become unmanageable and he physically exhausted by the strain of the lectures, by the end of the year he had to give them up.[27]

Another change during Fenwick's absence was the erection by Hill of a three-story brick building beside St. Peter's on Sycamore Street. Fenwick immediately took residence in the new building, which was a marked improvement from living in the half-cellar under the church. By this time the bishop's new recruits were already at work in the diocese. Bellamy and Dejean were in Michigan at the Indian missions and Rese was busy working with the German Catholics in Cincinnati. Moreover, Rese, with Hill's assistance, had helped find a home for Sister St. Paul. News of her forthcoming arrival in Cincinnati had spread rapidly. A number of people were anxious to greet the first nun ever in Ohio. Many of the individuals had never seen a religious woman and thus turned out to see, as one report put it, "what kind of a creature a nun was." Fenwick regarded Sister St. Paul "a gift from heaven." In 1825 she opened a private school for girls at the cathedral, the first Catholic school in Ohio. Besides a Catholic church in Cincinnati, Catholics now had a school of twenty-five girls taught by Sister St. Paul and her assistant Eliza Rose Powell. This was the beginning of the parochial school system in the diocese. She and the school, according to Fenwick, "live by charity." Encouraged by his initial success, Fenwick wrote to the superior of the Sisters of Mercy in France, respectfully requesting that two or three additional sisters be sent to assist Sister St. Paul in establishing a convent. But other French Sisters of Mercy were not forthcoming. This initial parochial school endeavor was on shaky ground.[28]

In addition to the positive influence of Hill's ministrations was Frederic Rese's missionary work in the German community. From the moment the German-speaking priest arrived in Cincinnati, his influence was felt, and he eventually served, along with Hill, as one of the vicars general. He appealed to the German immigrants with great success, causing numerous defections from Protestant denominations. "[H]e learns English very fast," Fenwick wrote, "and is working miracles with his Germans. . . . He preaches in German every Sunday, and will soon begin in English." Fenwick noted that when he became bishop in 1822 there were only ten or twelve Catholic families in the city. When he returned from Rome three years later, there were more than one hundred and ten families, of whom a number were converts. Rese alone had converted thirty-three German families. Because of this, observed Fenwick, the pastor of the Lutheran Church "is spitting fire and flame against him."[29]

By the mid-1820s there was considerable additional religious growth in the diocese. The local church displayed signs of vitality, and the bishop played no small part in it. On Easter Sunday in 1822 there were fewer than a dozen communions in the cathedral. Four years later there were at least three hundred on the same feast. Writing to the Association of the Propagation of Faith on the growth of the Catholic Church in Cincinnati, Rese acknowledged

Fenwick's positive influence. "One is justified," Rese wrote, "in expecting this from the zeal and piety of the saintly Bishop whom heaven has granted to the city, and whom the favors of God appear to accompany."[30]

Perhaps the most obvious sign of vitality in the young diocese was the movement for the erection of a new cathedral. Within two weeks of Fenwick's return to Cincinnati from Europe, he and his clergymen were busy planning the building of a new and larger place of worship. St. Peter in Chains had become too small to accommodate the growing congregation. During Fenwick's absence Hill had purchased a lot, adjacent to St. Peter's, for the sum of $1,200. The lot was to accommodate both the cathedral and a future seminary. However, not everyone was in full agreement with the idea of building a cathedral at this time. Stephen Badin, Fenwick's contact in Europe, was concerned that it would leave the bishop destitute of a livelihood and of a seminary. Because of the shortage of funds and alleged lack of honesty among the workers, Badin "knew not of any worse business," he wrote to Fenwick, "than that of building in our backwoods." Besides, he warned, "you will be incessantly in contact with masons, bricklayers, plasterers, painters, carpenters, joiners, sawyers, smiths," among others, "and often exposed to the vexatious insults and calumnies of unprincipled men." Badin had little interest in church buildings. He was much more interested in "saving souls."[31]

Even though there were a few critics, the cathedral congregation supported the idea of building a new cathedral. Construction began in the spring of 1825. It would stand 110 feet long by 50 feet wide and 30 feet in height. These were "vast dimensions for the house of God in this country," Hill wrote. The architect was the local Irishman Michael Scott. He did not accept any remuneration for his services. The cornerstone was laid on May 19. Before the church was completed, Mass was said in it on June 29, 1826. The "cathedral is nearly finished," Fenwick wrote at this time, "and is admired for its great simplicity." The plain style of religion was a dominant characteristic of American Catholicism throughout the 1820s and into the 1830s. The dedication of the new cathedral took place nearly six months later on December 17. The cost of the new church was between ten and twelve thousand dollars. A subscriber to the *United States Catholic Miscellany,* a weekly newspaper established by Bishop John England of Charleston, South Carolina, in 1822, described the cathedral as "a neat and elegant building . . . , distinguished on the outside only by the regularity of the brick work, fine Gothic windows, [and] a large cross formed by the pilasters, in front; . . . a handsome iron gate and railing separate it from the street." On each side were four handsome windows, fifteen feet high. The interior of the cathedral, the *Miscellany* continued, "is remarkable for grand simplicity and chasteness of design. . . . There is nothing light, frivolous or gaudy to be seen; dignity is sustained

FIG 3. Original Cathedral Complex, early 1830s

throughout, and imparts solemnity to the performance of divine service." It had a seating capacity of about eight hundred persons, with eighty-eight pews on the first floor, an organ in the large gallery, and thirteen large paintings, which Fenwick had brought back from Europe, on the wall.[32]

Upon completion of St. Peter Cathedral, the original frame church was moved to the rear of it and was converted into a temporary seminary. While Fenwick had been in Europe, his vicar general had started a seminary in the priests' house. The students as well as the priests were to live there. But the priest put in charge was there only temporarily. Belonging to the diocese of New Orleans, he was recalled in 1826. Thus, though the local church in 1826 had a seminary, it had one without a professor and a suitable building. In light of the fact that the erection of the new cathedral had exhausted his funds, Fenwick was unable to sustain a seminary. The *United States Catholic Miscellany* explained the following year that it "is a misfortune . . . that he has not a seminary, nor the means to erect one; and consequently no prospect of procuring suitable clergymen for the numerous and laborious missions within the limits of his jurisdiction." In time, all that would change. The bishop never gave up the idea, and before the end of the decade the diocese would have its theological seminary.[33]

LAYING A MORE SECURE FOUNDATION

F rom the mid-1820s to the end of his administration in 1832 Edward Fenwick helped lay a more solid foundation for the Catholic Church in the diocese of Cincinnati. Besides preaching and making conversions in the wilderness, the local church resolved its property dispute with the Dominicans and established a seminary, parochial school, college, and newspaper to help enhance the Catholic faith throughout the diocese.

During Fenwick's absence abroad his vicar general and two priests traveled and preached extensively throughout southern Ohio and the western half of the state as far north as Lake Erie. They did not often work together, but more so alone. Filled with religious zeal, they responded to the needs of non-Catholics as well as Catholics. "I have received," one of them wrote to London, "several invitations from large societies of Methodists and other Sectaries to go and preach the gospel to them."[1]

The life of the pioneer missionary was one of labor, trial, and self-denial. The missionary priest, often carrying vestments and altar supplies, at times fastened with a strap and tied on his back, forded streams and traveled narrow trails and dusty roads to minister to the people. He frequently had to pass through vast forests wherein no trace of road could be seen. When a missionary arrived at one of the sites, the news soon spread to other communities. The first family to meet him usually sent out one of the children to announce his arrival to the neighbors. By the next morning whole crowds assembled around the spot where the missionary stood. He would speak to them all day, sometimes well into the evening. "We instruct them . . . as much as possible," one of the missionaries wrote, "and leave among them" some catechisms, handbooks of questions and answers for teaching the tenets of Catholicism. "After three or four visits," he continued, "we receive them into the bosom of the Catholic Church." For the Catholics among them, the missionary would say Mass, hear confessions, and baptize the children. In some of the places there were forty to fifty houses, among which was a town house or someone's private home that served both as a church, a school, and a meeting place for the population. These occasional visits by traveling priests, who brought the sacraments, were by no means the limits of their spiritual lives. They met on Sunday mornings and holy days, especially during Lent, in the homes of various members of the community.[2]

Fenwick was most appreciative of the labors and apparent self-sacrifice of the missionaries. They "appear content," he wrote, "with their state of poverty, which obliges them to wear coarse homespun and at times even threadbare clothing." He was often reminded of their continued indebtedness, having to borrow, as one wrote, "for the postage of all letters being almost always without money." At times, Fenwick feared that the missionaries' incessant labors and oppressive poverty might ruin their health, leaving him, he feared, "without evangelical laborers."[3]

During his tenure, Fenwick was absent from Cincinnati a great part of the time. He made annual mission journeys, often going from house to house, "catechizing" in the forests, in taverns, in private homes, and in rural communities where Catholics were widely scattered. "At times," Fenwick wrote, "I administered to the same persons, and on the same day, all the sacraments, except holy orders and extreme unction. I often found people, married according to the laws of the land, who had been converted to the faith by reading good books or by conversing with good Catholics—and this without having ever seen a priest in their lives, or even having been baptized." These local missions were a form of Catholic evangelism. In the course of three months in the summer of 1825, Fenwick and a traveling companion baptized more than one hundred children and adults. Fenwick had the satisfaction of seeing his scattered congregation increase notably by frequent conversions. "At times," he noted, "in order to expedite the work and accomplish the greater good, we were obliged to separate for days, or even whole weeks. On one occasion, we brought back to the Church a dozen persons belonging to different families; on another, eight; and so on. . . . Wherever the missionaries go, conversions."[4]

By the end of the year Leo XII, who succeeded Pope Pius VII, proclaimed 1826 a Holy Year for the Catholic Church in the hopes of fostering during the year spiritual revivals that aimed at instructing the faithful and converting the sinners. It was customary for a new pope to proclaim a jubilee, a time for prayer and penance, in commemoration of his election. In December 1825 Leo XII extended it to the rest of the world. The jubilee, which had been deferred in Cincinnati by Fenwick until the cathedral was finished, was announced on Christmas Day 1826. This was the first time the Catholics of the diocese were called upon by the pope to unite with all Catholics in prayer and thanksgiving. The pope allowed Fenwick two years for the promulgation of the jubilee in the various portions of the immense territory under his jurisdiction. During the weeklong ceremony in the cathedral an observer noted that "two sermons in English and one in German were every day well attended, notwithstanding the extreme rigour of the season." Both congregations began the practice of worshiping at different hours in the cathedral, the Germans at seven o'clock in the morning followed by Mass for the English-speaking at ten o'clock. On the Sunday morning of jubilee week more than two hundred received communion. Even the secular press, Fenwick wrote, "lauded our zeal and enthusiasm, quite unknown before this."[5]

Indeed, there was reason for pride. In early February Fenwick, accompanied by Fathers James Mullon and Nicholas Young, traveled throughout parts of the diocese promulgating the jubilee. Fenwick left the episcopal city for Wheeling and from there journeyed westward, attending to the Catholics along the way. Mullon and Young took separate routes eastward and met at Lancaster where they opened the jubilee. From there they eventually joined up with Fenwick at St. Joseph parish, near Somerset. Within a radius of eight to ten miles people came to participate in the celebration, and for eight days they stayed on the campground during the mission. The number of communicants was about 400; 110 individuals were confirmed. The three missionaries then proceeded to Zanesville where they closed the jubilee at St. John the Baptist Church, a newly constructed brick church under the care of the Dominican, Stephen Montgomery. While in Zanesville Fenwick learned that Hill, who had been sent to Canton by the Dominicans as its first resident pastor, was ill. On horseback the bishop immediately went to visit his former vicar general, assisting him as parish priest.[6]

Along their route the three missionaries visited Catholics, administered the sacraments, brought dissenters into the fold, and opened and blessed some new churches. As they were invited to preach in Protestant as well as Catholic churches, in courthouses and other public places, their discourses were primarily designed to make people appreciate Catholicism. Consistent with the republican idea of religious liberty, through reason and intelligibility the missionaries promoted the doctrines of the church. As a result of the jubilee some four hundred converts may have joined the local church. The number of communions was more than seven thousand. Fenwick also urged Catholics in his diocese to observe the laws of fasting. In his first pastoral letter of 1827 he specified that they should eat meat only four days a week, though exceptions could be made for the working people, women, and travelers.[7]

Throughout his administration the distances that had to be covered by Fenwick and his missionaries were great. Because of the lack of priests the bishop was unable to station his clergy at any one locality, and because of the lack of funds he was unable to send two or more of them continually to preach to any particular congregation. Over an eight-month period in 1826, two missionaries, according to the *United States Catholic Miscellany,* "traveled on horseback 2,500 miles, exposed to the extremes of heat and cold." They feared that immigrants could become lax, drop Catholic practices, or convert to some form of Protestantism. The missionaries also had to contend with loneliness. In some cases the missionaries were deprived of the sacraments, not receiving absolution or extreme unction at the hour of death. The missionaries, moreover, received no fixed salary. They contented themselves, one commentator observed, "with the trifling collection made in the church on Sundays, . . . or what little the faithful are able or willing to spare."[8]

What became customary for the bishop was to perform the duties of his office in Cincinnati during the winter months, then attend to the rest of his diocese in the spring and summer. Besides visiting the missions in Ohio, he was especially attentive to the Indian missions. His 1829 tour of the northern region of his diocese was particularly noteworthy. One of the reasons for his trip was to deal with an alleged priest impostor at Green Bay. Earlier that year Fenwick had received word that a French Canadian by the name of Jean Baptiste François Fauvel, a seminarian who was never ordained, had deceived the Native Americans by pretending to be and performing the functions of a priest. The imbroglio at Green Bay very much concerned him. The moment Fenwick learned of Fauvel's escapades, he informed the Propaganda of his effrontery and requested that he be excommunicated. As standard operating procedure, Roman authorities declined to interfere in an issue involving lower clergy and expected Fenwick to deal with the matter himself. Fenwick eventually removed Fauvel.[9]

Many of the early bishops in the United States, including Fenwick, were concerned about the danger of accepting men of dubious character for priestly service. Even when the men were validly ordained, Fenwick insisted that they maintain high standards, that they be pious and compassionate, and that they not abandon their priestly life. Because there were very few places in Europe where the church had a surplus of clergy, there was reluctance by European bishops and religious superiors to let their priests, especially their most competent ones, go to America. Writing to Tommaso Ancarani, the Dominican Master General, Fenwick pointed out that "[t]epid or incapable religious . . . [are] extremely obnoxious to me." He wanted only worthy priests "who solicit nothing, whom a straw bed, food and garments of the coarsest kind quite satisfy, ready to attend the sick by night and day, who have no fear of danger nor fatigue."[10]

Fenwick's extensive missionary labors eventually took a toll on his health. For some time his health had been deteriorating, doubtlessly affected from years of exhausting travel. When he left Cincinnati for the northern region in the spring of 1829 he was in poor health. The young Dominican seminarian Samuel Mazzuchelli, who saw Fenwick earlier that spring, observed that the bishop was "not in good health; his journeys weaken him more and more and he very often forgets things of the greatest importance." There were those who feared that he would not return to Cincinnati alive. Commenting on a mistaken report received by a correspondent, the *United States Catholic Miscellany* wrote that "[w]e have frequently heard of the excellent private and public qualifications of the amiable and zealous Bishop of Cincinnati, . . . of the great benefits conferred on the American Church through . . . [his] instrumentality." But, it added, "we are indeed afflicted at the idea that there should exist any ground for apprehending his loss. We trust that the expressions of our correspondent are but those of tender and apprehensive affection."[11]

Concerned over the potential harmful effects of the Fauvel escapade at Green Bay, Fenwick headed directly there. He arrived on May 27, 1829. A large number of Catholic Native Americans flocked to greet him and receive his blessing. At Mass the next morning, he gave instructions to help increase the knowledge and revive the faith of the people. From Green Bay he began his journey back to Cincinnati, stopping at Mackinac and Arbre Croche, where he confirmed both whites and Native Americans. At Mackinac, approximately six hundred miles north of Cincinnati, there was a chapel and a congregation of American, Native American, and French Canadian fur traders under Father Samuel Mazzuchelli's charge. It was on this visit that Fenwick conceived the idea of providing priests for the Native Americans from among their own people. He invited two Native American youths, William Maccodabinasse and August Hamelin, to return to Cincinnati with him. He hoped that in time he could send them to the Urban College in Rome, so that they could receive an ecclesiastical education there, become priests, and then return to their Ottawa tribe in Michigan. For the education of Americans at the college, the American bishops paid nothing. The Propaganda assumed all the expenses.[12]

In the spring of 1832, Maccodabinasse and Hamelin accompanied Rese to Europe in order to pursue their studies. Pope Gregory XVI granted Fenwick's request, placing them under the care of the Urban College. Cincinnati was the first diocese in the United States to send American Indians to the college, and Fenwick may well have been the first of the American hierarchy to foster religious vocations among them. Pleased with the Cincinnati ordinary's overall work among Native Americans, the pope personally congratulated him on his success in the conversion of so many of them. Notwithstanding Fenwick's efforts, Maccodabinasse and Hamelin were never ordained.[13]

Whenever possible the local ordinary encouraged the establishment of schools in the Native American communities. Whereas the clergymen in the Cincinnati diocese ministered mainly to settlers of European stock, Fenwick, Gabriel Richard, and Samuel Mazzuchelli were missioners who paid special attention to Native American tribes in the northern region. For them the school was the major instrument in the Christianization and civilization of the Native Americans. Fenwick was particularly pleased with the Ottawa mission at Arbre Croche, where not only a Catholic school with sixty children had been started, but a society was formed to discourage the consumption of liquor. In the fall of 1830 a school was founded among the Pottawatomies on the St. Joseph River. It had approximately thirty pupils. A year later, another school was established on grounds that the residents at Green Bay presented him. By 1832, the school at Arbre Croche had upwards of one hundred children, St. Joseph's about sixty, and Green Bay's between eighty and ninety pupils. Fenwick was pleased in January 1831 when Father Frederic Baraga of Austria, with letters of high recommendation, arrived in Cincinnati, wishing to devote his life to their care.[14]

Throughout his term, Fenwick took a lively interest in the Native Americans' spiritual welfare. He felt a special bond with them. On one of his trips to Mackinac, where he participated in a procession of the Blessed Sacrament, he shared his feelings with Rese. "I believe," he wrote, "that I found more piety, faith and respect there than on any similar occasion among our American Catholics. . . . Truly, I would gladly exchange my residence in populous Cincinnati, together with my dignity, for a hut and the happy lot of a missionary among these good Indians." A year later Fenwick referred to the Native Americans as "the most interesting and important . . . portion of our flock and diocese. . . . At all events, it is the most simple, innocent and humble and docile part."[15]

As Fenwick expanded the local church's missionary work he was in dire need of more priests. But one of the major drawbacks of the early American church was the scarcity of priests. Though Fenwick had secured four priests while in Europe, the increase was not commensurate with the needs of the diocese. Shortly after his return home the Cincinnati ordinary appealed to Stephen Badin, still in Europe, to invite Jesuits and Benedictines in England to come to his diocese. Fenwick was particularly anxious to obtain both German- and English-speaking missionaries. It proved expensive and time-consuming to support priests until they could learn a new language. Badin, who believed that the Jesuits were the most supportive of foreign missions, presented a memorial to them to establish a foundation in Cincinnati. They declined, informing him that they could not at the time spare any missionaries for Fenwick's diocese. Badin received a similar response from the Benedictine order. During this period Fenwick and Gabriel Richard received more disappointing news by the departure of two priests in Michigan for missionary work in another province. Fenwick empathized with Richard's dilemma. "His situation," the bishop wrote to officials in Rome, "is painful for him and heartbreaking for me. He does not cease calling for missionaries. If you can send him a reinforcement of some good priests endowed with constancy and ardent zeal, you will relieve him very much and oblige me infinitely. As for myself, in Ohio, I can employ only those who know English well. To obtain such as these I depend on Rese [then in Europe] and Badin." In 1826 there were thirteen priests who assisted Fenwick in the diocese, nine in Ohio and four in Michigan. In 1827 and 1828 large numbers of immigrants from Germany, Ireland, and France, and a few from Switzerland, arrived in Ohio. This caused additional concern for Fenwick as he sought more missionaries who could speak the languages of the new arrivals. When many French settled in the general area of Canton, Fenwick sent the Dominican William Tuite, who had grown up in Belgium and could speak French, to minister to them. In the see city, Rese and John B. V. De Raymaecker continued to attend to the Germans.[16]

Though Fenwick had limited success in obtaining more priests from Europe, he did receive assistance from three women religious. Unsuccessful in his plea to secure more French Sisters of Mercy to assist Sister St. Paul, Fenwick did grant in 1826 two French Collettine Poor Clare Sisters, Francoise Vindevoghel and Mary Victoria de Seilles, permission to establish their order in the diocese of Cincinnati. While in Europe Fenwick and Badin had visited with them. Joining the two on their trip to the see city was Sister Adolphine Malingie from Ghent. In early fall the three sisters opened in Cincinnati a school for girls. By the turn of the year they were attending to approximately seventy girls in the school as well as instructing a large class of poor children on Sundays.[17]

In the summer of 1827, however, Sister Adolphine announced her intentions to give up her vocation and leave her two companions at the school. Rese, then in Europe, advised Fenwick to do what he could to keep the sisters together. If Sister Adolphine were to leave, Rese thought, it would hurt the diocese's efforts to recruit more sisters from Flanders. An even bigger disappointment and challenge to the bishop was the untimely death of Sister St. Paul in early September. Witnessing three years of her able work, Fenwick had hoped she would become the superior of the new community. "I am on the point," he wrote, shortly before her death, "of suffering an irreparable loss." Her death was a severe blow to him. With money that he received from the Propagation of the Faith, the bishop that year had built a brick school opposite the cathedral. Without her leadership the project was doomed to failure, the bishop thought, because the two Poor Clare Sisters alone were "not strong enough to make a foundation."[18]

The situation came to a head in the spring of 1828. In April Sisters Françoise and Victoria, after fourteen months of work yet unable to recruit any candidates to their community, left Cincinnati. When Sister Adolphine eventually withdrew from her order, the school closed for lack of teachers. Within a four-year period Catholic education in Cincinnati had started and ended. Fenwick nonetheless continued to try to attract other religious to his diocese to open schools.[19]

PROPERTY DISPUTE WITH DOMINICANS

Fenwick meanwhile wrestled with the issue of the ownership of property in the diocese, especially with the Dominicans who preceded the diocese in taking charge of the missions in Ohio. Who should own the bulk of the property, its bishop or the Dominican order? At the time Archbishop Maréchal was also engaged in a landholding dispute with the Jesuits in Maryland. Because of the chaotic condition of the Canon Law in the Catholic Church at the time, it was unclear exactly what were the rights of the bishops and what were the rights of the religious orders. Fenwick regarded himself as the proprietor of belongings of the Catholic Church under his jurisdiction. The money and articles given him by the pope and the Propaganda on his trip to Rome had been stipulated as property of the diocese and not as property of the Dominican order. Before leaving Europe he wrote a will, naming the bishop of Bardstown the heir in trust to all his property as bishop of Cincinnati. The property was to be passed on to his successor. However, with the exceptions of Frederic Rese and James Mullon, all the priests in Ohio were Dominicans. And as the Dominicans attended to the spiritual needs of their flock, they acquired titles to various church properties in the diocese in the name of the order. This created a difficult and awkward situation for Fenwick. He certainly did not want to be accused of favoritism toward his order. It also created potentially a more difficult situation for his successor should that person not be a Dominican. In April 1825 Bishop Dubourg of New Orleans advised Fenwick "not to leave to anybody the management of [his] money affairs. Your main object," he wrote, "is to build the establishment of an independent Bishopric; and that of your order is a secondary one, for which . . . you ought never to sacrifice any part of your capital."[20]

Francis Patrick Kenrick, the Dublin-born bishop of Philadelphia, expressed similar concerns. He pointed out to Rese that even though the land at Somerset had been given to the Dominicans before the establishment of the diocese of Cincinnati, its ownership by the order was "invalid or at least questionable." Although Fenwick was a Dominican, Kenrick did not question the Cincinnati ordinary's loyalty to the church. "I still respect his motives," Kenrick wrote, "and esteem his virtues no less than his talents; and I entertain a confident hope that his zeal for the true interests of our holy Religion will prove itself far superior to his solicitude" for the Dominican order.[21]

Wanting the delicate property dispute between the Dominicans and the diocese resolved, Fenwick turned to higher ecclesiastical authority. In the spring of 1826 he recommended to Archbishop Maréchal that the church authorities in Rome investigate the matter. Fenwick argued that all he owned legally in the diocese was the lot on which the cathedral and the adjoining buildings stood. Nearly all the ecclesiastical property in the diocese belonged to the Dominicans. Before he had left for Europe in the spring of 1823 he had appointed Hill, a brother Dominican, as vicar general, "expecting he would act in all temporal concerns for the interest of the B[isho]p of Cincinnati." While on his mission, more than a hundred acres of land that had been promised him in Brown County, Ohio, were deeded to the Dominicans. Similarly, at Canton and Zanesville he had encouraged and authorized the collection of money and building of churches. Yet there too the properties were deeded to the Dominicans and, as bishop, he had no claims over them. "All this was done in my absence," he wrote to Maréchal, "and by a *presumptive* or *tacit consent,* on which . . . my Brother Dominican acted. I wish to know from Propaganda if it is correct, and if I can consent to it; or what is to be done." The major point at issue had to do with respecting and adjusting the property rights of both the diocese of Cincinnati and the Dominican order.[22]

Mulling over the property issue, Fenwick also expressed concern over the lack of financial support. The income that he received from the whole diocese consisted, he wrote to Maréchal, "in the collection made in the church on Sundays, and amounts to 2 dol[lars] 50 c[ent]s and sometimes $3—rarely to 4 on those days—not a cent do I receive other ways, or elsewhere, except now and then for marriage, a rare and scanty fee. I have once or twice received retribution for mass—in all 5 ½ dol[lar]s since I live[d] in Cincinnati." By the end of 1826 the Propaganda enjoined Maréchal to investigate the matter.[23]

Early the following year Fenwick proposed a solution not only to the Dominican property issue but also to the shortage of clergy and funds in the diocese. He proposed making Ohio a prefecture apostolic, an area whose missionary jurisdiction would be almost exclusively under the care of the

Dominicans yet subject to the Holy See. He was hopeful that the order would provide much needed clerical and financial assistance to Ohio. The state of the diocese was distressing. There were few vocations to the priesthood, some religious were leaving, and funds were inadequate. Fenwick was also disappointed that Roman officials had failed to grant his request for a coadjutor. As a consequence, he sent Rese to Rome, giving him power to act for him and to serve as his emissary on the Dominican matter. Though part of Rese's mission was to raise money and secure additional religious, he took with him two letters written by Fenwick on the property issue, addressed to the pope and the Propaganda. He also delivered a third letter, written by Hill, to the general of the Dominican order urging him to support the bishop's requests.[24]

Fenwick's letters read the same. Wanting to put religion on a firm footing, he saw "no other means" than that the diocese be dissolved and "become a Dominican province." And for it to be effected successfully, he recommended that "the bishop be always chosen from the Dominican order." Having come to believe that Catholicism in the diocese needed the backing of a religious order, he felt the matter should be considered in no other way. "From the cradle of religion in this province," he wrote, "the Dominican Brethren were exclusively the only missionaries who were wont to plant in the vineyard of the Lord and to irrigate it with their sweat." Contrary to his earlier letter to Maréchal, he now argued that whatever donations or legacies were made, "they were given without a doubt to those Fathers and their churches." Fenwick was now convinced that this would be good for religion in the diocese and that the welfare of Cincinnati's bishops would be better safeguarded. The Cincinnati ordinary now thought it made sense for the bishop and his priests to belong to the same organization. As all but two priests in Ohio were Dominicans, it seemed only natural that most of the properties had been donated to the order. He further argued that a diocesan clergy "can by no means be introduced without great disturbance and danger to religion." Hill's letter to the Dominican order elaborated on the same points and outlined the status of the proposed Dominican province. It suggested maintaining a Dominican province in the United States with headquarters in Ohio.[25]

Nearly a year later Fenwick learned that Rome and the Dominican order had struck an agreement that covered six major points. First, there was to be only one Dominican province, located at St. Joseph, in the country. Second, Fenwick was put in charge of the province. He was to be both bishop of Cincinnati and superior for life of the Dominican order in America. Third, if the bishop of Cincinnati were not a Dominican, the order was to pay him $300 annually. Fourth, whatever gifts in the future might be given to the

Dominican fathers would belong exclusively to them; whatever gifts might be given to the bishop of Cincinnati or to the cathedral would belong exclusively to the bishop. Fifth, the cathedral at Cincinnati, including the lots and houses annexed to it, was to belong exclusively to the episcopal see. And sixth, ecclesiastical ornaments and furnishings, with the exception of vestments loaned to the diocese by the Dominicans in Kentucky, would belong to the cathedral.[26]

The agreement failed to grant Fenwick a number of his requests. The Propaganda made clear that it was not imperative that the bishop of Cincinnati had to be a Dominican; if he were not, he was to be paid an annual sum by the order. In addition to the usual diocesan duties, Fenwick now had to attend to the needs of the Dominican province. It was most unusual for a bishop, even in a missionary country, also to be head of a religious province. During the remainder of his term, Fenwick sought to remain loyal to both, hoping to do so without being detrimental either to the welfare of the Dominicans or to the growth of the diocese. When the Propaganda ordered a separation of diocesan and Dominican property, it instructed Fenwick to hold diocesan property in his name to be willed to his successor. This practice spread to other dioceses of the West and spared them many of the difficulties occasioned by the lay trustee system in the East.[27]

In January 1829 Fenwick received good news from his emissary Rese. While in Europe working on the Dominican matter, Rese helped establish the Leopoldine Foundation—an organization based in Germany and Austria—that raised funds for missionary work in North America. Having personally received support from the central councils of the Society for the Propagation of the Faith, Rese thought the organization should spread to other countries. For several months he promoted his plan to help form a society of generous individuals to help support the American missions. "I have now the happiness to announce to you," he wrote to the bishop in December, "that the well-being of our diocese and mission, together with that of many others, is . . . assured for the future." Authorities in Vienna established for the exclusive benefit of the church in North America the Leopoldine Foundation, which Leo XII approved by his bull of January 30, 1829. The German-based organization promised to be particularly helpful to the diocese because of its growing German Catholic population.[28]

CUSTODIANS OF THE CHURCH

Not long after the building of the new cathedral in 1826, the local church proceeded to build those institutions—seminary, parochial school, college, and newspaper—it deemed essential to preserving and enhancing the

Catholic faith in the diocese. Scores of people, religious and lay, played a critical role in laying the foundation. Fenwick made plans for a diocesan seminary-college to train his own priests-to-be, believing that a college and seminary were essential for the well-being of religion in his diocese. There was always a pressing desire for priests. In light of the fact that the Propaganda had rejected Fenwick's proposal for a new province of Dominicans in Ohio, which potentially would have supplied him with more priests, a diocesan seminary made very good sense. "Without a seminary," Fenwick wrote, "I see only distress for the future. I am, therefore, fully determined to direct all my efforts to this object, and to make no further delay." He thought it was "of the greatest necessity, if we do not wish to lose the result of all our labor." The total number of clergy under his charge being eleven in 1829, he felt he needed more personnel. Though he could obtain priests from Europe from time to time, he knew they would "always be too few in number," he wrote, "to answer the needs of the diocese." Moreover, he wanted priests who were sensitive to the American culture. "If I have a seminary," he added, "I shall be able to form a native clergy brought up according to the habits of the country, accustomed to the rough roads, [and] acquainted with the language."[29]

On May 11, 1829, Fenwick opened a theological seminary, dedicated to St. Francis Xavier, in the old wooden frame church in the rear of the cathedral. The seminary opened with ten seminarians, four in theology and six in the preparatory class. In little time the seminary served both as a diocesan seminary and a college for Catholic laymen. Only four other seminaries in the country antedated the establishment of the seminary in Cincinnati—St. Mary in Baltimore; Mount St. Mary in Emmitsburg, Maryland, from which the Cincinnati seminary later took its name; St. Thomas in Bardstown, Kentucky; and St. Mary in Perryville, Missouri. Fenwick appointed the Dominican Stephen Montgomery first rector of the seminary. He enlisted the best faculty possible. In addition to the newly ordained John Baptist Clicteur of Flanders and Martin Kundig of Switzerland, three other religious were brought in from St. Rose Convent in Kentucky to assist at the seminary. He saw benefits derived by making use of the European-educated clergy in the work of educating a home clergy. "If one may judge from the beginnings," Clicteur wrote, who had also just been appointed Fenwick's secretary, "this establishment promises happy results. . . . The regulations, which are already in full vigor, are patterned after those of the best seminaries in Europe."[30]

Fenwick kept a watchful eye on the seminary. Shortly after its opening he wrote a letter to Kundig, commenting on the latter's progress in learning to speak English. "You only need more practice in writing and talking English," he said. "Take courage therefore and you will do well in English. Write and speak freely." His letter also expressed concern over the behavior of two seminarians who failed to observe the rules of piety and obedience. "'Order is heaven's first law,'" he wrote. "Without it, no good can be effected in the house. . . . If those two gentlemen disturb that necessary order, . . . they shall both be dismissed—which shall be the fate of everyone who will not conform to the rules, and conduct himself as a good clergyman. I will prefer to have no Priests nor Seminarians if I cannot have such as are pious, regular and obedient." About a year later a resident of the seminary, Frederic Baraga, commented favorably on the seminary. "The rules of the house are as in a convent, and are to my taste," he wrote. "The Bishop is our guardian. We always say our prayers before and after meals in a monastic manner, and after the meals the pious prelate always leads us to the church, . . . and with us makes a short adoration of the Most Holy Sacrament." When in the summer of 1829 the diocese was, perhaps for the first time, "free of debt," the bishop contemplated building a new seminary. "I shall within a short time," he wrote, "purchase in the immediate neighborhood of the Cathedral another lot for the Seminary."[31]

In October 1829 Fenwick participated in the first provincial council in Baltimore. In fact, he had helped shape the agenda. The Baltimore Council was largely called for the purpose of bringing some degree of cohesion into the church. In the formative years of the Catholic Church in the United States there was a search for unity through ecclesiastical discipline and organization. Close to half of the thirty-eight decrees sent to Roman authorities for approval proposed uniformity in the administration of the sacraments, a few dealt with trusteeship and Catholic publications, and ten with priestly conduct or unqualified clergymen. The thirty-fourth and thirty-fifth decrees pertained to education. "Since it is evident," the Council fathers wrote, that "the children of Catholic parents, especially the poor, have been exposed . . . to great danger of the loss of faith or the corruption of morals, on account of the lack of . . . [Catholic] teachers . . . , we judge it absolutely necessary that schools should be established." They also stipulated that only books free from error and approved by the bishops should be used in Catholic schools. This action, which was the first important legislation on Catholic education in the country, was consistent with the traditional European model of Catholicism and church discipline. "Much good, we trust," Fenwick wrote, "will be effected [by the council], many salutary regulations adopted, abuses corrected, and uniformity adopted."[32]

Fenwick regarded the education of youth in the principles of faith and morality as well as in letters as one of the most essential duties of his office, especially in the face of the emergence of the public school system. In 1825 Ohio had passed its first law requiring the establishment of public schools. Assessing a tax upon property of one-half mill upon the dollar, the proceeds were to be used for the school fund. Four years later proponents of tax-funded schools in Cincinnati amended the city charter, which provided a structure and special funding for the common schools. Rapid increases in the city's population, from 2,320 in 1810 to 24,831 in 1830, made it imperative to increase the number of schools. Until the erection of the so-called "model schoolhouses" in 1836, the schools frequently used the facilities of local Protestant churches. In their attempt to build a Christian America, evangelical Protestants sought to regulate manners and morals in the community by controlling education. To resist the curriculum and evangelical proselytizing in the public schools, where many Catholic children attended, Fenwick saw the need for schools that would serve the Catholic clientele. Over time the formation of the local church and parochial school helped foster a separation of religion and Catholic education from public life.[33]

While Fenwick participated in the deliberations at the first provincial council, Father James Mullon, who had accompanied the bishop to Baltimore, returned to Cincinnati with four Sisters of Charity of Emmitsburg to reopen the Catholic school that had closed the previous year and establish a female orphan asylum. The Sisters of Charity were the first community of religious women native to the United States. Founded in 1809, it established the following year the first free parochial school and the first Catholic orphanage. In 1825 the bishop had tried unsuccessfully to obtain the sisters for his diocese. The Sulpician John Dubois, then the superior of the Sisters of Charity, insisted that the bishop secure funds to ensure the stability of the establishment by guaranteeing them constant financial support. That Bishop Fenwick could not do. Shortly after the Poor Clare Sisters left Cincinnati in 1828, the bishop tried again to get the Sisters of Charity to come to the see city.[34]

In October 1829 some sisters had stopped in Cincinnati on their way to St. Louis. Patrick Reilly, an influential Cincinnati layman and former trustee of the Christ Church Congregation, met with the sisters, gave them a donation, and expressed his desire to have some of them come to Cincinnati. Four months later another layman from Cincinnati traveled to Emmitsburg also to appeal to the order. On May 9, 1829, Fenwick wrote a letter to the mother superior, respectfully asking for three or four sisters to administer a female orphan asylum, pointing out "that great good may be done in this city by the establishment of a female orphan asylum under your zealous and charitable care." M. P. Cassilly, a Catholic layman in the diocese, arranged to furnish them "a good and comfortable house, rent free, as long" as they wished to occupy it. Though "unable to contribute anything in a pecuniary way towards your establishing yourselves here," Fenwick wrote, he promised to do all "in [his] power to give [them] spiritual comfort and advice" and endeavor to make them "happy and content."[35]

While in Baltimore in 1829 Fenwick also made a personal plea to the mother superior. By mid-October he was pleased to learn that the Sisters of Charity would establish a foundation in Cincinnati. On the 27th, only twenty years after Mother Seton had founded the community at Emmitsburg, Sisters Fanny Jordan, Victoria Fitzgerald, Beatrice Tyler, and Albina Levy arrived in Cincinnati after fifteen days of travel by stage and riverboat. For a week they stayed with a family and then moved into their promised rent-free residence, provided by Cassilly. It was a two-story frame house on Sycamore Street near the cathedral. The sisters immediately took charge of five orphan girls and reopened the girls' school. The orphanage, being part of the cathedral parish, was named St. Peter Academy and Orphan Asylum. The community's progress seemed assured, for the sisters were well prepared to assume their new duties. St. Peter's school was the first permanently established tuition-free school in Ohio and marked the beginning of enduring Catholic education in the see city. Moreover, the local church began, mainly through the work of women religious, an institutional approach to charity. Sister-run charities, particularly Catholic orphanages, would become a highly visible and effective response to social problems of nineteenth-century America.[36]

By 1830 the school already had 106 children. Much of the financial support came from collections taken during charity sermons and revenue raised from small private donations. In the early 1830s lay supporters of St. Peter's asylum moved to have the asylum separately incorporated and to form an association of "Ladies" who would manage its affairs. But the superiors in Emmitsburg and Cincinnati did not favor this. The sisters "should have the management and control" of the asylum, Sister Fanny Jordan wrote to one of the lay supporters. "We are not aware of any conditions that have been infringed in regard to the government of the house, as our immediate superiors left that to the prudence, piety and zeal of the Rt. Rev. Bishop of the Diocese and his clergy, who have been its governors." There was no change in management, and the institution continued to be owned by the diocese and conducted by the sisters. As early as 1832 a visitor to Cincinnati reported that the Sisters of Charity were doing "much for the advancement of moral and religious education in our city." Not only were the sisters among the pioneers in the establishment of the local church, they became the pioneer religious community of Cincinnati and the pioneer sisterhood of Ohio. The religious order also laid the foundation for various hospitals, asylums, protectories, and the homes for the afflicted and the aged in succeeding generations. In the process, they and succeeding sisterhoods in the archdiocese, like other women religious and Protestant and secular women's groups in the country, created—as a late-twentieth-century historian pointed out— "public space for women."[37]

Two and a half months after the arrival of the Sisters of Charity, Fenwick succeeded in bringing the Dominican Sisters to Ohio. In January 1830 four sisters left St. Magdalen monastery, near Springfield, Kentucky, traveled three weeks by stagecoach, and arrived at Somerset on February 5 to establish a foundation. Within two months of their arrival the four sisters opened a school with forty young women in a small house that had been bought for them. As the school changed from a day to a boarding one, and pupils of all denominations were admitted, enrollment increased. By the end of their first year in the diocese they began building a new three-story convent and school. They conducted additional schools in Canton and Zanesville.[38]

As the Catholic population and personnel grew, the local church also witnessed many conversions. "Very often," the bishop wrote to the Propagation of the Faith, "Protestants will attend our religious services with a view of ridiculing the ceremony. In most cases, they are amazed. . . . Then the conversions begin. The music and singing at the services also prove a strong attraction. Many come from curiosity, they hear a sermon, and there hear something inexplicable to them. They study, ask for information, and [before] long embrace the faith." Another reason that prompted Protestants to convert, Fenwick thought, was "the unwillingness of their preachers to attend the wants of the poor sick." There were a few reported instances when Protestants, "lying upon their death bed," sent for the Catholic priest. Fenwick cited the example of a poor dying black Methodist woman who "sent her boy to the preacher to call upon her in her sickness." With the preacher's refusal to come, Fenwick wrote, "the sick woman sent for a Catholic priest. He came at once." The bishop took pride over the fact that Catholic priests were willing to attend to the poor and the neglected as well as those who were influential. In particular, Fenwick was pleased with the conversions and the progress of Catholicity among German-speaking Catholics, especially since the arrival of the two young German priests, Henni and Kundig, "who have labored zealously to bring their scattered countrymen back to the fold." In 1829 he estimated the number of German Catholic families in Cincinnati to be eighty-seven, "and their conduct, attendance upon the services and frequent reception of the Sacraments," Fenwick wrote, was "truly edifying. The Germans are a great blessing for the country." That year alone, 150 Protestants in the see city converted. Hardly a day passed, Rese observed, without several people presenting themselves to the "good bishop to be instructed."[39]

To accommodate the growing Catholic population outside Cincinnati, more parishes were established. In the early 1820s more than thirty Catholic families had settled about thirty miles northeast of Cincinnati and east of the Little Miami River. On occasion Fenwick's missionaries visited the area. To encourage the growth of the community, General William Lytle donated a tract of land for ecclesiastical purposes. At the end of the decade Martin Kundig, then stationed in the area, helped organize a parish, prepare thirty-six of his parishioners for confirmation, and build a church, which was completed the following year. St. Martin's was the second parish of the present diocese of Cincinnati. About the same time, some of the inhabitants of Butler County took up a collection for the purpose of buying land and building another Catholic church. Though there was but one Catholic man then living in Hamilton, he and non-Catholics raised enough money to buy the ground. After presenting the deed to Fenwick, the inhabitants proceeded to build St. Stephen Church.[40]

While overseeing the growth of the local church, Fenwick acquired the reputation of being amiable and pastoral. According to one account, his "affability, gentleness, and noble bearing can never be forgotten by one who had the good fortune to know him." Even Frances Trollope, the noted English traveler and author who came to Cincinnati in February 1828 and who spent nearly two years in the community, had very kind words to say about the bishop, even though her general remarks about other clergymen were less than kind. She had never met "in any country," she wrote, "a priest of a character and bearing more truly apostolic. . . . His manners were highly polished; his piety active and sincere and infinitely more mild and tolerant than that of the factious sectarians who form the great majority of the American priesthood." Fenwick's apostolic and pious qualities were noticeable characteristics. Shortly after he got settled in Cincinnati in January 1831 Frederic Baraga noted that one "cannot easily imagine a more humble, amiable, pious and zealous ordinary than he is."[41]

The growth of the local church, due largely to increasing immigration and missionary work, generated uneasiness among some Protestants. The visit of Bishop John England of Charleston to Cincinnati in June 1830 contributed to the number of conversions. At the solicitation of Fenwick, England delivered a course of lectures on the doctrines of the Catholic Church. Attended by large crowds of Protestants, the lectures caused a large number of defections from the various denominations. Despite cordial relations of Catholics with Protestants in some communities, as a consequence of the ongoing growth of the Catholic population in Cincinnati there was increasing religious suspicion and prejudice expressed in Protestant pulpits and publications. Early-nineteenth-century Americans inherited a Protestant cultural tradition that had been bitterly anti-Catholic in the colonies. Like their Protestant counterparts, Catholics worked hard and wished to own their land. Also, like their Protestant colleagues, they had great interest in fostering learning as they sought to develop Catholic educational institutions. The very success of the Catholic Church itself helped create bitter opposition.[42]

Shortly after he returned from Europe in 1824, Fenwick noted that there were thirteen different Prostestant sects in Cincinnati, and all were "united against the Catholics." There were Protestants filled with bigotry and hatred who directed their antagonism against Catholics and immigrants. The principal opponents of the Catholic Church in Cincinnati were the Presbyterians. Their primary organ was *The Christian Journal.* The Protestant and sectarian press in the Midwest charged that the Republic was endangered by the growth of the church. Preaching the alleged corruption of the Catholic Church, they sought to prevent the Mississippi valley from falling into the grasp of the papacy.[43]

What in particular helped intensify the spirit of anti-Catholicism in Cincinnati was the fact that in the fall of 1830 there were more Protestant than Catholic pupils at St. Peter's school, and that the Sisters of Charity admitted Protestant children at the orphan asylum. In September the editor of *The Chronicle,* a secular newspaper in Cincinnati, criticized *The Christian Journal* for its anti-Catholic stance. "I have never been," he wrote, "the *emissary* of Popery except as far as to rebuke the intolerance that *The Christian Journal* is accustomed to exhibit towards the Roman Catholic Church" and the Sisters of Charity in particular. At the time the sisters supported eight "orphan children" in the asylum, besides teaching about one hundred and fifty day scholars. Most of them were "charity pupils." In the editor's judgment there was "[n]o effort . . . to inculcate the doctrines of the Roman Catholic church among the Protestant children placed in the asylum." Nevertheless, as Catholics took pride in the increasing number of conversions in the archdiocese, Protestant ministers had legitimate concerns about Catholics possibly influencing and taking some of their children. In the summer of 1831 *The Christian Journal* warned Cincinnati residents against the "increase of Papists in the United States," pointing out that "immense funds have been placed at their disposal." It urged Protestants not to place their children in Catholic schools, fearing that the West was fast becoming the pope's domain, and that it would soon be all under his control. In 1836 Catholics complained that Protestants "have filled every village store . . . with . . . vile, mendacious works" against Catholic priests and nuns. Notwithstanding these warnings and complaints, during the next twenty years, as one English traveler noted in 1852, "the education of all the first classes of Protestants seems to be entrusted to the Catholic priests and nuns. . . . The priests say that their children are better taught and looked after than they would be in any other schools."[44]

Although some Protestants expressed concern over Catholic growth, in the spring of 1830 plans for the building of a new college and seminary in the diocese were well under way. By this time the number of seminarians had increased to thirteen. The old frame church, which housed Fenwick's residence and the seminary-college, could not adequately serve their purpose any longer. A new and larger building was necessary. Funds obtained from European Catholics, especially from the Propagation of the Faith and the Leopoldine Foundation, enabled him to buy a lot of 100 by 195 feet, north of the cathedral. Despite the expense, he intended to build a college for laymen and a seminary on it. "I will do all I can to build there," he wrote to Father Montgomery, even if it meant he had "to go to Europe again to beg." Fenwick retained the services of Alphaeus White, a convert and one of Cincinnati's early renowned architects, to build the new college. Fenwick envisioned the seminarians teaching in the lower classes of the college. In the spring of 1830 the cornerstone for the new college, named the Athenaeum, was laid.[45]

On October 17, 1831, the Athenaeum, at a cost of about $11,500, was opened, with Fenwick as president. Even though his health and strength were failing, Fenwick felt "obliged," he wrote, to perform the duty of the presidency himself. A year earlier the old frame church had been razed and the new bishop's house and the seminary were completed. The college was built parallel to the cathedral and joined to the seminary and the bishop's residence. The bishop now had a college and seminary in operation, both under the direction of diocesan priests. Upon the completion of the Athenaeum, the seminarians were transferred to the two-and-a-half stories high building. The college consisted of classrooms, a study hall, library, students' chapel, rooms for the faculty, and an attic that served as dormitory for the seminarians. Catholic secondary and higher education had their beginning in Cincinnati with the founding of the Athenaeum. It became the first Catholic institution of higher learning in the Northwest Territory.[46]

Fenwick, like the other American bishops, was still in need of priests. He intended the Athenaeum to serve both as a day and boarding school as well as a nursery for vocations to the priesthood. A six-year classical course of studies was scheduled, as there was no formal division then of high school and college. The curriculum included mathematics, geography, history, rhetoric, moral, natural and experimental philosophy, chemistry, English, Latin, Greek, French, Spanish, Italian, and German. The absence of religion courses in the curriculum helped reassure some non-Catholic parents that their sons could receive a college education without being subjected to "conversion-to-Catholicism" tactics. "Like every similar institution, which much depend, for success, on the patronage of the Public," its prospectus read, the Athenaeum would "make every exertion to merit the patronage of a liberal and enlightened Public." On the other hand, Catholic parents were assured of a religious influence as there was a special students' chapel in the college and the faculty were mostly priests and seminarians. Initially all the members of the faculty were to come from the diocese. Though he wanted a native clergy, Fenwick realized that it would be difficult to staff the college only with diocesan clergy.[47]

On October 22, 1831, five days after the opening of the Athenaeum, the *Catholic Telegraph* was also founded with Father James Mullon, rector of the seminary, as editor. The diocesan paper was born on the same site as the Athenaeum, the western side of Sycamore Street between Sixth and Seventh Streets, the location of the present St. Xavier Church. The little eight-page weekly, its pages 9 ½ by 12 ½ inches, was printed on a hand press—given to Fenwick on his tour in Europe—in a building at the rear of the cathedral. The *Catholic Telegraph* was the first Catholic paper west of the Alleghenies, and the first diocesan organ and the second Catholic paper in the country. In its first issue the thirty-eight-year-old Mullon, a noted speaker as well as a talented writer, cited the main reason for its publication. "The primary object in issuing the *Catholic Telegraph*," he wrote, "is to aid in diffusing a correct knowledge of the Catholic faith," and to correct false notions about the Catholic faith often seen in the public press and heard from public platforms. In light of the fact that the custodians of Catholicism, namely, the church and the school, had been built, Catholics now had, as later reported, their own "arm of defense." Like other Catholic newspapers being founded at the time, the *Catholic Telegraph* served as the primary agency for the Catholic defense. "We do not wish to provoke controversy," Mullon wrote, "but we shall never shrink from it when our silence would be detrimental to the cause of religion and truth."[48]

In part, the purpose of the new weekly paper was not only to explain the Catholic doctrine to Catholics and to those potential converts seeking a better understanding of the Catholic Church, but it was also to respond to the bitter attacks from the enemies of the church. As early as 1829 Fenwick had hoped to start a paper to respond to the sectarian charges. Writing to the Propaganda he noted that "the Catholic Religion has been misrepresented and abused. As we have neither time to answer all their accusations nor a press of our own to combat their vilifying charges, we content ourselves to publish an occasional reply to these attacks in the columns of a local daily paper." Fenwick, who knew personally the need for a Catholic paper that would defend and explain the teachings of the church, believed it was imperative that the Catholics should have a paper to defend themselves against their enemies. In 1830 he had been accused of treason because of his correspondence with and acceptance of funds from the Propaganda. Over time articles in the *Catholic Telegraph* were not merely defensive. Occasionally they criticized and attacked Protestants.[49]

Expanding the local church with the establishment of a seminary and a diocesan paper, Fenwick again expressed interest in securing the services of a coadjutor with the right of succession. In light of his long vacancies from Cincinnati and his failing health he again thought a coadjutor would prove most helpful. Fenwick had never enjoyed robust health. A sign of his debility was his suffering from a polyp of the nose that was thought to cause frequent fevers. While in Europe in 1827 Rese sent Fenwick a prescription from the doctor who had treated the Bavarian King. This prescription, Rese wrote, "positively cures any polypus whatsoever." But it did not work. Because of his poor health and his humble estimate of his own abilities to serve as bishop, Fenwick wanted the assistance of a younger and more physically able man in the demanding labors of building up the Catholic Church in the diocese.[50]

In the mid-1820s Fenwick considered Francis Patrick Kenrick, then teaching in the seminary at Bardstown, for the position of coadjutor. Archbishop Maréchal also recommended Kenrick. Maréchal was concerned that Fenwick, who seemed depressed to him, might resign his see if he were not given some assistance. Bishop Flaget, however, not wanting to lose someone so learned and active in his diocese, successfully opposed the appointment of the Irish missionary. In December 1827 Fenwick wrote again to the Propaganda, this time requesting that Rese, his secretary, be appointed his coadjutor. Nothing came of his nomination.[51]

Though Fenwick had long been sick and fatigued by his work, and always believed he was not qualified to be bishop, he was delighted with the progress that the diocese had made within the short space of a few years. "The rapid progress of Catholicity. . . , not only in the city, but throughout the diocese, is very remarkable," the *Catholic Telegraph* editorialized in its second issue. In December 1831 Fenwick wrote to a friend in London that his "flourishing" diocese now contained "twenty-four priests, missionaries, twenty-two churches and several more congregations without churches, whereas fourteen years ago there was not a church, and I the only missionary in the State of Ohio." Furthermore, the diocese now had a seminary, a college, and a weekly paper.[52]

In the summer of 1832 the Cincinnati ordinary set out on his last pastoral journey through Ohio, Michigan, and the Northwest. While visiting St. Joseph's at Somerset, Fenwick gave Rese instructions for the administration of the diocese in the event of his death. Believing his health was fast deteriorating, he had exclaimed after saying Mass in the cathedral earlier in the spring that "[t]his is the last time in my life that I celebrate Mass in this church." That summer Cincinnati suffered deaths virtually every day due to the cholera epidemic. During one month alone 423 persons fell victims to the disease. The well-known contemporary physician, Dr. Daniel Drake, estimated that four percent of the population of Cincinnati died of cholera. As a consequence, the number of orphans attended to at St. Peter's increased to thirty-four. A number of impartial newspapers praised the religious who, putting their lives in danger, remained in the city to care for the sick. After making his rounds in eastern Ohio the bishop left by boat for Detroit. While sailing, cholera broke out on the boat. It had to stop for two days at Fort Gratiot on the St. Clair River.[53]

On July 14th, while at Sault Sainte Marie, the bishop came down with chills and fever. By the time the boat reached Mackinac three days later, his symptoms had gotten worse. While on the island he spent ten days with Father Samuel Mazzuchelli in his home. Though terribly ill and depressed, and incapable of traveling any farther, Fenwick began a course of spiritual exercises for the Canadian traders and inhabitants. Mazzuchelli tried to comfort him. Concerned over the bishop's depression, Mazzuchelli recorded in his *Memoirs* that the bishop "blamed himself for having accepted the episcopacy of which he was unworthy and incapable of carrying the burden." Notwithstanding the obvious growth of Catholicity in the diocese, he thought "he had governed his diocese badly," Mazzuchelli wrote, "and that he knew not how to answer before the supreme Judge." Shortly after he left Mackinac, Mazzuchelli sent a letter to the pope, describing Fenwick's weak physical condition. From mid-June to September 26, 1832, while quite sick and feeble and feeling himself "sinking under the weight of solicitude and infirmity," Fenwick traveled more than two thousand miles ministering to his flock. During the last two years of his life, he traveled nearly six thousand miles. Doubtlessly, all this traveling, which further demonstrated his commitment to his ministerial work, had worn him down and weakened his physical condition.[54]

In late July Fenwick journeyed to Canton where he and John Henni, the pastor of St. John Church, subsequently traveled to Steubenville and then to Pittsburgh. On September 25 the bishop and Eliza Rose Powell, a longtime friend and one of his converts, traveled to Wooster, Ohio. Powell, seeing the feeble state that the bishop was in, had decided to accompany him in the coach to Wooster and back to the see city. They arrived at Wooster in the evening. By morning the bishop's condition had declined to the point that he no longer recognized Powell.[55]

Fenwick, at the age of sixty-four, died about noon the next day on September 27, 1832, without an attending priest. He was buried the same day because of fear of the spread of cholera. Many doubtlessly empathized with the landlady's sentiments when she had come into his room on the last day and said, "Yes—he has administered to many, but there is no one to administer to him now." Though the bishop was buried at Wooster, his body was not to lie there long as plans were soon developed to bring it to Cincinnati. On February 11, 1833, his remains were committed to the vault under St. Peter Cathedral. Fifteen years later, his successor, Bishop John Baptist Purcell, had Fenwick's remains removed from the vault of what was then St. Xavier Church and placed beneath the altar of the new St. Peter Cathedral. On March 23, 1916, the remains were transferred to the mausoleum in St. Joseph cemetery in Price Hill, on the west side of Cincinnati.[56]

Though throughout his eleven-year tenure Bishop Fenwick's health was precarious at best and his self-confidence was almost always lacking, Cincinnati's first bishop organized mission activities and helped establish those institutions essential to a new diocese. There can be no question that under his supervision the new diocese experienced solid growth. In the process his ministry helped fulfill the American church's aspirations of attending to the spiritual and temporal needs of Catholics.

A New Bishop for a Growing Diocese

When the Irish-born John Baptist Purcell assumed direction of the diocese in the fall of 1833 he inherited a diocese that had under Edward Fenwick's leadership organized mission activities and established those institutions essential to a new see. From the cathedral and the Athenaeum branched forth many churches, seminaries, colleges, and academies in the diocese. The most spectacular growth of the local church occurred during Purcell's years in office. Besides building upon the visitation tours initiated by his predecessor, he helped secure more clergy and religious to operate the increasing number of churches, schools, and orphanages. To accommodate the growing Catholic population and institutions, the diocese by midcentury was raised to the status of an archdiocese. Following Fenwick's administration the local church under Purcell's guidance also helped bring the Catholic population and growing parishes into an organized and disciplined relationship with the church.

About a month before he died, Bishop Fenwick tried one last time to secure the appointment of a coadjutor for Cincinnati. Suspecting that Frederic Rese was now the likely candidate for bishop of Detroit, Fenwick requested as his coadjutor the Jesuit Peter Kenny of Georgetown College. The Jesuit General, however, opposed Kenny's appointment on the grounds of age and infirmity. The officials of the Propaganda shared these reservations. There was also the concern that the Dominicans, who still constituted the majority of the clergy in Ohio, would not welcome a Jesuit as their bishop. Having just appointed Rese bishop of Detroit, the Propaganda asked Bishop John England, then at Rome, for his opinion of Fathers John Hughes of New York and John Baptist Purcell of Maryland. Though England

FIG 4. Archbishop John Baptist Purcell, 1833–1883

thought either one would do well as bishop of Cincinnati, he leaned more toward Hughes. "There is one point . . . ," he said, "which may deserve to be considered. Mr. Hughes is emphatically a self-made man, and perhaps he would be on that account more acceptable to the people of a western diocese than Mr. Purcell."[1]

Archbishop James Whitfield of Baltimore, moreover, initially opposed Purcell's nomination. He did not want to lose him as president of Mount St. Mary's College at Emmitsburg. Whitfield also shared with his predecessor, Ambrose Maréchal, a distrust of Irish bishops. Convinced that both Bishops England and Francis Patrick Kenrick had "strong Irish predilections in favor of Irish Bishops & Irish discipline," he was concerned that if Purcell were named to Cincinnati he would be led by England as well as by Kenrick. Notwithstanding Whitfield's concerns and England's advice, the Propaganda chose Purcell. On the evening of May 12, 1833, Pope Gregory XVI named Purcell second bishop of Cincinnati. His selection appeared to have occurred partly out of a misunderstanding of England's statement by the cardinal prefect. "As soon as I told the Cardinals what you said about Mr. Purcell's being a self-made man," the prefect informed Bishop England, "they agreed upon him at once" and submitted his name to the pope for his approval. England had, of course, described Hughes as the "self-made man." Partly because of Whitfield's strong protestations the Holy See delayed Purcell's appointment for a few months.[2]

Purcell, a diocesan priest, officially received his appointment on the second day of August. Born on February 26, 1800, in Mallow County, Ireland, Purcell came to the United States at age eighteen. Two years later he entered Mount St. Mary's Seminary in Emmitsburg where he began his study for the priesthood. In February 1824 the slender, sandy-haired Purcell left the Mount to complete his theological studies at St. Sulpice Seminary in Paris, where he was ordained on May 26, 1826. Ten years later he returned to Mount St. Mary's as a professor and later president of the college. Shortly before he became a bishop Purcell was naturalized a citizen of the United States.[3]

Undoubtedly there were good reasons for Purcell to look forward to coming to Cincinnati. In about twelve years' time Fenwick, his clergy, religious, and faithful had laid the foundation for a viable Catholic Church in the region. But soon after the news spread of his appointment, Purcell received letters from fellow priests and laity urging him to hasten to Cincinnati. Bishop England, still in Rome, "strenuously" recommended to Father James Mullon, editor of the *Catholic Telegraph,* that he write to Purcell requesting he accept his appointment. "[I]t is by no means unlikely," Bishop England wrote, "that efforts will be made to urge his resignation." Mullon promptly wrote to Purcell and recommended that he assume the new post because the diocese was in a sad state owing to "Rese's want of energy and disposition to evade difficulties merely imaginary." Moreover, the layman M. P. Cassilly, a supporter of some local church activities and whose sons attended Mount St. Mary's College in Emmitsburg, complained to Purcell about the incompetence of some of the clergy in the diocese. The church and college were "in a retrograde state here," he wrote. "We have made priests of every one that has come this way."[4]

After settling his affairs at Mount St. Mary's, the bishop-elect made an eight-day religious retreat in Pennsylvania in preparation for his new duties. On October 13 Whitfield consecrated him in the Baltimore cathedral. The following month Purcell set out on his first trip to the West, arriving in Cincinnati aboard the steamboat *Emigrant* on November 14. Later that day Purcell was led by a procession to the cathedral where he was installed in his new see by Bishop Benedict Flaget. Purcell was one of eleven bishops in the American Catholic hierarchy. With no previous episcopal experience, the thirty-three-year-old Purcell became the bishop of Cincinnati, one of the youngest men to hold the episcopal office in the history of the country. The diocese had been without an ordinary for more than a year. It now had one, and he would serve the faithful for about fifty years.[5]

Though the diocese was in a much better financial condition in 1833 than when Fenwick came to it in 1822, it still had few material assets. There were numerous debts and scarcely any funds with which to pay them. Purcell soon discovered that the diocese had no adequate means of support for the clergy, the college, and the seminary, and the latter two were in need of physical repairs. Rese had had to borrow more than $500 simply to buy groceries and supplies. For three years the principal and interest on the mortgage of $750 for the cemetery lot at Liberty and Vine Streets had not been paid. The diocese also owed $1500 on property at St. Martin's in Brown County, where Father James Reid had recently built a brick school. For the maintenance of the cathedral house, the diocese was forced to use the money collected by the Germans and entrusted to Rese. The 5,000 or so German-born or second-generation German Catholics were members of the cathedral parish and had raised $720 to build their own church. As Cincinnati was without a bishop, Rese had delayed construction until a new bishop was installed.[6]

Shortly after his arrival to Cincinnati, Purcell confided to Bishop England that he was "under a debt of 6000 dollars" and was "badly disappointed." In the journal that he kept for the first six months of his administration, Purcell seemed to have recorded every possible defect he found in his diocese. Though filled with hasty and, perhaps, intemperate remarks, the journal does reflect Purcell's pessimism and perceptions of the state of the church. "Thousands upon thousands of Dollars," he wrote, "had been expended on buildings which are ill-constructed & inconvenient, of wretched materials, half-finished, leaking, mildewed roofs & walls; floors loose & badly laid, hydrants left insecure against external injury." He also noted that the president of the seminary had taken "the young Seminarians to Whiskey shops & to the Theatre" and returned "home drunk at midnight."[7]

One of the first problems that the new bishop encountered had to do with Fenwick's estate. Fathers Nicholas Young, Frederic Rese, and Anthony Ganilh were the executors of Fenwick's will. Both Young and Rese had turned over their papers to Ganilh. Before Purcell arrived in Cincinnati, Ganilh, who had recently been accepted by Bishop Flaget into his diocese, had brought all the diocesan legal papers with him to Kentucky. Notwithstanding Purcell's request that they be returned to the see city, Ganilh refused to send them, thus forcing the Cincinnati ordinary to travel to Bardstown to personally argue his case. Convinced that Rese had misused and embezzled funds, Ganilh instituted suit against Purcell for the property deeded to the Cincinnati bishop in Fenwick's will. The court later decided in favor of Purcell, giving him a clear title to the church property in the diocese.[8]

Purcell was also fundamentally concerned with the lack of priests. In 1833 the local church had fourteen diocesan and secular priests to attend to the scattered Catholics in Ohio, which in 1835 Purcell estimated to be between 25,000 and 50,000. Of that number, approximately 8,000 resided in Cincinnati. Among the sixteen Catholic churches in Ohio, three were within the present boundaries of the diocese of Cincinnati, namely, St. Peter Cathedral in Cincinnati, St. Martin in Brown County, and St. Stephen, which was under construction in Hamilton, Ohio. Nine of the sixteen churches had been deeded to the Dominicans in Fenwick's will. From the very beginning Purcell was hopeful that he would be able to secure enough competent priests to serve the growing Catholic congregations. A few days after his arrival in Cincinnati he wrote to his Philadelphia counterpart, John Hughes, that although he found the "astonishing" number of applicants to his seminary encouraging, it would always have room for "two or three truly eligible subjects." In addition to the presence of Dominicans in central and eastern Ohio, there were resident priests stationed at St. Martin's, Zanesville, Steubenville, Canton, Peru (near Norwalk), Tiffin, and Cincinnati. As interim administrator, Rese had stationed the Redemptorist Francis X. Tschenhenss at Peru, who was joined soon after by two other Redemptorist priests and lay brothers. A month after his arrival, Purcell sent Father William J. Horstmann of Osnabrück, along with his German congregation, northwestward where they established the town of Glandorf, in Putnam County. Horstmann also attended to the Catholic German settlement of Stallotown (now Minster) that had been established two years earlier. Seven priests resided at the cathedral in Cincinnati. They attended to the English-speaking and German congregations, the latter constituting at least half of the Catholics in Cincinnati. In addition, the priests in Cincinnati ran the seminary, the college, the diocesan paper, and visited neighboring missions, especially in Dayton and Hamilton.[9]

At the beginning of Purcell's administration there was only one German-speaking priest for the 5,000 German Catholics in Ohio. Though the cathedral held special services in German, the German Catholics thought they needed more German-speaking priests and their own separate church. Besides, the cathedral was too small to accommodate the growing congregation. After consulting with some of his clergy, Purcell expedited the ordination of Henry Damian Juncker, a German-speaking native of Lorraine, to the priesthood. Though he had not yet gone through a regular course of theological studies, "the situation of the German congregation," Purcell wrote in his journal, "seems to require his advancement to the Priesthood." On March 16, 1834, Purcell ordained Juncker, the first time the bishop had performed that ceremony.[10]

Even though by 1838 Purcell had seen the number of priests in the diocese increase from fourteen to thirty, there was still a dire need for English- and German-speaking clergy. Purcell, like other bishops in the Midwest, made repeated petitions to church leaders in Rome for European priests. On occasions, other provinces sent him priests, but they were not always satisfactory.

In early 1837 he complained to Archbishop Samuel Eccleston of Baltimore, his superior and friend from student days, about "the ungenerous conduct of the bishops of N[ew] York & Charleston" in sending him clergy with questionable credentials. "This," he argued, "is not honorable." Through his diocesan newspaper the bishop warned against clerical impostors, such as Fauvel in Fenwick's days. He was determined to have a competent staff. "[W]hatever be the dearth of Missionaries, or pastors, in this poor diocese," Purcell wrote to Bishop Joseph Rosati of St. Louis, "I am determined to receive none of the applicants from Europe . . . unless they are known to myself as well as unequivocally commended to me by those in whom I have confidence abroad."[11]

To help enhance the quality of the priests in the diocese, Purcell initiated the practice of holding synods, or meetings of the clergy, and clergy retreats. Joined by the Jesuit John McElroy of Maryland, who came to the diocese in early March 1840 to give retreats, Purcell sponsored an eight-day retreat in the cathedral. Thirty-eight priests attended the retreat. McElroy was impressed by the seriousness of the sessions, noting in his diary that "strict silence" was observed and that Purcell gave a daily exhortation on Catholic doctrine. The following year the Jesuit John Larkin conducted the retreat, and in 1842 the Vincentian John Timon did. The retreats were serious enough that the laity of the diocese were excused from attending Sunday Mass while the clergy were in session.[12]

VISITATION TOURS

In 1833 Purcell began his first of several three- to four-month visitation tours. Like Fenwick, the Cincinnati bishop felt the weighty responsibility of evangelizing and personally providing spiritual care to Catholics throughout the diocese. On his first tour Purcell began the practice of sending to the *Catholic Telegraph* detailed and candid accounts of his visitation. In the late spring of 1834 he left Cincinnati and traveled to Holy Trinity Church at Somerset, where he praised the fine work being done by the Dominicans. From the Dominican center he continued his ambitious journey to the Catholic settlements in western Ohio. He proceeded northwest to the Danville area in Knox County, south to Newark and Zanesville, further east to Guernsey, Noble, and Columbiana Counties, and then westward to Canton, another Catholic center. The latter and its surrounding missions, attended to by Fathers John Henni and John de Raymaecker, were increasing rapidly. There were already some 2,000 Catholics, mostly Germans, in the area, where ten years earlier, Purcell wrote, "there were scarcely thirty resident Catholic families." From there he and Henni left by carriage and visited

Wooster and Mansfield, and then went north to visit with Father Francis Xavier Tschenhenss's congregation in Norwalk. In their attempt to cross the flooded Mohican River, the carriage broke and the bishop and Henni got drenched. But they still made it to Peru, Ohio, in time for Purcell to bless the new St. Alphonsus Church on July 6. Purcell preached to the large congregation in English, and Henni and Tschenhenss delivered the German sermons. This was a custom that became standard procedure with Bishop Purcell.[13]

From Peru Purcell journeyed to Lower Sandusky (now Fremont) and Tiffin. Then he proceeded southward through the Wyandot Indian Reserve where he found, he wrote, "nothing to break the cheerless dreariness of the wilderness, but the recollection of the immense numbers of the fast disappearing sons of the forest, once the proud owners of the soil." From there he continued southward to Urbana and Dayton before entering his final leg back to the see city. He found Dayton to be "most advantageously situated" and had "no uncertain prospects of great increase in wealth and numbers." The Catholics in the community, he believed, were "among the most zealous and exemplary in the State," noting that a few families made generous contributions to the church and adorned "religion by their lives." From 1832 to 1834 the popular priest, Edward T. Collins from Cincinnati, lived in the home of Robert and Sarah Conway and their family, and then served as Dayton's first resident priest. As Father Emanuel Thienpont and the German Catholics in the region in the mid-1830s collected money to erect a German church, Protestants donated generously to the building fund. On November 26, 1837, Purcell dedicated Emmanuel Church. Days in advance of the dedication, Catholics and non-Catholics lined up at a bookstore on Main Street or at a home near the church to buy fifty-seven tickets to the event. The proceeds helped defray the remaining church debt. Seven years later it was estimated that the number of Catholics in Dayton and neighboring missions was about 1,650.[14]

Traveling by river steamer, canal boat, stagecoach, and on horseback, Purcell's annual trips were anything but leisurely. While visiting dozens of communities of settled or scattered Catholics each summer, he performed his pastoral and sacramental duties. In getting to know his diocese firsthand, he could identify the more pressing religious needs. He said Mass, baptized, gave communion, confirmed, heard confessions, and evangelized in private homes, in public buildings, and in the open air. Purcell had untiring energy. In one instance, while at a settlement near Danville, he replaced the sick pastor and preached nearly four hours every day for three days. His visitation tours contributed much toward the growth of Catholicity in his diocese, always seeking means to furnish his scattered flock with religious service.[15]

At times on his tours Purcell expressed concern over the Protestant influence in the public schools. "[I]n every town in the state, there are," he wrote, "sectarian free-schools, which the children of poor Catholics frequent for the purpose of learning to read, and where, under pretext of Charity. . . , the fountains of spiritual life are poisoned and those unsuspecting children have tracts placed in their hands, insinuating the vilest and most malicious slanders of our real principles." Very much aware of the practice of some Catholics to frequent Protestant churches when no Catholic service was available to them, he urged them not to do so. He felt "it was infinitely better [for parents] to stay at home on the Sabbath to instruct their children, to read good books, [and] to pray . . . [,] than to repair to scenes where all they could see or hear was mere human substitute for the [Catholic] doctrine."[16]

Purcell was not one to avoid doctrinal issues. His early sermons tended to be dogmatic and apologetic rather than moral, and his favorite topics dealt with the "Rule of Faith" and the infallibility of the Catholic Church. While at Mount Vernon in central Ohio, Purcell was invited to preach in the Methodist church. After speaking on the "vulgar prejudices against the Catholic Church," he rejected the notion that all religions were equal in the sight of God.[17]

Purcell's first year in office was a full and effective one. An optimist with an enormous amount of energy, the young bishop made an admirable start. "You have no idea," Father Stephen Montgomery wrote to him, "what deep root you have taken already in the hearts and affections of the good people of Cincinnati, Protestants and Catholics." Stephen Badin, who had come to Cincinnati to give the bishop a hand, commented in a letter to the recently installed Simon Bruté, bishop of Vincennes, on Purcell's extraordinary enthusiasm and dedication. "He is overpowered," he wrote, "by being obliged to attend to all sorts of offices & functions, which would keep several men very busy." While performing "all the functions of a parish priest, visit the sick not only in town but some times at a notable distance," he continued, "[h]e must & does preach (sometimes twice) on Sundays, [and] hear many confessions."[18]

Purcell was aware of the fact that he was trying to do too much. But the demands of the diocese were enormous. "The increase of Catholics keeping pace with our beautiful and flourishing city," the *Catholic Telegraph* editorialized in the fall of 1834, "renders a third and even a fourth church necessary, had we the means of erecting them." Besides the need for additional financial support and priests, the diocese was also in need of a "pious and learned professor of theology," Purcell wrote, "and a president of the seminary." Finding himself "distracted with a variety of duties" and concerns, the hardworking and zealous Cincinnati ordinary seemed unable to fulfill any one of them as fully and as quickly as he would have liked.[19]

DIOCESAN GROWTH AND TERRITORIAL CHANGES

Since the acquisition of the Louisiana Territory by the United States in 1803, the country had been consistently expanding westward. In 1845 John O'Sullivan, writing in the *New York Morning News,* coined the phrase "manifest destiny," suggesting that the country was destined to expand "from sea to sea." That year the United States annexed Texas. The following year, when the country waged war with Mexico, Purcell was optimistic about the growth of the state and of his diocese. At that time there were an estimated 65,000 Catholics in the diocese, one of the fastest growing sees in the West. He was equally optimistic about Cincinnati, speaking glowingly about its continued growth. The tremendous movement of people westward helped make the river metropolis one of the fastest growing urban centers in the country. In 1846 the Catholic population in Cincinnati alone was 25,000, approximately one-third of the city's total population. "Our city," Purcell wrote, "is increasing rapidly. I suppose 2000 houses in progress of building. Mechanics all employed—Journeymen, carpenters, masons, plasterers—from $1.50 to 1.75 per diem." The city's growing population and rapid economic development stimulated social and cultural growth.[20]

What also facilitated the economic development of Cincinnati were internal improvements. In addition to the Ohio River, two roads from the East gave access to Ohio for the immigrants. Zane's Trace ran from Wheeling, Virginia, through Zanesville, Lancaster, and Chillicothe. In the 1820s the National Road crossed through Ohio, passing through Cambridge, Zanesville, Columbus, Montgomery and Preble Counties. Paddle-wheel steamers plied the Ohio River and expanded river traffic. In the 1830s the Miami-Erie Canal and the Ohio Canal were built, connecting Cincinnati and Portsmouth on the Ohio River with Toledo and Cleveland, respectively, on Lake Erie. The Little Miami Railroad, chartered in 1836, ran from Cincinnati to Springfield, where it connected with another line that extended to Lake Erie. This gave Cincinnati access to the Great Lakes. By the 1850s railways crossed the principal towns and cities of the archdiocese. Migrants from Pennsylvania, Virginia, and North Carolina and immigrants from the British Isles and Germany made up most of the Ohio population. Most of the settlers in the diocese were Scotch-Irish Presbyterians, Congregationalists from New England, Baptists, Methodists, and Campbellites. In the midst of the various Protestant sects, Purcell had reason to be happy about the phenomenal growth of Catholicity in Ohio. In the 1830s and 1840s the new arrivals from Germany and Ireland would not only significantly change the size of the city but also its religious and ethnic composition. They were the two principal groups in the first thirty years of

Purcell's tenure from which the diocese received yearly increases to its population.[21]

Overwhelming as the lack of physical resources for the Catholic Church was in Ohio, it was not as serious as the shortage of personnel. With the growth of Catholicity Purcell needed more clergy, religious, and churches. In the early 1840s he estimated the number of Catholics to be at 50,000 in Ohio. The number of Catholics baptized in Cincinnati alone in 1843 was 1,156, an increase of 39 percent in three years. Purcell informed Father Louis Amadeus Rappe, who had just joined the diocese in 1840 and was sent later to Toledo, that the pastoral care necessary in the midst of so many Protestants and those without much faith was very great. He was concerned over efforts made by the Protestants by invitations, presents, and ridicule to take the Catholics away from their faith. He needed more clergy to combat these difficulties as well as more women religious to instruct the children. Hoping to make the faith available to the widely scattered Catholic flock throughout the diocese, he helped build up the church in the physical and institutional sense. Increasing immigration also put pressures upon the diocese to help foster religious solidarity among the immigrants and establish institutions to meet their spiritual and temporal needs. In conjunction with the city of Cincinnati, local Catholics often helped provide homes for the new immigrants.[22]

As Catholics in the eastern states in the early nineteenth century busily consolidated new urban parishes, in the Midwest they expanded the faith into the new frontiers. In many ways Catholics in the western communities drew upon the experiences of their counterparts in the East. Purcell was very much concerned with the ability of the diocese to establish parishes and build churches rapidly enough to meet the needs of the fast growing ranks of the Catholic population. He thought he could establish twenty new parishes if he had the priests. "From every little town, from settlements in almost every county," the *Catholic Telegraph* wrote in 1840, "there come continued appeals for clergy to direct the old and watch over the youth who are exposed to innumerable dangers for the want of a Pastor. . . . Like an army without a chief, Catholic communities are scattered over the land. . . . Fifty additional clergymen would find ample employment in Ohio." By the early 1840s Purcell had seen the completion of churches in twenty communities. By 1844 the diocese counted fifty priests. Among them were nine Americans, twelve Germans, eleven French, ten Irish, four Italians, three Belgians, and one Spaniard. Moreover, as the Catholic population grew and more churches were built, Purcell was optimistic. "[A] brighter Era," he observed in the early 1840s, "is now dawning on the United States and the day is not far distant when we shall have a Catholic house to stop at every ten miles and a Catholic Church every twenty miles, even in Ohio."[23]

The local church was also in need of more religious women. At the time they provided able service. The Dominican Sisters at Somerset were operating boarding and day schools for girls in the eastern part of the state, and the Sisters of Charity at Cincinnati were teaching 130 young girls in their school as well as caring for slightly more than thirty orphans. Living rent-free in a house owned by M. P. Cassilly, the Sisters of Charity expected to receive the property as a gift. By the time Purcell assumed his new post, however, Cassilly had changed his mind. Besides being influenced by his anti-Catholic wife, Cassilly was offended by the fact that his donations were published prematurely in the Catholic papers. At one point Cassilly instituted a suit against the sisters. Disappointed by Cassilly's behavior, Purcell recorded in his journal in 1833 that Cassilly's wife was "a bigoted and bitter Protestant [who] . . . has worried him and put him to great and unnecessary expense, reproaching him with reluctantly granting her articles of costly dress etc. when he could afford to squander 5000 Doll[ars] on Lazy nuns."[24]

The Cassilly incident forced Purcell and the sisters to search for a new home for the religious order. As the former president of Mount St. Mary's College in Emmitsburg, Purcell was familiar with the able work of the Sisters of Charity. A few weeks after his arrival in Cincinnati, he purchased a new home for them on Sixth Street for $4,000. For their support, the lay people in the community helped found on Christmas evening in 1833 the St. Peter Benevolent Society to aid in the education of the female orphans. Membership in the society, which in little time grew to approximately 400 members, required an initiation fee of fifty cents and a monthly contribution of twenty-five cents. As early as January 1833 a number of women had sponsored a fair for the benefit of destitute orphans under the care of the Sisters of Charity, raising more than $160. Along with charity sermons delivered by Purcell in support of the institution and continuing support from the members of the Benevolent Society, an annual fair, soon joined by such civic events as charity balls and concerts, constituted important sources of income for the work of the sisters at the orphanage.[25]

Though Purcell was most conscious of the need for parochial schools, he was unsuccessful in his early efforts to secure additional Sisters of Charity or a new religious order for the diocese. As the orphanage and school conducted by the sisters continued to grow, money and space became problems. In 1836 Purcell, with the aid of the St. Peter Benevolent Society, bought a mansion for $15,905 on the corner of Third and Plum Streets for an academy, school, and asylum for the female orphans of the city. During the cholera epidemic of the early 1830s, more children had become orphans and steps were taken to help provide shelter for them. The asylum, which by then attended to eighty-seven children, among whom were twenty Protestants, was found too small to admit more orphans. During the next fifteen years two additions to the orphanage were built. Alongside the asylum was St. Peter Academy, which was the first attempt to provide secondary education for girls in Cincinnati. By the summer of 1836 the sisters had taught nearly six hundred female children. The bishop also had to be pleased with the establishment of the Mary and Martha Society by the women of St. Peter congregation. These women, as well as local Protestant women, who had raised six hundred dollars in a fair to benefit the Catholic orphanage, made possible the establishment of this parish-based lay society. The members of the Mary and Martha Society paid $1.50 in annual dues and assisted the poor in the community. Members of the newly established lay societies across the country favored the traditional subscription method and low annual dues as they tried to get most parishioners, who were from the working class, to participate. Doubtlessly encouraged by the sisters' activities in his diocese, Purcell hoped to persuade the order at Emmitsburg to establish a separate orphanage for boys for the German-speaking Catholics of Cincinnati. The latter "would be rejoiced beyond measure, and generous to excess," the bishop wrote, "if they had an Asylum for their orphans and a school for their children." At that time, however, the Emmitsburg community could not spare any more sisters, nor were they willing to accept boys into an orphanage. In the first half of the nineteenth century many communities of women religious believed that they were not suited to teach or care for boys.[26]

In need of more priests, religious, and money, Purcell in 1838, like Fenwick before him, went to Europe seeking assistance. As bishop, this was the first of seven trips he was to make. "My chief object in going [to Europe]," Purcell wrote to Archbishop Samuel Eccleston of Baltimore, "is to obtain a colony of Jesuits for a college, . . . the Ladies of the Sacred Heart for an Academy, [and] the means of establishing both." For about a decade European contributions to the diocese of Cincinnati had been waning. Since Purcell's arrival in the see city in 1833 the local church had received only one donation from the Leopoldine Foundation, and contributions from the Society for the Propagation of the Faith continued to get smaller. Though Purcell had sent John Henni to do some diocesan begging in Europe in 1835, he had returned without any priests or money. To make matters worse, Bishop Rese of Detroit had arranged that all money from Germany pass through his hands. That raised the suspicion, as Father Stephen Badin had pointed out to Purcell, that it was unlikely Rese would be charitable to any diocese but his own.[27]

Before leaving Cincinnati, Purcell in May 1838 placed the care of his diocese in the hands of his two vicars general, Edward Collins and John Henni. Because of language differences in the diocese, Collins was appointed to the rank for the English-speaking Catholics and Henni attended to the German

Catholics. Furthermore, the bishop constituted his brother, Father Edward Purcell, his attorney with full authority to act for the bishop in financial matters. Born on March 31, 1808, in Ireland, Edward Purcell came to the United States in 1822, four years after his older brother did. After studying for a few years at Mount St. Mary's College in Emmitsburg, he left to pursue law studies and work in the East. In the summer of 1836 he gave up law and resumed his priestly studies in Cincinnati. On March 10, 1838, Bishop Purcell raised him to the priesthood. Having much confidence in his thirty-year-old brother's financial and legal abilities, he gave him full charge of the diocesan finances. The bishop, who had allowed some of the people of Cincinnati to deposit their savings with him following the nation's financial panic in 1837, now placed the entire business in his brother's hands. Edward Purcell operated the diocesan bank from his office in the episcopal residence adjacent to the cathedral. Before long the bishop also authorized his brother to open his letters when he would leave the city to visit parts of the diocese. Moreover, by the end of the decade Edward Purcell occupied the editorial chair of the *Catholic Telegraph*. He would serve as editor for almost forty years. When the bishop drew up a will during the cholera epidemic of 1849, he named his brother Edward his heir and administrator of the diocese in case of his death. He was to hold the property for the bishop's successor.[28]

Bishop Purcell sailed from New York on June 16, arriving at Liverpool on July 7. His trip took him to Ireland, Belgium, England, France, Germany, Austria, and Italy. His first major stop was in Dublin at the end of July. From there he visited his relatives at Mallow, whom he had not seen since he left Ireland in 1826. Entertained at a public dinner, he took the opportunity to respond to Bishop William Clancy's criticism of the United States. Clancy, who had served as coadjutor at Charleston, South Carolina, had returned to his native Ireland for a visit before he took on a new assignment in British Guinea. Critical of widespread American anti-Catholicism, Clancy sought to dissuade Irishmen from going to the United States. In his after-dinner speech, Purcell correctly minimized the extent of anti-Catholicism, countering that only a few Americans were guilty of the charge. Though he admitted there were "fanatics and bigots in religion" in the United States, as there were in other countries, he argued it was "unfair and illogical to conclude . . . that this religious rancour generally pervades the Union." He maintained that the very growth of Catholicity itself "contradicts forcibly" the assertion there were national prejudices against the church. In defense of his new country, Purcell praised the American principles of liberty, equality, and the separation of church and state. The latter, he argued, was contrary to the "unnatural connexion [*sic*] with the temporal power" that existed in many countries in Europe. The bishop's opposition to an established church and his defense of freedom of thought and speech arose from a sincere Americanism. Consistent with his evangelism, Purcell also endorsed both religious liberty and competition among denominations.[29]

While in France Purcell visited the Ursuline convent at Boulogne-sur-Mer, where he was well received by the sisters. The bishop was hopeful that the Ursulines would someday establish a foundation in his diocese. In early September he made a presentation to the Society for the Propagation of the Faith in Paris on the financial status of his diocese. With the exception of one year the Cincinnati see had been receiving annual donations from the Society. Following Purcell's visit the Society allocated 39,827 francs, which doubled the amount of the previous two years. Also, while in Paris, the Superior of the Sacred Heart Congregation promised Purcell that he would send sisters to Cincinnati to open a boarding school for girls. During the second quarter of the nineteenth century more and more orders of sisters in Europe viewed the United States as a vast field for missionary endeavor. Confident that the Sisters of the Sacred Heart would come, Purcell proved less demanding for the services of the Sisters of Notre Dame at Namur when he visited the motherhouse. He simply expressed his hope that someday they, too, would extend their ministry to Cincinnati.[30]

When Purcell left Paris for Germany and Austria, Father Hercules Brassac, a longtime friend, accompanied him. Brassac had recently left the diocese of New Orleans to return to France. He agreed to serve as Purcell's agent in Europe. Pleased with his reception in both countries, Purcell hoped that he would obtain additional financial assistance. From Munich he obtained a chest of church furnishings and books. From the Leopoldine Foundation he received 8,000 florins (about $3,200), which was double the amount Cincinnati had received in the past five years. Also, while in Munich, Purcell tried to obtain the services of Franciscan missionaries. He and his episcopal colleagues in the Midwest very eagerly sought the missionary services of the Bavarian Franciscans for the German congregations in the United States. Francis Louis Huber, a Franciscan, received permission from his superior to go to Cincinnati. He was one of seven priests who subsequently accompanied the bishop back to Cincinnati in 1839, the others being Michael Olivetti from Turin, and Joseph P. Machebeuf, John Baptist Lamy, Claude Gacon, William Cheymol, and Louis Navarron from the Province of Auvergne in France.[31]

In early February 1839, Purcell's journey took him to Rome, where he had a special audience with Pope Gregory XVI. Purcell also had profitable meetings with the General of the Society of Jesus and the General of the Dominican Order, respectively. In his meeting with the former, he extended an invitation to the Jesuits to take over Cincinnati's diocesan college. As Purcell wrestled with the problem of getting qualified priests and laymen on his college and seminary staff, he came to believe that the progress and stability of the Athenaeum would be better provided for by entrusting it to the care of a religious order. Purcell was ready to close the struggling school if the Jesuits did not take charge. The Jesuit General promised that the next house established by the order in America would be in the diocese of Cincinnati. In his meeting with the General of the Dominicans, Purcell was assured that even though the 1828 agreement between the Cardinal Prefect of the Propaganda and the Master General of the Dominicans was still being contested, the order would pay him the annual three hundred dollars. But that never came to be. When Richard Miles, the provincial of the Dominicans, consulted with his predecessor Nicholas Young on the matter, Young considered the agreement "a dead document" and nothing was ever paid. The issue dragged on for several years until Purcell dropped the claim in 1853.[32]

In July 1839 Purcell and the seven priests sailed from Le Havre for the United States, reaching New York forty-four days later. Upon his return to Cincinnati in September, after sixteen months' absence, the St. Peter Benevolent Society sponsored a public reception in his honor. The bishop informed his flock that he had "knocked, with the pilgrims and the beggar, at the gate of the rich, and the cottage door of the poor," and that he had done so successfully. The thirty-nine-year-old ordinary had helped rekindle the generous spirit of the societies of the Propagation of the Faith at Lyons, Munich, and Vienna. The generosity of the mission-aid societies enabled him to liquidate a large portion of the debts that the Catholics had contracted in the building of churches, in the purchase of the Orphan Asylum, and in the support of the seminary and clergy. This kind of foreign benevolence, consisting not only of monetary gifts but also the sending of clergy, and later religious, to work in Cincinnati and other dioceses in the United States, remained important throughout the nineteenth century.[33]

In the spring of 1840 the Jesuit general recommended to the Jesuit provincial in St. Louis, Peter J. Verhaegen, that the Jesuits take charge of the Athenaeum and thus relieve the diocesan clergy of the responsibility of operating the college. When Verhaegen in August wrote to Purcell, inquiring about the arrangement and conditions at Cincinnati, Purcell replied immediately. "I propose," he wrote, "to give you up forever, on condition that they should ever be held sacred for Church and School, the College, Seminary and Church" on Sycamore Street, "that you may have there a College and a Parish Church to be served by y[our] society in perpetuity." The Jesuits accepted Purcell's offer.[34]

News of the transfer spread quickly. In the fall of 1840 the *Catholic Telegraph* announced that the Athenaeum, now rededicated to St. Francis Xavier, would open under the auspices of the Society of Jesus, with Father John Anthony Elet, formerly president of St. Louis University, as its president. Purcell became the first person in charge of St. Xavier College's Board of Trustees. "No one," the *Catholic Telegraph* editorialized, ". . . ever regreted [*sic*] that their sons were educated under their direction, for the society is justly celebrated for success in developing the minds of youth, in leading them to the acquisition of every branch of knowledge, and sending forth men into the world, who have been enriched with the purest lessons of morality and fitted for the highest circles of society." In mid-October Purcell, pleased with the arrival of the Jesuits, wrote to Bishop Hughes that the "bigots have not so far shewn [*sic*] many of their teeth, but I presume they are on an edge."[35]

St. Xavier College, with six professors and five assistant tutors, opened on November 3, 1840. Before the end of the year there were seventy-six students enrolled. The Jesuits also assisted the diocese in attending to the Catholics at the city hospital and in doing parochial work in the community. To make room for the Jesuits at the college, Purcell moved the seminary to St. Martin's in Brown County. He liked the rural location for the seminary, thinking that the pastoral setting would be healthier for the seminarians. In 1842 the General Assembly of Ohio granted a temporary thirty-year charter to St. Xavier College. That year 217 students attended the college.[36]

Shortly after Purcell transferred the college and seminary buildings to the Jesuits in 1840, he embarked on the ambitious undertaking of building a new and more imposing cathedral at a new site. There were three Masses every Sunday and the crowds were getting larger. At each of the Masses there were individuals "compelled to remain out of doors," Purcell wrote, "for want of sufficient room" inside. It was estimated that "every day, for the last five years," he further observed, "there have been from thirty to fifty applications for pews, which notwithstanding the erection of galleries in the cathedral it has been impossible to satisfy." In addition, he wanted the new cathedral more centrally located. The city was now growing more to the west and the north, away from Sycamore Street. On December 1, 1840, he bought a lot 293 by 192 feet for $24,000 on Eighth and Plum Streets. By building "something uncommon" and majestic, Purcell thought, the new cathedral would help "put the heretics in good humour by beautifying the City. A fine steeple would command a view of ten miles down and up the river and be seen a great distance." For the next several months Purcell worked on the design of the cathedral. On May 20, 1841, he laid the cornerstone.[37]

The cathedral was an ambitious and daring financial venture. It was the bishop's major material concern between 1840 and 1845. Though funds raised on his trip to Europe helped him take the initial step, Purcell had to rely largely on local support, both borrowed and donated. Because Cincinnati was in the midst of an economic depression, and the monetary assistance from the Society for the Propagation of the Faith decreased by approximately thirty-three percent in the early 1840s, Purcell had to proceed more slowly with the building of the cathedral. Though a "heavy and oppressive debt still hangs over the churches," he wrote, the "first and most urgent want of this diocese is a suitable Cathedral." Through the newly formed diocesan Church Building Society, he urged each Catholic to contribute twelve and one-half cents per month. In order that sufficient time would be allowed to organize the Society in every part of the state, the first monthly contribution was taken on August 1, the feast of St. Peter in Chains. Because there is no documented evidence of the Society raising money during the next few years, there is every reason to believe that it failed in achieving its goal. Credit financing, made possible in part by people's savings entrusted to him and his brother, was also a source that Purcell tapped. Following the failure of several banks in Cincinnati in 1842, more people deposited their savings with the bishop. By offering competitive interest rates of four to six percent, Edward Purcell, with the approval of his brother, encouraged the faithful to deposit their money with him. Bishop Purcell's bank was not the only episcopal bank in the United States. Archbishop Peter Richard Kenrick of St. Louis eventually became engaged in a similar enterprise.[38]

On Sunday, November 2, 1845, Archbishop Samuel Eccleston of Baltimore consecrated the new cathedral. After "more than five years labor," the *Catholic Telegraph* wrote, "the Catholics of Cincinnati have crowned their hopes by the erection and consecration of a Cathedral." What added to the solemnity was the dedication of the German churches, St. John Baptist on the northern edge of the city, the day before, and Christ (later known as All St.s) in the northeastern end of the city the following Sunday. Several church dignitaries were in Cincinnati for the occasion. Seven bishops, sixty-seven clergymen, seminarians of the diocese, Jesuit scholastics, and lay people from various parishes took part in the four-hour services. With the dedication of St. Peter in Chains Cathedral, the old cathedral was turned over to the Jesuits. They and members of the old parish then formed St. Xavier parish.[39]

Designed by the architect Henry Walters, St. Peter in Chains Cathedral was a large-scale model of a Greek temple, a style very much in vogue at the time for public buildings. The elegant neoclassical cathedral asserted the substantial Catholic presence in the city. Cincinnati Catholics delighted in its design and ornamentation. Like its counterparts in New Orleans and Louisville, the new cathedral reflected the change in architecture in the immigrant church. Ornate European styles of design and ornamentation replaced the republican simplicity of the earlier years of the nation. As the

FIG 5. St. Peter in Chains Cathedral, 1890

shift to devotional Catholicism, imported from Europe and the heart of which consisted of devotion to Jesus, Mary, or one of the saints, began to take place in the 1840s, more American churches were filled with statues and stained glass. These changes reflected the majesty of the European Catholic past. The local historian Charles Cist praised the new cathedral as a worthy "ornament to our city. . . . It is the finest building in the West, and the most imposing, in appearance, of any of the cathedrals in the United States." It was also one of the material evidences of the growth of the Catholic Church in the community. The entire cost of the building was about $120,000. To sustain the new cathedral the parish repeatedly suggested the renting of pews "as the only effectual means of preserving" it.[40]

With the continuing growth of Catholicity in Ohio, Purcell began thinking of the diocese being raised to the status of an archdiocese. As early as 1840 the Cincinnati ordinary, aware of his own authority, expressed interest in seeing the "Queen City of the West," which he described as "a calm, beautiful City, having great facilities of access and as thriving as any other in the Republic," become a metropolitan see. No longer a frontier settlement, the burgeoning city had become an important western river community. Steamboats on the Ohio River and the opening of canals had provided the foundation upon which Cincinnati grew. Besides becoming heavily industrialized, Cincinnati was a place where banking services, hog slaughtering and packing, and furniture-manufacturing, clothing, and iron- and metalworking industries prevailed. By 1850 Cincinnati was the third largest manufacturing center in the United States. At this time there were twenty-six dioceses throughout the United States. As the trips to the metropolitan of Baltimore proved to be a great imposition on the dioceses and on the bishops, some of the ordinaries exchanged letters in which they discussed the possible creation of new archdioceses. Like other western bishops, Purcell minded more and more the inconvenience, expenses, and time of having to travel to Baltimore, the sole archdiocese, to attend the provincial councils every three years.[41]

At the Sixth Provincial Council of Baltimore in 1846, the American hierarchy discussed the possibility of establishing new metropolitan sees for New York, New Orleans, St. Louis, and Cincinnati. Though about a third of the group favored the erection of new provinces, nothing was decided. The Propaganda nevertheless went ahead the following year and established a western archdiocese in St. Louis. As Roman authorities attempted to centralize the authority in the Catholic Church, the Cincinnati ordinary and some of his confreres argued for some national episcopal autonomy. Purcell resented the way the Propaganda thought fit to decide on the matter without the recommendation of the American Council.[42]

Three years later at the Seventh Provincial Council of 1849, the American hierarchy petitioned authorities in Rome to establish new metropolitan sees in New Orleans, New York, and Cincinnati. Upon the recommendation of the Propaganda, Pius IX issued on July 19, 1850, the bull elevating Cincinnati, then ranked as the sixth most populous city in the United States and the largest west of the Allegheny Mountains, to an archdiocese. Both New York and New Orleans were also elevated, with John Hughes and Anthony Blanc, respectively, as archbishops. Doubtlessly pleased with the news of the elevation of his diocese and himself to the rank of archbishop, Purcell noted that in this instance, "at least, no underhand intrigue, or influence," he wrote to Blanc, "was allowed to interfere with the authentic and solemnly expressed will of our Prelates assembled."[43]

At the Sixth Provincial Council the American hierarchy had also discussed the possible erection of a see at Cleveland. After several visitations to northern Ohio, Bishop Purcell had realized his inability to administer the entire state. The subdivision of his diocese was a matter he discussed with Samuel Eccleston of Baltimore when the archbishop visited the see city in 1845. At that time Eccleston informed Purcell that he had placed the possible division of Purcell's diocese on the Council's agenda. At the meeting in Baltimore, Purcell persuaded the majority of the bishops to petition the pope for the establishment of a new see in Cleveland with Amadeus Rappe, the pastor of Toledo, as its first bishop. On April 23, 1847, Pope Pius IX, who succeeded Pope Gregory XVI upon his death, issued the bull erecting Cleveland into a diocese, thus dividing the diocese of Cincinnati into two parts, generally north and south of Holmes County. About six months later Purcell consecrated Rappe in the Cincinnati Cathedral. The diocese of Cincinnati that had covered about 41,000 square miles was now reduced to about 25,728 square miles. The division also reduced the number of churches in the diocese of Cincinnati from seventy to fifty and priests from seventy-three to fifty-seven. It was discovered later that the line cutting the diocese of Cincinnati into two parts inadvertently cut ten counties in such as a way as to make the interpretations of ecclesiastical jurisdiction difficult. The two bishops met and agreed to modify the demarcation. They constituted the counties of Mercer, Auglaize, Hardin, Marion, Morrow, Knox, Tuscarawas, Carroll, and Jefferson as the northern boundary of the diocese of Cincinnati, and Holmes County, which was for the greater part south of the line, was assigned to the diocese of Cleveland.[44]

As church building in the diocese continued during the 1840s, the Jesuit John McElroy of Maryland complimented Purcell in January 1848 on his "magic powers for church-building." Since his return from Europe in 1843 to the end of the decade, Purcell saw, in addition to the building of the new cathedral, the completion of churches in the northern, eastern, and western parts of Cincinnati, at Piqua, Sidney, Chillicothe, Russia, Frenchtown, Dayton, Springfield, New Richmond, and Freyburg. By 1850 there were eight Catholic churches in Cincinnati, six of which were German. There was a parochial school in each parish, ranging in size from 70 to 650 pupils, for a total of 2,607 children.[45]

The building and maintenance of new churches, asylums, and schools required additional financial assistance. And by the late 1840s, largely because of political disturbances in Europe, less money was pouring in from Europe. In 1847 and 1848 contributions from the Society for the Propagation of the Faith were cut in half. The Leopoldine Foundation made no contributions in 1848 and 1849, and the allocations from the nuncio of Vienna, done regularly up to 1847, were discontinued. Needing more money to meet the increasing needs of the diocese, Purcell tried to eliminate outside ecclesiastical beggars from Cincinnati. He proposed for the 1846 Provincial Council more effective policy against "indiscriminate begging." A year later Purcell published a signed statement in the *Catholic Telegraph* prohibiting outsiders from begging in Cincinnati.[46]

To staff the churches there were by the mid-1850s 110 priests in the archdiocese, second only to Philadelphia in the number of priests. By 1865 there were 163 priests. "One of the heaviest cares" assumed by his administration, Purcell wrote, "was that of providing for this diocese a sufficiently numerous body of saintly, learned and devoted priests. For this purpose," he told the clergy and laity, "we have spared no pains. We have incurred debts. We have written innumerable letters. We have made repeated voyages to Europe and knocked as suppliants at the doors of bishops and Seminaries." But his office could have been more successful. "Had we succeeded to the extent of our wants and wishes," he contended, "we would have, today, more priests and churches, and there would be fewer souls lost. . . ." Two years later, when there were seventy-nine students in the seminary being prepared for the priesthood, he was more upbeat about the number of priests in the diocese. The "diocesan vocations," he wrote, "are as many, we thank God, as the wants of the diocese require."[47]

In the first three decades of his tenure, the growth of the diocese of Cincinnati had gone on briskly. It grew in self-consciousness, both ecclesiastically and politically. When Purcell came to the diocese in 1833, there were sixteen parishes in Ohio. Five years later there were thirty priests, twenty-four churches, and 40,000 Catholics. By midcentury, seventy churches and seventy priests attended to 75,000 Catholics. Cincinnati was second to New York in the number of Catholic churches. The "vineyard" under Purcell's supervision, the *Catholic Telegraph* wrote, "has been enlarged beyond the hopes of the most sanguine." When the diocese of Cincinnati was established in 1821, there were approximately 7,500 Catholics in the three communities of Bardstown, Cincinnati, and St. Louis. The new ecclesiastical provinces of Cincinnati and St. Louis, encompassing the same general area, now had a population of 400,000 Catholics. By 1860 baptism registrations in the archdiocese of Cincinnati had increased to about 9,000 per year and marriages to nearly 2,000. During the same period, the number of Catholics in the United States increased from about two hundred thousand to a million and a half in 1850. Ten years later the Catholic population doubled to three million. Though in the United States Protestant denominations, when taken together, still outnumbered Catholics by about two to one, Catholicism had become the largest single denomination in the country.[48]

The metropolitan see of the Province of Cincinnati comprised the four states of Ohio, Kentucky, Michigan, and Indiana, with Louisville, Detroit, Vincennes, and Cleveland as suffragan sees, dioceses subordinate to the metropolitan. The see city of the bishop of Kentucky had been transferred from Bardstown to Louisville in 1841. After the erection of the new provinces, the first officially national, or plenary, council was held in Baltimore in 1852. It was at that session that the first suffragan see of the archdiocese of Cincinnati was divided. The Council Fathers, with the approval of Purcell and Bishop Flaget of Louisville, petitioned authorities in Rome that the eastern part of the State of Kentucky be erected into the diocese of Covington. The pope approved the recommendation in the summer of 1853. This solution helped resolve a controversy over the towns of Covington and Newport, Kentucky, which had been placed in 1847 in the jurisdiction of the diocese of Cincinnati. At the time Flaget and Purcell saw advantages to the transfer of the two border towns to Cincinnati because they were too distant from the episcopal seat at Louisville. Though in less than two years' time Flaget and his new coadjutor, Martin J. Spalding, had second thoughts about the transfer, the two towns continued to belong to the diocese of Cincinnati until an episcopal see was erected in Covington.[49]

Shortly after he received the papal bull erecting the Cincinnati Province, Purcell informed his friend Archbishop Blanc that he had "a mind to go to Rome" for the pallium, the insignia of an archbishop, for "it may be several months if we wait for an occasion to get it." Before he left Cincinnati in November 1850, his congregation gave him $1,000 for his journey. This was his third trip to Europe since his appointment as bishop, having gone in 1838 and 1843. He stopped first in New Orleans, where he visited with Blanc, then went to Mobile, where he preached at the dedication of the new cathedral. In early January he left New York for Europe, arriving at Paris later that month. Three months later, on April 25, Purcell received the pallium from the pope. Though Rome had already sent the pallium to Cincinnati, the pope went ahead with the presentation in his private chapel, instructing Purcell to destroy the first pallium upon his return home. While in Europe the archbishop again obtained financial assistance from the Association for the Propagation of the Faith and the Leopoldine Foundation. From the former he received $10,000 over three years, and $1,600 from the latter, one fourth of which was designated for the German Franciscans of Cincinnati to aid them in building a seminary.[50]

Not long after the formation of the archdiocese of Cincinnati in 1850, Purcell decided to further streamline the Catholic Church's organizational structure in the West. He recommended in the mid-1860s that the southeastern part of the state, with its 40,000 Catholics, be severed from the archdiocese. At that time, the area had forty-three priests divided among forty-one churches and twenty-three parochial schools. Purcell believed that this portion of the state would be administered better with its own bishop and more frequent visitations. On March 23, 1868, the pope, accepting the recommendation of the 1866 Second Plenary Council of Baltimore, issued the bull erecting the diocese of Columbus, the eighth suffragan see of the province. The new diocese consisted of that part of the state that lies between the Ohio River on the east and the Scioto River on the west, with the addition of the counties of Franklin, Delaware, and Morrow. Sylvester Horton Rosecrans, a native of Homer, Ohio, and Purcell's auxiliary bishop for six years, became the first bishop of Columbus. He served as bishop until 1878. With the departure of Rosecrans, Purcell was left without an auxiliary bishop until 1880, when depressing conditions in the archdiocese would occasion the appointment of a coadjutor. With this latest partition, the archdiocese of Cincinnati was now reduced to twenty-eight counties in Ohio. It covered about 12,043 square miles and counted 115 churches, forty-two stations, and thirteen chapels for a population of about 139,000 Catholics that were served by 135 priests. The establishment of the diocese of Columbus also meant the passing of the Sisters of St. Dominic and Dominican Fathers at Somerset from the territory of the diocese of Cincinnati to that of Columbus.[51]

ROLE OF THE LAITY AND PARISHES

In the early years keeping the faith alive in the diocese was mainly a lay responsibility. In the absence of a resident priest most Catholics had only occasional access to the sacraments. Whenever Purcell could, he would send the necessary priest to assist his flock. When the circumstances seemed ripe for growth and fund-raising, he encouraged them to form parishes and to build churches and schools. As more and more churches and schools sprung up, Catholics were more able to attend church regularly and to educate their children in the faith. These new institutions reflected the peoples' faith and also helped shape the faith and religious practice of the laity over many generations. Through his leadership Purcell helped bring the Catholic population into a more disciplined relationship with the church. A more structured and organized religious life gradually led, after the mid-nineteenth century, to greater episcopal and clerical authority. The coming of a resident priest to a hitherto isolated mission almost always meant that the parishioners ceded a great deal of authority to the priest. As the local church became more hierarchical, there was a gradual shift from a congregational model of the parish to a clerical model.[52]

In Fenwick's time Catholics had settled in various parts of Ohio, gradually organizing parishes and hoping to attract the services of a missionary riding a mission circuit. With the opening of better roads and canals in the 1830s and 1840s, new immigrants settled generally along the new thoroughfares. A priest in one of the neighboring communities would visit the newly arrived group and perhaps say Mass in a private home. When Purcell in the early 1850s learned from a resident of Greenfield, Ohio, who went to confession to him in Cincinnati, that there were several Catholic families in the area without the services of a priest, he asked Father John B. O'Donoghue of Fayetteville to serve the Irish town. In 1856 O'Donoghue became pastor of the newly formed St. Benignus parish. Not infrequently, a parish would pay a family to house the visiting priest and stable his horse. On one occasion a member of St. James parish at White Oak in Cincinnati in the 1840s had to send a bill for $5.50 because the parish had neglected to pay him for eleven Sundays. As the visits by missionaries to outlying districts became more frequent and the number of Catholics increased, money was raised and churches built, first as missions and then as parishes with resident priests. In many instances a parochial school or a combination church and school was begun contemporaneously, thus giving stability to the parish. As Catholics—like their religious counterparts, Baptists, Methodists, and Presbyterians—took to the frontier, they helped bring stability, education, and a sense of tradition to the Midwest. In the process, they would learn a valuable lesson in religious pluralism and adaptability.[53]

Though Catholics wished to live within the shadow of their church, many of them had to travel considerable distances to go to Mass. According to one account, in the early 1830s devout Catholics in Hamilton, Ohio, when there was no service at nearby Ross, would use the canal boats or even walk more than twenty miles to Cincinnati in order to attend Mass. Before Holy Name parish was formed at Trenton in 1871, every Sunday morning Catholics would climb on a farm wagon, upon which some chairs had been placed, and were driven to St. Stephen Church in Hamilton, eight miles away.[54]

As the Catholic population grew, more and more parishes were formed in the diocese. The core families in these new parishes took their religion seriously. Shortly after the St. Augustine parish at Minster was established in 1834, the lay trustees, elected by the congregation, drew up a constitution. It provided Mass would be said once each month, preferably on Sundays. When German and Irish Catholic families in Harrison, Ohio, in the 1840s arranged for Mass to be said once a month in the home of one of the residents, they scheduled prayer meetings on the other Sundays. Because a private home was sometimes not large enough to accommodate the Catholics in the parish, Mass was said in a rented storeroom or, as in the case of Catholics in St. Paul parish in Springfield, Ohio, in the bowling alley of a local hotel until a church was built.[55]

Steps taken to name a parish varied throughout the archdiocese. In July 1866 six men went to the home of Dr. Peter Liedel at Bridgetown in Cincinnati to organize a parish. Several months later they met to name the parish. The privilege of choosing a patron saint went to the highest bidder. When the bidding was over, a man with a bid of fifty-one dollars won and named the parish St. Aloysius, a patron of his grandfather. Similarly, laypersons at Taylor's Creek, Ohio, in 1867 took up donations and gave the highest donor the honor of naming the parish. Mr. Bernard Kielloeffer donated one hundred dollars and chose the name of St. Bernard. In another instance, because there were three Catholic families living at Coldwater in 1868, it was suggested to Purcell that the new parish be named Holy Trinity.[56]

Procedures adopted to build a church also varied among parishes. At mid-century members of St. Anthony of Padua parish in St. Anthony, Ohio, pledged four dollars per family and contributed labor and lumber toward the building of a log church. In most instances, however, Catholics, like the parishioners in Holy Name parish at Trenton, organized a building society and agreed to pay twenty-five cents per month to build a church and for the support of a pastor. But pledges were not always fulfilled. Even though forty-six families in Cincinnati's St. James parish at White Oak pledged from $2.25 to $9 in the early 1840s, they paid only $90.93. Moreover, though the parishioners promised to contribute $214.35 to the support of the pastor for one year, they paid only $145.30. By the 1850s, however, the parish agreed to pay $300 per year, payable monthly, to the pastor, as well as provide him with the necessary firewood and fifteen gallons of Mass wine yearly. At times other sources of revenue were tapped. To help build St. Clement Church at St. Bernard in Cincinnati in 1850, real estate agents donated the church property and gave $800, a local priest made a tour of Cincinnati and raised $1,200, and Purcell gave $400 from the Leopoldine Foundation. The parish borrowed the rest, approximately $3,000.[57]

Though over time more and more new churches were built to accommodate the increasing Catholic population, priests were often advised not to start building a new church where there was not a high probability that the congregation could raise sufficient funds for its completion. "Better worship our Creator in the humblest log," the *Catholic Telegraph* editorialized in 1846, "than be crippled with debt." In the 1870s William Bigot, pastor of St. Michael parish at Fort Loramie, began exploring the possibility of building a new church. At first he encountered some resistance from his flock. "With the increase of parishioners," he wrote, the church "was no longer large enough. On Sundays and holy days it was full to capacity, even the choir loft seats were occupied. Nevertheless the idea of building a new church did not want to take root. The farmers, especially, clung stubbornly to the old. They did think it nice when they could look over another's shoulder and read in their prayer book. Also there were many things to do. They wanted to save some money and wait for some good years." Before long, however, the congregation enthusiastically backed the idea. By the spring of 1878, a twelve-member committee began raising money for a new church. "Not one family or single person of the parish," Bigot wrote, "refused to give -$500 -$300 -$200 -$150 -$50 and some $1 were given, each according to his own means." In sixteen days $16,000 were pledged, and collected during the summer. "Besides this," Bigot also noted, "all had promised to give half of what they had given after 2 years. At the second collection some gave more than promised, for they felt they had not given enough the first time." All told they collected $24,000 in pledges and $1,800 from bequests and pew rent.[58]

What also grew in popularity in the United States in the second half of the nineteenth century was the parish mission, a special form of preaching that was especially effective in moving people's emotions and wills toward the goal of reviving the faith and moral conduct of the laity. Though the duties of the parish priest generally consisted of the sacramental and pastoral functions of baptizing, hearing confessions, celebrating Mass, attending to the sick and dying, and conducting marriages and funerals, at a mission he especially sought to awaken Catholics' consciousness to their sins and the need for forgiveness. The parish mission, which lasted from three to four days, sought to induce in Catholics a desire for confession and communion. During the spring jubilee of 1847, the diocese, under the guidance of the clergy, experienced what the *Catholic Telegraph* called a "spiritual fervor." The preaching at a mission contained many parallels with Protestant revivals. For two weeks, day and night, the churches were filled and confessionals crowded. More than twelve thousand people in Cincinnati alone received communion. By the end of the Civil War in 1865, the parish mission was a part of Catholic religious life in most regions of the country.[59]

A leading figure in the parish missions in the local church was the Jesuit and Austrian-born Francis Xavier Weninger. Shortly after his arrival in Cincinnati in 1848, the St. Xavier College teacher began preaching in local German parishes in his spare time. Generally he delivered two types of sermons: one directed to all parishioners, and the other to separate groups of married men, married women, single women, and single men. Weninger's first mission in the archdiocese took place at St. John the Baptist Church on Green Street in Cincinnati between Christmas and New Year's day in 1849. In time the Jesuit also wrote his own doctrinal and devotional literature.[60]

Ritual and devotionalism during Purcell's years of leadership came to play an increasing role in people's lives. Besides the official church rituals of the Mass and the administration of the sacraments, there was the forty hours devotion, which was a public exhibition of the Blessed Sacrament for a period of forty hours in memory of the forty hours Jesus's body spent in the sepulchre following crucifixion. Moreover, pilgrimages, increasingly emotional church-based devotions to the Sacred Heart and the saints, corporate recitation of the rosary, and the way of the cross were considered essential to the parish mission's goal of revitalizing and preserving the faith. In the process they generated closer attachments to the diocese. In the mid- to late-nineteenth-century music, hymns, and the sound of bells and booming cannon often contributed to the solemnity of the annual procession for the feast of Corpus Christi that was celebrated in some of the parishes. In 1852 a German Catholic noted that the "simple ecclesiastical chant [and] altars adorned with flowers and beautiful pictures" at the celebration at St. Clement parish in St. Bernard in Cincinnati "bore glowing witness of the honest faith of the parishioners." At St. Michael parish at Fort Loramie, Lenten devotions in the 1870s were held twice a week and were well attended. Because most of the farmers lived far from church, the devotions were held after Mass. On Palm Sunday there was a procession with the blessed palms and singing of the Passion. During the Corpus Christi Feast on Easter Sunday, bells rang and the choir sang while the people marched around the village and the four altars that they had built for the occasion. Among the many happy and festive events in the life of the parish were the first baptism and the first wedding. The entire congregation almost always took part in the celebration. Increasing emphasis on these rituals and external conformity were consistent with a European ecclesiology that stressed clerical authority. In addition, the devotions were approved by Vatican officials and were seen as a means of standardizing practices and of making the church truly universal.[61]

There doubtlessly was in every parish a core number of Catholics who were devout laypersons and active members of church organizations. But at the same time there were those Catholics who performed only the required religious observances, such as fulfilling the obligation to go to confession once a year and receiving communion in the Easter season. There were those individuals, moreover, who were indifferent and did not make their Easter duty. The clergy spent considerable effort and time promoting the devotional life. They tried to establish one devotional society for married women and one for married men. During and after the mid-nineteenth century, many Catholics in the diocese of Cincinnati as well as throughout the country were active in the various devotional and church-supporting confraternities. Parish-based confraternities and sodalities were often established in conjunction with the parish missions. The women, who were usually the first to organize when a parish was formed and were generally more attracted to these groups than men, centered mainly on the rosary and other Marian prayers. The men often belonged to church-sanctioned benefit societies. Seldom attracted to devotions outside of Sunday Mass, they were more likely to join a church society when it offered insurance benefits in the event of sickness and death. The parish societies tried to make sure that members received the sacraments at least once a year. The more devout members received them as frequently as once a month. Evidence suggests that in the nineteenth century daily attendance at Mass or daily communion was much less frequent than it was by the middle decades of the twentieth.[62]

Societies became the backbone of most parishes. Holy Trinity parish in Cincinnati served as the base of operation for such German societies as the Knights of St. Edward, Catholic Knights of America, Catholic Knights of Ohio, Catholic Order of Foresters, Ladies' Catholic Benevolent Association, and the Central Verein. Those women's societies that generally affiliated with parishes were the Ladies Auxiliary of the Knights of St. John, The Catholic Ladies of St. Frances, Ladies Catholic Benevolent Association, and Catholic Ladies of Columbia. Besides performing a variety of functions in the parishes, the societies gave financial assistance to the members and their families in sickness and death. The first society formed in St. Anthony parish at Madisonville in Cincinnati was the St. Michael School Supporting Society in 1861. It consisted of the young and married men who paid monthly contributions for support of the parish school. The following year some of the laywomen established St. Mary Ladies Society for support of the church. In the 1860s St. Carolina's Young Ladies Society of St. Anthony parish on Budd Street in Cincinnati donated a new pulpit, and St. Anthony's Men's Society donated an organ. The first sodality, or society, in St. Michael parish at Fort Loramie was St. Ann, established in 1874. It was initially composed of more than ninety married ladies. Shortly after its formation, approximately eighty young ladies also came forward and organized the Holy Mary Young Ladies Sodality and nearly one hundred young men formed the St. Lawrence Young Men Sodality. In the 1870s Father H. Brinckmeyer, pastor of St. Charles Borromeo Church at Carthage, worked among the youth and helped organize them into the Apostleship of Prayer and Devotion to the Sacred Heart Societies. In some parishes several hundred children also belonged either to the Society of the Infant Jesus or the Guardian Angel Society.[63]

Besides raising money and performing various committee functions, the parish societies played an integral part in the dedication ceremonies. At the cornerstone laying of St. Francis Seraph Church in Cincinnati on November 7, 1858, a lengthy parade preceded the ceremonies. As a sign of solidarity societies from several parishes took part in the program. Among these were the St. Aloysius Orphan Society, St. Boniface Young Men Society, St. Pius Men Society, St. Paul Society, St. Clement Society, St. Louis Society, St. Joseph Society, St. Aloysius Young Men Society, St. Charles Borromeo Society, and St. Augustine Society. Some six to eight marching bands, all wearing the distinctive badges of their organizations, furnished the marchers—who waved banners—with music. It was estimated that about twenty thousand people participated in or watched the parade. In the parish processions the marshals, often wearing uniforms of Knights of Middle Ages, rode proudly on their horses.[64]

Most nineteenth century parishes in the archdiocese depended for revenue mainly on weekly Sunday collections, sometimes taken at the door of the church, and on pew rents. Individuals and families who did not rent pews were expected to contribute. In principle, all but the poorest members of the parish were expected to rent pews, which was generally paid in four annual installments. Those pews closest to the altar were usually the most expensive. Laypersons in Cincinnati's St. Patrick parish organized the Church Debt Society in 1870. Members of the parish contributed no less than twenty-five cents per month. Within four years the entire debt was paid. Parish organizations and bazaars, fairs, and picnics, among other social activities, also supplemented parish income. Some of the social events proved quite profitable.[65]

As the Catholic population grew in the nineteenth century and more and more parishes were formed, lay people and parish-based societies became better organized and disciplined. Many Catholics in the diocese of Cincinnati as well as throughout the country participated in various devotional and church-supporting confraternities. In particular, German and Irish immigrants were especially active in the development of parish-based organizations and the diocese.

IMMIGRANTS
AND THE
GROWTH OF THE
DIOCESE

Purcell was an Irish bishop of a German city. Until after the Civil War, 75 percent of newly appointed bishops were foreign-born. From the 1830s to the 1860s thousands of German Catholic immigrants, unlike the Irish who tended to concentrate more in the East, made their way to the "German triangle," extending from Milwaukee to St. Louis to Cincinnati. Across the East and Midwest, Catholicism became an urban church as immigrants flooded the cities. Cincinnati's population nearly doubled every ten years in the first half of the nineteenth century. Whereas Catholicism in most nations of Europe and in the Middle East was influenced by their respective cultures and was culturally quite homogeneous, in the United States it was different. This was especially true in the diocese of Cincinnati. Well into the second half of the nineteenth century, among the German, Irish, French, and Dutch immigrants, the Irish and the German Catholics had the most visible impact on the local church. Catholicism in the diocese steadily moved in the direction of becoming a church of immigrants. Both groups, like later immigrants, had to adjust to the American ways of life while attempting to preserve their own unique European heritages. Because of the needs of immigrant life, local Catholicism increasingly developed religious and ethnic solidarity and institutional separatism.[1]

GERMAN CATHOLICS

In the diocese Cincinnati had the largest concentration of German Catholics. They, along with German Jews, Protestants, and freethinkers, were the dominant ethnic group to settle in southwest Ohio in the nineteenth century. For part of the 1840s German Catholics were coming into the city at the rate of two hundred or more a day. In 1841 the historian Charles Cist estimated the German population of Cincinnati to be 14,163 of the 46,382 inhabitants of the city. Whereas he estimated three-fourths of them to be Catholic, Purcell thought that at least two-thirds were Catholic. The estimate from baptismal statistics for 1840 indicates a total of 13,344, among whom were 8,800 Germans and 4,544 English, including the Irish.[2]

Catholic parishes traditionally had been organized territorially. People living in a designated area belonged to the same parish. As in other urban centers in the nineteenth century, this posed a problem for the local church. German and Irish Catholics did not want to worship together. Instances of ethnic conflict occurred between them. When the Irish and German Catholics shared St. Peter in Chains Cathedral in the early 1830s, one German chronicler wrote that the Germans endured "arrogant treatment" from the Irish. An example of such treatment took place in the fall of 1833 when Frederic Rese, who had been appointed bishop of Detroit, received episcopal ordination in the Cincinnati cathedral. The ceremonies were held at the time designated for the Sunday Mass of English-speaking Catholics. When the German Catholics arrived in a procession to participate in the episcopal ceremony, they were locked out of the cathedral. Undaunted, the Germans broke down the front doors. The following year they built their own church.[3]

Like some bishops in the East and Midwest, Purcell responded to the challenge of ethnic diversity in his diocese by allowing the establishment of national parishes. As more Germans arrived and faced the challenge of adjusting to the American situation while preserving their own religious heritage, the national parish became the norm. Purcell acknowledged the desire for the Germans to establish churches and organizations for their own use. For his part, he would do his best to recruit German-speaking clergy and religious. As more German-born priests, religious, and lay people came to the diocese, espousing a familiar and traditional European model of Catholicism, each decade saw a gradually increasing Europeanization of local church practices.[4]

In the see city most of the Germans occupied the northern territories. As a low-lying area surrounded by hills about 400 feet high, Cincinnati consisted of a flat "west end" on one side of the basin, flat "east end" on the other, and a northern edge. The Miami and Erie Canal, today's Central Parkway route, crossed the basin about halfway between the Ohio River and the hills. German Catholics established twelve parishes between 1835 and 1870, each with a parochial school, near the Miami and Erie Canal. The German laity had a central role in the organization and development of these parishes. Purcell accommodated this lay initiative by largely leaving the direction of the German Catholic community to its clerical and lay leaders. Under the directives issued by the pragmatic Purcell in 1851, which probably confirmed the already existing arrangements in the German parishes, each German parish was to have six elected laymen who were at various times called trustees, wardens, or counselors to assist the pastor in the operation of the parish. Elected annually by the men of the parish, the trustees were to be over thirty years of age, pewholders in the church, and of good character as demonstrated by making the annual Easter communion. The age of eligibility for election by 1865 was decreased to twenty-one. Though the bishop confirmed the trustees in office and could remove them, there is no evidence that this ever happened in the diocese. The trustees met with the pastor at least once a month. As they dealt largely with administrative matters, especially the expenditure of church income, the trustees were particularly advised to pay off the parish debts. The financial records were examined annually by the vicar general and two assistant priests. By asserting their lay rights and powers, these laymen helped establish the local churches on a democratic as well as on a sound financial and material basis.[5]

The self-government that the German parishes were permitted resulted from the positive and unique relationship the Germans enjoyed with the bishop of Cincinnati. In the process, the Germans developed a rich subculture distinctive in language. During the course of the nineteenth century they established organizations and institutions that helped them keep their traditions, beliefs, and language alive as they adjusted to their new environment. Most importantly, they preserved their language in their homes, churches, and neighborhoods. "The first movement of German Catholics in a new settlement," Purcell observed, was "to build a church and a schoolhouse." Whenever possible, they heard sermons in their mother tongue and practiced the devotions and customs of western Germany. Religious affiliation proved essential as an organizing force.[6]

Purcell often praised the German Catholic parishioners on their accomplishments. Their faith and schools impressed him. "The proximity of the churches to one another," Purcell wrote, "the length of the processions with banners and sacred music" that went to meet him from place to place, "and the great numbers confirmed as well as communicants and attendance at DAILY MASS" testified to their piety. Pleased with their initiative and support of educational and church functions, he permitted the German Catholic clergy and laity to direct their own affairs with rare intervention by his office. In each parish Germans established parish societies, or vereins, that helped support the "ornamenting and embellishing" of the church as well as connect the members more closely to the religious practices of the parish church. Cornerstone laying and church and school dedications in German Catholic parishes were always attended by public processions. While visiting the Minster congregation in the winter of 1840, the bishop commented in the *Catholic Telegraph* on some of the people's qualities. The German was "attached by association and grace . . . to the religious customs of his native land," he wrote, and "loves to hold a piece of ground that he can call his own; he suffers inconceivable privations that he may pay for it." Before purchasing a home or farm German Catholics were advised to take into consideration church and school, to purchase in those areas where a large Catholic population could be found. Without proximity to a church, Purcell argued, a family's property could lose "more than half of its value."[7]

When Canon Josef Salzbacher of Vienna visited the United States in 1842, he reported that the diocese of Cincinnati had more German-speaking Catholics than any other diocese in the country. Even though there were more Catholics in the eastern dioceses than in the western ones, Cincinnati was a center of German Catholicism. A decade later a visitor to the Queen City observed that the east side and northern periphery of the city teemed "with German faces" and that one could "hear the dialects of Baden, Swabia, Bavaria, Austria, Frankfurt, Berlin, Plattdeutsch, and also some Yiddish." Making reference to the German churches built from German money, he noted that "in no other city of the Union have I observed such a deep Catholicity, so much zeal for the glory of God, such beautiful harmony among our German brethren of the Faith, as in Cincinnati." Though the eastern side of the city never became exclusively German, the predominance of Germans and their culture had such an impact that it became known as "Over-the-Rhine," Cincinnati's little Germany. As in other mid-nineteenth century cities, most of the poor people and new arrivals tended to live on the outer boundary of the city, whereas the wealthier residents lived in the center.[8]

From the start Purcell established a good rapport with the German Catholics. Shortly after his arrival in Cincinnati, Purcell decided in 1833 to build Cincinnati's first German Catholic Church. In light of the fact that the diocese had already spent the money raised by the German Catholics to build a church, the bishop began soliciting pledges and recorded in his journal that "the Germans . . . subscribed liberally towards the erection of the contemplated church." Anticipating the spread of the German-speaking population to the northern edge of Cincinnati, as land there was less expensive than in the city, Purcell purchased land on West Fifth Street for $3,000. On Sunday, October 5, 1834, Holy Trinity Church, the second Catholic Church in the city and the first national parish for German Catholics west of the Alleghenies, was dedicated. It was built "in a high and healthy part of the city," the *Catholic Telegraph* wrote, "commanding a noble view of the green hills of Kentucky." The ceremony proved to be the most solemn event that so far

FIG 6. Holy Trinity Church in Cincinnati in the 1890s

had taken place in the see city. Bishops Purcell and Flaget, ten priests, sixteen seminarians, and members of the laity were in attendance.[9]

The dedication of Holy Trinity Church was a very special moment for the bishop. Less than a year after beginning his episcopal duties he had helped form a new parish, with Henry Damian Juncker as pastor, for the Germans. The total cost of building the church, including the lot, was $18,000. Shortly after its founding a parochial school was started in the church that recruited non-Catholic as well as Catholic Germans. In its first year the parish school attracted some 150 pupils. By 1840 there were four laymen in the school, teaching as many as 350 children per day. "It was amusing to see a little Irish boy," the *Catholic Telegraph* reported, "reading and praying in German, with as Saxon a tongue and as pure and intelligent a cadence as any of his young compeers."[10]

Shortly after the founding of Holy Trinity parish German Catholics again expressed the desire for a separate boys' orphanage for Cincinnati's German Catholics. Following the bishop's unsuccessful attempt in the mid-1830s to

get the Sisters of Charity to establish a separate boys' orphanage for Cincinnati's German Catholics, John Henni, now pastor of Holy Trinity Church,
interested several parishioners in the matter. In less than two years after the
establishment of the parish Purcell had summoned the twenty-eight-year-
old Henni, who had been serving the German parish at Canton and surrounding mission stations, to replace Juncker as pastor. There had been a
falling out over some now unknown issue between the trustees of the church
and Juncker. In January 1837 Henni called a parish meeting for the purpose
of forming the St. Aloysius Orphan Society. The thirty founding members
agreed to pay a membership fee of twenty-five cents per month for the care
of the orphans. The growth of the St. Aloysius Orphan Society, headed by
the layman J. B. Germann, was very rapid. In two months' time it had 155
dues-paying members. The organization placed the boys in its charge in
German family homes until such time an orphanage could be secured.[11]

Toward that end, the orphan society decided to publish the *Wahrheitsfre-
und,* the first German Catholic newspaper in the country, to help obtain
funds for the care of the orphans. The great increase of the German Catholic
population and its interest in preserving its own language led to the
Wahrheitsfreund publication. In the midst of German Protestants and a German-speaking Jewish community, the German Catholics in Cincinnati comprised the largest religious subculture. Henni had thought for some time that
they needed their own newspaper. Under the editorship of Henni, the first
publication of *Wahrheitsfreund* was on July 20, 1837. Its surplus funds were
regularly paid to the St. Aloysius Orphan Association. Even though Germans spoke a number of different dialects, the *Wahrheitsfreund* became a
valuable medium of communication among the scattered German-speaking
Catholics, instructing its readers in doctrine and religious practice and
informing them of the state of Catholicity locally and throughout the United States. By midcentury it was one of four German language newspapers in
Cincinnati. Catholic Germans were held together by a common consciousness of kinship and by a network of churches, schools, voluntary associations,
and newspapers.[12]

In the spring of 1839 the St. Aloysius Orphan Society succeeded in purchasing a nine-room house on West Sixth Street, close to the school, to
accommodate the orphanage for boys. The orphanage opened on June 21st,
the feast of St. Aloysius. Though two competent lay women were paid to run
the orphanage from 1839 to 1842, Purcell wanted religious personnel in the
institution. In the spring of 1842 the bishop again approached the Sisters of
Charity at Emmitsburg, requesting that the sisters, who spoke German, take
charge of the orphanage that then numbered twenty-seven. The orphan boys
"extend their hands to you imploring you not to abandon them," he wrote.

"[F]or God's sake, write soon to tell me that the Sisters are coming for St. Aloysius' Asylum." He assured the mother superior that even though the management of German congregations by lay trustees had been a source of much anxiety in some dioceses, there were no such problems in Cincinnati. By late summer three sisters were assigned to the orphanage. However, their stay was short-lived.[13]

The Sisters of Charity took charge of St. Aloysius Orphanage from 1842 to 1846, caring for as many as fifty-three boys per year. In late 1845, however, Louis Deluol, Sulpician superior of the Sisters of Charity, informed Purcell that by order of Emmitsburg authorities, who prohibited members of their order from operating a boys' orphanage, the sisters in Cincinnati were to leave the orphanage. Both Purcell and Bishop Hughes of New York, who was experiencing similar difficulties with the Sisters of Charity relinquishment of boys' orphanages in his diocese, appealed unsuccessfully to Emmitsburg. Like some other communities, the Sisters of Charity—who were at the time taking steps to become affiliated with the Daughters of Charity in France—clung to the letter of the French rule that described the work of the sisters as caring for girls. Some thought that contact with young boys endangered the virtue of the women religious. To the German Catholics' disappointment, in 1846 the Sisters of Charity were reassigned to other missions. Unsuccessful in replacing the sisters at the German orphanage with another religious order, the orphanage had to rely again on lay personnel, not unlike what the Catholic Germans continued to do in their parochial boys' schools. Henry Schulhof was appointed superintendent of the orphanage. He and his wife received a nominal salary per year in addition to their board and lodging. In 1850 the St. Aloysius Orphan Society opened a girls' orphanage on Abigail Street, now East Twelfth, with Mary Wiggermann in charge. In the fall of 1851 the St. Aloysius boys' orphanage was destroyed by fire, killing three of the 132 children. The St. Aloysius Orphan Society immediately resolved "to provide the children again with a convenient and comfortable home." In 1856 the boys' orphanage was moved to new accommodations on sixty acres of land in the suburb of Bond Hill. Five years later the girls joined them. In May 1877 the German-speaking Sisters of Notre Dame from Cleveland took charge of the orphanage.[14]

In 1840 Henni and his two assistants at Holy Trinity Church attended to the spiritual needs of approximately 9,000 Germans in the parish, nearly double the number of German Catholics in the city at the time of Purcell's installation. Almost twice as many German Catholics were being baptized each year than in the English-speaking church. The continuing influx of thousands of German immigrants into the city made it imperative that another church be erected for the German-speaking people. As more and more Germans settled in Over-the-Rhine, Holy Trinity Church, located in the lower part of Cincinnati, was far from the emerging German neighborhood. There was "scarcely a city in the United States where two new churches are wanted more than in Cincinnati," the *Catholic Telegraph* wrote. It argued that both the English-speaking cathedral and Holy Trinity Church were insufficient "to contain" the overflowing Catholic population. "[I]t is obvious to every observing mind," Purcell wrote, "that the places of our tents must be still further enlarged and their cords lengthened on every side." The *Catholic Telegraph* also expressed concern that the German-speaking people, who were better organized than the Irish and English-speaking Catholics, would more likely "outstrip us in the race" of building a new church.[15]

The diocesan paper's prediction was well founded. In 1841 a committee of German Catholics purchased land in the city in Purcell's name and selected the site for St. Mary Church on Thirteenth between Clay and Main Streets in Over-the-Rhine. Purcell made a substantial contribution of about $7,000 toward the building of the church, and the congregation assumed the debt for the remaining $7,000. What the parishioners could not pay in cash they contributed in work. The parishioners themselves as brick makers manufactured the bricks that were used for the church; the women fashioned them, and the men baked them in homemade kilns. A procession of the clergy, members of the St. Peter Benevolent Society and St. Aloysius Orphan Society, other laypersons, and schoolchildren dressed in white marched through the streets and attended St. Mary's dedication ceremonies on July 3, 1842. The ceremony involved the entire Catholic community, both German and English. Purcell addressed the congregation in English, Henni in German.[16]

Clement Hammer, a recent arrival from Bohemia and assistant to Henni at Holy Trinity Church, was appointed pastor of St. Mary parish. Having made acquaintance with Father Joseph Ferneding at Vincennes, Hammer prevailed on him to leave his diocese to come to Cincinnati and become his assistant. When Henni became the first bishop of Milwaukee in 1844, Purcell appointed Ferneding vicar general and put him in charge of St. Aloysius Orphanage. Henni's departure from Cincinnati was a great loss to the diocese. He had accomplished much, especially among the German Catholics. The local church had come to appreciate his ability and talents, especially as editor of the *Wahrheitsfreund*. Moreover, St. Aloysius had now lost not only his services but also his guiding spirit. Six years after the founding of St. Mary Church, three German-speaking Sisters of Notre Dame de Namur, who had arrived in Cincinnati in 1840 from Belgium, were placed in charge of the education of the girls of St. Mary's. The education of the boys of the parish was begun in 1852 when brothers of the Society of Mary, who had recently arrived in Cincinnati from France, agreed to conduct the school.[17]

As more German immigrants in the 1840s moved to Over-the-Rhine, Ferneding and parishioners at St. Mary's helped organize in the fall of 1844 another German Catholic congregation in the city. Statistics for 1844 reveal that at St. Mary's there were 521 baptisms, 167 marriages, and 252 burials as compared to 400 baptisms, 70 marriages, 150 burials in the cathedral parish and 270 baptisms, 78 marriages, and 118 burials in the Holy Trinity parish. That year German Catholics purchased land in Over-the-Rhine and established St. John the Baptist parish. On March 25 more than twelve thousand people, headed by Purcell and the clergy, marched in procession to lay the cornerstone of the new church. This was the bishop's first public appearance in Cincinnati in his episcopal robes. As the procession progressed along Vine Street, "every door, every window, crowded with respectful and seemingly delighted spectators," the *Catholic Telegraph* wrote, ". . . the crosses, banners, vestments sparkling in the sun-beams, the clergy chanting in solemn tone the psalms. . . . [And] two excellent bands of music, one in front, the other in the rear, alternately playing slow and measured marches," produced an effect that "was truly imposing." Five months later in a parish meeting the community resolved to build a school. In November St. John Baptist Church was dedicated. By 1860 St. John's had become the largest parish of the diocese. From 1849 to 1859 it witnessed 7,814 baptisms and 1,826 marriages, an annual average of 710 and 166, respectively.[18]

As the northern side of Cincinnati was filling with new arrivals from Germany, Purcell appealed for more German-speaking missionary priests and religious from Europe. In 1840 there were thirty-eight priests in the diocese. Five of them were from Germany. In addition to the five natives from Germany, there were five others who spoke German. Though all ten devoted their time to the care of the German Catholics in Ohio, the diocese needed more German-speaking priests. As most Germans did not understand English, it especially made confessions difficult. In the early 1840s Bishop Purcell requested German priests from the superiors of the Jesuit and Redemptorist Orders. Though neither request at the time was fulfilled, more individual German priests did come to the diocese. By 1844 there were five German priests and six German teachers at Cincinnati, and the communities at Glandorf, Minster, Columbus, Zanesville, Dayton, Lancaster, Canton, and Chillicothe each had a German priest and a German school. Though the local church reaped some success in attracting German priests, not every diocese was that fortunate. Bishop Peter Kenrick of St. Louis asked Purcell if he could spare one of his "excellent German priests," pointing out that his diocese did not have an "efficient" one, nor a separate church for the more than 4,000 German Catholics. Purcell did not oblige.[19]

It was this need for more German priests that brought the German-speaking religious order of Franciscans into the diocese of Cincinnati. On his visit to Europe in 1839 Purcell had obtained the brown-robed Franciscan, Francis Louis Huber of Bavaria. Huber, who five years later would become pastor of Holy Trinity parish, was one of seven priests who came to the United States with the bishop. Unable to secure further help from the Bavarian Province, Purcell appealed successfully to another German-speaking province, that of St. Leopold of Tyrol, Austria. As a consequence of that visit, Father William Unterthiner arrived in Cincinnati in October 1844 and became one of the most eloquent orators of the day.[20]

Over time Huber encountered difficulties with the German Catholics of Holy Trinity parish. Parishioners found him too authoritarian and accused him of controlling the parish money and making expenditures without authorization from the trustees. After Purcell asked him in 1848 to leave Holy Trinity Church, and he refused, the bishop removed him. Huber, who had some lay supporters, appealed both to Archbishop Eccleston of Baltimore and to Roman officials. Though they disapproved of his conduct, they refused to interfere. At the December 1848 diocesan synod, the thirty-seven priests in attendance condemned him and urged his departure in signed statements that were published in the *Catholic Telegraph* and *Wahrheitsfreund*. As tension mounted, Huber's Franciscan superiors ordered him to leave the diocese of Cincinnati and return to Bavaria. The case went to the religious courts and Huber was finally ejected from the rectory by force. He left Cincinnati in 1850.[21]

As the German Catholic population continued to grow in Cincinnati, more separate churches for the German Catholics were built. By 1847 Cincinnati had six German parishes, adding St. Philomena's on the south side of East Third Street, St. Joseph's on the west side of town below the western hills, and St. Michael's in lower Price Hill to the previous three. From 1843 to 1848 there was an increase of 111 percent in the number of baptisms in the German parishes of the city, from 787 to 1,661. That was twice the number of baptisms in Cincinnati's English-speaking churches. From St. Joseph parish there developed in the succeeding years the German parishes of St. Augustine, St. Anthony, St. Henry, and St. Stanislaus, all in the western end. Under the guidance of vicar general Ferneding, German-speaking Catholics formed St. Paul parish in 1848 in Over-the-Rhine. After the trustees of the parish purchased real estate, they subdivided it into residential lots that they sold, and with the proceeds they helped pay for the land and the construction of the church. Other German parishes like St. Michael in lower Price Hill and St. Anthony in Madisonville also sold lots to defray some of the parish expenses. The bishop, through the *Catholic Telegraph,* encouraged English-speaking as well as German parishes to speculate in lots "for the advancement of religion" in the diocese. By 1850 the Franciscans had also helped organize the parishes of St. Clement in St. Bernard and the Fourteen Martyrs in Reading.[22]

Under the supervision of Edward Purcell, the bishop's brother, the archdiocese in the early 1850s built St. Augustine Church near the convent of the Ursuline Sisters on Bank Street, serving both as a chapel for the Ursulines and as a parish church. The congregation consisted of English-speaking as well as German Catholics. Because of the influx of German immigrants in the community, however, in 1857 the parish was transferred to the German-speaking Catholics, for which they paid the archdiocese $15,000 in three years at six percent interest. Purcell also attached the condition that the English-speaking parishioners who remained in the area would "always have the right to assist at . . . Mass, to rent seats, to receive the Sacraments and to have the pastor . . . assist them with the holy rites of the Church when in danger of death." In the fall of 1869, German Catholics bought a meeting-house of the Disciples of Christ, a Protestant denomination, on the southwest corner of Walnut and Eighth Streets. The purchase price was $30,000, and the property was transferred to Purcell. After a few renovations it was named in honor of St. Louis on March 13, 1870. On the day of the dedication about 2,000 people marched in a parade, consisting of six divisions of German Catholic societies, two of English, and one of Italian. In the shelter of these parishes, German Catholics found nurture and care and a strong sense of identity. All of them, but the Church of the Immaculata, were the products of the initiative of German Catholics who participated in fund-raising and building committees.[23]

Wanting to dedicate a church to the Virgin Mary, Purcell in 1859 had taken the initiative in building for German Catholics Immaculate Conception Church, commonly called Immaculata, in Mount Adams, one of the city's oldest and most conspicuous hilltop neighborhoods. The archbishop provided the ground and the stone, donated $10,000, and urged Catholics to donate generously to its erection. "When this Beacon Light shines over the city," Purcell wrote, "let every one who sees it remember with pleasure the help he gave to place it on its watch-tower." Perched high above the surrounding countryside, Immaculata commanded a panoramic view and was removed from the noise of the city below.[24]

In 1871 the seventy-one-year-old Purcell was delighted to hear the news that the German-speaking Passionist Fathers agreed to take charge of Immaculata. In March 1872 the order also opened a mission at the cathedral for the Italian Catholics of the city. That same year they acquired the old observatory property, just two blocks west of the church. The land had formerly been a portion of the estate of Nicholas Longworth, who had given the four-acre plot to the Cincinnati Astronomical Society for an observatory. At the same time that the order in 1873 remodeled the observatory building into a monastery, it built Holy Cross Church in Mount Adams for the Irish and Italian Catholics residing there. The congregation of the Immaculata had been mixed, being composed largely of Germans, Irish, and a few Italians. The Passionist Fathers attended to both churches in Mount Adams.[25]

As the Franciscans searched for a location for a convent of their order, the St. Clement congregation in St. Bernard presented them with land and a contribution of $800. The Franciscans were resolved to combine the furthering of the monastic life and vocation with active work in the ministry. As early as 1851, Purcell had hoped the Franciscans, who had become increasingly more involved in the local German community, would establish a monastery in the see city. But when the Franciscan William Unterthiner died in 1857 there appeared to be no hope for the Franciscans to establish a monastery and firm foundation in America. Consequently, their superior ordered the recall of all the Franciscans from Cincinnati. But the local Franciscans, with Purcell's support, wanted to remain in Cincinnati. Not only did the archbishop give them permission to open an academy and seminary, but also transferred in perpetuity to them the property of St. John Baptist Church and land owned by the archdiocese at Vine and Liberty Streets in the east end of the city. The church and parish of St. Francis Seraph with a monastery and novitiate, a place where persons who had entered the order resided, were established on the site of the first Catholic church and cemetery in Cincinnati. In 1859 the Franciscans' mission was elevated to the status of a custody, or vice province, the first step in the foundation of a province. Father Otto Jair was appointed *custos,* or superior, of the new establishment.[26]

Throughout the remainder of Purcell's administration, the Franciscans were extensively involved in the expansion of the local church. Under the supervision of the Franciscan Candid Koslowski, the first Polish parish in the archdiocese, St. Stanislaus, was organized in 1873. After purchasing the Lutheran Church at the corner of Liberty and Cutter Streets in the west end in the spring of 1875, the St. Stanislaus Parochial Society immediately renovated the church for religious services. Until then the Poles had been scattered throughout Cincinnati and had been attending services at the nearest Catholic church within their reach. The Franciscans also provided chaplains to various archdiocesan institutions, such as hospitals, orphanages, prisons, and convents, which needed priests on a part-time basis. Otto Jair was a prominent figure in this period. In addition to working tirelessly on Franciscan matters, he also took part in archdiocesan affairs. He was appointed vicar general of the archdiocese of Cincinnati for German-speaking Catholics in 1872, a position he held until 1883.[27]

By midcentury German Catholics were also well concentrated in southern and rural western Ohio, in and around Norwalk in northern Ohio, in Canton in the northeastern part of the state, and in such communities as Lancaster, Columbus, and Chillicothe in central Ohio. In virtually every mission of the diocese, there were German Catholic families. In light of the scarcity of German-speaking priests, that posed a problem for the diocese. Father John Doherty, English-speaking pastor at Massillon, wrote to Purcell in the spring of 1844 that his parishes were "almost entirely German who can neither speak nor understand English and consequently are incapable of deriving any profit from my instructions." The diocese had to rely, especially during the Easter and Christmas seasons, on the priests from the larger centers of the German Catholic population to care for them.[28]

In the 1840s Purcell scored a coup. He obtained the priests of the Congregation of the Precious Blood from Alsace for the German parishes in the northwestern section of Ohio. On New Year's Day in 1844, seven priests and seven brothers of the congregation with their superior Francis de Sales Brunner arrived in Cincinnati. They took charge of St. John the Baptist parish and founded the convent of Maria Stein. The community then took over the Church of St. Augustine at Minster, which had been attended to by the secular clergy since 1834. During Purcell's administration the order played an important part in the development of the diocese, especially in the smaller towns and rural communities in Mercer, Auglaize, and Shelby Counties. In 1861 the Precious Blood priests, led by Father Joseph Dwenger and a Catholic layman, also founded and operated St. Charles Borromeo Seminary at Carthagena. The same year that the clergy arrived in Cincinnati, two sisters of the Precious Blood and a novice also arrived on July 22nd in the diocese and opened a school at the little mission of St. Alphonse in Peru. This was the beginning of the activity of the Precious Blood sisters in American education. Purcell's success in obtaining the Precious Blood fathers, brothers, and sisters helped address the needs of German Catholics in northern and western Ohio. Bishop Blanc of New Orleans probably echoed other bishops' sentiments when he wrote to Purcell in January 1845: "I congratulate you and your good German Catholics, for such an acquisition—indeed, you beat us all!"[29]

ESTABLISHMENT OF OTHER IMMIGRANT PARISHES

As the diocese of Cincinnati underwent expansion in the 1840s the bishop and members of his congregation also paid special attention to the potato failure in Ireland. The famine in Purcell's native land in the years 1845 to 1847 brought waves of Irish English-speaking immigrants to American shores, more particularly to Cincinnati. This immigration helped increase the proportion of English-speaking Catholics. Between 1843 and 1852 the number of baptisms in the Catholic English-speaking churches in the episcopal city jumped from 32 percent of the total number of baptisms to 44 percent. As the Irish famine worsened, the *Catholic Telegraph,* like so many other Catholic newspapers at this time, encouraged relief sent to Ireland. By August 1848 the diocesan paper, though cautious in its stance, became more supportive of the use of physical force in the revolution in Ireland, even suggesting financial assistance to help the cause. "[W]hen we consider the horrible character of the oppression to which the people have been subjected," it wrote, "we cannot condemn the appeal to arms no matter what may be the result." By the following month, however, Purcell put a stop to the editorial policy of the *Catholic Telegraph* on the Irish issue, indicating doubt about the success of the revolution. He argued that if the millions of Irish "at home" could not succeed, then "the hundreds, or thousands here, cannot accomplish more. Money sent to such a people, unless to buy bread for the starving, is absolutely thrown away. . . . [W]e can do [them] . . . no good."[30]

From that point on the diocesan paper advised the faithful to attend to the needs of the Irish settling in the diocese, arguing that charity should begin at home. The Irish Emigrant Society was formed to guard the newcomers "against vicious associations and to provide them with employment." Among those who came to the Queen City were the bishop's mother and his sisters Catherine and Margaret, arriving in the summer of 1847. The bishop was able to place them with the Ursuline Sisters, who had taken charge of St. Martin Convent in Brown County in 1845. Mrs. Purcell and Catherine remained with the Ursulines, whereas Margaret got married and subsequently moved to New Orleans.[31]

Before long the cathedral church was not large enough to accommodate the many newcomers. As many Irish Catholics resided in the first, third, and fourth wards on the southwestern edge and in the most undesirable parts of the see city along the riverfront, Purcell oversaw in 1850 the building of St. Patrick Church on Third and Mill Streets. Two decades later it also became necessary to relieve the overtaxed capacities of the two city's English-speaking churches. Out of St. Patrick parish and the cathedral came the parish of the Atonement on West Third Street in 1870. The church was completed in 1873. Another church that grew out of St. Patrick parish was the Blessed Sacrament Church in lower Price Hill, closer to the Ohio River and farther west than the Atonement parish, to accommodate the more than 100 Irish families that had settled below Price Hill. Father John Mackey, the pastor of

St. Patrick's, helped establish in 1874 a combination church, school, and parsonage.[32]

Like their German counterparts, religion for the Irish was central to their way of life. The parish church, which was a basis for group solidarity and pride, was an important identifying mark in their neighborhood. Whereas among German Catholics there was a strong tradition of lay involvement in parish affairs, the Irish had long been accustomed to being more dependent on the clergy on religious matters. They lacked a tradition of parish self-government, due in part to the leadership role played by priests in Ireland, where they served as guardians of Irish culture in the face of British rule. Moreover, since the transfer in 1822 of the ownership of ecclesiastical property to Bishop Fenwick by the Irish trustees of Christ Church, the system of lay trustees in the diocese of Cincinnati appeared to have been confined to the German parishes. Purcell's 1851 directives applied only to Germans. In 1865 Purcell distinguished between the operation of Irish and German parishes, noting that "without extending the [trustee] system where it is neither necessary, nor desired, we approve of it where it does exist." In contrast to German custom, the Irish tradition of an authoritarian clergy and deferential laity was commonplace. Though the Irish were not as active as the Germans in the organization and government of local parishes, they were by no means passive in parish life.[33]

In the mid-1850s the Jesuits began making plans to replace their little wooden St. Xavier Church, which largely attended to Irish and English-speaking Catholics, on Sycamore Street in Cincinnati. Even though a few years earlier Purcell had bought the Methodist Episcopal Church on Sycamore Street to take care of the overflow at St. Xavier, and had it dedicated to St. Thomas, the St. Xavier congregation needed a larger church. In February 1860 the work of dismantling and demolishing the St. Xavier Church began. During the demolition one of the walls fell, crushing thirteen laborers beneath its weight. At once the various Catholic congregations took up a collection for the relief of the families. In January 1861 the Jesuits held dedication ceremonies of the new St. Xavier Church. During the Civil War the archbishop bought property in the western end of the city and Catholics in the vicinity established another English-speaking parish, with St. Edward as its church.[34]

About two decades after the demolition of the old St. Xavier Church, the congregation experienced another tragedy. On Good Friday morning, April 7, 1882, a fire destroyed the interior of St. Xavier Church and steeple. William Henry Elder, then Cincinnati's coadjutor bishop, wrote about the church's "blackened walls and charred timbers." He noted that the crowds of English-speaking Catholics, who:

every Good Friday had made a pilgrimage to kiss the big crucifix, now gazed on ruins, bewailing, crying—not figuratively, but literally. The big wooden cross, 16 feet long, from the top of the steeple, falling and lying on the sidewalk, [was] muddy with the water of the engines. Spontaneously some good soul knelt and kissed the broken cross lying on the pavement. Others followed and almost all day they were kneeling on the curbstone, a dozen at a time, to kiss that cross; emblem of the ruin of their Church, and of the love of their Saviour.[35]

The total loss amounted to about $200,000. Under the leadership of the Jesuits and the pastor, Charles Driscoll, who would serve as pastor for more than thirty-five years, immediate steps were taken to rebuild the church. Contributions came in encouragingly and generously. Within two weeks, more than $40,000 were raised. By March 1883 the church had been rebuilt.

In the summer of 1852 the Lutheran Church at the corner of Liberty and Walnut Streets was purchased and converted into the first Dutch Catholic Church in the archdiocese. John Van Luytelaar was named pastor of St. Willibord Church in 1853. Seven years later the parish disbanded, and most of the few parishioners moved with Van Luytelaar to a new settlement in Missouri. Later that decade forty Catholic English-speaking families in the eastern part of Cincinnati broke away from Christ parish and helped organize in 1859, with Father Michael O'Sullivan's assistance, the parish of Holy Angels at O'Bryonville, which sat in suburban hills on the eastern side of town. Purcell provided a loan of $7,000 to help build a large church that was completed in 1861. In time Purcell cancelled the debt. This was not the first time that the archbishop assisted congregations by canceling debts owed to the archdiocese.[36]

In the midst of the growing Catholic population and increasing number of churches, the bishop's travels in the diocese in the 1840s proved more arduous and challenging. By the mid-1840s Purcell carried out his visitations in the alternate years 1844, 1846, 1848 and 1850, ranging from two months to four months in length. As before, these trips afforded him opportunities not only to strengthen relations with Catholic parishes and clergy but also to preach to non-Catholics. Throughout his life, Purcell was in demand for special occasion sermons. On his 1844 trip he preached in a Lutheran church at Lancaster, in courthouses at Woodfield, St. Clairsville, Mount Vernon, Tiffin, and Canton, and in a Methodist church at Wooster. In the odd years, he limited his visitations to about two weeks at a time, usually short trips generally in the vicinity of the see city.[37]

Purcell's visitations also enabled him to see some of the work of his missionaries firsthand. He was especially pleased with the pastoral work of the

French missionaries he had brought to his diocese from Europe. William Cheymol and Claude Gacon worked at St. Martin's in Brown County; Louis Navarron worked among the French Catholics about the present towns of Frenchtown, Versailles, and Russia in Darke and Shelby Counties and among the Irish and German workers along the Miami canal.[38]

At Greenville, southeast of Versailles, Father Navarron in late 1839 visited about a dozen Catholic families, who had built a log church that had not yet been blessed and contained no altar. Most of the settlers were French families. In the early 1830s, a number of people left France during the political storms and settled around the Versailles, Frenchtown, and Russia area in 1835. Two decades later the community purchased a United Brethren meetinghouse and was organized into a parish. Under the supervision of Navarron, who had been appointed Purcell's delegate over the large territory from Greenville to Lima, the St. Valbert log church was built three miles northeast of Versailles in 1840. Four years later, every fourth Sunday the congregation of 357 attended Mass and heard sermons in French, and occasionally in English and German as well. As the Catholic communities increased in size, owing largely to the increase of German Catholic emigrants, there was need for more and larger churches. The church at Tiffin, which Purcell visited in June 1841, "is so small," he reported in the *Catholic Telegraph,* "that not more than one third of the congregation can find place in it. This, indeed, is the case in nearly all the churches of Ohio. We are like a youth that has outgrown its clothes."[39]

The increasing number of English-speaking people in Dayton in the 1840s made possible the erection of the first English-speaking church in the city. The cornerstone of the church of St. Joseph was laid on July 11, 1847. The Benevolent Societies, one English, the other German, marched in procession to the new site. Notwithstanding the heat of the day, Protestant ministers of the various denominations attended the ceremony and listened to Purcell's talk that lasted about an hour. It was estimated that more than three thousand people from Cincinnati traveled to Dayton to witness the ceremony. The church was dedicated the following October. German Catholics and their Irish co-religionists also laid the foundation of Catholicism in the neighboring counties.[40]

Churches were being built throughout Ohio. By the time of the Civil War eighty-two churches had been built in the present diocese. When the Catholics of Wilmington intended to build St. Columbkille Church in the 1860s, a local newspaper aptly noted that the "well-known promptness and energy of that denomination in church building is a sure guaranty that they will accomplish whatever, in that line, they undertake." At times the mother churches resisted the founding of new parishes. For example, John Hahne, pastor of Emmanuel Church in Dayton, opposed the formation of Holy Trinity parish. He feared that if St. Mary and Holy Trinity were to become independent parishes Emmanuel would lose many families. During one of the tumultuous meetings Hahne declared that "all those who leave the mother church are going out of heaven." The parish was nevertheless organized and some of Emmanuel's parishioners transferred to Holy Trinity.[41]

ETHNIC ISSUES

The overwhelming majority of the newcomers to the diocese of Cincinnati clung tenaciously to the customs and language of their homelands. The deep commitment of the Germans to the preservation of their language was evident in their strong support of German instruction in both the public and Catholic schools. Separate schools were for the Germans a means of preserving the German language; preserving the German language was a means of preserving their Catholic faith. This interest on the part of the Germans, to maintain their native language, became an issue and a battleground within American Catholicism with those individuals who encouraged full assimilation into American life. Though concerned over the relationship of Catholicism with American society, Purcell did not push for full assimilation. "Here there is work enough for all Catholics of all nations," he wrote, "to do for their country and religion."[42]

Throughout Purcell's years of leadership, the diocese sought to maintain a balance on linguistic differences. In communities where there were English and German churches, "the language of the instructions," Purcell wrote, "should be only that spoken by the generality of the congregation," and that the sacraments "should be administered by English to English, by German to German." When German Catholics understood English, they had "a right," if they chose, to attach themselves to English congregations. "But English Catholics who do not understand German," Purcell argued, "are inexcusable for depriving themselves of the advantage of instruction which they can enjoy only in their own churches." At times during the course of the nineteenth century there developed feuds between English- and German-speaking Catholics in mixed parishes. Tensions between Irish and German Catholics at St. Brigid parish became apparent in the mid-1850s when the pastor forbade German priests from the Nazareth school, later named the University of Dayton, to minister to the thirty-eight German families and say Mass in the church more than twice a year.[43]

Overall, Purcell through his diocesan paper acknowledged the positive influence of Germans. "In faith," the *Catholic Telegraph* informed its English-language readers, the German and Irish emigrants "are one, [but] in almost every other disposition of mind they are distinct." In the late 1850s it also pointed out that the Germans generally supported their churches better than the Irish did. "All the German churches of the city," it wrote, "are reducing their debts." It wished it "could say the same of St. Patrick's and St. Thomas'." The *Catholic Telegraph,* likewise, praised the Germans in cultivating large tracts of land throughout the diocese. It attributed the accomplishment of this work to their "patience and frugality." It was "in these qualifications," the diocesan paper continued, "that our Irish brethren are deficient. Their minds are too quick for their hands; they do not seem to understand the only true 'progress' in which a Christian can indulge—the gradual but persevering toil by which day by day, and year by year, a man can build up a home for himself and family." The Irish tended to be poorer than the Germans, worked mostly in remote places on railroads and public works, and were less able than their co-religionists to adjust quickly to urban life.[44]

However, the Irish ordinary did come to the defense of the Irish Catholics. Though generally in favor of American political ideas and practices, Purcell criticized too much Americanization at the expense of certain ethnic traditions. At the same time that the American hierarchy contended with anti-Catholicism, there developed an internal dispute between some American bishops, including Purcell, and Orestes Brownson, a talented and famed lay leader from Boston and convert to Catholicism, on how to deal with the climate of fear and intimidation. Nativism set the stage for a vigorous defense of Catholicism by leaders of American Catholic thought. Two diametrically opposite thinkers on the subject in the 1850s were Archbishop John Hughes and Brownson. Whereas the more conservative Hughes favored a more hierarchically structured church that sought to protect the Catholic people in a frequently hostile environment, Brownson, as editor of his Boston quarterly *Brownson Quarterly Review,* consistently urged Catholics to become fully part of American life and culture. As an assimilationist, Brownson criticized the Irish Catholic immigrants for failing to distinguish sufficiently between their Catholicity and their being Irish, arguing that their lack of Americanization fanned anti-Catholicism. He told the Irish and other immigrants that they "must ultimately lose their own nationality and become assimilated in general character to the Anglo-American race."[45]

Brownson's critics, on the other hand, maintained that his extreme arguments played right into the hands of those anti-Catholics who feared excessive papal rule over American Catholics. Irish-born and native-born bishops were lined up on both sides of the quarrel. Purcell was particularly critical of Brownson's insensitivity toward the Irish. "That man," he wrote to Blanc, "is destined to be our worst enemy in these United States." Though relations between Purcell and Brownson were strained for a while, by the end of the year they dropped their quarrel, and relations between them improved. By 1857 the diocesan paper, now pleased with "the tone and spirit" of *Brownson's Quarterly Review,* expressed the hope that it would be found in the home of every Catholic family.[46]

Though Purcell criticized Brownson on his Irish insensitivity, the archbishop and the *Catholic Telegraph* occasionally reprimanded the Irish on their wakes and intemperance. Though the religious hierarchy was generally pleased with the "Sabbath-keeping character" of the Irish, there was concern over the disorderly conduct of the newly arrived immigrants. Even though there were complaints about German drinking and picnics, their communities were more stable. Church authorities disapproved of the "scandalous manner" in which the funerals of a certain portion of the Irish Catholic population were conducted. It condemned the "unchristian" practice of smoking tobacco, drinking whiskey, and "passing round indecent jokes and jests, at the waking of the dead, and not entering the church to pray for the departed . . . , and stopping on the way to and from the graveyard to drink." Purcell tried to put an end to these disorders. His understanding of ecclesiastical authority necessitated a strong approach to ecclesiastical discipline. The archbishop went so far as to establish a policy that there would never be more than six carriages at a funeral, preferably two or three. He urged all Catholics, with the exception of the family members of the deceased, to stay away from wakes and that the surviving relatives would walk gravely and prayerfully at the funeral. The fact that the diocesan paper often had to remind its readers of the church's policy suggests that the faithful did not fully adhere to the archbishop's directive.[47]

Though less faultfinding of the conduct of the German Catholics than that of the Irish, Purcell was critical of those German-speaking priests unable to understand or speak English. In the 1850s there were several places in the archdiocese where German-speaking priests could barely—if at all—understand English. Visiting Mercer County in the summer of 1852 Purcell observed that "hardly one of the German priests, though so faithful and devoted to those of their own tongue, is capable of hearing a confession in English." He was hopeful, he wrote in the *Catholic Telegraph,* that the German priests would master English, "as a powerful means of extending their usefulness to American Catholics and Protestants—for German priests should think not only of preserving but of propagating the faith." Ideally, thought Purcell, German priests would be able to speak the English language and be sympathetic to American values. Two years later the archdiocese sponsored a separate retreat for about twelve diocesan German priests who could not speak English. Like himself, Purcell wanted European priests to become Americanized.[48]

At the same time that he expressed concern over German parochialism, Purcell proved sensitive to German finances. Though the archbishop, like many of his fellow bishops, found some of the lay trustees too self-asserting, Purcell dealt with them prudently. His management of financial issues is a good example. As the number of Catholic churches and schools continued to increase, the American bishops tried to find regular means of support. In the early 1850s Archbishop Francis Patrick Kenrick of Baltimore suggested to his episcopal colleagues that one-tenth to one-third of the parish revenues be assessed for episcopal support. Though some of Purcell's suffragan bishops were receptive to it, Purcell thought otherwise. "The Germans, I am quite sure," he wrote to Kenrick, would "never consent to give a tenth of the revenues of their churches. And in my opinion it ought not to be expected from them, much less exacted." Although Purcell could have used the additional revenue, he felt there would be "a hue and cry raised against him . . . that would injure Religion and the bishop more than the money could do him good." Besides, he thought the German congregations should be assessed much less. He took into consideration not only their revenue, but their "indebtedness and liabilities for the support" of their own pastors, schools, and churches.[49]

Though Purcell overall was "[m]uch pleased" with the accomplishments of the Germans, occasionally on matters of church authority they displeased him. At the beginning of his administration he made reference to "the absurd pretension, especially of stupid & quarrelsome Germans, to elect their pastors like the heretics do." And at times he had to rebuke formally some German congregations for defying their pastors. Questions of authority and control within the church have been lively throughout American history. Purcell was well aware that one of the most challenging problems the American church faced was lay trusteeship in the German parishes. Throughout the nineteenth century, German lay trustees were actively involved in the decision-making process. Church congregations elected a board of trustees who were responsible for the management and disposition of church property. Many times these lay trustees felt they also had the right to select and dismiss their pastors at will. Unlike in Europe, where in some places lay patronage exercised that power, in the new nation, consistent with popular republicanism, congregations could exercise such authority. Though the local church in the nineteenth century witnessed a gradual shift from a congregational model of the parish to a clerical model, aided by the significant increase of a foreign-born clergy, the shift was slower and less noticeable in the German than in the Irish parishes. The latter generally accepted the hierarchical concept of the church.[50]

Though the uproar over trusteeship was largely in the East, Cincinnati was also touched by it. Cincinnati Catholics largely escaped the feuds between German trustees and the local bishop in such cities as New York, Philadelphia, Buffalo, and Cleveland. Instead of trustees or wardens owning parish property in the diocese of Cincinnati, Purcell did. This was consistent with the precedent set by Bishop Fenwick in the transference of the legal title to Christ Church in 1825 and the decrees passed by the first provincial council of Baltimore in 1829. The bishops had legislated against the laity holding titles to ecclesiastical properties. When forming a parish any land or buildings acquired were deeded to the bishop. His approval was also needed for any future construction. Though Purcell owned the property, its care was entrusted to the trustees. But not all German Catholics in the see city were pleased with the arrangement. In the early 1840s the diocese witnessed a battle between some German parishioners and Purcell over who should hold title to church property. In 1842 Bishop Purcell had purchased slightly more than nineteen acres of land in Price Hill for St. Joseph cemetery for all Catholics. In January 1843 Edward Purcell deeded one-half of the tract to a corporation directed by German laymen, the German Catholic Cemetery Association. The association then bought property in Fairmount, where St. Peter cemetery was established. In 1853 the archbishop bought more than sixty-one acres of land in Price Hill in the western portion of the city and consecrated most of it for cemetery purposes in August 1854, also calling it St. Joseph cemetery. In 1880 the two St. Joseph cemeteries, the old and the new, became incorporated as the St. Joseph Cemetery Association.[51]

Shortly after his return from Europe in 1843, Purcell encountered opposition to diocesan control over church properties from some of the trustees of St. Mary parish and of the German Catholic Cemetery Association of Cincinnati. This faction favored lay control of parochial fiscal concerns. Attempting to assert their independence from the bishop, the association secured more than sixteen hundred signatures and petitioned the state legislature for incorporation, changing its name in December 1843 to the German Catholic Congregation of Cincinnati. The following month about two thousand German Catholics met in St. Mary Church to protest the effort at lay incorporation. At this meeting, which according to the *Wahrheitsfreund* was "the largest that had ever been held by German Catholics in the West," strong presentations were given by Henni, at the time bishop-elect of Milwaukee, and other loyal German clergy. They successfully drew up resolutions condemning the efforts for independent incorporation, which Henni described as "highly uncatholic." The impending plans of the trustee group never materialized.[52]

In the February 1, 1844, issue of the *Wahrheitsfreund* an article appeared urging that the administration of the temporalities could be handled by a committee of lay people, but deeds for church property should continue to be held by the bishop. A few months later the *Catholic Telegraph* clearly expressed the diocese's position on the relationship of the Catholic Church and the authority of its people. "The line is broad and clearly marked where her power commences and the obedience of the people begins," the diocesan paper editorialized. "Every property of a religious character may be held in trust by the Laity, but the church MUST BE FREE. We will allow no encroachments on them. The INCOME of those churches is in the hands of the people; they see how the money is disposed of, that not one penny of it never [*sic*] comes into the hands of the Bishop; they have the administration of the affairs and the disposal of the money, but here they must stop."[53]

For some time Purcell had been concerned over the existing method of holding property in the name of the bishop. All property in the diocese except that of religious orders was held in his name. Purcell feared liability for parish debts. "I am frightened," he wrote to Bishop Hughes in 1840, "at the idea of 80 & 40's of acres, not to say 1000's, in my own name." In preparation for the upcoming Fourth Provincial Council of Baltimore that year, he proposed that the hierarchy discuss the issue of property. "Can anything be done," he wrote to Archbishop Eccleston, "to exonerate bishops from the care of Church property & the risk of loss if forced to pay debts contracted by clergymen, whom the law may look upon as their agents and by whose acts they are consequently bound?"[54]

At the same time that Purcell was engaged in the dispute with some of the trustees of the German Catholic Cemetery Association, some German Catholics in the United States complained that they were not receiving their proportionate share of contributions made by the Society for the Propagation of the Faith to the American hierarchy. In early 1844 the Society sent a circular to the American bishops, relaying the charges. Because of these complaints the Society now found it necessary to specify some of its allocations toward German projects. It sent 10,000 francs ($2,000) to Purcell for St. Mary's. Purcell, who did not want to jeopardize any assistance in the future, understood the delicate position that the Society found itself in. Upset over the accusations, Purcell responded angrily, yet cautiously, to the circular the same day that he received it. Two days later, still fuming over the complaints, he wrote a second letter to the French Society, stoutly defending the American hierarchy as the "most zealous, disinterested, [and] devoted" that he knew. On the eve of the Provincial Council of 1846, Purcell recommended to Archbishop Eccleston that he write "a strong" pastoral on "Church Authority & the obedience due to it, . . . to check the growing licentiousness of some perverse minds & enlighten the ignorant in danger of seduction by their bad example and persuasion."[55]

By the end of the decade he was again embroiled in controversy with the trustees of the St. Peter's Cemetery Association. The trustees defied the bishop's instruction to disallow the burial of persons not in communion with the church. On September 9, 1848, Purcell placed the St. Peter cemetery under interdict, which prohibited Cincinnati Catholics loyal to the church's authority from burying their dead in the cemetery thereafter. That day the ordinary's decree was read from all the pulpits of all the city's German parishes. Most German Catholics complied with the bishop's order. The dispute with the trustees continued for the next few years, forcing Purcell, as he put it to Blanc, to speak against this "small band of radical Germans, miscalled Catholics."[56]

Notwithstanding the few conflicts between German trustees and Purcell, overall relations between the Cincinnati ordinary and German Catholics were positive. In addition to allowing the creation of national parishes and the establishment of three more German cemeteries during the remainder of his term, Purcell helped foster an environment that was conducive to greater parish autonomy and lay powers among German Catholics.[57]

· 5 ·

THE LOCAL CHURCH
IN A NON-CATHOLIC
SOCIETY

When Purcell became bishop in 1833
Ohio's population was predominantly non-Catholic. He knew that Protestantism was the dominant force in the state, as was true of the whole country. The American principles of separation of church and state, freedom of religion, and religious tolerance permeated all his relations with non-Catholics and was evident in the public lectures of his diocesan visitations and in his participation at the First Vatican Council in 1870. Though firm in his opposition to bigotry, he was conciliatory toward the tolerant. While in Hamilton in the summer of 1835 he preached a strongly apologetic sermon in the courthouse and urged Catholics and non-Catholics alike "to cherish a feeling of benevolence and regard for all, whatever might be their religion, and to resist steadily, and energetically, any efforts to ally Church & State." In the process he challenged the teaching of the Bible in public schools and helped establish a separate school system for Catholics in the diocese. Overall, Purcell's relations with the community were concerned mainly with what affected the mission of the Catholic Church.[1]

Like many of his episcopal colleagues, Purcell was especially concerned over the growing anti-Catholicism in the nation in the 1830s. In his journal dated January 24, 1834, he recorded that "Bigots" were "growing fierce in their opposition to Popery. . . . Why do not Catholics awake?—Such apathy in the ranks of our own Clergy is inconceivable." Though he acknowledged "that prayer & Study & Visiting the Sick . . . [were] more meritorious and commendable, . . . we must descend sometimes," he wrote, "into the Plain & fight the Philistines with their own arms." When in early 1834 Father James Mullon, who had been managing the *Catholic Telegraph* and conducting the college, left Cincinnati for New Orleans to raise money for St. Peter's Orphan Asylum and to solicit subscriptions to the diocesan paper, Purcell became rector and professor in the seminary. He also took over the editorial management of the *Catholic Telegraph*. As editor he did considerable writing, hoping to counter Protestant charges and the developing nativism in the country. Anti-Catholicism, Purcell wrote to Bishop England, "begins to have noon-day apologists. A stronger tide than ever is setting in against us." Not everyone was pleased with the course of the diocesan weekly. Some thought it was a "party organ" and a bit too controversial. But Purcell had no intention of changing the policy. Refuting anti-Catholic charges and writing polemical pieces, the *Catholic Telegraph* also kept its readers informed on national and European Catholic matters. It also helped build a sense of community in the growing diocese.[2]

Organized anti-Catholicism became a major force in the 1830s. The significant increase in the Catholic population, churches, and schools doubtlessly reawakened fear and intolerance among some non-Catholics. As Protestant books and weekly newspapers played on Protestant fears, they invoked images of a church that was largely a traditional, hierarchical, undemocratic institution. A church that worshiped in a foreign tongue, namely Latin, and took orders from a foreign power, namely the pope. They viewed the Catholic religion as being irredeemably foreign and intrinsically opposed to the principles of American civilization. Could Catholics be loyal to the country and to the pope at the same time? Were the two identities compatible? Two works that received much publicity in the Midwest were Samuel F. B. Morse's *Foreign Conspiracy* (1834) and Lyman Beecher's *Plea for the West* (1835). In his attempt to show that the papacy, allegedly subservient to Austria, was out to undermine American democracy, Beecher printed in the appendix of his book an 1830 letter from Edward Fenwick to the Austrian emperor, thanking him for money he had received for his diocese. Beecher, who had left Boston in 1832 to take over the presidency of Lane Theological Seminary in Cincinnati, argued that part of his ministry was to fight the pope in the Midwest. At the same time, Morse, painter and inventor of the telegraph, maintained that Catholics threatened American liberties. He accused Bishops Purcell and Flaget of trying to subvert the American republic. These were not ecumenical times for American Catholics and Protestants.[3]

Cincinnati's *Western Christian Advocate,* a Methodist journal, and the *Cincinnati Gazette,* a secular newspaper, supported Beecher's and Morse's allegations and lashed out strongly against the Catholics. "What [did] the yearly erection of so many gorgeous temples, colleges, nunneries, and free schools [mean]? What," the *Advocate* asked, ". . . is meant by the sound of martial music, the military parade, the tramp of the footmen with the display of banners, at the laying of the cornerstone of each new Popish Church . . . in our Queen City?" To the editor it suggested that "Papal Rome is attempting to lay her foundations broad and strong in this great Valley, with the ultimate hope and design of the overthrow of all our free institutions." There were even rumors of ghosts inhabiting St. Peter's Orphan Asylum. Concerned over the increasing wave of anti-Catholicism and the "bigoted and misguided zealots" in the community, Purcell exclaimed that Beecher "is persecuting us fiercely, here. I seriously believe the hour of persecution," he wrote to Bishop Joseph Rosati of St. Louis, "is not far distant." Though anti-Catholicism in the Ohio Valley never reached the intensity that it did in the East, Catholics nevertheless felt the prejudice. There was "no country, claiming to be free, in which there is more underhand persecution than in America," the *Catholic Telegraph* editorialized, "nor is there a city in proportion to its population, where more instances can be produced of this vulgar bigotry, than in our own fair town of Cincinnati." Partly in response to nativism and to the needs of immigrant life, Catholics became increasingly defensive.[4]

PURCELL-CAMPBELL DEBATE

Purcell's early defense of Catholicism was very well illustrated in his debate with Alexander Campbell, a Baptist clergyman from Bethany, Virginia. Campbell was a founder of the denomination that would later become the Disciples of Christ. In 1836 Cincinnati's Western Literary Institute and College of Teachers, a voluntary organization of teachers more popularly called the College of Teachers, invited Purcell to address the Institute. Founded in 1832, the organization met for several days each year to debate various topics of interest to educators. On October 8 both Purcell and Campbell addressed the Institute. Following Campbell's morning presentation in support of Protestantism, Purcell challenged the minister's interpretation of the Reformation. Throughout the remainder of the day the College of Teachers debated various issues. Over the next three days Campbell and Purcell and their supporters continued their heated discussion at the Baptist Church on Sycamore Street. Through the *Cincinnati Gazette* Campbell in mid-October challenged the bishop to an oral debate on nine propositions he listed against the Catholic Church. After repeating the public challenge, Purcell accepted it.[5]

The Purcell-Campbell debate was the first time an American Catholic bishop held an oral debate with a Protestant minister. A few years earlier John Hughes, then a parish priest in Philadelphia, had engaged in two public debates with Reverend John Breckinridge, a Presbyterian minister. The Purcell-Campbell debate began on Friday, January 13, 1837, at the Baptist Church, ending on Saturday afternoon, January 21. It continued for seven

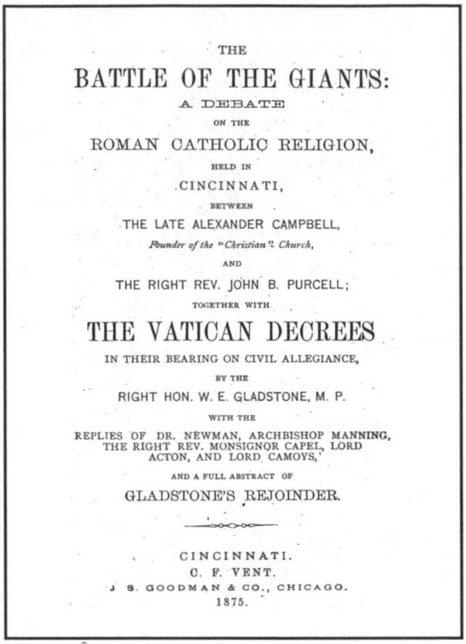

THE
BATTLE OF THE GIANTS:
A DEBATE

ON THE

ROMAN CATHOLIC RELIGION,

HELD IN

CINCINNATI,

BETWEEN

THE LATE ALEXANDER CAMPBELL,

Founder of the "Christian" Church,

AND

THE RIGHT REV. JOHN B. PURCELL;

TOGETHER WITH

THE VATICAN DECREES

IN THEIR BEARING ON CIVIL ALLEGIANCE,

BY THE

RIGHT HON. W. E. GLADSTONE, M. P.

WITH THE

REPLIES OF DR. NEWMAN, ARCHBISHOP MANNING,
THE RIGHT REV. MONSIGNOR CAPEL, LORD
ACTON, AND LORD CAMOYS,

AND A FULL ABSTRACT OF

GLADSTONE'S REJOINDER.

CINCINNATI.
C. F. VENT.
J S. GOODMAN & CO., CHICAGO.
1875.

FIG 7. Alexander Campbell and Bishop John B. Purcell
Debate, 1837

days, Sunday not included. There were two sessions each day: a three-hour
session in the morning that began at 9 A.M. and a two-hour session in the
afternoon that began at 3 P.M. Proceeds from the printed debate went to the
Protestant and Catholic orphanages. Campbell's propositions were published
in the *Gazette* in December, giving Purcell about a month's time to prepare
his general line of defense. Though familiar with the anti-Catholic literature
of the day, Purcell had the difficult job of responding to the various specific
charges and factual data that Campbell would present. Purcell pictured himself as David fighting Goliath. "I have only to say," he wrote, "that, however
low of stature, . . . I shall be found more than a match for this vaunting
Goliath."[6]

The debate was held before a packed audience. Though at times it
proved entertaining and provided an opportunity for both contestants to
inflate their language, it was generally conducted on a high level. In terms
of scholarship, both men were impressive. They demonstrated much scrip-
tural and historical information. Purcell, who had a flair for oratory, was
recognized as an authority not only on matters of religious doctrine, but also
on classical and literary subjects. He had a quick mind, retentive memory,
and a good command of the primary sources of Catholic Church history.

Campbell, on the other hand, more often quoted from secondary sources. The *Cincinnati Philanthropist,* which generally proved hostile to the bishop, acknowledged that Purcell "is evidently a well read man, especially in the history of the Roman Church, and his mind is handsomely enriched with the current literature of the day." The self-confident, assertive Purcell was diplomatic, witty, and possessed the necessary oratorical skills to win the audience. He proved himself a skillful and worthy opponent for the more experienced Campbell.[7]

The proposition that received the most attention and proved most controversial dealt with papal infallibility. Purcell strongly expressed his reservations, if not outright denial, of infallibility. "No enlightened Catholic," he said, "holds the pope's infallibility to be an article of faith. I do not; and none of my brethren, that I know of, do. The Catholic believes the pope, as a man, to be as liable to error, as almost any other man in the universe. Man is man, and no man is infallible, either in doctrine or morals." As Campbell kept pressing on the seat of infallibility and asked the bishop to name the "infallible expositor," Purcell countered that it was a "general council, or the pope, with the acquiescence of the church at large." Purcell argued that the "pope is the head—the council is the heart—and I have no objection to . . . [Campbell] calling the laity the members. . . . The true theory of the church, like that of the human body," he said, "is union. Ask not, does the heart alone, or the head, alone, or the members alone contain the vital principle . . . , they live and move and have their being together." On the matter of jurisdiction he denied the temporal power of the pope. He encouraged as much local autonomy as possible. Somewhat imaginatively, Purcell compared the Catholic Church with the planetary system. "The see of Rome," he said, "is as the sun and centre of the system . . . which gives us all, our proper impetus and coherency. But like the planets, we are not absorbed by it. We know its excellence, its usefulness, its destination, its limits."[8]

The debate received considerable national publicity both in the Protestant and Catholic papers. Most of the secular press of Cincinnati declared Purcell the victor, acknowledging his able defense of the Catholic doctrines. The lawyer and editor of the *Cincinnati Gazette,* Charles Hammond, pointed out that as a consequence of the debate "Protestantism gained nothing, Catholicism suffered nothing." To the *Catholic Telegraph,* "an event more propitious for Catholics could not have occurred." In February 1837 a committee of lay Catholics presented Purcell with gifts, including two large silver pitchers, as a testimonial of their gratitude for his performance. By summer the Congregation of Propaganda Fide in Rome congratulated him on his debate. The Cincinnati prelate had proven to be a brilliant and eloquent defender of the faith.[9]

Though Purcell's reputation doubtlessly benefited from his success, not all his fellow bishops were pleased by his participation in a public oral debate. Bishop England, whom Purcell greatly admired, was less than enthusiastic. "I have read with deep interest," he wrote, "the book of your controversy. . . . You had a formidable antagonist & were in a bad position & got out of it better than I could have imagined. I would not for anything that I could say be so placed." Purcell himself later expressed reservations about public debates. "I did not seek the controversy," he wrote a month after the debate, and "I am now, as I have ever been, averse to such exhibitions. Religion is not in need of them."[10]

NATIVISM

As a religious leader Purcell had made his presence known in Ohio. During the first few years of his administration, he had established solid relations with both German- and English-speaking Catholics throughout the diocese. He had also earned the respect of non-Catholics. Charles Peabody, a Protestant minister, who in 1846 rode a short distance with Purcell in a stagecoach on a trip to Louisville, found him to be a pleasant traveling companion. Purcell "is a scholar," Peabody wrote in his diary, "understands all the departments of literature well—has read almost everything—is familiar with history and poetry, and science—knows what is now going on in the literary, political and religious world. He understands the character of the pop[ulation] here better than almost any [one]. . . . Such men are to be feared in their influence." Three decades later Purcell was still "held in great esteem by all, even by those of different faiths," a French-speaking pastor from Northwestern, Ohio, wrote. "He likes to speak French as well as English. One feels at home with him at once so we were not lacking in conversation."[11]

On his diocesan visitations, the outgoing Purcell, who wanted Catholics to be accepted as full-fledged Americans, often gave public addresses in courthouses, public schools, and Protestant churches, where he defended the American tradition of religious freedom and the Catholic doctrines. His stance revealed how he thought about the relationship between Catholicism and American society. Purcell's debate with Campbell, along with his conciliatory approach and effective dealings with community leaders at the Western Literary Institute, helped elevate his status as a leader in the community. Moreover, he was becoming better known by his confreres in the West. Cincinnati's geographic position on the Ohio River was a natural stop for western bishops on their way to and from Baltimore and Europe. The national publicity given to the debate also helped enhance Purcell's status as the church leader in the Midwest.[12]

Like most of his colleagues in the American hierarchy, Purcell steered a neutral course in politics. His interest was in building strong community relations and remaining politically neutral. The editorials on voting in the *Catholic Telegraph* were also nonpartisan. Though some of Purcell's personal friends such as William Henry Harrison and Dr. Daniel Drake, founder of the Medical College of the University of Cincinnati, were Whigs, Purcell chose to remain noncommittal. "My time is too much occupied with the interests of a 'Kingdom which is not of this world' to admit of my devoting any portion of it to 'decided opposition' to any of the candidates for popular favor. . . . I have never that I am aware of," he said, "attempted to influence the vote of a single individual of my flock and in this course I am determined to persevere." When Harrison was elected president in 1840, Purcell was careful to continue his policy of neutrality. He regarded his attendance at a local dinner in honor of the president-elect as a civic function.[13]

One of the earliest political and social issues that Purcell and archdiocesan Catholics in pre–Civil War America faced was nativism. Although nativism subsided somewhat in the late 1830s, it was revived in the 1840s. The increased Catholic immigration in the 1840s and 1850s, which swelled the number of Catholics to record numbers, stimulated anti-Catholic and antiforeign sentiment. Expressing concern about a papist takeover, some Protestants and the Cincinnati press harangued against Catholics for their alleged "undemocratic" practices. Because many Catholic immigrants, especially the Irish, were poor, some people regarded them as an economic threat. They were seen as either taking jobs away from native-born citizenry or draining the coffers of public charity. In 1843 a branch of the American Protestant Association was formed in Cincinnati. Three years later the *American Protestant,* a No-Popery newspaper, was also started in Cincinnati. In August 1850 a mob in Chillicothe attacked the Notre Dame Convent, which had been established for the education of young girls. The convent had been attacked eight previous times and, to the disappointment of the 1,500 Catholics in the community, no arrests had been made. "Chillicothe," the *Catholic Telegraph* wrote, "is notorious for its hostility" to Catholics. Though most residents disapproved of the animosity, "there were enough people there," the diocesan paper editorialized, "to smile at the doings of the mob and to conceal the perpetrators." Chillicothe Catholics eventually passed a resolution pledging "not to vote for candidates who were not known to be favorable to an equality of rights." Though reluctant to mingle religion with politics, they saw no alternative.[14]

In the 1850s there were a few outbreaks against the Catholic churches in the archdiocese. Occasionally stones were thrown at the cathedral. In one instance, vandals shattered some stained glass in a window. On a more serious note, on August 20, 1855, the newly built Holy Angels Church in Sidney was blown up. A full keg of gunpowder had been placed under the small frame church and ignited by a string of powder leading nearly half a block away. Even though the mayor of the town offered a three-hundred-dollar reward for the apprehension of the perpetrators, they were never found. Within two years the congregation of Sidney rebuilt a larger church. In most communities, fortunately, there was no such violence. A good number of Protestants realized that Catholics were law-abiding citizens, shared important moral values, especially in charitable work, and were as much opposed to any form of European despotism as they were. At times Protestants even contributed to the building of Catholic churches, as they did in the erection of St. James Church at Wyoming in Cincinnati in the late 1860s.[15]

In light of the nativist frenzy, most American church leaders were understandably defensive. Their responses varied widely to the tension between American identity and the definition of the church. Bishop John Hughes of New York was the most well-known fighter. When New York City parishes were threatened, he urged pastors to arm themselves with muskets for the defense of parish properties. But he was not typical of the American hierarchy. When nativists burned churches and Irish homes in Philadelphia in 1844, Bishop Francis Patrick Kenrick was conspicuously silent. Purcell took more of a middle-of-the-road stance. Though critical publicly of anti-Catholic outbreaks, under no circumstance did Purcell sanction physical force. "We will not resist persecution with the weapon of our persecutors," he declared in an address before the Young Men's Catholic Literary Institute, "we will not stir up civil war."[16]

The most dramatic expression of anti-Catholicism in the archdiocese was Cincinnati's reaction in December 1853 to the visit of Archbishop Gaetano Bedini, the pope's nuncio, or ambassador, to the Imperial Court of Brazil. Sent by the pope to visit the United States, he was "to observe," the Propaganda wrote, "the state of religion . . . , the conduct of the clergy and the abuses that have crept in," and to investigate cases of trusteeship among German groups in Philadelphia, Buffalo, and St. Louis. On his tour Bedini was subjected to several anti-Catholic demonstrations. What doomed his journey from the start was the fact that Alessandro Gavazzi, a former priest, came to the United States at the same time as Bedini did. Gavazzi falsely condemned the archbishop for his alleged role in the suppression of the nationalist revolution in Italy and labeled him the "Bloody Butcher of Bologna."[17]

In mid-December Bedini arrived in Cincinnati. On Christmas day he preached in French and German in St. Peter in Chains Cathedral. That night a riot broke out. Some 800 to 1,000 German radicals marched from Free Men's Hall at Mercer and Vine Streets toward Purcell's residence near the cathedral, where Bedini was staying. Five days later Purcell described the incident to Archbishop Anthony Blanc of New Orleans. "Well! The Nuncio has been here. And at this peaceful season his visit has been made the occasion of death, and bloodshed, and riot & lawsuits. On Christmas night," he wrote, "from 500 to a 1000 [German] 'Freemen' marched in procession . . . to within a square of the Cathedral, with execrable charivari music, transparencies, a gallows, a stuffed & ready for hanging Nuncio, Mottoes infernal, clubs, dirks, [and] pistols" with the purpose of killing Bedini. The police, who were waiting for them, Purcell noted, "pitched into them." One German was killed, fifteen were wounded, including a policeman, and sixty-five were arrested.[18]

In spite of the riot and threats of personal violence to Bedini, there was not enough evidence to prosecute the rioters. The charges against them were dropped. The general public was sympathetic to the marchers and against the police. Area newspapers, with the exception of the *Catholic Telegraph,* defended the marchers on the grounds that they had been exercising their rights to free speech and assembly. Catholics, on the other hand, concurred with their archbishop that the demonstration had threatened Bedini's life. Both Purcell and the *Catholic Telegraph* viewed the Christmas night episode as one largely perpetrated by Gavazzi and German immigrants, who sympathized with the 1848 revolutions in Europe.[19]

While in Cincinnati Bedini, in the company of Archbishop Purcell, visited a number of Catholic institutions. On Sunday, January 1, he participated in the dedication of the new Holy Trinity Church. About a year earlier, Holy Trinity Church and the parish school had been destroyed by fire. All German parishes in the city had assisted in the rebuilding program. Two days after the dedication Bedini left Cincinnati for New York. Before leaving the country Bedini criticized some of the American bishops for not coming to his defense better than they did. Purcell felt hurt when he learned of Bedini's comments. Not only had he personally praised Bedini to the Vatican but had in fact publicly defended him. "I put myself a dozen times between him and death, while here," he wrote. "I covered him as well as I could with my little person to protect him from the dagger of the assassin when . . . visiting German Churches and schools."[20]

Less than two weeks after Bedini's departure, there was another anti-Bedini demonstration. About two thousand citizens marched through the streets of Cincinnati. They carried banners with such mottoes as "Down with Bedini!" and "No Priests, No Kings, No Popery." On a vacant lot they successfully burned the nuncio in effigy. The police broke up the rioters. A week later a demonstration in neighboring Covington, Kentucky, again successfully burned Bedini in effigy. Through all these anti-Catholic demonstrations,

Purcell observed, the Catholics had acted with "moderation, wisdom and firmness." By the middle of the decade the anti-Catholic demonstrations had subsided and Purcell was pleased to write that "[a]ll is quiet now."[21]

CATHOLIC EDUCATION

An important issue to Cincinnati Catholics in the nineteenth century was public education. As early as 1835 Lyman Beecher in *A Plea for the West* hoped that the Catholic children attending public schools would free themselves from the shackles of Roman despotism. As the public schools increasingly reflected Protestant teachings and values, the clergy, religious, and lay people, especially the German-speaking Catholics, who thought these values were subversive of Catholic faith and morals, committed themselves to Catholic education. This affected relations between Catholics and non-Catholics in the community.

As the head of the diocese, Purcell responded to the challenge. At the October 1836 meeting of the Western Literary Institute, Purcell criticized parts of Reverend Benjamin P. Aydelott's address on the study of the Bible in the public schools. Aydelott, a local physician, Episcopalian minister, and head of Woodward High School, recommended that the Bible itself, not selections from it, be the textbook in the schools. In light of the interest in the matter, the Institute put Purcell and Aydelott on a committee to report on it the following year. This was the first time that the issue of Bible usage in Cincinnati's public schools entered public discourse. Though Purcell realized that he was not among a friendly group, he faced the school question optimistically. In June 1837 he asked Bishop John Hughes of New York, who was gaining a national reputation for defending Catholic rights, to join him in a collaborative effort to determine the best use of the Bible in the public schools. Taking into account that the Western Literary Institute was "likely to prove a powerful engine for good, or for evil, I think we should take in hand, ourselves & work it," he wrote. "We could purge out much of the old leaven, if we mixed more with the mass. The only difficulty is how to mix with it & retain our religious identity." Purcell was hopeful that a compromise could be reached. But Hughes was skeptical of the whole matter. He felt a religious coalition in education would not work.[22]

At the 1837 meeting of the Institute, Purcell strongly opposed both the use of the whole Bible and a book of biblical selections. He did not want to place Protestant Bibles in the hands of the Catholic youth and disapproved of the "common-school teachers" influencing the pupils with their "sectarian bias." What he suggested, instead, was that separate days be set aside in the schools for the pupils of various faiths to be assembled together to be instructed by their own pastors. "If this were done," he thought, "our public schools would be a great benefit for this country." After considerable discussion, the Institute unanimously recommended that the Bible be read in all the schools as part of "a religious exercise, without denominational or sectarian comment." When attempts were made to affix amendments, giving the teachers opportunities to interpret the meaning of the Scripture, Purcell, Lyman Beecher, and other ministers rejected them. By allowing teachers to interpret the Scripture, Purcell argued, "would be to make religion a football and expose the youth frequenting these schools to change their religion as often as their teachers changed."[23]

Purcell was pleased with the October meeting. He detected no bigotry "as had been," Purcell wrote, "long the custom." Though the meeting went well, no real consensus was reached. Bible reading remained part of the curriculum in the public schools. The members of the Western Literary Institute, moreover, made no mention of Purcell's proposal to set aside separate days in the schools for students of various faiths to be instructed by their own teachers. Echoing the bishop's concerns, the *Catholic Telegraph* editorialized that the children should read the Bible "at home, under the eyes and direction of their parent, pastors, or circumspect tutors." Though Purcell continued to express concern over the policy of Bible reading in the public schools, an attitude that over time contributed to the secularization of public schools, he was pleased overall with the working relationship with public school authorities in Cincinnati.[24]

During this period Purcell and Hughes were the most vocal church leaders for Catholic schools. Their communities far outdistanced the other dioceses in the country in the percentage of children attending parochial schools. But unlike Hughes, who was abrasive and openly hostile to the public schools and clashed with city leaders, Purcell had a much more conciliatory policy toward them. Hoping to reach compromises with the public schools and their Protestant supporters, Purcell did not make a public issue of the school question. Though the Cincinnati public schools had a Protestant bias, as evident in the continuing use of the King James Bible and Protestant prayers and hymns in opening exercises, Catholics continued to work with public school officials. They believed that for the Catholic children to receive an education in the public schools was better than not receiving an education at all. "[H]alf a loaf," the *Catholic Telegraph* wrote, "is better than no bread." Purcell was also motivated partially by the desire to make Catholicism more acceptable and less threatening to non-Catholics. In 1840 Purcell was pleased to inform Hughes that the Cincinnati School Board "employed a Catholic Schoolmistress, the first, in one of the Com[mon] Schools." Besides, in some rural communities in Northwestern Ohio, like at Minster, public school funds in the 1840s were made available to St. Augustine parish boys' and girls' schools. Functioning as school directors, the parish trustees administered the funds. Because the instruction of the three Sisters of the Precious Blood, who had taken charge of the education of the girls of the parish in 1848, was entirely in German, the sisters were sent to receive tutoring in English from the Notre Dame Sisters at Dayton. This was done because the sisters were paid with public funds and the state then required instruction in English.[25]

In the early 1840s Purcell's conciliatory position enabled Catholics to make some progress in their relations with school board officials. Largely in response to the bishop's petition, the Cincinnati school board in 1842, at the same time that Hughes was battling the public school system in New York City, unanimously excused Catholic children from reading the King James Bible. Catholics were allowed to have separate readings from the Catholic Douay Version of the Bible. The board also made the children's visit to the school library, which contained anti-Catholic literature, dependent on parental consent. But Catholics soon learned that the policy was not forcefully implemented. There were contradictions in school practice. In 1847 a teacher in the public schools directed his students to bring their Bibles with them to class. When the Catholic students brought the Catholic edition, they were told to supply themselves with the Protestant edition. Most of the public school teachers at the time were Protestants, some being Protestant ministers or former ministers.[26]

The bishop's pragmatic and conciliatory attitude was clearly manifested at the diocesan synod of 1848. Purcell and his clergy did not want the school question "publicly agitated." Catholic parents were advised not to send their children to bigoted schools and to avail themselves of all the advantages that may be obtained in less bigoted districts, while "we quietly learn the state of public opinion and seek to obtain a change in the laws." The synod further recommended the appointment of Catholic teachers to public schools where possible.[27]

Cincinnati Catholics also complained about placing Catholic charitable institutions on the tax list. What especially irritated them was the policy of double taxation. The collection of taxes "from the Roman Catholic Asylum," the *Catholic Telegraph* editorialized, "has been a subject of astonishment for some years. It is an exhibition of bigotry." By midcentury the diocese had spent about one million dollars building churches, schools, and asylums, without receiving any public assistance. When the Catholic institutions in 1843 petitioned for public funds, they were denied on the grounds of sectarianism. Yet the Cincinnati Orphan Asylum, which was largely a Protestant institution, did receive public assistance. The diocesan paper repeatedly protested against a policy of double standards. At one point it urged Catholics not to vote for any politician who would not "pledge himself to remove the injustice."[28]

In the summer of 1852, Dr. Jerome Mudd, a Catholic school board member, decided to force the issue of Bible use in the public schools. After consulting with local church authorities, Mudd proposed that the Catholic children and teachers use the Catholic Bible rather than simply to be exempted from using the Protestant Bible. Though the majority of the members on the board preferred the King James Bible, arguing that the United States was "essentially a Protestant country," they settled on a compromise. In November the board agreed on a new policy for Cincinnati's public schools. It allowed the use of Catholic editions of scripture as long as notes and commentary were not read publicly. Though the King James Bible was still the norm, Catholics were now free to use their own edition of the bible. Purcell's diocesan weekly praised the board's decision. After a "display of anti-republican intolerance," it editorialized, "a respectable majority . . . has passed the resolution. . . . This is certainly a compliment to the Catholic population."[29]

By the middle of the century 80 percent of the parishes in the diocese had Catholic schools. At first these schools were usually in the damp basements of the churches. The absence of Catholic schools was more evident in the small towns and in rural areas. From the beginning, the diocese of Cincinnati tried to erect and maintain parochial schools for the education of its children. Immigrant Catholics and Purcell built upon that tradition. By the 1850s Purcell became the force behind Catholic schools and helped establish an alternative school system. A vast and inclusive parochial system was built primarily to teach children the tenets of the Catholic faith and provide a basic education similar to that of the public schools. It helped preserve the faith of young boys and girls of the parish who otherwise would attend the public schools. There was a deep suspicion of the public schools in the Catholic consciousness. Rather than try to change them, Purcell and his episcopal colleagues in the Midwest, unlike some of their counterparts in the East, spent their time and energy building parish schools. By building a separate school system, the local church also helped insure its unity in a pluralistic society. The parochial schools in the diocese became solidly united under Catholic rule. By 1860 there were sixty-one schools. Ten years later the number had increased to 103. The entire parish community, and not just the pupils' parents, bore the cost of educating the children. As Catholic children attended Catholic schools, they segregated themselves socially from the rest of the community. Furthermore, just as Catholic families were divided among themselves, most notably the English- and German-speaking families, their children were segregated from one another.[30]

In 1848, the first year that parochial school statistics became available, the six German schools and two English schools in Cincinnati had a combined enrollment of 2,527 pupils. Three years later there were thirteen parochial schools in Cincinnati with an enrollment of 4,494 students. In 1864 the parochial schools enrolled 9,544 students, constituting forty-one percent of pupils taught in the city. These figures do not include the students taught in the day and boarding academies run by the various sisterhoods. By 1870, due in part because of the substantial German-speaking population in the Queen City, between 12,000 and 15,000 children, whose numbers were equivalent to one-third of the city's total school population, attended the German and English Catholic schools. Four-fifths of the Catholic children of school age attended Catholic schools. The *Catholic Telegraph* could proudly boast "that there is not a city in the whole country where, in proportion to the Catholic population, there are so many parochial and select Catholic schools." Wherever Catholic parishes and churches were established, Catholic parochial schools were soon to follow. At that time the cathedral parish had four separate schools: a boys' school taught by lay teachers and three for girls under the guidance of the Sisters of Notre Dame, of Mercy, and of Sacred Heart. St. Xavier parish had three schools, and St. Patrick's and many of the German parishes had two.[31]

Some of the anti-Catholic sentiments in the archdiocese spilled over into education and politics. In 1853 the Ohio legislature debated a school bill that, if passed, would have required all school-age children to attend the public schools for a minimum of three months of the year. It threatened the existence of parochial schools. Purcell presented Ohio legislators with a petition, signed by eight hundred Catholics, arguing that parents have the right to educate their own children. "The school question is thickening on us," the archbishop wrote to Blanc. "We are in the midst of all manner of threats from all manner of Sects & infidels. . . . No one knows," he said, "how soon they may ripen into open, violent and prolonged persecution." Opposed to sending Catholic children "by force to the common schools," the *Catholic Telegraph* criticized the legislation for infringing on parental rights.[32]

During this same period Cincinnati Catholics, like some of their contemporaries in the East and Midwest, particularly in New York and Detroit, also petitioned the legislature for a share of the school fund. Consistently arguing that true education had to be based on religion, the archdiocese wanted each religious group to have its own schools. Throughout the remainder of Purcell's administration, the local church proposed that the state channel tax funds to the religious schools. There was also a practical side to the proposal. "We have sometimes thought," the *Catholic Telegraph* argued in 1850, "that if we were to close all our schools for a month, and send the thousands of Catholic youth to the 'District Schools,' the inspectors of the law-established institution would be a good deal puzzled what to do." Arguing that parents had the right to educate their own children and should be free to send their children to any school they chose, the local church presented its own plan for state aid to parochial schools. The proposal was a primitive form of the voucher system in which payments would be made to the school on the basis of the number of pupils enrolled.[33]

In the spring of 1853 Purcell published a forceful pastoral on the school issue. "Because we have asked for our share of the School Fund," he wrote, "we have been charged with a conspiracy to put down the Common Schools." He reminded the faithful that the local church was not opposed to the public schools. Catholics paid taxes for their support. In response to the legislative proposal to compel parents and guardians, under a penalty of $20 for every offense, to send their children to the public schools for three months in every year, Purcell became more defiant. "For ourselves," he declared, "we can only say, as Guardian of some three hundred orphans, that we pray God to permit that our life be trampled out by a mob in the streets of the Queen City before we obey it, if it ever sought to be enforced." The concerted efforts by Catholics proved successful. The Ohio bill was defeated and subsequently dropped.[34]

Mounting a campaign against mandatory attendance of public schools, Purcell's pastoral focused on the April 1853 elections and the issue of public funds for Catholic schools. Like in the diocese of Detroit the same year, the local elections centered on the propriety of state funding and developed into a significant confrontation between immigrants and "native Americans." The Cincinnati ordinary recommended an aggressive political course of action. Purcell's conciliatory attitude on the school issues changed. He gave up any efforts to gain accommodation. If Catholics "value their privileges as American citizens," he wrote, "they will assert them . . . in the selection of candidates who will fairly represent the wishes and requirements of their constituents" in the state legislature, city council, and school board. Though he did not want to sway Catholics away from any one political party, he made it clear that "if those parties value their support, and deserve to receive it, they will pledge themselves to redress the grievances of which they so justly complain. And if they refuse to do so, they cannot complain if Catholics are equally independent and refuse" to vote for them.[35]

Protestant and secular papers responded sharply and angrily to Purcell's pastoral. Even the *Cincinnati Enquirer,* the city's pro-immigrant paper, accused him of threatening the public school system. From the time of Purcell's pastoral to the election a week later, the area's newspapers, with the exception of the *Catholic Telegraph* and the labor paper, *Nonpareil,* endorsed the new mandatory legislation on public schools and urged the citizenry to let reason alone guide them on election day. The *Cincinnati Enquirer* referred to the Democratic slate as "the Pope's Ticket." By using the school question to mobilize voters, Purcell had helped make religion and schooling the principal issue of the election.[36]

The 1853 election marked the first time that an election hinged on the central issue of religion. The ideological dispute that had been brewing for some time between Protestants and Catholics on the development of schools was finally out in the open. The outcome of the election was not clear, as both Catholics and Protestants claimed victory. Religious newspapers like the *Western Christian Advocate* interpreted the election as a "Defeat of the Pope in Cincinnati," arguing that both Democrats and Whigs "forgot their peculiarities and voted for the schools." But some Catholics derived satisfaction knowing that the defeated Whigs in the election were among the most anti-Catholic of the candidates. In the end, though sixteen of the twenty persons on the regular Democratic ticket were elected, largely because the anti-Catholic vote was split among several candidates, anti-Catholics had outvoted Catholics for every major office.[37]

The heated election also took its toll on Purcell. He feared for his life. A month after the election Purcell sent his will to Archbishop Francis Kenrick of Baltimore. "Being frequently admonished that I may be put to a violent death," he wrote, "I have thought it my duty to make my will anew." A year later he again reiterated concern for his life. "For many years," he wrote, "I have never felt secure of my life, in this city, a single night."[38]

Throughout the decade there were renewed charges that Purcell interfered in local politics. In 1854 one newspaper ridiculed the Democratic Party with a mock "Holy Church Democratic State Ticket" and listed Purcell as a candidate for the board of public works. The following year the *Daily Gazette* published an article accusing the archbishop of controlling political votes. William F. Johnson, running on the Democratic ticket as a candidate for the state legislature and a former member of the Know Nothing Party, accused Purcell of controlling 6,200 votes in Hamilton County. Purcell denied the allegation. Johnson admitted later that he had spoken "from a rumor" that he had heard. Though the *Catholic Telegraph* became solidly identified with the Democratic Party on the education issue in the 1853 election, on most occasions the diocesan paper was neutral. It urged the faithful to vote on the issues and not to become identified necessarily with one political party. The political parties "love us," it reminded its readers, "where we have many votes."[39]

By midcentury Purcell had emerged as the Midwest champion of parochial schools. The elevation of the diocese of Cincinnati to a metropolitan see in 1850 doubtlessly increased the confidence of Catholics in the diocese. It also helped intensify their school policy. When Cincinnati hosted three provincial councils in 1855, 1858, and 1861, the archbishop, his suffragan bishops, and the superiors of the various priest and religious orders helped lay a solid foundation for a competitive system of Catholic education. In the process, they helped generate interest in the national movement toward parochial school education. Providing parochial schools became a matter of church legislation.[40]

At the 1855 and 1858 councils the Council Fathers passed a number of decrees on education. They wanted to see a parochial school in connection with every Catholic church in the province. In their pastorals the Council Fathers emphasized the importance of promoting the religious instruction of the children. In this "money seeking, and money making age," they wrote, there was need for religious education. They also emphasized the important roles parents had in the shaping of values. Reflecting the sentiments of the church hierarchy, the *Catholic Telegraph* argued that "Catholic homes must contribute to the training of our children more than Catholic schools. The children must learn truthfulness, obedience, self-denial, cleanliness, politeness, and fear of God, at their own firesides." Schools could never "supply the place of home teaching and example," it continued, "or make Christian gentlemen and ladies out of the scholars they send forth into the world." At the second council the ordinaries issued a decree obligating the pastors, "under pain of mortal sin," to establish a parochial school wherever conditions made it possible. This legislation was more rigorous than any previously passed by the dioceses in the United States. Throughout the archdiocese some pastors also began to deny the sacraments to parents who did not send their children to parochial schools, without prior approval by the bishop.[41]

Though in 1866 the Second Plenary Council at Baltimore benefited by the deliberations of the Cincinnati councils and emphasized the indispensability of parochial schools, its position on education was less stringent than the one issued by Cincinnati's second council. The Baltimore council merely recommended that in every diocese a school be built next to every church. It is clear that the majority of bishops were not prepared at the time, as were Purcell and Hughes, to launch a major campaign for parochial schools. That initiative came at the Third Plenary Council of Baltimore in 1884.[42]

At the Third Provincial Council of Cincinnati in 1861, the ordinaries attributed much of the "progressive demoralization" of the youth of the country to the public school educational system. "The system," the bishops wrote in their pastoral, "is well calculated to raise up a generation of religious indifferentists, if not practical infidels." Purcell maintained that the only public policy that would help correct the situation and would "be fair and equitable to all, would be that which would make education, like religion and like all other important pursuits, entirely free." He again argued that religious schools had a right to a share of the school fund. "If the State . . . will let us have our own money to make our own experiments, in our own way," he wrote, "we hope to succeed." He was also convinced that the proposed system would stimulate "competition," lessen the cost of education, and would "render the Schools," Purcell wrote, "really Public and Common—which they certainly are not at present except in name."[43]

Efforts to prevent Catholic children from attending the public schools were an uphill battle in a number of parishes. "Notwithstanding all that I have said to the people of this congregation to dissuade them from sending their children to these godless schools," the pastor of St. Patrick Church in Bellefontaine wrote to Purcell, "they still continue to set at naught all that I say, and send them there." Purcell saw the need to reinforce the hard-line tactic of compelling parents to send their children to a Catholic school. He reiterated the seriousness of the offense of those parents who neglected that duty. "The Catholic school is the nursery of the Catholic congregation," he wrote in his Lenten pastoral of 1872. "The one should stand under the protecting shadow of the other. . . . We see not how they, who wilfully [*sic*] and deliberately neglect this duty can worthily approach, or be conscientiously admitted to, the sacraments." William Bigot, pastor of St. Michael Church at Fort Loramie, could not have agreed more. "The religious instruction should take place every day for the children," he wrote. "A school without religion is like food without salt and pepper. About this principle nothing more need be said for the results of the parochial schools are clear to all reasonable people. In these days the spirit of the age . . . is . . . for slackness in religion and free thinking so all states and parishes must help themselves."[44]

But warning parents against sending their children to public schools was not enough. Purcell saw the proliferation of the rival public schools and programs as a threat to the parochial school system. He wanted the Catholic schools to be as thorough and extensive as the public schools. Uppermost on his mind was the deplorable student-teacher ratio in the parochial schools. In 1850 the ratio of students to teachers in the public schools of Cincinnati was 88-1, dropping to 62-1 in 1858. In the same period the student-teacher ratio in the Catholic schools was 94-1 and 100-1, respectively. In 1863 Purcell founded a diocesan school board. He hoped that it would help bring unity and uniformity in Catholic education in the diocese. It was empowered to improve academic standards in the schools, review credentials of teachers, and supervise the selection of textbooks. The German influence in the creation of the board was evident. All the appointed board members were German except the president, Sylvester Rosecrans, auxiliary bishop of Cincinnati from 1862 to 1868. Under the school board's auspices the diocese began teacher certification for the first time. To attract more competent teachers, the school board urged parishes to pay the teachers higher salaries, thus inducing them "to persevere in their profession, and not merely regard it as a stepping stone to something better." The archdiocese needed schools that "will be of such grade and character," the *Catholic Telegraph* wrote, "as will neutralize the inducements offered by the district schools. This character belongs not to our Catholic schools at present. They are not controlled by professional skill and experience of competent teachers."[45]

To rectify the situation, Purcell attempted to establish a normal school or teachers' college that would help train a much-needed corps of competent teachers. In August 1863 clergy, teachers, and delegates from several parishes attended a meeting for the foundation of a normal school. Opponents of the concept were probably Germans, as they more than likely viewed the school as a threat to their control of the parish school. For whatever reason, plans for a teachers' college were eventually dropped. The diocesan school board, moreover, was short-lived, as there are no records of its existence by the mid-1860s. The diocesan school board was a Midwestern innovation, the first permanent one being established by Bishop Joseph Dwenger at Fort Wayne in 1879. Though the above efforts for a teachers' college and a school board could not be sustained in the archdiocese, they point toward the eventual establishment of a highly centralized system of parochial education in the early twentieth century.[46]

One of the decrees issued by the diocesan synod in 1865 instructed the pastors to "work earnestly" to have the schools under their jurisdiction "excel the public schools not only in discipline but in secular instruction as well." The 1865 synod was the first formal synod of which there is record in the archdiocese. In the history of the archdiocese of Cincinnati there have been a few diocesan synods, meetings of ecclesiastics who come together with ecclesiastical authority to discuss and decide upon matters related to discipline and liturgy for their territory.[47]

In 1859, shortly before Purcell's attempt to establish the teachers' college, German Catholics proposed the establishment of the Catholic Institute. Through its educational programs and athletic facilities they hoped to serve the entire Catholic community. An association was formed and issued stock at fifty dollars per share. The Institute was entirely the work of Catholic laymen. Though most of the directors and officers were German, a significant minority was Irish. Purcell happily endorsed the project. He described the idea as "a noble one." Shortly after purchasing a lot at Vine and Longworth Streets, the association opened the three-story Catholic Institute in November 1860. In addition to providing a hall for public meetings, it had a library, museum, conference rooms, and a gymnasium. The Institute's most ambitious undertaking was the establishment of a Polytechnic School.[48]

Notwithstanding the initial enthusiasm over the Institute and its school, they did not last long. Though the *Wahrheitsfreund,* a strong supporter of the Institute, did not comment on its demise, which was sometime in 1864, the *Catholic Telegraph* speculated that it was due in part to opposition to it by the Catholic community. "We never could understand the motive of this opposition," the *Catholic Telegraph* editorialized. Because of it, however, "the Catholic Institute has ceased to be what it was intended to be. It is no longer identified with our faith or people." Dedicating a new faculty building for the Jesuits in the spring of 1867, Purcell told his audience that the Catholic Institute had proven "a grand failure" and that he had "lately signed a paper by which it was concluded that the entire concern should be sold. It has proved unworthy of our support. On Good Friday," he further explained, "there was performed in its hall a scandalous piece in which religion was ridiculed and scoffed at." He therefore concluded that he "would not have [his] name associated with it."[49]

When in 1869 several members of the Cincinnati board of education, led by R. W. Rauch, a Catholic, considered a plan to consolidate the public school system with the Catholic schools, German Catholics defended their parish schools from outside interference. The plan would have handed over control of the Catholic schools to the public school system with the understanding that the parochial school property would eventually be sold to it. In return, the archdiocese would have been permitted to use the buildings on the weekends for religious instruction. Toward this end the board opened discussions with vicar general Edward Purcell. In light of the close relationship of the two Purcell brothers, it is improbable that the archbishop did not approve of the meeting. What makes the discussions most unusual was the fact that it was inconsistent with the ordinary's opposition for more than thirty years to the integration of secular learning and religious values.[50]

In addition to anti-Catholic groups in Cincinnati who strongly opposed consolidation, German Catholics were quick to respond. In August 1869 twenty-four German priests, echoing the opinions of their respective parishes, signed a petition opposing any union of the Catholic schools with the public schools. They feared the schools would lose their unique German Catholic character. Moreover, they argued that valuable school property was being handed over at too low a price. The *Catholic Telegraph,* on the other hand, took issue with the conservative German clergy. Abandoning its usual anti–common school bias, it argued that Catholics "can not push back Niagara, and if we cannot all be of one religion, we can, which is the next best thing, be of *one nation.*" Despite the diocesan paper's efforts, the pressures on

Archbishop Purcell and his staff proved too great. In September Edward Purcell acknowledged defeat. "A little coquetting took place of late between the board of school directors and a few friends of the Catholic parochial schools," he wrote. "We were in hope that it would ripen into real affection. . . . In the meantime some of our German friends excited themselves terribly for fear this union would come to pass! When both parties forbid the banns there is no danger of marriage." Three weeks later Archbishop Purcell issued a public statement on the matter. "The entire government of the public schools in which Catholic youth is educated cannot be given to the civil power," he wrote. "We, as Catholics, cannot approve that system of education for youth which is apart from instruction in the Catholic faith, and teaching of the Church."[51]

During the course of discussions concerning possible union of the two school systems, the Bible controversy in Cincinnati was revived. In 1869 an attempt was made to make Cincinnati's public schools more acceptable to Catholics by de-Protestantizing its curriculum. A coalition of Jews, Catholics, and a few Protestants argued that because of the religious diversity in Cincinnati religion had no place in the public schools. That year Cincinnati's board of education decided to exclude Bible reading, religious instruction, and hymn singing from the public schools. At the time one-fourth of the members of the board were Catholics, a sign that Catholic political power had grown considerably in Cincinnati. The school board's decision caused a bitter feud among religious groups in the community and fueled a nationwide debate. About four years later the Supreme Court of Ohio upheld the board's decision as constitutional. The so-called "Bible War" further strained relations between Protestants and Catholics and helped hasten the secularization of public education.[52]

In 1873 the Catholic parochial school system encountered another challenge. The treasurer and auditor of Hamilton County attempted to collect taxes on thirty-three Catholic school properties. They charged that the parochial schools were not public schools, but denominational in nature, and therefore should not be exempt from taxation. Society "compels us to pay tax[es] for the support of common schools [and] conscience imposes a tax on us to build and support Catholic schools," the *Catholic Telegraph* argued, and "the State Auditor gives another turn to the screw and tells us that we must pay tax for having a conscience at all." In January 1873 Purcell filed a petition for an injunction against the treasurer and auditor from collecting the taxes. For three days in March, both sides presented their cases to the Superior Court of Cincinnati. In June the court decided for the plaintiff, preventing Hamilton County from imposing any taxes upon any of the school properties in the archdiocese.[53]

PURCELL AT THE FIRST VATICAN COUNCIL

An important development in the life of the church in the nineteenth century was the papacy's unprecedented assertion of authority over the internal life of national and local churches. In 1869 Purcell, who made his last of four trips to Rome in the decade, attended the First Vatican Council that reasserted the authority of the Catholic Church and defined the infallibility of the pope when speaking with authority on matters of faith and morals. The church became increasingly centered in Rome. A year before the council convened, the New York *Tribune* portrayed a growing struggle between conservatives and a more traditionalist element led by Purcell, Bishop Bernard J. McQuaid of Rochester, and Archbishops John McCloskey of New York and Peter Richard Kenrick of St. Louis. When the American ordinaries convened at the American College in Rome on December 8, they began working on a petition to the pope not to permit the subject of his infallibility to come before the council. Purcell played a prominent role in the deliberations. He and his American colleagues insisted that a definition of the infallibility of the pope would be inopportune. By reason of his seniority in the American hierarchy, Purcell was regarded as dean of the American bishops. The American bishops feared that assertion of the pope's infallibility would impede the work of the American church, diminish the role of the bishops, and possibly revive anti-Catholic sentiments of nativist days. Purcell, whose opposition to the doctrine dates back to his debate with Alexander Campbell in 1837 and his public criticism in the 1850s of Orestes Brownson's strong defense of the pope's temporal power, drafted the petition. It was submitted on January 15, 1870, with the signatures of twenty-seven English-speaking bishops. All of them but three were Americans. About half of the forty-eight American bishops and one abbot at the council, including William Henry Elder, bishop of Natchez, favored the definition. In light of the fact that more than 500 fathers at the council wanted the definition, the subject remained on the agenda.[54]

On the last day of May 1870, Purcell delivered a learned address in Latin. Objecting to the lack of clarity and confusion on the doctrine, he cogently argued that the pope was not necessarily infallible unless he spoke in his official capacity as teacher of the church on matters of doctrine or morality. He argued that not every papal utterance was to be taken as infallible. Agreeing with some of his colleagues, Purcell sought to limit the authority of the church and pope to spiritual matters. He was particularly concerned over the consequences in the United States if a pope were to speak infallibly against republicanism. "I believe," he said, "that kings are nothing but representatives of the people; I believe that the king is established for the people, and not the people for the king."[55]

The responses to his address were mixed. One of the delegates expressed surprise that Purcell had "preserved intact amid the distracting missionary" work of forty years "the elegance of deep scholarship." Bishop James Goold of Melbourne, Australia, on the other hand, was not impressed by Purcell's talk. He noted in his diary for May 31 that the Cincinnati ordinary had "addressed the council feebly and incoherently." Writing to a friend in Germany on June 2, Lord John Acton of England reported that he found Purcell's speech interesting, especially his defense of popular sovereignty. Building upon Purcell's line of argument, he suggested that perhaps the pope existed for the church and not the church for the pope.[56]

The Council Fathers accepted the pope's infallibility and jurisdictional primacy. Shortly after the close of the council, the major focus of interest among the returning ordinaries was on the inopportunists who had challenged the definition and had been allowed to leave Rome to avoid casting negative votes. Purcell was the first to draw attention. A few hours after he arrived in New York City on August 10, 1870, he agreed to an interview with a reporter from the *Herald*. "The Archbishop declared himself an anti-infallibilist," the reporter wrote, " . . . [and] expressed himself to the effect that the Roman Catholic mind in America is not prepared to accept the doctrine of infallibility." During the next week some of Purcell's episcopal colleagues expressed concern over his alleged position expressed in the interview. Bishop Patrick Lynch of Charleston urged Purcell to consider his position carefully and to weigh the potential harm of his remarks. He pleaded with him to subject his "own opinions and if need be personal judgments . . . to the yoke of Faith." Sylvester Rosecrans, his longtime friend and bishop of Columbus, also suggested to his metropolitan that he accept the definition. It should be noted, however, that in the American tradition of episcopal collegiality, some ordinaries, such as Bishop McQuaid of Rochester, believed that the bishops, as they did at the Second Plenary Council at Baltimore in 1866, acting in unison with the pope could teach infallibly.[57]

On August 21, three days after his return to Cincinnati, the seventy-year-old Purcell read the decree on papal infallibility at a public ceremony. All the Catholic societies of the city and adjoining suburbs were present. "[N]o one," the *Catholic Telegraph* wrote, "expected such an outpouring of citizens, Protestants as well as Catholics, old and young, that gathered in thousands around the Cathedral, and Railroad Depot, and along the line of march, crowding the streets." Purcell began his address by praising American political liberties. As he did throughout his administration, he argued that the United States had "the best form of human government." A longtime proponent of the separation of church and state, he pointed out that the U.S. Constitution "grants perfect liberty to every denomination of Christians." That was, he insisted, "infinitely better for the Catholic religion, than were it the special object of the State's patronage and protection." What Catholics want, he argued, "is a free field and no favor. Truth is mighty and will prevail."[58]

Purcell then tried to undo the confusion surrounding his remarks in the *Herald* interview. He denied the allegation that he was insincere in his acceptance of papal infallibility. "I am here," he said, "to proclaim my belief in the Infallibility of the Pope." But when he tried to explain his initial position as stemming from certain theological distinctions on papal pronouncements that had been made over the centuries, he inadvertently added to the confusion. Purcell ended his talk by declaring his unswerving loyalty to the pope and to the church. "I am," he said,

> a true Roman Catholic, as I said in Rome. . . . I have vindicated the rights of the Pope, and the infallibility of the Church in the strongest language I was capable of using in Rome, and I am not going back on this. . . . I want the editors of newspapers and reporters to send it on the wings of the press, North, South, East and West, that John B. Purcell is one of the most faithful Catholics that ever swore allegiance to the Church. Let them say what they please of me and my course in Rome; for that I have received the thanks of those who do not think exactly as I do. It is by free discussion that much is elicited, and without such discussion it can not be.

The audience appeared content with their archbishop's proclamation of loyalty to the pope and the church.[59]

Though Purcell made public his approval of the decree on papal infallibility, Cardinal Alessandro Barnabò, prefect of the Propaganda, nonetheless advised him to communicate his acceptance directly to the pontiff as an example to other bishops. In his December 5 letter to the pope, Purcell acknowledged the primacy of the Roman See and the infallibility of its occupant in matters of faith and morals when speaking *ex cathedra*. The following month the pope expressed his appreciation of the archbishop's support.[60]

At the same time that he affirmed the mission of the Catholic Church and acknowledged the infallibility of the pope, Purcell during the next decade continued to promote strong community relations. Since the earliest days of his administration, the ordinary had proven sensitive to educational and social issues by adopting a pragmatic and conciliatory stance. During this time the archdiocese further enhanced its image in the community by becoming steadily involved in social and charitable programs that benefited non-Catholics and Catholics alike.

· 6 ·

RELIGIOUS AND SOCIAL ISSUES

F rom the 1830s to the 1870s Catholics under Purcell's leadership expanded their charitable and educational programs for the needy, largely made possible by the pioneer efforts of women and men religious orders and benevolent lay societies. Though childcare in the archdiocese, as in other urban dioceses, still dominated Catholic priorities in the second half of the nineteenth century, other areas increasingly attracted concern. Moreover, through Purcell's leadership the local church took an unequivocal stand on the abolition of slavery, opposed secession by the South, and was consistently loyal to the Union during the Civil War. While the Cincinnati ordinary's stature among his episcopal colleagues increased in the nineteenth century, his episcopal authority in the archdiocese also grew. By midcentury Purcell, who presided successfully over a vast spiritual empire, also began building a new seminary, hoping to provide more American and diocesan clergy. Two decades later the dean of the American bishops suffered a devastating blow. Because of erratic banking practices by his brother, Edward Purcell, the archdiocese faced a severe financial crisis.[1]

CHARITABLE PROGRAMS AND TEMPERANCE

In the early years of Purcell's administration the diocese's social work programs focused on schools and orphanages. By the 1850s the archdiocese began developing new social programs. The economic depressions of 1854 and 1857 and the continuing influx of immigrants called for more organized charities. Furthermore, the six archbishops and twenty-six bishops who met in 1852 for the First Plenary Council of Baltimore had affirmed in their pastoral letter the increasing need to "found Hospitals, establish orphanages and provide for every want of suffering humanity, which Religion forbids us to neglect." The Catholic poor in the archdiocese populated the city's poverty zones in far greater proportions than the general population. When in 1855 the Cincinnati Relief Union informed the archbishop that three-fourths of the individuals on their relief rolls were "poor Irish people," they inquired what the Catholic Church was doing for its needy. Purcell responded by pointing out that the local church supported four orphan asylums and spent about $10,000 annually "on the poor members of her communion, and of others not of her communion," including twenty of eighty-six children in St. Peter's Orphanage.[2]

To help support charitable causes members of the St. Peter's, St. Joseph's, and St. Aloysius's male and female orphan societies paid twenty-five cents per month to support charitable causes. Those of the Mary and Martha Society, a charitable organization established in 1836 for the benefit of the poor, the sick, and the elderly, paid twelve and one-half cents per month. Money was also raised by fairs for the benefit of the orphans and by collections taken up in the churches and by fairs, balls, and concerts. As in other dioceses, local benevolent societies often turned to crowd-pleasing social events to raise money. While officially ordinaries presided over all the charitable enterprises in their dioceses, responsibility for the administration of financial success rested primarily on the voluntary efforts of the lay members.[3]

Moreover, in the early 1840s the Sisters of Notre Dame established sodalities under the patronage of the Blessed Mother. The lay women at these sodalities, which met at the Sixth Street convent, worked among the poor and orphans in their own parishes. In the German parishes a committee of two in each city ward investigated the claims of applicants and drew upon their parish treasury for such sums as were required to help the needy. These efforts by the laity constituted the beginning of the Catholic lay ministry in the diocese of Cincinnati.[4]

Purcell's commitment to the needs of the sick and the poor was equally well respected. Throughout his tenure he "always found an hour or two to visit the sick," William Bigot, pastor of St. Michael Church at Fort Loramie wrote in 1873, "and devote some time to the poor. His bishop's ring was pawned many times to get money to be used for the needy. Some found out about it and got it back for him."[5]

In particular, the Cincinnati ordinary was concerned over the living and working conditions of the Catholic poor. In Purcell's judgment, intemperance, low wages, and general economic conditions contributed to their plight. In the early years of his tenure the local church addressed the issue of alcoholism. It was the most enduring reform movement that local Catholics became identified with in the nineteenth century. The temperance crusade continued into the early twentieth century. By 1840 Bishop Purcell, along with a few other bishops, supported the cause. In March of that year the Catholic Total Abstinence Society of Cincinnati was formed, with Edward Collins, the Irish vicar general for the English-speaking Catholics, as president. About two weeks later Purcell joined seventy-seven members of the cathedral parish in taking the pledge. Though Purcell was generally abstemious, he had an occasional drink. When the Jesuits arrived in Cincinnati in early September, Purcell invited them to his house where he served, he wrote, "red & white wine, in spite of Teetotalism." He and the diocesan paper criticized the American Temperance Union for its advocacy of prohibition. In the 1840s and 1850s more and more parish communities sponsored local temperance societies. Throughout his administration Purcell saw the Catholic temperance movement as essential. In 1874 the seventy-four-year-old archbishop addressed the Catholic Total Abstinence Union that convened in Philadelphia. "Having enjoyed, thank God, very fine health for the ten years when I was totally abstinent . . . ," he said, "now I can, though a teetotaller once more, work with as little inconvenience as ever." He was pleasantly surprised that his health did not suffer from abstinence.[6]

While supporting the Catholic Total Abstinence movement, Purcell made it exclusively a Catholic crusade. When invited to preach a temperance sermon in two Methodist churches in the early 1840s, he declined. He had no objections, however, to the participation of the Catholic Total Abstinence Society in local temperance parades, regarding them as purely civic in nature. Though fully committed to the cause, Purcell stopped short of attempting to force the German and French Catholics, who generally did not endorse the abstinence movement, to take the pledge. Instead, Purcell and his clergy focused on the Irish poor. They were generally more hospitable to the temperance cause. While visiting the public works at St. Mary's Lake on the Miami Canal in the fall of 1850, he described it as "the Irish laborers' graveyard in Ohio." Only "they who have lived among the 'shanties,'" he further noted, "can conceive the hardships there endured by a people whom oppression had driven from their own healthy homes to seek an honest livelihood where the very air is darkened with the shafts of the pestilence! Alas for poor, human nature, when this evil is frightfully aggravated by intemperance madly resorted to as a refuge from disease!" Aware that some canal workers were served as many as seventeen glasses of hard liquor a day, Purcell derived pleasure to see people come forward to take the pledge. Their experience of the "evils of intemperance convinced them," he wrote, "that they could not otherwise avoid the miseries of this life."[7]

Like most of his episcopal colleagues, however, Purcell did not consider the pledge as binding under pain of sin. One of the more ardent pastors who ministered to the workers on the Erie Canal was Emanuel Thienpont, pastor of Emmanuel Church at Dayton. On one of his visits to the canal near Piqua, seventeen workers took the pledge. Though many of the bishop's clergy crusaded for the cause, not all of them were strong temperance men from the start. Father Joseph Machebeuf, who took care of several counties in northwestern Ohio, admitted to Purcell that, not unlike other priests he knew, he was not at first a friend of total abstinence. But he eventually felt compelled to abstain. On St. Patrick's Day, 1842, he took the pledge.[8]

Besides participating in the temperance movement, local Catholics also addressed a number of social issues. When in the summer of 1849 Cincinnati experienced another cholera epidemic, the worst since 1832–1833 when Bishop Fenwick succumbed to the disease, the local church expressed particular concern over the plight of the Catholic poor. In a nine-day period, June 18 to June 26, 398 of 505 burials in Cincinnati were victims of cholera. In his July 2, 1849, pastoral letter to the diocese, Purcell estimated that more than seventy Catholics a day died of it. He attributed the high rate of Catholic deaths to the fact that the Catholics were among the poorest in the city. They "must put up," he said, "with the damp cellar, the ill-ventilated garret, the loathsome alley, . . . the wet, unchanged garments after toil and rain." As the supreme pastor of the diocese Purcell reminded the faithful that the innocent must suffer with the guilty in the face of God's wrath. He pointed out that the cholera was also due to the "crimes of intemperance, profane swearing, desecration of the Sabbath, contempt of religion, dishonesty, and oppression and insensibil[it]y to the wants of the poor."[9]

As before, the Sisters of Charity responded heroically to the cholera epidemic. While the sisters attended to the sick and provided rooms at St. Peter's Orphanage to a large number of new destitute orphans, Purcell urged Catholics to be as generous toward the facilities as possible. "We are all very much exhausted by fatigue and anxiety of mind," Purcell wrote. "Fourteen of our little orphan girls have died and some others may follow owing to the inherited weakness of their little frames." Some German Catholic families responded by renting a house to accommodate additional children.[10]

Purcell concluded his July 1849 pastoral on the cholera epidemic on an uncharacteristic note, in which he suggested substantial social reforms. Believing that Americans had the capacity to effect reforms in society to improve living conditions, he recommended that "the filthy and disgusting hovels where the penniless are compelled to congregate . . . be reduced to ashes and grounds." Purcell hoped that community funds would be allocated "to build up whole streets of comfortable cottages, or houses, in sufficient number for all who may require them! This good thing can be done." What was needed, he argued, was "a 'Creating Spirit,' a hearty good will on the part of our citizens to realize this moral and physical phenomenon for which no city, or nation, hath a parallel."[11]

A year earlier Purcell had recommended that a "prudent, legal, thorough reform of the Social System" be implemented to give a ". . . sufficient share to every man of the good things of this life." He blamed "the lazy, the vicious, the dishonest, the unprincipled usurpers of the hard earnings of the virtuous poor" for much of the social malaise. Purcell also warned his flock that the "bursting storms" in Europe in 1848 were such that they and other Americans should not "let the evils of society become so aggravated by . . . neglect and indifference as to require such a terrific explosion. . . . Let us save, if possible," he continued, "our country from the calamities of the old world. Better do this while it is yet time. Better vaccinate society, than let it take the small pox."[12]

Though the local church expressed concern over social ills, it frowned upon direct government assistance. While criticizing those individuals who made a profit by raising fuel prices due to a shortage during the economic depression of 1857, Purcell and the diocesan paper emphasized more the importance of self-help. "The Spirit that is evidently growing in our large cities of looking to government for bread in hunger, or for employment in idleness," the *Catholic Telegraph* editorialized, "seems to bode the decay of the republican sentiment among our people. . . . In a true republic the people take care of themselves, and ask nothing but justice from the law, and the moment government becomes the father of the people, republicanism is effete."[13]

RELIGIOUS ORDERS, EDUCATION, AND SOCIAL CONCERNS

Under the auspices of various women religious communities, Catholic social work expanded in the diocese during the Purcell years. By midcentury American women religious were among the strongest advocates for health, education, and social service institutions. The local ordinary, like his episcopal colleagues, praised their efforts and constantly encouraged them to expand their works and attend to the people who need them. As they did, it was nevertheless through their schools that the greatest number of people came into contact with the women religious. Notwithstanding the earlier anti-Catholic warnings of some Protestants, by midcentury some wealthy Protestants contributed to financing the Catholic schools and sent their children to them. Writing about the work of the women religious, Purcell noted that the "Protestants are forced to acknowledge the solidity of instruction given by these ladies. Consequently, a goodly number of them have confided to them their children."[14]

To accommodate the increasing numbers of children under their care, by 1850 the Sisters of Charity from Emmitsburg, who had moved their academy, school, and orphanage to Third and Plum Streets in 1836, had made three additions to the building. At that time there were more than three hundred children in St. Peter's, about half each in the school and the orphanage. In 1850 the superiors of the Sisters of Charity at Emmitsburg affiliated with the Daughters of Charity in France. Two years later five of the eight sisters in Cincinnati under the leadership of their superior, Margaret Cecilia Farrell George, one of the original founders of the American Sisters of Charity and friend of the founder Elizabeth Seton, declined affiliation. Like their sister counterparts in New York, who had already withdrawn from the Emmitsburg community to form their own separate community, they disapproved of the changes in dress, customs, rules, vows, and the limitation of the exercise of charity to females in the orphanages and parochial schools.[15]

Having witnessed the work and spread of the order in his diocese, the archbishop eventually supported Sister Margaret and those sisters who wished to retain the initial dress, rules, and regulations, which were more symbolic of American customs and practices. Purcell, like some of his episcopal colleagues, sought to promote religious communities that would attend to local needs without needing approval from authorities outside the diocese. In February 1852, after saying Mass for the Sisters of Charity in their chapel, Purcell declared that his "Brother ecclesiastics" and he had decided that the sisters should remain Mother Seton's Daughters of Charity. "I shall establish here in my Episcopal City a Motherhouse and open a Novitiate for training the young," he said. The following month, the five sisters, joined by Sister Sophia Gillmeyer, a native of Maryland who had stayed in Cincinnati after a visit two years earlier, disevered their connection with the community at Emmitsburg. They made their vows to Purcell and became an independent diocesan community. Another sister from St. Louis soon joined them.[16]

The seven sisters became the founding members of the Sisters of Charity of Cincinnati. The ordeal was not an easy one for them, as they had to decide between loyalty to the community at Emmitsburg and the needs of the American community and the local church. A year after the break, Sister Margaret George was elected the first mother superior of the community. St. Peter's academy, orphan asylum, and school served as the first motherhouse until 1853, when a two-story building was renovated on Mount Harrison in Price Hill. There they opened Mount St. Vincent Academy and boarding school the same year. In addition to the founding of St. Xavier College and the church schools established in the various parishes, the archdiocese also saw during the next thirty years of Purcell's tenure an increase in female academies. The Sisters of Charity, soon to be joined by other women religious

FIG 8. Sister of Charity with her class at Mount St. Vincent in Price Hill in Cincinnati in the late 1800s

orders, regarded the moral and religious training of the girls as future mothers as essential to sustain the sanctity of the home. This was a view widespread generally in American society during the nineteenth and first half of the twentieth centuries.[17]

In 1857 the Sisters of Charity acquired thirty-three acres on Glenway Avenue, where the motherhouse and Mount St. Vincent Academy were relocated. This area became the center of community activities for the next twenty years. As the number of students and novices increased and the academy became overcrowded, the Sisters of Charity in 1869 acquired Biggs Farms in Delhi, on the outskirts of the city. When new buildings were erected across the road from the farmhouse in 1884, the sisters' motherhouse was moved there. The farm became known as the Mount St. Joseph. The sisters used the farmhouse as a novitiate, the place of training for those who were preparing to enter the order.[18]

Following the diocesan organization of the Sisters of Charity and the addition of more personnel to their community, the ministry of the sisters expanded rapidly. The order was the most important of the religious orders in the archdiocese with regard to charity and social service. The same month that they became an independent diocesan community, local lay Catholics organized St. Joseph's Benevolent Society to help support an orphanage for boys. Two months later they opened St. Joseph Orphanage on George Street, with Sister Anthony O'Connell in charge of the 23 boys. In the fall of 1852 the archdiocese acquired nearly twelve acres of land in Cumminsville at a cost of $8,000 for the purpose of building a new orphanage. Two summers later the sisters and 160 orphan boys moved to their new site. The following year the girls from St. Peter Orphanage were also transferred to Cumminsville. On the eve of the Civil War, St. Joseph Orphanage took care of 400 children.[19]

In February 1853 two Sisters of Charity also took charge of the Mary and Martha Society. Later that year the Sisters of Charity opened St. Mary Academy, a select boarding and day school, on the southeast corner of Sixth and Park Streets. Two years later the school was closed in order to open pay and free schools on George Street. Not uncommon among most women religious communities in the pre–Civil War period was for a free school to be conducted side by side with the select school. The select or "pay school" often provided the funds that made possible the free school.[20]

In the fall of 1852 Purcell helped expand the ministry of the Sisters of Charity by purchasing a hotel for invalids in Cincinnati and giving it to them. On November 13 the sisters opened the first private hospital, St. John's Hotel for Invalids, on Broadway and Franklin Streets in the east end of the city. Increasing immigration and periodic epidemics pointed to the need for Catholic hospitals. Providing care for twenty-one patients, St. John's, which was one among approximately twenty-five Catholic hospitals opened in the country by 1860, was also the first such Catholic hospital in the community to have a teaching faculty associated with it. Three years later the sisters moved the hospital to the property vacated by the girl orphans at Third and Plum in the west end. In 1866 two generous non-Catholic benefactors, Joseph Butler and Louis Worthington, bought the U.S. Marine Hospital at Sixth Street for the Sisters of Charity. They handed over the deed of the property on the fiftieth birthday of Sister Anthony, who had joined the staff of St. John's and was often referred to as the "Florence Nightingale of America." The donors requested that the name of the hospital be changed to the "Hospital of the Good Samaritan" in remembrance of Sister Anthony's kindness. That year the sisters abandoned St. John's and opened Good Samaritan Hospital. The latter, with a ninety-five-bed capacity, remained there until 1915, when it was moved to Clifton Avenue, northeast of the city. In the fall of 1873 the Sisters of Charity also founded in the east end the St. Joseph Infant Asylum, later known as the St. Joseph Infant and Maternity Home, as a branch of Good Samaritan Hospital. The property was another gift to Sister Anthony from her friend Joseph Butler. As one of twelve Catholic infant homes and maternity hospitals opened in the United States between 1870 and 1900, St. Joseph cared for expectant, unwed mothers and their babies.[21]

Besides the expansion of the Sisters of Charity's social ministry, by the late 1850s more parochial schools in the archdiocese came under their guidance. In 1857 the order took charge of St. Mary Academy connected to St. Joseph Church in Dayton. This was the Cincinnati order's first institution outside Cincinnati. Two years later they staffed St. Patrick school in Fayetteville. Over time other cities in the East and West invited the Cincinnati sisters to establish a branch of Mother Seton's community. By 1870 there were more than 180 Sisters of Charity, staffing seventeen parochial schools in Ohio alone.[22]

In the nineteenth century other women religious came to the diocese and helped enhance the social and educational work of the local church. It was Purcell's understanding after he returned from Europe in 1839 that the superior of the Sisters of the Sacred Heart would soon be sending him sisters for his diocese. He was doubtlessly disappointed to learn that new regulations in the order had forced the superior to postpone indefinitely sending any sisters to Cincinnati. Purcell then immediately appealed to the Sisters of Notre Dame de Namur in Belgium. Though the sisters appeared willing to come to the diocese, they would do so only if certain conditions were met. They requested financial assistance, a suitable house with a garden, and the opportunity to conduct classes for poor children. Though unable to meet the first two conditions, Purcell assured them that they could choose a proper location at Cincinnati, Fayetteville, or Chillicothe, and conduct parochial schools for poor children. The sisters accepted the bishop's invitation.[23]

On October 31, 1840, eight sisters of Notre Dame de Namur, with Sister Louise de Gonzaga as local superior, arrived in Cincinnati. Purcell went to the river and personally greeted them on the steamer. Not wanting to be insulted and ridiculed, the French-speaking sisters were not wearing their religious habits because they had chosen to be inconspicuous on the journey. This was an age when, in some circles, women religious who, unlike their Protestant contemporaries, wore distinctive clothing, took lifelong vows of poverty, chastity, and obedience, and subjected themselves to regulations governing every aspect of their lives, were considered suspect. During the next six weeks the Notre Dame Sisters stayed with the Sisters of Charity. Though Purcell offered them two hundred acres of land in Brown County, Sister Gonzaga declined the offer, preferring to stay in the city in order to comply with the established customs of the religious community and attend to the education of the poor children. By late fall the sisters purchased a thirty-room mansion on Sixth Street for $24,000 and occupied it Christmas day. Immediately they began preparing the property for a select school for girls. This decision was well received by Purcell, who had wanted a boarding school in the diocese to compete with Nazareth Academy in Kentucky where many Cincinnati girls were being sent. On January 19, 1841, the Sisters of

Notre Dame opened the Young Ladies Literary Institute and Boarding School, later known as Notre Dame Academy. Classes for those students unable to pay the tuition were opened at the same time as the boarding school. A month after its opening there were thirty pupils in the day school, between thirty and forty in the free school, and one boarder. By summer the Sisters of Notre Dame had five boarders, about sixty day pupils, and the same number of poor.[24]

Catholics were "mightily pleased," the *Catholic Telegraph* editorialized in 1841, with the Sisters of Notre Dame that "grace our Queenly City." When in 1845 the old cathedral on Sycamore Street became the Jesuit Church of St. Francis Xavier, the children of the parish enrolled in the sisters' free school. The children were accommodated in the convent classrooms and taught gratuitously by the sisters, until the Jesuits erected two decades later the St. Xavier parochial school. In 1846 the Sisters of Notre Dame erected their first school building adjoining their residence on Sixth Street. But that soon proved insufficient. To accommodate the 125 boarders and day students and the six additional sisters and postulants from Europe, a two-story building, containing a refectory, schoolroom for the boarders, a dormitory, and music rooms, was built. With the arrival of German-speaking Sisters of Notre Dame from Belgium, the order then undertook the task of teaching girls in the German parish schools. Shortly after the Civil War, the sisters opened an academy at Court and Mound Streets for young girls in the western parts of Cincinnati. It became the cherished alma mater of hundreds of Catholic, Protestant, and Jewish women. This academy remained open until 1920.[25]

By midcentury the Sisters of Notre Dame extended their ministry outside Cincinnati. In the fall of 1849 four sisters went by canal boat to Dayton and laid the foundation of the second oldest house of the sisterhood in the country. The following year they opened a free school and a boarding school. For the next several decades the sisters in Dayton devoted their time to the parish schools. It was not long before they had flourishing academies and parochial schools at Reading, Hamilton, and Columbus in the Midwest and cities in the East. Pupils and postulants multiplied rapidly. The order's plan of having a boarding school, a day school, and a free school taught simultaneously, wherever possible, was followed from the beginning.[26]

Another boost to the educational efforts of the diocese was the arrival of the Ursuline Sisters in 1845. Bishop Purcell had first established relations with the Ursulines on his trip to Europe in 1838 when he visited their convent in France. When in 1844 Father Joseph Machebeuf received word that his father had died in France, he obtained permission to visit his family. Acting as Purcell's agent, Machebeuf was successful in obtaining from the mother superiors at both Boulogne-sur-Mer and Beaulieu, France, the services of eleven Ursuline Sisters. Three were English-speaking sisters and eight French-speaking. They left Le Havre in May 1845, arriving in Cincinnati on June 19.[27]

Though Purcell offered them a choice in location between Brown County and Chillicothe for their new academy and convent, the Ursulines left the selection to him. Purcell chose Brown County. For over a decade more and more Catholics had moved from the city and settled in the county. The Catholic settlement in Fayetteville was one of the largest in Ohio. The diocesan paper encouraged such movement, pointing out that "the country is a thousand times preferable to the city for the laboring Catholic population. . . . The country is better for soul and body than the crowded cities; there is more peace of mind and tranquility to be there enjoyed." Shortly after the Ursuline Sisters took possession of the St. Martin's Convent, located in the vacant seminary quarters in Brown County, they opened an academy where, on October 4, 1845, they received three boarding pupils. The following year they established "The St. Ursula Literary Institute," and by September 1847 a new convent was built.[28]

By midcentury several religious orders ran schools for girls in the archdiocese. The Ursulines conducted the boarding and day school at St. Martin's and the Sisters of St. Dominic the boarding and day school at Somerset. Meanwhile, the Sisters of the Precious Blood operated the German schools at Wolfscreek settlement in Crawford County, St. Michael's in Seneca County, St. Alphonso in Huron County, and a girls' boarding school at Minster. At all these schools for girls, those who could not pay, those who could pay a little, and those who had ample means were "equally suited."[29]

Regrettably, the *Catholic Telegraph* wrote, "similar advantages are not afforded to the boys. In this respect our German brethren, at least, in this city, are far ahead of us." Purcell and his staff were hopeful that the opening in the late 1840s of the St. Francis Xavier and cathedral parish schools for English-speaking boys would provide "equal, if not superior advantages."[30]

In the spring of 1849 the pastor of Holy Trinity Church, through his Jesuit missionary friend, Francis X. Weninger, invited the Brothers of the Society of Mary, founded in 1817 at Bordeaux, France, to come to Cincinnati and conduct a school for boys at the Holy Trinity parish. The Society accepted the invitation and sent Father Leo Meyer and Brother Charles Schultz to the diocese. When they reached Cincinnati in mid-July there was a cholera epidemic raging in the Midwest. Purcell asked Meyer to assist temporarily Father Henry Juncker in Dayton, then a community of 16,000 inhabitants. For a month the forty-nine-year-old Meyer aided the sick and dying in all parts of the city. While there he met John Stuart, a parishioner at Emmanuel Church, who owned 125 acres of land southeast of Dayton.

Given the opportunity to buy the estate, Meyer related the offer to the superior general in France.[31]

When Meyer returned to Cincinnati in mid-August, Purcell gave him and the order the opportunity to open schools anywhere in the diocese. Though Purcell tried to get the Brothers of the Society of Mary to provide teachers for the English-speaking schools, Meyer worked with the pastors of the German-speaking parishes of Holy Trinity and St. Paul. On December 3, four Brothers from Alsace arrived in Cincinnati; two were stationed at Holy Trinity school, whereas the other two were reserved for the foundation that Meyer was planning for Dayton. In February 1850, following the departure of Juncker for Europe, Purcell placed Meyer in charge of Emmanuel Church, the mother church of the city. Like his predecessor, Meyer impressed upon the German Catholics the close link between religion and language. By late March the Marianists purchased the Stuart estate for $12,000 with a six percent annual interest. Meyer intended to make the property, later christened "Nazareth," the headquarters for the Brothers of Mary in America. On September 1, 1850, Meyer and three Brothers of the Society of Mary opened St. Mary's School, a boarding school for Catholic boys, with fourteen in attendance. Three years later the school had an enrollment of fifty students, among them twenty boarders.[32]

On the evening of December 26, 1855, tragedy struck the school. A fire destroyed the central house, including the dormitory, classrooms, and several rooms of the Marianists. Temporary quarters were provided the students. Within three months the Brothers of the Society of Mary were back on the school grounds and began the work of rebuilding. School buildings were ready for classes by September 1857. Among the twenty students who attended the school, nine were boarders. Before the end of the school year, there were thirty students. In 1857 the school became known as St. Mary's College, which later became the University of Dayton. Like St. Xavier College in Cincinnati, the second college in the diocese of Cincinnati opened as a day and boarding school. During the next two decades the college continued to grow and several new buildings were added to the Dayton property. The additions included a three-story building in 1860, new wing in 1865, chapel in 1868, and St. Mary's Hall in 1871.[33]

At Purcell's request the Brothers of the Poor of St. Francis, founded in 1857 at Cologne, Germany, and dedicated to the care of orphans and the education of youth of the poorer classes, came to Cincinnati in 1868. Five brothers opened the protectory for homeless and wayward boys in the abandoned St. John's Hospital on Lock Street. "If all their efforts tend to prevent one mortal sin," Purcell wrote, "all their labors and sacrifices shall have been fully compensated." In its first year the home cared for more than 130 boys.

As the problem of providing sufficient food for the increasing number of boys became more acute, Father Richard Broering of Holy Trinity Church conceived the idea of establishing the St. Margaret Society. By 1870 several parishes established branches of the ladies' aid society in order to help provide food and clothing for the young boys. In one instance the Society sponsored a three-day social and raised $6,000 for the protectory. In need of larger accommodations, Purcell donated $10,000 as a down payment and the brothers, in 1870, obtained and moved to a farm of more than 100 acres at Mount St. Peter in Delhi Township. When Purcell visited the facilities and said Mass at the family mansion he renamed the site Mount Alverno. At times as many as 250 boys were in the Mount Alverno Protectory for Boys.[34]

During Purcell's tenure Mrs. Sarah Worthington King Peter helped arrange for other orders of sisters from Europe to come to Cincinnati to help expand organized Catholic educational and social work in the archdiocese. Daughter of Thomas Worthington, one of Ohio's first senators and governors, Sarah married Rufus King, who died in 1836. Eight years later she married William Peter, British Consul at Philadelphia. After his death in 1853 she traveled extensively. Fascinated by the Christian traditions and shrines of Jerusalem and Rome, Sarah Peter eventually converted to Catholicism and began a long career of service not only to the Catholic Church but also to the arts in Cincinnati.

The first order of sisters that Sarah Peter, with Purcell's approval, helped bring to Cincinnati to do social work was the Good Shepherd Sisters from Louisville. Upon arrival in Cincinnati in February 1857, the sisters took possession of a little frame house adjoining St. Augustine Church in the west end. Sarah Peter brought them eighteen female prisoners for the opening of their class. Taking charge of the Women's Prison on Front Street in the early 1860s, the sisters took care of more than 3,000 "poor prisoners" over a six-year period. A few years later they established a new convent on Baum Street, in the eastern section of the city. In 1866 the Good Shepherd Sisters also opened an industrial school and a day asylum for the children of working mothers. They soon outgrew their facilities. By 1870 the white-robed sisters bought a farm at Carthage, where they established their provincial headquarters and school for girls as well as two industrial schools, one for whites and the other for blacks. Some of the older women prisoners followed the sisters from Front Street and spent the rest of their lives in the Magdalen Retreat of the Good Shepherd institution at Carthage. The ministry of the Good Shepherd Sisters proved controversial as they often worked with delinquent girls and reformed prostitutes. The community of "Magdalens," established in 1859, provided a regular, religious life for penitent, reformed women, who wished to remain forever cloistered. They followed the rule of the Third Order of Mount Carmel and wore brown habits similar to the Carmelite habit. Their chief occupations were fine needlework, embroidery, and sewing altar linens and church vestments.[35]

The same year that Sarah Peter helped Purcell obtain the Good Shepherd Sisters, she went to Ireland to procure the Sisters of Mercy to also engage in social work. To help obtain them Purcell assured the sisters that they would never be without food as long as he had "a crust" of bread to share with them. More than two decades after Mother Catherine MacAuley founded the order in Ireland in 1831, eleven Sisters of Mercy, with Mother Mary Teresa Maher as the superior, arrived in Cincinnati on August 18, 1858. Sarah Peter provided temporary residence for them at her home. The sisters, who trained nurses and social workers as well as teachers, immediately engaged themselves in numerous social work activities. Consistent with the mission of their society, they instructed young girls in the useful branches of education, took care of the very young children of working mothers, visited the jails and hospitals, and provided temporary accommodation to distressed, unemployed women. In October they opened a night school in the basement of St. Thomas Church on Sycamore Street for uneducated adult Irish immigrants. The following day they opened the Infant Boys' School in the same quarters. Within a month approximately two hundred working girls attended night school, eighty infant boys were registered in the day school, and the sisters paid some 360 visits to the sick, destitute, and dying in the neighborhood.[36]

In the spring of 1860 the Sisters of Mercy, with Purcell's approval, purchased and moved to the former German orphanage on Fourth Street for their future convent and schools. They paid $6,000 from the proceeds of a fair and picnic and mortgaged the property for the remaining $23,000. There they cared for needy children and homeless women and opened a laundry to enable the women to earn a livelihood. They also conducted married women's classes, a day school of nearly two hundred students, and a Sunday school.[37]

By September the sisters opened a new school for girls on Third Street, which was readily reached from their convent by a flight of outdoor stairs. Though the Third Street property was to serve largely as a house of refuge and academy, it also served as a hospital during the Civil War, the cholera epidemic of 1866, and the flood of 1883. By the 1870s the Sisters of Mercy, who would become the largest female religious community in the world, had expanded their work to schools not only in Cincinnati but also to other communities in Ohio.[38]

While visiting the Sisters of Mercy in Europe in 1857, Sarah Peter was also successful in getting a delegation of Sisters of the Poor of St. Francis in Germany to work with the poor, the aged, and the sick in their home. On September 7, 1858, five sisters and a postulant arrived in New York, where they were greeted at the wharf and escorted to Cincinnati by the archbishop's brother and chancellor, Edward Purcell. Thus within a month's time Sarah Peter had managed to secure two orders of sisters, one Irish—Sisters of Mercy, who had arrived in August—and one German. After the Franciscan Sisters of the Poor stayed a few days in a temporary home in Cincinnati, three trustees of the St. Aloysius Orphan Society offered the use, rent free for six months, of the building that had served as St. Aloysius' Orphanage on West Fourth Street. The sisters' first establishment was the old orphanage on Third Street that was remodeled for that purpose. On Christmas day 1859 they opened the city's second Catholic hospital, St. Mary's, on Betts Street in the west end of the city in a predominantly German neighborhood. Early in 1860 Sarah Peter put them up, as she had the Sisters of Mercy, in her own house. A short time later she deeded over to them half her property, which then became a convent, as did the other half upon her death. In 1878 some sisters went to Dayton at the request of John F. Hahne, pastor of the Emmanuel Church, and founded St. Elizabeth Hospital, the third Catholic hospital in the archdiocese. Ten years later, because of the overcrowded condition of St. Mary's in Cincinnati, the Sisters of the Poor of St. Francis also established St. Francis Hospital on Queen City Avenue in the west end.[39]

The fourth order of sisters invited to the archdiocese by Sarah Peter was the Little Sisters of the Poor. She induced some of the sisters to leave their motherhouse in Brittany, France, in 1868 and come to Cincinnati to work with the elderly. Shortly after their arrival in October of that year, six sisters, in their black dresses, kerchiefs, and white bonnets, began their work in an old abandoned schoolhouse on George Street in the southwestern section of the city. Five years later they built on Florence Avenue in the eastern end the St. Joseph Home for the Aged, one of thirty-four homes for the poor the Little Sisters of the Poor opened in the country by 1900.[40]

After the arrival of the Sisters of the Poor to the archdiocese, Cincinnati obtained the services of three other orders of sisters to run parish schools. At Purcell's request Sisters of the Sacred Heart from Paris came to Cincinnati in 1869 and opened the Sacred Heart Academy and Convent in the downtown area with Mother Ellen Hogan as superior. In 1874 the convent was transferred to Echo Place on Grandin Road in the eastern end of Cincinnati. In the mid-1870s the Franciscans invited Sisters of the Third Order Regular of St. Francis, located at Oldenburg, Indiana, to teach in their parish school. Four years later they ran a second school in Carthage. In 1880 the sisters were called to St. John parish at Middletown. During the next twenty years they took charge of several schools in the archdiocese. In August 1881 four Sisters of Christian Charity, upon the invitation of Father George Steinlage at Piqua, Ohio, took charge of the teaching duties at St. Boniface.[41]

During the second half of the nineteenth century the various sisterhoods became the backbone of the educational and social work in the hierarchical and male-dominated archdiocese. In the 1860s the girls' schools were conducted by the Sisters of Notre Dame, the Ursuline Sisters, the Sisters of Charity, the Sisters of Mercy, the Sisters of St. Dominic, and the Sisters of the Most Precious Blood. The latter and the Sisters of Notre Dame were the only ones who taught in the German girls' schools. As teachers, fund-raisers, choir directors, sponsors of religious organizations, coaches, active caregivers, and social service providers, women religious helped pioneer the growth of the Catholic Church, contributing their share to the religious and intellectual life of the archdiocese. In the process, their myriad activities afforded many of them leadership opportunities not available to most women in America at the time. Through their communities, which served as family and work for them, the sisters combined faith and labor to help build and shape a distinctive Catholic culture and American society.[42]

Though Purcell was always very much interested in obtaining more women religious for his archdiocese, he developed reservations regarding the Oblate Sisters of Providence, a congregation of black sisters in Baltimore. Early in his administration he had tried unsuccessfully to get them to establish a school for African Americans in the diocese. Again in 1850 he requested their services, only to find that they could not come for a year. The "Superior seems, if I may judge from her Letter," Purcell wrote to Archbishop Eccleston of Baltimore, "to have an imperfect knowledge of English Grammar. She tells, or asks, me to 'pray for I'. . . . Many of our blacks here c[oul]d beat that." When the sisters in 1857 expressed interest in establishing a colony in Cincinnati, Purcell again had his doubts. The letter "they write," he wrote, "is fresh proof of their want of the English language, which many of our Colored folks read and write correctly. Still I hope I can find a place for them. We lately baptized twenty four colored children in Mercer County, where there is a large settlement of that race, and many adults are there preparing for baptism." But the sisters never established a foundation in the archdiocese.[43]

SLAVERY AND THE CIVIL WAR

Though institutional energies of Cincinnati Catholics in the antebellum period were mostly devoted in providing poverty relief, health care, childcare, and employment assistance, the diocese did address the issue of slavery. Bishop Purcell, who personally "condemned slavery," was in full agreement with the bull issued by Gregory XVI on December 3, 1839, denouncing the slave trade. One of the advantages of having his diocese in Ohio, he wrote in 1840, was "the absence of slavery," for the Ohio River formed the border between the slave states in the South and the free ones in the North.[44]

Though Ohio was a free state there were differences of opinions regarding the institution of slavery and African Americans. In the mid-1830s prominent individuals in Cincinnati, led by the mayor, sponsored antiabolition meetings on the grounds that abolitionists pursued a course that hurt trade, threatened "to spread desolation and murder throughout the peaceful borders of our sister States," and would cause disorder within the union. When residents, including some Irish Catholics, staged anti–African American demonstrations in Cincinnati, Purcell publicly disapproved of them. While congratulating Bishop Anthony Blanc of New Orleans, perhaps his closest episcopal friend, on the founding of the *Propagateur Catholique,* he criticized the publication for placing advertisements on the hiring of slaves. "It is afflicting," he wrote in 1841, "to read such advertisements in a political journal. . . . It is not necessary to be an abolitionist to condemn a practice so repugnant to Catholic feelings." But not all the U.S. bishops thought alike on this subject. Purcell was reminded by Peter Kenrick of St. Louis that it "requires less courage" to oppose slavery in Cincinnati, where there was no slavery, than in his slave-owning state. Purcell was sufficiently concerned about the institution of slavery that he suggested it be discussed at the Fifth Provincial Council in Baltimore.[45]

Almost three weeks before South Carolina voted to secede from the United States in December 1860, the *Catholic Telegraph,* reflecting Purcell's sentiments, decried the principle of secession and urged Catholics to remain loyal to the nation. In his January 13, 1861, address at the Catholic Institute, Purcell hoped "that the hideous rattlesnake of secession may be crushed to death." When the Civil War broke out the following April, the archbishop flew the U.S. flag over the cathedral. "The President has spoken," he said, and argued it was the duty of Catholics "to walk shoulder to shoulder" with all Americans in support of the nation. A few days later Bishop Martin John Spalding of Louisville shared with Purcell his disappointment that Cincinnati Catholics favored war. Archbishop Francis Patrick Kenrick of Baltimore informed Purcell that he chose not to comment publicly on Purcell's "views on the topics which agitate the country." It may have been just a coincidence, but in his visit to Rome in 1861 Purcell requested permission to retire. Either the negative reactions he received on the Union issue drove him to make the request or the sixty-one-year-old archbishop's sheer desire to spend his remaining years in retirement did. Five years earlier he had written to Blanc that he would "on the slightest hint of a want of confidence in my administration, tender my resignation." Notwithstanding the motive, the pope did not accept his resignation. Shortly after Purcell's return from Rome,

Spalding informed the Cincinnati ordinary that he was pleased the pope had refused his resignation.[46]

When the Civil War broke out in 1861 the American hierarchy consisted of seven archbishops and thirty-seven bishops, among whom three-fourths lived in free states. The giant in the hierarchy was Hughes of New York. Purcell's prestige, influence, and loyalty to the Union were also widely acknowledged. Some of Purcell's fellow bishops advised him against taking sides. Martin Spalding, a southerner by birth and himself a slave owner, was disappointed to learn that Catholics in Ohio had fallen with the black Republicans favoring the Civil War. Purcell's natural impetuosity and aggressiveness nevertheless led him to become an outspoken advocate of the northern cause. He, his brother, and Auxiliary Bishop Sylvester Rosecrans, who was assistant editor with Edward Purcell of the *Catholic Telegraph* and whose brother would become a general in the Union army, were strong Union men. Rosecrans, a convert from the Episcopalian Church, was appointed the first auxiliary bishop in the archdiocese in 1862. Because of the many labors entailed in administering the archdiocese, Purcell had petitioned Rome several times for an auxiliary bishop.[47]

Consistently loyal to the Union, the Cincinnati ordinary and his supporters denounced those Catholics who resisted being drafted into the Union army. "Something may be necessary in the way of manifesto," Rosecrans wrote to Purcell, "to prevent . . . this mutinous spirit." Ten days later on August 20, 1862, the diocesan paper editorialized that Catholics who refused to serve deserved "scant mercy. It is the same as if your house was on fire, and your neighbor would cut the hose, so that the water could not reach the burning building." A year later when Cincinnati and New York experienced antidraft riots, the diocesan paper urged Catholics to uphold law and order. Though the *Catholic Telegraph* generally supported the Union's cause, it nevertheless allowed some southern views to be published in the paper. It reminded its readers that though Catholics were divided on the issue of the Civil War, "in religion they are ever one in mind and heart."[48]

On the abolition of slavery issue, most American bishops during the Civil War were of the opinion that the issue was fundamentally political and economical, arguing that it had no bearing on the church's mission of salvation and grace. Purcell thought otherwise. Five months before President Lincoln issued the Emancipation Proclamation on New Year's Day, 1863, Purcell issued a call for the abolition of slavery in the editorials of his diocesan paper. The *Catholic Telegraph* was the first Catholic paper in the country to come out unequivocally for emancipation of the slaves. At a time when most of the Catholic press in the North viewed the union as more important than the abolition of slavery, it was bold for the Cincinnati archbishop, situated on the borders of slave states, to denounce in vigorous tones the institution of slavery. Arguing that the Catholic Church had always been the friend of liberty, Purcell hoped that everyone, regardless of color, would be free. "He who tries to perpetuate slavery," he wrote, "disrespects the doctrine and example of Christ."[49]

Known to be "impulsive," at times "explosive," Purcell took an unequivocal stand on emancipation. He supported full emancipation. As a consequence, the archbishop lost a good deal of support, even among his suffragan bishops, and the diocesan paper lost subscribers. The overwhelming majority of Catholic newspapers in the country supported slavery. In the summer of 1864, the New York *Tribune* took issue with Purcell's views on slavery and the Civil War. "We differ . . . in politics from Archbishop Purcell, as we have a right to do," it wrote; "we are no Abolitionist as he is; we are no unconditional loyalist as he is." Through all this, Purcell did not retreat from his position.[50]

At the same time that the New York *Tribune* took issue with Purcell, Bishop William Elder of Natchez, Mississippi, criticized Purcell's pro-Union and abolitionist stance. Elder, who would some twenty-five years later become Purcell's coadjutor bishop and successor, thought the Cincinnati ordinary and the *Catholic Telegraph* helped prolong the war. "We have felt pained," he wrote, "of hearing of bishops and priests publicly urging the vigorous prosecution of the war, and giving their influence to the enlistment of volunteers." When Elder wrote to Purcell in January 1864 he expressed concern about the North sending a particular young priest south, because southern law exempted from conscription only priests who had been duly licensed. Purcell or the editorial staff of the *Catholic Telegraph* or both misinterpreted the information. The diocesan paper warned all priests not to go south because a southern bishop had indicated that they would be drafted. Elder denied the allegation and demanded a retraction from Purcell and his paper. He felt that such a false report could do significant damage to the Catholics in the south. Writing to Purcell, Elder argued that the Cincinnati ordinary's "zeal for the abolition of slavery and . . . the success of certain political views" had too "much control over both . . . [his] judgment and . . . [his] feelings and that the consequences are injurious to religion." Though Purcell and the *Catholic Telegraph* never issued a retraction, Elder sent a correction to the *Baltimore Mirror.* A month later Elder apologized to Purcell for the strong language in his last letter. He hoped there would "not be any division between" them. Time eventually healed the wounds of these two longtime friends.[51]

During the Civil War Purcell, Rosecrans, and some of the local clergy visited the war camps, where they preached and administered the sacraments.

Wanting to make sure that the soldiers did not have only Protestant texts at their disposal, Catholic literature was taken to them. In one instance Purcell lent $40 to a Confederate soldier. "It is to me a source of no little consolation," he wrote to Archbishop John Odin of New Orleans, to "comfort prisoners and sick and wounded soldiers from the South as well as from the North."[52]

In the fall of 1864 Purcell also wrote a letter to President Lincoln in behalf of General William Beall, a Confederate general, who was a prisoner of war on an island in Lake Erie. He did this at the request of an old friend, Miss Catherine Todd, Lincoln's sister-in-law. "Miss Kitty Todd," he wrote, "begs me to intercede with you for the exchange of General William Beall. . . . Surely it is time to show him at least so much mercy when much more has been extended to many others. So do good Mr. President," he continued, "grant me this favor and let me feel that we have a President who has some little regard for the old Archbishop of Cincinnati." The president eventually ordered General Beall's release.[53]

Thirty-six Sisters of Charity, eleven of Mercy, and ten of the Poor of St. Francis from the archdiocese also generously volunteered their services during the Civil War. Like the other sister nurses in the United States, they contributed tradition, experience, skills, and religious commitment to Civil War nursing. They were unique among the few thousand women who cared for the sick during the conflict. Sister Anthony O'Connell, who was foremost among the Sisters of Charity, helped organize sisters for nursing on the battlefields. The Irish-born sister came to Cincinnati as a young teenager in 1837 and, during the next sixty years, became connected with all the many charitable institutions her order established in Cincinnati. By June 1861 Sisters of Charity were at Richmond, Virginia, and at Camp Dennison near Cincinnati, taking care of the wounded soldiers. At times they had to walk in mud and water over their shoe tops in heavy rains. During the war some of the sisters from Cedar Grove and St. John's Hospital moved with the army and went to Cumberland, New Creek in Virginia, Nashville, Shiloh, and Pittsburgh Landing, and a group went to the Army Hospital at Gallipolis, Ohio. It was at the battle of Shiloh in 1862 that Sister Anthony won for herself the surname "Angel of the Battlefield." There she demonstrated exemplary valor and mercy while gathering the wounded and assisting the surgeons in their work.[54]

From their Fourth Street convent the Cincinnati Sisters of Mercy also helped in the military hospitals and on the battlefield by dressing wounds and giving medicines. Following the battle of Shiloh, three sisters went to the battlefield and attended to the wounded and to cases of smallpox. Besides performing their nursing duties at St. John's Hospital and aboard river ships that were converted into hospital transports, they also rented their house in

Cincinnati to the government to serve as a hospital for the wounded until the end of the war. The women and children under the charge of the sisters were taken into the convent.[55]

At the beginning of the war three Sisters of the Poor of St. Francis supervised for six months the Federal Military Hospital in Cincinnati. In May 1862 three other sisters and two postulants, accompanied by Sarah Peter, attended to the wounded soldiers on a hospital boat. Two years later Archbishop Purcell requested some of the sisters to visit the soldiers at Camp Chase near Cincinnati to provide both material and spiritual support to the men. Because of prejudice against the clergy by some of the officers, priests were not allowed at the camp. He was hopeful that the sisters, who by then had established a solid reputation to providing generous service to the soldiers, would be accepted.[56]

The various sisters' involvement as nurses, as one in five Civil War nurses were women religious, gave them more exposure to the lay public and helped enhance their public activities and image. Sister Anthony and the more than six hundred women religious, representing twelve religious orders, who nursed on the battlefields and in army hospitals, helped change, though some stereotypes persisted, the tide of public sentiment toward the sisters from one of suspicion to one of respect and high praise. Gradually the sisters, who first saw themselves as missionaries promoting religion, became more identified with their commitment to Christian living and humane concerns and, in the process, they helped enhance a more positive view of Catholicism.[57]

After the war the archdiocese, through its archbishop and diocesan paper, called upon the faithful to extend the hand of charity to the newly freed blacks to enable them to earn their own living and preserve their faith. In their philanthropic work toward African Americans, Catholics nationally in the immediate post–Civil War period lagged far behind that of Protestants. They had no organization resembling the American Missionary Association. Catholics had a responsibility, the *Catholic Telegraph* wrote, "to educate and christianize the freedmen." In 1866 the Jesuits, under the leadership of Francis Weninger, helped organize St. Ann's Colored Church and School in the west end, the first parish organized in the archdiocese to meet the needs of African Americans. At the time there were fewer than 6,000 blacks in Cincinnati, and only a small number of them were Catholic. Weninger, who devoted his life to helping the poor and had seen whites discriminate against blacks when they worshiped with them in some of the local parishes, believed that the blacks should have their separate parish. He raised more than $4,000 to help build a combination church and school on Longworth Street between Elm and Race in the west end. The Holy Trinity Church parish donated one thousand dollars for the purpose. In 1871 St. Ann's was one of only six Catholic churches established exclusively for blacks in the United States. Two years later the archdiocese purchased the African Methodist Episcopal Church on New Street, near the Jesuits at St. Xavier Church, and transferred the operations of St. Ann parish there. The Sisters of Notre Dame, who had been giving convert instructions to blacks, began teaching in St. Ann school in 1867. The following year Weninger founded the St. Peter Claver Society, named after the Jesuit who, in the early 1600s, converted thousands of slaves in Colombia to Catholicism, to help spread the Gospel to blacks as well as help provide money to support a school for both boys and girls. Though at first members contributed one dollar per month, by 1874 they reduced the amount to twenty-five cents per month in order to increase membership. Purcell's contribution of one hundred dollars made him a lifetime honorary member.[58]

NEW SEMINARY

Shortly after his return from Europe in 1851, Purcell began making plans to build a new and larger theological seminary to educate young men. As in other dioceses in the United States, the archdiocese of Cincinnati had a predominantly immigrant clergy to care for pastoral needs. Like his episcopal colleagues and other church leaders who founded or expanded seminaries in the nineteenth century, Purcell sought to provide a clergy trained in the United States. Though indebted to the European priests for their services, Cincinnati Catholics lamented not having more of their own local and American seminarians. Moreover, it became evident to Purcell that if the seminary were to provide more priests, it needed a fixed location and more financial support. Unlike the European church, the American church, including the archdiocese of Cincinnati, had no revenues from endowments to help support the operation of a seminary.[59]

In its brief history the diocesan seminary had undergone several changes of location. In 1842 Bishop Purcell had persuaded the Congregation of the Missions (more popularly known as Vincentians or as Lazarists) to operate the seminary, then located on a donated farm near Fayetteville in Brown County. The seminary had moved there when the Jesuits took charge of the college in Cincinnati. From 1842 to 1845 the Vincentians discharged all the duties of the seminary. Because of the distance of about forty miles from the city and the difficulties of slow travel, some thought Brown County was an undesirable location for an ecclesiastical seminary. Purcell and the Vincentians, furthermore, did not always agree on the operation of the seminary. The Vincentians resented the bishop's interference. The final blow came in the summer of 1845 when Purcell placed the newly arrived Ursuline Sisters in Brown County and, without consulting the Vincentians, brought the seminarians back to Cincinnati. He housed them temporarily in the scholasticate attached to St. Xavier College on Sycamore Street. Displeased with the bishop's treatment, the Vincentians immediately withdrew from the seminary. The seminarians stayed with the Jesuits for about two years. In 1848 seminary classes were conducted at the episcopal residence at West Eighth Street. After consulting with the clergy at the diocesan synod of 1848, Purcell the following year inaugurated an annual seminary collection in each parish of the diocese. Up to that time Catholics had made contributions for the building and support of churches, schools, and orphanages, and the relief of the destitute. Now they would also provide financial support for the seminary. At a time when the number of local seminaries in the United States under the direct sponsorship of the individual ordinaries decreased, largely because of the need to build more churches, Purcell challenged local Catholics to build a new seminary.[60]

Through the generosity of several Catholic laymen, a new seminary building was built on top of Price Hill on the west side of The Mill Creek. Michael and Patrick Considine, two Irish brothers, donated five acres of land. John and James Slevin, two other Irish brothers, built a four-story building at their own expense. The new location provided, as Purcell put it, a "delightful Panoramic view" of Cincinnati and its neighboring communities. While the seminary was under construction, Purcell withdrew the seminarians from St. Xavier College and placed them temporarily in the attic of the bishop's new episcopal residence at Eighth and Plum Streets. Father Michael M. Hallinan, an Irish priest who had just completed his doctoral studies in theology in Europe, was put in charge. On October 2, 1851, the new diocesan seminary, at a cost of $22,116, opened with twelve seminarians in residence. In grateful remembrance of Mount St. Mary in Emmitsburg, where Purcell had served as rector for three years, the name of the seminary was also changed at the time from St. Francis Xavier to Mount St. Mary's of the West. The scholarly Purcell took a lively and close personal interest in the seminary. He often solicited books in his travels for its library.[61]

At Purcell's request, Cincinnati's first provincial council in 1855 proposed making Mount St. Mary's of the West a provincial seminary. The idea had received enthusiastic support from Bishop Michael O'Connor of Pittsburgh and Archbishop Peter Kenrick of St. Louis. Though this acknowledgment would make no difference in Mount St. Mary's day-to-day operation, it was a vote of confidence by the bishops in the newly formed Province of Cincinnati, which had been established in 1850 when Cincinnati was made an archdiocese. In addition, the bishops petitioned the pope to make Mount St.

Mary's a pontifical seminary, enabling it to confer doctorate degrees in philosophy and theology. The bishops also proposed making St. Thomas Seminary in Kentucky a provincial preparatory seminary. The hierarchy was hopeful that in time the clergymen trained in the seminaries would prove as competent as those educated in Europe. "We seek not to disguise the fact," Purcell later informed his clergy and laity, "that we aim, above all things, at the education of . . . a native born clergy."[62]

The petition for a provincial seminary came up at a time when the pope, attempting to tighten its rule and authority in the Catholic Church, was considering the idea of establishing a college specifically for American seminarians in Rome, similar to those of other nations. A Roman education would help assure loyalty to the Holy See and provide some assurance for advancement of Roman centralization and authority. At first even Purcell was warm to the idea. "I shall be most happy at the realization of the Nuncio's inspiration of having a College founded for American students in Rome," he wrote in 1854. He promised to do what he could "towards its success." He even contemplated donating some money from the sale of a piece of land for it. When the project of the Roman College came up at the Provincial Council in 1855, however, the bishops, including Purcell, voted against it. They feared it would divert money raised in the various dioceses that were needed to build up their own seminary and a "Little Seminary" for the Cincinnati province. "The Roman College," Purcell wrote, "would withdraw from those two institutions much of the support they will need."[63]

A strong supporter of an American pontifical college in Rome was Archbishop Hughes, who went so far as to solicit pledges from his episcopal colleagues. It did not surprise Purcell that New York Catholics, "with their comparatively vast resources," he wrote, would want it. "They may as well found the College and underwrite it, and let us who are poor, or poorer, send students there at a stipulated stipend for each one we send." He also had his doubts about the wisdom of sending seminarians to Rome to be educated. In light of the political unrest in Italy, he felt Rome was "not healthy." More importantly, he argued, "vocations are not fostered there with the same success with which they are elsewhere. Of eight sent to Rome from this Diocese by my Predecessor and myself only two became priests there."[64]

Approximately two years elapsed before the Propaganda denied Cincinnati's request for a pontifical seminary. The Prefect of the Propaganda informed Purcell that the project for an American College in Rome had been approved and that the American bishops were to come up with ways of financing it. Reprimanded a little for not being more supportive of the Roman College, in the fall of 1858 Purcell unenthusiastically sent to Rome a contribution of $5,000 for the new college. When it opened in December

1859, with twelve seminarians enrolled, Purcell was still concerned about the unrest in Rome. So much so that he refused to send any of his students there the first year. But gradually he became more cooperative. Though he did not want his "American clergy . . . educated, as a body, anywhere but at home," he wrote in 1868, "it is both practicable and desirable that, like other nations, we should have a college in Rome, where American bishops, priests and tourists" might have a place to visit. Even though each year, throughout the remainder of his administration, an archdiocesan collection for the American College in Rome was made on the first Sunday in November, Purcell still had reservations. He preferred seminary training in American seminaries. In 1871 he advised a potential donor not to give $5,000 to the American College. Pointing out that the archdiocese had already paid $5,200 and had derived no benefit from it, he urged her to consider making the donation to Mount St. Mary's of the West Seminary.[65]

Even though the Cincinnati seminary enjoyed steady growth in the 1850s, seeing its enrollment grow from twenty-three seminarians in 1854 to ninety seminarians and lay students in 1858, Purcell was concerned over the lack of financial support. "While our people have responded most generously to every appeal in behalf of the orphans and other charities," he wrote in his pastoral letter of January 1864, "the education of the Clergy . . . has never enlisted their sympathy to the extent required. There are not more than six families, in all the Diocese, who have 'done well' for its foundation."[66]

In an effort to obtain students for the seminary, in the fall of 1856 Purcell established Mount St. Mary's College in connection with it. It remained in operation until 1862, when circumstances during the Civil War forced its discontinuance. From that point on, Mount St. Mary's of the West Seminary was a strictly theological seminary. Its history has been closely linked with the history of Catholicity in the West and South. Staffed with a learned faculty of diocesan priests, Mount St. Mary's of the West Seminary not only helped produce competent priests for the archdiocese, but from it many priests carried on the work of the church in the western and southern states of the nation. Notwithstanding Purcell's concerns over the paltry parish contributions in support of the seminary in the early 1860s, until 1879 Mount St. Mary's enjoyed a period of financial stability largely because of the support of the parishes of the archdiocese and an increasing enrollment of seminarians.[67]

Purcell's interest in building a seminary to provide a much-needed diocesan clergy also reflected his attitude toward the religious orders. Part of the reason the Vincentians left the diocese had to do with the strained relations between James Burlando, the Vincentian superior of the bishop's seminary in Brown County, and Purcell. Burlando often complained to his superior that the Cincinnati ordinary wanted to retain full control of the seminary.

Though Purcell had assured the Vincentian provincial that he was satisfied with the administration of the seminary, Burlando countered that Purcell had a "very poor opinion of [religious] communities," and would "not so easily give any chance that might be advantageous" to religious communities. It is clear that the Vincentian superior wanted his order to have a parish and seminary of its own. When Purcell moved the seminary into his own house in 1845, the provincial finally decided to withdraw the congregation from the diocese.[68]

At the same time that Purcell appreciated and often praised the work of the religious orders in his diocese, having been personally involved in bringing some of them to the diocese, he was concerned over any diminution of his episcopal authority. His concern was typical of a diocesan clergyman's reaction to the separate orders. The local Jesuit superior, John Elet, observed that at times Purcell appeared indifferent or cool toward the order. Nevertheless, Purcell often praised the Jesuits for their work. Writing to Archbishop Eccleston in December 1845, Purcell noted that the Jesuits "are, individually, most exemplary & edifying priests. . . ." But, he added, "it is their too great zeal . . . for their society that is at fault." Notwithstanding some early disagreements between the Jesuits and Purcell, relations between them improved. By 1847 Elet described Purcell as "every day more and more benevolent" toward the order.[69]

Also, during this period, Purcell opposed the Dominicans' effort to start a college at their headquarters at Somerset. Differences between Purcell and the Dominicans date back to the bishop's inability to collect the annual $300 from them. When the Society for the Propagation of the Faith at Lyons requested Purcell's advice on the establishment of a Dominican college, the bishop's response was emphatic. Not only did he think that such a proposal first should go though him, he felt the Dominicans were trying to do too much and should confine themselves to parochial work. But at the same time that Purcell denied the Dominicans' request to start a college, he gave permission to the Fathers of the Holy Cross, who had founded the University of Notre Dame in 1842, to establish St. Joseph College on West Eighth Street in Cincinnati. Founded on October 2, 1871, it was incorporated under Ohio laws in 1873. Because of the national bank crisis of 1873 and the ensuing economic depression, the college experienced financial difficulties from the start. Due to mounting financial liability, the order closed the college in 1920.[70]

FINANCIAL CRISIS OF 1878

In 1876, when the country celebrated its one-hundredth birthday, Purcell celebrated his Golden Jubilee—fifty years—as a priest on May 21. A weeklong celebration began on that day. Though common in Europe, the Golden Jubilee of Archbishop Purcell's priesthood may very well have been the first celebration of the kind in the American church. As the country celebrated its many accomplishments, Purcell also had much to celebrate. Catholic churches were increasing in number, newer and larger ones were replacing smaller ones, educational institutions and religious communities were growing, and the seminary had 130 students. Yet, two years later a financial crisis occurred in the archdiocese that drove the archbishop from power.[71]

For about three decades the bishops of the Cincinnati Province had expressed concern over the tenure of church property and the loans of money by individuals to priests for safekeeping. Wanting to preserve church property, the bishops at their provincial council meetings in the 1850s decided that all diocesan church property be held in fee simple by the bishop of each diocese. Some of the bishops, moreover, disapproved of the practice of making loans to priests, while others argued that the money was useful for building churches. A compromise was reached prohibiting priests to accept loans and to receive money on deposit without the permission of the bishop. Since Purcell held parish property in his name, not only did he approve of the compromise but he also directed his clergy to inform the faithful that the bishop was not responsible for parish debts. "We should prefer that churches should never be built," Purcell wrote to his suffragan bishops in 1858, "rather than to see the priest involve himself in debt for their construction."[72]

At the same time that Purcell expressed public concern over the acceptance of loans by parish priests, he was, through his brother Edward, operating a banking enterprise out of the cathedral residence. Besides being a church leader, pastor, and builder, the archbishop was also a banker. "I have reason to bless God," he wrote to Archbishop Kenrick, "that my brother has been enabled so well to meet all the demands made on him in the crashing of banks and the failure of so many mercantile houses during the past year— and this notwithstanding [he made] a most heavy outlay for our orphan asylum." The archdiocese used some of the money to help build the cathedral, churches, schools, and orphanages, loan money to individuals, and finance episcopal projects. Though Purcell had his doubts about the practice of accepting deposits, he had great faith in his brother's financial acumen. In the wake of several bank failures in the country in 1854, Purcell at the time considered the possibility of liquidating the bank and selling some of the property that had "no special use for any religious or charitable objects . . . as soon as times [would] improve" in order to pay some of his debts. When a more severe financial panic occurred in 1857, resulting in the closing of many more banks, there were heavier deposits with Edward Purcell. "Thank God," the archbishop wrote to Blanc, "we, of the cathedral, are getting through the 'epidemic financière' bravely." But the Purcell brothers did not survive the next financial panic.[73]

In 1878 a devastating financial failure struck the informal private banking operation of Edward Purcell. For approximately forty years the archbishop's brother, whom Purcell entrusted with total responsibility on financial matters and control of the "purse strings," had been accepting deposits for safekeeping from Catholics in the archdiocese and other Ohio residents. As confidence in the private banks was shaky and news spread of Edward Purcell's banking business, more and more people found comfort in placing their savings in the hands of the archbishop and his brother. Over a forty-year period perhaps as much as twenty-five million dollars were deposited in the bishop's bank. Archbishop Purcell always claimed that as they accepted these deposits the perceived needs of a growing diocese were uppermost on their minds.[74]

There had been, since the national panic of 1873, a series of financial crises in Cincinnati. By 1878 a number of small banks were forced to close their doors. A panic ensued and there was a run on Purcell's bank. To make matters worse, the city's leading bankers no longer accepted Purcell's notes. The archbishop's priest-brother had used personal notes from his debtors, individuals to whom he had loaned money, as collateral to secure loans from banks to help meet demands from his depositors. Although by November Edward Purcell, on the brink of a nervous breakdown, had paid out more than $100,000, he could not meet all the requests from the depositors. "This dull, gloomy, day," he wrote, "makes me long for heaven."[75]

The following month some of the clergy in the archdiocese met at St. Xavier College to draw up plans to help the archbishop in this time of crisis. They formed a committee, consisting of William J. Halley, pastor of the cathedral and chancellor of the archdiocese, John Albrinck, pastor of Holy Trinity Church, Ubald Webersinke, Provincial of the Franciscans, and Edward A. Higgins, president of St. Xavier College, to meet with the archbishop. As a way of restoring public confidence, the committee urged Purcell to make a public statement "to the effect that he holds himself . . . responsible for all financial claims against his brother." They also proposed that he provide "as security for such claims and liabilities, . . . all the assets, of whatever kind or value, that belong to him, as well as all the properties" that belonged to the diocese. If there appeared "an excess of liabilities over the assets," the four clergymen assured Purcell that "the clergy present at this conference pledge themselves . . . to cooperate cordially with the Most Reverend Archbishop in providing means to meet all the demands, and pay off all debts." Later they realized that in their resolve to pay the entire debt they had, as Albrinck put it, "undertaken a fool's task." Moreover, their recommendation to pledge the local church's property as security for the liabilities of the bank failure would later be discounted by the court.[76]

Three days before Christmas Archbishop Purcell, consumed with worry, suspended any further payments to creditors. He announced that his brother could no longer meet the immediate demands of those wanting to withdraw their money. Unburdening himself, he assured the faithful that he had not spent the money "in waste or extravagance." Purcell insisted that the deposits had been accepted to help build churches, orphanages, seminaries, as well as help finance other episcopal projects. If Rome could not help him resolve the financial crisis, he hoped to rely, he said, "in the charity and goodness of the laity to pay all." Quite unexpectedly, the seventy-eight-year-old Purcell, who was showing signs of age and wear, also announced that he had sent his resignation to Rome, asking to be relieved on account of his age and the increased labor in administering the finances of the church. In an attempt to quiet the storm of protests by creditors, that same day Edward Purcell informed the press that church property could be sold to help pay the debt. "A very small fraction of the Church property in our Diocese would pay all the debts," he said, "but we will not, I think, need to call upon the Church for any."[77]

The response to the archbishop's resignation was immediate. Prominent Catholic businessmen, who did not want him to resign, promised to help. "Catholics of this diocese," one of them told reporters, "would rise up to a man and do their utmost to have him remain at the helm." The clergy of the diocese wired a telegram to the pope, urging him not to accept Purcell's resignation on the grounds that it "would be a deplorable loss to religion." Purcell also received several letters of encouragement and sympathy from his episcopal colleagues. Archbishop James Gibbons of Baltimore informed Purcell that the news of his application to resign made him "really sad. I would like to see the Prelate die at his post," he wrote, "who has been an example to all of us in singleness of purpose, and apostolic heroism." Bishop Joseph Dwenger of Fort Wayne was "extremely sorry," he wrote to Purcell, "that after a long life of glorious and successful labours you should have to pass through this adversity."[78]

For several months the clergy and laity raised money through benefit concerts, bond issues, and bazaars. Individual gifts ranging from $1,000 to $5,000 also came in. Though more than $40,000 were raised in a short period of time, that amount would prove inadequate in the face of the mounting debt. In one instance, the Montana Lottery Company offered to raise three million dollars in one year, contingent on the repeal of a state law forbidding lotteries. Many priests and members of the laity, however, opposed the lottery on moral grounds.[79]

As efforts were made to raise money to help pay the debt, creditors persisted in their efforts to get their money. Though most waited in paralytic disbelief, some went to the cathedral residence and demanded their money. They were forcibly ejected. On another occasion, a priest at the residence was threatened with his life.[80]

When it came time for Edward Purcell to disclose records of the financial transactions, he "had no books to turn over to them, only a bundle of notes." After spending six weeks auditing Edward Purcell's accounts, the diocesan trustees were appalled by what they found. Though they saw "no reason to suspect any dishonesty," they did find, in addition to the large amount paid as interest, "bad investments, shrinkage in value, misplaced confidence and unbusiness-like management." At first the loss was estimated to be approximately $100,000. By February 1879 auditors estimated the loss to be in excess of a million dollars. Three months later it reached $3,697,651.49. As the amount of the indebtedness grew, Purcell kept reassuring the creditors that not one of them "would be wronged out of a dollar." He wanted them to know that the diocese was ultimately responsible for repayment of the debt.[81]

But as the debt mounted, support from the clergy steadily eroded. Many were fearful they could lose their property. In February 1879 the Franciscan Otto Jair pointed out that the German parishes had received very little financial assistance from Purcell. "We have raised the money to build our churches by the sweat of our brow," he said. "I have not received a cent toward the creation of these churches from the Archbishop, nor have I asked for any." A year later many priests no longer believed that the diocese was obligated to repay the debt, arguing that Edward Purcell had run the bank as a private individual.[82]

All along the archbishop supported his brother and reiterated the diocesan nature of the debt. As divisions grew among the clergy, the *Catholic Telegraph* repeatedly expressed and supported Purcell's position, declaring that the "Catholic Church never repudiates. It may take years to wipe out this heavy debt . . . , [but] Catholics of the whole country, poor and rich alike will soon form themselves into a vast army of charity." It mistakenly assumed that Catholics everywhere would regard the affliction in the diocese of Cincinnati as their own. Cardinal John McCloskey, the highest-ranking church official in the United States at the time and Purcell's former student at Emmitsburg, launched a national campaign to assist Purcell. While he did, he also made it clear that the effort was done out of "charity." He argued that each diocese was responsible for its own financial administration and that the church was under no obligation to pay the debt. McCloskey's campaign, however, fell far short of its expectations, raising approximately $60,000. Bishop Francis Silas Chatard of Vincennes perhaps captured the mood of many when he noted that the debt "is simply impossible to pay. . . . I don't see anything but inevitable failure and bankruptcy. . . . We don't want to throw our money into a swamp where it will be lost entirely. . . ."[83]

In the spring of 1879 Purcell finally heard from Rome. The pope did not accept his resignation. He decided, instead, to assist him by appointing a coadjutor to the archdiocese. The financial disaster of 1878 and Purcell's declining health, which had deteriorated more during the crisis, made imperative the appointment of a coadjutor. Because of his weak eyes Purcell was also unable to do much reading. Although in financial difficulty, and obviously weakened physically, Purcell in October 1879 nevertheless traveled to Fort Loramie and helped celebrate the laying of the cornerstone of the new St. Michael Church. After the ceremony he spoke a few words. "When the people of this parish finish this according to plans and the rough work is paid for," he said, "after two years I will return and consecrate it to the honor of God and praise of the parish." But that trip would never take place. At the end of November 1879 Purcell, upon the advice of his friends, left the city and went to the Ursuline convent in Brown County. The archbishop initially interpreted the pope's decision to provide him with a coadjutor as a vote of confidence. But when the Propaganda on January 16, 1880, wired Purcell that it had named Bishop William Henry Elder of Natchez as his coadjutor, he also learned that he was to be archbishop in name only. Elder was put in charge of the archdiocese. Disheartened, Purcell went to the convent's chapel and laid himself "almost prostrate on the altar." After finishing his prayers, he informed Sister Mary Baptista Fraener that "it would have been a fitting end to his life could he have died on that altar step—were it God's will." In reality, the financial crash and woes of the archdiocese undermined Purcell's administration, drove him from power, and retired both him and his brother to the Ursuline convent.[84]

The bishops of the Cincinnati province had unanimously recommended the nomination of Elder. Archbishop James Gibbons also felt that Elder, because of his administrative experience at Natchez, was the strongest candidate to attend to "the desperate state of affairs in Cincinnati." As coadjutor and administrator of the archdiocese, Elder was entrusted with the responsibility of straightening out the unresolved financial crisis. Finding someone to take on this challenge had not been an easy task. Bishops Edward Fitzgerald of Little Rock, Arkansas, and Bernard McQuaid of Rochester, New York, had also been considered for the Cincinnati post. They both indicated to authorities in Rome that they would not accept the appointment. In April 1880 Purcell resigned all his affairs to Elder.[85]

While the archdiocesan hierarchy underwent an administrative change, the creditors, who had gotten restless with the state of affairs, instituted a number of civil suits. The court appointed J. B. Mannix, a Catholic attorney, as Purcell's assignee to handle his financial affairs. A number of creditors unsuccessfully petitioned the court to appoint another assignee, claiming that he was too close to Purcell and the church. Mannix tried to appease the creditors by filing a motion in the courts requesting permission to sell 211 churches, convents, schools, orphanages, among other institutions in the archbishop's name, and to use the proceeds to help liquidate the debt. Meanwhile, the priests of the diocese retained the services of three lawyers to help prevent the sale of the local church's property. The clergy also passed resolutions declaring that Purcell held the church property in his name in trust for the various parishes and institutions. They further argued that such property could not be sold to pay off the debt unless it could be shown that it had "been acquired by moneys furnished by . . . Edward Purcell, or by . . . J. B. Purcell, and not repaid. . . . " Legal and social issues related to the financial crisis would drag on throughout much of Elder's first decade in office.[86]

Notwithstanding the stigma associated with the banking crisis, the Purcell years saw unparalleled growth in the diocese. In the nineteenth century the massive network of educational and charitable institutions, which benefited from parish fairs and pageants and male and female benevolent organizations, was largely built by a working-class, immigrant population. No population has had a more decisive influence on the history of the local church, and which is true of the American church as well, than that of its many teaching orders. In particular, women religious in the archdiocese, like many of their counterparts in other dioceses, established a remarkable record of achievement. Living in religious communities that prepared them for a perpetual life of service, they created and operated numerous educational, charitable, health care, and social service institutions. They, the clergy, other religious, and the Catholic laity played a critical role in institution building in the Midwest.[87]

PART
TWO

BUREAUCRATIZING
CATHOLICISM
IN THE ARCHDIOCESE
OF CINCINNATI
1880s–1920s

Introduction

After the dark days of the Purcell bank failure, Archbishops William Henry Elder (1883–1904) and Henry Moeller (1904–1925) helped put the archdiocese back in fiscal order. Elder's successful management of the archdiocese in the 1880s would have to be his most significant accomplishment during his tenure. He dealt with the crisis with steadfastness, skill, and diligence.

During Elder's and Moeller's administrations episcopal and clerical authority continued to grow and the archdiocese of Cincinnati became more centralized. Up to this time rather informal methods had been followed in the various channels of episcopal and parochial administration. The two Provincial Councils of 1882 and 1889 and two synod meetings of 1886 and 1898 helped greatly improve the administrative organization of the diocese. Elder also helped systematize the inner workings of the archdiocese by introducing reforms that created system and order. Under his leadership the local church collected annual reports from all the pastors and administrators. These reports covered such items as the number of families and their ethnic and racial backgrounds, the number of teachers and pupils in the parochial schools, the parish debt, property holdings, and the parish's annual collections and rental pews. He also instituted the office of Chancellor, established ecclesiastical tribunals and counseling bodies, organized examinations and conferences for the promotion of theological studies among the clergy, and created a matrimonial court and diocesan consultors. Increasingly, lay people were less involved in decision making in the government of the local church. Moreover, though in the wake of the First Vatican Council there was more Roman direction, the local church continued to seek greater autonomy. Both Elder and Moeller resented too much interference and meddling by Vatican officials in diocesan affairs.[1]

As Elder and Moeller, like many of their episcopal colleagues, tightened their rule and exercised more authority over parishes and the regular clergy, there were parish feuds over territorial lines and parish raiding as well as tension between German- and English-speaking churches. As they dealt with these issues they wanted German Catholics to become more Americanized. Boundary feuds and parish raiding also intensified tensions between the archbishops and regular clergy.

During Elder's twenty-four-year tenure the clergy and laity established twenty-six parishes and six new missions. At the time of his death, 294 priests attended to the spiritual needs of a population of about 200,000 Catholics. The archdiocese consisted of 151 churches with resident pastors, thirty missions with churches, and twenty stations. It had 103 parochial schools taking care of 26,281 students. Furthermore, during his years the archdiocese established St. Gregory Preparatory Seminary in Mount Washington, east of Cincinnati, and reopened Mount St. Mary's of the West Seminary. Besides becoming involved in the labor movement and attending to some of the needs of African Americans in Cincinnati's west end, the local church, under the leadership of the Sisters of Charity, inaugurated the Santa Maria Institute, which began as a mission among Italian immigrants.[2]

Although Henry Moeller did not become official head of the Cincinnati diocese until 1904, his long-term assistance to Elder as well as his tenure as archbishop meant that he helped administer affairs in the archdiocese for forty-five years. He devoted practically all his time to the cares of his apostolic office, seldom taking time for social relaxation. As a churchman, Moeller occupied a high place among the Catholic hierarchy, serving as president of the American Board of Catholic Missions from its inception.

The physical side and visible part of the archdiocese grew much during the Moeller years, manifesting itself in stately and monumental places dedicated to the worship and service of God. New buildings for religious and educational or charitable purposes were constructed, costing in excess of five million dollars. By the end of his tenure in 1925 the archdiocese had overcome its financial problems and streamlined much of its administration. While thirty-nine new parishes were also organized during his administration, the number of churches increased to 190 and priests to 450. Among the building projects sponsored in the first quarter of the century was the new Mount St. Mary's of the West Seminary, which was the crowning achievement of Moeller's administration. The charitable and social welfare efforts undertaken by the clergy, religious, and laity kept pace with the work in education. A central bureau of Catholic charities helped coordinate the activities of the various charitable and social welfare institutions in the archdiocese. It also helped foster youth programs through the Boy Scouts, Girl Scouts, summer camp, and other recreational services. In addition, the national headquarters of the Catholic Students' Mission Crusade was established in Cincinnati with Francis J. Beckmann, the rector of Mount St. Mary's of the West Seminary, as its executive chairperson. The archdiocese also witnessed the growth of the Holy Name Society. During the last year of his term Moeller was working toward the establishment of central Catholic high schools.[3]

On January 5, 1925, the archbishop, who had been a sick man for two years, died at his episcopal residence. After meeting in the afternoon with the Sisters of Charity at the motherhouse and visiting with his own sister, Sister Henry Marie, the seventy-six-year-old prelate returned home and had dinner. Two hours after retiring to his study, Moeller complained of illness and his physician was notified. He died later that evening. The next day, at a meeting of the consultors at the archbishop's residence, Monsignor Louis J. Nau, rector of Mount St. Mary's of the West Seminary, was chosen administrator of the archdiocese.[4]

THE DIOCESE UNDER STRESS

In the beginning of 1879 Bishop William Henry Elder of Natchez received notice from Rome that he would soon receive the bulls of his appointment as coadjutor to Archbishop Joseph S. Alemany of San Francisco. Because of the ravages of yellow fever in his diocese, which had killed six of his twenty-five priests, he was allowed to stay at Natchez until the plague subsided. When Elder heard again the following year, he now was directed to move to Cincinnati. On Sunday, April 18, 1880, almost three months after his appointment as coadjutor to Purcell, Elder arrived at a railroad depot in Cincinnati. From that moment on he dealt with the bank crisis. In the process of attempting to straighten out the financial difficulties, the archdiocese at the end of the nineteenth and early twentieth centuries—consistent with the general trend in society—became more centralized. As clerical authority grew and the Cincinnati ordinaries tightened their grip on local parishes, there also developed feuds among parishes over territorial lines and tension between diocesan priests and various religious orders.[1]

Because of the financial difficulties in the archdiocese Elder had had reservations about taking the Cincinnati position, but he accepted the appointment out of obedience to the pope and as a personal favor to Purcell. Elder's bishop colleagues also knew of the precariousness of the situation in the "afflicted diocese." Bishop James O'Connor of Omaha was reluctant to congratulate Elder on his appointment. "I really could not find it in my heart to do so," he wrote. Richard Gilmour of Cleveland tried to reassure Elder that "God will see you through. . . ." The archdiocese of Cincinnati was no sinecure. It needed a man of administrative ability, prudence, diplomacy, and piety.[2]

FIG 9. Archbishop William Elder, 1883–1904

Elder was born in Baltimore on March 22, 1819. One of thirteen children, Elder attended a private Catholic school in his native city. At the age of twelve he enrolled in Mount St. Mary College at Emmitsburg, where the president, John Purcell, greeted him. After graduating from Mount St. Mary Theological Seminary in 1837 he was sent to Rome to finish his theological training. He was ordained to the priesthood in the chapel of the Propaganda in 1846. Elder then returned to Maryland and became professor of Dogmatic Theology at his Alma Mater in Emmitsburg. He aided in the management of the college, taught the seminarians, and did pastoral work in the community. He remained there until his appointment to the see of Natchez in 1857. As the youngest ordinary in the American hierarchy, Elder took charge of a large and sprawling diocese that embraced the State of Mississippi. He was bishop of the diocese for twenty-three years.[3]

Elder's tenure received national attention during the Civil War. When Union troops occupied Natchez in 1864, Elder, whose sympathies lay with the South, refused to obey the commands of Brigadier General James M. Tuttle to offer prayers in the cathedral for the Union army. Not wanting to subordinate his episcopal power to the military authority, Elder respectfully declined to obey the command on the ground that Tuttle's order both violated religious liberty and usurped his episcopal functions. Appealing to President Abraham Lincoln for exemption, Elder argued that civil or military authorities had no right to intrude upon purely ecclesiastical matters. "My resistance," he wrote, "is based simply on the ground that our church service is a matter to be regulated exclusively by the authorities of the Church." Because of his refusal to comply with the General's command, Elder was arrested and sent to Vidalia, Louisiana, where he was confined under the custody of the Union commander. But he did not stay there long. When Secretary of War Edwin M. Stanton learned of the arrest, he ordered Elder's release. All told, Elder spent seven days in prison.[4]

The main challenge that Elder faced upon his arrival in Cincinnati was to straighten out the financial affairs of the archdiocese. The Purcell bank crisis had grown to gigantic proportions. When Elder arrived in the see city, Archbishop Purcell was in seclusion at the Ursuline convent. About a week later the archbishop went to the cathedral, celebrated Mass, and spoke briefly to those present. He praised Elder and urged the faithful to show their "gratitude to God for sending such a good pastor to atone for all my deficiencies." Then he addressed the debt issue. "I can appeal to you all today, in the presence of God and of the new Bishop," he said in a "tremulous" voice, "that there has been no waste and no abuse of your money."[5]

Relations between Elder and Purcell began on a friendly note. They attended episcopal functions together and collaborated on several appointments. But the relationship gradually deteriorated over the issue of repaying the creditors and the question of Purcell's salary as archbishop. In his May 1880 deposition before the Hamilton County Court of Common Pleas in the suit, *Mannix v. Purcell,* the archbishop made clear once again that the deposits that had been entrusted to him had provided much of the capital necessary for the growth and expansion of the archdiocese. Thus, it had an obligation to repay the creditors. He testified that when Edward Purcell contracted the debt, money that was now owed the creditors, he had "acted as his agent and with his consent, and that the debt is his [the archbishop's]." More specifically, he contended that several churches "had received or borrowed money" from his brother. On January 21, 1881, Edward Purcell died suddenly before testifying about the loans and his role in the running of the bank. Elder's disagreement with Purcell over the payment of the debt would strain relations between them indefinitely.[6]

After Archbishop Purcell suffered a stroke in the fall of 1880, Elder also became concerned over the amount of influence Father James F. Callaghan, the archbishop's secretary since 1870, had on him. Over the years a close relationship had developed between Purcell and his secretary, who was on loan from the New York province. Callaghan gave the aging Purcell unswerving loyalty and devotion. A few days after Elder's arrival in Cincinnati, Bishop Joseph Dwenger of Fort Wayne had urged him to watch Callaghan. Finding the "good old archbishop sometimes vigorous, sometimes absolutely in his second childhood," Dwenger found him too dependent on his secretary. He cautioned Elder "that the hasty and inconsiderate counsels of Callaghan are not always the wisest." As Purcell's condition worsened, Callaghan and Sister Ursula, Superior of the Brown County order, assumed full responsibility of attending to the archbishop. When Elder tried to persuade Callaghan to let someone else take care of Purcell, he refused. Elder also learned that in the spring of 1880 Callaghan had gone to Europe to make a personal effort to restore Purcell's powers as well as to help pay off the creditors. He accomplished neither. Elder now regarded the priest as a troublemaker.[7]

When Callaghan requested Elder's help in paying off the debt, Elder refused. He did not believe the archdiocese was liable and thought it would be best to wait for the decision of the court. This angered Callaghan. He and his supporters used the *Catholic Telegraph* to uphold Archbishop Purcell's position on the debt issue. Callaghan had served on the editorial staff of the diocesan paper from the spring of 1869 to 1881, at which time Owen Smith, as publisher, and Harry W. I. Garland, as editor, took over its management. Sympathetic to the archbishop and the creditors, these two laymen became a thorn in Elder's side. The newspaper's editorials consistently criticized Elder for mishandling the banking dilemma and for his poor treatment of the archbishop. "[I]t is somewhat worse than cowardly," the *Catholic Telegraph* editorialized, ". . . to seek to shun the question of the debt any longer. . . . If no one will heed the broken words and heartbroken wish and prayer of the venerable old man, . . . the PAPER which has been his Diocesan organ for half a century . . . will voice with no uncertain sound his last dearest, earthly wish . . . that our Catholic debt should be paid." The paper insisted that if the debt were not paid, the "dishonored diocese will go down in history . . . a curse. . . . " It would "be better," it wrote, "that every church be sold to pay the debt, and the priests' vestments given to clothe the poor, and the chalices melted down . . . to buy them bread."[8]

In the fall of 1882 the *Catholic Telegraph* also launched a national campaign to raise money to help pay off the debt to the creditors. With his "deepest gratitude" Purcell thanked his supporters and wished them success in their efforts "to pay [his] debts." Toward that goal he made a personal contribution of sixty dollars. "Like the 'Widow's Mite," he wrote, "it is very small; yet, like the Widow's Mite, it is literally all I have." But not everyone approved of the diocesan paper's fund-raising scheme. Some local priests withdrew their subscriptions to the *Catholic Telegraph*. They referred to the debt as exclusively the Purcell debt. "Whether we call it Father Purcell's debt, or the Archbishop's debt, or the Diocesan debt," the *Catholic Telegraph* replied, "there it is. Its odour cannot be kept out of the Church." The diocesan paper continued its effort on behalf of the archbishop well into 1883. He "is still our Archbishop; he is still the head of the diocese; and, if his authority can no longer enforce obedience," it wrote, "his prayer and wish ought to win compliance."[9]

As the split between Elder and the archbishop widened over the debts' issue, Elder learned that Callaghan, Sister Ursula, and several priests were spreading the rumor that he had not paid Purcell his cathedraticum. The latter was a tax paid annually to the church ordinary by all churches and lay confraternities in the diocese. In the spring of 1882 two anonymous letters to the editor of the *Cincinnati Commercial,* printed under the name of "T," accused Elder of paying Purcell an inadequate amount for his stay at the convent. Elder denied the allegation. He also assured Sister Ursula that he had every intention of paying any additional funds, when needed, for his support at the convent. In response to charges against Elder, a large contingent of priests came to his defense. In a signed petition they pledged their loyalty and support to him. In May they also joined Elder in his celebration of the twenty-fifth anniversary of his episcopal consecration. "I rejoice that your priests," Gilmour wrote to Elder, "have at last held up their hands. They should have done so before to strengthen your hands in your heavy and thankless task."[10]

Increasingly, Elder suspected that Callaghan, Sister Ursula, and Harry Garland, out of devotion to the archbishop, were fueling the opposition against him. In one instance Garland made clear his unreserved loyalty to the archbishop. When a reporter from the *Cincinnati Commercial* asked him to clarify his relationship as editor of the *Catholic Telegraph* with Elder, he responded that it was "certainly not those of master and servant. The *Catholic Telegraph,*" he said, "is private property, in which the Bishop has not a single red cent of interest. I am my own master and use my own judgment, outside of faith and morals." Then he went on to say that the "*Telegraph* is and has been for half a century the official organ of the Archbishop, who remains to this day the head of this ecclesiastical province. . . . My allegiance is due first of all to the Archbishop, and he has it with all my heart, soul and strength." The day after Garland's interview in the *Cincinnati Commercial,* Elder instructed Francis Dutton, pastor of St. Martin parish, to go to the convent and ask Purcell to sign a receipt that would show he had received compensation. Sister Ursula denied him admission. Callaghan had to personally check all of Purcell's correspondence before presenting it to him. When Elder learned of this, he informed Callaghan that his personal correspondence with the archbishop must go directly to him. Similarly, Elder instructed Sister Ursula that no one "can be allowed to interfere between the Archbishop and me—or any one to whom I may give a commission for him."[11]

After fighting off paralysis for almost three years, Archbishop Purcell suffered his fourth and final stroke on June 29, 1883. Five days later on July 4 he died. A week later Elder held the solemn obsequies in the cathedral. His remains were then sent back by train to St. Martin's, where they were laid to rest in the convent cemetery. At the cemetery also lay the remains of his mother, brother, and one of his sisters.[12]

On Purcell's death Elder succeeded him as archbishop. On December 13 he was invested with the pallium, a vestment conferred by the pope on archbishops, at the cathedral. This was the first such instance in Cincinnati. Fearing that Callaghan would continue to work against him, Elder—who was attempting to establish his own legitimacy—ordered Callaghan to stay out of the archdiocese. Bishop Dwenger assured Elder that Roman authorities understood Callaghan "fully," and that Callaghan would not be able to harm him. After Archbishop Corrigan of New York recalled Callaghan to his home province, there were still a few priests in the archdiocese, like Francis Goetz, pastor of Holy Trinity Church in Dayton, who complained of Elder's unwillingness "to pay the dead Archbishop's debt." They accused him of being insensitive to the financial woes of the creditors.[13]

THE TRIAL OVER THE PURCELL BANK FAILURE

The trial of the celebrated *Mannix v. Purcell* case against the archdiocese, known as the "Church Case," began on April 4, 1882, and ended about nine weeks later on June 24. The judges then deliberated on the matter for almost a year and a half, rendering their decision in December 1883. The court decided in favor of the archdiocese of Cincinnati, declaring that the local church was not liable for the bank's debt. It concluded that Archbishop Purcell had held various churches' "properties . . . in trust for charitable and pious uses." The decision was clear. Though head of the local church, Purcell was the trustee and not the actual owner of the properties and therefore could not sell what he did not own. The judges rejected the creditors' argument that all property in the diocese held in Purcell's name as archbishop could be auctioned to pay the creditors. They accepted the defense argument that parish fairs and picnics, along with individual donations and offerings, had helped raise money for various churches in the diocese.[14]

Though the court's decision favored the local church, the creditors were nevertheless entitled to recover some of their money. In the opinion of the presiding judge in *Mannix v. Purcell,* creditors had advanced some money to the archbishop or his brother to help buy or build certain church properties and it had not been repaid. Displeased with the overall legal decision, John Mannix, who sought full compensation for the creditors, then appealed to the Ohio Supreme Court. To make matters worse for the creditors, however, Mannix's report in November 1885 listed $444,793.54 in receipts and $370,000 in expenditures. The creditors, who had not yet received a penny, were outraged. They petitioned the court for an accounting of the financial affair. The court-appointed Mannix immediately resigned his stewardship of Purcells' personal estates, and the court named two new trustees. By the spring of 1886 the court ordered Mannix to repay the personal estates in the amount of $406,655.16. He had lost it speculating in stocks and bonds. Even though the judge of the Court of Common Pleas reduced the amount of Mannix's indebtedness to $314,413.91, he was unable to come up with the money. With the help of a hung jury, he avoided going to jail.[15]

In their efforts to recover their money the creditors also appealed in vain to Rome. Moreover, they distributed placards, both in English and in German, throughout Cincinnati, highlighting the severity of the financial crisis. Many Catholics had lost most or all of their savings in the calamity. Notwithstanding the court's decision, the creditors maintained to the end that the archbishop had used their money mainly for the benefit of the diocese. They were also resentful that Elder while in Rome in the fall of 1885 gave "a goodly sum of the poor creditors' money to the Pope in Peter Pence." They argued repeatedly that hundreds of families, especially the elderly, had "been reduced to destitution" and that many "had lost their faith."[16]

During this long ordeal Elder was faced with a major personal dilemma. From the start he empathized with the creditors. Within a few days of his arrival in Cincinnati, he distributed a few hundred dollars among a few poor creditors. The money was a gift he had received from the faithful of Natchez before leaving them. In the early years of his administration he acknowledged privately that for many years the people, businessmen, and clergy of Cincinnati and the bishops of the province saw the business carried on by Edward Purcell to be "in the house of the Archbishop." Besides, Purcell himself acknowledged the debts to be his own. He always insisted that his brother was his agent in the whole matter. The faithful had trusted both Purcells. They believed that "the Church was not only infallible in doctrine," Elder wrote, "but she was also the infallible guardian of justice, and so their money was safe."[17]

Though sympathetic to the argument that the archdiocese had a moral obligation to repay the debt, Elder thought it advisable to go along with those priests and episcopal colleagues who advised him to pay the creditors only the amounts ordered by the courts. Bishop Casper Borgess of Detroit urged Elder not to allow his sympathy for the creditors get the better of him. He feared they would interpret his actions as an acknowledgment that the entire debt belonged to the archdiocese. "I know very well," he wrote, "yes the Catholic world knows, that you are in a sad plight, that you are harassed by the plottings of the evilminded, . . . that your charity impels you to relieve the sufferings of the poor as far as it may be in your power. [B]ut all that," he continued, "should not drive you into indiscretion under such an unholy pressure as they exercise over you." Archbishop James F. Wood of Philadelphia, a former priest of the Cincinnati archdiocese, also advised him against assuming Edward Purcell's debt. "Don't think of such a thing," he wrote. "The action of your predecessor in assigning what did not belong to him," he further argued, "was a desperate and crazy act, in my opinion of no force or value. . . . He had nothing; he owned nothing; all was a trust—unfortunately shamefully abused, but this abuse you have nothing to do with." Dwenger, also formerly of Cincinnati, concurred with his episcopal colleagues that the debt belonged to Edward Purcell and not to the archdiocese.[18]

In the summer of 1884, eight months after the lower court decided that the archdiocese was not liable for the Purcell debt, Elder wrote a letter to the clergy and laity under his jurisdiction on the matter. Though he expressed his desire to do all that he could for the liquidation of the debt, he did not view it a debt owed by the diocese. "I have repeatedly consulted Advisers, in civil and Canon Law, and in Moral Theology," he wrote, and "I have not found one, who on a consideration of the whole case would advise me that I had a right to declare this a diocesan debt binding in justice. It is not a question of magnanimity on my part. I have no right to be magnanimous in imposing obligations on other persons, . . . unless it were very clearly established that the debt was theirs." He hypothesized that if it were a debt of the diocese, then every Catholic in the diocese would be bound in justice to contribute his full share for paying the whole debt. Though he acknowledged there were times when Purcell used portions of the creditors' money for the churches and other works of religion, he was convinced that fund-raising events, individual donations, and parish contributions helped purchase most of the lots and build most of the churches in the archdiocese. From that point on the archbishop nevertheless urged the clergy and the faithful to do all they could personally to help the creditors. On the last day of the diocesan synod of 1886, Elder appealed to the clergy to help raise money for the creditors' benefit. As a result of his plea, a commission was established. By 1887 the archdiocese had raised close to $60,000 for the benefit of the sufferers.[19]

Elder then tried that year to secure a more substantial gift from church leaders in Rome. He asked Cardinal James Gibbons of Baltimore and Bishop Camillus Maes of Covington, both then in Rome, to intercede in behalf of the archdiocese. Gibbons, a realist, offered the archbishop little hope of receiving any assistance from Rome. "Your Grace is well aware," he wrote, "that the Holy See is not in the habit of coming hastily to the relief of embarrassed foreign missions, . . . still less is it disposed to help a suffering diocese in a country like ours[,] which . . . is regarded as rolling in wealth." At the end of the year Maes informed Elder that the archdiocese's request for assistance had been refused. "There is not a doubt," he wrote, "that the Congregation of Cardinals was in favor of giving us a million, but . . . Leo XIII has seen fit not to grant it."[20]

With slight modifications, the Ohio Court in January 1888 upheld the lower court decision that Purcell had held the church property in trust. It decreed that the cathedral was liable for $114,182.92; the cathedral school for $15,442.48; Mount St. Mary's of the West Seminary for $8,635.18; and St. Patrick Church in Cumminsville for $4,901.30. With the sale of lots in St. Joseph cemetery and other assets collected from the Purcell estates, the amount awarded to the creditors was $409,384.61. Those creditors, still living, recovered seven and one-eighth percent of their money. For twenty-five years, 1880 to 1905, legal action against the archdiocese of Cincinnati ensued in State and Federal Courts. Both Elder and his successor, Henry Moeller, felt that the creditors had been paid the total legal amount due them and that the archdiocese had "discharged its obligation of justice." During his tenure, Moeller also occasionally gave aid to destitute and elderly creditors. Especially through his pastors, he came to the aid of destitute creditors in the twilight years of their lives. Moeller always felt that Archbishop Purcell "was not to be blamed for the financial cloud that darkened the last days of his life."[21]

Concerned over both the payment of the debt and the image of the local church, the seventy-eight-year-old Elder in 1895 refused the offer of the palatial residence of Mrs. Bellamy Storer to serve as his archiepiscopal residence. Storer offered her residence and two acres of land, on prestigious Grandin Road, as a gift in commemoration of Elder's golden jubilee of his priesthood in 1896. "Both my feelings and my judgment," he wrote, "dispose me to live as near the cathedral as possible. . . . I would do a wrong to the diocese and to every congregation and to each individual Catholic, if I were to weaken the ability of the cathedral congregation to collect and pay" its portion of the debt. He thought that his presence near the cathedral helped solidify the work and fund-raising activities of the congregation. Elder also argued that the residence that had satisfied his predecessor was quite sufficient for him. Though the Jubilee Committee and the clergy in the community petitioned the archbishop to reconsider the Storer gift, he remained firm in his decision. Such "a declination," the New York *Independent,* a leading Protestant paper, wrote, "is both unusual and honorable." Elder never moved out of the two small rooms under the shadow of the sanctuary.[22]

Modest in appearance and small in stature, Elder was never ostentatious. He never seemed proudly conscious of his high title. "Notwithstanding his exalted position," the Jesuit Francis J. Finn wrote, "he was, from the time I first knew him, the most humble of men." He also seldom made use of a carriage. He preferred to walk. A non-Catholic journalist commented on the archbishop's modesty and gentleness. "He is a character worth knowing— one worth studying," he wrote. "His time is more valuable and more sought after than any public office holder in the city of Cincinnati. Yet it is a fact that there is less red tape in gaining admission to shake the kind hand of the highest Church dignitary in the central part of the United States, than it is to gain for a moment the ear of the average public official." Elder never had much interest in the pomp and privileges enjoyed by ordinaries in comparable or more established sees.[23]

In the end, how much harm did the Purcell bank failure bring to the local church? Evidence suggests that some Catholics, scandalized by the affair, turned away not only from the bishop but also the church. Henry Moeller, who had worked out of the Cincinnati chancery for more than twenty years, estimated that between one hundred and two hundred people left the church in consequence of money that they lost by the financial failure. In addition, for almost two decades there was a slowdown in the building of new Catholic churches and schools. The "dead carcass of the debt," Anthony H. Walburg, pastor of St. Augustine Church in the west end in Cincinnati, wrote to Elder, ". . . is paralizing [sic] all our energies." With time, however, the diocese weathered the storm and recaptured some of its old energy. In 1887 Mount St. Mary's of the West Seminary, which had been forced to close its doors in 1879, reopened. By the next decade new parishes were slowly formed and schools opened. Doubtlessly, the bank failure caused grief and hardship to many of its depositors and had a devastating impact on a number of them. It is impossible to assess the hurt and feeling of betrayal, especially among the creditors, caused by it. It also had its toll on Archbishop Purcell. Having lived to see the creation of a vast spiritual empire, he received a blow that utterly crushed him.[24]

ARCHBISHOP HENRY MOELLER, NATIVE OF CINCINNATI

For nearly three years as coadjutor administrator and more than twenty-one years as an archbishop, Elder ably managed the affairs of the archdiocese. On October 28, 1904, he celebrated Mass at Mount St. Joseph Convent in Cincinnati, returned to his residence, and shortly after dinner he was found in his room lying on the floor in a semi-comatose condition. He died two days later. The city pastors tolled the church bells daily at noon for ten minutes until

FIG 10. Arhbishop Henry Moeller, 1904–1925

after the funeral. On November 8, following his solemn funeral services at St. Peter in Chains Cathedral, Elder's remains were transported to the priests' lot in St. Joseph cemetery in Price Hill.[25]

Henry Moeller succeeded Elder as archbishop of Cincinnati. At the cathedral on February 15, 1905, Cardinal Gibbons invested him with the pallium. A man of scholarly attainments and a profound theologian, Moeller became the fourth and first locally born bishop to preside over the diocese. The son of German immigrants, he was born on December 11, 1849, in the west end of Cincinnati in St. Joseph parish. His parents, Bernard Moeller and Teresa Witte, had emigrated from Germany. They had six children, five sons and a daughter. One of the sons died in infancy, three of the four became priests, and the daughter entered the convent.[26]

After attending St. Joseph elementary school, Moeller graduated from St. Xavier College in 1869. Wanting to become a priest, he attended the American College at Rome to complete his studies in philosophy and theology, where he was awarded the degree of doctor of divinity. In the competitive examinations Moeller earned the highest distinction, winning three first prizes in theology. On June 10, 1876, Moeller was ordained to the priesthood in the Basilica of St. John Lateran at Rome. Largely because of his scholarly accomplishments and theological studies, eight years later he was one of three candidates considered for the rectorship of the American College in Rome.[27]

Upon his return to Cincinnati in December 1876, Archbishop Purcell assigned him to the pastorship of St. Patrick Church in Bellefontaine, Ohio. In October of the following year, he joined the faculty of Mount St. Mary's of the West Seminary. In 1879 Bishop Silas M. Chatard of Vincennes, who lived in Indianapolis, asked him to become his personal secretary. Moeller spent only a few months in Indianapolis. When Elder arrived in Cincinnati he recalled the native Cincinnatian and made him his own secretary in July 1880. Six years later Elder promoted Moeller to the position of chancellor, an office he filled until April 6, 1900, when he became bishop of Columbus. Elder informed Cardinal Gibbons that in losing the services of his confidant of twenty years "he lost his right arm."[28]

Two years later Elder, then eighty-one years old and lacking vigor and strength, requested the assistance of a coadjutor. The duties of the office weighed heavily on him. "My old age," he wrote to a relative, "is having its effects . . . [on] my eyesight, my stiff fingers and my memory." His administrative papers often got "out of order," he wrote to a local pastor, "and sometimes letters get entirely mislaid." In January 1903 the consultors and rectors of Cincinnati met at Elder's residence. For the first time and in accordance with the decree issued by the Third Plenary Council of Baltimore about two decades earlier, local consultors, official advisors in matters of diocesan administration, participated in the selection of nominees for archbishop of Cincinnati. In six successive ballotings, the result was always the same: Four votes each for Bishops Moeller of Columbus and Camillus Maes of Covington, Kentucky. Both names were sent to Rome. Though Moeller had been Elder's longtime friend and confidant, the archbishop favored Maes as his heir apparent because of Maes's "acquaintance & influence with men of prominence . . . in the Church and out of it." Elder shared his thoughts with Moeller. He preferred the Covington ordinary "not because of personal preference. No one," he wrote, "can have preference over you." But if "our Holy Father should send you to me," he added, "I will be happy to learn my judgement was mistaken."[29]

On April 27, 1903, Henry Moeller was appointed coadjutor to Elder. He was known in Cincinnati for his "irreproachable character" and executive ability. Pleased that Moeller would soon assist him again, Elder urged him to come as soon as he had "authority to do so." When Moeller returned to Cincinnati on June 26, Elder relinquished many of his administrative duties to him. The diocese purchased a separate residence for Moeller on West Eighth Street.[30]

DIOCESAN GROWTH AND CHANGES

During the course of the nineteenth century the archdiocese of Cincinnati grew in size and became more centralized. In the process clerical control grew and lay involvement in the parishes waned. Priests became more involved in the operation of the parishes. Though the shift from parish control to clerical control came more slowly in the German parishes, by the end of the third quarter of the nineteenth century the trustee system had been considerably weakened. Fifty years later, by the end of Moeller's term, Catholics in the archdiocese, like most Catholics in the United States, accepted the hierarchical concept of the church. Following the first Vatican Council's declaration on papal primacy and infallibility, the Third Baltimore Council in 1884 gave a ringing endorsement of the pope's infallibility. It also renewed emphasis on church authority. Like most U.S. bishops, Elder and Moeller stressed loyalty to the archdiocese and strengthened their grips on local parishes. The archdiocese witnessed the growth of authoritarianism, of centralization, and of increasing influence by Vatican officials. During Fenwick's and Purcell's administrations the lay people, especially the German Catholics, were involved in the management and administration of church affairs. They had an enormous responsibility for the development of the archdiocese. In the late nineteenth and early twentieth centuries, however, when the authority of the local church, like that of society in general, became more centralized, more and more power shifted from the parish to the chancery. The American bishops insisted that the laity had no rights with regard to parish government. Increasingly, parishes and charities were brought more directly under the archbishop's supervision. In the process, notwithstanding the clerical strengthening of authority with regard to the laity, this weakened the autonomy of parish priests. In a society that celebrated the principles of freedom and independence, Catholics were expected to submit unquestioningly to the external authority of the church. As a religion of authority, the church continued to offer stability and expected the faithful to obey.[31]

In the spring of 1881 the diocese of Nashville was assigned to the province of Cincinnati. The following year the tenth suffragan see to Cincinnati was added when the diocese of Grand Rapids was created out of the diocese of Detroit. In April 1910 Pius X approved the division of Cleveland, and Toledo, with a Catholic population of one hundred thousand, was elevated to an episcopal city with Joseph Schrembs as its first bishop. Toledo was the third suffragan see established in the state, where less than a century earlier there was no Catholic church to be found. This was another illustration of the remarkable growth of Catholicity within Ohio.[32]

In the period 1883 to 1925 the growth of the local church slowed somewhat from the Purcell days. Whereas 142 parishes were formed during Purcell's tenure, 66 were established during Elder's and Moeller's terms. Moreover, the archdiocese witnessed a remarkable growth in Dayton and neighboring communities. Sixteen parishes were formed, which was more than three times the number since the creation of Emmanuel, St. Joseph, St. Mary, and Holy Trinity before the Civil War. During the first quarter of the new century, industries in Dayton were attracting a number of foreign immigrants, especially from Eastern Europe. They found the German Catholics and their pastor, Charles Hahne, at Emmanuel parish friends who made them welcome to their church. Through the efforts of Ladislas Lipski, pastor of St. Stanislaus Church in Cincinnati, and Our Lady of Czestochowa Society, Polish Catholics helped establish St. Adalbert parish in the northern part of Dayton in 1902. Three years later St. Adalbert Church was dedicated with Boleslaus F. Strzelcokas as pastor. In 1915 four Polish Franciscan School Sisters from St. Louis took charge of the parish school. Over the next decade Holy Name and St. Stephen parishes were formed for the Hungarian congregations in 1906 and 1909 respectively, Holy Cross for the Lithuanians in 1914, and St. Gabriel for the Romanians in 1916.[33]

Among the thirteen metropolitan sees in the United States in 1892, Cincinnati ranked ninth in Catholic population with 200,000 Catholics, eighth in the number of priests with 238, ninth in the number of parochial schools with ninety-three, and seventh in the number of churches, stations and chapels with 166. Among the 188 churches in the city of Cincinnati, Catholics had the most with fifty-six places of worship, followed by the Baptists with twenty-six. By 1920 the archdiocese had 186 churches with resident priests, thirty-three missions with churches, and sixty-three chapels. There were 391 priests who served a Catholic population of about 210,000. The archdiocese, with its ten suffragan sees, comprised an area of almost 200,000 square miles with a population of approximately 2,010,447 Catholics, served by one archbishop, ten bishops, and 2,573 priests, diocesan and regular.[34]

In the late nineteenth and early twentieth centuries the *Catholic Telegraph* also underwent changes. As the secular press became less combative toward Catholics, the *Catholic Telegraph* concentrated less on anti-Catholic sentiments and more on the news of the local church and the faithful. After the death in 1882 of its editor, Harry W. I. Garland, the diocesan paper's owner, Owen Smith, conducted the paper until 1890, when failing health forced him to relinquish his duties. Joseph Schoenenberger, former manager of the

Wahrheitsfreund, then purchased the *Catholic Telegraph.* Within a few years, however, Schoenenberger found the paper, which had long been burdened with debts, a financially unprofitable enterprise. Bishop Camillus Maes of Covington feared that the diocesan paper was, he wrote to Elder, "on the verge of disappearance." It seemed for a time that the *Catholic Telegraph* would join the many other Catholic papers that were discontinued in the nineteenth century.[35]

In November 1896 Elder asked his clergy to help increase the number of subscribers and do whatever they could to support the paper. Even though the *Catholic Telegraph* was not an official organ of the archdiocese, in the sense of being conducted by it, it was, he wrote, "the ordinary channel in the English language of the official utterances of the Archbishop." Late in 1897 Schoenenberger was forced to hand over the paper to his creditors. But a group of Catholic laymen headed by Dr. Thomas P. Hart, a medical doctor, formed the Catholic Telegraph Publishing Company and purchased the paper early in 1898. Hart, who gave up his medical practice to own and publish the diocesan paper, became editor. He served the *Catholic Telegraph* for almost forty years.[36]

Although they supported the diocesan paper, Archbishops Elder and Moeller maintained a close watch over its publications. In July 1889 Elder reprimanded Owen Smith for publishing articles critical of the action of the Provincial Council of Cincinnati. The archbishop's action was in keeping with the judgment of the Third Plenary Council of Baltimore that forbade the clergy or laity of assailing ecclesiastical persons by offensive words in the press. Elder demanded that Smith publish a letter of apology and "promise that hereafter" he would not allow anything to appear in the paper that went against "the rules and the spirit of the Catholic Church." Smith replied that he had been "under the care of a physician" and that the columns of his paper were opened to the archbishop to say what he pleased in regard to the articles. Elder responded by sending him a prepared letter for Smith to sign and publish under the editor's name. "In offering me the use of your columns," Elder wrote, "you forget your respective position. I am not arguing a case as litigant. I am giving judgment as Bishop." Smith published the proposed draft. Appreciative of Elder's overall support of the diocesan paper and perhaps wanting to stay on his good side, the *Catholic Telegraph* wrote approvingly of him in the summer of 1893. "[A]s priest, as bishop, as administrator, as theologian, as scholar, as friend, as man," it editorialized, "William Henry Elder stands in the very front rank and is conspicuous among his equals. This province is proud of him. . . . Long may he live to rule over us."[37]

Early in Moeller's term there was also friction between himself and Thomas Hart. Moeller thought that the editor did not always "deal in an honest straight-forward manner with him" and that a "'half-hostile' spirit" dominated the management of the paper. He assured Hart that they would get along "very amicably" if he demonstrated "[l]oyalty to authority, readiness to accept advice, and irreproachable conduct," which he regarded as the "befitting traits" of the editor of a Catholic newspaper. Midway through Moeller's term relations improved between the *Catholic Telegraph* and the archbishop. From this point on the diocesan paper's news coverage and editorials never deviated seriously from chancery policy.[38]

CLERGY AND PARISH ISSUES

Like the bank crisis, feuds among parishes during Elder's and Moeller's terms over respective territorial lines called for administrative and diplomatic skills. Since the founding of the diocese in 1821, its good fortune intertwined with that of the industrial city. The many churches built in Cincinnati in the middle decades of the nineteenth century were intended to accommodate a stable Catholic community. By the last third of the nineteenth century, however, more and more people left the older parts of the city and moved to hilltop neighborhoods and suburbs. Such technological improvements as the horse-drawn omnibus, electric streetcar, incline, and automobile helped facilitate the movement away from the city. In the face of commercial expansion and aging housing, like other middle-class Cincinnatians, Catholics who could afford to move gravitated to new parishes on the hilltops and more distant suburbs and the church followed them. In the process, the movement contributed to clerical infighting for parishioners, stipends, and territory.

In the wake of the Purcell bank failure, part of Elder's task was to keep alive the parishes and institutions affected by it and to help rebuild and refinance the various works of the archdiocese. Shortly after his arrival in Cincinnati Elder issued a memorandum against parishes raiding other parishes for members. He instructed the pastors to settle territorial disputes among themselves and to "avoid interfering with persons and places belonging to another Pastor's jurisdiction." He also directed them to send him a description of their respective territories. Elder always hoped that the feuding priests would resolve their problems in a friendly manner. He argued it was "very important both for our own peace, & for our due respect from the people, & for our influence over them—that we ecclesiastics carefully avoid all appearances of difference among ourselves. . . . We ought to be very delicate & courteous in our relations with each other." Notwithstanding Elder's admonition, parish raiding continued. In the face of the bank crisis Elder considered it inadvisable for him at the time to openly challenge the pastors on parish raiding. Besides, he was unsure how much backing, if any, he would receive from Roman authorities. In the latter part of the nineteenth century the Propaganda occasionally served as a court of final appeal for aggrieved priests. Furthermore, he was very much aware of the disputes Bishop Louis Amadeus Rappe of Cleveland had had with his German- and English-speaking priests that contributed to his resignation in 1870.[39]

In accordance with Canon Law the clergy could appeal to the Holy See for relief if they believed that local church leaders treated them unfairly. Despite the Roman legislation on clerical discipline in 1878, American ordinaries were determined to maintain their rights over priests. Archbishop Gibbons of Baltimore advised Elder in 1882, who was about to convoke the Fourth Provincial Council of Cincinnati, to endorse the broad principle that pastors and priests may be removed without trial by the bishop. "We cannot too much insist on the rights of Bishops on this point," he wrote. Gibbons felt the exercise of that right was "essential to the discipline" of the local church and to securing episcopal control. Even though the prevailing theology of the church suggested that the bishops were in control, in reality they often had to contend with clerical independence. As the archdiocese, in compliance with Rome, placed more emphasis on church authority in the late nineteenth and early twentieth centuries, it became more organized and centralized. Gradually the archbishop acquired more and more control over both priests and people.[40]

At the same time that Elder and a number of his episcopal colleagues tried to consolidate their hold on local activities, they sought more local autonomy and greater independence from the decrees issued in Rome. They wanted no interference. But the intent of such interference was to limit what Roman authorities perceived as the growing independence of the American hierarchy. In a letter to his suffragan bishop, James Gilmour of Cleveland, Elder argued that the welfare of the American church rested upon granting it as much autonomy as possible. Gibbons became concerned in the 1880s that the pope would use the complaints and appeals of priests "as a pretext" for installing a permanent delegate, or papal representative, to the United States. If that were to happen, he feared, the "dignity and authority of the [Church prelates] would be seriously impaired." Elder concurred. He believed that Vatican authorities often sided with the priests to check the authority of the American hierarchy. An apostolic delegate, Elder thought, would not only jeopardize the authority of the American bishops but "if he acted as a tribunal to receive complaints, would be an occasion of multiplying dissatisfactions among loose priests." Indeed, the pope enhanced the role of the papal representative precisely in order to exercise greater control over every diocese and ensure more uniform teaching and practice throughout the church in the world.[41]

The American hierarchy split into "liberal" and "conservative" factions in the late nineteenth and early twentieth centuries. They were divided on the appointment of an apostolic delegate to the United States, labor, the necessity of parochial schools, the founding of Catholic University, the separation of church and state, and the status of the American church. In general, the liberals, often designated as Americanists, advocated more autonomy from authorities in Rome, moderate social reforms to remedy social inequities, and a more active role for Catholics in society. They argued that American Catholics should embrace the principles of the new culture and bring the Catholic faith to its fullest realization in the United States. Freedom, equality, democracy, separation of church and state, and liberty of conscience were far more advanced in the United States than any place else in the world. At times the liberals accepted almost uncritically America's sense of mission in spreading its liberties and system of government around the world. In general, Archbishop John Ireland of St. Paul and Cardinal James Gibbons of Baltimore led this group. Ireland, who took the lead on some of the issues, would become one of the more dominant and controversial figures in the American church, especially in the area of education. Those who favored this liberal approach also tended to support the growing labor movement, recommended greater cooperation with other faiths, and promoted more mainlining of Catholics, especially immigrants, into American society. They believed that national differences among Catholics in the United States should be minimized.[42]

The conservatives, on the other hand, were deeply skeptical of the relationship between American life and Catholicism. A few Jesuit theologians, German clergy, and bishops, most notably Archbishop Michael Corrigan of New York and his longtime mentor, Bishop Bernard McQuaid of Rochester, were convinced that the liberal ways of the Americanists compromised the Catholic faith in order to make it more acceptable to Protestants and secularists. Many Catholics of German-American communities opposed efforts toward cultural and linguistic assimilation. Concerned over the negative and modern influence of socialism, secularism, and Protestantism on the church, conservatives also supported the hierarchical and institutional concept of the church. They became more identified with authorities in Rome and stressed the need for greater authority, discipline, and uniformity. Conservatives argued that the principle of independence in the United States fostered a spirit of individualism, and thus weakened the respect for authority regarded as necessary in the church.[43]

When Archbishop Francesco Satolli, who was appointed the first apostolic delegate to the United States in 1893, arrived in Washington the previous year a number of bishops viewed him as an "Ecclesiastical Spy." As the voice of the pope in America, he helped him exercise a more direct role in American church affairs. Believing that the American church was in disorder and that it should be brought more into conformity with European practice, Leo XIII in his famous 1899 apostolic letter *Testem Benevolentiae* to the archbishop of Baltimore attempted to restrain enthusiasm for republican principles in the church. Eight years later Pius X in his encyclical *Pascendi* strongly condemned theological modernism. Modernism, which developed in the 1890s principally in Western Europe, attempted to blend Catholicism with modern thought, especially in such areas as psychology, evolutionary biology, pragmatism, and critical biblical scholarship. Roman authorities made it clear that the American church, especially its liberal faction, should be less supportive of republican ideals and limit its contact with modernism and the secular culture. Pius X further institutionalized the antimodernist stance by prescribing that all seminary, college, and university professors of theology take an oath against modernism. Moreover, the Roman Code of Canon Law, which took effect in 1918, provided a legal framework attempting to insure uniform church life. Though the pontiff's and other Roman officials' actions at the turn of the century generated a spirit of Roman authority and discipline and had considerable impact in weakening "Americanization," they did not kill it. The influences of American life on the American church continued into the twentieth century.[44]

Like most church ordinaries, neither Elder nor Moeller identified totally with the liberal and conservative factions. On the subject of maintaining a separate Catholic school system, the two Cincinnati archbishops sided with the conservatives. Writing to the pope in January 1893, Elder joined Archbishop Corrigan and others in refuting Archbishop John Ireland's proposal that Catholics, who he thought needed to become more a part of American life, participate more in public education. Acknowledging publicly the benefits of public education, Ireland went so far as to say that he wished that the need for the parish school "did not exist. I would have all schools for the children of the people be state schools." Elder strongly disagreed with the archbishop of St. Paul on this matter. When in 1892 Archbishop Francesco Satolli issued a statement endorsing Ireland's attitude toward the public schools, Elder and all the bishops of the Cincinnati Province but one signed a letter of protest. During their administrations, Elder and Moeller vigorously supported and maintained a separate Catholic school system in the archdiocese.[45]

On most major issues Elder, and later Moeller, sided with the liberals. On the issue of maintaining separate German parishes and schools, they endorsed the assimilationist position. They wanted the German Catholics to become more Americanized. Elder also opposed the appointment of an apostolic delegate. He was skeptical and resentful of interference by officials in

Rome. In the 1880s Elder thought that the future welfare of the American church rested upon being granted more autonomy. An advocate of home rule, he did not want Vatican officials or the apostolic delegate to impinge upon his jurisdiction. Sensitive to the needs of American Catholicism, both Elder and Moeller attempted to create a distinctive and united Catholic culture. That meant keeping authorities in Rome out of their affairs. When in 1905 the apostolic delegate, Archbishop Diomede Falconio, offered to come to Cincinnati to invest Moeller with the pallium, Moeller selected Cardinal Gibbons instead. A few months later, however, upon the request of German Catholics in the community, Moeller reluctantly invited Falconio to come to Cincinnati and help celebrate the fiftieth anniversary of the German Roman Catholic Central Society.[46]

Moeller's concern over the apostolic delegate's potential intrusion in diocesan affairs was not unfounded, as Archbishop Satolli was a party to a number of conflicts between priests and their ordinaries, and in a number of cases he forced bishops to accept compromises. Early in his administration Moeller had to deal with a conflict between the leaders of the Ursuline Order at St. Martin's in Brown County and those at the Oak Street convent in Cincinnati. Mother Fidelis, the Ursuline superior headquartered in Cincinnati, and Mother Margaret Mary, her assistant in charge of the convent at St. Martin's, feuded over Mother Fidelis's authority. At the outset the archbishop sided with Mother Fidelis and was critical of those who behaved "outrageously" toward her. He urged the Ursulines at St. Martin's to acknowledge Mother Fidelis as the duly elected superior of the order. There was also evidence that because of the friction between the two groups some young women hesitated joining the Ursulines. "The sooner harmony is restored," Moeller wrote, "the better." The sisters at St. Martin's, however, paid no attention to his advice and continued to challenge Fidelis's leadership.[47]

By August 1908 both sides voted for a formal separation. Realizing that all hope of reconciliation had vanished, the archbishop reluctantly agreed to the existence of two separate and independent Ursuline communities in the archdiocese. On the subject of property ownership, Moeller sided with the Cincinnati group and insisted that the convent on Oak Street be turned over to them. Once again the St. Martin sisters disagreed with Moeller. They appealed to Falconio, the apostolic delegate, for assistance, insisting that the archbishop had forced them to sign a property agreement favoring the Cincinnati Ursulines. Moeller, on the other hand, urged Falconio to regard Fidelis as the superior of the Ursulines. He also argued that there was no need for two separate schools run by two separate groups of Ursulines in Cincinnati. Whereas the Ursulines in Cincinnati had never given him any trouble and that he had "misgivings" about the community at Brown County, he thought any "support" given to the St. Martin sisters "will make them," he wrote, "belittle my authority." But Moeller's appeals were in vain. Falconio sided with the St. Martin Ursulines and awarded them the Oak Street convent. In return, Mother Fidelis received a dowry of $52,700 from the Brown County branch. With this money Fidelis and nineteen of her supporters started St. Ursula convent and academy on McMillan Street in Walnut Hills. The Ursulines of Cincinnati later opened the parish schools of All St.s and Our Lady of Visitation in Cincinnati and St. Henry in Dayton. Just as Moeller had predicted, relations between the two Ursuline communities remained strained for years.[48]

Elder, Moeller, and their episcopal colleagues were of the opinion that Vatican officials unnecessarily meddled in other affairs of American dioceses, such as in cases of priests charged with gross subordination, alcoholism, or sexual deviation. The issue between priests and bishops over the rights of the clergy and the trials of clerics was a national one. Unlike in Europe, priests had no tenure in office until the Holy See intervened at their request. Elder, as one of the archbishops more outspoken on the matter, was critical of Propaganda's procedures in handling priests' cases. In the summer of 1885 he complained to Bishop Richard Gilmour of Cleveland that a number of Catholics were "'destroyed by scandal," due to the misbehavior of certain priests. Because of the strict judicial procedures that tended to favor the priests, "people are afraid to testify . . . in any formal way," he wrote, "though they will talk about them freely & the Bishop sees clearly they are true." Elder argued that even though he could gather evidence on the behavior of certain priests that would "convince," he wrote, "any impartial judge," the evidence was often regarded insufficient according to the "'judicial form' demanded by Rome." To prevent Vatican intrusion into the affairs of the diocese, it became advisable to have a clear-cut case before prosecuting a priest in the diocesan court. The appointment of an apostolic delegate a few years later was in part designed to keep the Propaganda informed of disputes between bishops and priests as well as perhaps to help deter bishops from proceeding irregularly.[49]

Another issue of contention was the pope's insistence that the bishops in established dioceses make certain churches "irremovable" posts. When a priest became the pastor of an irremovable parish, the archbishop could not arbitrarily remove him without serious cause. This assured the pastors a certain amount of independence. It gave them security of tenure by making them irremovable pastors. Elder always maintained that by not being free to remove any priest, his authority was diminished. But during the Third Plenary Council of Baltimore in 1884 Gibbons urged Elder and other American ordinaries to assign irremovable rectorships to prevent papal intervention.

Elder reluctantly went along with his recommendation. The Council also provided for some clerical consultation in diocesan administration and in the election of bishops. The powers of the bishops, then almost unquestioned, were curbed by the decrees adopted by the Plenary Council.[50]

At the archdiocese's second synod in 1886, nine parishes were made irremovable. The synod also reorganized the structure of the archdiocese, giving Elder and his administrative staff greater control over the spiritual and temporal welfare of all the parishes. This was a period in American history of consolidation and centralization in business, politics, and education. Increasing developments in transportation and communication made it possible for a greater integration of social systems. Using standards of efficiency that were characteristic signs of the era, Elder and Moeller, like some of their urban counterparts, centralized diocesan matters from their chancery headquarters. With increasing centralization the diocese was divided into four deaneries, with a trusted priest as dean overseeing each part. The synod further restructured the diocese by designating ten synodal examiners and six diocesan consultors.[51]

The duties of a dean were extensive. He visited all the churches and Catholic schools of his deanery. In view of the fact that the archbishop frequently recruited his vicars general, deans, and consultors from among the pastors of big parishes, many priests aspired for promotion to a prosperous parish. What many priests dreaded was being assigned or banished to a small rural parish or "to any inferior petty little town." The *Catholic Telegraph* observed that "[a]lmost all the priests of the diocese are . . . looking for big parishes. There is no concealing this fact. It seems to be a perfect mania among them." During Elder's administration pastors also began submitting to the chancery annual reports on the size of the parishes as well as on their debts, income, and expenditures. Since the Fourth Provincial Council of 1882 the pastor submitted a financial report at least once a year, which was read to the parishioners after Mass. Increasingly pastors appointed church wardens to assist them in administering the parishes.[52]

In the midst of the administrative changes, interparish disagreements and raiding were rampant throughout the archdiocese. As there was considerable infighting among the clergy for stipends, parishioners, and territory, there were charges of priests invading other priests' domains to steal parishioners or to perform a baptism, wedding, or a funeral. When the commotion over the Purcell bank failure had abated by the 1890s, Elder began addressing the issue more forthrightly. In his letter to the diocesan clergy in the fall of 1896, Elder took a firm stand against parish raiding. No one was allowed to rent pews in another congregation without the knowledge of the pastor of the parish in which the person resided. It was also regarded as unlawful for any person to attend a church of a language that he did not understand. By doing so he was not fulfilling the Catholic duty of hearing the Word of God. Furthermore, no one was allowed to hear Mass in the chapels of hospitals or religious communities, excepting the inmates of those institutions. Elder informed the clergy in 1897 that if he had not received the description of their boundary lines by the end of the summer, he would "regard the delay as evidence of [their] negligence, and make note of it for future reference." The archbishop tried to establish clearly defined borders for all the parishes. About half the parishes responded.[53]

When Moeller succeeded Elder in 1904, boundary fighting and parish raiding continued. The clerical disputes were so intense, especially in the newly created parishes on the fringe of older and more established parishes, Moeller decided not to press the issue. By the end of the decade, however, he attempted to resolve some of the interparish quarrels. "I have never seen," he wrote in 1910, "greater selfishness displayed than in regard to boundary lines." A good illustration of a boundary dispute at the time was the quarrel between Holy Angels Church, which lay midway between East Walnut Hills and Hyde Park east of downtown Cincinnati, and St. Mary, the new Hyde Park parish formed in 1898. In the early 1900s the two pastors, James Moore of Holy Angels's and Patrick J. Hynes of St. Mary's, fought over families and boundary lines, both wanting the lion's share of the wealthy families in a square in Hyde Park. Moeller formed an impartial committee of priests to investigate the pastors' claims. Acting on the committee's recommendation, Moeller allotted the square to Hynes and allowed Moore at Holy Angels to keep two families who lived in the disputed area and had been attending his church.[54]

When a group of laymen in the northwestern section of Dayton in 1911 attempted to form a new parish without consulting with him first, Moeller took exception. He argued that the responsibility of establishing new parishes belonged to him and not to laymen who were unable to assess adequately the spiritual and temporal needs of various communities. Moeller informed the Corpus Christi congregation that the committee to establish a new parish in Dayton View, which he deemed too close to the Corpus Christi line, did not have his approval. After three years of quarreling, Moeller allowed the Catholics of Dayton View to have their own church but not on the original sites proposed. Moeller dedicated the new parish to St. Agnes and assigned John M. Sailer as pastor.[55]

As they attempted to resolve parish feuds, some priests in 1913 blamed Moeller for some of the boundary disputes. They charged that he and other diocesan officials allowed the laity, especially real estate promoters, to multiply parishes needlessly. This issue became particularly acute in Dayton when

Moeller approved a petition submitted to him by a group of laymen to establish St. Anthony parish on the east side. Charles Kemper, the pastor of neighboring St. Mary's, accused the supporters of the proposed new parish of wooing parishioners away from his parish. Moeller advised Kemper to meet with representatives of the St. Anthony congregation and settle the dispute amicably, which they eventually did. He knew from experience, Moeller wrote to Kemper, that "pastors of the Mother church are, as a ru[l]e loath to give up territory and people and are generally unreasonable. They picture all kinds of disasters unless their views are complied with, but disasters never materialize when their views are disregarded."[56]

The issue that helped trigger a resolution of the boundary disputes in the archdiocese was the rivalry between English- and German-speaking parishes. Since the end of the nineteenth century the distinction between these parishes had broken down significantly and disputes between the pastors over boundary lines and parish raiding increased significantly. At the same time that German parishes found it increasingly more difficult to find German-speaking priests or even candidates interested in learning German, more and more young German Americans attended English churches, where many priests welcomed them. The number of German-speaking parishes declined with the passage of time. Though many older German Americans clung to the customs and language of "the old country," their sons and daughters frequently did not share their parents' enthusiasm. By the 1880s most of them were American-born, and many came from homes where some English was spoken. Some of the pastors complained that it did not seem right to preach German during the Mass for only a few. Upon the death of the Irish-born William J. Halley, vicar general of the English-speaking churches, Elder in 1886 discontinued the practice of having two separate vicars general for the German- and English-speaking Catholics. He made John C. Albrinck vicar of the entire diocese. Moreover, on June 19, 1907, after over seven decades of staunchly defending the church, the *Wahrheitsfreund* came to an end, due to the gradual decrease in the use of the German language in the archdiocese.[57]

Though more slowly than the Irish in the archdiocese, Germans eventually became more fully integrated into American life. As the German congregations declined, however, some German priests conducted some of their services in English and welcomed non-Germans in neighboring communities to their churches. But this effort violated ecclesiastical law. Though Vatican officials permitted Germans to join an English congregation, they prohibited English-speaking Catholics to join a German parish even if the priest conducted his services in English. In the late nineteenth and early twentieth centuries a number of German Catholics, especially in the Midwest, complained to Roman authorities that they were treated as second-class citizens. Father Peter Abbelen, vicar general of Milwaukee, went to Rome carrying a petition to that effect from German priests of Milwaukee, Cincinnati, and St. Louis. As German pastors complained that the ecclesiastical law was unfair and contributed to the decimation of their parishes, English pastors encouraged diocesan officials to enforce the law. Though Elder expressed sympathy with some of the Abbelen demands, he deplored the underhanded method employed by him. Abbelen and the German pastors "should be made aware of how unfair has been their conduct in this matter," he wrote to Archbishop Gibbons, "and how grievous injury it threatens to our peace & unity, & consequently to the deepest interests of religion."[58]

The approach American bishops took against the German Catholics resembled the stance Orestes Brownson and others had adopted a half-century earlier. They accused German Catholics of perpetuating through its schools a foreign nationality in the United States and, in the process, hurting the church by giving credence to the allegation that Catholics were not true Americans. Moeller responded to the rift among German- and English-speaking parishes in the archdiocese by attempting to reclassify as English parishes all parishes that no longer used German as their main language. Many pastors in charge of English parishes, however, complained that they would lose parishioners for the sake of maintaining semidefunct German parishes. German nationalists also opposed Moeller's scheme. They accused the archbishop of trying to anglicize their parishes and contributing to the decline of their Catholic faith. For over three-quarters of a century German Catholics had built and maintained their own separate parishes and neighborhoods.[59]

In the tradition of the German priest John Henni, Father Anthony Walburg, pastor at St. Augustine Church in the west end of Cincinnati from 1877 to 1910, reflected the belief of many of his parishioners that true Catholicism was tied together with language and cultural heritage. The first person of German descent born in Cincinnati to be raised to the priesthood, Walburg publicly criticized attempts to Americanize German Catholics. A longtime champion of the cause of perpetuating the speaking of the German language among those of German extraction, he eventually established an endowment of fifty thousand dollars from his own fortune for a chair of German language, literature, and history at Catholic University in Washington, D.C. Even though Moeller's parents were also from Germany, the archbishop was not sympathetic to Walburg's argument. He did "not believe," he wrote in 1906, "that the Faith is bound up in the language, and that if the German language goes the Faith will go with it. I am inclined to believe and my belief is based on experience," he argued, "that the children of German parents are lost to the Faith because they have not learned their religion in the English language." During his tenure Elder had expressed similar concerns, protesting against the overidentification of the German language and customs with faith. Although the German language and customs helped bring up "children in piety and in the family spirit," he wrote to Gibbons in 1886, they were "in many respects a hindrance to the development of many Christians and a vehicle of many irreligious influences . . . after they get out in the world."[60]

Both Elder and Moeller opposed demands for ethnic separatism and through the schools, parishes, and other institutions they promoted the Americanization of Germans and other immigrant Catholics from Eastern Europe. Wanting Catholics to be accepted as part of mainstream America, the two Cincinnati ordinaries encouraged immigrant Catholics to get rid of their immigrant stigma by shedding foreign loyalties, customs, and languages. Moeller, like his predecessor and other American church leaders, feared for the "church in America if either foreignism or national antagonism" were established. He was also of the opinion that when all Catholics under his jurisdiction spoke English, it would help bring them "closer together and enable . . . [him] to organize the diocese." By the turn of the century the *Catholic Telegraph* also wrote several articles in favor of assimilationism.[61]

In mixed parishes, such as St. George's in Cincinnati, the archbishop insisted that catechism be taught in English. Though he stressed the importance of the English language, Moeller was not opposed to knowing a second language, such as German. He thought his views in that regard were misrepresented. "One of the matters that has always grieved me," he wrote in 1916, "was that . . . I have so often been accused of acting out of a spirit of 'Anti-Germanism.'" Though at times Moeller proceeded more cautiously in his criticism of the German language, perhaps hoping that the matter would "gradually adjust itself," his Americanist stance was evident. When it came to choosing between the German language and the Catholic religion, his position was unmistakably clear. Though German was taught in some public schools during World War I, it was not in parochial schools. During the war the German language was also banned from church services. When a parent inquired about sending her child to public school to learn German, Moeller replied "that if a choice must be made between giving the child instruction in German, and giving him a thorough drilling in Religion, the former must be sacrificed, and not the latter." By the end of the war Moeller came to the conclusion that "for the good of the state and of religion . . . all the foreign languages ought to be excluded from the primary grades."[62]

As the rift among parishes grew and some of the priests complained that Moeller and his staff seemed unable to settle the boundary feuds, the archbishop thought that his hands were tied. "If you knew the obstacles in the way of establishing territorial boundary lines in the Archdiocese," he wrote to one of his critics, "you would soon realize that you are mistaken in your contentions." Moeller appealed to the apostolic delegate several times for his support to discontinue the ethnic division of the diocese into German and English parishes and establish territorial boundary lines. Local church officials concluded that as long as the issue remained unresolved, the confusion and constant quarreling among the parishes made it "impossible to organize the Diocese or take proper care of souls." Following a meeting of the archdiocesan consultors in the spring of 1919, the local church again proposed to officials in Rome that territorial parish limits be drawn for the whole diocese.[63]

In the summer of 1921 the pope finally allowed Moeller to establish territorial boundary lines. By this time nearly all the former German parishes used the English language. To smooth matters, some German-speaking families, such as those from St. Mary's and St. Paul's in Cincinnati, were not compelled to attend an English-speaking church. The following year Moeller also took a firm stand on parish raiding. For those parishes that could not reach an amicable settlement, Moeller and his staff appointed a special court of four judges to resolve the disputes.[64]

RELATIONS WITH REGULAR CLERGY

Boundary disputes and parish raiding in the late nineteenth and early twentieth centuries in the archdiocese of Cincinnati also intensified tensions between the archbishop and the regular clergy, priests who were members of religious orders. Not unlike the tension and conflict between bishops and religious orders in other dioceses, a number of controversies flared between the Cincinnati ordinary and religious orders. Though Purcell had had his struggles with local Dominicans, Jesuits, and Vincentians, Elder's and Moeller's relations with the regular clergy were tense. What helped trigger the conflict was Elder's effort, like that of many of his episcopal colleagues, to revamp the organizational structure of the archdiocese, foster more centralized control over church affairs, and strengthen his position as the supreme authority in the local church. When Elder in 1896 appointed a diocesan priest, Francis Quatman, as dean of Montgomery, Fayette, Greene, Madison, Darke, Shelby, and Mercer Counties, he alienated relations with the Precious Blood priests. Elder sought to exercise greater control over the spiritual and temporal welfare of the parishes in the deanery. Some Precious Blood priests countered that the appointment of a dean in their portion of the archdiocese encroached upon the authority of their provincial. They also feared losing their best parishes to the diocesan clergy. They provided the order with a good income and a wonderful source for recruiting new members.[65]

To protect their vested interests the Precious Blood priests wanted the provincial of the order to control both the internal affairs of the community and also all the parishes under his care. Through his chancellor, Henry Moeller, Elder made clear that Dean Quatman, and not their provincial, was their immediate superior in parochial affairs. Acknowledging that matters regarding their community life fell under the jurisdiction of their provincial, he stressed that it was not so in matters pertaining to the administration of parishes. The issue became more heated in 1898. In an effort to end all the bickering over parish borders, Elder directed his deans to get the pastors to cooperate in establishing more clearly defined borders for their respective parishes. When Quatman attempted to canvass all the parishes in his deanery, some Precious Blood priests, suspicious of the archbishop's intentions, believed that this was probably "a scheme" on Elder's part to get their parishes. Some feared that the archbishop and his staff would do "anything to kick out religious and get these parishes for themselves."[66]

In the midst of the mistrust and suspicion between the Precious Blood priests and the secular clergy, Elder also grew suspicious of the Franciscans' motives. He thought they were interested less in the spiritual needs of the diocese and more in increasing the status and prestige of their own order. As more and more German parishioners moved away from downtown Cincinnati to the hilltops and suburbs, Franciscan parishes in the city, like St. John the Baptist's and St. Francis Seraph's, lost many members. From the 1880s to the turn of the century the sizes of the two congregations decreased from 1,400 and 900, respectively, to about 800 each. As the Franciscans expressed concern over their future role in the archdiocese, they were accused of parish raiding and placing obstacles in the way of establishing new parishes adjoining theirs. When they requested to be relieved of their duties at St. Charles Borromeo, a small parish on the northern periphery of Cincinnati, the archbishop suspected that they wanted to get rid of their smallest parish in order to focus on larger parishes. Elder consented on the condition that the order would continue to provide chaplains at various public and private institutions. Because the ranks of the diocesan clergy continued to increase, the archdiocese became less dependent on the religious societies. As a consequence, the Franciscan Lucas Gottbehoede, the local superior of the order, asked Elder in 1885 to sign an agreement that would place Cincinnati's parishes of St. Clement, St. Stephen, St. Bonaventure, St. Joseph, and St. George permanently under the supervision of the Franciscans. The archbishop agreed to give them the first two, but he deferred decision on the others until such time they assured him that they would continue to staff St. Aloysius Asylum, the hospitals, and the prison.[67]

Even though Elder questioned some of the Franciscans' motives, he nevertheless supported the movement for the erection of a Franciscan Province, a territorial division of the religious order. Before the end of Purcell's administration, the Franciscans had requested the archbishop to petition the general of the order for the erection of a province. By 1885 the Franciscans had three convents or monasteries, fifteen residences in nine dioceses, and 130 members, including fifty-seven clergymen. They felt their establishment warranted being erected to a fully constituted province. Pope Leo XIII approved the Franciscans' establishment of the Province of St. John the Baptist. In the spring of 1886 Elder implemented the papal decree with Hieronymus Kilgenstein as the first American-born friar to be elected superior of the Cincinnati foundation of Franciscans.[68]

Moeller, like his predecessor, also had an abiding suspicion that religious orders cared less about the needs of the archdiocese than upon their financial status and power. The "grasping spirit of the religious," he wrote in 1922, "is really amazing." Throughout his administration the archbishop attempted to secure diocesan rule over the separate religious orders. Though titles of various religious institutions were often invested in the religious orders in charge of the institutions, Moeller made it clear that the institutions were nevertheless diocesan because they were "under his control and jurisdiction."[69]

Boniface Russ, the Provincial of the Precious Blood Order, and his clergy distrusted Moeller even more than they had Elder. When the Precious Blood priests in 1904 expressed interest in establishing a parish in Cincinnati, Moeller gave them permission on the condition that they relinquished some of the places they now had in the archdiocese. "[T]his I am sure," he wrote to Russ, "would satisfy the [diocesan] clergy." The following year the order was given permission to establish St. Mark parish in Evanston, one of Cincinnati's newer middle-class suburbs. There were more than one hundred Catholic families in the region. In return, the secular priests acquired four parishes, St. Henry and Holy Trinity in Mercer County and St. Sebastian and St. Patrick in Shelby County. Before they could establish schools in their new parish in Evanston, however, the order also had to establish a mission house to help out the diocesan clergy. Russ would doubtlessly have agreed with the comment Moeller later made to a parishioner that "Bishops are human and sometimes have some vanity and selfishness in their make-up."[70]

When in 1911 Moeller asked Russ to surrender the chaplaincy of institutions in the archdiocese to the diocesan clergy, Russ, concerned over the erosion of the holdings of the Precious Blood Order, became more convinced that Moeller was unreasonably partial to his priests. He wrote to the archbishop that he should "care for the Religious in his diocese as well as he does for the [diocesan] and even more so because the former are as it were his body guard." Though Moeller acknowledged the contributions of the Precious Blood priests and assured them they were needed in the archdiocese, he admitted that he was partial to his clergy. Being "directly under me," he wrote, "I naturally feel a greater solicitude in providing for them. Whilst the Religious may rightly be called the body-guard of the Bishop, the [diocesan] clergy may . . . be said to be members of his household."[71]

Relations between Moeller and the Precious Blood priests improved significantly following the election of a new provincial, George Hindelang, in 1914. More diplomatic than his predecessor, Hindelang worked on improving relations by frequently seeking the archbishop's approvals on various parochial matters, by rendering clerical assistance whenever he could, and by urging his priests and parishioners to contribute generously to the archbishop's special collections. No longer did the Precious Blood priests seriously question the archbishop's authority in running the parishes. Similarly, Moeller praised the "laudable services" they rendered religion in the archdiocese and their efforts to build a new seminary at Carthagena.[72]

When Moeller announced in 1904 that he planned to establish Holy Name parish for the Catholics living in Mount Auburn in Cincinnati and expected the Franciscans' St. George parish to surrender the eastern portion of its territory, he encountered resistance from the friars. They appealed to the apostolic delegate. Before the delegate had an opportunity to investigate the matter, however, Moeller and the Franciscans worked out an agreement. But Moeller's selection of a diocesan priest as pastor of Holy Name Church and his partition of St. George parish intensified the Franciscans' suspicion that the archbishop favored the diocesan clergy over the religious in the distribution of parishes. This suspicion became even more intense in the fall of 1910 when Moeller revived plans, which had started under Elder, of establishing St. Monica parish in Fairview Heights. Moeller expected the Franciscans at St. George and St. John parishes to relinquish parts of their territory. The Franciscans perceived this latest move as posing a severe threat to the survival of St. John. During the next three years Moeller, the Franciscan Provincial, Eugene Buttermann, and the pastors of St. George, St. John and St. Monica parishes deliberated over the boundary lines. By the summer of 1913 Buttermann and the pastors reluctantly agreed to a boundary settlement.[73]

In 1918 the controversy between the Franciscans and the secular clergy became more heated over a dispute regarding St. Stephen parish for Hungarians in Cincinnati. After several years of searching for a Hungarian priest who could speak both Hungarian and German, in the fall of 1914 Father Edmund Neurihrer from Hungary came to the city to minister to the spiritual needs of the parish. At the time there were about four thousand Hungarians in Cincinnati, among whom approximately two hundred families spoke Hungarian and German. A few spoke Slovak. Though Moeller believed that the days of forming an ethnic parish in the see city were numbered, a year after Neurihrer's arrival he nevertheless authorized him to organize a parish and to make repairs on the former chapel of the Good Shepherd Sisters in the west end for their use.[74]

Neurihrer made plans to remodel the rest of the Baum Street property into a priest's house and thirty-nine apartments for Hungarian families. Underestimating the cost of the renovation, he had to borrow $65,000 from the Philadelphia Fire Insurance Company to cover the total cost for repairs and alterations. To make matters worse, few Hungarians occupied the apartments or attended St. Stephen Church on a regular basis. They preferred attending neighboring St. John the Baptist and St. Francis Seraph Churches. Meanwhile, Neurihrer accused the Franciscans of stealing marriages and funerals from him and denying Hungarian children the opportunity to attend the Franciscan parochial schools unless their parents rented seats in one of their parishes. Rudolph Bonner, the new Franciscan Provincial, not only denied the charges as "calumny pure and simple," but accused Neurihrer of having alienated many of the Hungarian families. Bonner also urged Moeller to assign the friars to the Hungarian parish. Though the archbishop generally liked the idea and initially promised the new parish to the order, he chose instead to appoint Henry Meyer, a diocesan priest, who had already been working with the Hungarians.[75]

But Meyer had no more success with St. Stephen parish than did Neurihrer. When he tried to borrow money from the archdiocese to help pay Neurihrer's debt, Moeller refused. "St. Stephen is insolvent," the chancery wrote, "and the Archbishop had no power to require the other congregations of the Archdiocese to assume its obligations." Each parish was expected to shoulder its own debts without expecting any help from the other parishes. Moreover, when the Philadelphia Fire Insurance Company appealed directly to Moeller for repayment of the loan, he refused. Moeller contended that the loan was not given to him personally, nor to the Catholic Church, but to St. Stephen parish. When the company appealed to John Bonzano, the apostolic delegate, Bonzano backed Moeller. The loan was eventually settled out of court.[76]

As the issue over the Hungarian parish unfolded, the Franciscans, intending to embarrass the archbishop, complained to the apostolic delegate that Moeller had used some of the funds earmarked for missionaries and for Catholic University in Washington, D.C., for diocesan purposes. Moeller did not deny the use of funds but indicated that it had not been his intention to mislead the laity or the clergy. Because of this incident, a Franciscan parish chose to contribute little in the diocese's annual collection for the pope. In his attempt to improve relations with the Franciscans, Moeller now allowed them to staff the new parish for the Hungarians. In the spring of 1919 the Hungarians, with the archbishop's assistance, secured St. Joseph of Nazareth Church at Liberty and Elm Streets in the west end. But when it came time for Moeller to transfer the parish to the order, he chose not to hand it over directly to the provincial but to his representative. "[U]ntil you apologize for your unfairness towards me," Moeller wrote in April 1919, ". . . your presence would be undesirable." That spring Bonner apologized. The archbishop, in turn, asked him to "obliterate from [his] mind the sharp things" he had said.[77]

During Moeller's tenure the Jesuits, like the Precious Blood priests and the Franciscans, also ran into problems with the secular clergy. The Jesuits had two parishes in Cincinnati, St. Francis Xavier on Sycamore Street and St. Ann on New Street. St. Francis Xavier was the largest parish and one of the most prosperous in the archdiocese, whereas St. Ann was among the poorest. Because of Cincinnati's commercial and industrial expansion, the people who lived within the boundaries of St. Xavier parish gradually took up their residence in the suburbs. As the number of resident parishioners slowly decreased, the prestige of the church attracted transient worshippers. The diocesan clergy complained to the chancery that Jesuits at the St. Xavier Church stole marriages, funerals, and parishioners from them. Though the Jesuits may not have actively solicited Catholics from other parishes, they did not turn them away when they sought membership on their own.[78]

Because the religious orders at the turn of the century had "charge of quite a number of churches," Moeller granted permission to the Jesuits to build a new parish and college in one of the suburbs on the condition that the St. Xavier parish in the city "be given up." When the Jesuits purchased twenty-six acres of land east of Cincinnati from the Avondale Athletic Club in 1911, they chose to keep St. Xavier Church rather than form another parish. Eight years later St. Xavier College was transferred from Sycamore Street to its new location, marking an epoch in the history of the institution. The college and the high school were now separate. The buildings on Seventh and Sycamore Streets were reserved for the high school and the evening extension classes. In 1920 two new college buildings, Alumni Science Hall and Hinkle Hall, were erected in Avondale.[79]

By the end of Moeller's tenure in 1925 the archdiocese had fostered over four decades more centralized control over church affairs. In the process, Archbishops Elder and Moeller in their relations with the separate priests' orders strengthened the local ordinary's position as the supreme authority in the archdiocese.

CATHOLIC EDUCATION
AND CHARITABLE WORKS

A s the archdiocese of Cincinnati at the end of the nineteenth and early twentieth centuries became more centralized, it built upon its educational programs and became more actively engaged in community outreach programs. At the same time that it sought to improve the efficiency of parochial schools, it promoted the development of Catholic secondary education, reopened Mount St. Mary's of the West Seminary, started a preparatory seminary, and launched an ambitious plan for a planned Catholic residential community. The laity and men and women religious, moreover, became more involved in social and charitable work.

Shortly before the Fourth Provincial Council convened in Cincinnati in 1882, Elder, as administrator of the archdiocese, reminded the pastors that the children "are the prize for which the opposing armies of God and the World are contending. The schools are the battle-field." The day before the opening, a dense crowd filled every available seat in St. Peter's Cathedral for the Mass. "The only mournful episode," the *Catholic Telegraph* wrote, "was the sad sight of the vacant throne of the Most Rev. Archbishop Purcell." In the absence of the archbishop Elder acted as metropolitan, assisted by the seven suffragan bishops of the ecclesiastical province of Cincinnati. At the time the province embraced more suffragan sees than any other province in the country. At the session the bishops spent most of the time underscoring the importance of Catholic education. In light of the Purcell bank failure ecclesiastical finance also constituted part of its deliberations. The council made clear that no pastor was to owe more than one hundred dollars or incur a debt on behalf of his church, and no new churches, renovations of old ones, repairs or restorations to school buildings were to be started without approval of his bishop.[1]

Building upon Purcell's educational legacy, it was the council's wish "that the Church and school go hand in hand; that where the one is, there also shall the other be." Wherever there were sufficient Catholic schools, parents, under serious moral obligation, were exhorted not to send their children to public schools unless excused by the bishop. Poverty was no excuse. If it could be shown that it was absolutely impossible for parents to buy the books used by the Catholic schools, the parish assumed the cost. Whereas Catholics in the first fifty years of the history of the diocese were primarily concerned with the influence of Protestantism in public education, in the latter part of the nineteenth century they worried over a society, including public schools, that was becoming increasingly secular. When the Third Plenary Council convened in Baltimore in November 1884, in response to a directive by the Holy See, it set forth more strongly than ever the necessity of Catholic education, devoting close to one-fourth of its decrees on it. Encouraged by Vatican officials since the issuance of instructions by the Propaganda in 1875, the sixty-nine ordinaries at the council took a strong separatist stance and directed that parochial school systems be developed in every diocese in the country. They required the erection of a parochial school near each church and mandated the attendance of Catholic children at these schools. Schools were also a way of strengthening parish loyalties as well as the religious beliefs of the children.[2]

Concerned about the quality of education the Council Fathers thought they had to mobilize educational resources. They passed legislation stating that sisters had to pass examinations that tested their competency. Each diocese, furthermore, was to form a board of examiners to administer the exams as well as to establish a normal school to train teachers properly. There was concern about the inferiority of parochial schools to public schools. The council also established the famous uniform national catechism known to generations of Catholics thereafter as the *Baltimore Catechism*.[3]

Throughout their administrations Elder and Moeller stressed the importance of parochial education. They argued that religion should be a part of a child's education. Believing that it was not enough to teach reading, writing, grammar, geography, and arithmetic, many Catholics argued there had to be "the careful training and development of the *moral*, as well as the intellectual, faculties."[4]

Though most Catholics preferred to send their children to Catholic schools for religious reasons, the archdiocese did not oppose the public school system. It believed that all children had a right to the education necessary to fit them for their future stations in life, and that the state had the right to compel parents or guardians to give their children sufficient schooling. Though he acknowledged the state's right to sponsor public schools, Moeller contended that the "chief objection to the public school system is that it is essentially defective. True education must be based on, directed and guided by religion." Arguing that the exclusion of religious training in the public schools was "radically wrong," Catholics sponsored their own separate schools. Catholic parents were generally pleased with the powerful religious and cultural influence of the environment in the parochial schools. In addition to the morning Mass, the opening and closing prayers, the recitations in Christian Doctrine, the presence of sacred images and pictures, and an adequate curriculum, there was an ever-active influence of religious teachers.[5]

When the bishops of the Cincinnati Province met at Elder's residence in the fall of 1892, they passed a resolution decreeing that the Catholic children not attending parochial schools should receive catechetical instruction during the week. A few weeks later Elder and his episcopal colleagues met at Archbishop Michael Corrigan's residence in New York. There they declared that the sacraments of the church "should be denied only to such parents as neglect efficient means of having their children taught the Christian doctrine." It was no longer imperative that it was the duty of Catholic parents to send their children to parochial schools. If unable to enroll them in Catholic schools, they were expected to send them to Sunday schools, generally taught by the sisters—who staffed the parish schools—and lay women volunteers, as well as teach them "the Christian doctrine in their homes." Wanting to emulate the success of the Protestant Sunday schools, the local church increasingly recruited "ladies of leisure" who had had training in the Catholic teachings in the various convents. Throughout the United States the work of catechizing children was largely given over to women, both lay and religious. During Moeller's term Pius X promoted the Confraternity of Christian Doctrine (CCD), which helped standardize religious education programs nationally. In the spring of 1921 Moeller authorized the Jesuit John M. Lyons to establish in the archdiocese the Catholic Instruction League, designed to give religious instruction to Catholic children attending the public schools. As before, Catholic women volunteered to teach the children.[6]

Continuing to work to promote Catholic education, the local church sought to improve the efficiency of Catholic schools. By the early twentieth century, local church ordinaries approached the organization and the search for order in the development of Catholic schools in a manner similar to administrators in the public schools. In the summer of 1904 Elder, consistent with the decrees of the Third Plenary Council of Baltimore, appointed a Board of Examiners. The board was authorized to hold an examination annually and issue credentials to qualified teachers. The establishment of boards of education in most dioceses from 1885 to 1920 was the first significant step to standardize as well as establish control over parish schools. For the 1904–1905 school year the archdiocesan board accepted the testimonials of religious superiors and pastors as to the fitness of members of religious orders and lay teachers. But thereafter the Board of Examiners certified the teachers in the parochial schools. This forced women religious, who did the bulk of the teaching, to upgrade themselves professionally. In addition to their heavy teaching schedules, the large classes, the obligation to teach catechism after school hours to public-school children, and other religious obligations, many had slighted their formal educations. All too often, the young sisters were expected to acquire their teaching skills on the job as well as learn from experienced teachers and mentors in the schools. Notwithstanding their lack of professional training, the teaching sisters compared favorably with their secular female counterparts. The latter's average age was twenty-six years or younger and worked about five years before marriage, whereas the sister-teachers often spent decades of their lives teaching, gaining much experience and expertise. In time more and more women religious took college-level courses and some even received their college degrees. Throughout his priestly and episcopal career, Moeller had a predilection for education. His ideal was having free schools, with modern equipment and standardized training, conducted by fully qualified teachers. To fulfill this ideal, he encouraged the archdiocesan teaching communities of the religious to increase their efficiency by intensive study at normal schools and teachers' institutes. Attempting to enhance the competence of teachers in the parochial schools, Moeller contended that in order to compel parents to send their children to a Catholic school, the parochial school "must be up to the standard of the public school." A few weeks before the 1904 school year, Moeller urged the pastor of St. Patrick Church in Cumminsville to replace its "unhealthy" school, "so that your people will have no . . . reason for sending their children to the public school." Consistent with the directives of the Third Plenary Council and instructions from Propaganda, he forbade confessors "to give absolution to parents" who, without his permission, "sent their children to non-Catholic schools."[7]

To provide for more efficiency in the administration of the parochial schools, Moeller and his staff also encouraged more uniformity in education and better record keeping. In 1906 the archbishop appointed Father Otto B. Auer as the archdiocesan superintendent of schools. The cultural trends of centralization and professionalization, so evident in society and in the church at the turn of the century, influenced Catholic educators. The Cincinnati ordinary and other Catholic leaders were of the opinion that superintendents, like school boards, were important to the future success of the parochial school system. The larger urban dioceses of New York, Philadelphia, and Cincinnati led the way. By 1910 there were school boards in more than 55 percent of parishes across the country and superintendents appointed in seventeen percent of these dioceses. Whereas throughout much of the nineteenth century parish schools in the archdiocese of Cincinnati were independent of one another, and each pastor was the neighborhood superintendent of schools, the archdiocese by 1906 had a superintendent to oversee the administration of all the Catholic schools. A school board, consisting only of clergymen, was also organized for the archdiocese. In his first year Auer initiated a program of school visitation. After personally visiting nearly two-thirds of the schools, he submitted a report and a list of recommendations to the school board. The *First Annual Report of the Superintendent of the Parish Schools of the Cincinnati Archdiocese,* issued in 1908, showed that there were 110 parochial schools, with an enrollment of 27,233 pupils, in the eighteen counties of the archdiocese. More than 90 percent of the parishes in Cincinnati, and more than 70 percent of the parishes outside the city, supported their own elementary schools. Twelve years later there were 123 schools attended by 33,900 pupils.[8]

At the time the cost of sending a student to parochial school was estimated to be from $12 to $17 a year, as against $24 to $45 in the public school system. The main reasons for the difference in cost were the facts that some teaching religious taught without salary and that the few lay teachers in the parochial schools were paid much less than those in public schools. Moreover, the pastors, who served as principals of their respective parochial schools, received no compensation for their supervision. The primary reason that the parochial schools succeeded financially was because the sisters, who constituted the bulk of the teaching, subsidized them through their low salaries. Though at times pastors were displeased if superiors of religious communities did not grant their requests for sisters in their schools, Moeller cautioned superiors against yielding to the pastors by sending them novices unqualified for the tasks. He insisted that novices should have their full novitiate of two years before being sent out in the community.[9]

During this period Auer and the school board also warned against the danger of overcrowding the schoolroom, especially in the primary grades. Overcrowding was a common complaint. Inadequate facilities and large class size supported the view that the parochial schools were inferior to their public counterparts. Class size ranged from seventy to one hundred students, with the lower grades larger than the upper levels. They recommended that the number of pupils of any one room be fixed at fifty. "It is unfortunate," Auer wrote in his second report, "that the importance of the primary grade is so commonly misunderstood . . . ; for this is the foundation period—the time for impressions right or wrong."[10]

Notwithstanding the legitimate concern over class size, by the fall of 1908 the archdiocese had nevertheless made considerable progress in regard to parish schools. Cincinnati became one of the first dioceses to establish a centralized school system. It had established a diocesan superintendent, a diocesan school board, a system of teachers' examinations, and uniformity of schoolbooks. Moreover, many of the schools had become free schools, new buildings replaced old ones, and a parish without a school was a rarity. In the east end of Cincinnati all the Catholic schools were free schools. Our Lady of Loretto, St. Stephen, St. Rose, and Holy Angels schools charged no tuition and were supported by the ordinary revenue of the respective churches. "We believe the day will come soon," the *Catholic Telegraph* wrote, "when every parochial school will be a free school, supported by the parish as a most necessary and judicious expense." Some people were hopeful that over time there would no longer be Catholic children in public schools. In July 1920 Moeller ordered that the parochial schools under his jurisdiction become free schools.[11]

The archdiocese was pleased with the fiscal initiative taken by St. Brigid parish in Xenia in the spring of 1898. Under the leadership of Isaac Hocter, its pastor, and St. Brigid's school board, the parish adopted a new method of raising money for its school. The school board provided sufficient funds to maintain the school without drawing from the ordinary income of the church. It had its own bank account, and the pastor and treasurer of the school board signed all checks. A monthly collection was taken in church for this special school fund. It was also the duty of the board to visit individuals who did not contribute to the fund and try "to induce them" to contribute to the monthly school collection. All moneys collected appeared in the annual church report. This new plan "on the part" of St. Brigid's congregation, the *Catholic Telegraph* wrote, evidenced "a laudable spirit of lay cooperation."[12]

As they attempted to build and upgrade the parochial school system, largely financed by working class families, church officials in the archdiocese regarded it as "unjust" that Catholics were forced to support their own schools as well as the public school system. Acknowledging the right and obligation of the state to assist education, they insisted it should do so without violating denomination freedom. By the turn of the century, Catholics were no longer alone in their stand for denominational schools. Many Lutherans, Methodists, Episcopalians, Baptists, and Orthodox Jews insisted that religion be inculcated concurrently with secular instruction. Convinced that the parents and the denomination were the proper determining parties of a child's education, they maintained that the respective churches, and not the state, should have the authority to choose the teachers, the books, and the curriculum. The archdiocese regarded a state-supported denominational system as an ideal solution to its financial difficulties.[13]

Moeller was always of the opinion that Catholics should receive a share of the Ohio funds for the support of their schools. "My idea," he wrote in

January 1910, "is that the State should give us our share per capita for the children in our schools for their secular education and that we look after the religious part of their education ourselves." When in the summer of 1899 the Cincinnati Board of Education asked for a special appropriation for the purpose of supplying free textbooks to children in the public schools, the *Catholic Telegraph* opposed it. It countered that "an attempt was made to hold up the Catholics again, and force them . . . to buy irreligious school books for godless schools." There should be "NO TAXATION WITHOUT PARTICIPATION." The diocesan paper urged Catholic voters in Cincinnati to defeat "any candidate for office who favors the free school-book scheme."[14]

As Catholics demanded a fair share of Ohio's school fund, there were several attempts by Protestant ministers and members of the Ohio legislature to obstruct Catholic education. When in the spring of 1915 efforts were made to provide for the compulsory reading of the Bible in Ohio's public schools, Moeller and his episcopal colleagues in the state sent a representative to the public hearing in Columbus to oppose the idea. How would the Catholics and Jews and Protestants agree as to which edition to use? Since children of various denominations and sects attended the public schools, it seemed unlawful to compel children of one denomination to read or listen to the reading of the Bible of another denomination. "I am afraid," Moeller wrote to one of the state senators, "that it might be a[n] entering wedge for a denomination or a sect in the public schools." The Ohio bishops were doubtless pleased with Governor A. Victor Donahey's veto of the bill. When in 1919 a member of the Ohio legislature lobbied for a bill requiring parochial schools to conduct all religious instruction outside of the regular school hours, again the Catholic hierarchy responded. They countered with the argument that there was no evidence religious instruction imparted in the parochial schools interfered "with proper training in the secular branches of learning." The bill was defeated. Four years later when the U.S. Congress debated bills that would create a federal department of education and grant federal aid to public schools, Moeller opposed the legislation. He and other church leaders feared that by excluding religious or privately owned schools, the proposed legislation would strengthen the public schools at the expense of the private institutions. Catholics also argued that they would be made to pay more taxes to implement the new legislation.[15]

SECONDARY SCHOOLS AND HIGHER EDUCATION

When Moeller became archbishop in 1904 Catholic secondary education in the archdiocese, as in the public sector, was still in its infancy. Most of the education of Catholic as well as Protestant children in the United States in the nineteenth century had centered on primary grades. Although the Jesuits, the Sisters of Charity, and the Notre Dame Sisters had secondary schools, they generally charged tuition. Most Catholic families could not afford to send their children to the schools. These schools, moreover, were mainly college preparatory schools for men and finishing schools for women. In response to the need for greater education for a larger number of students, about a dozen of the parishes began adding secondary courses to the curriculum of the existing parochial schools. At the same time, however, the nineteenth-century pattern of combining secondary and collegiate training in one school gradually disappeared. As part of the move in American education toward standardization and uniformity, Catholic educators recommended more secondary schools. In the first half of the twentieth century the modern Catholic high school, though not as extensive as the elementary school, became an integral part of the archdiocese's educational enterprise.[16]

The trend of parochial high schools serving only one parish seemed unrealistic and impractical to Moeller. He proposed instead that Catholics from several parishes pool their resources and build modern, well-equipped high schools. In the summer of 1909 pastors and lay Catholics of six parishes in Hamilton, Ohio, helped organize Hamilton Catholic high school for boys on Sixth and Dayton Streets, the first central Catholic high school in the archdiocese and in Ohio. Since 1889 Notre Dame Academy in Hamilton had been offering secondary education for girls. Until the establishment of the new Catholic high school, there were no such opportunities for Catholic boys in the city. Throughout the country most graduates of Catholic or public secondary schools before 1914 were mostly female. The new Hamilton school, under the charge of the Brothers of Mary, opened in the fall of that year with an enrollment of sixty-three students. The Catholic central high school concept, first established in Philadelphia in 1890, proved so successful in Hamilton that the chancery urged priests elsewhere in the archdiocese to consider the same.[17]

It took almost thirteen years, however, before another central high school opened in the archdiocese. In 1920 Moeller decreed that in the larger cities in the diocese a central high school for several parishes should be built, thus providing greater administrative efficiency. He intended the central high school to become the norm in the archdiocese. At the time there were more than a dozen central Catholic high schools in operation in the country. When in 1920 the parishioners of Price Hill and vicinity realized that St. Lawrence High School could no longer handle the increasing student population, they formed a corporation for the purpose of erecting a new high school. The following year pastors representing eleven parishes on the west side of Cincinnati met to plan for a central high school in their area. The new school, dedicated to Archbishop Elder, began its operations in the fall of 1922. It used St. Lawrence school and a nearby Knights of Columbus hall as temporary facilities until the permanent school was completed in 1923.[18]

Following a meeting with his consultors in the summer of 1924, Moeller in his July circular insisted on two central Catholic high schools in Hamilton County, Elder on the west side and Purcell High School in Walnut Hills. Pastors and parishioners on the east side to Walnut Hills had been making plans for a central high school for about two years. Elder and Purcell High Schools became free schools in the sense that the expense was paid *pro rata* by the parishes assigned to them. No tuition was collected from the pupils. Sensing that many Catholic parents did not feel the same sense of urgency to send their children to Catholic high schools as they did to the primary grades, Moeller argued that they were "even more necessary for the preservation of the faith" of the children than the elementary schools. Though the archdiocese had initially intended to build a third high school in the heart of Cincinnati, Moeller and his staff were dissuaded to do so because it was believed by some that two high schools would be sufficient to accommodate the Catholic children in the high school grades. Besides, they thought the inner city was not a desirable locality for a central high school. It was thought that the preponderance of poor Catholic families would not have been able to support a high school.[19]

In the late nineteenth and early twentieth centuries the archdiocese also continued to promote institutional separatism in education by urging Catholic young men and women to attend Catholic colleges. Both Elder and Moeller, like their conservative episcopal colleagues, argued that religion should permeate the education of the children from kindergarten up to the university. But the number of Catholics in secular colleges grew during this period. A national survey taken in 1907 of Catholic students in college revealed that approximately two-thirds of them were enrolled at secular institutions. Throughout this period the two Cincinnati ordinaries expressed concern over the secular teachings at the University of Cincinnati. During Elder's administration, the diocesan paper portrayed the University as "a sectarian Protestant seat of learning," guilty of spreading a "materialistic philosophy." Moeller personally viewed the University of Cincinnati as a fortress of atheism. He privately criticized the University officials for trying to raise money through tax levies and putting an unfair "burden . . . on the tax payers . . . for boosting . . . the infidel University of Cincinnati. . . ." He suggested, moreover, that if the tax levy for the University were ever put to a vote, it "ought to be objected to by every Catholic congregation."[20]

When in 1908 Charles W. Dabney, president of the University of Cincinnati, invited Moeller to give the benediction at its commencement, he declined. Though he had another engagement that evening, he pointed out that he did "not approve of some things taught in the University and I fear I would compromise my position by attending." Moeller never visited the University of Cincinnati, fearing that he might inadvertently create the impression among the Catholics that he approved of it. Concerned over the University's secular teachings, Moeller encouraged Catholics taking classes there to "take down verbatim the statements of those conceited and half-baked professors." He encouraged the students to "be alert and write out accurately the unsound teachings of the professors, giving their names and the date of their utterances." The archbishop's posture toward the University of Cincinnati was consistent with the request of officials in Rome that the American church limit its contact with modernism and secular culture.[21]

SEMINARIES

In the early days of Catholicity in Ohio the theological and preparatory departments of Mount St. Mary's of the West Seminary operated as a single unit. Though plans for a preparatory or minor seminary, separate and distinct in location and administration from the theological seminary, had been discussed, not until 1889 were the plans realized. Every year officials in the archdiocese had argued "more pressingly" the need for one. When Purcell in 1853 was offered a farm of 320 acres and about $10,000 worth of property for a "petit seminaire," he declined the offer largely because of his preference for a "mixed" college. As more and more students of the preparatory grades were admitted to Mount St. Mary's of the West Seminary in the early 1870s, again plans were discussed for a college and preparatory seminary. Father Bernard H. Engbers, who was a strong advocate for a separate preparatory seminary and later became pastor at St. Rose Church, suggested to Purcell the formation of a preparatory college where the students who intended to live in the community would be educated. "It is said," he wrote, "that our young men do not know life and its realities, that they are unacquainted with the world, [and] know nothing of business and practical undertakings." Plans for a preparatory seminary, however, were again shelved. But at the Third Plenary Council of Baltimore in 1884, however, the bishops saw the need to help develop qualities for the priesthood from boyhood and adopted legislation calling for a minor seminary.[22]

The first time that Elder met Archbishop Purcell after his arrival in Cincinnati in 1880, the elderly archbishop pleaded with him to try to open Mount St. Mary's of the West Seminary, which had been forced to close due to the financial disaster of 1878, as soon as possible. Elder saw obvious advantages to reopening the seminary, but the bankruptcy of the archdiocese caused him to evaluate his options. Bishop John Lancaster Spalding of Peoria, Illinois, proposed to Elder in 1880 the purchase of Mount St. Mary's Seminary for $125,000. Spalding hoped to acquire a set of buildings at a reasonable price for the "opportunity," he wrote, "to make a beginning towards founding a Catholic University." He hoped to use the property as a national "theological high school." Though Elder was warm to the idea, Cardinal McCloskey of New York and Archbishop Gibbons of Baltimore opposed it. The matter was subsequently dropped. Elder needed no persuasion on the merit of the seminary. "A diocesan seminary," Elder later wrote to the clergy and laity, "is the nursery, we might say, for all other institutions of religion." Although the churches, schools, asylums, and hospitals were the work of all the faithful, "they only become realities," he argued, "when there are priests to lead the way." Like Purcell, he thought it was advantageous to educate most of the students in the diocese. The pastors would have an opportunity to know the seminarians, and they in turn would become more familiar with the local needs of the people. On September 12, 1887, Mount St. Mary's of the West Seminary, after having been closed for eight years, was reopened due largely to the generosity of Reuben Springer, a longtime benefactor. Springer was an avid supporter of Catholic institutions, the arts, Music Hall, and other public institutions in Cincinnati. In his will he bequeathed to Elder the sum of $100,000 for the education of priests. Springer's bequest made possible extensive repairs to the building, which had suffered the physical effects of having been closed. In the first year of its reopening, twenty-seven students enrolled, fifteen of whom came from the archdiocese. "It cheers our hearts and revives energies," Elder wrote, "to see the lights of science and piety again burning in those halls." Within six years of its reopening, sixty-three priests completed their theological studies at the seminary. By 1897 enrollment reached 152.[23]

Shortly after the reopening of Mount St. Mary's of the West Seminary and inspired by the impetus for opening minor seminaries stemming from the legislation of the Third Plenary Council, Elder in 1889 revived discussion for a preparatory seminary. He commissioned Engbers to prepare a class of students at Holy Trinity school. Elder also approved the plans of his vicar general, John C. Albrinck, to purchase, with the bequest of Reuben Springer, fifty-seven and one-half acres of land for $5,625 at Cedar Point, now Mount Washington. Approximately ten miles from downtown Cincinnati, the location seemed ideal for seminary purposes. "[I]f an imposing building were placed on it," Albrinck wrote, it "would show well far and wide and would give the inmates a grand panoramic view in all directions." In the fall of 1891, St. Gregory's minor seminary, exclusively for residential students, opened its doors with an enrollment of twenty-three young men. Albrinck served as president until the appointment in the summer of 1892 of Father Henry Brinkmeyer as rector. Throughout its twelve years existence as a boarding school, the seminary's annual enrollment numbered between eighty-five and one hundred students. The seminarians represented the dioceses of Cincinnati, Columbus, Covington, Grand Rapids, Louisville, Vincennes, Nashville, and Detroit.[24]

Operating a second seminary, however, compounded the financial woes of the archdiocese. As early as 1892 Elder conferred with some prominent businessmen in the city regarding the local church's financial difficulties. A few years later the archdiocese's Auditing Committee reported that the chancery was "laboring under a great and ever increasing difficulty in its financial connection with the Seminaries." The expenses of keeping up both seminaries proved too great. In spite of the collections from the parishes, which some parishes had trouble making, the seminaries got deeper into debt to the chancery "with little, if any hope of ultimate repayment." Remembering the Purcell bank failure, the committee feared that if this practice continued it would "hamper the chancery seriously, and in a possible case of panic among the depositors[,] history may, to a certain extent at least, repeat itself." Two viable options seemed opened to the diocese: Combine both seminaries and place them under one management, which would have required keeping the preparatory students separated from the theologians, or keep the two seminaries separated and make the preparatory seminary a day college. After much consultation the archbishop chose the latter course.[25]

In the summer of 1904 Elder found it necessary economically to transfer the theological seminary from Price Hill to the Mount Washington property and move St. Gregory's to West Seventh Street, where it operated as a day college. But from the start this arrangement met resistance from a number of faculty and pastors. The faculty wanted a boarding school for the preparatorians in a rural setting where they could more closely supervise them. Many parents who lived outside the city were also reluctant to send their boys to the city to board with private families. As a consequence, attendance at St. Gregory's was small and the plan of the day school was eventually abandoned. Though it was suggested once again that the theological and preparatory seminaries be united under one management, Archbishop Moeller and his consultors took exception. After corresponding with the rectors of several seminaries, who all favored a separation of the preparatorians from the theologians, Moeller in 1907 closed "St. Gregory Seminary for a time" while the archdiocese raised enough money "to erect a preparatory seminary at Norwood," northeast from the downtown area. For the next sixteen years the archdiocese had no preparatory seminary. Local aspirants to the priesthood received their college education at St. Xavier College, University of Dayton, or St. Joseph College in Indiana. Meanwhile, the Mount Washington property, which now housed Mount St. Mary's of the West Seminary, was remodeled. With the addition of a new wing the building could now accommodate one hundred and twenty-five students. The old and attractive seminary building in Price Hill was sold to the Good Shepherd Sisters. There they consolidated the operations of their Baum Street and Bank Street convents under the title of "Mt. St. Mary Training School for Young Girls."[26]

THE NORWOOD HEIGHTS PROJECT

Early in his administration Moeller began a grandiose building program for a planned Catholic residential community, built around a new cathedral, bishop's residence, and theological seminary. Concerned over the deterioration of the west end of Cincinnati, he thought there was need for a new location for the cathedral. Having been connected with the cathedral for more than twenty years, Moeller knew personally that attendance and receipts were getting smaller. In 1880, when he was an assistant at the cathedral, it was necessary to have six Masses every Sunday, two of these in the basement, in order to accommodate the parish. All these Masses were crowded. Twenty-five years later the basement was no longer used, and only five Masses were said, with smaller numbers of people in attendance. In 1881 the cathedral membership numbered eight hundred families. By the turn of the century the number had dropped to six hundred. Moeller had seen during his work at the chancery more and more Catholics leave the west end and move to the suburbs while more and more businesses and blacks moved in. Seeing no end in sight to the falling off in attendance and receipts, in 1905 Moeller asked Vatican officials to extend the cathedral's boundary limits in order to draw more parishioners. Generally predisposed not to extend territorial boundary lines, the pope said, "No."[27]

The following year Moeller appointed a committee of priests to consider a new location for the cathedral. After considering several sites, the committee settled on approximately 156 acres in Norwood Heights in Norwood, a suburban community completely surrounded by the city of Cincinnati. To help finance the project the archbishop and a group of close friends organized a private company, the Norwood Heights Company, a real estate development corporation. To raise capital to finance construction, then sell lots, the company offered its stock to the priests and laity of the archdiocese with the assurance that the accruing profits would become the "personal property of the shareholder." From the start Moeller and several priests became the largest stockholders in the company. As more and more factories were moving to Norwood and employing substantially more people, Moeller and his staff hoped that the new facilities would entice Catholics to move into the area and thus create a boom in the sale of lots. The Norwood Heights Company deeded approximately sixteen acres of its acquired property to the Cincinnati ordinary. The transfer was made on the condition that within twenty years a seminary and episcopal home were built on it and, if conditions warranted it, also a cathedral.[28]

Though Canon Law required a bishop to build his cathedral within the territorial boundaries of the episcopal city, Moeller was hopeful that in the near future the city of Cincinnati would annex Norwood. The addition would make Norwood Heights the "center" of Greater Cincinnati, thus providing an ideal location for the cathedral. But Norwood fought for its independence, and Cincinnati never annexed it. That forced Moeller to give up his dream of building a cathedral there. The Catholics of Norwood subsequently built St. Peter and Paul Church on property acquired from the archbishop. For the remainder of his tenure Moeller kept an eye on the cathedral parish, resolving never to allow neighboring congregations because of their declining numbers "to incroach [*sic*] on the Cathedral in order to keep alive."[29]

On the subject of a new episcopal residence in Norwood, Moeller had no doubts that a larger house was needed for the archbishop of Cincinnati. He felt that the honor and needs of the archdiocese called for one. "Priests and [l]aity, when visiting Cincinnati," he wrote, "have often expressed to me their surprise that the Archbishop of Cincinnati has not a larger and more commodious residence." The archdiocese needed a residence spacious enough to accommodate the bishops of the province who met in Cincinnati from time to time as well as to have adequate meeting and reception rooms to conduct diocesan business. Moeller also had a personal reason for wanting his new residence in Norwood. For years he had suffered from a "delicate throat" and his physicians recommended that he remove himself from "the smoke of Cincinnati" and move to the suburbs. In 1908 a new archiepiscopal residence, the fifth such residence in the history of the archdiocese, began to be built at Norwood Heights. The large palatial Italian renaissance building was ready for occupancy in 1911.[30]

The main reason the archdiocese acquired the Norwood Heights property was to build a new seminary. From the beginning, however, the seminary project encountered problems. Besides a depressed real estate market, there were rumors that the directors of the Norwood Heights Company were speculating for their own personal gains. As sales of the lots declined, the directors grew uneasy and tension among them increased sharply. Eventually Moeller himself accused some lay directors of being in the project "simply to get all the money out of it" they could. When some of the investors suggested that Moeller should bail them out, he became more indignant and

FIG 11. Mt. St. Mary's Seminary of the West in Norwood, Ohio, in the 1950's

regretted that he had joined the venture. Along with other stockholders Moeller lost money in the project.[31]

Notwithstanding the fact that the building project failed to live up to its expectations, Moeller kept his promise to build a new seminary and residence in Norwood Heights. The new diocesan seminary, which adjoined Moeller's new residence, was completed in September 1923. Upon its completion the theological faculty moved to Norwood and St. Gregory Preparatory Seminary reoccupied the Mount Washington property. Mount St. Mary's of the West Seminary opened with 182 students. Costing slightly more than one million dollars, which was more than double the original estimate, the new seminary was a most imposing structure, combining classical and renaissance elements. It contained four classrooms, a lecture hall, a chapel in the center, five small chapels at the rear of the sanctuary, and enough room to accommodate 180 students. By the end of Moeller's term the two diocesan seminaries, the new episcopal residence, along with the hundreds of church steeples throughout the archdiocese constituted an impressive visual presence. As Cincinnati Catholics manifested greater self-confidence, it was a matter of pride to have magnificent buildings.[32]

The celebration of the one hundredth anniversary of the founding of the diocese was delayed two years so that the celebration of Mount St. Mary's could be joined with it. On October 21, 1923, the centenary was observed. Two days later the new seminary was dedicated. The double celebration was fitting. More than one hundred years earlier, the protobishop of Cincinnati, Edward Fenwick, had dreamt of a school to train candidates for the priesthood. Archbishop Peter Fumasoni-Biondi, the apostolic delegate to the United States, officiated at both ceremonies. At the banquet following the dedication of the seminary, Moeller thanked the many priests and people who had contributed to the building of the seminary. St. Raphael parish in Springfield alone had raised $10,000 for the new seminary. In addition to contributions from the various parishes and individual donors, the Knights of Columbus Councils from Cincinnati, Norwood, Dayton, Celina, Versailles, among other places, made generous gifts. Moeller, who had hoped to have the seminary entirely paid for before its dedication, realized his wish. He was pleased to announce there was a balance of slightly more than $100,000 in the seminary fund.[33]

In the midst of the celebration, however, the new theological seminary in Norwood had its share of critics. Instead of transferring the preparatory seminary to Norwood, as the archbishop had originally intended, the local church transferred the operations of Mount St. Mary's of the West Seminary from its rural and spacious setting in Mount Washington. A number of people criticized the move, arguing that a major seminary needed more than the twelve acres of land adjoining the archbishop's residence. The critics that annoyed Moeller the most, however, were those who questioned the quality of instruction at Mount St. Mary's. From the beginning the archbishop had high hopes that the bishops in the Cincinnati Province as well as in the neighboring provinces would send their students to his seminary. He was disappointed to learn that Bishop Ferdinand Brossart of Covington sent his philosophy students to the seminary in Baltimore. Having heard negative remarks about the quality of instruction at Mount St. Mary's, Brossart felt it his "sacred duty," he wrote to Moeller, to secure as good an education for the priests as possible. Moeller was hurt and disappointed by Brossart's remarks. It was unlikely that other bishops would support the provincial seminary if the bishop in its own backyard did not send his students there. There was nothing, Moeller wrote to Brossart, "that has given me more pain as the information that you intend to discriminate against Mt. St. Mary Seminary. I all along flattered myself with the belief that the Bishop of Covington would be one of the staunch supporters of the Cincinnati Seminary." When Brossart became ill a year later and could not ordain his deacons to the priesthood as scheduled, he asked Moeller to perform the ceremony for him. The archbishop refused, declaring that he "could not in good conscience ordain men that he regarded as not prepared for the sacred ministry."[34]

REFORM OF CHARITY AND SOCIAL WORK

Like other urban centers, Cincinnati in the late nineteenth and early twen-tieth centuries witnessed a quarter-century of humanitarian and social reform. Like many Americans, Catholics were caught up in the spirit of urban reforms. A group of bishops, clergy, religious, and lay social thinkers inaugurated a movement to restructure the philanthropic sector at both the national and diocesan levels. In the archdiocese of Cincinnati the Catholic crusade for charity intensified and the local church became more of a force in the community's social and economic life. Responding to increasing immigration, industrialization, and urbanization, it developed an extended network of institutions and services aimed at taking care of those people in need. Various religious and lay communities established hospitals, homes for the aged, remedial institutions, orphanages, industrial schools, and homes for working boys and girls. As in other urban dioceses at the time, modern medical and social facilities of the religious and ethnic institutions were anchored in the traditional Catholic subculture. As they intensified their care for the poor, the sick, the elderly, and the orphaned, the growing Catholic population and continuing influx of immigrants strained the church's resources to its limits. In particular, Elder and Moeller, like their confreres, looked to the communities of women religious to assume the greatest share of the burden of attending to the physical and spiritual needs of the people, especially Catholic immigrants. Their spirituality, training, and lifestyles affected positively the lives they touched.[35]

By far the most impressive aspect of the local church's response to the social problems of the period was the founding of homes for the aged, hos-pitals, and orphanages. This response involved more women than previ-ously. Sisters of various religious orders were the main support of the charitable work of the archdiocese and were, in many ways, as one histo-rian put it, "the force holding the Church together." They "exercised the major influence on the growing immigrant population, and bore the eco-nomic brunt of selfless service." In the early 1880s fourteen Little Sisters of the Poor operated Cincinnati's St. Joseph Home, which accommodated 220 elderly inmates, men and women more than sixty years of age. Three years after building a new home on Dayton Street, the order bought a piece of land on Riddle Road in Clifton for a second home. Upon comple-tion of St. Peter's Home for the Aged in 1889, which sheltered about 185 elderly, the Dayton Street home was turned over to the Dominican Sisters of the Poor. By 1890 more than thirty Little Sisters of the Poor in the two homes watched over the elderly, providing them with food, clothing, and medicine.[36]

In August 1910, under the direction of Mary Shanahan, the St. Teresa's Home for the Aged was opened at Estelle and Auburn Avenues in Cincinnati. Unlike St. Joseph's and St. Peter's Homes, St. Teresa's was established as a diocesan institution. Shanahan, with the assistance of a lay board, managed the institution for six years without the assistance of a religious community. The home permitted membership upon payment of $500 to $1,000, for which the residents were to receive care for their remaining days. Twenty years later a number of the older residents still received care at the home. Though the newer residents were charged more realistic monthly rates, Archbishop Moeller appealed for assistance in covering the expenses of the earlier residents, whose initial payments did not meet the growing expenses. By the end of Moeller's term, Cincinnati Catholics had four homes for the aged: St. Joseph, St. Peter, St. Teresa, and St. Francis of the Poor in Fairmount.[37]

On the Feast of the Sacred Heart, June 22, 1882, Elder dedicated the Sacred Heart Home for Working Girls, the third of its kind in the United States. Under the direction of Margaret McCabe, a pioneer of social work among the Catholic laity of Cincinnati, a four-room house was rented on Sycamore Street for the young, homeless, working girls of the city. By the fall the boarding home had ten inmates. Opened to young girls of all denominations, the home was not a charitable institution in the ordinary sense. McCabe frowned upon the word charity and referred to it as a "hateful sound." Those individuals who could pay for board or lodging could do so, and those who could not were just as welcomed. "*Our* . . . purpose," McCabe wrote to Elder, "is the protection of the most exposed and endangered class of the community, . . . young girls who come from a distance to secure work in a strange city." In less than two months after its founding the house was found too small, and a house with twelve rooms was rented. This too became overcrowded, and a twenty-room house on Sycamore Street was purchased. By August 1887 the home was transferred to a four-story building on Broadway. For eleven years McCabe, assisted by ten lay women, guided the destiny of Sacred Heart Home.[38]

In February 1893 eight of the women applied to the mother superior of the Sisters of St. Joseph at New Orleans for affiliation as a group to the religious community. McCabe had written to Elder several times, hoping that her "little community" would become religious. The following month Elder supported their request. He was "very much satisfied," he wrote to the archbishop of New Orleans, "with their work, . . . with their conduct, and the spirit of religion and humility which they manifest." By June four Sisters of St. Joseph came to Cincinnati to take charge of the home and to open a novitiate. Within six months the sisters had some forty girls in residence. In addition, about eighty working girls from factories joined them for dinner. Over the years Sacred Heart Home sheltered thousands of girls.[39]

The limitations of the home for a novitiate, however, led the community of sisters in the fall of 1893 to purchase a house and seventeen acres in Mount Washington. The previous year thirteen Catholic families had helped organize Guardian Angels parish in the area. When the sisters arrived, they responded to the needs of the congregation. Prior to the completion of Guardian Angels Church in 1893 there had been no church in the locality. Catholics of Cedar Point, as Mount Washington was then called, had to travel to distant churches to attend Mass, and their children's nearest schools were also several miles distant. The sisters arranged their apartments in the convent as classrooms for the accommodation of the children. With the assistance of a benefactor they erected a small frame schoolhouse, Guardian Angels school, across the street from their property. As the number of children increased, the new school no longer sufficed and work on a new building began in the fall of 1914. St. Joseph Academy was ready for occupancy a year later. This was the sixth academy established in the Queen City.[40]

In addition to the work of the Sisters of St. Joseph, Sisters of Charity, and Sisters of Mercy, who also managed Cincinnati's Mount Carmel Home for young working girls and women, three Dominican Sisters of the American Foundation at Albany, New York, arrived in Cincinnati in the summer of 1912. With the assistance of Josephine Schwind, the three sisters established their community in Dayton, where they opened the "Dominican House of Retreats" and provided a home for working girls. Women in Dayton joined the newly formed "Auxiliary Loretto Guild," paying $1.20 annually in support of the home. Five years later they established the "Loretto Guild" for employed women. Sisters of the Second Order of St. Dominic, more popularly known as the Cloistered Dominican Sisters, came to Cincinnati in 1915 and conducted the Holy Name Monastery in Walnut Hills for perpetual adoration of the Blessed Sacrament.[41]

In December 1885 the Jesuit John N. Poland, with the able assistance of his father and Margaret McCabe, opened the Home for Working Boys on East Fifth Street in Cincinnati. The following year it was turned over to McCabe to manage. In five years' time, the home, which opened with 25 inmates, cared for more than 780 boys. It accommodated a group of youngsters that the orphanages and children's homes could not reach. As enrollment increased the Boys' Home moved three times over eight years, always to larger accommodations. It settled on Sycamore Street in 1893. The young boys, some of them newly arrived immigrants, were sent to the parochial schools where they could stay until they were fifteen years old. Volunteers in the newly established Mission of Our Lady of Pity worked for the support of the Boys' Home. Each month the home published its paper, *The Homeless Boys' Friend.*[42]

In February 1915 Charles F. Baden, chaplain of St. Mary Hospital, and some prominent lay people in Cincinnati visited Moeller and proposed the idea of establishing a Catholic young men's club similar to the Y.M.C.A. Baden had conceived the plan. He hoped to provide a home where self-supporting Catholic young men would have opportunities to avail themselves of Catholic teachings and activities. Moeller enthusiastically endorsed the idea. About a month later three hundred Catholic laymen attended a meeting at a local hotel. This meeting laid the groundwork for the establishment of the Fenwick Club on Broadway on March 19, 1915. Named in memory of the first bishop of Cincinnati, its membership was limited to Catholic men between the ages of seventeen and thirty. The Fenwick Club was the first institution of its kind under Catholic auspices in the United States. It served as a model for other cities in the country.[43]

The following year the Boards of Trustees of the Fenwick Club and of the Boys' Home of Cincinnati decided to build a new Fenwick Club and Boys' Home. The latter's building, which accommodated thirty-five members, proved too small. During Margaret McCabe's able administration the Boys' Home had been the haven for more than five thousand homeless boys. In 1915 feeble health had caused McCabe to relinquish the management of the Home. Baden was then appointed chaplain and manager. On April 28, 1918, Moeller dedicated the new Fenwick Club and Boys' Home on Pioneer Street, east of Broadway, within three blocks of the heart of the city. In addition to a gymnasium, recreation facilities, and a classroom for a night school with practical courses, the six-story building had 150 rooms for the Fenwick Club. The dormitories of the Boys' Home accommodated about one hundred. During the next two decades approximately 10,000 young men annually entered and resided in the Fenwick.[44]

During his administration Elder also emphasized the necessity of religious instruction for the deaf. In the 1880s interest in educating Catholic deaf children of the diocese grew, especially after an intimate friend of Archbishop Purcell had in the 1870s a son, Edward Cleary, who lost his hearing at the age of six years. Not having a Catholic school for the deaf in the community, the child attended a local day school for the deaf. After class hours he received religious instructions from Father John M. Mackey, pastor at St. Patrick Church. By the fall of 1887, the Springer Institute, the first Catholic School for the Deaf in Ohio, was opened on Eighth and Plum Streets in Cincinnati. It opened as a free school in the cathedral parish and later moved to the rectory. Within a year there were thirteen pupils on the roll. The school operated for only three years. In 1890 the Sisters of Notre Dame de

Namur opened a day school for the deaf in their academy on East Sixth Street. They attended to the deaf for more than thirty years, teaching them both by sign language and by vocal sounds and lip reading. Alexander Graham Bell praised the instruction when he visited the school in 1893.[45]

Notwithstanding the early efforts made by the Springer Institute and the Sisters of Notre Dame, there was still in the 1890s a large percentage of deaf-mute Catholic children in the city and surrounding communities who were not receiving the benefit. This was because of "the inability of parents," Edward Cleary wrote to Elder, "to bear the expenses of bringing them to the school and paying for the board." The archbishop urged the pastors and the parishes to do what they could to identify those who needed assistance. When the Jubilee Committee of Elder's ordination reported a surplus of $2,000, Elder suggested it be used for the education of the deaf. By the end of the nineteenth century Jesuits and Franciscans also conducted programs of religious instruction for deaf-mute children.[46]

Building upon the work of his predecessor, Moeller thought a permanent home "for the deaf mutes" was necessary. In 1907 the archbishop urged all the parishes under his jurisdiction to assist in the establishment of a deaf-mute school. Five years later Father Henry J. Waldhaus, assistant pastor at St. Philomena Church on Third Street in Cincinnati, took up the work. He and some of his parishioners sponsored a bazaar to help raise funds for a school. In the spring of 1914 the Catholic Mission for the Deaf, with an efficient corps of willing workers under Waldhaus's direction, was opened on West Fourth Street in Cincinnati.[47]

After visiting nearly all the Catholic schools for the deaf in the country, Waldhaus recommended a farm in the country as the most advantageous spot for the new school. Moeller supported the idea. A farm, they thought, would give the children an "opportunity to learn the art of farming, stock-raising, poultry-raising, [and] truck-gardening." In the summer of 1915 Moeller and his staff selected a picturesque site along the Glendale-Milford Highway, thirteen miles from downtown Cincinnati. The money set aside by Elder on the occasion of his priestly Jubilee, coupled with funds raised in local ceremonies and the annual collection, made possible the opening of the internationally renowned St. Rita School for the Deaf in Cincinnati. It opened as a boarding school with an enrollment of eleven children. The following year, the number increased to twenty-four. Because a rule of the order prevented the Sisters of Notre Dame from operating a boarding school of any sort, the Sisters of Charity agreed to take on the charge. Two sisters, along with a number of Catholic lay women and men, assisted Waldhaus, who was named director of the school. Lack of accommodations, however, prevented the acceptance of more than thirty children at a time. Accordingly, plans were drawn for a new building. The First World War, together with a disastrous fire that destroyed the barn and other outbuildings, delayed the realization of these plans until the fall of 1921 when William Hickey, vicar general of the archdiocese, laid the cornerstone of the new school. Three years later, on Labor Day, clergymen from various parts of the United States and laity attended the dedication of the St. Rita School for the Deaf at Lockland. The institution, with its four main buildings, was one of the finest of its kind in the country. When parents were unable to pay the price to send their children to the school, arrangements were made through the pastors and Waldhaus to take the children "without discrimination and without humiliation."[48]

In the 1880s the Sisters of Notre Dame in Cincinnati alone taught in ten German-speaking schools, conducted their new academy on Sixth Street, and were in charge of the six hundred boys and girls attending St. Xavier's parochial schools. Anticipating the need for more commodious quarters for the religious community and school on Sixth Street, the Sisters of Notre Dame secured on East Walnut Hills a tract of land overlooking the Ohio River. In 1890 they began construction of a new convent and academy, known as "Our Lady's Summit," on Grandin Road. The sisters also expanded their work by building academies in Dayton and in Hamilton, Ohio. By the end of the decade, Notre Dame Academy in Hamilton offered secondary education for girls. These institutions played an important role in the history of education in the archdiocese of Cincinnati.[49]

During this period, religious and lay persons also became increasingly more involved in social work. By the 1880s there was a marked increase in the involvement of laywomen in charitable activities. In 1899, Emily Callaghan and other Catholic lay women met at the Boys' Home and helped organize the Visitation Society. These women comforted the sick and the dying and helped prepare the room for the priest when he came to administer the sacraments to them in their homes. Moreover, women religious expanded their ministry in hospital work. Two days after Christmas in 1888, the Sisters of the Poor of St. Francis opened St. Francis Hospital on Queen City Avenue, their second hospital in Cincinnati. The ground had been donated to the Sisters of the Poor two years earlier by St. Peter's Cemetery Association. Planned as an extension of St. Mary Hospital, the new hospital took care of the aged, infirm, and chronically ill, especially those suffering from tuberculosis, cancer, and incurable diseases. In the latter part of the nineteenth century it earned the distinction of being the only hospital west of the Appalachians to receive patients suffering from cancer. As the number of long-term patients increased, two additions to the hospital became necessary within the next decade.[50]

In 1890 the Sisters of Charity erected an addition to Cincinnati's Good Samaritan Hospital, which was larger than the original building. At this time the community of the Sisters of Charity consisted of about five hundred sisters, under whose care were thirteen parochial schools, five hospitals, two orphan asylums, one infant asylum, and two academies. In 1881 the religious community had purchased property adjacent to the novitiate in Delhi Township for a new motherhouse. In May 1884 the motherhouse, built of blue limestone on the high bluff overlooking the Ohio River, was completed. A year later the sisters began construction of an east wing to house the boarding school that was subsequently transferred from Cedar Grove. On July 16, 1885, a fire destroyed the new motherhouse. The limestone burned quickly and little could be salvaged. As Mount St. Mary's of the West Seminary was closed at this time on account of financial troubles, Elder offered the premises to the sisters. There the novitiate was continued for a year until the new building at Mount St. Joseph in Delhi was ready for occupancy. This new location would serve the sisters well, providing religious training and professional education to many of them.[51]

In 1915 Good Samaritan Hospital was moved from its initial location on Sixth and Lock Streets to a new building on Clifton Avenue across from Burnet Woods Park. Almost a decade earlier, Moeller and Mother Superior of the Sisters of Charity, M. Blanche, had discussed the advisability of erecting a new Good Samaritan Hospital. The old neighborhood no longer served its purpose, thought Moeller, as it was "occupied by many negroes, by factories and Rail Roads." At the turn of the century the order also opened Seton Hospital on West Eighth Street, later moved to West Sixth Street. But the hospital was short-lived. In December 1924 the sisters found it necessary, largely due to the "disreputable neighborhood," to close the hospital. It subsequently merged with Good Samaritan Hospital. In 1891 the Sisters of Mercy, on the invitation of the priests and people of Hamilton, Ohio, opened Mercy Hospital. They converted a fifteen-room house on Dayton Street into the hospital. Two years later they acquired additional property, increasing the number of beds by twelve to thirty-six. As the number of patients at the hospital continued to increase, totaling two thousand in its first ten years, the old buildings were torn down and a much larger hospital was completed in 1905. By 1915 three additional houses were acquired, forming an annex to the hospital.[52]

During the administrations of William Henry Elder and Henry Moeller the archdiocese made vast strides in the amount of charity it provided. In the fall of each year it had a collection for St. Joseph Orphan Asylum in Cumminsville. The diocesan orphanage, which averaged in the 1890s about 375 English-speaking children annually, was almost entirely dependent for its maintenance on the annual collection and the proceeds of the Fourth of July Picnic held on its grounds. The orphanage, which extended its benefits not only to orphans but also to children neglected by their parents, accepted children between the ages of four and twelve of whatever nationality. At times crowded conditions forced the children at St. Joseph to sleep two in a single bed. In need of additional financial support, Elder formed a committee of clergymen to develop a remedial plan that led to the establishment of the St. Joseph's Orphan Asylum Association. Its membership consisted of the clergy and three lay delegates for every three hundred families from each parish in the archdiocese. To widen the base of financial support, the Association initiated a contributing membership enrollment in every parish, making it the duty of the lay representatives to collect the dues. During this time St. Joseph Orphanage in Dayton, which traced its beginning to the organization of the St. Joseph Orphan Society in 1849, fell under the supervision of the Sisters of the Precious Blood. St. Aloysius Orphan Asylum in Bond Hill, conducted by the Sisters of Notre Dame since 1877, continued to care for the German orphans from Hamilton County.[53]

The two decades after 1900 saw Catholic charitable projects and social work agencies increase rapidly. St. Joseph Infant Asylum in Norwood took boys up to age four and girls up to age six. Mount Alverno Protectory continued to attend to dependent boys from twelve to eighteen. The Boys' Home cared for dependent and working boys, fourteen to twenty years of age. During Moeller's first year as archbishop, the Brothers of the Poor of St. Francis bought the property of the Good Shepherd Sisters on Bank Street and opened St. Vincent Home for delinquent boys seven years or older. The archbishop and the brothers had become concerned at the prospect of Catholic boys being sent to the Ohio State Reformatory. When a disastrous fire swept the Mount Alverno Protectory in the spring of 1906, destroying all the buildings, St. Vincent Home became the haven for more than two hundred boys and brothers made homeless by the incident. Three years later the Franciscans organized on Vine Street, opposite St. Francis Monastery, the Friars' Athletic Club for boys. For the next half-century the brothers cared for more than ten thousand boys and young men in the archdiocese. The Good Shepherd Convent in Carthage received black girls and white juvenile delinquents who needed protection. Mount St. Mary's in Price Hill admitted delinquent girls, whether orphans or not, usually five years of age or older. The Sisters of Mercy ran the House of Mercy for dependent children.[54]

Throughout his tenure Moeller strongly encouraged the laity to become involved in social and charitable work. "A layman, who truly loves his Church, . . . and is concerned about the salvation of his neighbor," Moeller wrote, "will give his time, his talents to anything and everything that promotes these purposes." There were also Catholics, like Ernest F. DuBrul, one of Cincinnati's leading manufacturers, who thought that lay Catholics had "shirked their work" and shifted their responsibility to the clergy. Very much concerned over the rift between those at the top of the economic ladder and those at the bottom, Moeller urged personal service by the more affluent in society. "It is true beyond all doubt," he said, "that there is a rather strained feeling today between those who live in comfort and those who have to struggle for every scrap they eat. This yawning abyss is becoming wider and deeper, day by day, and threatens to subvert all in a dreadful catastrophe. The imperative thing to do is to bring these two classes closer together; and this great good the rich can effect by generously giving their personal service to the alleviation of those, who are in dire poverty or sore distress . . . . Let the poor see that you have a heart that feels for them."[55]

Notwithstanding the amount of charity provided by various Catholic organizations, many poor Catholics turned to the Salvation Army for assistance. In December 1914 Brigadier David E. Dunham informed the archbishop that "65% of the families that apply to us for assistance are Roman Catholics." He hoped the local Catholic organizations would attend to these families who were "in a starving condition. . . . We are not making any complaint to you, Reverend Sir," he wrote, "for we understand there are difficulties in every organization. . . . I believe your big heart will make a response to this letter and you will investigate it. . . ." To help remedy the situation, Moeller established in 1916 the Bureau of Catholic Charities of Hamilton County, with Father Francis A. Gressle as director.[56]

By that time most large cities in the country had diocesan bureaus of charities. Ever since the founding in 1910 of the National Conference of Catholic Charities, which stated its intent to conduct "a war on the causes of poverty" and to accommodate the expanding urban and suburban communities, charity bureaus were considered a necessity to deal with modern social conditions. There was also a demand for Catholic charities to become better organized. Big city ordinaries, and Moeller was no exception, became consolidating bishops. Like corporate developments in American business, labor, and government in the progressive era, centralization and efficiency became the watchwords in welfare work in the archdiocese of Cincinnati. As the local church looked upon its field of service among the poor as essential, more and more Catholic leaders saw the need for better coordination and organization of relief efforts. It was assumed that the parish was no longer an adequate unit for the care of the poor. "We realized," Moeller wrote, that "in order to take proper, efficient and effectual care of all charity cases, it would be absolutely necessary to establish also in Cincinnati a Central Bureau of Charity." As Moeller took up the drive for consolidation, he assumed direct control of diocesan charitable organizations and services. The bureau helped coordinate and systematize the many and varied activities of the institutions and parish societies engaged in charitable work throughout the archdiocese. It provided Catholics a sense of solidarity in responding to social issues. Working in conjunction with the various agencies, the Bureau of Catholic Charities served as a "clearing house" for the charitable organizations.[57]

A close union developed between the Bureau of Catholic Charities and the St. Vincent de Paul Society, whose spiritual director also was Father Gressle. Founded in France, this benevolent society was first organized in America in St. Louis in 1845. Forty years later St. Francis de Sales parish in Walnut Hills in Cincinnati instituted a Conference of the Society of St. Vincent de Paul to assist the poor in their area. The parish was the center around which neighborhood charitable societies were developed. Though the Society had been initially founded in the St. Xavier parish in 1870, after about ten years of work the conference was discontinued. Following the lead of St. Francis parish, St. Xavier revived its conference in 1886. The laymen of the two conferences collected money and visited the homes of the poor, providing them with food, clothing, fuel, and religious assistance. Four years later the St. Xavier and St. Francis Conferences applied to the Superior Council in New York for the institution of a council composed of the presidents and vice presidents of the two conferences. In 1892 parishioners at the cathedral also established a conference. There was a quickening interest in charity work among a small group of Catholic men. By 1900, when the St. Vincent de Paul Society had become the major charitable agency in the church, there were thirteen conferences of the Society serving the poor of the city. That year alone the conferences distributed more than $7,000 among the needy and supplied clothing to more than five hundred persons. Among the societies in the Catholic Church at the turn of the century, the Conference of St. Vincent de Paul merited "to be ranked," Elder wrote, "among the first in dignity [and] in the importance of its work." It was the best expression of the lay ministry in the archdiocese at the time. It had expanded its operations and developed into a prime source of aid for individuals in economic need. Moeller urged every pastor to do his utmost to establish a conference in his parish. "[H]ow can the priest better display . . . sentiments toward the poor," he wrote, "than by securing for them all the assistance possible, both as to body and soul?" The conferences, which drew their members largely from the ranks of the Catholic middle and upper-middle classes, were largely English-speaking and were concentrated largely in the Irish parishes. Those cases that could not be handled by the forty-five conferences in the city were turned over to the Bureau of Catholic Charities. Among the German and Eastern European parishes, the mutual benefit society provided comparable relief in times of economic need.[58]

Moeller continually exhorted the parishes "to take a deep and active interest in the poor." Parishes that had not yet established a St. Vincent de Paul Conference were asked to do so without delay. "Any further procrastination in this matter is inexcusable," he said, "and will be taken cognizance of." In 1921 Vincentians made 4,694 visits to needy families in Cincinnati, disbursing approximately $20,000 worth of supplies. The expansion of the work of the Bureau of Catholic Charities necessitated the establishment of a branch in Dayton. By the end of Moeller's administration the bureau had evolved into a major diocesan institution divided into four departments: a family department, a children's department, a department of protective care, and a recreational and community work department. All Catholic charitable institutions were placed under the supervision of the bureau's central office on East Ninth Street in Cincinnati.[59]

A year after its founding the Bureau of Catholic Charities became a member of the Hamilton County Community Chest. The local church fully endorsed the Community Chest Drives to raise funds for promoting charity and welfare work in Cincinnati. It urged Catholics to contribute according to their means. "As citizens of the Queen City of the West," Moeller wrote, "we should take particular pride in showing that we are members of one large family." Not only did some of the Catholic agencies benefit financially by being connected with the Community Chest, but it also enabled them to relate more with secular and other denominational organizations. Though archdiocesan social programs, like Catholic philanthropic works nationally, had always existed for the common good and had never been totally denominational, avoiding the acute separatism that characterized education, they now welcomed even more intergroup relations. Many American bishops and Catholic charity workers alike argued that greater cooperation with mainstream organizations would help enhance the image and work of the American church. As the century progressed an increasingly heavier proportion of the archdiocese's charities budget would come from public sources.[60]

During the First World War Catholics, like their religious counterparts in the community, not only fought in the war but also supported and participated in a number of war-related activities. Catholics nationally constituted a larger proportion of the armed forces than they did of the general population. The war aroused the mass of Catholics to a sense of their immense resources and gave them an opportunity to demonstrate their patriotic Americanism. When the United States entered the war in the spring of 1917, Moeller made a strong plea for loyalty to the country. The time had now come "when we must put aside our personal and private views," Moeller wrote, "and . . . generally assist in carrying out the national designs of our government." Like their Catholic counterparts during the Civil War and Spanish-American War, Catholics once again rallied to their nation's support. They placed American flags in churches, sang the "Star Spangled Banner" after Mass, bought war-savings stamps, and became involved in war-bond drives, fund-raising rallies, and recruiting-drives for the military. "In Red Cross activities, in preparing bandages, in knitting and sewing," the *Catholic Telegraph* wrote, "our women and girls labored with a diligence that was unsurpassed by any others in the great civil army of volunteers." At home and overseas the Knights of Columbus, a national Catholic fraternal organization founded in 1882, rendered commendable service. It was the preeminent Catholic lay organization during the War. First established in the archdiocese in 1898, the local chapters provided assistance to Catholics in the armed forces. Moeller praised the work of the Knights of Columbus for "the moral uplift and spiritual good of the soldiers" at the cantonments, on the battlefield, and in the hospitals. Catholics also sent contributions to the Cincinnati Catholic Women's Association, which numbered 16,000 persons. "These self-sacrificing women," Moeller wrote, "are doing splendid work, for they are preparing various articles most necessary for the comfort and relief of the stricken soldiers." They sent their articles to the Cincinnati Red Cross, which shipped more knitted garments for the Catholics than did any other chapter in the country. Sensitive to the charges of disloyalty, the war afforded Catholics the opportunity to affirm their Americanism. As local parishes conserved food during wartime, children in the parochial schools participated in 1918 in a School Tagging Day to encourage economy in the use of coal. They tagged shovels with the slogan "Save a shovelful a day for Uncle Sam." These wartime experiences doubtlessly helped Catholics become more fully integrated into the larger society.[61]

On November 29, 1918, Cincinnati witnessed one of the most memorable Thanksgiving Day exercises ever held in the city. An immense throng of people attended Music Hall, thanked God for the victory for American arms, and participated in Cincinnati's first ecumenical expression. Clergymen, representing Judaism, Catholicism, and Protestantism, delivered patriotic addresses. "Bigotry and prejudice," the *Catholic Telegraph* wrote, "were forgotten; and rabbi, priest and minister were roundly and impartially applauded." William D. Hickey, dean of the Cincinnati Deanery, was the Catholic representative on the program. "How naturally and fittingly then today," he said, "that Jew and Protestant and Catholic of this fair city, forgetting their differences, laying aside prejudices, united in love and adoration of one God." After the war local Catholics also generously helped war orphans in Europe. A number of laymen banded together and formed the Hamilton

County European Relief Committee to aid Father Francis Gressle in collecting clothing and food for the war sufferers, especially the women and children in Central Europe.[62]

The archdiocese by the 1920s was engaged fully in educational, social, and charitable programs. Throughout their administrations Archbishops Elder and Moeller stressed the importance of education and social work. Through various religious and lay activities and organizations, the local church figured more prominently in the community's social and economic life. Moreover, Catholics worked more closely with secular and other denominational agencies.

· 9 ·

RELIGIOUS AND SOCIAL ISSUES

In the last quarter of the nineteenth century the archdiocese of Cincinnati assumed a more imposing and consolidating form. Since midcentury its churches and schools had doubled. Though the missionary character that the church once had in Ohio had lessened, it nevertheless continued its missionary and community outreach. It attended to the spiritual needs of African American Catholics in the inner city and the new immigrants from Eastern Europe as well as becoming more involved in the labor movement. But at the same time that the Catholic Church grew, church leaders feared religion was losing its influence on society and that parishioners were becoming too worldly. In response, parishes formed devotional organizations and lay men and women gradually become more involved in social issues.

As the chancellor's office exercised greater episcopal control over archdiocesan matters, it legislated against church fairs, picnics, and bazaars on Sundays. Not unlike in other dioceses, most parishes were supported in part by these activities, which were usually the work of parish women. When Elder arrived in Cincinnati in 1880 it was not uncommon for individuals in some of the parishes to organize church entertainment independent of the pastors. Detecting excesses, he prohibited Catholics in the archdiocese from taking part in any parish picnic or excursion unless approved by the pastor. Moreover, he ordered that no money be accepted for the benefit of any church or school unless the entertainment had previously been sanctioned by the pastor and was under his control. It was commonplace in this period for ordinaries to restrict parish entertainments. Both Elder and Moeller also admonished the faithful not to go to those public places where night dances were held. "You know our rule," Elder said, "there is to be no dancing after dark." During Moeller's tenure the local church continued to regard dancing as a "dangerous diversion." It advised organizations like the Knights of Columbus "to exercise great vigilance" at their dances.[1]

As archbishop, Moeller was also particularly critical of those parishes that found it expedient to sponsor fairs, picnics, and excursions to secure funds to help build and maintain their buildings. He felt it was inconsistent "with the dignity" of the Catholic religion "to resort to methods for raising money which foster the inclinations of pleasure seekers." Moeller repeatedly urged pastors to induce their people to contribute directly to works of charity and religion solely for the love of God and for the sake of charity, because it was "far more dignified and meritorious." In that same spirit Moeller directed the *Catholic Telegraph* not to publish notices of fairs, bazaars, or "any of the other catch-penny devices for obtaining money from the faithful."[2]

The local church also forbade the practice of some pastors of charging an entrance fee at the door of the church. Moeller reminded the pastors in his January 1905 pastoral that to exclude the faithful from the church because they could not or did not wish to pay the amount asked was strictly forbidden by the Third Plenary Council of Baltimore in 1884. He also considered it "indecorous" for a priest to stand near the door of the church either to collect money for mere entrance or for a seat in the church. Though the archbishop approved of pew rents and felt that persons should be assessed according to their means, most parishes did not adopt the pew-rental system. They felt it discriminated against the poor.[3]

In the late nineteenth and early twentieth centuries, Elder and Moeller often expressed concern over declining morality in society. High on the list was their concern over the broken family. During their administrations they helped regularize the institution of marriage. In compliance with the laws laid down in the synods of 1886 and 1898, marriages were now solemnized at Mass, rather than taking place in the afternoon and evening, as had often occurred, and funerals were also conducted with the solemnities of the Mass, rather than conducted in the afternoon. During his term Moeller published two significant pastorals on marriage. Concerned over the fact that the divorce rate nationally more than doubled between 1880 and 1910 and that one out of every nine marriages in the United States ended in divorce, Moeller reiterated that the church forbade divorce. His pastoral letters on these doctrinal matters were considered classics in their genre and were used as texts in many seminaries.[4]

In keeping with the teachings of the official church, mixed marriages, which were in the Elder-Moeller years on the rise nationally, were also forbidden. The church advised Catholics not to become engaged with non-Catholics without first ascertaining from the pastor if there were suffi-cient reason for obtaining dispensations.[5]

The archdiocese also opposed any form of sexual activity outside of mar-riage, birth control, and abortion. In anticipation of a talk by Margaret Sanger, president of the American Birth Control League, at the first Ohio Conference on Birth Control at the Hotel Gibson in Cincinnati in 1922, the *Catholic Telegraph* editorialized that Sanger "should not be permitted to spread her disgusting teaching in our city." Two days before her talk, Moeller issued a mandate forbidding Catholics, "under grave censure," from attend-ing the lecture.[6]

As the archdiocese waged a battle against what it defined as declining morality, it protested strongly against blasphemy and intemperance and established rules for the conduct of Catholic societies. In 1898 Elder and other religious leaders in the community were asked by a local newspaper to write an article on Cincinnati's needs from a moral and spiritual point of view. When asked to delete his critical remarks on the press, Elder refused and published his piece in the *Catholic Telegraph*. He articulated his vision of what may appropriately be called, as one later twentieth-century historian aptly put it, a "new urban Gospel for Catholics." Elder insisted that what Cincinnati needed was a reformation of its daily papers and saloons, "sup-pression" of immodest theatres and sensational posters, and "good" citizens in public office and in its schools. Those theaters and posters that exhibited immodest pictures as well as acts of violence had a "sad effect," he argued, on the children. "[T]heir young plastic imaginations," he wrote, "get filled with scenes of wickedness or coarseness, that obscure . . . their sense of what is beautiful and true." To help counter those effects every morning, after the usual prayers at the beginning of school, the children recited the versicles—short sentences usually spoken by a priest and followed by a response, given as an act of reparation for profane language.[7]

The *Catholic Telegraph* also often reminded its readers of the principle that the political and social prosperity of a community was in direct "pro-portion to the morals of the people" and that the "cultivation of literature and industry" was an essential "safeguard of morality." It argued that in terms of intellectual activity American Catholics were weak. Studies showed that Catholics had little influence on the community by their writings. Though they counted by far the largest number of members of any single religious denomination in the United States, they exercised less influence in the affairs of the country than did any of the smaller denominations. In the archdiocese the Jesuit Francis J. Finn, who presided for many years over St. Xavier school in Cincinnati and wrote juvenile fiction, was an exception. His books, espe-cially *Tom Playfair* (1891) and *Percy Winn* (1891), received a very wide reading throughout the country and the world, being translated into many foreign languages. The heroes tended to be boys of good family who combined piety and industry and either joined the Jesuit order or dedicated themselves to Catholic good works as laymen. Concerned over the low quality of secular literature generally available in the community, Elder urged the faithful to supply their families with Catholic newspapers and books. In 1885 George A. Pflaum, Sr., began in Dayton the *Young Catholic Messenger,* a general magazine for youth. In time the magazine reached more than a million Catholic pupils every week. Eight years later the Franciscans began *St. Anthony Messenger,* the second Franciscan periodical during Elder's tenure.[8]

At the Fourth and Fifth Cincinnati Provincial Councils of the 1880s, Elder and his suffragan bishops, who were concerned over declining morality in society, identified intemperance as "one of the great evils" of the time. Not opposed to the moderate use of liquor, they disassociated themselves from the "fanatical advocates" who tried to do away with all liquors. They sought, instead, to restrain the abuse by appeals to reason. Church officials applauded efforts of parishes that formed temperance societies. Elder fully supported the Total Abstinence movement. As a total abstainer, he was a member of his own cathedral society. In keeping with the directives of the Third Plenary Council of Baltimore, the archdiocese also criticized those who sold any intoxicating liquors at social events. Elder made clear in his pastorals to the laity that the pastor was to be held personally responsible for such incidents. In the summer of 1889 he removed a pastor from his pastoral charge for a week for allowing beer to be sold on the occasion of the blessing of his new church. When he learned that the St. Aloysius Orphan Society had also sold beer at a social event, Elder directed the Society to get his permission before sponsoring any entertainment in the future. Furthermore, the Cincinnati ordinary frowned upon the opening of saloons in the vicinity of cemeteries. He appealed to all Catholics not to patronize those saloons when going to or returning from a funeral, as well as when making visits to the graves of relatives or friends. In his address at the 1896 convention of the Catholic Total Abstinence Union, the seventy-six-year-old Elder also supported the idea of working for appropriate legislation. "By the enacting and enforcing of good laws," he said, "we can hinder the selling of liquor to men who are drunk, we can preserve the sanctities of the home, we can hinder the destruction of the children. All this is the work of Catholic societies. Politics is only to be influenced by organization."[9]

Moeller also recommended the formation of total abstinence societies and opposed prohibition. To drink alcohol "with moderation is not wrong," he wrote to the Ohio Temperance Union in the fall of 1915, "nor is a respectable saloon a public nuisance." Though he praised the total abstainer and advised his priests to become such, he opposed the use of compulsion to enforce total abstinence. "I am as much of a total abstainer . . . as any one," he wrote in 1917, "yet I am not a prohibitionist." To impose prohibition on the community, he thought, was a violation of man's liberty. Like Purcell and Elder, Moeller urged his clergy to induce people to practice abstinence "voluntarily."[10]

In the late nineteenth and early twentieth centuries the Cincinnati ordinaries helped enhance the role of the laity in activities outside of parish management and diocesan hierarchical affairs. Catholic laymen, due in part to growth in the Catholic middle class, formed several fraternal societies. Generally national organizations, these societies, which had ethnic, cultural, and religious dimensions to them, had local chapters based in individual parishes. Germans generally belonged to the Central Verein, whereas the Irish tended to belong to The Ancient Order of Hibernians. Adult males joined these societies with some regularity. Increasingly, the local church also realized a need for the establishment of societies for Catholic young men. Though there were a number of young ladies' sodalities, those of the young men were comparatively scarce. In January 1886 the Young Men's Sodality of St. Xavier parish established the Xavier Lyceum. Under the leadership of its first president, James L. Keating, it sponsored debates, and literary and musical exercises. The following year the Springer Institute in Cincinnati hosted the fourteenth annual convention of the Catholic Young Men's National Union.[11]

In his Provincial Council pastoral of 1889 Elder proposed "a flying battalion of Apostolic men." Archbishop James Gibbons of Baltimore liked the idea. "We need such a force," he wrote to Elder, "which would fill a place not occupied by the local clergy or regular missionaries." In the 1890s several Catholic organizations in the archdiocese supported the movement for an American Federation of Catholic Societies (AFCS), enthusiastically promoted by Bishop James A. McFaul of Trenton, New Jersey. In little time the AFCS, which held its first national convention in Cincinnati on December 10–12, 1901, established a bond of close friendship among the Catholic societies and gave them unified strength in protesting against anti-Catholic measures and affirming Catholic principles. In the early 1900s, the *Catholic Telegraph* editorialized that "[l]ay co-operation on the part of the men of the church is of the first importance, if our religion is to grow and flourish." Building upon the rich tradition in the archdiocese, especially among the German Catholics, the diocesan paper argued that men's "heads just as well as their hearts should be enlisted in the holy cause of religion. Utilize their business abilities, interest them in the active work of the parishes, place responsibilities upon them, let them manage the temporalities and they will surprise you with the results." During his tenure Archbishop Moeller also expressed publicly the need for a Catholic lay ministry of "fairminded, fear-less and prominent laymen." In his address on the "Layman's Duty in the Church" to the Knights of Columbus in 1917 he argued that a "staunch Catholic will take a manifest and active interest in all that concerns the wel-fare of the church."[12]

Moeller also thought that the laity could refute many accusations hurled against the church "more effectively than either the Bishop or priests." More aggressive than Elder he proposed the formation of a "vigilance committee" in order to help reduce immorality in the community. Moeller, who like his predecessor subscribed annually to the local Society for the Suppression of Vice, personally felt obligated to publicly condemn whatever was potentially detrimental in society. "This duty," he argued, was "incumbent on all author-ity. . . . [A]nything that is indecent, anything that is vulgar, anything that is food for man's unruly appetites, they should not only never countenance, but with all their energy and power stop." Moeller was hopeful that the commit-tee would advise the public not to patronize "indecent plays" as well as "induce the owners of theatres not to rent their houses to companies" that would put them on the stage. Catholic laymen, through the American Fed-eration of Catholic Societies, responded to Moeller's proposal by establishing a Committee on Public Morals in 1913. This committee, which reflected the sentiments of the AFCS's national crusade, called for a national crusade against public immorality, gathered information on plays and shows, and reported anything objectionable to civil authorities.[13]

Though he urged cooperation between laity and clergy in parish and diocesan affairs, Moeller thought at times that he was "walking on the ashes that cover a smouldering fire." He realized there was "some danger when undue power of directing ecclesiastical affairs" was placed in the hands of the laity. But he insisted that "just as much harm will come to the Church from the apathy and supineness on the part of the laity in this important matter." In his mind there was no doubt that the laity were in a position to give pru-dent advice and much needed help in those things that "concerned the mate-rial good of the parish." More lay people began to take a more active role in parish organizations as well as to help raise money for church and school. This helped relieve pastors from performing some of those functions , thus enabling them to spend more time attending to the spiritual needs of the parishes. Though the pastor remained solely in charge of ecclesiastical affairs, he and the laity were expected to work side by side on temporal mat-ters. Moeller maintained that such "united effort will bring the clergy and laity more closely together, . . . will produce a community of interest and aims, and will tend to unity and harmony, so important for the peace and welfare of the parish."[14]

As a consequence, the local church witnessed the birth of a number of grassroots lay ministries. Significant among these groups was the Catholic Students' Mission Crusade (CSMC). Mount St. Mary's of the West seminarians, who constituted a unit in the national movement of the CSMC, were among the founders of the Students' Crusade in Illinois in 1918. Under the leadership of Father Francis J. Beckmann, who later became bishop of Lincoln, Nebraska, and archbishop of Dubuque, Iowa, after his years in Lincoln, Mount St. Mary's of the West Seminary became the cradle of the Catholic Students' Mission Crusade movement. The organization, with its national headquarters at the Crusade Castle in Cincinnati, helped generate thousands of vocations to the priesthood, the religious life, and service to the church. The success of the Crusade may be attributed in part to its constitution as a society of students. The students passed their own laws at national conventions and elected their own national officers. Through *The Shield,* the official magazine of the CSMC, "Mission Crusaders" sought to awaken the Catholics' consciousness to the myriad ways lay people may "know the missions" and lend a helping hand to them. Moeller likened the interest in the missions implanted in the hearts of the students of the Catholic Students' Mission Crusade "to the mustard seed, of which Christ spoke, that grows into a large and mighty tree, whose branches reach out into many lands." Related to the missionary work of the CSMC was the American Board of Catholic Missions (ABCM), organized in December 1920 under the chairmanship of Moeller, who held the office until his death. Inspired by the U.S. bishops' pastoral letter of 1919, the ABCM, designed to coordinate all American mission activity under one body, made a special plea to Catholics to do missionary work at home and abroad. Through this board the entire hierarchy now supervised the missionary projects of the country.[15]

As more and more lay people and parish organizations became involved in social programs, there developed in the archdiocese a lay ministry to counter the resurgence of organized anti-Catholicism in the Midwest. The hard times and unemployment that accompanied the national panic of 1893 helped foster religious bigotry. Some people attributed much responsibility for the high level of unemployment and low wages to foreign immigration. In February of that year the *Catholic Telegraph* reported that the pre–Civil War anti-Catholic sentiments were returning through the work of such inflammatory and "un-American" organizations as the American Protective Association (APA). Founded in 1887 at Clinton, Iowa, it was committed to stopping immigration. The APA also tried to keep Catholics out of politics and Catholic teachers out of the public schools. It developed considerable strength in the Midwest. "We are keeping tabs on your movements," the APA wrote to Elder, "and that of your Romish Scoundrels of cut throats of priests." Partly in response to the bigotry, Catholics in the archdiocese formed a number of social organizations that stressed the defense of the Catholic faith and compatibility of Catholicism with American life. In 1898 Thomas E. Gallagher, an insurance salesman who came to work in Cincinnati from New York, sowed the seed of the Knights of Columbus Cincinnati Council No. 373, with fifty-eight members. This fraternal organization developed an extensive educational program aimed at religious and civic education. The Irish Ancient Order of Hibernians, designed to help support and defend Catholic priests, also proved quite active.[16]

A local incident that agitated a number of Catholics occurred in 1903. In the spring of that year, Moses Goldsmith, a Cincinnati businessman, gave a reception in honor of his son and his son's bride. Several prominent Cincinnati politicians and judges were present. Ballet dancers, robed as religious sisters, acted as ushers. When the party was at its height the dancers threw off their sisters' habits, appeared in pink tights, and performed Oriental dances. Catholics in the archdiocese were outraged. Protestant ministers and Jewish rabbis were equally upset by the Goldsmith scandal. A Jewish delegation made a formal apology to Elder, and through him to their "Catholic fellow-citizens." Elder wasted no time exonerating his Jewish neighbors for all responsibility. He was hopeful that Catholics and Jews would "live together in the future in the same peace and amity that they have until now."[17]

By the time of Moeller's tenure as archbishop, education and experience had driven much political bigotry from the country. In contrast to earlier times when Catholics were practically barred from holding political office, by the turn of the century more and more Catholics held political seats. In November 1905 Edward J. Dempsey, a Catholic, was elected mayor of Cincinnati, the first Catholic elected to that office. What helped dispel much of the prejudice was the growing acquaintance of Protestants with Catholic principles, as well as the cooperation of Catholics and non-Catholics in social work and in mutual business and social relations. Many Catholic officials, moreover, had proven themselves exceptionally well in their posts.[18]

Though bigotry had abated, anti-Catholic sentiments and suspicions of foul play by Catholics were still current. In July 1906 an article in a local political newsletter accused Moeller of entering into an agreement with Mayor Dempsey to have a voice in the city's political appointments. More specifically, it accused the archbishop of having ordered the mayor to appoint a Catholic to the Board of Trustees of the University of Cincinnati. Moeller denied both allegations. There was no foundation to the charge. At times, Protestants openly attacked the candidacy of Catholic candidates, such as in 1914 when they opposed Ohio Attorney General Timothy S. Hogan for the

U.S. Senate. Both the diocesan paper and Moeller acknowledged the benefits Catholics brought into politics. "Catholics are bound," the *Catholic Telegraph* wrote, "to bring their religion with them into politics, just as well as they are bound to bring it into every phase of family, social and business life. The principles of Catholic morality . . . apply in the street as well as in the home, in political office as well as in private trust." In Moeller's judgment America had nothing to fear from the Catholic Church. "Even if it should come to pass that a Catholic were to occupy the Presidential Chair," he wrote in 1914, "the Pope would not meddle in the political and temporal affairs of this country." American church leaders consistently argued that they were not pawns of a foreign potentate.[19]

As Catholics constituted an integral part of the local war effort in 1917 and 1918, Moeller was upset that the Red Cross, which he claimed "had not been friendly to Catholics," had no Catholic on the committee, even though Catholics constituted approximately forty percent of the Cincinnati population. Similarly, he was disappointed that the May Festival Association excluded the Knights of Columbus from participating in the May Festival in Cincinnati's Music Hall. What made it "more strange," he noted, was that Reuben Springer, a Catholic, was one of the main supporters of Music Hall, and that Mrs. Bellamy Storer, one of the founders of the May Festival, was also a Catholic.[20]

Partly in response to the resurgence of nativism since the 1890s, representatives of parishes in the various deaneries met in early 1921 to form a diocesan branch of the National Council of Catholic Men (NCCM), a national federation of organizations of Catholic laymen. A year earlier Bishop Joseph Schrembs of Toledo had invited parish societies of Catholic men to send delegates to a conference in Chicago in May 1920. That group scheduled a national convention held in Washington, D.C., four months later, out of which was formed the NCCM to promote the development of the lay ministry. "Our enemies," Moeller wrote in 1922 to A. M. Boex, secretary of the new Archdiocesan Council of Catholic Men, "are very active and we must organize on principle to frustrate their villanous [*sic*] and organized assaults." Though the archdiocesan branch of the NCCM helped fight the Ku Klux Klan and resist the political proscription of Catholics, its agenda was much broader. As one of the most vibrant branches in the country, it helped develop and coordinate the Catholic resources of the archdiocese. With a view to enhancing the Catholic presence in the community, it sponsored talks on labor issues, countered attacks against parochial schools, and addressed taxation issues related to church property. When Cincinnati hosted the Third Annual Convention of the National Council of Catholic Men in mid-October 1923, Moeller, who tried to draw more interest in the organization, argued that a "thorough organizing of our Catholic forces is imperative [in order] to protect our civil and religious rights."[21]

DEVOTIONAL CATHOLICISM

In the wake of the First Vatican Council the Holy See's direction of the internal life of local churches advanced steadily. The decree *Pastor Aeternus,* issued in 1870, affirmed the pope's power over all churches. Over a forty-year period Leo XIII and Pius X used the powers of their office to increase devotional activities in local churches by means of encyclicals and other decrees. In addition, Pius X's policy of promoting frequent communion helped enhance religious life in local churches.[22]

To late nineteenth- and early twentieth-century Catholics, ritual as part of religious life continued to be very important, and the most important ritual was the Mass. Then followed the rituals of the sacraments of baptism, communion, confession, and marriage. Next in importance was devotion to the saints, who occupied an important place in the lives of Catholics. In the archdiocese of Cincinnati, as in other urban dioceses at the time, the Irish tended to honor St. Patrick, the Germans, St. Boniface, and the Polish, St. Stanislaus. During this period devotional Catholicism, which supported tradition and authority in the church, was also rampant in the local church. The faithful manifested their faith in the parishes, and the devotional confraternity or sodality was the most important parish society. Some of the more popular services were the Marian, Sacred Heart, and Rosary devotions; during Lent, the Way of the Cross; the Forty Hours devotion to the Eucharist; the benediction of the Blessed Sacrament; devotion to particular saints; and novenas, recitations of prayers and devotions for nine consecutive days. Every first Friday the churches were filled with monthly communicants. The priests of the archdiocese often preached the need for Catholics to go to confession and receive communion. Shortly after the founding of St. Clare parish at College Hill in Cincinnati in 1909, John Stein, the pastor, and the trustees helped organize four lay groups to promote monthly reception of communion. In many parishes, like at St. Monica's in Cincinnati, the Men's, Young Men's, Ladies', and Young Ladies' societies had their monthly or quarterly group communions. At St. Louis Church at North Star, every society had a Communion Sunday each month. On the appropriate Sunday the members of the society were the first to receive communion in a group followed by the rest of the parishioners. Moreover, a number of Catholic homes in the archdiocese, especially in those parishes where Mass could not be celebrated weekly, had "prayer rooms" for private devotions. This made it possible for families to come together to pray the rosary.[23]

After the turn of the century Roman authorities helped revive the church's inner life by initiating religious practices that encouraged more frequent confession and communion by the mass of American Catholics and reforms in church music. Catholics in the archdiocese became a more disciplined population with regard to religion. Following Moeller's return from a four-month trip to Europe in 1910, the bishops of the Cincinnati Province issued a joint pastoral letter on the importance of the First Communion. Earlier that year the pope had issued a decree instructing pastors to admit children to communion at the "age of reason." The following year Catholic children in the archdiocese now received their First Communion at the age of seven, allegedly the time when they began to reason. One of the reasons it had been delayed until the children had attained the age of twelve or thirteen was to prevent parents from withdrawing them from the Catholic schools before their religious instruction had been completed.[24]

In July 1916 the Archdiocesan Music Commission, which had been instituted during Elder's administration and helped revive the Gregorian chant—a vocal chant used in musical worship—in the churches and seminaries, opened its first Musical Institute at St. Xavier College. More than three hundred people, consisting of priests, members of various sisterhoods, organists, and directors of choirs and singers, attended the Institute. Its purpose was to help bring church music in the archdiocese into closer harmony with the liturgy of divine service. The archbishop and clergy had long criticized some of the music that had been allowed to creep into church choirs, which led eventually to the banishment of choirs from religious services. Just as "liturgical vestments, worn by the priests, are entirely different from the common garments, worn at home or on the street," Moeller said in his address at the Institute, ". . . so also is it most desirable and befitting that the music for the Sacred Liturgy should be distinct in character from that used and heard in concert halls and temples of profane music." The following summer the Society of St. Gregory was formed and held its first convention in the cathedral. Under the guidance of John Fehring, organist and choirmaster at the cathedral, the Society published in its official organ, *The Catholic Choirmaster,* a list of compositions for church use.[25]

Part of the devotional revival in the second half of the nineteenth century was the growth of tabernacle societies. Through the Tabernacle Society in Cincinnati, Catholic laywomen provided material assistance to more than fifty poor churches and missions in Cincinnati. In February 1897 a large and enthusiastic crowd attended the first general conference of the Tabernacle Society at "Our Lady's Summit" in Walnut Hills, run by the Sisters of Notre Dame. Father Francis X. Lasance, who compiled various devotional volumes, prayer books, and retreat manuals, and who was the resident chaplain at the sisters' convent and academy, helped firmly establish the Tabernacle Society. Three months later the diocesan conference of the Priests' Eucharistic League, founded in Germany in 1879, convened at the cathedral and began using their influence toward the personal sanctification of the priest and the revitalization of the faith among the laity. In 1887 Father Beder Maler, a priest of St. Meinrad Abbey and Seminary in southern Indiana, started the movement in the United States. The first convention, attended by six ordinaries, including Elder, and 150 priests, was held at the University of Notre Dame in 1894. Through the League, the priests encouraged the people to spend at least one hour a week in prayer before the Blessed Sacrament. Cincinnati's diocesan branch of the League was one of the first of its kind in the country. In early spring 1897 Elder, who was one of the main episcopal supporters of the Eucharistic League, was the first U.S. ordinary to appoint a local director, Henry Brinkmeyer, then president of St. Gregory Seminary. During the next two decades the work of the League expanded. In the fall of 1911 Cincinnati hosted the Fifth National Eucharistic Congress. Seven archbishops and more than ten thousand people participated in the solemn benediction of the Blessed Sacrament in the closing ceremony. Through the procession Archbishop Moeller carried the Blessed Sacrament, and a body of uniformed knights from various parishes formed the guard of honor. Parish outdoor religious processions, such as those in honor of the Blessed Sacrament and the Blessed Virgin Mary, were an outward expression of religious piety. An event of note every year for the Catholics in Cincinnati and from outlying communities, and which has continued to the present, was the Good Friday pilgrimage to the Church of the Immaculata on the brow of Mount Adams. Whether in the cold, bleak, and wet weather or in warm sunshine, the two long flights of steps were crowded with Catholics reciting the rosary as they climbed slowly to the shrine.[26]

During Elder's administration a number of parishes established Holy Name Societies. The Society, whose object was to discourage profanity, indecency, and vulgarity in speech, "and to cultivate a greater reverence for the name of Our Savior," was originally founded in the thirteenth century. In the 1890s the American Dominican, Father Charles McKenna, began the spread of the parish-based societies in the United States. It grew so rapidly in the late nineteenth century that in 1900 a National Headquarters for the Holy Name Society was established in New York City. As a special activity of the Dominicans, the Societies spread rapidly in the early twentieth century. This organization was for men only. Until that time devotional societies were largely the sphere of women, and mutual-aid and charitable societies were largely under men's rule. The first Holy Name Society in the area was organized in January 1900 in the Immaculate Conception parish in Newport,

Kentucky. Shortly thereafter the Passionist Order established one in the Holy Cross parish in Mount Adams. As more and more pastors and parishioners realized the amount of good being accomplished, Holy Name Societies began springing up throughout the archdiocese. Growing numbers of middle-class men were drawn to the disciplined piety associated with the Society. On the eve of the First World War there were more than seventy units in the archdiocese.[27]

The first Holy Name rally on record in the archdiocese was held in 1907 in Mount Adams when members from four parishes conducted a march from Holy Cross school to the church for benediction. Three years later the *Catholic Telegraph* observed that there was probably no Catholic organization, among the wide variety of fraternal organizations, which had taken a stronger hold on the affections of the laity of the archdiocese than the Holy Name Society. That fall some six thousand men participated in the city's Holy Name rally. The parade formed on Auburn Avenue and marched to the grounds surrounding Holy Name Church, where the archbishop and other dignitaries addressed the crowd. In 1911 twelve thousand men marched in the rally. Reporting the event, the *Catholic Telegraph* noted that black Catholics from St. Ann parish, joined by their pastor, Edward T. Cleary, "turned out one hundred strong and . . . attracted considerable attention." One of the benefits of the Holy Name rallies and other popular devotions was to help serve—at least on the surface—to unify a Catholic population divided by ethnic and racial differences. In 1912 Holy Name Societies of Dayton held their first rally on Pentecost Sunday. By this time there were Holy Name rallies in large cities across the country. In the fall of the following year it was estimated that thirty-five thousand men marched the streets of Cincinnati to Redland Field where, together with thousands of others that filled the stands and grounds of the Cincinnati Reds Baseball Park, they joined in the benediction of the Blessed Sacrament.[28]

During America's involvement in the First World War there were no annual rallies. In the fall of 1919, when the war clouds had finally passed away and the Holy Name rally was resumed, Cincinnati witnessed the single largest gathering of Catholics at an event ever in its history. It was perhaps the largest demonstration ever witnessed in the city up to that time. Moeller led the march of more than forty thousand Catholics to Redland Field. Four years later more than thirty thousand men, representing about eighty parishes, marched eight abreast in the Holy Name parade. The parade stopped momentarily at St. Augustine Church in the west end where Moeller left the head of the procession with his escort. There he vested and waited until the last parish division arrived, followed by hundreds of little boys and girls carrying lighted candles. From this point on the men marched in fours, and in this formation they entered Redland Field where the grand-stand, pavilion, and bleachers were filled. Once inside, each section circled the field and then escorted the Blessed Sacrament to the platform and altar in the center. It took close to two hours for the procession to enter the park. Moeller was hopeful that these rallies, which helped bring thousands of men to the sacraments on a regular basis, would "stir up" the Holy Name Society members' "enthusiasm, rekindle their love, and make them staunch, living, active members." In the judgment of the *Catholic Telegraph,* the rallies reflected an "increase of religious zeal" and were a public manifestation of the Catholics' religious faith.[29]

NEW IMMIGRANTS AND AFRICAN AMERICANS

In the second half of the nineteenth century, a wave of new immigrants from southern and eastern European countries flowed into the United States, many of them settling in the Midwest. Italians, Poles, Hungarians, Rumanians, Syrians, Greeks, and other Catholics of the Oriental rite poured into Cincinnati. Building upon the institutions of the immigrant church, the new immigrants brought a rich ethnic diversity to the local Catholic population.

When the first group of Italians arrived in Cincinnati in the 1850s and 1860s, the archdiocese was not prepared for them. They were expected to worship in existing church buildings. As their numbers increased, Italian Catholics wished as early as 1860 to have a church of their own where they could worship in their native language. They resented being second-class members in a parish. Besides, they were not always well received. On occasion the *Catholic Telegraph* came to their defense. "[T]here is none," the paper wrote in 1888, "that has been the butt for more accusations and aspersions than the Italian." Slowly, efforts were made by the Italians to organize themselves into a parish. By the closing decades of the century more Italians from other provinces of Italy migrated to Cincinnati.[30]

It was not until 1890 that an Italian parish in the archdiocese began to take form. That year Father Angelo Chiariglione, a member of the Pious Society of the Missionaries of St. Charles, commonly called the Scalabrinians, founded in Italy in 1887 for the spiritual and social care of Italian emigrants, came to Cincinnati at the request of Archbishop Elder. Obtaining the ordinary's permission to organize the Italians of the city into a special parish, he held religious services for them in the basement of St. Clara's chapel of the Sisters of the Poor of St. Francis at Third and Lytle Streets. Before long, Chiariglione said Mass for the Italians in the basement of St. Peter in Chains Cathedral and then in the chapel of the Sacred Heart Home on Broadway. "The little Italian Congregation is doing well," the social worker Margaret

McCabe wrote to Elder. "The chapel is well filled, and the members seem to be in earnest." In 1893 Sacred Heart Church for the Italians was built on Broadway, between Fifth and Sixth Streets. As more and more second- and third-generation immigrant Catholics were moving out of the city into the economic middle class in the suburbs, Italians largely settled where the Irish once lived. By this time there were approximately four thousand Italian immigrants in Cincinnati. For them, Sacred Heart parish became far more than a place of worship. It became the major cultural and social center in the neighborhood. In preparation for the dedication of their new church, a delegation of Italians went to Washington, D.C., and invited Archbishop Francesco Satolli, apostolic delegate to the United States, to come to Cincinnati and bless their new church. He accepted their invitation and officiated at the dedication on August 27.[31]

In the summer of 1897 Mother Superior Mary Blanche Davis of the Sisters of Charity combined Christian education with industrial and domestic training for the Italian youth of the archdiocese. With Elder's approval, she commissioned Sisters Blandina Segale and Justina Segale, Italian immigrants themselves and sisters by blood, to do mission work among the Italian Catholics. As young girls, Blandina and Justina had seen Sisters of Charity working among the poor, the sick, and the orphaned. Now their intention was to help their own people and to counter the Protestant proselytism among the immigrants by preserving the true faith among the Italians. In the fall the two Italian sisters, with the assistance of vicar general John Albrinck, started a class at the Holy Trinity school in the western part of Cincinnati for the Italian children. By the end of the year, one hundred girls and boys were enrolled in the kindergarten and primary classes. In time, branches of the school were established at the St. Xavier's and St. Edward's parochial schools and at the Springer Institute. Besides caring for the children, the two sisters attended to the sick and provided instruction in domestic economy.[32]

As their welfare work expanded, Sister Blandina, regarded by a representative of Cincinnati's secular Associated Charities as "the very best social worker in Cincinnati," organized the Willing Workers. This group consisted of Catholic laywomen whose primary goal was to help raise money for the sisters' work. On December 8, 1897, "The Santa Maria Italian Educational and Industrial Home," more popularly known as The Santa Maria Institute, was incorporated. The Santa Maria, the first Catholic settlement house in the country, became the pioneer Catholic social center of Cincinnati, providing a multiplicity of services primarily for Italians, but also for Hungarians, Poles, Syrians, Mexicans, Germans, Irish, Syrians, and blacks. Two years later the two sisters took possession of the former convent of the Sisters of St. Francis at Third and Lytle Streets and established permanent residence. The following year the Sacro Cuore school was opened for Italian children in the eastern portion of Cincinnati.[33]

By 1904 there were some four hundred Italian families in Cincinnati, with a few scattered families in other parts of the diocese. This led to the establishment of several Italian colonies, whose members were of the poorer classes and almost all of the Catholic faith. By the turn of the century the German and Irish Catholics, who had constituted the Catholic working class poor half-a-century earlier, had achieved greater economic and social mobility. Situated below them were the new Catholic immigrants. "The poverty of [the Italian] colonies," the *Catholic Telegraph* wrote, "make them a tempting field for Protestant proselytizers." It was argued that notwithstanding the good work performed by the Sisters of Charity, there had to be an increase in the ranks of the Willing Workers. "The danger of 'leakage' from the Church," an annual report of the Santa Maria Institute read, "is greatest when among strangers, not understanding the language of the country, . . . [they] discontinue the practices of religion, and finally drift away with the crowd of the indifferent." By 1920 there were approximately sixteen hundred Italian families in Cincinnati. Nine hundred belonged to Sacred Heart, attended by two priests from Italy, and five hundred and two hundred to the Italian missions in Walnut Hills and Fairmount, respectively. In 1922 a small group of Italians, led by Sisters Blandina, Justina, and Euphrasia, established San Antonio di Padova parish in Fairmount in Cincinnati. They raised $3,400 and bought a building on Queen City Avenue. The parishioners took up collections among themselves and bought statues, chairs, and carpeting. Two years later Italians in Walnut Hills founded Our Lady of Mount Carmel parish.[34]

Conducting welfare work among the new immigrants in the congested districts of the city, the Sisters of Charity in the early 1900s established a temporary home for stranded working girls. In addition, they formed an employment bureau, a domestic service department, a kindergarten, a day nursery, a boys' club, a girls' club, and Sunday Schools. Complementing the work of the parishes, which sponsored classes that taught the immigrants how to read and write, Santa Maria's activities included night school with classes in Americanization, English and Italian languages, sewing, dressmaking, and art craft. At the same time that the Sisters of Charity ran a day nursery at the Institute, a day nursery at the east end of Cincinnati flourished under the directorship of a Jesuit and the Ladies' Aid. The Children of Mary Sodality at Sacred Heart Academy in Clifton also established one for the northwestern portion of the city.[35]

Among the new immigrants in the see city at the turn of the century were the Syrians. Upon the arrival of Father Kayata in 1910, they organized a parish and struggled to establish a church of their own. For some time the Syrians had petitioned Moeller for a priest, and he had endeavored since 1905 to obtain one of the Maronite Rite. The Maronites, who had first come to Cincinnati around 1895, did not celebrate Mass in their own rite until Kayata's arrival. With the increasing Syrian population living in the depressed areas of Pearl Street and Central Avenue, the diocesan paper appealed to the faithful to come to their aid. Their greatest single source of help came from the Sisters of Charity of the Santa Maria Institute. A number of Catholic lay women assisted the sisters in the work. Moreover, the Sacred Heart parish generously placed the basement of their church at the disposal of the Syrian Catholics until such time as they would have a church of their own. A number of the Syrian children were placed in parochial schools.[36]

An unexpected problem arose when Moeller learned that Kayata had a wife and three children in Syria. Though the Maronites were accustomed to seeing married priests in Syria and would not be surprised to find the same condition in the United States, local Catholics of the Latin Rite were scandalized. In accordance with the wishes of the U.S. bishops, who did not want to receive into their dioceses priests who were married, Moeller requested the newly arrived Syrian priest to leave. By the summer of 1911 Moeller secured a replacement, Father Tobias Dahdah. Once again Moeller encouraged the faithful to assist the Syrian Catholics in their effort to have a church of their own. Some of the pastors gave permission to Dahdah to take up a collection for this purpose in their churches. By the year 1913 the Atonement Church on Third Street, which had been closed, was given to them. They remained there until 1920, when they occupied their new church on Third and Ludlow.[37]

By the late nineteenth century, Cincinnati, like other major cities in the country, had become increasingly more segregated residentially along ethnic, class, and racial lines. As Catholicism had also become more divided along those lines, the local church reached out to African Americans. The "colored people," Purcell had written in 1877, "are not favorably received in the midst of the congregations of the whites." More specifically, the Jesuit Francis Weninger, associated with St. Ann Church since its founding in 1866, noted that "neither the Irish nor the Germans like to see their children mixed up with colored children in schools; adults, too, are neither welcomed . . . in the churches of the whites. Nay, many whites have a natural aversion of the colored race." To help raise money for St. Ann parish, Weninger turned to diocesan officials for assistance in order to secure a "continuous and regular source of revenue" for the parish. Funds provided by the parish's St. Peter Claver Society were not enough. The archdiocese took up an annual collection in every church, with half of the proceeds going to St. Ann. Weninger continually urged Elder to support the parish. *"Have mercy with those needful*

FIG 12. St. Ann Church for African Americans in the late 1800s

negroes!!" he wrote. Hoping that other bishops would patronize the St. Peter Claver Society, Weninger also urged Elder to launch a national collection for the poor blacks and Native Americans in the United States. Under Elder's leadership, the bishops at Cincinnati's Fourth Provincial Council in 1882 agreed to take up a special collection each year for missionaries working with them. In October 1884 Weninger sent Elder a copy of his text on "The Care of the Indian and African Races," which the archbishop more than likely shared with his episcopal colleagues at the Third Plenary Council of Baltimore the following month. The Council ordered that on the first Sunday of Lent a national collection should be taken up in all the churches to assist the missionary efforts for African Americans and Native Americans. Weninger, who became a national spokesman for the cause, later wrote with some pride that "St. Ann's was the chosen *'point de depart'* for the whole movement in regard to the most *consoling* and *energized* stepps [*sic*] taken by the Council in regard to the Colored." Despite these efforts, most bishops were unenthusiastic about this collection and amounts raised nationally were small and a failure in contrast with the generosity of Protestants at this time.[38]

Weninger also urged Elder to transfer St. Ann to the diocesan clergy or to some order that could oversee the parish on a full-time basis with a resident pastor. Acknowledging that what the Jesuits had done for the blacks in St. Ann parish "was no doubt very useful," Weninger did not think it was "sufficient to answer the wants of the colored race. They want their own Pastor. . . ." In the early 1890s Elder explored the possibility of turning over the parish to the Holy Ghost Fathers, whose mission was the evangelization of the poor, in Pittsburgh, but nothing came of it. He continued to rely on the services of the Jesuits.[39]

Archbishop Elder also supported the pioneer efforts of Daniel A. Rudd in sponsoring national Black Catholic Congresses in the 1880s and 1890s. Born of slave parents in Kentucky, Rudd moved to Cincinnati after the Civil War. Besides emphasizing the importance of devotion, education, and racial pride, the black Catholics at their assemblies protested against segregation and discrimination in church and school. Disappointingly, few American bishops endorsed their work. The national African American congresses praised only two ordinaries between 1890 and the 1920s, John Ireland of Minnesota and Elder. Rudd personally thanked the Cincinnati archbishop for his support of the publication of the black newspaper, *American Catholic Tribune.* "It was your approval," he wrote, "that gave us standing among the prelates and clergy of the country." Notwithstanding the efforts of the black congresses and of the *Tribune,* separate Catholic institutions for the blacks remained intact.[40]

Though during this period the *Catholic Telegraph* wrote extensively in support of the blacks in the community, there were times when it reflected a general cultural bias. In 1909 the diocesan paper criticized Harvard University's President Charles Eliot for "having characterized the Irish in Boston as constituting a racial problem comparable" to that of blacks in the South. "When Dr. Eliot put the intelligent, law-abiding, and virtuous Catholics of Massachusetts on a level with the lazy, ignorant, depraved Negroes that have given rise to the race question in the south," it editorialized, "he uttered a deliberate and malicious lie." But this editorial was not typical. Even though the diocesan paper generally endorsed segregation, it did not as a rule write condescendingly or derogatorily of blacks.[41]

In the fall of 1907 during Moeller's administration, workers building the Heekin Can Company in a lot adjacent to St. Ann seriously damaged the church's foundations, causing the city inspector to condemn it. As trustee of St. Ann parish, Moeller appealed to the Heekin Can Company for relief. With settlement money received from the company and a grant of $11,000 from Katherine Drexel, Mother Superior of the Blessed Sacrament Sisters in Pennsylvania, and heiress to the Drexel banking fortune, Moeller searched for a new site for St. Ann. But the archbishop was not enthused about relocating the parish. He doubted "whether or not the work among the colored people . . . [would] succeed." Wanting some assurance that he could "get the money back" if the parish should fold, he made certain that the new combination church and school, built in 1909 on John Street in the west end, could without much expense be converted into an apartment house. Though Moeller had preferred property on Eighth Street for the new church, he rejected it partly because the residents in the neighborhood "would be highly incensed at me for securing it for a Colored Church." As much as Moeller wanted a new church for blacks, he insisted the school was more important. He doubted much could be done for the "old folks. If we can get hold of the young," he wrote, "and thoroughly drill them in their faith, there is hope that we will have after some years a good Catholic Colored Population."[42]

The status of St. Ann parish came up again when the Jesuits began to make plans to move their college out of the city as well as establish a new parish out in the suburbs. The downtown location, surrounded by office buildings and factories, restricted the development of the college. In March 1905 Albert J. Dierckes, president of St. Xavier College, met with Moeller to discuss the idea. The archbishop, who had no intention of allowing the Jesuits to expand their operations in the archdiocese, informed Dierckes that a new college was "scarcely necessary." But unable to find anyone to take charge of St. Ann parish, Moeller was willing to consider the relocation of their college on the condition that a more effective priest be put in charge of St. Ann. Though Moeller found the current pastor to be a "very good man," he was, in his judgment, "old and not able to do the work that is required to make the colored folks do their duty. Besides, he thinks it is useless to try to convert the darkey." The Jesuit Provincial informed Moeller that the terms were acceptable and that he had a priest that understood "the negro character" for St. Ann parish.[43]

But in the end, Moeller appointed Edward Cleary, a white diocesan priest, pastor of St. Ann. When Cleary took over St. Ann parish in 1909, it had approximately seventy-seven adults as members and sixty-two children in its school. Within four years St. Ann's membership grew to about three hundred, with one hundred students enrolled in the school. The parish also introduced several innovations, including a free luncheon program in the school, sewing and cooking classes for the girls, and a dramatic club. Moeller was pleased with Cleary's work. "He likes the Darkies," he wrote to Drexel, "and they like him." He noted that the parish had shown its appreciation by increasing its contribution on Sunday from four dollars to nine. Hoping to obtain additional funds to help carry on the work in the parish, Cleary also reorganized the St. Peter Claver Society. During Easter Week in 1914 there was a Bazaar in Holy Trinity hall on Fifth Street for the benefit of St. Ann.

Moeller directed the pastors of Cincinnati parishes to announce the Bazaar at all the Masses and urge their people to patronize it.[44]

For almost fifty years St. Ann school had been conducted by the Sisters of Notre Dame. Owing to the inability of these sisters to visit the African Americans in their homes, Cleary met with Mother Drexel and worked out an agreement. In 1891 Drexel and the Sisters of the Blessed Sacrament had established a national home missionary movement to assist blacks and Native Americans. In addition to teaching school, they worked among the black residents, visited the elderly and the sick in their homes, and conducted evening classes for adults and instruction classes for converts. In the summer of 1914 five Sisters of the Blessed Sacrament came to Cincinnati to replace the Notre Dame Sisters at St. Ann. St. Ann parish saw an increasing number of neophytes coming for instruction to the Sisters of Blessed Sacrament as well as an increasing number of baptisms. Within six months after the sisters' arrival, fifteen black adults were baptized. By October 1914, 115 pupils were enrolled in the day school. At the end of Moeller's term the parish had increased to 547 and the enrollment in the school to 237. In 1915 two members of the St. Ann parish volunteered their services to the Juvenile Court to help black Catholic children. Moreover, a group of young white women organized a club for the purpose of aiding the Blessed Sacrament Sisters in their work. At first they taught Sunday school; by 1924 the lay women were conducting evening classes in typewriting and shorthand for the seventh and eighth graders.[45]

Notwithstanding the gains made in St. Ann parish, church officials encountered problems in trying to attract blacks to the Catholic Church. The Catholic policy toward blacks as they moved into the northern cities in the nineteenth and early twentieth centuries, and Cincinnati was no exception, had been to segregate them into their own separate parishes. This hardened the color line separating blacks and whites. There were blacks who viewed St. Ann as a symbol of segregation and criticized local church authorities for not encouraging black Catholics to attend the churches and parochial schools closest to their homes. At the end of Moeller's term in 1925 only a few blacks attended white parishes in Cincinnati. Henry J. Richter, the new pastor of St. Ann in the early 1920s, warned the archbishop "there is much agitation among non-catholic [*sic*] colored about this and some of the Catholics are bound to be affected. The less said to them about this the better as little good and much harm would come of it." Another problem facing the local church was the substantial number of black Catholics who left the church. Richter observed in 1920 that many of them were former stranded inmates of the Good Shepherd Convent. He knew "personally of nearly one hundred," he wrote, and according to former inmates in the convent there were "probably several hundred."[46]

Throughout his tenure Moeller had to deal with charges of abuse levied against the Sisters of Good Shepherd. In addition to their convent in Price Hill, the sisters had their motherhouse and school at Carthage. There the sisters had about two hundred black children in their St. Peter Claver Industrial School, allegedly the largest institution of its kind in the country for black girls. In the "reformatory department" the sisters had more than one hundred younger adults, ranging in age from twelve to twenty-six. At Carthage the sisters had two principal means of support, the charity of the laity and workshops operated by the sisters and the black girls. To sustain their operations the sisters relied on public charity and on revenue from their commercial laundry and sewing rooms where the inmates and the sisters produced shirts for various businesses.[47]

Not unlike the anti-Catholic propaganda aimed at the House of the Good Shepherd in Detroit during the First World War, the Good Shepherd school at Carthage came under attack in 1916. In the spring, *The Cincinnati Times-Star* published a letter signed by A.K.N., condemning the State of Ohio for sending delinquent girls to private sectarian schools where they were treated as virtual slaves. Five days later the paper published a rebuttal letter signed by "Fair Play." When Francis A. Gressle, director of the Bureau of Catholic Charities, also sent a letter to *The Cincinnati Times-Star* to refute the charges against the Sisters of Good Shepherd, the paper refused to print it on the ground that it did not want to perpetuate the debate. Furious over the denial, Moeller issued an ultimatum to the paper. He threatened the loss of Catholic advertisements if Gressle's letter were not published. Charles P. Taft, the paper's owner, assured Moeller that he had agreed to the publication of A.K.N.'s letter without taking into consideration "its hidden import." Though he felt his paper could not succumb to threats, he nevertheless agreed to print Gressle's statement. Expressing his gratitude to Taft, Moeller admitted that in his "exasperation" he was perhaps "a bit hasty. But calumnies of the nature of the letter," he wrote, ". . . have been so frequent of late, that I was highly incensed."[48]

In his letter in *The Cincinnati Times-Star* Gressle denied the allegation that the girls in the convent had to work late at night. Thirty years earlier Elder had put a stop to any night work in the convents. Gressle also argued that "A.K.N. does not seem to have the welfare of the colored race at heart." Pointing out that Ohio had no refuge home for black girls, he argued that the "wayward and incorrigible colored girls sent from every section of the State" would have no place to go if places like the convent at Carthage did not exist. Both Gressle and Moeller invited "any fair-minded person" to inspect "every nook and corner" of "any of the Catholic institutions anytime." What Moeller did not make known publicly, however, was that both he and Elder had received a number of complaints about the conditions in the Good Shepherd Sisters' convents. Though many consisted of anonymous letters, some came from some Good Shepherd Sisters themselves, usually complaining about the poor relationship with their superiors and the carelessness or exploitation of the inmates entrusted to them. When in 1913 Moeller had learned that the sisters operated their convent laundries on holy days, he informed the Mother Superior that "working on a day of obligation in a Catholic institution would give disedification and scandal." Two years after the A.K.N. incident, Moeller reminded the Good Shepherd Sisters that the girls should not work "like slaves." If "the girls have to work very hard and nothing is done to bring any sunshine into their lives," he wrote, ". . . I fear there will be serious trouble. These girls when they leave the institution will surely speak of the harsh treatment they received."[49]

LABOR

In the 1870s and 1880s Catholics, who were predominantly a working-class people, became increasingly involved in the labor movement. At the time most U.S. bishops and priests were suspicious of labor organizations. They were especially critical of their secrecy and propensity to violence. Gradually, however, some clerics warmed up to the cause of labor. Cardinal Gibbons of Baltimore became one of organized labor's strongest supporters. Believing that it should be on the side of the workers, the local church eventually supported labor unions. The "strong arm of the poor man and the skill of the mechanic," the archdiocesan council of 1882 argued, "is as much his stock in trade as the gold of the rich man, and each has a right, as he pleases, to sell his labor at a fair price. Men have also a right to band together and agree to sell their labor at any fair price within the limits of Christian justice." The Council Fathers, led by Elder, acknowledged the right of workers to form voluntary unions. The *Catholic Telegraph,* moreover, often wrote of the responsibilities of the employer to his workers. There was, it editorialized, "a moral bond between the employer and the laborer . . . which, while it obliges the one to work faithfully and industriously for his master, obliges the other in turn to provide for his servant the possibility of keeping a home and bringing up his family decently." Elder and his staff generally favored a reduction of the hours of labor, improvement in working conditions, and an increase in the workers' wages. This concern about social justice and the lives and rights of the working people would become one of the special marks of Catholicism in the history of the archdiocese.[50]

Because of ongoing controversy and violence involving labor, American bishops called upon Roman authorities for guidance. Elder echoed the sentiments of his colleagues when he requested in 1888 a "clear statement of Catholic doctrine," one that could be used "with confidence in our instruction to the people." Encouraged by Gibbons to write a second letter, Elder, who had earlier proposed to him that he recommend to the pope that he issue an encyclical on labor, again emphasized that "[m]any Catholics do not know what to believe . . . in regard to property[,] labor[,] wages etc." On the issue of labor and capital "there are errors on both sides," he wrote. "Property owners and employees have false notions about their rights and many have *no notions* about their duties. And indeed the very root of these difficulties out of which the dissatisfaction and extravagance of the poorer classes grow is the unchristian spirit of the rich." When Bishop James Gilmour of Cleveland expressed concern that the Catholic Church in the United States was "drifting within a large, large [*sic*] stream into the ranks of the wealth," Elder assured him that he did not detect any trend toward the wealthy on the part of the American church.[51]

By endorsing the right of workers to form trade unions and offering a program of reform based on the concept of social justice, Leo XIII's 1891 encyclical *Rerum Novarum* gave added encouragement to Catholics to take part in the labor movement. But at the same time that local church officials supported the right of workers to unionize, they insisted that no man should attempt to force others to join a union. They also were critical of labor strikes. To deny the workingman a just and fair compensation for his labor "is a sin," Moeller wrote in his January 20 pastoral, but "it is also a crime for laborers, hastily and thoughtlessly, to resort to strikes for obtaining their demands." Though the *Catholic Telegraph* consistently took the side of labor and argued the justness of its cause, it too deplored the frequency of strikes and warned against their overall usefulness.[52]

When in the spring of 1886 workers went on strike in Cincinnati, New York, and Chicago, among other cities, the *Catholic Telegraph* agreed with President Grover Cleveland that federal legislation could do much to avert labor disputes. During the railroad strikes of 1888 it further urged the federal government to resolve major differences between capital and labor. At a time when federal intervention in industrial disputes almost always meant action on behalf of employers, the *Catholic Telegraph* highlighted the need of the workers. "Until a great social regeneration takes place to adjust on a sound basis the difficulties of the question," it wrote, "the interference of Government may not be amiss." Just as the government provided for the soldier "disabled by the labors of war," it further argued, provision should also be made "for the disabled of that large army of laborers who make our railroads, pave our streets, build up our cities, [and] expend their muscles in our manufactures."[53]

Though Elder and his staff in general disapproved of strikes, in 1902 local Catholics, with the archbishop's encouragement, established a fund for the benefit of the 150,000 striking anthracite coal miners in the fields of Pennsylvania. The *Catholic Telegraph* was one of the earliest, if not the first, Catholic paper to start a collection for the striking miners. When in the spring of 1913 there was a streetcar strike in Cincinnati, Moeller urged the pastors to provide whatever assistance they could to help bring about a settlement between the company and its employees, nearly 80 percent of whom were Catholic. He felt they were being led "blindly" by individuals who were "actuated by personal and selfish motives." Moeller also wrote a confidential letter to each pastor, encouraging each one to speak to the employees belonging to his parish.[54]

During the national reform period of the late 1890s and early 1900s, a growing number of Protestant and Catholic clergy noted a discrepancy between the ideals of Christianity and prevailing attitudes toward the poor. Washington Gladden, a Congregationalist minister in Columbus and spirited leader in the Social Gospel movement, urged his congregation to take an active part in the fight against social injustice. In the spirit of the movement, archdiocesan officials contended that the Catholic Church had "always been the church of the poor," and that "the hope of the Church everywhere lies in the plain people." It urged landlords to provide better housing in the inner city. "It is a sin and it ought be made a crime," the chancery argued, "to herd people together as often those helpless beings are herded. Why does not somebody think of preaching the gospel to owners of buildings arranged like so many shambles?" In the summer of 1898 John Mackey, then rector of St. Peter in Chains Cathedral, criticized the deplorable working conditions of the women in the Cincinnati laundries. Compelled to work sixteen and seventeen hours a day, six days a week, for one dollar a day, the women suffered under conditions he described as amounting to "tyranny."[55]

In 1918 Peter E. Dietz, the American church's strongest advocate for the unions in the first half of the twentieth century, came to Cincinnati from North Carolina and established his American Academy of Christian Democracy on a ten-acre tract near Ault Park. He felt the unions were the surest means of securing justice for the workers of America and of preventing the growth of socialism. In his first two years in the archdiocese, Dietz gained both Moeller's support and that of labor. When in January 1920 there developed friction between Dietz and a local Jesuit regarding industrial and social activities, Moeller backed the labor priest. "I deem it fitting," he wrote, "that the industrial field in the Archdiocese of Cincinnati be entirely left to him." During the next several months, however, Moeller's opinion of Dietz changed.[56]

Shortly after Dietz in his November 29, 1920, letter to the *Cincinnati Times-Star* criticized the local Chamber of Commerce for not being more supportive of his plan to form an industrial council, Catholic businessmen met with Moeller and charged that Dietz's work harmed the best interests of the Catholic Church. Moeller quickly reprimanded Dietz, pointing out that he had acted "imprudently" in writing the letter. Fearing that Dietz's writings "might fan into mighty conflagration the flames of excitement existing between employers and employees," Moeller forbade him in the future to publish in the papers any article without first getting his approval. From this point on Dietz's actions were suspect. Moeller, furthermore, found him to be "stubborn, self-willed," and impulsive, rushing "into projects that are beyond his reach." On December 15, 1920, the archbishop requested him to leave the archdiocese.[57]

Dietz ignored Moeller's request, and took steps to become more firmly established in the archdiocese. As friction between Dietz and Moeller intensified, the archbishop incurred the odium of the local unions. Though Moeller attempted to assure the unions that his action was "not prompted by any hostility to organized labor," their protests persisted. When Moeller learned that Dietz intended to appeal to Archbishop Giovanni Bonzano, the apostolic delegate, he immediately informed Bonzano that the "labor priest" had "been the cause of some friction." Though he had no evidence that Dietz taught any erroneous doctrines or advocated unsound principles, Moeller considered him to be an "enthusiast," not "easily governed," and "too intensive in his support of the labor organizations." By April 1922 Moeller, after conferring with his diocesan consultors, commanded Dietz to leave the archdiocese. As late as March 1923 Father John A. Ryan, a highly respected national social reformer, tried unsuccessfully to meet with Moeller on behalf of Dietz. The following month Archbishop Sebastian Messmer called Dietz to Milwaukee.[58]

WOMEN'S SPHERE

During Elder's and Moeller's administrations there was considerable concern by the Catholic hierarchy over the changes in the woman's sphere and their likely adverse effects on the family and society. In the process the archdiocese presented mixed and at times conflicting views on women's issues. This was especially apparent in the publications of the *Catholic Telegraph*. Though the diocesan paper disapproved of what it regarded as the extremes of the "Women's Rights" position, it adopted a more understanding view of the working woman. It argued in 1888 that since women often had to earn bread for themselves or as single mothers for their children as well, "they should receive as much pay as a man would receive for the same work." Although it advocated equal pay for women, it expressed concern in 1899 that the young woman "does not promise to equal her mother in scarcely any woman trait." Reflecting the sentiments of the official church that a woman's primary place was in the home and that her main obligations were to her husband and children, it suggested in 1902 that women were "somewhat at fault." The diocesan paper further contended that the dislike for housekeeping sent "great numbers of girls to seek employment as saleswomen and office work[ers] which unfit them for the duties of wives to the industrious workingmen, who would in other circumstances give them a comfortable home which they could make happy." That view was consistent with Catholic moral theology at the time, which subordinated the wife to the husband.[59]

Though the *Catholic Telegraph* expressed concern over the increasing presence of women in the workplace, it nevertheless took the stand that women should be well educated. It criticized those individuals who believed "that the only training necessary for the gentler sex is such as would fit the fair daughters of Eve to be . . . capable housewives, patient and loving mates, tender and watchful mothers. . . . This sentiment," it wrote, was similar to "the degraded position of slave occupied by the weaker sex among the uncivilized races." In 1889 the diocesan paper proudly observed that the intellectual life was becoming increasingly more attractive to women than to men. "The weaker sex," it editorialized, "appears to be becoming the more intellectual sex," based on the fact that a greater number of local Catholic women were attending lectures, summer schools, and pursuing higher education than Catholic men.[60]

In the late nineteenth and early twentieth centuries the *Catholic Telegraph* also supported the effort to organize Catholic women. Out of the Catholic Women's Congress, held in Chicago in the early 1890s, grew a National League to promote the involvement of Catholic women in temperance activities, day nurseries and kindergartens, protective and employment agencies for women, and social clubs and residences for young working women. The diocesan paper argued that there was no reason why Catholic women's societies, like their non-Catholic counterparts, could not continue to unite among themselves for mutual support. For many years Catholic women in the archdiocese had rendered distinguished service to the National Red Cross, the League of Service, and various parish organizations. The power of Catholic women, the *Catholic Telegraph* editorialized, "is ineffectual without organization."[61]

Archbishop Moeller, on the other hand, doubted the "advisability" of having a federation of Catholic women societies. Besides arguing that it would "draw them away from household duties," he insisted that it would "be difficult" for the women "to keep it up." But if there were to be a federation of women societies, Moeller wanted it totally separate from the male organizations. Notwithstanding the archbishop's reservations, in 1913 several fraternal organizations of women formed the Federation of Catholic Women Societies of Cincinnati. Helping to bring Catholic women and Catholic women's societies into closer union, the Federation's main object was to foster works of religion, education, and charity. By this time the chancery encouraged the pastors "to see to it that their Women's Societies join the Women's Federation." In the spring of 1921 a small group of women also established the Cincinnati Catholic Woman's Association. This Association, which sponsored two large social events yearly, a theater party in the winter and a card party in the spring, got involved in various religious, educational, charitable, and humanitarian activities in the archdiocese.[62]

The social issue that received most attention in the secular and religious realms during Moeller's term was women's suffrage. Although some church leaders, such as Archbishop John Ireland of Minneapolis and Bishop Bernard McQuaid of Rochester, supported it, the majority of the hierarchy was opposed. In an official letter read in the archdiocesan churches in the spring of 1914, Moeller publicly opposed women's involvement in politics and the ballot. He implored Catholic women to sign antisuffrage petitions. Moeller was concerned that the voting franchise would "lower" rather than "uplift" women. "It is a movement that does not apply to Us," he wrote, "because We feel that it will bring women into a sphere of activities that is not in accord with their retiring modesty, maidenly dignity and refinement." Reflecting the opinion of the official church that a woman's primary place was in the home, Moeller feared paradoxically that if the woman suffrage movement were successful, women "would cease to be the Queens of the House. Let the women," he argued, "devote themselves, as far as their duties will permit, to works of charity for which Nature has so well fitted them."[63]

Shortly after the woman suffrage amendment was ratified in August 1920, there was a complete reversal of attitude about it by Moeller and his staff. "We have always been opposed to female suffrage," the diocesan paper wrote in September, "and, in principle, we are as much opposed to it as ever; but, now, that the vote has been given to the gentler sex, we are convinced that Catholic women should qualify themselves to exercise their franchise intelligently and for the best interests of home and country." Previously opposed to the ballot, the chancery now entreated Catholic women to vote. When various sisterhoods inquired whether the sisters should also vote, Moeller urged them to make use of the privilege. Partly in response to the passage of the Nineteenth Amendment and the need for higher education for women, the Sisters of Charity established the College of Mount St. Joseph on the Ohio for Women in 1920. It was an outgrowth of Mount St. Joseph Academy, which had been offering pre-collegiate courses for several years. The few Catholic women's colleges that had opened by this time had started as an extension of secondary academies, which had provided in Cincinnati, as was true of other private female academies in the country in the nineteenth century, the only Catholic secondary education available to Catholic girls. As more Catholic women were going to college, and many were attending state or secular institutions, there was a perceived need for Catholic women's colleges. Mount St. Joseph was the second Catholic women's college in Ohio. Even though women's colleges under secular and Protestant rule had been thriving since after the Civil War, their Catholic counterparts in the United States developed mainly after 1920. This might be due in part to the fact that Catholics, largely because of their poverty, were slower to come to the realization that higher education could benefit women as well as men.[64]

By the mid-1920s more Catholic women, like their male counterparts in the archdiocese, were actively engaged in various religious, educational, and charitable programs. Notwithstanding the growth of episcopal and clerical authority during the Elder-Moeller years, the laity—though less involved in decision-making in the management of the local church—gave birth to a number of grassroots lay ministries. Doubtlessly, the growth of the Catholic middle class and more educated laity helped expand the local ministry. Increasing concern about social justice became one of the distinctive characteristics of Catholicism in the history of the archdiocese of Cincinnati.

PART
THREE

MODERN CATHOLICISM
IN THE ARCHDIOCESE OF
CINCINNATI
1920s–1960s

Introduction

During the administrations of John Timothy McNicholas (1925–1950) and Karl Joseph Alter (1950–1969) the archdiocese attained a new level of institutional growth and became more assertive on social issues and confident of its own Americanism. Both ordinaries attempted to develop a specific Catholic culture, hoping to influence American culture with their religion. While solidifying its position in American society, the local church over a forty-year period saw a significant increase in the number of churches, schools, hospitals, and charitable agencies. During McNicholas's tenure alone fifty-two new churches were built. Under his supervision a regional Catholic high school system was established and all Catholic charity and social service agencies were reorganized under Catholic Charities. Before the end of McNicholas's term, Archbishop Samuel Stritch of Chicago wrote to him and praised him on his accomplishments. "Your balance sheet is probably one of the very best," he wrote, "and the beauty of it is that you have done things."[1]

McNicholas was considered one of the more influential and preeminent American churchmen of his time and was widely regarded as the leading theologian in the American hierarchy. He was an effective, energetic, and persistent leader in many national movements, especially in the fields of apologetics and of social and racial justice. He achieved national prominence as spokesperson for such causes as the Legion of Decency, labor movement, and welfare of African Americans, education, and anticommunism. He also helped inspire the Catholic national program of rural evangelization in the United States. Regarded as one of the ablest minds among the American hierarchy, he served in many capacities in the National Catholic Welfare Conference, having been chosen many times by his episcopal colleagues for membership on the administrative board of the conference. From 1929 to 1935 and again from 1941 to 1950 he was a member of the NCWC administrative board, serving as its chairman from 1945 to 1950. He also served as episcopal chairman of the NCWC education department from 1930 to 1935 and again from 1943 to 1945 and was president general of the National Catholic Educational Association from 1946 to 1950.[2]

McNicholas had a refined intellect and was one of the brightest American ordinaries. He was a rigorous thinker and in his twenty-five years in Cincinnati he made known his views on a variety of subjects, ranging widely from immoral movies, tax-supported education, and capitalism to labor, peace, and totalitarianism. The most important ground that he chose to occupy as archbishop was that of defending traditional morals, never ceasing to speak consistently for morality and Christian principles. Concerned over declining morality in American society, McNicholas continually addressed issues that hit close to home. Indeed, he did not hesitate to address the burning issues of his day. From his earliest years McNicholas's strength and solidity on moral matters was irrefutable, continually valuing religion, education, family, and human rights. As a shrewd administrator he was unafraid to take an unpopular stand if he thought that he was standing for what was right and best for the people. He did not shy from controversy. "Those who believe in eternal truth and age-old morality," he wrote in 1938, "have a duty to voice their faith in them rather than stand supinely by while they are challenged by the forces of irreligion, or immorality, and atheism rampant in the world today." In his efforts after World War II to inspire Catholics to help restructure American society, he was a staunch and conscientious worker for the improvement of public morals.[3]

As Cincinnati's fifth archbishop Karl Alter was a builder. By the time he resigned in 1969 the building program of the archdiocese under his leadership had included more than one hundred and thirty projects. True to their tradition, lay Catholics generously contributed their time and money toward their completion. Chief among these projects were the restoration and expansion of St. Peter in Chains Cathedral, expansion of St. Gregory Seminary, a new orphanage, St. Joseph Villa, and St. Margaret Hall, a new home for the aged. The restoration of the cathedral, Archbishop Joseph Bernardin of Cincinnati later wrote, was Alter's "pride and joy." It was his single greatest triumph. Alter was also the prime mover in the archdiocesan campaign that netted thirteen million dollars to build seven Catholic high schools. During his nineteen-year tenure there were forty-one elementary schools, fourteen high schools, seventy-nine rectories for priests, and fifty-five convents for nuns built. In addition, more than fifty elementary schools were enlarged. Parochial school enrollment soared during his tenure, growing from 48,000 in 1950 to over 100,000 students in 1963, increasing more than 100 percent. But in the face of an increasing shortage of women and men religious teachers, declining vocations, increasing number of lay teachers, and mounting expenses, the archdiocesan school system by the mid-1960s faced substantial financial problems and declining enrollment. This posed a new challenge to church officials.[4]

A major thrust of Alter's career was also to encourage the lay ministry. He helped reorganize the structures that gave lay men and women the means to help shape the philosophy of Catholic Action in the Cincinnati archdiocese. Throughout his administration Alter, who helped reorganize the Archdiocesan Councils of Catholic Men and Women, was one of the leading ordinaries in the United States who encouraged the development of the National Council of Catholic Men and the National Council of Catholic Women and their respective diocesan affiliates.

CATHOLIC ACTION AND
DIOCESAN GROWTH

At the quarter mark of the twentieth century Catholics in the archdiocese and throughout the United States were more confident than they had been previously of their own American identity and of their ability to contribute to the growth of the country. As the nation was experiencing unprecedented economic growth and the Catholic population became increasingly affluent, Catholics generally made their way into the American middle class and helped define their place in American culture more explicitly. It was also a period of administrative reform in the American church. In 1919 U.S. bishops organized the National Catholic Welfare Council as a standing secretariat. Three years later the title changed to the National Catholic Welfare Conference (NCWC). This organization gave the Catholic hierarchy an effective agency in Washington to safeguard and advance American Catholic interests.

Social and cultural changes in the 1920s, the economic depression of the 1930s, the rise of totalitarianism in Europe, World War II, social ferment in America in the late 1950s and 1960s, and the Second Vatican Council also had an impact on the growth of the church. During this period the institutional church kept pace with the economic growth of the country. Under the leadership of Archbishops John McNicholas and Karl Alter, the local church experienced substantial growth and change. Their skills in financial management and in "brick and mortar" policies characterized the administrative style of American Catholicism in the first half of the twentieth century.

Although in May 1925 Bishop John McNicholas of Duluth, Minnesota, was named to Indianapolis to succeed Bishop Joseph Chartrand, who was to be elevated to the see of Cincinnati, McNicholas never occupied that post.

FIG 13. Archbishop John Timothy McNicholas, 1925–1950

Chartrand opted to serve out his years in the Indiana capital, and the pope, uncharacteristically, reversed his decision and appointed the Irish-born McNicholas on July 8 of that year to Cincinnati. More than two hundred priests greeted McNicholas when he arrived at Eaton, Ohio, from Duluth on August 11. Together they traveled on a special train to Cincinnati. At every crossroads on the train ride groups of people gathered and waved their welcome. Upon his arrival in the Queen City, where more than ten thousand people lined the streets to greet him, McNicholas was escorted to his archiepiscopal residence. He was installed as Cincinnati's archbishop in formal ceremonies in St. Peter in Chains Cathedral on August 12, with Cardinal George Mundelein of Chicago as the officiating prelate. The province, then embracing five states, again had a metropolitan. Like Cincinnati's founding bishop, Edward Fenwick, McNicholas was a Dominican. But the comparison stopped there. Unlike the mild-mannered Fenwick, the new archbishop would prove to be an outspoken, forceful, and at times controversial church leader.[1]

McNicholas was born in Kiltimagh, County Mayo, Ireland, on December 15, 1877. He was the youngest of eight children. When he was three, his parents, Patrick and Mary Mullany McNicholas, emigrated to the United States, establishing a home in Chester, Pennsylvania, in 1881. After attending parochial school and a four-year preparatory course, McNicholas attended St. Joseph College in Philadelphia. He was a student at the college only a short time when he decided to become a priest. Religion seemed to run in his Irish blood as a brother and two nephews also became priests. In 1894, at the age of seventeen, he entered the Dominican Order at St. Rose Priory in Kentucky. He took his scholasticate at the Dominican Order's house near Somerset, Ohio. On October 10, 1901, Moeller, then bishop of Columbus, ordained him a priest.[2]

In the same year of his ordination, McNicholas went to Rome to study at Minerva University, where in 1904 he received a doctorate in sacred theology. The following year the twenty-six-year-old McNicholas went to Washington, D.C., where he taught philosophy and theology at the Dominican's house of studies at Catholic University. In 1909 he was appointed National Director of the Holy Name Society with headquarters in New York City, and the first editor of the *Holy Name Journal.* Through his efforts and organizational skills, the first national convention of the Holy Name Society was held in Baltimore, with representatives of more than 3,000 branches in attendance. While stationed in New York, he was put in charge of St. Catherine of Siena parish. In 1917 the Dominicans recalled him to Rome, appointing him assistant professor of theology and canon law at Angelico College and assistant to the Master General of the order. While in Rome he renewed contact with his old and influential Dominican friend, Cardinal Tommaso Boggiani, whom he had escorted a few years earlier around New York. As head of the Consistorial Congregation in Rome that controlled the nomination and appointment of bishops, Boggiani was instrumental in 1918 in persuading Pope Benedict XV, who referred to McNicholas as the "Dominicanetto," to appoint him bishop of Duluth. In 1925 McNicholas became Cincinnati's fifth ordinary.[3]

At the same time that Catholics during McNicholas's tenure emerged from the experience of World War I filled with self-confidence and optimism about the future, and the local ethnic divisions that had persisted in the late nineteenth and early twentieth centuries steadily diminished, American Catholicism nevertheless was a little defensive. This was partly in response to the bigotry of the Ku Klux Klan and an aggressive Protestant crusade to promote one hundred percent Americanism. It opposed African Americans,

Catholics, and Jews. In the 1920s the Ku Klux Klan burned crosses in the archdiocese in the front of churches, such as in full view of St. Aloysius Church at Shandon, and on the front lawns of some parishioners' homes. In a parade in downtown Xenia a model of St. Brigid school was set on fire to protest the existence of the school. When the Klan had planned a parade to march past the front of St. Raphael Church in Springfield, Monsignor Daniel Buckley stood in front of the church and would not let them pass. After a few tense moments the parade turned around. Overall, the struggle over prohibition, the immigration restriction quotas of the 1920s, Oregon's legislative attempt to prohibit private schools, the activities of the Ku Klux Klan, and the defeat of Alfred E. Smith in 1928, the first Catholic presidential candidate, reinforced the Catholic sense of alienation.[4]

Between the two world wars Catholic churchmen reiterated the more than half-century argument that moral persuasion, rather than legislation, was the most effective strategy to combat intemperance and alcoholism, and they continued to strongly oppose immigrant restriction quotas. McNicholas thought, as had previous local church leaders, that there was nothing inherently evil in the consumption of alcoholic beverages. Like Elder and Moeller before him, he expressed concern over the fanaticism associated with prohibition. When prohibition was repealed in 1933, the *Catholic Telegraph* editorialized that it "never should have been foisted upon the people." U.S. church leaders also opposed the immigrant restriction quotas of the 1920s on the grounds that they discriminated against southern and eastern Europeans, many of whom were Catholic. In 1922 Oregon passed a law requiring all children between the ages of eight and sixteen to attend public schools. This new legislation, which challenged the independence of the entire Catholic school system, raised the fears of Catholics across the country. Joined by Lutherans, Seventh Day Adventists, and the American Civil Liberties Union, Catholics charged that the Oregon law violated religious freedom and educational diversity. In 1925 in *Pierce v. The Society of Sisters* the U.S. Supreme Court handed down a landmark decision for religious liberty. Although it acknowledged the responsibility and rights of the state to oversee public education, the court protected the rights of private and parochial education.[5]

When Alfred E. Smith ran for the presidency his candidacy brought out into the open America's widespread anti-Catholic sentiment. It brought to the fore the whole question of double allegiance. Could a Catholic remain loyal to the church and, as president, be loyal to his country? In a radio talk, McNicholas, who resented the fact that he and other Catholics had to demonstrate their loyalty to the country, refuted the allegation that American Catholics would give their civil allegiance first to the pope and only a secondary allegiance to the United States. "We, as American Catholics," he said, "owe no civil allegiance to the Vatican State." The Cincinnati prelate was particularly critical of those who accused the church of supporting Smith because he was Catholic. A few weeks after the presidential election, McNicholas addressed some of the charges at the annual meeting of the National Council of Catholic Men. "As an American citizen," he said, "I protest against the insinuation made that my Church, because of a Catholic candidate, . . . attempted to control my political affiliations or to give me the slightest indication as to how I or any other Catholic citizen of my jurisdiction should vote. This is not the province of the Church. It is not her affair."[6]

The renewed attacks on the Catholics and the defeat of Smith reinforced the feeling of alienation among a number of church leaders. McNicholas considered the attacks to be a slander of the Catholic Church and reacted with a stirring call for Catholics to come to her defense. His understanding of the place of Catholicism in America was continually influenced by lingering anti-Catholic sentiments. Going to great lengths to defend the faith against external attacks, he also helped Catholics rise out of their nineteenth-century, second-class status. From the moment he first arrived in Cincinnati, he argued that as far as citizenship was concerned, there was no inherent conflict between being Catholic and being American. What baffled the archbishop was the fact that notwithstanding the "glorious record" of Catholic patriotism in war and in peace, many Americans still feared the Catholic Church.[7]

Throughout his administration McNicholas repeatedly called upon Catholics to exercise their rights as citizens to vote, especially when there was certainty or serious doubt of moral turpitude in questions. Urging his clergy to get people to vote, he reminded them never to "interfere with their liberty of action with regard to their party affiliations or the selection of candidates." Though archdiocesan officials did not allow a discussion of political issues and political candidates from the pulpit, church and school halls were used for the free discussion of all issues affecting the general interests of the community. At the same time that the *Catholic Telegraph* generally refrained officially from endorsing specific candidates in political campaigns, its editorials during McNicholas's episcopate generally were sympathetic to the Democratic Party.[8]

More than thirty years after Smith's presidential race the issue of religion and politics surfaced once again with the presidential candidacy in 1960 of Senator John F. Kennedy, a Catholic from Massachusetts. Karl Alter, then archbishop of Cincinnati, reiterated the church's position that a man's religious beliefs should not be a factor if he sought the highest public office in the nation. Like his predecessor, he felt that voters should consider only two criteria, a candidate's ability to do the job and his integrity of character. "The only interest which we as Catholics have in the question," he wrote in the fall of 1960, "is that no disability be levied against a Catholic because of his religion." Significantly, Kennedy's victory was symbolic in the sense that as more and more Catholics were gradually becoming more bourgeois-minded and were moving up the economic ladder, this was another barrier that Catholics had overcome.[9]

LAY APOSTOLIC WORK

During their terms Archbishops McNicholas and Alter thought more could be done to awaken the laity and parishes to the needs of the local church. In his first year as archbishop McNicholas was of the opinion that the members of the Cincinnati Conference of the National Council of Catholic Men (NCCM) had very little responsibility. The NCCM was a national federation of organizations of Catholic laymen established in 1920 by the National Catholic Welfare Conference to promote the development of the lay ministry. "While I am anxious to see [the Cincinnati Conference] continued," he wrote to Archbishop Austin Dowling of St. Paul, "I do not think I should supply it with the oxygen of authority to make it live." Generally, McNicholas, like some of his episcopal colleagues, such as Archbishop Michael J. Curley of Baltimore, was displeased with the limited achievement of the NCCM and regarded it as impotent. From the time it was formed in 1920 some of the bishops had viewed it with suspicion and did not think the council was necessary. Writing three years later to Bishop John Noll of Fort Wayne, McNicholas also blamed himself for not constructing something "very definite" for the men of the NCCM in the archdiocese. They felt "hampered," he wrote, having "no freedom of expression." Besides, he thought that if the priests were "not hostile" toward the lay Catholics, they were "at least apathetic." Convinced that the lay people in the various societies were also too much "under the jurisdiction of the Church," he felt they no longer had to "stand in awe of the Bishops and priests." He suggested to Noll that it would be best to have the NCCM become an organization of lay societies for which "we Bishops will not assume responsibility."[10]

By the fall of 1929 the Cincinnati Conference reorganized itself. Becoming a federation representative of all parishes and societies in the archdiocese, it served as an inspirational force to various Catholic societies. In October McNicholas, who had considerable drive and flair, urged the Catholic men at the Annual Convention of the NCCM at Fort Wayne to participate more in community outreach programs and to take more of a leadership role in society. "Our aloofness, our silence, our refusal to make contacts with those who misunderstand or differ with us, when it is in our power to show the sanctity of the Catholic position," he said, "cannot be justified." What he proposed was "a legion of Catholics" who would be "spiritual athletes for Christ and for the Church." Also inspired by Pius XI's encyclical *Mens Nostra* issued in December 1929 and his program of Catholic Action, more and more lay Catholics by the 1930s became identified with the Catholic Action movements. Catholic Action generally entailed on the part of the laity a more fervent religious practice, a study of Catholic doctrine and social principles, and a fuller involvement in community organizations.[11]

As leader of the archdiocese at midcentury Alter also urged greater lay participation in the life of the church. On June 21, 1950, Pius XII named Alter, then bishop of Toledo, archbishop of Cincinnati. The grandson of a stagecoach driver and all-around athletic star as a young man, Alter became the sixth ordinary and fifth archbishop of the Cincinnati see. He enjoyed the reputation of being a great organizer, a forceful and forthright speaker, and a national leader of the church in social welfare.[12]

Alter was born in Toledo on August 18, 1885. After receiving his early education in the community, he completed his studies for the priesthood at St. Mary's Seminary in Cleveland. He was ordained a priest on June 4, 1910. Between his ordination and the time he became bishop, Alter served in varied capacities. Following his parish assignments at Leipsic and Lima, Ohio, Alter, a sturdy man of about medium height, was appointed the first director of Catholic Charities in the diocese of Toledo. During the next thirty years he became keenly interested in child care and family welfare. In 1935 he became associated with the social work of the National Catholic Welfare Conference. Following his election to the Administrative Board of the Conference in 1948 Alter, as chairman of the Social Action Department, lobbied in Washington for the increase of the federal minimum wage, passage of the full employment bill, and the promotion of a national health program.[13]

Of German extraction Alter was expected to find himself at home in the Queen City. In some ways he reminded Catholics in southwest Ohio of McNicholas, particularly in his stand on social and family welfare issues. Though both were reform-minded archbishops, they differed greatly in personality and administrative style. Intimates among the clergy referred to McNicholas simply as "the Boss," in recognition of his leadership qualities. A headstrong administrator, McNicholas may have alienated many of his clergy by his authoritarian style. He was regarded by some as an abrasive autocrat. To many, however, this lover of dogs who enjoyed collecting rare works of art had a friendly, fatherly personality. Though Alter, a diocesan priest, resembled his Dominican predecessor, Cincinnati Catholics expected him to participate more in public life than McNicholas, whose interests had been more in the intellectual realm. At the same time that he was a gentleman and a leader, Alter was also flexible and amiable. He was not a man of quick judgments. He impressed his colleagues with his firm and questioning mind. Alter's appointment brought to Cincinnati the dean of American archbishops, since rank in this regard dates from consecration as bishop. He had served for nineteen years as the supreme pastor of the diocese of Toledo.[14]

On September 26, 1950, Alter was installed archbishop of Cincinnati. Shortly after his arrival in Cincinnati's Union Terminal, he went to the episcopal residence in College Hill where he changed from black to the red robes of his office. Then he went immediately to the chapel of the residence. After praying quietly, he turned to the archdiocesan consultors who were present to hear the reading of the papal bulls that appointed him archbishop of Cincinnati and gave him official possession of his archdiocese. At the time St. Monica Church had replaced St. Peter in Chains as the cathedral church. Largely because of the decline of the neighborhood on Eighth and Plum Streets and the uncertainty of the future of the inner city, McNicholas reduced St. Peter in Chains in 1938 to the status of a parish church. At St. Monica's, Cardinal Samuel A. Stritch of Chicago, Alter's immediate predecessor as bishop of Toledo, escorted Alter in 1950 to his throne and a Solemn Pontifical Mass completed the installation ceremony. Forty-three archbishops and bishops, and hundreds of priests, religious, civic leaders, and laity crowded the cathedral to witness the formal installation of the new archbishop. Alter was the first and only prelate to be installed in St. Monica's.[15]

The year 1950 was the centenary of the establishment of the Cincinnati ecclesiastical province. The past one hundred years had witnessed an astounding growth of the Catholic Church everywhere in the United States. As an archdiocese Cincinnati shared second place after Baltimore with New York, St. Louis, and New Orleans. When the Cincinnati Province was established in 1850 there were two dioceses in Ohio—Cincinnati and Cleveland— and one in each of three states—Detroit in Michigan, Louisville in Kentucky, and Vincennes in Indiana. One hundred years later there were four provinces and eighteen dioceses in the same area. In 1850 there were only 160,000 Catholics in the territory; in 1950, there were more than 3,000,000 Catholics.[16]

As Cincinnati's new archbishop Alter had in his charge a well-organized archdiocese with 332 priests, 219 parishes, and a Catholic population of 294,493. Fifteen months after his arrival he wrote to Cardinal Guiseppe Pizzardo in Rome and praised "the splendid work accomplished by [his] predecessor." It was gratifying to Alter to see so many Catholics attending Mass and receiving the sacraments. A survey of all the parishes on five successive Sundays showed that almost 90 percent of Catholics in the community attended Mass regularly, and approximately thirty percent of them received Holy Communion. Though he realized there were other criteria by which to

FIG 14. Holy Name Parade in Crosley Field in Cincinnati in the 1940s

judge "the vigor of Catholic life," he was pleased to see the faithful tapping "these two great sources of divine grace."[17]

In 1952 and 1953 Alter, with the assistance of his vicar general Clarence Issenmann, a native of Hamilton, Ohio, oversaw the reorganization of the Archdiocesan Councils of Catholic Men and Women. These two organizations, along with the Knights of Columbus and Holy Name societies, among other lay groups, provided opportunities for lay people to mobilize their resources and help bring about social change consistent with Christian principles and values. When in May 1955 more than 1,200 women representing nearly every parish of the archdiocese met in Dayton for the third annual convention of the Archdiocesan Council of Catholic Women (ACCW), their main goal was to help "revitalize parish activities" and make the parishes "living cells of Catholic Action." It should be noted that both McNicholas and Alter focused almost exclusively on the expansion of the laity's leadership influence in society and not so much on their influence within the church. Leadership within the church itself was still essentially the realm of the clergy. The Second Vatican Council in the 1960s would help change that somewhat.[18]

Working in conjunction with the clergy, lay efforts were also made in the decades after the First World War to stimulate piety through parish missions, forty hours devotions, novenas, May crownings, Marian devotions, Eucharistic processions, Confraternities of the Blessed Sacrament and of Christian Doctrine, and public recitation of the rosary. These along with attending Mass and receiving the sacraments became more frequent and occupied a central place in the religious life of the mass of Catholics throughout the United States as well as locally. Parishes such as St. Susanna's at Mason conducted rosary devotions and benedictions each Friday evening. In 1950 Cincinnati's Resurrection Church in Price Hill began an around-the-clock, seven-days-a-week program of adoration of the Blessed Sacrament. During the next five years, twenty-four more churches in the archdiocese adopted the program, thirteen of them with day and night schedules, and twelve with daytime adoration. More than two million hours of adoration were offered. As a result of information supplied by promoters of the program in Cincinnati, adoration programs were initiated in more than seven hundred churches in the United States. In the early 1960s St. Bartholomew parishioners in Springfield Township in Cincinnati met one evening a week for communal prayer.[19]

There was throughout the archdiocese an intense effort on the part of the lay people to develop their spiritual lives. In 1931 the Legion of Mary, which had originated in Dublin ten years earlier and became one of the largest lay associations founded in the twentieth century, entered the United States. Formed to promote veneration of the Blessed Virgin Mary, members often prayed the rosary at their weekly meetings and participated in special novenas. Organized on a modest scale it gradually became an effective lay organization of the local church. Charter legion groups were formed in a number of parishes. Legion members undertook various tasks assigned by their pastors. Some took the parish census, looked after the pamphlet rack in the back of the church, promoted retreats, and conducted religious classes for children attending public schools, and others visited the sick in hospitals and homes. In 1941 Cincinnati hosted the first Legion of Mary congress in the Midwest. Approximately two hundred spiritual directors and officers, representing fifty-six legion groups from Ohio, Indiana, and Kentucky, participated in the congress. In 1945 the legion established a group devoted entirely to visiting the blind and preparing braille copies of prayers and religious literature for distribution. By midcentury there were forty-two parish legion groups, consisting of 417 active members, with an enrollment of 11,210 auxiliary or "praying" members who promised to recite a rosary and the legion prayers every day.[20]

Pope Pius XII designated 1954 as the Marian Year, a year set aside so that people could exercise special devotions to the Blessed Mother in observance of the centennial of the definition of the dogma of the Immaculate Conception in the Church. Alter chose St. Mary Church in Over-the-Rhine in Cincinnati, the oldest consecrated church named for the Virgin Mary under his jurisdiction, as the principal pilgrimage center in the archdiocese. On December 8, 1953, Alter opened the Marian Year by celebrating Mass, with almost two thousand people in attendance. During the year, more than fifty thousand people made pilgrimages to St. Mary's. In the summer children from St. Clement parish at St. Bernard in Cincinnati assembled at the St. Clement Church each afternoon at 4 P.M., Monday through Friday, to pray the rosary. Laypersons throughout the archdiocese also met weekly for corporate recitation of the rosary. For an enduring memorial of Marian Year, St. Joseph parish in Hamilton erected a shrine to Our Lady of Fatima next to the church. In 1917 three children in Fatima, Portugal, claimed to have seen a vision of a woman who identified herself as "Our Lady of the Rosary."[21]

As novenas and Marian devotions took on new popularity in the 1930s, the Holy Name Society continued to thrive. Nearly every one of the large cities in the country witnessed Holy Name processions. Some parishes in the archdiocese, such as St. Antoninus's in Covedale in Cincinnati, had two divisions of the Holy Name Society, one each for the married and single men. Each year McNicholas made the Holy Name parade one of the outstanding public events in Cincinnati. As many as 40,000 to 50,000 men would turn out for the annual event. Though essentially a religious organization, it doubtlessly helped create the image of Catholic political solidarity. In October 1934, 45,000 men, including thirty-five bands and drum corps, marched through the streets of Cincinnati. About one hundred parishes were represented in the procession. The demonstration culminated at the Crosley Field, the new home of the Cincinnati Reds baseball team, where Archbishop Amleto Giovanni Cigognani, apostolic delegate, Alfred E. Smith, former governor of New York, and McNicholas reviewed the marching men. In the stadium, the archbishop led the huge congregation in prayer. Smith then led in the pronouncement of the antiprofanity pledge of the Holy Name Society. The *Cincinnati Enquirer* estimated that close to 250,000 people either witnessed or participated in the parade and in the religious exercises. During the last year of McNicholas's administration, more than 100,000 men took part in the Holy Name public observances in seven cities in the archdiocese. All these demonstrations concluded with benediction of the Blessed Sacrament. The women annually on the Sunday before the Holy Name parade celebrated Marian Day for the Blessed Mother. Though crowd sizes at Holy Name rallies grew during the 1950s, by the mid-1960s their numbers declined sharply. As more and more Catholics became involved with various social issues in the sixties, they lost interest in the Holy Name processions. The last rally in downtown Cincinnati was in 1969.[22]

For most parishes, the various parish organizations provided the principal sources of extra revenue and volunteer labor. Virtually each parish had a Holy Name Society and Rosary Society. In order to raise money for necessary expenses, the Holy Name and St. Margaret Mary Societies of All St.s Church at Kenwood in Cincinnati gave rummage sales, held card parties in the homes of some of the members, and sponsored luncheons and dances. St. Anne's Altar Rosary Sodality at Cincinnati's St. Bartholomew parish in Springfield township sponsored fashion shows, dinner dances, bridge games, and 500 Marathons. The additional parish revenue helped buy pews, student desks, and liturgical items. Besides sponsoring some of the more familiar activities, Our Lady of Lourdes's St. Mary's Ladies Sodality in Westwood in Cincinnati conducted white elephant sales, penny drills, a minstrel show, and a Christmas walk. Through the Crusaders of Mary Society, the youth of Cincinnati's St. Antoninus parish raised money for various charities, taught Bible school, and assisted in renovating buildings in the inner city.[23]

Perhaps the most lucrative source of extra parish revenue in the second quarter of the twentieth century was the introduction of the weekly bingo game. The games were almost always initiated to pay debts, which were especially difficult to liquidate during the hard times of the depression. St. Mary parish in Springfield held its first bingo in 1936 and netted two hundred dollars. Impressed by the financial success of bingo at St. Bonaventure Church at Fairmount in Cincinnati, St. William parishioners at Price Hill inaugurated a weekly bingo in the mid-1930s in order to liquidate a mortgage. It was an instant success. "The crowds," the pastor wrote, "come over by the hundreds." One night it had close to two thousand people. It was reported that buses came down from Indianapolis and that the city railway company had to put on ten to fifteen extra streetcars on bingo night. At St. Joseph Church in Hamilton, bingo drew patrons from as far north as Piqua and Toledo in Ohio and as far west as Fort Wayne in Indiana.[24]

The weekly bingos, however, were controversial. When St. Lawrence parish in Mason introduced the game in the town hall in January 1940, the following month *The Warren County News* printed criticisms from citizens. They objected to using public property for such an activity. A local Baptist pastor also criticized the game by citing the evils of gambling. Believing that no harm was done, the Mason officials allowed the games to continue. When in 1943 there were movements by Cincinnati officials to ban church bingo, McNicholas in his August pastoral defended with some frustration the right of people to play bingo. "As the public official moral teacher of the Archdiocese of Cincinnati," he wrote, "I deem it my duty to assure priests and people that an innocent game of chance doing an injustice to no one is not morally wrong in itself." Pointing out that there was gambling that was sinful and criminal and that all Catholics were bound in conscience to avoid it, he argued that no reasonable person could possibly misconstrue an innocent game of amusement "in which there happens to be an element of chance" with gambling. Bishop James Hartley of Columbus commended McNicholas on his "good judgment and common sense" in his defense of bingo. In the face of possible legislation, parishes that held bingo games helped bear the expenses incurred in the legal battle for the right of the people to continue to play them. Bingo games have continued in the archdiocese to the present.[25]

Though it encouraged various parish programs and activities, the local church—in keeping with the teachings of the church—affirmed the sanctity of the family and the home. When in December 1930 the *Cincinnati Enquirer* published statements that appeared to ridicule the Catholic position on the indissolubility of the institution of marriage, McNicholas reacted. In an official letter to his clergy, published in the *Catholic Telegraph,* McNicholas criticized the article and its publication. Though he acknowledged that the views expressed were not necessarily those of the editor, in his judgment that fact could not "excuse a reputable paper for giving space in its columns to a most vicious attack upon what Catholics accept as belonging to the very substance of their religion." McNicholas further argued that the article could not be justified on the plea of liberty of the press. "Would the business interests of this community and the property owners of our city tolerate the publication of . . . a series of articles . . . advocating the abolition of the rights of private property . . . ? Would they," he continued, "allow papers printing such articles to come into their homes?"[26]

Throughout their years of leadership McNicholas and Alter contended that the degradation of the home and the family in the United States threatened the very existence of society. In an address at the National Convention of Catholic Women at Fort Wayne in 1935, McNicholas stressed the importance of family life. "The measure of the strength of any country," he said, "is the strength of its homes." Local church leaders maintained that divorce, birth control, and abortion threatened the unity and stability of marriage and social life. Many Catholics in the archdiocese participated in the Christian Family Movement (CFM), a group for men that started in Chicago, South Bend, and New York in the early 1940s and was transformed into an organization that included women four years later. Condemning in the 1950s the increasing social acceptance of divorce, CFM argued that broken homes and multiple parents were fertile sources of juvenile delinquency. Although Alter generally applauded the work of diagnostic clinics and social workers, they failed, he suggested, to come to grips with the underlying causes. He always believed that the chief cause for juvenile delinquency was found in the home. "To prescribe remedies is good," he wrote, "but to remove the cause of evil is better."[27]

During this period lay Catholics also protested against the Planned Parenthood Associations or maternal health societies and clinics that promoted artificial birth control or abortion. Throughout the 1930s and 1940s the archdiocese also lobbied in Columbus against sterilization bills. "The basic trouble with the confused world of our day," McNicholas wrote to his clergy on January 11, 1949, "is the ever-increasing determination to reject fixed principles of morality in every sphere of human activity." When in the late 1950s the Planned Parenthood Association and other groups accelerated their campaign for artificial birth control, Alter joined U.S. Catholic bishops in the fall of 1959 in issuing a statement in opposition to it. When six years later the Ohio Legislature held hearings on a bill to liberalize the state's abortion law, Alter spoke out against it. "At a time when oppressed minorities in the United States are finding the courage and the resources to protest their lot," Alter wrote in 1965, "the most helpless minority of all is facing more serious threats than ever. The members of this group are the thousands of unborn children who each year are killed before they can draw a single breath." The archbishop supported the efforts of local Catholic leaders in their antiabortion campaign. "I send you my blessing," he wrote in 1967, "with the hope that you will continue to do good work for the higher moral education of our young people as well as for their parents." The following year Alter endorsed Pope Paul's encyclical on birth control. Like most of his episcopal colleagues he issued a pastoral letter reaffirming the church's traditional teaching that there was a birth control, namely conjugal abstinence, that was virtuous, and there was a birth control that was sinful.[28]

In the 1930s and 1940s, young men and women through the Catholic Students' Mission Crusade (CSMC), a national federation of mission societies founded in 1918 to acquaint Catholic students with the work of the Missionary Church in the United States and in foreign countries, also became engaged in missionary work. The CSMC, which made annual contributions to the Pontifical Society for the Propagation of the Faith, grew throughout McNicholas's tenure. Cincinnati became the national center for the Crusade. On May 29, 1927, fifty thousand adults and students participated in the first annual rally and Mass of the CSMC at Corcoran Field, the athletic stadium of St. Xavier College. McNicholas, as national president of CSMC, which at its peak claimed approximately one million student members, often raised students' consciousness to national issues. After fifty-two years of stimulating thousands of vocations to the priesthood, the religious life, and special service to the church, in the fall of 1970 the CSMC went out of existence.[29]

Like his predecessor Alter continually emphasized the importance of the laity of the church. He felt it was impossible for a bishop to do all that was required to meet the problems confronting society without help from the lay people. In his first sermon in Cincinnati Alter acknowledged "that no prelate of the Church has ever stood alone when the cause of religion has made progress. He is merely the sentinel on the mountain-top—the captain who devises the strategy or organizes their advance. The unsung heroes of the army of the Church," he said, "are the zealous priests, the devoted religious, and the faithful members of the laity. Without their devoted efforts and unselfish sacrifices, the Church would be poor [or inadequate] indeed."[30]

A year after his ordination as auxiliary bishop to Alter in 1958, Paul F. Leibold delivered the same message at the first convention of the Dayton Deanery Council of Catholic Men. He argued that every Catholic had a moral obligation to take part in Catholic Action. "Individual action by itself," he said, "cannot reform the social habits of men in the world. Organized united action is necessary." Leibold, who eleven years later would succeed Alter as archbishop of Cincinnati, made it clear that this united effort was to begin at the grassroots level with the individual parishioner. Though he praised Catholics for their generosity with money, he felt they should also be motivated to attend a parish meeting one evening a month. Whereas at the beginning of the twentieth century a parish was not considered active unless a different society met every night of the week, the parish itself now became the center of the organized lay apostolate. The plan of the archdiocesan councils was essentially a parish plan of action so that a deanery council of Catholic men "is totally ineffective as the Bishop's arm of Catholic Action," Leibold wrote, "unless it is rooted in the parish unit."[31]

Though parish missions were popular during McNicholas's and Alter's administrations, another pastoral technique, the retreat, was also developed in the archdiocese in these years. Developed in the nineteenth century and designed, like the eucharistic movement, to revitalize the religious fervor of the laity, the national retreat movement, an idea that originated among the laity in New York in 1911, was another significant religious revival in the first half of the twentieth century. Promoted by Piux XI in his encyclical *Mens Nostra,* the retreat movement was defined as the "soul of Catholic Action." On December 7, 1926, McNicholas initiated the laymen's retreat movement. He was hopeful that the weekend retreats would "do an immeasurable amount of good in making all our laymen Catholic-minded and Catholic-spirited," he wrote to William Albers, the first president of the retreat movement in Cincinnati. McNicholas thought that the lay retreats, rooted in the spiritual exercises of St. Ignatius Loyola, would contribute to each retreatant's "own personal sanctification" as well as get the men interested in the affairs of the diocese. Every group of laymen that he spoke to "seemed uninterested in diocesan matters," he wrote to Archbishop Austin Dowling of St. Paul in 1926, "but wholly taken up with the affairs of the

Jesuits." Jesuit retreat ministry had begun in the archdiocese a few years earlier. Believing that building lay support "was never more urgent," McNicholas was convinced that the diocesan retreats would help "intensify" the
interest of laymen in local parish work and deflect their interest away from
the Jesuits. "Every bishop realizes," he wrote, "what a force for good he
would have in his diocese if a group of staunch laymen, Catholic in every sentiment, earnestly strove to further his plans for the extension and preservation of the Church." The first diocesan retreat was held at Crusade Castle in
Cincinnati on January 21 to 23, 1927. There were five retreats that first year
and McNicholas preached them all. From that point on the retreats constantly gained in popularity. By the 1930s attendance ranged from 225 to 250
retreatants annually. Though the Jesuits were the main promoters of the
retreat movement in the country, the Passionists, Franciscans, and the priests
of the Society of Mary also conducted retreats for men.[32]

In the 1950s Alter regarded the retreat movement among the laity as
"[o]ne of the most significant religious developments in modern times." Half
a century earlier it would have been regarded as some sort of "devotional
vagary," he wrote, for lay people to retire from the activities of the world and
seek seclusion for a number of days in order to meditate on the spiritual
truths of faith. Like his predecessor, Alter believed the retreats benefited the
retreatant as well as the whole church. "It is," he thought, "like leaven in a
parish. It gives vitality and purpose where before there was spiritual inertia."
When in 1955 the Society of Mary established a men's retreat house at Mount
St. John's in Dayton and the Jesuits a new retreat house in Milford, Ohio, it
brought to eight the total number of retreat houses in the Cincinnati archdiocese. In January 1950, at the request of McNicholas, a community of sisters of the Society of Mary Reparatrix from New York established a convent
in Clifton. They promoted retreats and days of recollection for women. By
the end of Alter's term there were four major retreat houses for women in
the archdiocese, namely the Convent of Mary Reparatrix and Friarhurst at
Cincinnati, Dominican Retreat House at Dayton, and Maria Stein Retreat
House at Maria Stein. The close cooperation between laity, religious orders,
priests, and ordinaries helped foster the growth of the retreat movement,
locally as well as nationally, and reflected a growing stability and maturity in
the Catholic community.[33]

During their administrations McNicholas and Alter also helped promote
the religious education of the laity by supporting the work of the *Catholic
Telegraph*. A few months into his term, McNicholas asked the clergy to help
increase the number of subscribers. "It is our obvious duty," he wrote, "to
cultivate . . . a taste for the reading of Catholic newspapers." In his May
1929 address at the Convention of the Catholic Press Association, McNi-

cholas also pointed out that to make the Catholic people an interested body of readers, the strongest hope lay, he thought, in the youth. "We must cultivate in them," he said, "a taste for everything that is worthwhile in our Catholic papers and periodicals."[34]

In the summer of 1937 arrangements were made for the archdiocese to take over the *Catholic Telegraph*. Dr. Thomas Hart, who had published the paper for nearly forty years and had made many personal sacrifices, turned the paper over as a gift to the archdiocese. During Hart's tenure, the paper had proven to be a conservative organ, generally supporting the ordinaries on their political, economic, and theological views. Praising his dedication and great abilities, McNicholas appointed Hart editor emeritus. To the time of Hart's death in 1947, the archdiocese "carried him on a little pension," McNicholas wrote, "for he had nothing on which to live." The paper now came under direct control of the archbishop and its direction was again committed to diocesan priests. McNicholas thought "the interest of religion" demanded that "the priesthood of the Diocese take up the Apostolate of the Press." The work of printing it was transferred to the Register publishing house in Denver, Colorado. The paper, under the editorship of Father Edward A. Freking, was now called *The Catholic Telegraph-Register*. The first issue appeared on September 16, 1937.[35]

In January 1967 the diocesan paper ended its nearly thirty-year tie with the Register. For more than a decade the Executive Board of the *Catholic Telegraph* had been considering severance and giving the paper the independence it had lacked. "Primary reasons that move us to a local operation," Monsignor Lawrence C. Walter, business manager, said, "are problems of distance and control that have been with us for some years." The *Catholic Telegraph* had experienced a number of delayed deliveries brought on by accident of inclement weather between Colorado and Ohio. Moreover, the Executive Board was displeased with the increasing errors with news and advertising copy. Though similar errors could be made in Cincinnati, the chances seemed smaller. Throughout his administration Alter and his staff also explored ways to increase circulation of the *Catholic Telegraph*. "[I]t is my conviction that our Catholic paper," he wrote to the clergy, "belongs in every home in our jurisdiction." He welcomed the initiative taken by some pastors who placed the diocesan paper in every home in their parish.[36]

LEGION OF DECENCY

In the early 1930s some of the energies of archdiocesan officials were directed toward implementing papal teachings on social issues. McNicholas took an aggressive stance on morally suspect motion pictures and helped launch a national crusade to clean up the cinema. Viewing themselves as part of the moral conscience of the nation, American bishops and priests not only condemned birth control and abortion but also indecency and immorality in the entertainment industry. As the majority of American Catholics became more and more part of mainstream America, the archdiocese, part of the official church, increasingly presented itself as the true conservator of American moral values. Building upon the tradition of Archbishops Elder and Moeller, McNicholas warned people, especially parents, to be aware of the dangers of film. His campaign led quickly to the formation of the Catholic Legion of Decency, a national organization aimed to raise the standards of public entertainment.

Part of the impetus for this crusade was supplied by remarks of the newly appointed apostolic delegate to the United States, Archbishop Amleto Giovanni Cicognani, to the National Conference of Catholic Charities held in New York in October 1933. He called for a movement to counteract the evil influence of "salacious cinema." McNicholas interpreted Cicognani's words as a "clarion call" to concerted action. The following month Bishop John Cantwell of Los Angeles and San Diego, whose diocese included Hollywood, urged his colleagues at the annual bishops' meeting to start a crusade. The Administrative Board of the NCWC formed the Episcopal Committee on Motion Pictures (ECMP), with McNicholas at its head, to help improve the tone of the movies. Bishops Cantwell, John Noll of Fort Wayne, and Hugh Boyle of Pittsburgh joined McNicholas on the committee. Together they helped coordinate the Legion of Decency.[37]

In March 1934 the archdiocese of Cincinnati launched its first Legion of Decency pledge campaign. Catholics were urged to stay away from all movies that offended "decency and Christian morality." McNicholas drew up a written pledge that was printed in duplicate and distributed in the parishes with one copy to be returned to the chancery. The signer kept the original as a reminder of his or her obligation. The following month the ECMP, at its first official meeting in Washington, D.C., approved of its distribution nationwide. Legion members protested against those producers and actors who allegedly promoted the belief that marriage, the purity of women, and the sanctity of the home were "out-moded [*sic*] sentimentalities." Perceiving certain movies as corrupting society, McNicholas unhesitatingly undertook the duty of urging all church members to sign the pledge and send it to local theatres. A number of parishes formed committees to ascertain and make known the character of movies in their respective areas. As head of the Legion of Decency, McNicholas also threatened a boycott of Hollywood in order to safeguard the moral standards of society. The archbishop's language was strong, blunt, and uncompromising, reminding

Catholics that such aggressive action was only taken after years of false hope that Hollywood would correct itself on its own.[38]

Shortly after the first ECMP meeting, Martin Quigley of *The Motion Picture Herald* from New York, a Catholic who worked for the motion picture industry, informed McNicholas that any effort to curb the production of objectionable movies must include New York to be effective. Most movies were distributed through New York rather than Hollywood. By June producers themselves, concerned that a major grassroots campaign was under way, were contacting various bishops asking to participate in the upcoming ECMP meeting in Cincinnati on June 20 and 21, 1934. The national character of the Legion of Decency movement was having an immediate impact at the box office as revenues declined. The meeting in Cincinnati proved to be pivotal. Two representatives of the movie industry met with the four bishops on the porch of McNicholas's residence in Norwood and offered the producers' plan for self-regulation of the moral content of the movies.[39]

Though McNicholas and his colleagues were hopeful that this new plan of self-regulation would work, they decided not to leave matters entirely in the hands of the movie industry. In the August issue of *Ecclesiastical Review,* McNicholas continued to stress the need for aggressive campaigning to arouse the public to make their ire felt publicly. Because Hollywood had previously broken its promises, the ECMP felt it was important to sustain public interest in the cause. In addition to editorials and articles in diocesan newspapers there were addresses on local radio stations. McNicholas also directed Auxiliary Bishop Bernard Sheil of Chicago to arrange with NBC a hookup on national radio for four allotments of time for the Legion of Decency. On September 21, McNicholas gave one of the radio addresses. He emphasized the church as "the relentless foe" of those who corrupt morality and innocence, especially that of children.[40]

The Legion of Decency took off quickly. It had a branch in every diocese. Though the response in the archdiocese of Cincinnati may not have been all that McNicholas had hoped for, it was nevertheless substantial. Of the 84,150 pledges sent out to city parishes in the spring of 1934, 23,408 were returned; of the 113,300 to parishes outside Cincinnati, 26,083 were returned. It is estimated that by the fall of 1934 more than seven million pledges were received nationally, and there was "activity," McNicholas wrote to Cardinal Patrick Hayes of New York, "in 80 or more dioceses." Members took the pledge each year during a Sunday liturgy. For some Catholics the pledge became morally binding in conscience. The Legion of Decency, furthermore, gained support from other faiths. "The fact that all groups, Protestants, Catholics and especially the parents of children, have entered into a crusade for a clean screen," McNicholas said approvingly, "is proof that the rank and file of

Americans stand for decency." Many rabbis also approved of the work of the Legion of Decency. Though the bishops were gratified by and accepted this support, they chose to retain their independence rather than collaborate with non-Catholic groups on the matter.[41]

By the summer of 1935 the results of the agreement with the movie producers proved encouraging. Only three or four movies during the past year had been condemned. Notwithstanding the marked improvement, the bishops continued to call for constant vigilance. Denying the implication of censorship made by some critics, McNicholas repeatedly argued that the Legion of Decency was not a censoring organization. He pointed out that the Legion was only interested in monitoring the morality of films after they had been made. The success of the campaign, he felt, stemmed not from reliance on legislative restriction or censorship but by making the movie industry realize its responsibility to produce wholesome films. From McNicholas's perspective, movies presented or implied "a moral thesis," and it was his duty as a religious leader to protest immoral or corrupt theses presented in movies. As a consequence of the Legion's pressure on the film industry, filmmakers changed dialogue, cut scenes, and there were topics and scenes that Hollywood never filmed in order to avoid problems with the Catholic Church.[42]

McNicholas's action against Hollywood stemmed largely from his concern over the morality of children and the powerful effect movies had on them. What the American bishops found particularly objectionable was the way that many movies tended to glamorize sin and crime. Because McNicholas feared movies would influence people to accept more immorality in life, he insisted that a loss of morality in one area of life meant a loss of morality as a whole. On matters of morality McNicholas was unbending. He was never reluctant in taking a resolute moral stance against immorality. "He is as uncompromising in his condemnation of what he considers the pagan tendency of modern movies," an interviewer wrote in 1934, "as he is when denouncing divorce, birth control, or unscrupulous business ethics."[43]

McNicholas always stressed that public opinion was the most effective means of combating immorality in movies. In the fall of 1936 the ECMP published an eight-page guidebook on "How to Judge the Morality of Motion Pictures." Distributed to dioceses all over the country, it provided a practical guide for Legion of Decency use in discerning the quality of the moral content of movies. Though McNicholas was eventually relieved of the burdens of the chairmanship of ECMP in 1939, throughout the remainder of his term he remained vigilant on the subject. In the late 1940s he continued to urge the faithful to show their power by staying away from all motion pictures condemned by the Legion of Decency. Warnings about the immoral nature of films were found in the *Catholic Telegraph* each week, a practice that has continued to the present. From the time of its establishment in 1934 to the early 1950s, the Legion had been remarkably successful in achieving its goals, as only a few films produced by major Hollywood studios had been condemned. In the mid-1950s, however, during Alter's tenure, there were efforts made to renew the Legion of Decency pledge. In 1955 the Legion had seen the largest percentage of morally objectionable films in two decades. Though the Cincinnati Chancery Office directed that the Legion of Decency program be reactivated in every parish of the archdiocese and, in 1964, prepared a new pledge, the movement did not get the popular support nor attain the results of earlier years.[44]

In the fall of 1953 parish units of the Cincinnati Archdiocesan Council of Catholic Men (ACCM) also promoted good reading. Two years later the Archdiocesan Council of Catholic Women at its third annual convention in Dayton pledged full cooperation with the ACCM in the formation of a decent literature committee in each parish. By 1960 the group, headed by Charles H. Keating, Jr., a local Catholic attorney, emerged as a nonsectarian national organization with its headquarters in Cincinnati. In the spring of that year four hundred delegates from all parts of the country participated in the two-day National Conference of Citizens for Decent Literature in Cincinnati. Addressing an audience of six hundred persons at the Netherland Hilton Hotel, Archbishop Alter called pornography "a serious moral problem" that attacked "the home, the family, and . . . the well-being of the entire community."[45]

HOME MISSIONS AND RURAL LIFE

Within a year of McNicholas's installation in 1925 the archdiocese hosted the fourth National Catholic Rural Life Conference. As the main speaker, McNicholas expressed concern that there were too few Catholic rural parishes and schools. Since his days as bishop of Duluth, McNicholas had come to believe that the American church's "greatest problems" were in the "rural parishes." It was at the first Catholic Rural Life Conference in St. Louis in 1923 that McNicholas first proposed the establishment of a society of diocesan priests and women religious dedicated to the rural missions. Like many political and social reformers during the economic depression of the 1930s, the Cincinnati ordinary attempted to arouse bishops, priests, religious, and lay people to America's rural problems.[46]

With the assistance of Father Peter J. O'Callaghan, head of the Catholic Home Mission Society of America, McNicholas in the 1930s began making plans to establish a foundation in the archdiocese. By 1937 he secured the services of Father Howard Bishop from the Baltimore archdiocese to lay the groundwork for the establishment of the Catholic Home Missioners of America. Bishop had been a visionary and activist in rural ministry since 1920 and had started a community for that purpose. Because Bishop was not allowed to establish his home mission society in Baltimore, McNicholas invited him to come to Cincinnati. Bishop referred to his generous host "as the soul of kindness" who had "deep, constructive interest in my plans." The Society, whose purpose was to seek converts and to serve the rural areas that were without priests or were very much undermanned as far as priestly ministration and the teaching of religion were concerned, was formally established on property in Glendale in the summer of 1939. It seemed appropriate that it would start in the archdiocese of Cincinnati. It was to Kentucky and Ohio that the first Catholic pioneers came to settle and began to spread the Catholic faith westward. A philanthropic family in Dayton gave Howard Bishop a trailer for mission work. Within ten years of its founding the Home Missioners of America, named Glenmary Missioners by McNicholas, consisted of nineteen priests and twenty-two seminarians who dedicated their labors to poor mission localities in six dioceses. By the early 1940s some Glenmary Sisters approached Howard Bishop with their offer to render social service in caring for the needs of the rural areas. They became catechists in the mission field and teachers in the mission schools.[47]

Even though by 1944 the archdiocese had built about sixteen rural chapels, McNicholas saw the need "for a hundred chapels" to help seek converts and lay the foundations of religion. There were five counties in the archdiocese in which there were no Catholic schools. A survey revealed that in Adams County alone, which had a population of more than twenty thousand, there were approximately fifteen persons who were Catholic. "The hatred of everything Catholic in this county," McNicholas wrote to the apostolic delegate in December 1945, "is almost incredible." When the Glenmary Missioners first began their endeavors there, a man shot at one of the priests.[48]

In addition to the work of the Home Missioners of America, McNicholas praised the accomplishments of the Workers of the Grail, an important lay woman movement for rural reform. Founded by a Dutch Jesuit in 1921, the Grail came to the United States in 1940. The first center was in a Chicago suburb. Not able to remain profitably in the archdiocese of Chicago, Lydwine van Kersbergen, founder of the Grail "novitiate" in the United States and a spokesperson for the group, approached McNicholas as a likely patron. In January 1944 McNicholas, who was very much interested in the work of the Grail, invited the movement to establish its national center in his diocese. That spring, with considerable financial assistance from the Cincinnati ordinary, it moved to a 183-acre farm in Loveland, Ohio, about thirty miles northeast of downtown Cincinnati, and established a school to train Catholic young women for their apostolic work in the church. McNicholas called the new headquarters "Grailville." The Grail was devoted to attracting women to the land. "We can and we must through the Workers of the Grail," McNicholas wrote, "convince our young American women that it is natural and wholesome, noble and supernatural, to live on the land where we can have the highest expression of Christian living and of happy, blessed homes." In the late 1940s McNicholas helped dedicate a new Center of Womanly Arts at Grailville as well as establish an agricultural school in Mercer County to help prepare individuals for rural leadership. McNicholas's commitment to rural reform was unwavering. He had "neither peer nor rival when it comes to charity," Bishop William T. Mulloy of Covington and president of the National Rural Life Conference wrote. "I have never met a man more charitable."[49]

A good example of the growth of the church in the rural areas was at Millville in Butler County. In 1940 Millville was a village of approximately three hundred residents, and three Protestant churches served the overwhelmingly Protestant population. In spite of the non-Catholic atmosphere of the village, some of the Catholics felt that there were enough Catholic families for a parish. They took a census of the area and discovered forty Catholic families. With the aid of a priest in a neighboring town, they asked McNicholas to consider the establishment of a parish. McNicholas granted their request and appointed Father Joseph V. Urbain, a teacher at St. Gregory Seminary, to organize the Queen of Peace parish. Released from his teaching duties, Urbain took up residence at Mercy Hospital in Hamilton. As soon as the needs of a chapel were made known, people began donating equipment and supplies. One woman farmer from a neighboring parish sold enough eggs to buy a chalice and an organ. In a short time the parishioners also built Urbain a home adjoining the chapel and parish hall. To encourage Catholics to find the social stability and economic independence that came with home ownership in a rural community, the Queen of Peace parish laid out a 140-acre tract of land near the church in acre and half-acre plots. Parishioners then developed the plots into small farms. McNicholas hoped that these lots would entice more Catholic families to move to the land. By midcentury Millville had a Catholic church, eighty families in the parish, and 105 children enrolled in the parish school, which had been opened in the fall of 1946. "We cannot urge Catholic families to found homes in the country," McNicholas wrote, "if their children are to be deprived of a Catholic education." Two Sisters of the Precious Blood were engaged as teachers. The children as well as the adults took part in the parish's work program. Crews of school children were appointed each evening to clean up the classrooms under the direction of the sisters.[50]

Activities at the Queen of Peace parish were designed to strengthen parish solidarity. One of the most colorful of these activities was the observance of the Rogation days, commonly prescribed in Western Christendom as days of prayer and fasting to implore God's blessing on farm crops. These days were celebrated at the farm of a different member of the Queen of Peace parish every year. On Rural Life Sunday, observed on the Feast of Christ the King, the children marched in a procession before the Mass and the pastor blessed symbols of the harvest. The church was decorated with rural symbols, emphasizing the relation of rural life to the liturgical life of the church. Frequently, a social program that featured a covered-dish dinner and folk dancing in the parish hall followed Mass. It was often mentioned that one of the admirable qualities of the rural parish was the spirit of cooperation usually found there. When a fire razed the home of a parishioner of St. Bernadette's parish at Amelia in November 1950, the parish responded with contributions for the fire victims. "The people don't regard this as something extraordinary or heroic," Father Bernard Piening, pastor of St. Bernadette, said. "To them it's just the decent, neighborly, Christian thing to do."[51]

In early 1952 the archdiocese, with Alter's approval, helped organize the Catholic Rural Youth Organization (CRYO). It was designed to provide for Catholic rural youth opportunities for religious, cultural, and social activities similar to those offered through the Catholic Youth Organization. Father Urbain of Queen of Peace parish was named director. CRYO had existed in limited form in the archdiocese under Urbain's direction since the late 1940s but had been localized to half a dozen rural parishes in the southern part of the archdiocese. In the 1950s the archdiocese also established a Rural Life Conference for priests. It provided the clergy in rural areas with a means of discussing their common problems and fostering greater understanding of the problems of rural people. The Conference paid special attention to the liturgical movement, the development of credit unions, and the promotion of health programs.[52]

DIOCESAN CHANGES

During the McNicholas and Alter years seventy-four new parishes were formed in the archdiocese, bringing the number of parishes to 262. Within two years of McNicholas's installation, five new parishes were opened in Cincinnati alone. One of the parishes, St. Thomas's in Avondale, brought the Dominican Fathers in 1927 back into the archdiocese from which they had been absent since Bishop Fenwick's time. That same year the white-robed friars took charge of St. Gertrude's, founded four years earlier, in Madeira. By 1943 they also oversaw St. Andrew parish in Avondale. Besides the formation of new parishes, the archdiocese in 1947 opened the 240-acre Gate of Heaven cemetery in Cincinnati.[53]

When McNicholas laid the cornerstone of St. Monica Church on West McMillan Street in Cincinnati on August 22, 1926, he did not know the special role the church would eventually play in the history of the archdiocese. At the time he expressed sorrow at the passing of some inner-city churches due to business growth and people moving to the suburbs. "A great change is coming over our city so far as many of our Catholic churches are concerned," he wrote in 1926. "Not a few of our old parishes, with their splendid temples, have, in the natural growth of the city, lost their people and are no longer the great centers of religious activity they once were. It is not, indeed, that the membership of the church has decreased," he explained, "but rather that the faithful have been driven by the encroachments of business to less congested portions of Cincinnati." Largely because of these changes, on Sunday, September 18, 1938, St. Monica Church replaced St. Peter in Chains Cathedral as the cathedral church. St. Peter in Chains was reduced to the status of a parish church.[54]

Among the sixteen churches that closed during this period were three religious landmarks in Cincinnati. Once-thriving parishes in the inner city now found themselves with smaller and poorer congregations. In 1958 Holy Trinity parish in the west end, the second oldest parish in Cincinnati, was discontinued. Five years later the church was torn down. In 1962 St. Joseph Church on Lincoln Park Drive and Linn Street was taken down to permit the widening of Linn Street by the city. St. Edward Church, three blocks away, served St. Joseph parishioners until a new church was completed in 1965. In 1963 St. Anthony Church was the third church of the old west end in ten years to be torn down. German parishes had built all three churches a century earlier.[55]

During this period of overall growth in the archdiocese, church officials reopened St. Gregory Seminary in Mount Washington. Shortly after McNicholas came to Cincinnati, he decided to continue the work of his predecessor in arranging to have the preparatory seminary reopened in order to help improve priestly vocations in the diocese. In September 1928 the preparatory seminary became a unit of the newly incorporated Athenaeum of Ohio. Graduates of the college program could now be awarded the bachelor of arts degree. Realizing the need of enlarged accommodations for the work of the seminary, the archdiocese secured approximately twenty-eight additional acres of land, immediately adjoining the seminary property. Constructed of stone in a Lombard style of architecture, the new building, erected at a cost of $1,200,000, contained classrooms, laboratories, student dormitories, and apartments for some members of the faculty. Writing to William Albers, who proved to be the biggest lay benefactor of the seminary since its conception almost a century earlier, McNicholas pointed out that the preparatory seminary had been a "great burden" to him. Not merely because he held "every string in [his] hand during its construction," he wrote, "but chiefly because of my grave anxiety lest I might be imposing too great a tax upon the people. This has worried me more than any one knows." The new St. Gregory Seminary was dedicated on October 6, 1929, the centennial year of the seminary. Approximately ten thousand priests, religious, and lay people from all parts of the archdiocese attended the ceremony.[56]

At the time approximately five hundred students were enrolled at the Mount St. Mary's of the West and St. Gregory Seminaries, with 230 of them, representing thirteen dioceses, at Mount St. Mary's in Norwood. In the first fifteen years of McNicholas's term, approximately eight hundred students entered St. Gregory's. One hundred and fifty of these were ordained. During the Depression years the enrollment slowly declined to 222 students in 1941 from a high of 260 a decade earlier. During the war years enrollment declined to slightly under 200. After the war the trend was reversed and by midcentury the enrollment had grown to more than 300 students.[57]

Seminary life in the pre–Vatican II church was a matter of total involvement and total commitment on the part of the seminarians. Both Mount St. Mary's of the West and St. Gregory Seminaries were committed to tight clerical education and socialization. The young men were separated from the laity and general population. Wanting his priests to be trained well in scholasticism, McNicholas sent a record number to Thomistic centers in Europe. At the local seminary he helped establish a specialized course in the *Summa Theologica,* wanting his priests to become highly skilled in the *Summa* itself. He was "convinced," he wrote to Archbishop Edward Mooney of Detroit, "there is no training superior to this in developing an analytical mind."[58]

Within months of his installation in 1950, Alter launched a project to renovate and enlarge the historic St. Peter in Chains Church as well as restore it to its cathedral status. At the time the former cathedral was in a state of neglect. Alter wished to "return home," he said. In accordance with the Cincinnati Metropolitan Master Plan of 1948, urban renewal now ensured that the old cathedral neighborhood would be restored. Local Catholics in 1952 received with enthusiasm and approval his announcement. In his pastoral letter to the clergy and the faithful, Alter also announced a campaign for funds to resume the building operations at St. Gregory Seminary. "In justice to our need for more priests and in justice to the students themselves," he said, "we must provide more ample facilities for their care and ecclesiastical training." Though Alter may have thought as had McNicholas that a bishop had "no more disagreeable duty than that of constantly asking for funds to sustain the many works of religion and charity," he strongly promoted both projects. On August 31, 1952, posters and cards were distributed in the 235 parish churches of the archdiocese in the month-long Cathedral-Seminary drive. From 1955 to 1963 St. Gregory's was expanded at a cost in excess of $5 million.[59]

The renovation of St. Peter in Chains Cathedral was completed in 1957 at a cost of $5 million. The parishes of the archdiocese contributed a proportionate share of the cost. According to Alter, the canonical reestablishment of the stately, Greek Revival church was "an event of major significance in the history and religious life of the archdiocese." Three years later on Alter's golden anniversary as a priest, Cardinal Richard Cushing of Boston complimented the archbishop on his perseverance to restore the historic cathedral church. "It is rather easy for a bishop of the present day to be persuaded," he said, "that a cathedral is a medieval luxury, and that the greatest need of the church is for schools and centers of social action." In the judgment of the leading authority on Greek Revival architecture, Talbot Hamlin, the cathedral with its great square tower, surrounded on three sides by a Corinthian colonnade of twelve columns, was "the handsomest and most monumental of Greek Revival churches."[60]

Throughout his tenure Archbishop Alter also expressed concern over the growing shortage of religious and priests. In the fall of 1959 he focused on the clergy, pointing out that there was a "threatening shortage of priests for the immediate future." At the time there were forty-two priests of the archdiocese who were well over seventy years of age. Because past experience indicated that the number of deaths among priests under seventy averaged four to five each year, it was anticipated that the next ten years would require a replacement of ninety-two priests to maintain the existing number. Since 1950 there had been an increase in the Catholic population of approximately 150,000. Thus, by looking ahead ten years, it was estimated that the archdiocese would need a minimum of one hundred newly ordained priests for replacement alone; "but to meet expanding growth," Alter wrote, "the number should be nearer 150 priests, or a rate of 15 ordained each year." Unless something was done to increase the number of vocations, he anticipated that the enrollment of seminarians in the ecclesiastical college and major seminary would provide little more than one hundred priests over the next ten years.[61]

Because of the increasing Catholic population there was also need for more religious sisters and brothers. In the 1950s the Vocations office sponsored Vocation Day Programs both in Cincinnati and Dayton, making it possible for the young people to talk to representatives of the various religious groups. During the 1951 school year alone, the office visited 208 schools and gave 408 talks on religious vocations. In 1962 Alter asked Father John P. Boyle, then the Vocation Director, that something be done about the vocation problem for the religious communities of sisters. In turn, Boyle asked three sisters to draw up a plan, which was eventually sent to each of the major superiors of the thirty-three communities in the archdiocese, requesting them to send two representatives to a meeting in the spring. Out of this meeting grew the Archdiocesan Vocation Endeavor (AVE), a cooperative enterprise of the religious communities of women in the Cincinnati archdiocese. Through this organization, sisters encouraged religious vocations and enhanced their communities' understanding of the various ministries of the religious sisters.[62]

To address some of the changes in the local church since the 1920s, the archdiocese on December 14, 1954, sponsored its fifth synod. More than three decades had passed since the last diocesan synod was held. Though new diocesan decrees had been issued to meet emergency situations, Alter thought that the time had come for a general review and the enactment of permanent synodal statutes. Preparation for the recodification of the diocesan statutes took about three years. During this period, six commissions met regularly for several months. The regulations of the archdiocese were amended, and new legislation was proposed. Copies were distributed to all the priests of the diocese, who met in a series of regional meetings to make their suggestions.[63]

Besides changes in diocesan statutes, the archdiocese underwent territorial and administrative changes. When Detroit became an archdiocese in June 1937, with Edward A. Mooney as the first archbishop of the created see, Detroit and Grand Rapids were severed from the Province of Cincinnati. That reduced the province from eleven to nine dioceses—four in Ohio, two in Indiana, two in Kentucky, and one in Tennessee. To help streamline the administrative and ecclesiastical divisions of the archdiocese, seven new deaneries were added during McNicholas's and Alter's administrations, bringing the number to ten.[64]

In the 1940s two new dioceses were established in Ohio. The diocese of Youngstown, formed in 1943, also embraced former Cleveland territory. The diocese of Steubenville, the last of the Ohio dioceses, was formed in 1944 of thirteen counties cut from the Columbus diocese. In the fall of 1944 Pope Pius XII also transferred five counties and portions of four others that were formerly in the Cincinnati archdiocese to the Columbus diocese, thus reducing the archdiocese to its present area of nineteen counties in southwestern Ohio. At the same time the pontiff erected the new ecclesiastical Province of Indianapolis, thereby reducing the Cincinnati province to the confines of the state of Ohio. In 1946 the bishops of Ohio formed the Ohio Catholic Welfare Conference, designed in part to deal with urgent matters in Ohio and to help develop and clarify their ideas in preparation for the national conference of bishops.[65]

SOCIAL ISSUES

F rom the 1920s to the 1950s the archdiocese of Cincinnati worked more closely with secular social agencies and expanded its charitable programs, defended the poor and the rights of workers, condemned totalitarianism, and expanded its ministry among African Americans. During McNicholas's first years as archbishop it began reorganizing its charity and social service agencies. In November 1926 the Cincinnati ordinary appointed Father R. Marcellus Wagner as his vicar in the direction of charities in the archdiocese. The Bureau of Catholic Charities, established in 1916 and of which Wagner had been director, was replaced with the Catholic Charities. In Cincinnati, as in other dioceses, the various Catholic charitable institutions and organizations had developed without much centralized direction and full-time personnel. Each organization had been designed by its founders to attend to some specific area of need. In 1926 there were nine institutions that cared for dependent, neglected, and delinquent children away from their own homes. This care occupied the premier place among the charitable organizations of the archdiocese. Besides forty-two conferences of the Society of St. Vincent de Paul with two thousand active members who ministered to the poor in their own homes, there were five Catholic hospitals, three homes for the needy, three community houses, three day nurseries, and two large clubs for men and boys.[1]

The Cincinnati Bureau of Catholic Charities, one of the pioneer organizations of its kind in the country, had accomplished much in its ten-year history, especially in its work with the Society of St. Vincent de Paul. But due to the bureau's lack of authority, full-time personnel, and funds necessary to render effective service to the poor and to other Catholic organizations of the archdiocese, a change was needed to bring the central organization up to the highest standards. It had been difficult to secure trained personnel for Catholic charities. Social and charitable work on a full-time basis was a new field for the Catholic laity. Until the establishment of the bureau, archdiocesan officials had depended entirely on the religious and volunteers to carry on the works of charity. The bureau had shown that full-time workers were essential for adequate service to families in their own homes. Furthermore, Catholics had not been accustomed to spending large sums of money for the types of work in which the bureau had been interested. Most of the money had been devoted to the care of children away from their own homes. It had been assumed that the parishes through the aid of volunteer groups of men and women could be depended upon to care for the needs of the poor. Over time, however, Catholics realized that the funds of the parish conferences of the Society of St. Vincent de Paul were not entirely adequate. Studies of poor families in the community revealed that relief represented only one element in their needs. There was also a need for adequate and sustained service. "If we allow our charities to go on . . . without direction, without conferences and without analysis," McNicholas said in support of the establishment of the Catholic Charities, "we can readily see, in this day of organization, [that] we cannot make the progress we should." The new structure, moreover, gave the individual organizations and institutions sufficient freedom to sustain a progressive diocesan program. Its work fell into four main divisions: Family, Children's, Protective Care, and Recreational and Community Work.[2]

During the economic depression of the 1930s, when the archdiocese expanded its relief activity, Catholic Charities had four priests and about fifty trained lay workers. Each year Catholic Charities provided financial and other services to approximately four thousand families. By the middle of the decade the archdiocese had three institutions for dependent children. These were St. Aloysius Orphanage in Bond Hill, operated by the Sisters of Notre Dame, St. Joseph Orphanage in Cumminsville, run by the Sisters of Charity, and St. Joseph Orphan Home in Dayton, conducted by the Sisters of the Precious Blood. It also had two institutions for the care of young girls, Mount St. Mary's Training School for black girls in Price Hill and Our Lady of the Woods Training School in Carthage, both under the supervision of the Sisters of the Good Shepherd. In Cincinnati St. Joseph Infant Asylum and Maternity Home on Tennessee Avenue, under the auspices of the Sisters of Charity, cared for children under the age of four years and for unmarried mothers. Mount Alverno School for Boys in Price Hill was under the supervision of the Brothers of the Poor of St. Francis. The Catholic Big Brothers took care of an average monthly total of 151 boys and the Catholic Big Sisters gave service to about eighty-seven girls per month. In the 1960s St.

Joseph Orphanage moved to a forty-acre site on North Bend Road in Mont-fort Heights and the St. Joseph Maternity Home moved from its ninety-year-old institution to a twenty-acre site in Sharonville.[3]

During McNicholas's tenure women's religious orders expanded their social outreach in the community. By 1926 the Sisters of Charity had developed the Mount St. Joseph motherhouse and college, conducted Good Samaritan Hospital, St. Vincent Academy, St. Joseph Orphanage, St. Joseph Infant Asylum and Maternity Home, and taught in thirty-five schools of the archdiocese. In 1932 the sisters opened Good Samaritan Hospital in Dayton, made possible by a gift of four acres of land by a local physician. At the time there were nearly one thousand sisters in the religious community working in several dioceses. In the 1920s the Sisters of Charity, with McNicholas's eventual backing, had decided to affiliate with Rome, transforming the diocesan community into a papal community. Final approval of their Constitution came in 1928. This "gives us," Mother Superior Irenaea wrote, "greater prestige in the Church and strengthens our Organization."[4]

The Sisters of Notre Dame de Namur maintained their convent home on Sycamore Street, their academy on Grandin Road in Walnut Hills, Notre Dame Academy at Reading, Notre Dame Academy in Dayton, and the convent on Mound Street in Cincinnati. The sisters taught in twenty-five parish schools of the archdiocese. Another branch of the Sisters of Notre Dame, the Cleveland community, had come to the archdiocese on May 1, 1877, and had taken charge of St. Aloysius Orphanage. In 1926 they taught in five parish schools of the archdiocese. The Sisters of the Precious Blood, whose mother-house was in Dayton, had convents at Maria Stein, Cassella, and Minster. In addition to teaching in twenty parochial schools and operating St. Joseph Orphan Home in Dayton, they provided domestic service at the Fenwick Club, St. Teresa Home, and Mount St. Mary's of the West Seminary in Cincinnati. At the time there were about six hundred sisters in the community. In 1930 the sisters established Maria Joseph Home for the Aged on Salem Avenue in Dayton. A group of lay women had started the building fund with profits from street fairs and other public benefits. From 1891 to 1967 the Sisters of the Precious Blood conducted the St. Joseph Home for Children, formerly called St. Joseph Orphan Home. In 1967 the School Sisters of the Third Order of St. Francis from Pittsburgh assumed this responsibility.[5]

The community of Ursulines, which still had its motherhouse at Brown County in Ohio, was in charge of two academies, the boarding school at St. Martin and the day school for students from kindergarten through high school at Oak and Reading Road. Some of the sisters also taught in St. Vivian's grade school at Finneytown and conducted Sunday school classes at

St. Martin, Blanchester, Wilmington, and Hillsboro. The Ursulines, with headquarters in St. Ursula's convent on McMillan Street in Cincinnati, taught in four parochial schools. At the McMillan convent the sisters conducted a private day school that numbered, at midcentury, about 840 pupils of grade and high school levels.[6]

The Sisters of Mercy, who had their motherhouse and academy on Freeman Avenue in Cincinnati, conducted the Mother of Mercy Academy at Westwood, the Mount Carmel Home, and Mercy Hospital in Hamilton. During the second quarter of the twentieth century the sisters taught in twelve parochial schools. In June 1929 the pope expressed the desire for the union of all the Sisters of Mercy in the United States. A majority of the sisters consented to the amalgamation into one larger institute, constituting the largest congregation of religious women in the United States. Two months later the apostolic delegate convened the first general chapter of the united congregation in Cincinnati. The Sisters of the Poor of St. Francis conducted a total of twenty institutions in the archdiocese, including a central retreat house, homes for the incurable, tuberculosis, and hospitals, among which were St. Francis Hospital for Incurables in Cincinnati, St. Elizabeth Hospital in Dayton, and a central retreat house. Since the establishment of the first house in the United States in 1858 in Cincinnati, the congregation enjoyed a rapid growth, spreading first to the East and then to the West. In the early 1930s the congregation numbered approximately three thousand members in ninety establishments.[7]

The Little Sisters of the Poor had their convent home on Florence Avenue and the St. Peter Home on Riddle Road in Cincinnati. On average, the sisters in the two institutions took care of four hundred elderly people annually. For more than half a century two Little Sisters of the Poor usually rode a black horse-drawn wagon to make their rounds of the city on their daily mission of begging alms and food for the elderly poor in their institutions. By mid-twentieth century they made similar calls in a station wagon. The Sisters of St. Joseph maintained their convent home and a novitiate at St. Joseph Academy in Mount Washington in Cincinnati. Besides teaching in a parochial school, the sisters operated a home for young businesswomen in the community. In 1926 they built the Fontbonne on East Fifth Street, the outgrowth of the Sacred Heart Home on Broadway. The name of the home was changed to the Fontbonne in memory of Mother St. John Fontbonne, founder of the congregation of the Sisters of St. Joseph in France. The Sisters of the Third Order Regular of St. Francis, whose motherhouse was at Oldenburg, Indiana, taught in about thirty parochial schools of the archdiocese. The Sisters of the Blessed Sacrament, who taught black children, were in charge of Cincinnati's St. Ann school. The Sisters of Christian Charity conducted St. Boniface school in Piqua, and the Polish Sisters of St. Francis of St. Louis had charge of St. Adalbert school in Dayton.[8]

In the fall of 1927 a new order of women religious, the Dominican Sisters of Memphis, Tennessee, arrived in Cincinnati to take charge of the school in the new St. Thomas Aquinas parish in Avondale. Seven years later they also began teaching at St. Gertrude's in Madeira. In 1927 McNicholas also put fellow Dominican Fathers from the Province of St. Joseph in charge of the Avondale and Madeira parishes. This was clearly an effort on the part of the archbishop to give the Dominican Order some permanence in his diocese. In 1929,at the request of McNicholas, the Dominican Sisters of Adrian, Michigan, also came to Cincinnati and made themselves available for parochial visitations and parish census-taking. Though some pastors resented the idea of sisters making parochial visitations, arguing that the priests should do this work, McNicholas disagreed. He was convinced that his clergy, preoccupied with many other duties, could not or would "not do it as thoroughly as the Sisters." Other members of the order took charge of St. Teresa's home for the aged in Silverton in 1936. During the depression eight Sisters of Mercy of the Holy Cross, whose motherhouse was in Switzerland, took charge of St. John's school in Deer Park. In 1942 the Benedictine Sisters of Duluth, Minnesota, came to the archdiocese and took charge of the new school of Our Mother of Sorrows parish in Roselawn.[9]

In addition to the great contribution of the women religious in the educational enterprises and Catholic charities of the archdiocese, the laity gave generously of their time and means. Among the active organizations of Catholic women engaged in charitable work, the largest and most prominent was the Catholic Women's Association. In the fall of 1928 lay women representatives from all parts of the archdiocese organized the Cincinnati Archdiocesan Federation of Catholic Women with Mrs. R. K. LeBlond as president. The federation was the medium of uniting Catholic women and coordinating their social and charitable work. It was the organization to which all women's societies turned for guidance in Catholic Action. It involved more than 10,000 women. In McNicholas's judgment, it was the most important group of women in the archdiocese. Speaking at the National Council of Catholic Women in Cleveland in October 1928, McNicholas praised the "awakening" of Catholic women to their social responsibilities. They "have unquestionably a public duty to their respective communities," he argued, "in the moulding[sp] of public opinion." In their charitable work, American Catholic women were able to expand their role in society and exercise more influence.[10]

In March 1928 St. Joseph Mission in Dayton was opened as a residence for homeless men and women. Ten years later the building was converted into a community center for the youths and adults of the neighborhood. In April 1930 the Dominican Sisters opened the Loretto, a nondenominational home for girls, on West Fifth Street in Dayton. In 1912 Josephine Schwind, a Dayton resident who was instrumental in bringing the sisters to the area, had presented to the order two fully equipped properties on Franklin Street. Within a year of its founding, the Loretto accommodated 120 residents who were generally self-supporting and of modest means.[11]

During the early years of the depression the Sisters of the Poor of St. Francis opened a house on East Ninth Street. Besides providing care for the sick poor in their homes, they helped show mothers how to take care of many domestic affairs. A decade later the sisters also opened St. Raphael Convent at Hamilton, Ohio, for social service. Under the leadership of the Sisters of Mercy, the Mercy Braille Club was founded in 1937. It would operate until 1993. The sisters' work began by transcribing books into Braille and then opening a free Braille library, providing textbooks, and preparing blind children to receive the sacraments.[12]

Perhaps the most active Catholic charitable organization during the depression years was the Society of St. Vincent de Paul. In 1934 it had approximately 450 active members in the fifty parish conferences. The conferences met weekly and attended to the immediate needs of the poor. At midcentury U.S. church officials thought, as did Archbishop Alter, that Catholic parishes could manifest the spirit of charity in no better way than through the activities of St. Vincent de Paul Conferences. By the 1960s some parish conferences, like St. Bartholomew's in Springfield Township in Cincinnati, regularly sought donations of used clothing and furniture and conducted blood drives.[13]

At the celebration of the twentieth anniversary of the Fenwick Club in 1935, Archbishop McNicholas announced that the groundwork had been laid for a Catholic Youth Organization (CYO) for the archdiocese. Charles F. Williams, Knight Commander of St. Gregory, was its first president. The CYO council was composed of four priests and three laymen. Inspired by the accomplishments of the Catholic Youth Organization in Chicago, the new archdiocesan organization provided spiritual, intellectual, and recreational activities for Catholic youths. Also in 1935 a Boy Scout group launched the Dayton CYO. Two years later Monsignor Charles A. Ertel, first director of the Dayton CYO, established the organization on a broader basis. In 1939 the archdiocese hosted the first National Conference of the Catholic Youth Organization in the United States. Ten years later the CYO in the archdiocese served approximately 9,500 young Catholics, ranging in age from seven to twenty-six years. For several generations the CYO proved to be one of the major elements of the local church's ministry to Catholic youth. With the expansion of the work of the Catholic Charities, the archdiocese opened central branch offices in Hamilton in 1953 and in Springfield in 1957.[14]

As the local Community Chest expanded its services in the late 1920s and 1930s, greater sums of money were asked for the various charities of the Catholic Church. In 1928 the Catholic Charities received approximately $300,000 from the Community Chest; by 1940 the amount was more than $350,000. In Dayton the Community Chest provided more than $80,000 in assistance to six Catholic agencies. But as more and more Catholics became associated with the fund drives, not all the Catholic charitable institutions were beneficiaries of the Community Chest. The rules of the Little Sisters of the Poor, who conducted two homes for the destitute and aged in the archdiocese, required them to be mendicants and to independently seek support for their aged wards by daily soliciting money and merchandise. Increasing relationships with the Community Chest and other secular agencies, furthermore, helped break down "prejudice," McNicholas wrote. They helped generate "good feeling in the community" toward Catholics as well as establish financial contacts for them. By midcentury there were a few occasions when parishes gave a pulpit announcement in favor of the Community Chest and the Red Cross. Though not specifically under church auspices, these organizations worked closely with the Catholic charitable institutions.[15]

By the second quarter of the twentieth century, the archdiocese made available to Catholics all the new kinds of social agencies developed by non-Catholic civic organizations. Since the arrival of the Little Sisters of the Poor in 1862, when homes for the aged began in the archdiocese, church officials had gradually provided more resident care for the elderly. In 1943 the archdiocese purchased Orchard Springs sanitarium and its twenty-two acres on North Main Street at Shiloh Springs as the site of another home for the aged in Montgomery County. When McNicholas appealed for a group of religious sisters to take charge of the new home, the Sisters of Mercy offered to staff what became known as the Siena Home. The following year the religious community bought property from the Knights of Pythias in Springfield and established Mercycrest as a home for the aged. For more than fifty years the buildings had been used as an orphanage by the Pythians. In addition to Siena and Mercycrest, the archdiocese by midcentury had five other institutions dedicated to caring for the aged. These homes were St. Joseph's on Florence Avenue, St. Peter's on Riddle Road, St. Teresa's in Silverton, Mount Carmel's on Freeman Avenue, all in Cincinnati, and Jarla-Joseph's in Dayton. In 1962 the Carmelite Sisters for the Aged and Infirm of St. Teresa Avila Convent in Germantown, New York, opened St. Margaret Hall on Madison Road in Cincinnati for retired persons.[16]

At midcentury the Catholic hospitals in the archdiocese provided care for a total of 64,476 patients. This record number of patients was an indication of the growth and expansion that had marked the work of the various sisterhoods in the care of the sick since the founding of the first hospital in Cincinnati in 1852. In September 1942 the Sisters of Mercy opened Our Lady of Mercy Hospital in Mariemont in a building erected by Mrs. Mary Emery. Eight years later the sisters and residents of Springfield and Clark Counties provided three million and two million dollars, respectively, and built Mercy Hospital. With the opening of Mercy Hospital in Springfield in January 1950, the religious sisterhoods conducted nine hospitals in the archdiocese. There were the Good Samaritan, St. Mary's, St. Francis, and St. George hospitals in Cincinnati, Mercy Hospital in Hamilton, Our Lady of Mercy Hospital in Mariemont, Mercy Hospital in Springfield, and St. Elizabeth and Good Samaritan Hospitals in Dayton. The following year the Sisters of Mercy also operated hospitals in Coldwater and Urbana. In 1956 there was a local financial campaign to raise $17,500,000 for the eleven hospitals in Hamilton County. A substantial part of the total was designated for the five Catholic hospitals. As the Catholic hospitals became increasingly drawn into relationships with state and federal agencies and with programs of hospital care and insurance, the archdiocese in 1958 established the Office of Archdiocesan Superintendent of Hospitals to help coordinate the hospitals' operations. In 1965, for the first time in Hamilton County, it became possible for privately operated hospitals to receive building money from public funds. That year Alter urged passage of a bond issue in order to build Providence Hospital, a new St. George Hospital, and additions to Our Lady of Mercy Hospital and Bethesda Hospital. Hamilton County voters passed the $19.8 million bond issue; of that amount, Providence Hospital received $8.6 million.[17]

LABOR AND INDUSTRY

During the economic depression of the 1930s many Americans became preoccupied with national social reform programs. The participation of Catholic Church leaders, the clergy, and the laity in the burgeoning reform movement made the church less parochial, drew it closer to the American liberal tradition, and helped make Catholicism more of an American religion. Catholics' involvement in the era's progressive social programs and their full-fledged participation in World War II were signs that they were becoming more a part of the American mainstream. During this period McNicholas became a staunch defender of the poor and the rights of workers as well as an outspoken critic of the excesses of capitalism. By no means a radical, as he was a greater critic of communism and socialism than capitalism,

he believed the church was justified morally and religiously in speaking out
on capitalism and industrialism. Much of his criticism of the excesses of capitalism was derived from the church's teachings on justice, as found especially in papal social encyclicals.[18]

In his fall 1931 pastoral, read in every church throughout the archdiocese
and given wide circulation by the press, McNicholas urged his pastors and the
faithful to allow none to hunger. The economic depression was deepening
and was widely regarded as a serious depression. To McNicholas it was
unthinkable in the light of Christian principles that "in this land of plenty,"
where there were "superabundant harvests" and excess food held in storage,
the bread lines were lengthening in the cities. He argued it was the duty of
local, state, and federal authorities to attend to the needs of the poor. "Just as
in time of war the Government is justified in resorting to emergency measures to meet a crisis," he said, "so in our present circumstances civil authority
has not only the right but the duty to adopt relief measures." But he was not
hopeful in 1931 that President Herbert Hoover and the national government
would soon come to the aid of the poor. "Government officials have lost," he
wrote to Bishop Hugh Boyle of Pittsburgh, " . . . all sense of democracy and
a representative form of government, and are selfishly concerning themselves
about their own political fortunes and personal interests rather than the general welfare of the people." Issuing an appeal in 1932 for the Community
Chest, McNicholas warned that unless there was "a speedy reconstruction of
the social order" the nation would "face great social disorder."[19]

Shortly after President Franklin D. Roosevelt's inauguration and
announcement of his New Deal policy in 1933, Americans became more
hopeful and supportive of the promising new legislation. A number of
Catholic Church leaders and lay people became involved in reform programs. Calling for economic justice, McNicholas praised the new administration for having courageously begun a program to address the needs of the
masses. He spoke out forcefully on the needs of workers and urged Catholics
in the archdiocese to do whatever they could to help the poor, especially those
who wanted to work but could not find it and were deprived of their means
of livelihood. Because of his concern over the plight of the poor, McNicholas
took a strong stand against proposals for various state sales taxes on essen-
tials. Preferring to see the burden fall on the wealthy, he supported a tax on
luxuries and an income tax on those individuals best able to pay. A sales tax,
he argued, would place "an intolerable burden upon our poor Negro population, who not only in our locality but throughout the whole country during
the depression have suffered most and have complained least."[20]

McNicholas often criticized the affluent for not doing enough during
the economic crisis. "In this aristocracy of wealth, too many seem to feel

themselves set above the average of humanity. There is something in the mere possession of great wealth," he wrote, "which tends to give men an entirely false outlook on life. It warps their judgment and too often renders them incapable of realizing the value and the essential dignity of every human being, regardless of race and color." Although he acknowledged the natural inequality of men and the right to private property, he condemned "the monstrous injustice of the distribution of wealth" due to the injustice of the economic system.[21]

McNicholas consistently urged capitalists and workers to abide by moral principles. He warned of impending ruin if Christian principles and morality were not adopted by industry. There was, he argued, a "potential for revolution in the hungry masses." Believing that capitalism was "on trial before the world," he thought it could reform itself only according to Christian justice. "It if does not so reform itself," he wrote, "the end must be revolution and confiscation." His views on labor were consistent with his position on capitalism. He argued that the unions "must also realize that social justice obliges them to work for the common interests of the community and country." For McNicholas the common good was more important than the profit motive. He always maintained that both capitalists and workers were "in conscience bound to consider what is for the best interests of the majority of our citizens rather than seek advantages for their own particular group." In practical terms, he thought that industry should provide a wage that would "enable the employee to live in a manner befitting the dignity of a human being." Just as industrialists had a right to a fair return for their investments, he insisted the workers should be allowed their fair shares as well.[22]

As the depression worsened, the archdiocese focused its energies on the victims of the depression. The archbishop insisted that no appeals for money should be made at the time "except for the hungry, the homeless and the sick poor." The Catholic Charities and the St. Vincent de Paul Society alone cared for about one thousand families in the archdiocese. Though some parishioners helped take care of needy families, their resources were limited. Income in parishes by 1932 had fallen off from 30 to 60 percent and there was increasing difficulty on the part of the parishes to pay interest on loans. Because some of the parishioners in St. Louis parish at North Star were unable to pay their pew rent, the chancery lent $2,200 to help meet parish expenses. Based on a study done of high school finances, McNicholas in the fall of 1932 felt compelled to reduce the salaries of priests and lay persons at Elder and Purcell high schools. Hoping to make it possible for as many Catholics as possible to subscribe to the *Catholic Telegraph,* the diocesan paper reduced the subscription rate from $3 to $1 per year.[23]

As he assessed the social malaise of the 1930s, McNicholas became a forceful speaker on moral matters. Acknowledging that he could not discourse on specific economic issues, such as the fluctuation of the dollar, with much authority, he thought he could on moral matters. "[I]f I say anything about moral questions," he said in his first newspaper interview as archbishop, "I expect it to be understood that I am talking on a subject about which I presume to know something." He believed there was a need for a fixed moral code. Consistent with Thomas Aquinas's teachings on the moral principles by which the wealthy were obliged to share their abundance with the poor, McNicholas argued that the destitute were entitled to what they needed and that their right to live was greater than any right to possess.[24]

Holding high standards for himself as a leader, McNicholas was also a fighter. "I wish to live on amiable terms with everyone," he wrote, "but when a principle is at stake and I am convinced I am on the right side, I enjoy nothing better than a good fight." The five foot five prelate was quite pugnacious and his strong voice carried all around the archdiocese and beyond. A 1934 interviewer for the *Cincinnati Post* pointed out that "the priests and laity are well acquainted with the Archbishop's candor. His public utterances give no evidence of hedging." Local Catholics "frequently writhed," another writer wrote, "under the pungent, hard-hitting pastoral letters that flowed from his busy pen."[25]

Early in his term McNicholas vowed that the Catholic Church had a special duty to help the poor and the working classes. It was clear where his sympathies lay. He maintained that the strength of the country was not to be measured by the wealth of its corporations, "but by the number of its happy homes." Advising workers to hold fast to their unions, he assured them "that their Church will always be their spokesman; that she will never remain silent in the presence of injustice." During the depression the editor of *The Labor Advocate,* a national labor publication, referred to Cincinnati's activist archbishop as "the one voice" that was "looked up equally" by both the working people and the business community. In 1940 McNicholas made the front page of *Social Justice,* a national publication. Though in general he supported labor causes, he was concerned over the use of sit-down strikes and the influence of radicals and communists in the unions. During a sit-down strike in Cincinnati in the 1930s, McNicholas warned that strikers could undo the progress of labor unions over the years and retard efforts to get the country out of the depression.[26]

At the same time that McNicholas advocated more federal government assistance for the poor, he did not believe that the government should do everything. Throughout his administration he expressed concern over too much federal control. He lamented the multiplicity of laws and "the mania that lawmakers have for enacting them." Though he realized social legislation could be of great benefit to the working class, he warned labor "against the loss of that liberty" that belonged to individuals. "The tendency of governments today," he said in his address at the American Federation of Labor in 1939, "is towards totalitarianism. We cannot expect our country to be an exception. The democracies of the world are facing a great crisis."[27]

Building upon the work of such labor-priests as John Mackey and Peter Dietz in the archdiocese, in 1937 McNicholas appointed nineteen priests to assist and defend workers and the poor. They offered their services to all groups regardless of creed, color, or race. Eight years later he again called upon his clergy to know the conditions of the poor and to help workers see the advantages of unions. He thought that unions were the best way to help workers. In another effort to reach the urban working class, a group of diocesan priests in the summer of 1940 began the practice known as street preaching on the south side of Court Street in downtown Cincinnati. Every Friday night two priests preached on popular subjects and answered questions from the audience. Throughout the 1940s street-preaching during the summer months proved to be an effective means of reaching the urban poor, especially non-Catholics. The involvement of priests in the social and labor causes of the 1930s and 1940s was substantial and exerted considerable influence on the future of the local church in social activism.[28]

In the early years of the depression the Detroit radio priest, Charles Coughlin, was the idol of thousands of people. He convinced much of America that the Catholic Church was not the particular friend of the privileged classes. Though Coughlin's popular polemics were for some time reported favorably in the *Catholic Telegraph,* in March 1933, "The Observer," a weekly unsigned column in the diocesan paper, expressed concern over some of his anti–New Deal views. It warned its readers that he was not an official spokesman of the Catholic Church. For the next several weeks people telephoned and wrote letters chastising the diocesan paper for rebuking Coughlin. Believing the criticism was not justified, the diocesan paper reminded its readers that it had carried many news items condemning "the sins of the profiteers." When Coughlin spoke in Cincinnati in 1936, McNicholas, who had argued for some time that Coughlin was "not grounded in the fundamentals" of Catholic theology, thought he had to respond to some of his remarks. Though he espoused the right of free speech, the Cincinnati ordinary protested on "moral grounds" Coughlin's reference to the possibility of using "bullets" and suggestion that the ballot was useless.[29]

During the next several years, the American Catholic hierarchy expressed concern over Coughlin's statements. By this time the Detroit priest had turned against the New Deal, criticized President Roosevelt at every available opportunity, and had become openly anti-Semitic. As a member of the Administrative Board of the National Catholic Welfare Conference, the hapless McNicholas disapproved of Coughlin's "unguarded, . . . unmeasured and inaccurate statements." Though it was suggested to McNicholas that he bring the matter up before the church authorities in Rome, he preferred not to. He was of the opinion that if Coughlin were to be censured, "a formula must be found by which an American Bishop, or Bishops, can do it." He thought it inadvisable for Vatican officials to tell Coughlin to stop speaking. He was convinced that "a great cry" would go up against the pope meddling in American affairs. Preferring that the matter be dealt with exclusively within Coughlin's diocese, he urged Bishop Michael Gallagher of Detroit to "insist on moderation" in the radio priest's statements.[30]

During and after World War II, McNicholas continued speaking on behalf of labor. Shortly after the war he announced that arrangements had been entered into between a local radio station and the archdiocese to give a series of dialogue addresses on various public issues under the guiding caption of "Catholic Position." In the fall of 1945 the chancery selected fourteen priests to give these addresses. Following McNicholas's opening talk on November 4 on the importance of taking a Catholic position on various issues, the station broadcasted talks on the next three Sundays. But the station rejected talks on the "Rights of Labor," scheduled for December, as too controversial. The archdiocese protested. "If there is not true freedom of speech over the radio," Chancellor Clarence Issenmann wrote, "then we should realize the dangers that are in store for us." The United Automobile Workers and the Congress of Industrial Organizations also protested against the station's policy. Unable to resolve the conflict, they cancelled the radio broadcasts. The following spring the archdiocese inaugurated a new radio series of religious programs over another local station.[31]

Archbishop Alter was also very concerned with economic and social justice issues. Even though, unlike McNicholas, he pulled away from being in front of the issues, he was not shy in addressing political questions of social welfare. This was especially evident, as will be discussed later, in his involvement in civil rights issues in the 1960s. In an interview aboard a train en route to Cincinnati for his installation in 1950, he urged that the church's interest in labor-management affairs be continued. Before long he recommended "profit participation" plans as a sound approach toward resolving many employee-management differences. He also thought such plans would give workers more incentive. In 1958 the Ohio Catholic Welfare Conference, headed by Alter, opposed proposals by the business community to ban the union shop in Ohio. Heads of industries and businesses protested against the bishops' statement, forcing Alter to meet personally with a committee of seven prominent Catholic businessmen. Alter and the other Ohio ordinaries stood firm. Near the end of his term Alter, acting on behalf of the local church, also endorsed the efforts of California grape workers to win collective bargaining rights. He argued that the farm workers in the table grape growing industry were "among the forgotten Americans suffering the privation and human indignity of poverty and social injustice." The Archdiocesan Council of Catholic Women, like many of its counterparts across the country, took the lead in supporting the boycott in the archdiocese.[32]

TOTALITARIANISM AND WORLD WAR II

Between the world wars American Catholics became increasingly concerned with the rise of Russian communism and the governmental persecution of Catholics in various countries. This Catholic protest was another sign that Catholics were emerging from their earlier conclaves of ethnic separatism. By the mid-1930s McNicholas, who had great interest in international as well as national affairs, was one of the foremost members of the militant hierarchy in the United States. As Adolf Hitler gained power in Germany, Benito Mussolini consolidated his hold on Italy, and Joseph Stalin maintained his iron grip on the Soviet Union, McNicholas found it necessary to address the growth of totalitarianism and its possible effects on the United States. In the process, McNicholas, as archbishop and member of the NCWC Administrative Board, engaged the church with the larger American culture.[33]

At a talk in May 1938 before the Medievalists, primarily a group of prominent Catholic businessmen and professionals in Greater Cincinnati who met monthly, donned medieval garb, and staged a medieval-style banquet, McNicholas alluded to some of his responsibilities as head of the local church. In response to the growing voices of irreligion, atheism, and immorality in the world, he believed it was his duty to bring to his peoples' attention the truths of religion and morality. "I would be unfaithful to my trust," he said, "if I did not have the courage to give voice to these views when they are challenged." Similarly, he urged his listeners to stand for the things they believed in and to use their influence "in furthering true morality. . . . I do not ask you to be obnoxious in this," he continued, "but on the other hand, you should not sit by supinely and let the forces of evil prevail." McNicholas was indefatigable and unswerving once he had set his course. Never tiring in his defense of morality, he developed his theology around the idea of the Catholic Church's role as the central bulwark of morality.[34]

The rise of anti-Semitism on a national and international scale during the 1930s generated a response from the archdiocese. McNicholas prohibited his flock from joining or supporting any organization expressing hostility to Jews. Throughout his years of leadership he proved to be a tireless campaigner against anti-Semitism. "God forbid," he said early in his term, that "I should remain silent if the religion of any man not of my faith were attacked." As the Second World War approached and the persecution of Jews became more apparent and frequent, McNicholas declared that the persecutions "should be condemned by sane men everywhere." Besides criticizing anti-Semitism on humanitarian grounds, there was also the practical realization that if persecution were allowed to take place against the Jews, Catholics may very well be next. Many Catholics were very much aware of their own history and remembered only too well the anti-Catholic outbursts of the nineteenth and early twentieth centuries.[35]

At the same time that articles and editorials appeared in the *Catholic Telegraph* condemning anti-Semitism and the persecution of Jews, there were Cincinnati Catholics ambivalent about Jews. This attitude was reflected in the diocesan paper, especially in the early 1930s. In the spring of 1933 the *Catholic Telegraph* cautioned its readers against overreacting regarding the "alleged persecution of the Jews in Germany." Urging the faithful to be certain of the facts, the diocesan paper suggested that recent cablegrams on the persecution of the Jews by the Hitler government were "greatly exaggerated." Suggesting that Hitler was "a practical Catholic" and that his vice chancellor was an "exemplary Catholic," it concluded with the unbridled assertion "that an era of persecution of the Jews in Germany is out of the question." A few months later "The Observer" column in the diocesan paper also noted that even though there was some persecution of Jews in Germany, the Jews had "brought [it] upon themselves . . . by their exploitation of labor in sweatshops." Later that decade "The Observer" further blamed the Jews for offensive movies through their ownership of the major film studios. By the time of the Second World War, the inconsistency in the *Catholic Telegraph* stopped. From that point on it consistently condemned anti-Semitism and Hitler's persecution of Jews. It remains somewhat of a mystery as to why McNicholas, who vehemently opposed anti-Semitism, did not put a stop to this ambivalence in the diocesan paper earlier.[36]

Although McNicholas was concerned over the rise of Nazism in Germany, his preoccupation with totalitarianism had largely to do with communism. Because of its officially expressed atheism, he regarded communism as a special threat to Catholics and Catholicism. It gave him "much anxiety," he wrote to Bishop John Cantwell of Los Angeles and San Diego. He believed the communists could not be trusted. "I think our country," he wrote as early as 1932, "is much more seriously menaced by Communism than we realize." In the summer of 1936 McNicholas helped launch the Marian Brigade, a national crusade of prayer among Catholic students against the growing menace of communism. Duties incumbent upon members of the new crusade were the daily recitation of the *Memorare*—a late medieval prayer that asked the intercession of Mary—the weekly recitation of the rosary, and the reception of Holy Communion on the feast of the Most Holy Rosary on October 7. Catholics prayed for the conversion of Russia, which had begun under Pope Leo XIII, after every Mass, and Marian devotion became an integral part of their faith lives. Anticommunism also became a means for Catholicism to begin shedding its separatism, to express its loyalty to the American way of life, and to help draw Catholics together with Protestants and Jews in a common cause. Like the fight against immoral movies, local Catholics in their assault against communism defended traditional American values. In response to the request of Bishop Joseph Pinten of Grand Rapids that McNicholas write a text on the evil of communism, the Cincinnati ordinary wrote a pastoral that was published in 1937 in leaflet form. The NCWC had copies of it distributed nationally.[37]

As McNicholas rose to prominence in the 1930s over moral, social, and international issues, there were rumors of a possible cardinalate. The first rumor to reach the papers came in 1934, and the rumors continued right on through the reign of Pius XII. Not until 1939, however, did the rumors become widespread, making the front page of Cincinnati newspapers. That year McNicholas was considered the leading candidate among three ordinaries mentioned as a possible successor to Cardinal Patrick Hayes of New York. McNicholas knew personally Pope Benedict XV, who died in 1922, and was also a personal friend of Cardinal Eugenio Pacelli, Papal Secretary of State. It was rumored that Pacelli had recommended McNicholas's elevation shortly after the Cardinal's visit to Cincinnati in 1936. Pacelli, who had gotten to know McNicholas during the latter's residence in Rome, wrote glowing reports on McNicholas's leadership in the Legion of Decency, in his expansion of the Holy Name Society into a worldwide institution, and in his administration of the Cincinnati see. By late November 1938 it was rumored, as Bishop Francis Spellman of New York noted, that the Cincinnati ordinary was "cleaning his desk preparing to go to N.Y. as Archbishop." With the election of Pacelli as pope in 1939 the speculation as to McNicholas being bestowed a red hat grew stronger. Later that year, however, McNicholas was passed over and Bishop Francis Spellman of Boston was appointed to the New York see. It is difficult to assess how McNicholas's outspokenness on national and world issues affected his chances to becoming a prince of the church. At the same time that it may have hurt him, it may also have been the cause for consideration. Moreover, sources maintain that McNicholas was actually named archbishop of New York, but Pius XI died before officially appointing him ordinary.[38]

In addition to being an inveterate foe of communism, McNicholas was a strong advocate for peace before, during, and after World War II. Until Japan's attack on Pearl Harbor on December 7, 1941, he was openly critical of those who encouraged U.S. entry into the war. The December 1938 issue of *The Catholic World* made reference to McNicholas's appeal "for a mighty League of conscientious noncombatants of all informed Christians who have the best interests of America at heart." Though critical of the Nazi invasion of Poland in 1939, like various Catholics in Congress and other church leaders he remained adamant that the United States should remain aloof from the war. While addressing Catholic high school graduates at a ceremony at Music Hall in the summer of 1940, he urged them to form "peace brigades" to stand for peace, justice, and morality. As late as December 1940 McNicholas argued that America was being pushed into war against her will. Claiming that ninety percent of the American people were for peace, he urged Americans to stand up to the ten percent who wanted war.[39]

But the moment the United States entered World War II the day after the attack on Pearl Harbor on December 7, 1941, McNicholas informed the apostolic delegate that the American bishops should go on record supporting their country. At the Christmas Midnight Mass at Sts. Peter and Paul Church in Norwood, McNicholas pointed out in his sermon that while the United States was "involved in a titanic war," Americans were to serve it loyally. They should do so with "only one end in view," he argued, "that through our war efforts the blessing of peace may come to us and to the whole world." Throughout the war McNicholas urged the faithful to participate in war bond drives.[40]

During and after the war McNicholas presented peace plans and proposals. He envisioned the United States playing a leadership role in concluding and maintaining a just peace. In an address on a CBS national radio broadcast in 1942 McNicholas emphasized the importance for leaders to build a strong front against the danger of world chaos after the war. His 1942 plan called for the churches to help establish a new world order, arguing that peace without morality and a moral structure was pointless. Some of his episcopal colleagues applauded his work. On the eve of the annual meeting of bishops in the fall of 1942, Archbishop Edward Mooney of Detroit, then chairman of the Administrative Board of the NCWC, complimented McNicholas on his fertile mind. "You know that you are our starter," he wrote to him. "Some of the rest of us have more talent in criticism than in creation! . . . Please do jot down what thoughts come to you as you look out on the world at war and we shall have something to work on." McNicholas had great respect for Mooney. He, Archbishop Stritch of Chicago, and McNicholas constituted an intimate and influential trio in the American hierarchy and exercised considerable influence in the domestic affairs of the American church.[41]

On the subject of world peace, McNicholas was practical as well as spiritual. He realized that it could not be accomplished if physical needs were not met. McNicholas maintained that the end of hostilities would not assure peace unless the whole world were organized for the task of helping the overwhelming masses that would be in a condition of hunger and disease. "The profit element in the world of industry and commerce," he wrote to Archbishop Mooney, "must be made subservient to the common good if we are to have a lasting peace with justice and with a sense of true brotherhood." In a national radio address in the fall of 1943, he listed several conditions for world peace, among which were arms limitations, an international regulating body, a more equitable distribution of basic necessities, and freedom of religion. Above everything else, McNicholas was convinced that there could be no world peace so long as atheistic communism existed. A year later, speaking on "The Crisis of the Ages" at the annual religious service conducted by the Holy Name Society in New York City, McNicholas, in his usual candid and forceful manner, identified an ideological struggle in the making. He foresaw "a long struggle . . . for generations after the war, over the God-given freedom, dignity, and security of man on the one side, and the man-denied freedom, dignity, and security of his fellow man on the other side." That year he and nine other U.S. bishops, including Bishop Karl Alter of Toledo, warned of a postwar era without God and issued statements in opposition to the policies and attitudes of the Soviet Union. By 1945 American bishops were already concerned over the specter of Soviet control over Eastern Europe. Catholics in the preconciliar era were as much convinced that the world needed saving against Godless communism and secularism as did Catholics in post–Vatican II who campaigned against the evils of poverty, race, and war.[42]

When President Truman issued his famous foreign policy doctrine in the spring of 1947, advocating the containment of communism in Greece, McNicholas praised his efforts. "I feel," he wrote to the president in May of that year, that the Truman Doctrine "will resound through succeeding ages." The following January McNicholas again wrote to Truman. He hoped that his containment policy would not be restricted to southeastern Europe but would be "expressed in terms that will be world-embracing." Acknowledging that "the material cost of preventing world war may be very serious," it would be, he argued, "infinitely less costly than our engagement in a global conflict."[43]

As McNicholas grew older and the world situation looked increasingly bleak to him, his tone became a bit more strident. His views of the Soviet government hardened, and he repeatedly warned his flock of the spread of communism. It was "a world octopus," he argued, "with tentacles reaching out to every nation of the earth." McNicholas's views on communism doubtlessly mirrored that part of the American public that had a strong conspiratorial cast. As he spoke out against communists, materialists, agnostics, and secularists, he freely criticized—without naming names—legislators, teachers, and members of the press as their allies. Before McCarthyism became a national phenomenon, McNicholas argued that America was "standing by and allowing Communism to sweep the country, . . . to place their agents in every pivotal position." He maintained that the most effective means to counteract communism was to provide moral training and instruction in America's schools.[44]

In the fall of 1946 McNicholas was aghast at the arrests of Archbishop Alojzije Stepinac and fifteen others in Yugoslavia on the charge of having collaborated with the Germans. Denouncing Marshall Tito's "Red Fascist" rule, the archbishop asked his pastors and people to request the American government to voice its protest against the arrests. As head of the National Catholic Welfare Conference, McNicholas sent a telegram to President Truman, disapproving of the condemnation of Stepinac to sixteen years of imprisonment. Two years later the archdiocese also came to the defense of Cardinal József Mindszenty of Hungary. The Cincinnati Archdiocesan Union of the Holy Name Society, representing 50,000 Catholics, sent a telegram to Secretary of State Dean Acheson in opposition to the despotic imprisonment of Mindszenty. Five weeks earlier McNicholas had urged President Truman to protest the arrest. "The utterly false and stupid charges against the Cardinal by a Communist government," he wrote, "do not hide the real purpose of attacking, persecuting, and liquidating religion." In the spring of 1949, when Mindszenty was tried and sentenced to life imprisonment, McNicholas led local Catholic groups in adding their voices to the thousands who protested throughout the country.[45]

Before and during World War II, a number of American Catholics became less parochial and increasingly interested in issues beyond their parishes and dioceses. By the end of the war more and more Catholics and church leaders became preoccupied with world peace, the spread of communism, and relief of war-torn Europe and the Far East. Among the 33,691 Catholic men and women of the archdiocese who served in the armed services during World War II, 886 were killed, 938 were wounded, and seventy-four were missing in action. One hundred and two religious and diocesan priests of the archdiocese served as chaplains. After the war the Catholic War Veterans Association offered every Catholic veteran man and woman fraternal and social activities. Catholics in all the parishes, moreover, gathered food and clothing to be shipped to the war-stricken areas in Europe, in the Philip-

FIG 15. Archbishop Karl Alter, 1950–1969

pines, and in the islands of the Far East. Volunteers, like The Clement Helpers at St. Clement parish at St. Bernard in Cincinnati, met once a week in the basement of their church to sort clothing and pack boxes. The trucks of St. Vincent de Paul collected items directly from the parishes and took care of the shipping to the warehouse. Through the archdiocesan resettlement council, under the directorship of Monsignor August Kramer, Catholics offered home and job opportunities to approximately two hundred refugees. McNicholas, as chairman of the administrative board of the NCWC, spearheaded the campaign in 1946 for the Bishop's Fund for Victims of War. The fund, used to finance work in Europe, was collected in Catholic churches and in more than 10,000 Catholic elementary and high schools nationally. Within a year's time more than $500,000 were raised. Since 1943 War Relief Services had maintained a vast program of relief and rehabilitation in the war-torn countries of Europe and the Far East. At the end of the war the program concentrated on the problems of displaced persons, the sick, the aged, and children.[46]

When the sixty-five-year-old Karl Alter succeeded McNicholas in 1950 he affirmed the local church's anticommunist stance. The day after his installation he backed the national Crusade for Freedom and urged local Catholics to sign the Freedom scroll. At the annual Marian Day celebration at Xavier University on October 1 of that year, he described the conflict between U.S. democracy and Soviet communism as a "struggle between freedom and slavery." The following month the bishops gathered in Washington, D.C., and elected Alter treasurer and vice chairman of the National Catholic Welfare Conference Administrative Board. Three years later Alter left Cincinnati for Europe where, as the new chairman of the NCWC Administrative Board, a position he held from 1952 to 1956 and 1958 to 1961, he visited NCWC relief centers.[47]

As head of the NCWC, Alter urged Catholics to contribute generously to the annual Catholic Bishops' Thanksgiving clothing campaign for war victims throughout the world. The campaign continued through the 1950s. Throughout his tenure Alter also urged the faithful to continue the good work of supporting the worldwide program of Catholic Relief Services. Laetare Sunday became associated in the minds of Catholics with the annual appeal of the Catholic Relief Services. By 1962 the agency had brought aid and religious instruction to some thirty million hungry and homeless people in more than seventy countries.[48]

THE BLACK APOSTOLATE AND RACIAL ISSUES

During their administrations McNicholas and Alter also made the apostolate to African Americans one of their special causes. The local church moved from convert making in the 1920s to community organization and direct action on behalf of African Americans by midcentury. Within two months after his installation, McNicholas, who believed that the most fertile field for conversions in the United States was among blacks, established Holy Trinity parish in the lower west end near the Ohio River in Cincinnati as a church dedicated to work among black people. Ninety-one years earlier almost to the day, October 5, 1834, Holy Trinity Church had been established as the first Catholic church for German-speaking people in Ohio. During its many years Holy Trinity parish grew in importance, always retaining a large preponderance of German Catholic families. By the turn of the nineteenth century the parish's mostly white population was declining rapidly due to the removal of many middle- and upper-middle class German Catholics to the suburbs. The parishioners felt keenly the passing of the glory that was once theirs. Whereas in the fall of 1922 Holy Trinity school had an enrollment of 137 pupils, three years later it had less than thirty-five. The provincial of the Sisters of Notre Dame withdrew the teachers, arguing that it was impractical "to supply teachers for so small a number of children." In 1925 the school closed.[49]

Moreover, the neighborhood surrounding Holy Trinity Church had badly deteriorated, as well as largely populated by blacks. The black population of approximately seventeen thousand in the lower west end had almost doubled since the migration of blacks from the South during and after World War I. Holy Trinity parish consisted of forty-eight white and two blacks. Though advised to sell the church and school, the newly arrived McNicholas asked Father Leo M. Walsh, then at St. Gregory Seminary, to spend a few days a week in the neighborhood, study the situation, and help decide what to do. When Walsh told the archbishop that he "knew nothing about Negro work," McNicholas reminded him "that souls are neither black nor white and that the same general principles apply to all phases of conversion work."[50]

In late September Walsh distributed about nine thousand handbills throughout the city's west end, inviting the residents to attend Mass at Holy Trinity Church on October 4. More than eight hundred persons responded, among whom were about four hundred blacks. A number of local church leaders attended the services, including Henry J. Richter who, as pastor of St. Ann Church in the west end, had been working among the city's blacks for several years. During the ceremony Walsh read a letter written by McNicholas. Pointing out that the mission of the Catholic Church was the sanctification of all souls regardless of race, McNicholas protested "against the race prejudice which has done so much injustice to the colored people." He extended an invitation to local blacks to investigate and consider the teachings of the Catholic Church. Forty-eight blacks applied for instruction. In the meantime all but one of the Catholic white families in the parish moved out of the neighborhood.[51]

In November 1925 Holy Trinity Church, with Walsh as pastor, was reopened for blacks. At first the work was difficult and slow. Walsh helped build up a parish composed almost entirely of converts. Most of the first new members were children and the elderly. The following year five additional Sisters of the Blessed Sacrament came to Cincinnati to work at Holy Trinity. The newly arrived sisters went from house to house in the west end, asking the parents—white and black—to send their children to the Catholic school. Their efforts paid off. On registration day, long lines of children waited to be enrolled. Because the school could accommodate only two hundred, the sisters had to refuse admission to about a third of the applicants. At a large gathering of people, mostly black, at an outdoor meeting on the church grounds in August 1926, McNicholas again encouraged blacks to join the Catholic Church. "Can we find in any other Church," he said, "the inspiring democracy that we witness at the Communion-rail every Sunday . . . , where the master and the servant, the powerful and the lowly, the millionaire and the paupers, the colored man and the white man, kneel side by side to adore God and to receive His sacred Body and Blood [?]" Though there were a few instances of blacks and white kneeling at the same communion rail, the archdiocese at this time largely discriminated against blacks. Most blacks were segregated into their own parishes and schools and were almost never allowed into white Catholic institutions. During the next four years there were more than two hundred children baptized in Holy Trinity parish each Easter. By the year 1935 more than 1,300 blacks had been baptized.[52]

In September 1927 the archdiocese acquired the property of the Sisters of Notre Dame at the corner of Court and Mound Streets in Cincinnati's west end. Formerly used as an academy, it now served as a home for the Sisters of the Blessed Sacrament and for Madonna high school, a coeducational high school for the children of Holy Trinity and St. Ann grade schools. Madonna High, which opened that fall with twenty-three students, was the first high school for African American Catholic students in Ohio and one of the few black high schools in the country. For the next eighteen years the sisters were in charge of the school with an average enrollment of approximately seventy students.[53]

During those early years of McNicholas's administration, Catholic African Americans participated in several parish activities. In the spring of 1927 the parishes of St. Ann and Holy Trinity organized the McNicholas Convert Club and provided club and recreation rooms at the Holy Trinity school. Blacks in the west end also organized a forty-piece band, composed of boys from St. Ann, Holy Trinity, and Madonna schools. The band was known as the Father Cleary Band, in honor of the pioneer priest in his work with the black people in the archdiocese. In the fall of 1928 the local church hosted the fourth annual convention of the Federated Colored Catholics of the United States. At the time there were approximately twelve million African Americans, among whom—a 1928 survey showed—were 203,896 black Catholics. The object of the federation was to bring about a closer union among black Catholics and to stimulate them to a larger participation in the racial and civic affairs of the country.[54]

In the spring of 1930 four Franciscan Sisters from Providence, Rhode Island, arrived in Cincinnati to establish another religious foundation to aid in the black apostolate. They located their convent at St. Anthony parish on Budd Street in the west end and reopened the school that had been vacant for three years. The limit of expansion had been reached in St. Ann and Holy Trinity parishes due to the fact that the Sisters of the Blessed Sacrament, who had been in charge of all the Catholic schools for blacks in Cincinnati, could not spare any more sisters from their religious community. The arrival of the Franciscan Sisters promised to enhance the Catholic work among the blacks. St. Anthony school, with an enrollment of 109 students, most of whom were

Protestants, admitted only the younger black children. In "taking older children," McNicholas thought, there was "naturally the great danger that they may have acquired bad habits."[55]

By 1933 the archdiocese had opened Madonna high school, schools in Holy Trinity, St. Anthony, and St. Ann parishes, and the Catholic Mission at Lockland for blacks. In 1935 St. Ann parish school cared for 250 pupils in the six elementary grades. Holy Trinity Junior High had 350 students, and Madonna High numbered seventy-five. The number of black children in Catholic schools had increased from fewer than two hundred to approximately seven hundred in about four years. Moreover, approximately one thousand blacks attended Sunday Mass at Holy Trinity Church and four hundred went to St. Ann. When offers were made in the 1930s to buy the St. Anthony Church property, McNicholas and his advisors declined because of the successful work that was also being conducted there among the blacks. In 1945 archdiocesan officials decided to transform Madonna High School into a school for only black boys and changed the name to De Porres High, named after the Dominican lay brother, Martin de Porres, who had cared for slaves brought to Peru from Africa in the early seventeenth century. The increasing number of converts to the Catholic faith had made the high school inadequate as a coeducational institution. Diocesan priests replaced the sisters on the faculty. The first class at De Porres High School numbered thirty-five students. The girls, who had initially attended Madonna High School, attended other interparochial high schools for girls in the city.[56]

During the depression of the 1930s the archbishop also worked for the welfare of poor blacks in the archdiocese in other ways. Besides recommending low cost and better housing for blacks, he backed slum clearance projects. At the 1933 National Catholic Interracial Federation Convention in Cleveland, McNicholas, as the spiritual director of the organization, criticized ill-conceived slum clearance and redevelopment programs. He strongly urged the delegates to be leaders in Catholic Action. Concerned over the proposed removal of blacks by the all-white Cincinnati Metropolitan Housing Authority for the renovation of the west end of Cincinnati, he was outraged that no provision had been made for the "helpless" blacks who had been dispossessed. Convinced that the condition should "be brought to the attention of the public by a militant group," he urged Catholic lay leaders and priests to "assume the responsibility of bringing this condition to the attention of the city and the State of Ohio."[57]

Throughout his administration McNicholas expressed concern over the deplorable housing conditions of whites and blacks in the see city. In a letter to his clergy on April 14, 1945, he referred to the slum areas in the west end as "a disgraceful blot in the metropolitan area of our city." Believing that the "poor people themselves could not solve the problem," he repeatedly argued it was the responsibility of city, state, and national officials to deal with it. It was not enough to hope that the black poor would have the same sense of responsibility that working whites did. McNicholas pointed out that the "degrading state of affairs" in the city, he wrote, "is crime-promoting, disease-propagating, and destructive of all the values, to which we attach importance in the intellectual, moral, and spiritual order." If the west end had only "poor White dwellers in it, and if they were condemned to live as our Colored people are now living," he insisted that "conditions would be many times worse."[58]

McNicholas joined African American Catholics in calling for racial justice both in the local church and in the community. In spite of efforts by some Catholics to lessen racial prejudice, there were recurring examples of it. The chancery received allegations of St. Xavier's Commercial School and Cincinnati's Good Samaritan Hospital denying admission to blacks and St. Joseph cemetery refusing to sell lots to them. In response to McNicholas's plea for more assistance to blacks in the inner city, a number of schools began contributing a fixed part of their yearly mission contributions for the maintenance of segregated black missions and parishes. Students from Catholic high schools engaged themselves in catechetical work for the benefit of black children in the community. Pleased with the work of the Sisters of the Poor of St. Francis in taking care of blacks in hospitals, McNicholas hoped to see African American doctors and nurses also given an opportunity to care for them. He also wanted to see more priests and sisters, as well as more black parishes, schools, and missions, working with the black population in the archdiocese. Though gratified to see women religious communities doing missionary work in "far-off China," he hoped to see more of them "undertake some work among the Negroes of this Diocese." At the same time that church officials wanted to see more done for blacks in the archdiocese, they did not favor integrating the parishes. There were those who believed, as did Walsh of Holy Trinity Church, that there would be "no social problem in our churches if we will but give the Negro his own buildings and his own priests. The average Negro," Walsh argued, "does not want to mix with the White Folks any more than the Whites want to associate with the Colored." He also insisted that the work of the church "would be twice as effective if it were conducted by a Negro priest."[59]

In 1939 four Dominican priests of Sinsinawa, Wisconsin, came to Cincinnati at the request of McNicholas to work among blacks in a black neighborhood in the newly founded Mother of God Church in Walnut Hills. The following year McNicholas welcomed to the archdiocese the Sons of the Sacred Heart of Verona, Italy, whose special apostolate was African Missions.

After taking up residence at Holy Trinity, the Camboni missionaries took charge of St. Henry, St. Anthony, St. Michael, and St. Pius black churches. McNicholas was pleased with the "extraordinary success" they had, he wrote, "in bringing the Colored people into the Church." The Congregation of the Holy Ghost, stationed at St. John's parish in Dayton since 1928, was also active in African American missions. Their work at St. John's was devoted almost exclusively to the blacks that formed the bulk of the parish. By the end of the decade there were nine diocesan priests who labored among blacks.[60]

In 1941 there were 2,821 blacks registered in the parishes in the archdiocese. All but one of the parishes had their own grade schools. In Cincinnati, the Sisters of the Blessed Sacrament, Sisters of Charity, and Franciscan Missionary Sisters of Mary conducted the schools. The Blessed Sacrament Sisters taught at Holy Trinity and at the school attached to St. Edward's, which was known as St. Ann's mission, and the Franciscan Missionaries of Mary taught at St. Anthony's School. Though Mother of God Church had no school, it had a catechetical center. The Dominican Sisters from Sinsinawa taught religion both in the evening and in the day. Sisters of Mercy undertook similar work at the catechetical center at Hamilton. At Lockland, on the northern outskirts of Cincinnati, St. Christina Church and a school for blacks were built. In addition, St. Joseph and St. Henry Churches in Cincinnati were made parishes for blacks. St. John's school in Dayton, conducted by the Sisters of Notre Dame de Namur, was also turned into a parochial school for black children. In 1942 the Queen of Angels parish in Hamilton was reorganized for blacks in the community. Four years later the new Church of St. Richard of Chichester was opened in North College Hill. It was the seventh black church in Greater Cincinnati. Jerome Wolf of the Congregation of the Precious Blood was named pastor. The Precious Blood Fathers were in charge of two other missions for the blacks in the archdiocese, Queen of Angels mission in Hamilton and St. Martin in Springfield. In 1941 the De Porres Welfare Center in Cincinnati was established to serve the needs of blacks in Hamilton County. Three years later the archdiocese incorporated the DePorres Welfare Center into Catholic Charities.[61]

Throughout the 1920s and into the 1930s most Catholic colleges, secondary schools, monasteries, convents, and seminaries in the country were segregated. American bishops as a national body did not speak out against segregation until during World War II. In 1943 McNicholas urged the priests of the archdiocese to integrate Catholic high schools and colleges, though there was no mention of the parishes. This concern for integration and equal rights for blacks represented a new direction in American Catholic action. McNicholas suggested to President Celestin J. Steiner at

Xavier University that if there were objections from the student body, he should "get a number of students to organize in favor of the admission of the Negroes." Steiner replied that he saw "no reason why Xavier [University]. . . should not admit some deserving Negroes." Efforts to integrate some of the elementary and high schools, however, met considerable resistance. There was loud protest by some of the white parents at St. Francis de Sales School in Cincinnati. In "retaliation" of the archbishop "ruining our homes overnight, putting Negroes in our schools, where it is unnessary [*sic*]," 'Disgusted Catholics' from de Sales parish wrote in November 1946, "we are going . . . to cram your beloved Bingo Game full of Southern Negroes." They demanded that the black children be immediately taken out of the school. McNicholas rejected their demand and the children stayed. When white parents in 1947 threatened to take their children out of some high schools, McNicholas and his staff "quietly urged" the student body to accept black students "whenever there was an expression of indignation."[62]

In the spring of 1946 a group to aid blacks in the archdiocese established the Apostolate of the Negro, with John M. Cronin, a Cincinnati insurance agent, as its president. The new organization launched a membership campaign designed to reach every parish in the archdiocese as well as make appeals to the clergy and laity to help underwrite the activities of the African American missions. It was estimated that among the 128,000 blacks in the archdiocesan area, 4,500 were Catholics, approximately one out of every twenty-eight blacks. The organization helped the black missions not only financially but also in the social, educational, and athletic phases of their work. It also attempted some work in race relations through the promotion of discussion groups and the staging of black choral groups. Within five years the Apostolate of the Negro, with a membership of approximately 14,000, raised more than $70,000 for support of black parishes.[63]

As head of the archdiocese, McNicholas urged support of the Apostolate. "The condition of the Colored people," he wrote in 1947, "is very pitiable in the archdiocese. We ask our priests and their parishioners to pay even a casual visit in the Negro sections of Cincinnati, Dayton, Hamilton, and Springfield so that they may see for themselves the inhuman conditions under which the Negroes' abject poverty forces many of them to live." Shortly after his installation in 1950 Alter directed Monsignor August Kramer, spiritual director of the Apostolate for the Negro, to phase out the organization. Two years later the Apostolate was completely dissolved. Alter thought that the men would accomplish more by working through the parishes instead.[64]

By midcentury the archdiocese had come a long way on the race issue in a quarter century. The black cause was no longer the preserve of one parish, but the work of many priests and parishes. Notwithstanding the progress, however, racism still remained a serious problem in the archdiocese. The majority of the white lay people, religious, and clergy lived in outer city neighborhoods and in the suburbs, far removed from the problems in the city and largely inattentive to racial problems. At times, by today's standards, McNicholas also appeared somewhat patronizing to blacks, subscribing to the stereotypical beliefs that most whites had about blacks. Openly challenging the view that blacks were inferior to whites, he nevertheless thought that their "simplicity and childlike nature" would make the apostolate attractive to priests. He attributed their resistance to communism to "their superstition, . . . their innate cheerfulness and also their improvidence. . . ." But McNicholas nonetheless had a genuine concern for the spiritual and material well-being and a sense of justice for blacks that was ahead of his time. From the time he arrived in Cincinnati, a black layman observed, McNicholas had become "a loyal, faithful and devoted friend of my group."[65]

One of the foremost social issues during Alter's administration was racial segregation in churches, schools, and recreational facilities in the archdiocese. In the early 1950s seventeen priests and thirty-seven religious sisters served African Americans in these institutions. Though the local church addressed some of the needs of blacks, it was reluctant to publicly challenge discrimination. By its silence it probably helped fan racism. Most African American Catholics in the 1950s were still segregated into their own parishes and schools and were seldom allowed into white parishes, schools, and hospitals. When in 1953 some Protestant clergymen protested against discrimination at Coney Island in Cincinnati, the editor of the *Cincinnati Leader,* a business newsletter, asked the Chancery Office to state its position on the matter. Responding on behalf of the local church, Chancellor Paul F. Leibold insisted that no one should be discriminated against because of color. Nobody in the community did more "for the real advancement of [African Americans] . . . than the Archdiocese of Cincinnati," he argued. Then he maintained that it was not in the church's province "to publicly condemn any individual or group for not promoting a private venture or business in the same way [the Church] . . . might conduct it."[66]

By the end of the decade, however, and especially during the urban riots of the 1960s, the archdiocese took a more aggressive stance on the race issue. Alter became deeply committed to social justice and took strong stands against racism and any form of bigotry. Throughout the sixties he issued statements and pastoral letters promoting interracial justice. On October 1, 1961, at a Mass connected with the "Rally for Interracial Understanding" sponsored by the Third Order Franciscans, Auxiliary Bishop Leibold labelled race discrimination a "spiritual disease," and urged the faithful to help eliminate it by prudent and courageous action. When the Catholic

Interracial Council of Dayton informed Alter in 1963 that a black child was refused admission at Fort Scott Camps, run by the archdiocese, the archbishop ordered the director to begin admitting blacks. In the wake of the Birmingham, Alabama, summer race riots of 1963, Alter issued a pastoral urging Catholics to support legislation that would grant all citizens, regardless of race and color, equal rights. He called for an end to discriminatory practices in voting rights, employment, housing, and education. At the same time that he urged real estate agents to promote open occupancy, Alter recommended that neighborhoods be integrated in ratio to the population of white and black citizens in Cincinnati. In 1963 archdiocesan officials also began awarding two four-year college scholarships annually to black students graduating from Catholic high schools. The students received a sum covering the cost of books and tuition at any of the Catholic colleges or universities in the archdiocese. Through the work of the De Porres Center the archdiocese also helped provide more educational and employment opportunities for black youths.[67]

To help eliminate legal and social barriers for blacks, the archdiocese looked to the laity, and they responded. Shortly after Alter's 1963 pastoral on interracial justice, the Archdiocesan Councils of Catholic Men and Women pledged concrete action. Within a year there was a substantial increase of Catholic participation in neighborhood and citywide interfaith efforts for racial justice. Members of both lay organizations wrote to their political representatives in support of the Civil Rights bill. Through their speakers' bureaus, the Catholic Interracial Councils of Cincinnati and Dayton distributed thousands of copies of Alter's pastoral in parish societies and other organizations. Catholics also joined Protestants and Jews in the 1963 Cincinnati March for Jobs. In the fall of that year some parishes conducted pilot home visit exchange programs, called Living Room Dialogues, for white and black families. By the following spring a full-scale program in Cincinnati drew 1,800 participants, including several priests and women religious. In the first year after the issuance of the pastoral, there was a substantial increase of Catholic participation in neighborhood and citywide efforts for racial justice. Throughout the archdiocese lay men and women echoed the spirit of the time as they became more involved in social action work, housing, education, job discrimination, health, public welfare, voter registration, migrant workers, and peace. In January 1965 Front Line, a lay movement that prepared volunteers for foreign and domestic mission work, established a service in Dayton's predominantly African American west side. The movement, which concentrated its effort within the black apostolate, had been initiated in 1962 by the Society of Mary at the University of Dayton under the name Chaminade's Auxiliaries of North America.[68]

By 1965 there was no doubt where the archdiocese stood on the issue of race. That year the Cincinnati Catholic Interracial Council, joined by Protestant and Jewish groups, called on City Council to support the passage of "an effective and comprehensive state law" that would prohibit discrimination in the sale or rental of housing because of race, religion, or national origin. In the summer needy students in Catholic high schools of Hamilton County benefited from a federal government grant of $138,954 for the neighborhood summer youth program of the De Porres Center, conducted in Cincinnati's west end. This was the first instance of direct federal aid to students attending Catholic schools in the archdiocese. On Labor Day the chancery placed nondiscrimination clauses in all building contracts for churches, schools, and other institutions in the archdiocese. Auxiliary Bishops Leibold and Edward A. McCarthy, assisted by a committee of priests and lay people, were put in charge of the program.[69]

As interracial tensions mounted throughout the United States in the mid to late 1960s, there was increased rioting in many American cities, including Cincinnati. Blaming part of the unrest on the high rate of unemployment among young blacks, Alter in 1967 called for more job and educational opportunities, open housing, and relief of the poor. Consistent with the liberal agenda of the times, he urged individuals to get involved by bringing social and political pressure that would lead to government action. "Only government through taxes," Alter argued, "can supply the many millions of dollars needed for relief." Campaigning for more government initiative, he insisted that individual efforts were also needed because the national government could not do it all. In early February 1968 Alter launched Project Commitment, a grassroots program in human relations designed to communicate the teachings of the church on racial justice to local parishes. The project helped bring together white and black citizens to engage in serious dialogue. Modeled after a similar program in the Detroit archdiocese, Project Commitment started officially as a pilot effort in St. Francis de Sales deanery. It consisted of an eight-week series of discussions of community problems by civic and social welfare leaders. In addition, the Knights of Columbus, which made generous grants to the Catholic Youth Organization and the Newman Clubs at area secular colleges and universities, became more active in assisting the local church in the fields of interracial justice, antipoverty programs, and general social welfare. Catholic high school and college students, moreover, volunteered their time in community action programs in predominantly black neighborhoods.[70]

In response to Alter's pastoral on the civil disturbances in Cincinnati, the local church's Commission on Human Relations organized "top-level dialogue" with Catholic real estate agents, building and loan directors, and other professionals. The Commission also called for support for integrating neighborhoods in Cincinnati and in nearby communities, for placement of at least one black faculty member in each Catholic high school, for use of schools and gymnasiums in after-school hours, and for greater efforts to eliminate segregation in schools. In 1967 black students were enrolled in fifty-nine of the 148 elementary schools in the archdiocese and in twenty of its twenty-six high schools. Among the 65,862 students in the elementary schools, 2,123 were black; among the 21,768 high school students, 492 were black. There were nineteen black teachers in the elementary schools and eight in the high schools.[71]

In May 1968 the De Facto Segregation Committee in Dayton, headed by Thaddeus Regulinski of Corpus Christi parish, presented a report to Monsignor Edward A. Connaughton, superintendent of Dayton area Catholic schools. For nearly a year the committee had studied the problem of racial imbalance in parish schools. In the summer the archdiocese responded to the increasing needs of the black community by establishing an "open enrollment" policy for Dayton that allowed black Catholic children to attend the Catholic school of their choice. The church's plan also initiated a voluntary student exchange program to bring white children into two predominantly black schools: St. James and Resurrection. To facilitate matters, no tuition assessment was made against pupils going outside of their parish boundaries to attend either black school.[72]

During the decade a number of priests from urban parishes began meeting to exchange ideas on what actions should be taken by the parishes to enhance interracial relations. At the end of Alter's term the Urban Apostolate, building upon the success of the Negro Apostolate of the late 1940s, was formed. It focused on the inner city of metropolitan areas in the archdiocese. As early as September 1959, Franklin Shands and Father August Kramer had asked that the Negro Apostolate be revived in order to promote "good racial relations." By the fall of 1968, fifty-four priests, mostly pastors, belonged to the Urban Apostolate. Alter put Clement Busemeyer, pastor of St. Joseph parish in Cincinnati's west end, in charge. Busemeyer stressed that the religious and lay people in urban parishes with black parishioners had "a special mission in the Church." A core of committed priests, sisters, and lay persons came together into serious collaboration and helped promote programs with mixed success on race and poverty in the parishes. The group represented parishes in Cincinnati, Dayton, Middletown, Hamilton, Lebanon, Batavia, Piqua, and Xenia.[73]

Acknowledging that race and class issues often intersected, the archdiocese also focused on poverty. In 1964 a growing concern for the poor led a group of Mount St. Mary's of the West seminarians to open Bible Centers in the inner city of Cincinnati, a project that afforded a new witness in the local church, especially in the Appalachian white community. In the summer the 120-year-old St. John the Baptist Church at Green and Republic Streets became the center of a mission to the Southern Appalachian migrants. The center helped serve Appalachians who had for the most part displaced the old German Catholic families of the area. Concerned over the level of poverty in Cincinnati, where one-fourth of the total number of families had incomes of less than $3,000 a year and lived below the poverty line, the archdiocese in 1966 established a Poverty Commission, headed by Bishop McCarthy. The seventeen-member commission, composed of clergy, religious, and laity, leveled charges that the state was "guilty of breeding poverty." It urged the implementation of programs to help improve welfare assistance. In October the local church took another concrete step toward improving interracial relations by establishing the Catholic Commission on Human Relations. The commission, also headed by McCarthy, expanded the work of the Cincinnati Catholic Interracial Council.[74]

The archdiocese in 1968 took another important step and established and staffed a Central Planning and Budget Commission for the funding of Catholic and ecumenical programs and projects in the areas of race and poverty. The local church pledged $1.25 million over a five-year period. The new Commission also helped coordinate the work of the Poverty Commission, Project Commitment, and community centers. This new and innovative archdiocesan response to urban unrest influenced the larger national Catholic Campaign for Human Development in establishing a similar fund in 1970 for human development. By the end of Alter's term the archdiocese also joined Project Equality of Ohio. Based in Columbus, Project Equality was part of a nationwide, interreligious effort to promote fair employment practices through the hiring and buying policies of religious institutions. The local church along with nine other churches in the state committed their multimillion-dollar purchasing power to equal opportunity in all aspects of employment, especially for the African American workers.[75]

The McNicholas-Alter years saw significant improvement in the expansion of the ministry among African Americans. At the same time that it addressed some of the needs of the poor, the rights of workers, and inequities against African Americans, the local church increased and reorganized its charity and social organizations. The increase in the number of social agencies was due, in part, to the leadership of the two ordinaries and to the contribution and sacrifices made by devout lay people, parishioners, and the charity of the various religious orders.

· 12 ·

CATHOLIC EDUCATION

U nlike the Catholic activists of the immigrant period who sought to adapt religion to the American culture, Archbishops McNicholas and Alter along with other Catholic leaders from the 1920s through the 1960s attempted to develop a specific Catholic culture and hoped to influence American culture with their religion. The Cincinnati ordinaries were of the opinion that Catholics were a distinctive group with a distinctive view of the world. As McNicholas and Alter promoted Catholicism they had a great interest in education. They both had much to say about the roles of the church, the state, and the parents in education. They fought against increasing secularization of education from the primary to the university levels. Sharing rather standard Catholic views for their time, both archbishops saw an ongoing struggle between Catholic education and secular education, consistently arguing that the latter undermined the moral ends of education.

McNicholas's leadership and activities in education were widely recognized and resulted in his election as chairman of the Department of Education of the National Catholic Welfare Conference (NCWC) from 1930 to 1935, 1943 to 1945, and as president general of the National Catholic Education Association (NCEA). Keenly interested in the NCEA, which he headed five times beginning in 1946, he was reelected for the last time at a meeting in New Orleans just a week before he died in 1950. In this role he articulated a very definite philosophy of education. True to his Thomistic training, McNicholas advocated a thoroughly Catholic education, one that integrated the natural and supernatural. Revived in Catholic intellectual circles in the late nineteenth century, following Leo XIII's 1879 encyclical *Aeterni Patris,* neo-Thomists argued that the individualism, secularism, and relativism of the modern mind were incongruous to the Catholic ethnic's sense of tradition and community. No other American ordinary reflected as much the teachings of his thirteenth-century confrere, St. Thomas Aquinas, as did McNicholas.[1]

When the Cincinnati ordinary broke ground for the new Notre Dame high school for girls in Dayton in 1926, he emphasized the importance of imparting "a specific moral discipline" that was "spiritualized." Though preoccupied by issues of war and peace in the 1940s, as episcopal chairman of the Department of Education of the NCWC McNicholas spoke often on the moral bankruptcy of state supported schools. He accused school boards of acting like "drunken sailors" in taxing the poor to support a public school system that drove religion from the curriculum and prevented both the development of the moral character of children and their spiritual formation. Examining the parameters of a postwar peace, he noted that a new world order would not necessarily mean less crime and more righteous living unless there were a revolution in education. To McNicholas, religious instruction in all schools was essential.[2]

Moreover, the Cincinnati ordinary recommended formal religious instruction to Catholic children attending public schools. McNicholas was inspired by the work of Bishop Edwin V. O'Hara of Crest Falls, Montana, the first chairman in 1934 of the Episcopal Committee of the Confraternity of Christian Doctrine (CCD), whose purpose was to provide religious education for individuals who had never had formal catechesis in a church-sponsored school. In 1938 McNicholas appointed a priest to organize a CCD program locally. But it was short-lived. Three years later, however, the first regular religious instruction during school hours for Catholics in public high schools in Cincinnati began at Woodward High School. The class was taught during the students' free periods from other classes. Sister Agnes de Sales of the Sisters of Charity and four assistants taught the class of seventy-five Catholics.[3]

Under the auspices of the Bishops' Committee of the CCD, O'Hara also launched in the mid-1930s a revision of the Catechism of Christian Doctrine, more commonly known as the *Baltimore Catechism,* inaugurated in 1884 as the official text for religious instruction in the Catholic schools. O'Hara conferred with a few of the American church leaders, including McNicholas, who readily agreed that the language of the catechism could be clearer as well as more succinct and contemporary. Forty theologians at the New York Catechetical Congress of 1936, presided by McNicholas and Archbishop Mooney of Detroit, studied the suggestions of more than one hundred theologians on the "archane theology" of the *Baltimore Catechism.* O'Hara asked

McNicholas, a trained theologian, to oversee the preparation of a draft to be sent to all the bishops of the United States. Thirty bishops worked on subsequent revisions, resulting in six subsequent printings of the revised text. After several years of research, the *Baltimore Catechism* for the primary grades was finally completed by 1942 and the high school version in 1949. Though McNicholas had found the work "slow and tedious," it had been, he wrote to the apostolic delegate, "a real relaxation from routine duties and from perplexing problems." Up until the 1960s, the revised *Baltimore Catechism* remained the primary text for religious instruction in the schools of the archdiocese from elementary to college.[4]

The question that had occupied the minds of local church leaders, the clergy, religious, and the laity in the nineteenth century was whether Catholics should join a system of state schools without religion or build their own elementary schools. They chose the latter course. Education without religion became unthinkable. When Ohio in the 1920s extended compulsory education to the high school level, again archdiocesan priests, religious, and laity responded to the challenge. Catholics demanded that their children be given the same benefits of a religious education on the secondary level as in the elementary schools.

At the same time that he underscored the importance of religious instruction both at the primary and secondary levels, McNicholas thought that the time was ripe for closing most of the small, mostly two-year parish high schools and for revising Moeller's concept of a centralized school system. During the second quarter of the twentieth century Cincinnati Catholics became steadily better educated and more prosperous. This growth was reflected in the increasing number of suburban parishes and in the establishment of a widespread network of Catholic high schools. When McNicholas first arrived in the archdiocese he looked at Moeller's detailed plans for a very large high school on the eastern hills of Cincinnati. After several conferences with the area priests, McNicholas inaugurated a plan for citywide extension of Catholic high schools. Instead of two big high schools in Cincinnati, one on the western side and the other on the eastern side, providing for three thousand students each, it was decided to have smaller high schools that would each handle between five to eight hundred students. Each school was to serve a number of parishes and all students of a given parish were to be assigned to a given school. In this manner, parishes would have more identification with the respective high schools.

During McNicholas's first five years in office several Catholic high schools were either restructured or built. In Cincinnati Mount St. Vincent Academy, a high school founded in 1850 by the Sisters of Charity and moved to Glenway Avenue in 1857, was renamed Seton High School. It served the girls in the Price Hill community. Notre Dame Academy on Sixth Street, under the direction of the Sisters of Notre Dame, became a diocesan high school for girls and was renamed Notre Dame High School. Mercy Academy on Freeman Avenue, conducted by the Sisters of Mercy, became Mercy High School. In Norwood, Regina High School for girls was built and run by the Sisters of the Precious Blood. The Franciscan Sisters of Oldenburg, Indiana, operated Our Lady of Angels High School for Girls in St. Bernard. This was the community where, fifty years earlier, the sisters had begun their work of elementary education in the archdiocese. For boys, two new high schools were built. The archdiocese erected Purcell High School on Victory Parkway. The Society of Mary and diocesan priests of the neighboring parishes conducted the school. The Franciscan Fathers built and conducted Roger Bacon High School in St. Bernard. Another central high school for girls, formerly St. Mary's Parish High School in Hyde Park, was also opened. The Sisters of Charity conducted it as a diocesan high school. In 1928 St. Rita High School for the deaf, established five years earlier and the first Catholic high school for the deaf in the United States, had its first graduation exercises. In Springfield St. Raphael parish built the Catholic Central High School, conducted by the Sisters of Charity. Pupils of all parishes in the community could attend it. A decade later there were Catholic high schools in Botkins, Celina, Chillicothe, Glendale, Marion, Middletown, Piqua, and Sidney. In addition to the regular high school subjects, each high school allotted a full scholastic period daily to the study of religion and sponsored a yearly retreat for students.[5]

In Dayton McNicholas, like his predecessor, initially encountered some difficulties. Convinced that Moeller had been "broken in spirit because of the endless" disagreements over the proposed centralized school system, McNicholas had about fifteen meetings with the priests of Dayton before a decision was finally reached. In 1927 two diocesan high schools opened. The reorganization of the Catholic high school system resulted in the transformation of Notre Dame Academy, renamed Julienne High School, into a diocesan central high school for girls. The new school inherited a rich tradition extending over eighty-seven years. Chaminade, a central high school for boys, was opened and operated by the Brothers of Mary. In their first year the two schools combined had more than one thousand students.[6]

Continuing a rich archdiocesan tradition of support for Catholic education, many sacrifices and contributions were made by the religious and the laity in the cause of Catholic secondary education. Millions of dollars were expended in the building of the high schools. By conducting the various schools, the religious orders relieved the archdiocese of a great financial obligation. McNicholas acknowledged the "extraordinary outlay" made by religious communities. In his judgment, the women religious were "especially desiring of the highest commendation," he wrote to Archbishop Joseph Ritter of St. Louis, "because it is due to the life of sacrifice to which they are habitually accustomed that we have been able to continue our schools." Complementing the work of the religious, the parishes largely supported the system of the new free high schools. Pastors established a monthly collection for education in order to help meet the finances of the high schools. Each parish paid a certain amount for each student from the parish attending one of the high schools. The system for financing the regional Catholic high schools in the Cincinnati archdiocese attracted national attention. It assured a high school education to every capable boy and girl, regardless of the ability of the individual family or parish to bear the financial burden. For more than half a century, separate high schools for men and women became the pattern. This was the ideal repeatedly expounded by papal encyclicals on education. Women religious taught in the female academies and high schools, and religious brothers and clergy taught in the schools for boys. Initially opposed to coeducation at the high school level, McNicholas helped establish separate high schools, with the single exception of the establishment of Madonna High School for black students of both sexes in 1927. Although private schools operated by religious orders have continued to the present day, a number of independent ventures either closed or became incorporated into the central archdiocesan system. Consequently, religious of various orders often found themselves on the same faculty with diocesan priests and lay teachers.[7]

By 1944 McNicholas, as chairman of the NCWC Department of Education, pointed out that a reorganization of the Catholic secondary system of education was "long overdue." He thought that Catholics had delayed too long in coming to grips with the real purpose of the secondary school. McNicholas argued that the church with its meager resources could not hope to duplicate all the educational facilities that the state made available to public schools. It would be unwise, he thought, for the church "to embark on any large program of vocational education." As far as the archbishop was concerned, 90 percent of the secondary school problem was pastoral and 10 percent educational. Believing that most of the young people would make up the "great bulk" of the future Catholic population, he contended the church had a pastoral duty for the sanctification of their souls.[8]

As he attended to the pastoral needs of the students and provided some vocational education, McNicholas did not want to sacrifice the minority of Catholic students who had the capacity for an academic education. Since it was impossible for the church to do everything "we can at least," he wrote, "concentrate on what we know is most important. Academic [or] . . . liberal arts education . . . should be made as excellent as possible." He was of the opinion that the gifted young people should be given opportunities so that they would become "the priests, the scientists, the lawyers, the doctors, the writers, and the artists who will command attention and respect." As a member of the NCWC administrative board in the 1940s, the Cincinnati ordinary consistently argued that the American church needed thinkers and scholars. Advocating an education that was primarily intellectual, McNicholas was critical of any curriculum that was "diluted and broadened so as to make it adaptable to those of a different intellectual competence." He further argued that the Catholic schools began their secondary education too late. The archbishop thought that students should begin learning Latin as early as twelve years of age. He was aware of the success of the two Latin schools in the diocese of Covington. McNicholas proposed that Catholics experiment "with the idea of taking boys and girls of superior talents at the end of the sixth grade and affording them the opportunity of beginning secondary work of an academic nature." By 1941 four Latin schools for boys were operating in the archdiocese, two in Cincinnati at St. Francis de Sales and St. Lawrence, a third at Sacred Heart in Dayton, and a fourth at St. Bernard in Springfield.[9]

When Karl Alter became archbishop in 1950, the archdiocese had twenty-six high schools for boys and girls. It had a larger proportion of its Catholic children attending diocesan and parochial high schools than any other of the larger dioceses in the United States. Only the dioceses of Nashville and Lansing, both considerably smaller than that of the Cincinnati archdiocese, had a larger proportion in the schools. A steady stream of students from the 150 Catholic elementary schools in the archdiocese maintained the comparatively large enrollment in Catholic high schools. At the time the parochial schools accommodated approximately one-fourth of all the children—Catholic and non-Catholic—in the nineteen counties of the archdiocese. In some areas 30 or 40 percent of the entire population of grade-schoolers were in the Catholic schools. More than four of every five children who graduated from a Catholic elementary school went on to a Catholic high school. In addition to the founding of Fenwick High School in Middletown and Holy Angels High School in Sidney in the 1950s, St. Joseph's Academy, founded in 1915 by the Sisters of St. Joseph, became McNicholas High School in 1951, then the only coeducational high school in the archdiocese. Shortly before he died, McNicholas had written to Archbishop Ritter that he had "lost all the inhibitions [he] had about high schools that are coeducational."[10]

A study made by the archdiocesan school office in the 1950s projected enrollments of Catholic high schools in the Cincinnati area to increase by about two-thirds by 1964. Speaking to an overflow crowd at the dedication of the new church-school building and convent of Our Lady of Good Hope parish at Miamisburg in the fall of 1956, Alter noted that the Catholic school population was growing faster than the church could build and equip schools. "Today we no longer see the Bishops and clergy pleading with the people to build schools," he said. "Instead, the people are pleading with the clergy to build them." But, he cautioned, "there is a limit to how far we can go into debt." By the year 1955 the accumulation of parish reserves deposited with the chancery for investment in the parish building program had been exhausted. For several years new parish buildings had been constructed through this fund as well as from individual savings of certain parishes. Because the chancery could no longer help finance any new projects, each parish had to secure its own bank loans to meet the costs.[11]

In a confidential report to the pastors of Hamilton and Clermont Counties in January 1957, Alter emphasized the immediate need to expand Catholic high school facilities in their area. He proposed a fund drive to cover the costs of new construction. Two months later he appointed Harry J. Gilligan, a prominent Catholic layman, to head the Archbishop High School Fund Campaign. In a pastoral letter read in all the churches, the archbishop called upon the faithful to continue the rich tradition of support for education in the archdiocese. Although "Catholic educators have no bone to pick with the public schools," Gilligan said, "Catholic educators must, in conscience, make their own schools consistent with Catholic belief." Priests and laymen formed a general committee, and parish chairmen in each area enlisted thousands of laymen to carry the high school appeal into every Catholic home in the two counties. The goal of the campaign was to raise more than $6,000,000 in order to erect three new high schools—LaSalle, Moeller, and McAuley—in the northwest and northeast sectors of Hamilton County and to make substantial additions to Elder, Roger Bacon, and McNicholas High Schools. Even though St. Xavier High School for Boys on Sycamore Street had already made plans to campaign in 1956 to build a new school on sixty-one acres of land on North Bend Road, it agreed to postpone a separate drive in favor of a joint campaign.[12]

Though the building of Catholic elementary schools was the responsibility of the individual parishes, and more than 500 parochial elementary classrooms had been built in the period 1947 to 1956, building and maintaining high schools was the responsibility, Alter argued, "of the entire Catholic community." The Cincinnati ordinary reminded the parishes, as had Moeller and McNicholas before him, that no one parish had adequate resources "to operate a well-organized and departmentalized high school." Alter issued the unusual order for priests in the 121 parishes in Hamilton and Clermont Counties to exchange pulpits to show their solidarity for the project in their pleas for financial donations. The fund campaign topped its goal by more than two million dollars. "The resounding success of your high school development campaign is almost incredible," Bishop George Rehring of Toledo wrote to Alter. In the end Alter paid tribute to "the intense loyalty" of Catholics to their religious schools, calling it "one of the most consoling phenomena in our Catholic social life in America." Catholics were making their presence known in the archdiocese not only religiously but socially as well. Because of the success of the campaign, a portion of the surplus was distributed among the girls' high schools in the city.[13]

The Society of Mary, Sisters of Mercy, and the Brothers of the Christian Schools, newcomers to the archdiocese, agreed to staff the three new high schools in Cincinnati. In 1961 the Society of Mary, which operated the University of Dayton and Chaminade, Purcell, and Hamilton Catholic High Schools, staffed Moeller High School for Boys on Montgomery Road. The same year the Brothers of the Christian Schools took charge of La Salle High School for Boys on North Bend Road. McAuley High School for Girls was built and operated by the Sisters of Mercy on Oakwood Avenue in College Hill. The three high schools, each erected at a cost of about $1,250,000, were constructed to accommodate about one thousand students each. Outside of Cincinnati, Carroll High School in Dayton opened its doors in 1961. The following year Archbishop Alter High School in Kettering was founded. In 1963, St. Mary's High School in Hyde Park in Cincinnati was moved to a new location on Madison Road and became Marian High School.[14]

In April 1959 the archdiocese launched the Archbishop's Greater Dayton High School Campaign among thirty-one parishes in Montgomery County and three parishes in Greene County. More than six thousand laymen were organized in the various parishes to solicit every Catholic wage earner in the area. The main goal of the campaign was to build a new high school for one thousand pupils in the eastern section of Montgomery County and a new high school for eight hundred to one thousand students in the southern section. The campaign, moreover, sought to raise money to purchase land for a proposed high school in the northern section and make additions at Chaminade and Julienne High Schools. "Our obligation," Auxiliary Bishop Leibold wrote, "extends to thousands now and to thousands yet to come." Pointing out that he represented five generations of the Leibold family in Dayton, he warned that "for the first time in five generations they now hear the warning: 'There is no room in the Catholic school for you.' Are the children of today less dear to us than we were to our grandparents, when they did their fair share with no little sacrifice to educate us?" By December 1962 the archdiocese was pleased with the results of the campaign, "and not least the fact," Alter wrote to Monsignor Edward A. Connaughton at the Parochial Schools Office in Dayton, because "we will be able to fulfill all the promises which we made to the people of Dayton."[15]

In 1965 the archdiocese also took steps to consolidate and refinance the indebtedness of approximately $5 million of eight high schools in Cincinnati and Dayton. The borrowed money was paid off in accordance with a new plan of high school tuition payments. In addition to each student paying an annual tuition payment of $170 and the student's parish $30, each parish paid $40 a year for each of its high school students into a common fund to be used for the reduction of the debt. In the mid-1960s a new addition was made to Mother of Mercy High School in Westwood and two new high schools were built, Stephen Badin in Hamilton and Mount Notre Dame in Reading. Mount Notre Dame Academy, which was founded in 1860, had become a centralized high school for girls in 1957. The new high schools now made the archdiocese only second to Philadelphia in the number of high school students in ratio to the Catholic population. Funds for the new buildings were paid out of the reserve from the high school debt fund. During Alter's nineteen-year administration Catholics donated more than $13 million for seven new high schools in Cincinnati, Dayton, Middletown, and Springfield.[16]

GOVERNMENT AID

During his administration McNicholas foresaw the impossibility of long maintaining the growing Catholic school system without some form of aid from the state. During the depression of the 1930s local church officials became more vocal. Through its auxiliary bishop, Joseph H. Albers, the archdiocese participated in meetings and discussions with the legislators in the Ohio legislature. Catholic schools, which at the time were free to all students, were hurting financially as was true of many other institutions in society. Fearing that some of the schools might have to be closed, McNicholas called for a just and fair share of tax revenues. His main object was to gain for Catholic schools a share of the school fund.[17]

The archdiocese often pointed out that because of the Catholic parochial school system, local and state taxpayers realized an enormous financial saving. It was estimated in 1933 that each year the local church saved taxpayers in Hamilton County alone more than $4 million for education and about one million dollars for social service. One-sixth of the children of Ohio were educated in Catholic schools, providing the state not only a service but saving it approximately eighteen million dollars per year. It was further argued that if the Catholic schools were compelled to close because of the depression, the public schools would be responsible for educating those students. Surely, McNicholas thought, it was in the state's interest to provide "some help" and enable the Catholic schools to continue in operation. Catholics requested aid for such basic educational necessities as textbooks, building maintenance, and other general operating costs. When proposals for tax-based state aid failed, the archbishop in 1935 proposed a system in which parents would be given money in the form of vouchers that "they could give to the school of their choice for the education of their children." What McNicholas asked for the Catholic Church, he also asked for all denominations.[18]

The Cincinnati ordinary argued for state-based aid in education to Catholics, which he also asked for all denominations, and he consistently fought also for the rights of all parents regardless of creed, color, or race in the education of their children. "Parents' rights and duties," McNicholas said, "are not surrendered to the State, nor can the State lawfully take them away when children are placed in school." He often cautioned parents against transferring too much of the responsibility for their children onto the schools. Viewing parents as "co-creators and co-conservers with Almighty God, not in a temporary, but a life-long contract," he urged them not to shirk their responsibility. The assumption that teachers and priests were better qualified than parents were "to develop the characters of their children," he said, "is not true. The greatest character builders in the world are parents." Emphasizing the sanctity of the family and parents' responsibilities in rearing their children, the local church thought parents had no duty so important as that of caring for the spiritual, intellectual, and physical welfare of their children.[19]

In his "Official Column" in the *Catholic Telegraph* in August 1935, McNicholas, who had become by that time a national leader in the field of education, warned against the danger of too much state control in public education. Pressing for state money for Catholic and other denominational schools, he urged parents not to surrender their rightful authority on educational matters to the state. He insisted that the more authority in public education was centered in Columbus, parents would have that much less to say about the instruction and training of their children. He charged public officials, especially those at public colleges and universities, of being "usurpers of the rights of parents, . . . kidnappers of the minds of children." Fully aware that his language was strong, McNicholas had lost "all patience," he wrote to Bishop James Hartley of Columbus, with those "professors who try to rob the youth of our day of their faith." McNicholas also thought it was good political strategy to emphasize the rights of parents. "I think we Bishops," he wrote in 1936, "should build up constructively a program that show parents' rights. We have got to be realists in education. . . . It seems to me that we have a chance to get a hearing in the country if we insist on the rights of parents." The archbishop was convinced that by genuinely fighting for parents' rights in education the church was building a strong political base of support.[20]

As resources became scarce during the depression, the archdiocese was forced to abandon the idea of free Catholic high schools. It required pupils attending some of the Catholic high schools to pay part of the tuition. "We now face," McNicholas wrote in 1937, "the impossibility of conducting free high schools." The parents or guardians of each student now had to pay forty dollars a year and the parish to which the pupil belonged paid an additional forty dollars. Due to the sacrifices made by parents, parishioners, and various teaching orders, the parochial schools were able to survive the economic crisis. But not all families could afford to pay tuition. Partly because of the new regulations, about three-fifths of high school students in Holy Trinity parish in Dayton attended public high schools.[21]

The strong possibility of federal aid to Catholic or religious education arose during and after World War II. Though American bishops had opposed federal aid to education consistently before and after World War I, by 1944 they began to change their minds. Positive experience with government relief programs in the 1930s and 1940s doubtlessly helped diminish some concerns regarding federal assistance to education. Even though McNicholas continued to express concern over governmental interference in local issues, he anticipated a radical change in the educational status of the country. "Federal aid to public schools," he wrote to the apostolic delegate in the fall of 1944, "is, I think, inevitable." He now thought Catholics "should not express further opposition, but should cooperate" as far as they could "in framing a measure in Congress which would be fair to all schools."[22]

In February 1945 McNicholas sent a telegram to Ohio Senator Robert Taft, who was a sponsor of a federal education bill that came to be associated with his name. The archbishop adamantly opposed certain provisions of the bill that excluded children from Catholic and other denominational schools. McNicholas feared that Taft's proposal would create a system of "secularist" schools and "would indirectly abolish freedom of education for the poor and religious-minded parents." Touting parents' rights over the education of their children, he argued that any federal aid for education should be based "on the proved need of the educable child." He contended that the aid should be equitable to all children of a community, regardless of color, origin, or creed. Hurling lightning bolts at Taft's education bill, McNicholas maintained that more than 200,000 children in the nonpublic schools of Ohio would be "treated unjustly." Wanting to avoid the entanglement of church and state, which many Catholic and non-Catholic critics objected to, he was convinced that Catholics should not ask for direct aid for their schools. There was, in his judgment, "too much propaganda about union of Church and State," he wrote to Cardinal Francis Spellman of New York. Protestants and other Americans united for separation of church and state were nevertheless critical of McNicholas's outspokenness. They accused the Catholic Church of "playing with fire" by violating the principle of separation of church and state. McNicholas and his episcopal colleagues consistently denied the charge. In one instance the chancery had full-page ads published in daily newspapers throughout the archdiocese, denying any interest on the part of the Catholic Church for union of church and state.[23]

Believing that private schools were "needlessly duplicating the needs of the public school," Senator Taft thought the Catholic Church was "making a tremendous mistake in seeking government money" for its schools. Admiring some of Taft's capabilities, McNicholas regretted that he should "have a closed mind in the field of education." Those who knew Taft spoke of him "as a man with a most unfortunate personality," he wrote to Bishop Michael Ready of Columbus in May 1946. "He has exceptional gifts, but also the most extraordinary limitations. He has no patience in listening to the arguments of others. . . . He apparently has nothing of scholarly patience, which is so necessary to get an objective view of things. If you think as he does, you are right; if you differ with him, you are wrong. Does it not seem tragic that a man of this mental calibre should aspire to the Presidency?" McNicholas became convinced that the senator's "twisted reasoning" would make him "a very dangerous man . . . in the office of the President." Although McNicholas was "deeply saddened and puzzled" by Taft's stand on the question of federal aid to education, it did not stop him two years later from recommending to Roman authorities that he be granted a private audience with the pope. "The Senator," he wrote, "is a man whose integrity and love of America command the highest respect of our citizens. His family life is an edification to the country."[24]

During the remainder of the decade McNicholas, as head of the NCWC, waged a powerful campaign for public aid to parochial schools. In his lobbying efforts he had several visits with President Harry Truman, whose "friendship he valued highly." McNicholas consistently argued that it was the duty of the federal, state, and local governments to safeguard the rights of all parents to educate their children in the schools of their "conscientious choice." In a radio address in the summer of 1946, he pointed out that the public school system was not the only American system of education. That system "included," he said, "public schools, private schools, and schools under the auspices of religion." McNicholas cited the post–World War II GI Bill and the National School Lunch Act as examples of fair legislation. The GI Bill, which provided a college education to those who had served in the military, allowed individuals to attend either public or private universities, and the federally funded School Lunch Program applied to children in all schools. McNicholas called on both state and national governments to pass school aid legislation to cover all schools.[25]

Debate over the issue of government aid to nonpublic schools continued during the tenure of Karl Alter. The archbishop carried on McNicholas's fight for Catholic students in much the same terms, though he added his own insights and arguments. Alter had long argued that Catholics were not opposed to public schools, but readily supported them by their taxes. What they objected to was discrimination. "If there were no public schools," he wrote, "we would have to create them." In full agreement with McNicholas's July 1947 pastoral that the "Catholic and public schools are partners in American education," Alter added in 1957 that the public and private schools were "parallel and not opposed to each other."[26]

Like his predecessor Alter left his footprints on church-state relations. He believed that federal aid to education should "be free from control by the Federal Government and free from discrimination against any group of school children." He, too, thought that the best way to secure justice and fair play for all without violating the First Amendment was not to subsidize the school, "but to provide instead a subsidy for all school children and their parents" by means of scholarships or vouchers. Believing that the state had the same responsibility toward Catholics that it had toward those who were not Catholic, Alter advocated a public-supported private school system wherein parents would be able to choose the education they desired for their children and at the same time pay for it. Catholics should not be "penalized by being forced to bear a double burden of taxation," he wrote. Catholics contended that such social services as bus transportation, health services, lunches, textbooks, and vouchers should be regarded as "civic benefits" and be made available to all children. Echoing the sentiments of most Catholics, Alter thought it was a matter of justice and equity. By this time it was estimated that Catholics of the Cincinnati archdiocese provided an annual savings to the public of more than thirty-one million dollars.[27]

In 1964 the Citizens for Educational Freedom (CEF), a grassroots organization of mostly Catholic parents interested in the fair and equal treatment of all schoolchildren, held a meeting of priests and lay people in each deanery of the archdiocese. It promoted passage of the Fair School Bus legislation in Ohio to provide bus transportation for religious or private school pupils. The CEF had 320 chapters spread throughout Ohio's eighty-eight counties. The archdiocesan chapters joined those in other dioceses to help defray the expenses of the CEF program. The chancery encouraged pastors to make appropriate pulpit announcements and to get parishioners to circulate petitions and obtain signatures at the church doors in support of the Fair School Bus Bill. This was "a matter of principle," Cincinnati's Chancellor Henry Vogelpohl wrote, "that involves the common good." In the summer of 1965 archdiocesan Catholics wrote to Governor James Rhodes in support of the Fair School Bus Bill. Later that year the legislation was passed. Two years later Ohio also allotted funds for supplemental services and materials.[28]

GROWTH OF EDUCATION

In the second quarter of the twentieth century Catholic educators in the archdiocese and in other big dioceses encouraged greater centralization, standardization, professionalization, and state certification of teachers in order to improve education. In the process, the measures helped American-ize Catholic schools. In 1925 Father Urban Vehr became the superintendent of schools. He served until 1929 when Father Francis J. Bredestege replaced him. During Bredestege's tenure, the school system experienced substantial reorganization of its high schools and the founding of the Athenaeum and the Teachers' College. In 1932 Father Carl J. Ryan succeeded Bredestege, serving as superintendent of schools until 1969. Under his leadership, Catholic schools realized unprecedented growth and consolidation. The archdiocese fully implemented the certification of all teachers, introduced diocesan supervisors, and organized the School Lunch Program. In compli-ance with the standards of the Ohio Department of Education, each bishop in the state maintained a central teacher-training institution to prepare teachers for all schools of his diocese. Each diocese, furthermore, had a dioce-san Board of Examiners. The pastor, who had direct charge of the parochial school in his parish, could not permit a teacher who did not hold a certificate from the Board of Examiners to teach in the school. It was the pastor's responsibility to maintain and staff the school with qualified teachers. Though the majority of the courses conformed in general to those of the pub-lic schools, the study of religion received an all-important place in the cur-riculum of the parochial schools. Students attended Mass each morning during the school year and recited prayers at intervals throughout the day.[29]

When Ohio in 1927 imposed more rigid requirements in teacher training and preparation, McNicholas in the spring of that year called a meeting of the various teaching orders in the archdiocese to discuss the establishment of a Teachers' College. "I have not sought to do this," he wrote, "but it rather been forced upon me by the State" because of its more stringent standards. Until then the various religious communities and the local Catholic colleges largely undertook the training of teachers in the Catholic schools of the arch-diocese. But the idea of a Teachers' College had been introduced earlier. Besides the unsuccessful effort of Archbishop Purcell in 1863 to form an archdiocesan normal school, the Jesuits in 1920 had also proposed to establish a Teachers' College. Because Moeller at the time wanted to retain the own-ership of the proposed buildings as well as control of the faculty and cur-riculum, the Jesuit Superior General in Rome disapproved of the project. Though by 1927 the Jesuits at St. Xavier College finally conducted a normal school for the various religious teaching communities in the archdiocese,

McNicholas eventually thought it was necessary for the archdiocese to take it over. In March 1928 he organized the Teachers' College, with Bredestege as dean. Housed in the building formerly occupied by St. George parochial school on Calhoun Street in Cincinnati, the college provided a complete teacher training program for the teaching communities of sisters, lay teachers, priests, and seminarians. It also helped prepare organists and music teachers for the archdiocese. In its first year the college had an enrollment of thirty-three full-time students and 116 part-time. As the archdiocese reorganized and expanded the high school system, the Teachers' College helped enhance the education and preparation of teachers in the schools.[30]

In the summer of 1947 the Teachers' College vacated the old quarters on Calhoun Street and moved into the newly remodeled archbishop's former residence on Moeller Avenue next to Mount St. Mary's of the West Seminary. Earlier that year Louis Richter, a local Catholic, had bought the twenty-acre Peter G. Thomson estate on Belmont Avenue in College Hill for the archdiocese. McNicholas then made the estate his new residence. Contrary to his relatively ascetic life, the archbishop's new home had eight bedrooms, a swimming pool, and a greenhouse. Though not as large as his Norwood residence, McNicholas found it "more homey." Moreover, it became clear that the conversion of the former residence to the archdiocesan Teachers' College would represent a considerable saving over the cost of erecting a new structure. The college operated at this location until 1953 when it was discontinued. Area Catholic colleges and universities now assumed the responsibility of preparing the teachers.[31]

One of McNicholas's early goals was the consolidation of Cincinnati's Catholic institutions of higher education under the corporate umbrella called the Athenaeum of Ohio. Legally incorporated in 1928, it was initially designed as a governing body to direct and supervise the colleges, seminaries, academies, and institutions for training priests, sisters, and lay persons in the archdiocese. It was called the Athenaeum of Ohio after the Athenaeum, founded by Fenwick as the first institution of higher learning in the archdiocese. The archdiocesan seminaries were the first two units of the Athenaeum at the time of its incorporation. St. Gregory Seminary, which comprised the high school and college programs, was empowered by the state to confer the bachelor's degree, and Mount St. Mary's of the West Seminary conferred the master's degree in scholastic philosophy. In 1950 the Athenaeum of Ohio was reorganized and all affiliates were dropped, except the two seminaries and the Teachers' College.[32]

Catholic higher education experienced continued growth during McNicholas's episcopate. On August 4, 1930, by an act of the state of Ohio, St.

Xavier College, with approximately one hundred lay faculty and Jesuits and more than one thousand students, became known as Xavier University. In 1935 Our Lady of Cincinnati College in Cincinnati, a new college for women, was opened with the Sisters of Mercy in charge. During McNicholas's tenure the archdiocese also thought it had a responsibility for Catholic students attending secular colleges. "The safeguarding of the faith of our Catholic students attending secular universities," McNicholas wrote, "is a pastoral anxiety that weighs heavily upon us." Archdiocesan officials approved of the Newman Club and the establishment of the Newman Foundation of Cincinnati, composed chiefly of Catholic men and women of the archdiocese who were interested in the welfare of Catholic students attending the University of Cincinnati. In Oxford, Ohio, the Newman Club at St. Mary Church attended to Catholic students at Miami University.[33]

Appointed chairman in 1934 of a Roman-appointed visiting committee for the ecclesiastical faculties of The Catholic University of America, a pontifical university founded in 1887 in Washington, D.C., McNicholas emphasized the importance of teaching and educating people in theology. The Cincinnati ordinary insisted that the university ought to confine itself to its "real work," by which he meant graduate education and theological training. Convinced that the university was "a mess" in its overemphasis on research, he and his episcopal colleagues wanted a group of priests who had "a thorough knowledge of theology, even though they never produce a thing for publication." McNicholas, who had also presided over a committee to investigate the differences between the rector and the faculty of theology, was instrumental in the eventual removal of Father James Hugh Ryan as rector and the selection of his successor, Father Joseph Moran Corrigan.[34]

An educational project dear to Archbishop McNicholas was the Institutum Divi Thomae, founded in 1935 at St. Gregory Seminary to train students in postgraduate science work under the direction of Dr. George Sperti, formerly a professor at the University of Cincinnati. McNicholas, who served as president for its first seven years, saw in the scientific work at the Institutum great promise for the unity of science and philosophy, the natural and supernatural. In his address on "The Present Opportunity of Scholastic Philosophy" at the annual meeting of the American Catholic Philosophical Association in 1938, McNicholas argued that "a closer and stronger bond should exist between philosophy and the positive sciences." The archbishop had high expectations and often praised the work of the new scientific institute, which sought not only to reconcile differences between science and philosophy but also to search for cures for various diseases. "The whole project may seem like a dream," he wrote, "but God help the world if there were not Celtic dreamers in it." A year after its founding he sent some of the Sperti therapeutic sun lamps to Archbishop Michael Curley of Baltimore. "It is perfectly safe," he wrote, "to sleep under it for several hours at a time or all night if you wish to do so." McNicholas kept one of the lamps at his bedside and used it for reading purposes. He also found it very helpful for colds and sinus trouble. In addition to sending vitamin tablets and cleansing cream, known as "Sperti Cream," to episcopal colleagues, shipments of vitamin tablets were sent to foreign mission fields. A million tablets were sent to the Vatican to be distributed under the direction of the Holy See. McNicholas was also hopeful that Sperti would find a cure for cancer. Revenues derived from the sale of Sperti's inventions funded educational programs and helped support a number of priests and sisters in graduate school. The Institutum remained under diocesan control until 1950, shortly after McNicholas's death. At that time it fell in disfavor with Archbishop Alter and the local church officials, and it eventually went its separate way.[35]

McNicholas died of a heart attack at his College Hill home a little after 7 P.M. on April 22, 1950. About an hour earlier he had complained of being ill and lapsed into a coma. His nephew, Father Timothy McNicholas at Mount St. Mary's of the West Seminary, gave the last rites. The silver-haired prelate was seventy-two. McNicholas had been in ill health for two years, several times confined to bed. The fourteen priests comprising the archdiocesan board of consultors met on April 23 and elected Auxiliary Bishop George J. Rehring administrator of the archdiocese. He served in that capacity until Pius XII named Karl Alter the new archbishop of Cincinnati.[36]

One of the early decisions of Alter's administration was the establishment in 1954 of the Archbishop Choir School, headed by John J. Fehring, archdiocesan music director. Boys enrolled in grades five through eight at the school received training in music as well as a regular educational curriculum. The school, originally located in Holy Angels school, occupied part of St. Francis de Sales school in 1965. The boys' choir sang at Sunday Mass and other services at the cathedral with the Cathedral Men's Choir. Difficulty in recruiting students and finding a suitable location for the school led to its closing and the disbanding of the Cathedral Boys' Choir in 1970.[37]

By the middle of the 1950s Alter decided to establish a thirteen-member archdiocesan Board of Education to help determine matters of policy for the parish elementary and diocesan high schools. Until 1959 all members of the school board were clergy. At that time the board was reorganized and eight lay persons were added to it. By the 1950s, moreover, lay teaching in Catholic schools became the norm rather than the exception. In the fall of 1957 alone there was an increase of only four religious in the parochial elementary school system of the archdiocese. In contrast there was an increase of more than eighty lay teachers. Like many parochial school systems in the country at the time, the archdiocesan system was growing every year. In 1958 there were more than 93,000 students in attendance in the Catholic schools of the archdiocese, from kindergarten to the post-graduate level. There were more than 2,900 teachers and of these almost one-fourth were lay teachers. In the fall of 1959, despite the expected increase of approximately 3,500 pupils in the parochial schools, there were fifteen fewer sisters available to staff the classrooms. The continued increase in enrollment, felt mostly in the suburban districts, dramatically reflected the shortage of religious vocations. Moreover, the 139 lay teachers in the diocesan high schools represented approximately one-fifth of all the high school teachers. "How long," Alter argued, "can we continue to operate our Catholic school system under such conditions?" It was evident "to any thoughtful person," he said in his fall 1959 pastoral, "that a voluntary and self-supporting system of education cannot continue to exist without the donated services of religious men and women." He went on to point out that the financial burden on a parish of the employment of one lay teacher was equivalent to "the services of four sisters. When the number of lay teachers reaches a fifty per cent ratio and more, as it does in some parishes, then a Catholic parish school system ceases to be a possibility." There was need, he argued, for more vocations. Because of the shortage of religious teachers and the sharp decline in enrollment in certain schools, in 1959 three basin area schools in Cincinnati, St. Ann's on John Street, St. John's on Green Street, and St. Michael's in Price Hill, were closed. Each school had fewer than ninety pupils.[38]

In 1962 there were 152 parish elementary schools, twelve private and institutional elementary schools, twenty-nine central high schools, and seven private and institutional high schools, for a total enrollment of 94,589 students. Fifty-four of the schools were within the Cincinnati city limits and another thirty-four lay within Hamilton County. Among the teaching staff in the archdiocese, 695 were sisters and members of religious societies; 446 were lay teachers. The enrollment in the fourteen interparochial high schools in Hamilton County was 13,238, with a teaching staff of 595. Among the teachers were 159 laymen. Over a five-year period, the elementary school enrollment had increased by 14,000, a 23 percent increase. Thirty-five percent of all teachers were lay teachers. In the fall of 1961 the Chancery Office, upon the recommendation of the archdiocesan school board, set a maximum limit of 50 children to a classroom in parochial elementary schools. The average class size in 1962 was forty-one pupils per class. The following year the total enrollment in the elementary and high schools of the archdiocese went over 100,000 students. This represented a growth since Alter's arrival in 1950 of more than 100 percent. It had required about 130 years to provide for the first 50,000 students, and only twelve years for the second 50,000. "Obviously," Alter wrote to Monsignor Ryan, "we have strained all our resources, and a similar effort cannot be expected within the next decade. In consequence, any further growth will have to depend upon some new sources of revenue as well as some new sources of staff recruitment."[39]

In the face of mounting school expenses, the archdiocese was in need of more revenue. For the first time since the diocesan high school system was set up in the late 1920s, Alter in the early 1960s attempted to get any kind of figures on the cost of operating the high schools. Part of the problem was the lack of uniformity among the various high schools in keeping financial books. On assuming office in 1950, Alter had found hundreds of thousands of dollars of unpaid tuition. He ordered an assessment of the parishes and instructed each school to secure a bank loan to pay its arrears. It took more than a decade before the parishes paid all the loans to the banks. In 1961 the tuition fee in archdiocesan high schools was raised from $120 to $160 a year. The parishes continued to pay the high schools $60 a year for each of their students attending the schools. The parents paid $100. Before that the parents had paid half the cost of tuition and the respective parishes the other half. The parishes' share was not increased because of the growing burden of maintaining parish elementary schools. The growing proportion of lay teachers on the high school staffs and other factors continued to push the costs upward.[40]

On March 5, 1964, the members of the archdiocesan school board, with Alter's approval, instituted a new program designed to strengthen the school system. They dropped the first grade of parish elementary schools, increased lay teachers' salaries by an annual increment of $100, raised sisters' salaries from $1,000 to $1,500, increased high school tuition to $200 a year, and proceeded to reduce class size. The elimination of the first grade, which involved twelve thousand children, underscored "the burden we've been carrying all these years," Alter said, "in operating our schools without outside help." Though unhappy with the dropping of the first grade, the archbishop asked the parishes to keep a correct perspective by taking into consideration the facts that the archdiocese was raising sisters' salaries, proceeding with four new high schools, and decreasing the number of pupils per classroom. In order to reduce to forty the maximum number of children in a class, a drop of ten, the school board had retained most of the teachers. Total enrollment in the elementary schools of the archdiocese in 1964 was 68,332 or 8,644 less than in 1963, which was the peak enrollment in the history of the archdiocese. By the spring of 1966 the pupil-teacher ratio in the elementary schools had gone down from 40-1 to 36.4-1.[41]

Whereas in 1964 the national average of Catholic children in parish schools was approximately 50 percent, the ratio in the archdiocese was nearer

75 percent. The percentage in the Catholic high schools was higher than in any other diocese of the country except one. Notwithstanding the high ratio, by the mid-1950s the number of Catholic children in the archdiocese attending public schools had increased. In October 1956 Alter had appointed Father James Shappelle as an assistant to the superintendent of schools to help organize a Confraternity of Christian Doctrine (CCD) program for Catholic students in the public schools.[42]

By the mid-1960s more than 50,000 Catholic boys and girls in the archdiocese were enrolled in public schools, twice as many as five years earlier. This meant that about a third of the Catholics of school age in the archdiocese were not attending Catholic schools. What contributed to the sharp increase were the dropping of grade one by parochial schools, the difficulty of transportation, especially in rural areas, and the fact that about one hundred parishes were without a parochial school. One-fifth of the children of school age lived in these parishes. What also contributed to the problem was the flight from established city parishes to suburbia, where a number of the schools were overcrowded. Shappelle, as director of the Catechetical Office, urged the establishment of a strong CCD program in every parish. "[T]he vigor of the faith in the archdiocese," he insisted, "depends upon a concentrated parish effort. . . . The strength of the Church in America in 15 years will depend largely on the strength of the CCD now." In 1964 alone more than five hundred of the Catholic laity took courses in catechetics in order to prepare themselves to teach religion to the children. By the end of his term Alter nevertheless surmised that the CCD program had not been "truly effective," primarily because there were few staff teachers who could give continuity to the program and insufficient time to instruct the children.[43]

In 1965 the archdiocese consolidated four parochial schools in the Cincinnati area. Pupils from St. Andrew in Avondale, Holy Angels in Walnut Hills, Holy Name in Mount Auburn, and St. Aloysius in Elmwood were reassigned to neighboring parochial schools. When Alter gave permission to close St. Aloysius elementary parish school, he did so because it seemed "to be somewhat of a waste of effort," he wrote, "to utilize the services of three Sisters" for seventy-five children. The children were subsequently cared for in the neighboring St. Charles parish at Carthage. The following year the Sisters of Christian Charity, because of the shortage of sisters, relinquished their convent in St. Boniface parish in Piqua, thus terminating eighty-five years of service in the archdiocese. They turned their teaching duties over to the Sisters of Mercy, who at the time staffed Piqua Catholic High and St. Mary's grade school in the city.[44]

The financial problems confronting Catholic schools in the 1960s represented the chief pastoral concern of the archdiocese. At the time parishes expended 70 percent of all their revenues for education. What made the problem particularly acute was the high ratio of eligible children attending archdiocesan schools, the rising costs of salaries and operation expenses, and the rapid turnover of lay teachers. Since 1950, the ratio of lay teachers had continued to increase. By 1967 lay teachers outnumbered religious in the elementary schools of the Cincinnati archdiocese for the first time. Of the 2,044 full time elementary teachers, 1,004 were religious and 1,040 were lay teachers. In the high schools there were 629 priests and other religious and 465 lay teachers, with the latter comprising 42.5 percent of the total. Though lay teachers were still in a minority in the high schools, there were forty-nine more in 1967 than the previous year, and thirty-nine fewer religious. Ten years earlier lay teachers in the elementary schools represented about one-fourth of the total number of teachers. In the 1950–51 school year they comprised less than 12 percent of the total.[45]

In his talk at the Ohio Catholic Educational Association's convention in the fall of 1967, Alter acknowledged that he was concerned over the future of Catholic education in the archdiocese. Even though there was more government aid to Catholic schools, the future was still a matter of "growing anxiety." He was troubled by the continuing decline in the number of religious vocations, the rising costs of operating schools, and the limitations of financial resources. "Only an extraordinarily optimistic person," he said, "would assume that we can grow in the future as we have in the past and solve the problems of meeting the educational needs and demands of our Catholic population. If we must curtail our efforts," he added, "shall it be in the early years of our elementary program or shall it be on the secondary level?" Wanting to keep schools opened to the extent that the resources of the archdiocese permitted, he was certain that "extensive collegiate and university ventures [were] a thing of the past."[46]

In the fall of 1968 Catholic schools in the Cincinnati archdiocese recorded an enrollment loss of 1.6 percent as compared to the previous year. The local figures reflected a national trend. Part of the loss stemmed from the closing of three more elementary schools, namely St. Peter in New Richmond, St. Denis in Versailles, and St. Patrick in Bellefontaine. What again contributed to the closing of the schools was the withdrawal of religious orders. A survey of fifty-nine elementary schools in 1968 revealed that there were three factors that weighed heavily in the determination of the economics of a parish school: rate of growth, proportion of religious to lay faculty members, and the contributions of the parishioners. The survey showed that more than two-thirds of their total expense was on salaries. Because of the increasing proportion of lay teachers, which was 52 percent in 1968, and the "constant escalation of salaries," Alter wrote, "I don't see how we're going to make it."[47]

In January 1969 the archdiocese endorsed a "Master Plan for a State-Wide Focus on Catholic Education." Proposed by the Catholic Conference of Ohio, the plan listed several financial objectives, including a drive for greater governmental assistance in the operation of Catholic schools. Theodore Staudt, executive director of the Catholic Conference of Ohio pointed out that the enrollment in Catholic schools in Ohio had decreased by more than twenty thousand students, adding a tax burden of approximately $12,250,000 to Ohio citizens for 1969 alone. Overall the archdiocese saved taxpayers of southwestern Ohio more than $50,000,000 a year. It was in the best interest of Catholics in Ohio to lay "the red figures of deficit financing before [their] own people and the general public," Staudt argued. Otherwise, they would "wake up one morning without a Catholic school system and with a public school system unable to take [their] children."[48]

In the spring of 1969 Governor James Rhodes and public school leaders in Cincinnati promised their support to help obtain a share of education tax benefits for Catholic schools. Dr. Paul A. Miller, superintendent of Cincinnati public schools, acknowledged the "major contribution to this community" made by parochial schools and pledged to work jointly with the archdiocese for state aid to nonpublic as well as public school students. Consistent with the Catholic practice since the mid-nineteenth century of backing taxation for the support of public schools, Alter and the Citizens for Educational Freedom reciprocated by strongly endorsing the Cincinnati public schools tax levy. Despite the "desperate financial situation" of parochial schools, Alter wrote, "no one possibly can gain by curtailing the educational services to children in the public schools." In June the Archdiocesan Board of Education published a booklet entitled "Why," which contained a letter by the archbishop. In June Alter again cautioned Ohioans that if the nonpublic schools closed, it would be a disaster for public schools as well. "Self-interest alone," he wrote, "would urge every citizen to keep the nonpublic schools alive."[49]

In August 1969 Governor Rhodes signed the education bill that provided $50 a year for each child in nonpublic schools. It helped ease the financial crisis facing Catholic schools in the archdiocese. Though pleased with the bill, Father Lawrence R. Strittmatter, coordinator for the Cincinnati archdiocese of the Statewide Focus on Catholic Education program, pointed out that in "no way can these benefits . . . be thought to solve the financial problems of the parochial schools." But, he added, "they may keep the wolf from the door for a while."[50]

PART

FOUR

LOCAL CHURCH
TRANSFORMED
Of, by, and for the People
1960s–1996

Introduction

During Karl Alter's tenure in the 1960s the nation and the Catholic Church were shaken by the social and political tumults raging across America. Americans lived in a society full of paradoxes, in a culture that involved confrontation and interchange between differing ideas and values. Women's rights, concern for the environment, racial justice, and a desire for peace were part of the American mainstream. The local church was affected by the ferment in society. The dominant issues of race, poverty, and war had an immense effect on it. When Pope John XXIII convened the Second Vatican Council in 1962, no one could foresee its impact on the church and its influence on society. There were profound changes in the structure and practices of the church, reinvigorating the role of the laity and transforming the people's experiences of worship. Moreover, at the same time that the church was influenced by the cultural crisis of the 1960s, it also influenced it. Issues within the church reflected the revolution in culture in the larger society. Catholics were practically everywhere on the political landscape, as they explored new ways of being both Catholic and American. The clergy and women religious became familiar figures in racial justice marches and peace protests.[1]

During the succeeding administrations of Paul F. Leibold (1969–1972), Joseph L. Bernardin (1972–1982), and Daniel E. Pilarczyk (1982–present), the post–Vatican II archdiocese of Cincinnati underwent a period of consolidation as well as stabilization and adjustment to the changes that had swept the church. In the face of a substantial decline in the number of clergy and religious, Catholics in the archdiocese witnessed an unprecedented number of church closings and mergers. Simultaneously, however, there was greater involvement of the laity and parishes in the life of the church, expansion of social programs, as well as increasing Mass attendance and enrollment in Catholic schools. A new model of church and authority emerged that replaced the more authoritarian and clerical concept that prevailed throughout the second half of the nineteenth and first six decades of the twentieth centuries. There was more shared responsibility in the governance and administration of the local church and the various parishes by the clergy, religious, and laity. As it celebrated in 1996 the 175th anniversary of its founding, the archdiocese braced itself for the challenges of the new millennium.

· 13 ·

IMPACT OF THE SECOND VATICAN COUNCIL

T he Second Vatican Council, which sent winds of change throughout the church, intersected with the social and cultural upheavals of the sixties. The council, held in Rome over four years, was the major event of the twentieth century for the Catholic Church. Its goal was, in one word, *aggiornamento,* to bring the church into line with the modern world. It sought to revitalize Catholic teaching and Christian living, reform certain ecclesiastical practices and structures, and promote Christian unity, social justice, and world peace. Moreover, as a result of Vatican II, a new vocabulary came into existence. Catholics would now speak of "ministry," "People of God," and "shared responsibility."

Religious communities, like the rest of the church, underwent self-examination of internal structures and of ministerial duties, resulting in sweeping changes. With these changes came tension and strife. As it did everywhere, the forces unleashed by the Second Vatican Council brought many changes to the archdiocese of Cincinnati. The ecumenical council brought about what appeared to be the virtual end of Tridentine Catholicism, the beliefs and practices of Catholics between the Council of Trent in 1545 and Vatican II, and ushered in a new Catholicism. Mass was celebrated in English, at times to the accompaniment of folk or contemporary music performed on the guitar rather than the organ. An increasing number of priests, seminarians, women religious, and brothers blended into the secular world to fulfill their mission. As the lifestyles of many clergy and religious changed in the sixties, some replaced religious habits and clerical collars with secular dress. Some, upon reexamination of their life decisions, left their respective religious orders.[1]

Many of the changes paralleled the questioning and reexamination of values and institutions in America. Catholic individuals and families were divided over the response to such issues as Vatican II, racial justice, and Vietnam. Interest in social justice nevertheless found many avid supporters among the laity and religious. Though not everyone welcomed the changes enthusiastically or approved of the new spirit, the archdiocese was filled with activity undertaken to fulfill the ideals of Vatican II. It established a liturgical commission, an ecumenical commission, a poverty commission, a human rights commission, a senate of priests, parish councils, and a Pastoral Council. Alter was also the first in the history of the archdiocese to appoint lay persons to the archdiocesan Board of Education. His support of parish boards of education, furthermore, attracted attention throughout the country.[2]

There were areas of conciliar renewal in the local church well before the Second Vatican Council. The liturgical movement that originated in the nineteenth century in French Benedictine monasteries first appeared in the United States in the 1920s. Its goal was to create a better understanding of the Mass through a more active participation of the laity. Virgil Michel, a Benedictine monk at St. John's University in Collegeville, Indiana, Martin Hellrieger of St. Louis, and the Jesuit Gerald Ellard spearheaded the movement. Though most Catholics still clung to devotional Catholicism, the liturgical movement, which was strong in the Midwest, began to challenge its relevance. Moreover, Pius XII's 1943 and 1947 encyclicals also encouraged the laity to participate more actively in the celebration of the Mass. Liturgical changes began occurring in the archdiocese in the 1950s. Though most bishops in the United States were raised in the novena and private rosary tradition and did not question their value, Alter was in the forefront of reform. He was instrumental in creating the climate and structures that made it possible for the priests, religious, and laity of the archdiocese to take a more active role in the life of the church.[3]

Over the course of the Alter years and in the decades that followed, lay leadership reemerged in the archdiocese. Alter helped reorganize the Archdiocesan Council of Catholic Men (ACCM) and the Archdiocesan Council of Catholic Women (ACCW), and entrusted to these federations a voice in planning and in implementing programs in the areas of liturgy, education, social action, legislation, decent literature, and family life. The success of Catholic Action movements over three decades doubtlessly gave rise to generations of educated, talented, and confident lay leaders. By 1957 the work of the ACCM and ACCW had developed to such a degree that a layman became assistant to the executive secretary, Monsignor Earl L. Whalen. The local church's move in this matter was to be followed later by a growing number of dioceses that employed laymen in executive positions. The increasing emphasis on lay work was also reflected in the growth of the family life and social action apostolates. A Family Life Bureau was established in the archdiocese in 1962, and lay faculties gave many of the courses for engaged and married persons.[4]

That same year Alter also helped bring the Cursillo Movement to the archdiocese. In the process, he helped shape the course of the movement in the country. First presented in the United States in Texas in 1957, the Cursillo made it possible for laymen to participate fully in a course designed to awaken personal awareness of Christian ideals and a renewed commitment to Christ. Under the tutelage of the Franciscans, the first Cursillo in the archdiocese was held in February 1962 at St. Anthony Friary in Cincinnati. Shortly thereafter St. John the Baptist Church in the Over-the-Rhine section then served as the Cursillo home until 1969, when it was announced that the church would be torn down. At that time the Cursillo returned to St. Anthony. From the start, teams of lay people from Cincinnati under the direction of the Franciscan Fidelis Albrecht took the Cursillo to a number of cities in the United States.[5]

Partly in response to papal pronouncements for the establishment of diocesan liturgical commissions, Alter became "greatly interested," he wrote to Cardinal Samuel Stritch of Chicago, in liturgical changes. He thought that priests and faithful alike had lost much of the significance of the liturgy. In January 1956 he established the Archdiocesan Liturgical Commission. Chaired by Monsignor John E. Kuhn, the Commission was charged with the responsibility of bringing about a right understanding and use of the liturgy. Before the end of the decade, the Englishhand missal at Mass and the dialogue Mass with its congregational responses were two signs of the increasing participation of the laity. More and more pastors taught their parishioners to participate actively in the Mass through the dialogue Mass. The liturgy was now seen as public worship, an act in which all the faithful were full participants. Alter did not want the faithful to be "mute onlookers." The liturgy was no longer seen as something with which the priest alone was involved.[6]

The dialogue Mass proved a great success. It became a common practice in a growing number of churches throughout the diocese. But practices varied. Sometimes the leader stood at the Communion rail facing the people or stood at the back of the church; sometimes the leader was a woman. The leader read in English the verses read by the priest in Latin, and the leader and people recited together the *Confiteor,* the *Gloria,* the *Creed,* the *Sanctus,* the *Pater Noster,* and the *Agnus Dei* in English. Some parishes recited together the prayers of the Offertory. Others also added the Communion prayers and the *Confiteor* before Communion. Active participation in reciting the responses and prayers in English helped deepen the laity's understanding and appreciation of the Mass.[7]

During the next few years Alter continually showed interest in liturgical reform. In 1957 he served on the Committee of Bishops to define the function of a proposed National Liturgical Commission of the Hierarchy. The following year Cincinnati hosted the annual North American Liturgical Week, designed to promote the participation of the laity. Thousands of Greater Cincinnatians joined the thousands of visitors from many states and several nations who packed Music Hall. Following the convention Alter called for congregational singing of the Sunday High Mass in parish churches.[8]

A survey conducted by the Archdiocesan Liturgical Commission in 1959 showed that the Mass participation program had generally good results. Though there were pastors who had met with opposition from parishioners who had grown accustomed to the "silent" Mass, which was especially the case with older parishioners, the survey revealed that most parishes were taking a more active part in Sunday Masses. "It seems evident," Monsignor Kuhn observed, "that the people are well-disposed to the idea of more active participation in the Mass. Even those who are slow to understand the reasons behind it accept it willingly as the mind of the Church. . . . Our greatest hope lies with the children." With thousands of children learning to make the responses, the future of the program of active participation in the Mass looked promising.[9]

CHANGES IN THE LOCAL CHURCH

In 1959 John XXIII announced the establishment of the Second Vatican Council, scheduled to open three years later. By virtue of Alter's stature in the American hierarchy and his chairmanship of the Administrative Board of the National Catholic Welfare Conference since 1958, he was one of four American prelates among the sixty-two members of the hierarchy appointed to the Central Preparatory Commission in 1961. Alter had also earlier served as chairman of the Administrative Board of the NCWC from 1952 to 1955. Meeting for ten days in June, the Commission acted as a clearinghouse for agenda material submitted for the Vatican Council. The following year Alter participated in two more series of preparatory meetings. When the Second Vatican Council finally opened in October 1962, Alter was elected to the Commission on Bishops and Government of Dioceses, one of ten specialized working commissions formed by the worldwide assembly of 2,700 prelates. On this Commission he helped produce the schema "Pastoral Function of Bishops in the Church." After participating in two-month work sessions in the falls of 1962 and 1963, his views toward liturgy, the laity, ecumenism, and religious freedom expanded. He returned from Rome enthused about the prospects of renewal. Anticipating less dependence on Rome and a movement away from the centralizing tendency that had, he stated, "perhaps been carried as far as is helpful in the Church," he looked at the council as focusing mainly on the inner renewal of the church. He stressed the need for greater use of the vernacular in worship, for more emphasis on Scripture, and for more lay participation in the liturgy. The call for lay responsibility was not new to the many men and women who had worked resolutely to make the Archdiocesan Councils of Men and Women with their parish counterparts vital organizations.[10]

Liturgical renewal was the first fruit of Vatican II. Before the third session of the council began in the fall of 1964, Alter had implemented some of the liturgical changes. He was among the first ordinaries in the nation to begin the gradual implementation of the council decrees. Earlier that year Alter had expanded the Archdiocesan Liturgical Commission to thirteen priests and five laymen. Serving as a council of advisers for the archbishop, the Commission helped organize in the parishes study groups for better understanding of Sacred Scripture. In August Alter authorized the use of the vernacular in all sacramental rites and directed Father Paul Leibold, chair of the Liturgical Commission, to instruct the clergy to encourage active participation by the laity in the liturgy through songs and prayers in their own language. In a number of parishes, liturgy committees worked with the pastor and lectors and musicians received special training. On the first Sunday of Advent, November 29, 1964, English was used in the Mass in the archdiocese for the first time. That day Alter gave the sermon at a special televised Mass he offered in St. Peter in Chains Cathedral.[11]

The most visible changes in the postconciliar period took place in the Mass. Before Vatican II, Mass was said in Latin, the priest faced the wall and prayed the prayers of the Mass silently and alone, and the parishioners prayed the rosary and recited prayers. No one except the priest was supposed to talk in church. The revised rite stressed the importance of community celebration and of enlightened lay participation. The laity were now visibly and audibly involved in the liturgy. Though using English, saying Mass facing the people, and distributing Holy Communion to people who were standing instead of kneeling constituted a distinct departure from the past, they did not in any way "affect the substance of the Mass. That," Alter said, "remains forever the same." The archbishop always insisted that in the midst of change in the outward forms, "the integrity of the faith must be maintained. . . . Customs can change; but the substance of faith, never." The archdiocese began using English in the High Mass on March 7, 1965, the first Sunday of Lent. It also introduced that spring the first use of concelebration and communion under both species. Two years later the local church authorized Sunday afternoon or evening Masses in any parish within the archdiocese, as long as the Mass was not scheduled after 8 P.M. The first evening Mass in the history of the archdiocese had been celebrated, with special permission from Rome, fourteen years earlier by Archbishop Alter at the opening of the Marian Year. By the year 1969 the Mass was said entirely in the vernacular.[12]

Overall, the pastors and laity responded well to the liturgical changes. A survey conducted by the Archdiocesan Synod Committee on Worship in 1970 revealed that the Catholics in the archdiocese approved of the liturgy renewal. But in some parishes, such as St. John the Evangelist's at Deer Park in Cincinnati, controversy arose regarding the pace of liturgical reforms. Because of some parishioners' dissatisfaction, there was a decline in weekly collections. In St. Philomena parish at Stonelick, Catholics at first resented the replacement of the handcrafted, white wooden altar with what seemed to be an austere, steel-legged table.[13]

In the spring of 1968 the parish councils and their liturgical commissions began to consider ways of involving all the people of the parish in the Prayer of the Faithful, prayers offered during Mass in which the celebrant and congregation pray for a series of intentions. They promoted, moreover, greater participation of the parish in wedding and funeral ceremonies. Dan Shannon and Mrs. Frederick R. Bohlen, who headed the liturgical program of the archdiocesan councils, also called attention to Alter's decree on Masses in homes and for small groups. "We urge parish liturgical commissions to study this decree," they said, "and work to promote" Masses in the home. St. Antoninus parish at Covedale in Cincinnati was the first congregation in the archdiocese to begin the program of home Masses. The Liturgical Commission also recommended that spouses of members of the parish commission should participate in parish activities, pointing out there were too many local organizations that tended to divide the family.[14]

During the interim sessions of Vatican II Alter also prepared religious groups for upcoming changes. In the summer of 1963 he spoke to more than three hundred religious superiors representing more than two hundred communities at the Conference of Major Superiors of Women's Institutes in the United States at the College of Mount St. Joseph. He urged sisters' communities to review their purposes and methods and to "set aside traditions and customs that are out of touch with the world." At midcentury the sisters had largely been limited in mobility to convent, church, and school. He urged them to take those practices that were "obsolete and no longer being practiced out of [their] rules." In particular, he cited the hardship imposed upon all members of a family by a rule that prohibited a sister to visit her home. "I know from 30 years as a Bishop," he said, "what it means to families to be denied the comfort of a visit from a daughter they've given to religion."[15]

Moreover, Vatican II helped bring church teaching into closer conformity with dominant American values. Whereas there were some who were more comfortable with the absolutist claims of the church, there were those who had high expectations of continued change and a more democratic Church. The pre–Vatican II Church forbade eating meat on Friday and receiving communion without absolutely fasting. Though Pius XII modified practices of fasting and abstinence, by November 1966 Paul VI dropped altogether the prohibition against eating meat on Fridays. The Lenten rules, likewise, were lightened. Ash Wednesday and Good Friday were now the only days of fast and abstinence from meat. A change that occurred rather inadvertently in the 1960s was the decline of the practice of women covering their heads with hats or handkerchiefs pinned in their hair when entering church. The change took place without any directives or assistance from church leaders.[16]

When the Second Vatican Council had completed its work in 1965, Alter encouraged Catholics to give practical application to the principles it had enunciated. The questions that particularly concerned the archdiocese were those affecting the liturgy, ecumenical relations, the ministry of the laity, and a better distribution of the church's resources in personnel and in finances. As a consequence, Alter and his staff felt obliged to rethink the organization of the archdiocese and of its parishes. Like many of his episcopal colleagues the Cincinnati ordinary eventually convoked parish councils, a diocesan priests' senate, and a diocesan pastoral council. The archdiocese responded to the Council Fathers' call for dialogue and shared responsibility by taking into account much more than ever the voices of priests, religious, and laity on ecclesiastical matters.[17]

In 1965 the Archdiocesan Councils of Catholic Men and Women began self-studies of their operations with particular emphasis on the parish organizations. The following January the executive boards of the two groups held their first joint meeting since the reorganization of the archdiocesan councils nearly fifteen years earlier. They adopted a new program that enabled them to unite their efforts at the parish level. That same year Alter took a major step toward greater lay involvement when he issued a decree in September, establishing the Archdiocesan Pastoral Council (APC). The archbishop also gave evidence of his commitment to the development of lay leadership when he appointed twenty-five lay men and twenty-five lay women from the ACCM-ACCW boards to the Council, along with ten deans and representatives of religious orders of men and women in the archdiocese. A chief advisory group to the archbishop, the APC's purpose was to investigate pastoral problems and propose solutions. Responding to the demands of a new generation of lay persons, parish councils were also established as the new parochial structure. Cincinnati was one of the first dioceses in the American church to establish the APC and parish councils.[18]

By the end of 1966 more than one hundred parishes in the archdiocese had formed parish councils. A year later there were 215. The parish council was seen as a new structure for shared responsibility and parish renewal. Membership in the council included all the priests of the parish, the parish school principal, at least one lay teacher, the lay heads or representatives of parish organizations, and five to ten members-at-large. The council shared with the pastor responsibility for the quality of parish life, for policies and programs of the parish, and for securing financial resources. In 1969 Alter also encouraged and gave approval to the formation of the Archdiocesan Council of the Laity (ACL), governed by a 42-member board of directors. The new organization replaced the Archdiocesan Councils of Catholic Men and Women. Mrs. Andrew Hellmuth of Springfield, who formerly presided over the ACCW, headed the new Council. The members of the ACCM and ACCW drew up the constitution and bylaws. The Archdiocesan Council of the Laity, along with the APC and parish councils, enabled the laity to become more involved in making decisions about pastoral and financial priorities. The decision to establish the ACL helped lay the seed to the establishment in 1971 of the National Council of Catholic Laity.[19]

In May 1966 a special committee of the archdiocesan school board recommended, with Alter's support, that every parish have a board of education "broadly representative" of the parish membership. The committee pointed out that pastors who consented to the establishment of a parish board of education needed to recognize that they were accepting "a limitation of their autonomy," but one that reflected what Vatican II had said concerning the increasing role of laity in the church. A few weeks later Alter called for equal representation of laity and priests on the boards of interparochial high schools of the archdiocese as a way to help meet the schools' growing financial needs of higher salaries for lay teachers and increasing operating costs. By the end of the decade Catholic colleges in the archdiocese also began inviting lay people to serve on their boards of trustees.[20]

In the summer of 1966, in direct response to the Vatican II Decree on the Ministry and Life of Priests, Alter established a Senate of Priests. Ballots were distributed to all the clergy serving in parishes, and each priest was asked to submit three names for the Senate. From these the thirty priests with the highest number of votes were elected, and ten additional priests were appointed by Alter to insure a representation of all areas and all ranks. As a consultative body, the new priests' council helped improve communication between priests and the archbishop on pastoral concerns. It addressed some of the tensions and morale problems among the local clergy and provided a greater forum for clerical expression. It held its first meeting on October 3 at St. Peter in Chains Cathedral. The group elected Monsignor August J. Kramer, pastor of St. Cecilia's Church in Cincinnati and former director of Catholic Charities, chair.[21]

That fall seminary reform was also under way at Mount St. Mary's of the West Seminary. Under the direction of Monsignor Joseph Schneider, the rector, the seminary allowed for greater personal freedom among the seminarians in their academic studies and in the selection of mentors from the faculty. Though appreciative of the relaxation of internal rules, in May 1967 three-fourths of the students signed an open letter calling for more open discussion of the issues. The letter was sent not only to Alter but to the students' respective bishops in other dioceses. Feeling "humiliated . . . before his suffragans," the archbishop informed the students that their action had caused "serious harm" to the seminary. During the next two years other changes occurred. The most significant change took place in July 1969. Students were now free to come and go as they pleased at the seminary, provided that they attended classes and were in their rooms by midnight.[22]

During implementation of Vatican II reforms, the Liturgical Commission had to contend with both resistance to change and overzealous innovation. At the same time that there were priests who went along very slowly without educating people or providing meaningful celebrations with full lay participation, there were those who did "their own thing" without authorization, resulting in questionable theology or liturgy. The archdiocese found it difficult to get everyone to comply with its many directives. This challenge to authority in itself was perhaps one of the most unexpected consequences of the Second Vatican Council.[23]

At times the archbishop cracked down on people he thought were getting carried away by the spirit of Vatican II. There were instances when the religious were so involved in their own self-study and discussion that they did not have the time or opportunity to keep authorities in the local church fully informed of their activities. Some of the parishes, moreover, struggled to gain control of their own renewal processes and implement social justice programs. In 1965 Alter placed the 102-member order of Glenmary Sisters in the archdiocese under restrictions on the hours they kept and the books they read. They were also prohibited from attending night school outside the convent. The restrictions were imposed after a group of five to seven Glenmary sisters complained to the archbishop that they believed the order was too liberally interpreting the new role of sisters. Members of the order, one of the youngest in the United States, worked mostly in the poverty-stricken areas of the Appalachians. They were at times unconventional in approach, some-time wearing secular clothing and going into the fields with their sleeves rolled up. To Alter their activities seemed unbecoming or too radical for sis-ters. He instructed them to keep proper religious spirit and reserve in their relations with the laity. The order, which had been set up as a diocesan order and not a pontifical one, was also forbidden to start new houses or accept new members in the fall's postulant class. In the end about half of the Glenmary Sisters left the order to form a lay group.[24]

It was not surprising to Alter that the ferment of recent changes had dis-turbed "somewhat," he wrote to the religious in 1965, "the serenity of reli-gious life." He argued that it "is good not to be too quick to discard the past, nor too slow to make adjustments here and now. Prudence must not be an excuse for inaction." He further contended that order could not "exist with-out authority, and obedience is a necessary correlative of authority. Freedom is the soil in which responsibility develops," he wrote, "but there is no freedom from God's law and from the legitimate authority [that] He has established."[25]

UNIVERSITY OF DAYTON CONTROVERSY

Another example of ferment within the archdiocese that allegedly defied church authority was the issue of academic freedom at the University of Dayton. In October 1966 members of the University of Dayton's philosophy department charged that four of their colleagues in the philosophy and the-ology departments were advocating positions contrary to the teachings of the Catholic Church. They maintained that Catholic professors dealing with moral and religious matters had an obligation to respect the magisterium in their teaching. A subsequent investigation by the university's Ad Hoc Com-mittee cleared the accused faculty members. But five days later, on Decem-ber 8, 1966, eight faculty members termed the action of the administration a "classic whitewash." The university's Faculty Forum then censured the eight professors for "conduct unworthy of the University of Dayton faculty." As a consequence, a number of pastors and lay persons in the archdiocese wrote letters to Alter. Members of the philosophy department, furthermore, sub-mitted a formal canonical appeal from the decision of the university's admin-istrative committee that had cleared the faculty accused of violating the magisterium to Archbishop Alter. A letter was also sent to the apostolic del-egate in Washington.[26]

Six months earlier a Marianist priest and head of the theology department at the University of Dayton had complained to Monsignor Henry Vogelpohl of the archdiocese of Cincinnati that two faculty members, who were among the four subsequently accused, ridiculed the church and were guilty of "questionable principles and teaching." He had further alleged that the authorities at the University were aware and "failed to do anything about it." In December 1966 Alter, concerned about the "pastoral implications" of the "expressions of concern" in the letters, established a committee to conduct an informal, nonjuridicial, fact-finding inquiry into the doctrinal controversy. "Normally," he later wrote, "Church authority need not take the initiative, but it cannot reject an appeal for a decision, when made from within the university or from the Catholic community." The committee of inquiry was composed of four professors, the head of the philosophy department at Xavier University and three from Mount St. Mary's of the West Seminary.[27]

During the course of a month the committee interviewed the professors accused, those who made the accusation, other professors, and members of the administration. As the investigation unfolded, the local chapter of the American Association of University Professors alleged that Alter's investigation abridged the academic freedom of the faculty. The university's Student Council also passed a resolution calling the intervention of the archbishop's committee as "unnecessary seizure of power and an undesirable precedent for future intrusion." On the other hand, the Marianist and university president Raymond A. Roesch defended the archbishop. He argued that Alter was acting completely within his rights and responsibility when he showed pastoral concern for Catholic doctrine. "Canonically speaking," he said, "the local ordinary may under pain of excommunication forbid any faculty member, lay or religious, in a Catholic or public institution, to teach what the bishop considers an heretical position." Though he regarded the 1918 law "antiquated," he nevertheless acknowledged its legality. Although he affirmed the church's right to guard against anything that would be taught in the name of the church "in opposition to faith and good morals," he concluded that "matters which are on the academic level can be properly be debated and controlled within the halls of a university."[28]

On February 13, 1967, the fact-finding commission submitted its report to Alter. It confirmed the decision of the university's Ad Hoc Committee. Though the faculty members' teachings "may not have been contrary to defined doctrines," the report said, "in some public lectures a lack of respect for the Magisterium of the church was manifested." The report also acknowledged that the philosophy faculty had every right to make a canonical appeal to the archbishop for it was based on church law and on the stated objectives of the university. The University of Dayton official bulletin and faculty handbook identified the institution as "committed to the upholding of the deposit of faith and Christian morality." The commission made no suggestion pertaining to the possible discipline or dismissal of any of the accused professors.[29]

Upon receipt of the report, the archbishop sent a copy to the chairman of the university's board of trustees. Alter was hopeful that the University of Dayton would "quietly solve its own problem," he wrote, "now that it has been exposed and the students and community are alerted to it." Throughout the ordeal, Alter made it clear that the university was an independent corporation with its own board of trustees and administration and had no legal responsibility to pay "attention to any of the authorities in the Church." When Alter spoke at Xavier University's commencement exercises the following June, he addressed the issue of academic freedom. Describing it as "a two-way street," Alter pointed out that both the institution and the faculty "have a claim on academic freedom, and both have duties as well as rights. . . . Every private institution of higher learning," he argued, "should be free to choose its own specified goals and make its own commitment to a system of education [that] will enable it to achieve its declared and distinctive purpose." Alter further insisted that "every member of a faculty who freely accepts a contract to teach at an institution of higher learning under these conditions thereby limits voluntarily his academic freedom so as to bring it in conformity with the purpose of the institution." He thought that neither the institution nor any of its faculty should trespass upon one another's rights and duties.[30]

When in the fall of 1968 some Catholic laymen urged Alter to intervene in the selection of questionable speakers in Xavier University's Speakers Forum, he declined, indicating that his "authority over the academic program . . . is practically nil." But if "it were a question of teaching in the class of Theology some doctrine contrary to the official teaching of the Church," he said, "I might intervene." He also pointed out that sometimes "pocketbook resistance is a much more persuasive argument than words alone." When the Jesuit Paul O'Connor resigned as president in 1972, Alter praised him on his "steadfast devotion to the Church." He also took the opportunity to note that "the problem of academic freedom and the safeguarding of Christian truth and Church loyalty still stand in need of a more satisfactory definition, and hopefully of true reconciliation."[31]

CHRISTIAN UNITY

As Alter and the clergy prepared the faithful for changes in the interior spiritual life of the local church, the archbishop also encouraged promotion of Christian unity. As a leader in the ecumenical movement, Alter worked with the Christian and Jewish communities in affirming common religious values. In 1961 virtually every church and school of the archdiocese sponsored an open house program to let non-Catholics know what Catholics were doing. The following year the Archdiocesan Council of Catholic Men invited Protestant lay leaders to participate in a panel on "Christian Unity." In late January 1964 Alter appeared before an interfaith audience at United Theological Seminary in Dayton. It was an event without parallel in the history of the city. The meeting brought together both Catholic and Protestant church leaders in a Protestant seminary to hear a Catholic archbishop. He led a group of some four hundred persons of all faiths in the recitation of the Lord's Prayer. During the session one questioner referred to an article in *Newsweek* magazine that characterized Alter as a conservative at the Vatican Council. He asked the archbishop if he thought the label was correctly applied. Alter turned to his audience and asked them whether they would describe him as a conservative or "the opposite." The audience applauded and cried out, "the opposite."[32]

Ever since the pope first called for a Second Vatican Council, Alter's views on Christian unity had solidified. He had pointed out in his talk to the Archdiocesan Council of Catholic Women in Dayton in April 1959 that the church's interest in the world community stemmed from its recognition of the unity of the human race. During the next several years Alter spoke of the spirit of charity needed to promote Christian unity. His outlook toward ecumenism now relied less on doctrinal arguments and showed more of an acceptance of other churches in a dialogue over religious differences. Although Alter never changed his view of the true church or the desirability of attracting or drawing other religions to the Catholic Church, he had a different attitude toward non-Catholics. He now embraced an approach based more on dialogue and mutual understanding than on polemics, even though he hoped that all true Christians would come to see the one true church.[33]

Alter consistently argued that ecumenism was not based on compromise, but sought to reach "an agreement on the basis of one organic living Church." When in March 1964 Alter addressed the annual convention of the Protestant Episcopal Diocese of Southern Ohio, marking the first time a Catholic prelate appeared before the Ohio Episcopalians, he suggested that adherence to the scripture and tradition could more easily unify the Christian religions. When later that spring he received the annual Good Neighborhood award from the Isaac M. Wise Temple in Cincinnati, Alter stressed in his acceptance remarks the common religious heritage of Jews and Christians.[34]

Postconciliar openness to other religious traditions helped decrease the Catholics' separatist identity. By 1965 Protestant and Catholic clergy in the archdiocese held joint study days in several communities, young Christians participated in ecumenical study days, Protestants joined Catholic parishes for prayer during Church Unity Octave, and a Catholic layman spoke in the

Calvin Presbyterian church in Amelia on Reformation Sunday. That year St. Mary of the Woods Church at Russells Point celebrated three ecumenical Masses. All three were well attended by the Protestant ministers in the area. The collaboration of Catholics, Jews, and Protestants in social action programs led to the establishment of the Greater Cincinnati Interfaith Commission in 1966, followed by the establishment two years later of the Metropolitan Area Religous Coalition of Cincinnati. In the fall of 1966 the Archdiocesan Ecumenical Commission was organized under the chairmanship of Monsignor Ralph A. Asplan, with several lay members and Protestant advisors. On January 25, 1967, Alter presided at the first ecumenical service held at St. Peter in Chains Cathedral. Protestant ministers joined Catholic priests in the service.[35]

The following spring the Taft Broadcasting Company began telecasting the weekly television program, *Dialogue.* The panelists consisted of a Roman Catholic priest, a Protestant minister, and a Jewish rabbi. On October 8, 1967, for the first time in the fifty-five-year history of the Holy Name Rally, Protestant men joined Catholics in the annual procession. With a theme of "Brotherhood in Christ," marchers made their way to the new Cincinnati Convention Exposition Center for an interfaith prayer service with Catholic and Protestant clergymen participating. In November a joint Thanksgiving service was held at the Immanuel United Church of Christ on Queen City Avenue in Cincinnati. The Franciscan Jerome Kirchner, pastor of St. Bonaventure Church, delivered the sermon. That year the Southeastern Ecumenical Ministry was formed and the Councils of Catholic Men and Women cosponsored with Protestant and Jewish groups concerts by the Cincinnati Symphony Orchestra at Music Hall. A chorus of men and women from Cincinnati churches and synagogues also participated in the concerts. On April 7, 1968, three days after the assassination of Martin Luther King, Jr., Alter presided at the ecumenical prayer service held in his memory. For the first time in the history of the cathedral, a Jewish rabbi took part in a prayer service and a Protestant minister preached the sermon to an overflow crowd. Another step toward uniting Christians was taken in September when a number of Protestant and Catholic churches sponsored the Twelfth Community Prayers for Peace Service at St. Bonaventure Church.[36]

Alter's reputation as an authority on church-state relations and religious liberty and his membership on key commissions of the Second Vatican Council enabled him to play a leadership role in the drafting, presenting, and promoting of a very progressive document on ecumenism and freedom of conscience in religion. This issue was very important to Alter, who was the first American bishop to call for a document on it, and to many of his fellow American bishops. Beginning in 1963 Alter, a member of the Theological

Commission, participated in the discussion of the issue of religious liberty at the meeting of the Central Preparatory Commission. Cardinal Alfredo Ottaviani of the Theological Commission and Cardinal Augustin Bea, S.J., a scripture scholar of the Secretariat for Christian Unity, presented divergent views on the issue. Ottovani presented the traditional view that "error has no rights." In Alter's opinion that "left much to be desired." Bea, on the other hand, defended the right of freedom of conscience and religious liberty. The Preparatory Commission was evenly divided on the issue. Alter, representing America's tradition, supported Bea's position. To the Cincinnati ordinary religious liberty meant "immunity for individuals or groups of individuals from any outward compulsion by public authority in the area of religion."[37]

During the next two years Alter remained active in its cause. In 1964 he and the Jesuit John Courtney Murray, a peritus at the Council and an acknowledged authority on church-state relations, exchanged views on the matter of religious liberty in proposed schemata for presentation at the fall session of the Second Vatican Council. Shortly after his arrival in Rome in mid-September, Alter spoke before the council in support of the declaration on religious liberty. Though he disclaimed the "personal right of any individual to teach error or to do harm," he defended "the right of every human being to be free of outside force in his worship of God." Alter was very much aware of the difference of opinion between those who interpreted "the Catholic ideal" as better than "U.S. freedom of religion" and those who did not. This difference formed the heart of the disagreement between the American bishops and some of their European counterparts. Cardinal Arriba of Spain, where Catholicism was the state religion, was the main spokesman for the European position. He argued that only the Catholic Church could preach the Gospel and proselytize in a predominantly Catholic country. He maintained that the views and efforts of non-Catholics should be suppressed. Warning the Council against ruining Catholic countries, he urged the members not to issue a declaration on religious liberty. Rather, the matter should be left to each national conference of bishops. This was a position shared by a number of European bishops and supported by many centuries of Catholic tradition. Reminiscent of Archbishop John Purcell's position on church-state relations at the time of the First Vatican Council, Alter and his American colleagues debated against this position and defended the American tradition of separation of church and state and freedom of conscience. The matter was finally resolved in favor of religious liberty at the fourth and final session in 1965. The efforts of Alter and the American hierarchy to frame a cogent position on religious liberty were instrumental to the final promulgation of one of the significant texts of the Second Vatican Council.[38]

On January 31, 1969, less than four years after Vatican II, the eighty-three-year-old Alter offered his resignation to Rome. He was the oldest Catholic bishop in the United States. Having served the church for almost sixty years as a priest and for thirty-eight years as a bishop, he thought that "a young man with dynamic energy and creative initiative should assume the responsibility" of his office. In the process he complied with a Second Vatican Council decree that advised bishops reaching an advanced age to voluntarily resign. By spring his resignation had been accepted. On April 17, 1969, Alter sent a letter to the six hundred priests in the archdiocese, requesting that they submit recommendations for his successor. The ordinary asked that each priest nominate no more than three bishops or priests for the office of archbishop and no more than one priest for a possible new auxiliary bishop for Cincinnati. At the time the archdiocese had one auxiliary bishop, Edward A. McCarthy. The usual manner for the nomination of new archbishops was for all the bishops of the province to present three names to the Vatican. The pope normally selected the new ordinary from that list. On July 23, 1969, Alter called a press conference in St. Peter in Chains Cathedral and officially announced his resignation. Paul Leibold, bishop of Evansville, succeeded him. Upon his retirement Alter continued to live at his home on Belmont Avenue. Leibold occupied the former episcopal residence next to the seminary in Norwood. "I have taken this action now while still blessed with good health and strength," Alter stated, "for fear that the wisdom of acting in time might not be as easily recognized later on."[39]

The former head of the archdiocese of Cincinnati remained a strong supporter of the changes stemming from Vatican II as well as an optimist about the future of the church. When he was interviewed in 1975 at the age of ninety, he argued that there was still a solid layer of belief among the church faithful. "There is always a certain element who do not accept change," he told the interviewer. "But they will in due time accept the liturgy as it is organized. The Latin Mass was considered a novelty before the Council of Trent." Similarly, he was critical of those who were impatient with the pace of change, calling them a "fringe element" that "run after novelties." Upon Alter's death, Archbishop Joseph Bernardin said: "He became archbishop of Cincinnati when one era of the history of the church was ending, and he led us with confidence into an era that was beginning." On August 23, 1977, Alter died at the age of ninety-two. Except for poor eyesight, which had plagued him in his later years, Alter had been generally in good health. He certainly remained mentally active until his death.[40]

· 14 ·

The Post-Vatican II
Archdiocese
of Cincinnati

Cincinnati Archbishops John McNicholas and Karl Alter were seen as great builders and developers of beautiful church and educational edifices in the archdiocese. The next three Cincinnati ordinaries—Archbishops Paul F. Leibold, Joseph L. Bernardin, and Daniel E. Pilarczyk—were largely consolidators. The parish building process was reversed during the post–Vatican II era. In the period 1969 to 1996 the local church saw fewer churches built than was true in any previous twenty-seven-year period in the history of the archdiocese. Experiencing an unprecedented number of church closings and mergers, the laity and parish organizations assumed myriad tasks in the day-to-day activities of the church, and the local church witnessed increasing Mass attendance and enrollment in Catholic schools, and involvement in social programs.

Leibold, a native of Dayton, was the first of the triumvirate to succeed Alter as archbishop. Born on December 22, 1914, he was reared and spent his priestly life in the archdiocese. Leibold attended Dayton's Holy Trinity elementary school, Chaminade high school, and the University of Dayton for two years. He completed his studies for the priesthood at St. Gregory and Mount St. Mary's of the West Seminaries in Cincinnati, and was ordained on May 18, 1940, by McNicholas. He was with the chancery, located above St. Louis Church at Eighth and Walnut Streets in Cincinnati, from 1942 until his appointment to the Evansville see in April 1966. He served under Alter for sixteen years as chancellor and then as auxiliary bishop. When he became archbishop of Cincinnati on July 23, 1969, the fifty-five-year-old Leibold had a reputation as both a warm-hearted, approachable pastor and a hard worker. Though an efficient administrator, the humble Leibold was not in the

358

FIG 16. Archbishop Paul Liebold, 1969–1972

mold of his two immediate predecessors, Alter and McNicholas, who had been exceptional churchmen and national spokesmen for the hierarchy.

During his tenure Leibold helped give vigor to the Priests' Senate, the Archdiocesan Pastoral Council (APC), and the parish councils. The priests, religious, and laity increasingly shared congregational responsibility for the local church's mission. In December 1969 the Senate of Priests, composed of forty priests, dissolved itself to make way for a smaller and entirely elected senate of twenty-five priests, auxiliary bishop, and vicars general. Leibold was hopeful that the reduced number of priest-senators "would enable the senate to act more efficiently." The new structure provided for more adequate representation. Ten members of the new senate represented the diocesan clergy, another ten the deaneries of the archdiocese, and the remaining five were elected by religious communities of priests, with the Franciscan, Jesuit, Marianist, and Precious Blood communities electing one each of their members. The archdiocese, moreover, found the seventy-member Pastoral Council too large for effective action. In the spring of 1970 the Council adopted a restructuring plan that reduced its membership to forty. During his brief tenure Leibold also emphasized the importance of parish councils. Since their beginning in 1967 there were by the end of Leibold's term in 1972 more than two hundred parish councils in the archdiocese. In October 1970 the new archdiocesan Sisters' Advisory Council (SAC) was formed. More than six hundred sisters from the archdiocese voted to accept the group's constitution at the sessions held in Dayton and in Cincinnati. Developed from the old Archdiocesan Vocation Endeavor (AVE), which was officially dissolved in 1969, SAC served as a voice for the more than 2,000 sisters in the archdiocese. The new organization complemented the Archdiocesan Council of the Laity (ACL) and the Priests' Senate.[1]

In the aftermath of Vatican II the archdiocese also had interest in a reforming synod, the last one having been held in 1954. On May 3, 1970, at the first assembly of the Council of the Laity, Leibold launched the archdiocese's sixth synod and, in the process, gave new impetus to collegiality. About 1,200 to 1,400 priests, religious, and lay men and women were present at the ACL assembly that day, and heard the archbishop outlining his plans for the proposed synod. The synod, which did not convene until 1971, was preceded at every stage of the proceedings by a period of thorough discussion by members of the clergy, religious, and laity. It became a great educational experience for the more than one hundred persons who from June to September 1970 drafted the documents. The eleven commissions consisted of fifty-five priests, twenty-four sisters, four brothers, and sixty lay members. The priests of the archdiocese and the members of the Priests' Senate, the Pastoral Council, the ACL, and the Sisters' Advisory Council then evaluated the documents in November. From January to March 1971 more than 16,000 parishioners in the archdiocese reacted to the documents in ten parish "speak up" sessions. Whereas only a few lay persons had participated in the 1954 synod, the laity in 1970 and 1971 took an unprecedented role in shaping the synod's agenda as well as at the synod itself. On May 16, 1971, more than three thousand elected delegates voted on the final drafts of the documents at the Cincinnati Convention Exposition Center.[2]

The synod, with Father John L. Cavanaugh as coordinator, developed a set of guidelines for the archdiocese in full accordance with the spirit and teachings of the constitutions, decrees, and declarations of the Second Vatican Council. The eleven commissions, with a vicar at the head of each, provided some restructuring of the diocese. The archdiocesan Bureau of Information continued in operation until 1971 when the local church called for a new Archdiocesan Communications Office with a full-time director and staff. The appointment of a layman, Daniel J. Kane, as vicar for communications represented a departure from tradition. The document on laity stressed the role of the parish, deanery, regional, and pastoral councils as structures in which the laity could best exercise leadership in the local church. Lay men and women were to share in community decision-making. They were to be not just advisors, but parties "at interest, sharing in both decision and responsibility." In January 1972, in compliance with the guidelines of the sixth synod, the chancery issued in the *Catholic Telegraph* the first public annual financial report of the archdiocese.[3]

The synod's document on religious also called on the archdiocese "to involve religious in the decision-making processes of the diocese." They were "not merely hired servants," the document read, "but collaborators in the vineyard of the Lord." In May 1974 the new thirty-six-member Archdiocesan Council of Religious was launched. Comprised of nine priests, four brothers, and twenty-three sisters, the Council advised the archbishop and the Commission of the Religious on the needs and priorities of the apostolic ministries. That same month the newly formed SAC dissolved itself in order to participate in the broader concept of the Council of Religious. In the 1980s the archbishop and approximately one thousand men and women religious met twice at one of four locations over a month's time to discuss the future state of religious life. One of the biggest challenges facing all the religious orders in the post–Vatican church was taking care of their aged members. In 1975 the archdiocese pledged $3 million to help pay retirement costs of nineteen religious communities of women whose members had worked in schools or institutions of the archdiocese. In the 1980s Archbishop Pilarczyk along with other U.S. bishops launched ten annual appeals to help religious orders meet their retirement debts.[4]

In 1971 Byzantine Rite Archbishop Nicholas T. Elko was named the seventh auxiliary bishop of Cincinnati, the first Eastern rite bishop to serve as an auxiliary bishop in a Roman rite diocese. Six months later Elko took up residence in Dayton to coordinate the work of Dayton area diocesan offices, including a new Dayton branch of the archdiocesan chancery. The move was part of a plan, in response to the recommendation of the synod of 1971, to provide for the special interests of the local church in the northern part of the province. The Dayton area already had independent offices of Catholic Charities, Catholic youth, the *Catholic Telegraph,* social action, and Catholic education. In 1972 there were thirty-five Catholic parishes in Montgomery County, a Catholic university, two Catholic hospitals, two homes for the aged, two retreat centers, an orphanage, five high schools, a home for women, and a motherhouse for women religious. To the east, west, and north of Dayton in an eleven-county area, there were seventy more parishes together with hospitals, high schools, and other institutions. Leibold was hopeful that with all these offices in Dayton the voice of the church would

FIG 17. Archbishop Joseph Bernardin, 1972–1982

"be heard much more clearly" in the area. But this experiment did not prove to be totally successful. Having an archbishop stationed in Dayton and serving as vicar general created another level of bureaucracy between the clergy, religious, and laity in the Dayton area and the chancery in Cincinnati. In April 1985 Pope John Paul II accepted Archbishop Elko's resignation.[5]

After serving almost three years as head of the Cincinnati archdiocese, Paul Leibold, at the age of fifty-seven years, suffered a stroke and died on June 1, 1972. Though his tenure was too short to engender a significant growth in the local church, he was instrumental in revitalizing the Priests' Senate, the APC, and the parish councils and in launching the sixth synod. He was succeeded on November 21 by Joseph Bernardin, general secretary of the National Conference of Catholic Bishops (NCCB). Bernardin was born in Columbus, South Carolina, on April 2, 1928, to Italian immigrant parents. Following studies at St. Mary's Seminary in Baltimore, he was ordained in 1952 to the priesthood for the diocese of Charleston and later served as parish priest and chancellor. In 1966 he was named auxiliary bishop of Atlanta, vicar general, and rector of the cathedral. Two years later he became general secretary of the NCCB. At the age of forty-four the new Cincinnati ordinary was the youngest archbishop in the United States. More polished and cosmopolitan than Leibold, Bernardin served from 1974 to 1977 as NCCB president. In 1974, 1977, and 1980 his fellow bishops appointed him one of four American delegates to the World Synod of Bishops in Rome. On July 10, 1982, Bernardin was appointed archbishop of Chicago. About seven months later he was named to the College of Cardinals.[6]

At the beginning of Bernardin's second year as archbishop of Cincinnati, the process of electing deans, who visited all the churches and schools of his deanery, took place for the first time. The election helped get the people more fully involved in the life of the local church. First to be elected by representatives of all the people in his deanery was Father Bernard H. Bruening, pastor of St. Francis de Sales Church in Cincinnati. In the spring of 1974 the Pastoral Council helped establish an archdiocesan secretariat to help keep the lines of communication open both to and from the deaneries and to provide services to the restructured deanery councils. By the early 1990s the archdiocese established St. Andrew deanery, its eleventh deanery. The St. Francis de Sales and St. Martin deaneries had gotten too large geographically and represented a wide diversity of socioeconomic elements. The two deaneries were rearranged to make them smaller, more coherent, and efficient.[7]

During his tenure Bernardin also helped revitalize and reorganize the archdiocese. A year after he established a planning and research office, Bernardin in 1975 introduced a new archdiocesan-wide program to promote increased financial support for parish operations. Rather than substantially increase the assessments of the parishes to meet the growing needs of the local church, the archdiocese decided to raise more money by sponsoring an annual drive. At the time Cincinnati was one of the few dioceses in the country that did not have a development fund campaign. One of the goals of the Archbishop's Fund drive, conducted for the first time in the spring of 1976, was to provide adequate funds for retired priests and religious of the archdiocese. In the fall of that year the Clergy Relief Union of the Cincinnati archdiocese, after fifty-six years of service, was dissolved. Most of the funds paid out by the union had been for sick benefits, as few priests had retired. The phasing out of the union began in 1972 when U.S. Internal Revenue Service rulings prevented it from continuing as a retirement and sick-benefit agency for the clergy. In 1978 Bernardin also approved budget cuts of more than $250,000 for offices and agencies of the archdiocese to offset deficits caused by inflation and increasing demands for services. Six new departments of Community, Educational, Executive, Financial, Pastoral, and Personnel services were established, each department headed by a director reporting to the archbishop.[8]

Following Bernardin's appointment to Chicago in July 1982, the forty-eight-year-old Daniel E. Pilarczyk, who had served as administrator of the archdiocese since August, was named archbishop of Cincinnati on November 2, 1982. He was the ninth individual and third native son to serve as leader of the local church. Born in Dayton on August 12, 1934, he attended Our Lady of Mercy and St. Anthony elementary schools and Sacred Heart Latin School in Dayton and then enrolled in St. Gregory Seminary high school. After graduating from the high school Pilarczyk stayed at St. Gregory's for two years of college, until he matriculated in the Roman College of the Propagation of the Faith in 1953. He was ordained in Rome in 1959 and later earned a doctorate degree in sacred theology. Upon his return to Cincinnati in 1961 he was named assistant chancellor and served as an assistant pastor of St. Louis Church. In 1963 Alter appointed him to the St. Gregory Seminary faculty to teach Latin and Greek. Five years later he became rector, the youngest in the history of the seminary. One of his major interests is classical languages and civilization, and he received a master's degree in classics from Xavier University in 1965 and a doctorate in the same field from the University of Cincinnati in 1969. In 1974 he left his seminary post to become the vicar for education. In December of that year he was named the archdiocese's second auxiliary bishop.[9]

Pilarczyk is known for his dry wit, drive, intelligence, and cautious temperament. Devoted to education, evangelization, and priestly vocations, he is a prolific writer and preacher. He has published books on the church's social teachings, sacramental life, and scripture. Though in the summer of 1988 the fifty-three-year-old archbishop suffered a ruptured aneurysm while on vacation in Tennessee, he successfully underwent brain surgery. The following year his episcopal colleagues elected the fully recovered ordinary president of the National Conference of Catholic Bishops and the U.S. Catholic Conference. In the spring of 1991 Pilarczyk was also elected to head the Episcopal Board of the International Commission on English in the Liturgy.[10]

RELIGIOUS GROWTH

On January 15, 1970, Catholics in the Cincinnati archdiocese could begin fulfilling their Sunday and holy day obligation by attending Mass the preceding evening. Though most of the pastors cited convenience of the parishioners as the main reason in the request for permission, a few cited the fact that a number of workers on Sundays could more readily attend a Saturday Mass. The pope had granted permission to make the privilege available to parish churches. Within a week seventy-six parishes, close to a third of the parishes in the archdiocese, exercised the new option. No parish was to have more than one

Saturday liturgy for the Sunday obligation. Moreover, some people thought an evening Mass would help bring back many of the young people who had been "gradually slipping away" from the Sunday Mass attendance. In the spring of 1981 the archdiocese also issued new guidelines for parish Mass schedules. In hopes of consolidating liturgies, pastors were advised to examine any Mass that utilized less than 50 percent of a church's seating capacity. By the end of the decade Pilarczyk granted permission to those in the archdiocese who longed for an older style of liturgical observance for regular celebrations of the Tridentine Mass, the eucharistic liturgy celebrated in Latin.[11]

Statistics taken from a head count of persons attending weekend Masses in October of each year showed that from the late 1960s through the 1980s Mass attendance continually declined in the archdiocese. Before Vatican II many people felt they were committing a "grave sin" if they missed Mass, whereas by the 1980s that belief was less prevalent, reflecting a change in attitude among the laity toward serious sin. The fear of hell was largely gone. Many Catholics no longer spoke the theological language of their parents and grandparents. Other reasons for missing Mass varied from being dissatisfied with liturgy and the quality of preaching to the "erroneous" assumption, Pilarczyk noted, that "if you don't get anything out of Mass, it's okay not to go." In the summer of 1980 three priests of St. William Church at Price Hill in Cincinnati celebrated liturgies outdoors in twenty-two parish neighborhoods in an effort to help rekindle their religious faith as well as their family solidarity. Notwithstanding the decline in Mass attendance, Catholics were still more regular in their attendance at church than the members of other denominations. Also, most practicing Catholics received communion on a regular basis.[12]

Specialized programs for growth in holiness also arose in the archdiocese. In the 1970s some parishes began sponsoring parent sacramental preparation classes to help adults teach their children as they prepared them for the Sacraments of Holy Communion and Penance. Courses were also available to prepare new parents for baptism given to their infants. Among other programs were the continuation of the Cursillo, parish renewal programs, prayer groups, spiritual groups, and various types of retreats. The archdiocese built upon the Marriage Encounter program, a worldwide movement that aimed at the spiritual renewal of married couples, and helped strengthen programs of marriage preparation and marriage support. Through the archdiosean Marriage Tribunal it also helped facilitate the annulment process, the formal declaration that a marriage was null and void from the beginning. In 1979 Sister Marilyn Gohs became the first woman to serve on the Tribunal. Four years later the archdiocese appointed the first lay woman to serve as a canon lawyer on it. In January 1976 the Pastoral Council established a Task Force on Evangelization. The following month at the annual Mass for the area's fifty-seven prayer groups Bernardin extended an invitation to members of Greater Cincinnati charismatic groups to join him "as active partners in the Church's evangelizing mission." He also made a special plea to priests and religious "to be involved in the activities of the charismatics." By the late 1980s the archdiocese launched an evangelization program, with a full-time evangelization coordinator, designed to bring people back to weekly liturgies.[13]

By this time it appeared that the decline in Mass attendance had bottomed out. Since 1960 there had been a decrease of almost 100,000 people attending Mass in the archdiocese. By 1989 the decline in Mass attendance in the local church was a mere 0.2 percent from 1988. In light of the 1.3 percent decrease in attendance from 1987 to 1988 and the 2.8 percent the year before that, the negligible decline in 1989 appeared indicative of a break in the more than twenty-year trend. Whereas nationally in 1991 not quite 27 percent of Catholics attended Mass, figures showed that about 44 percent of Catholics in the archdiocese were going to church. Though the numbers were disappointing, the archdiocese did better than most large dioceses in the country where attendance was around 30 percent. Along with Milwaukee, Cincinnati appeared to be the top ranking big-city diocese in Mass attendance. In the 1990s a number of parishes in the archdiocese began a "Come Home" project for inactive Catholics. The plan stemmed from a national plan for Catholic evangelization developed by the National Conference of Catholic Bishops.[14]

Following Vatican II lay participation at Mass also increased. In February 1970 the pope authorized Leibold to give laymen the privilege of distributing communion at Mass. On March 22 in St. Peter in Chains Cathedral, more than 150 men and women from fifty parishes were commissioned to serve as eucharistic ministers, lay people with the privilege of distributing communion. The option of receiving communion under both species—bread and wine—was introduced in parishes within the archdiocese on the first Sunday of Lent, March 4, 1979. Until that time Catholics had been receiving communion under both species only on special occasions.[15]

In the fall of 1974 fifty men enrolled in the archdiocesan permanent deacon program, with Father John L. Rea as director. Candidates ranged in age from thirty to over sixty-five. Within five years, fifty-seven men were ordained deacons. Besides assisting at the Eucharist and reading the Gospel, permanent deacons preached, baptized, blessed and assisted at weddings, administered last rites, officiated at funeral and burial services, and presided at prayer services. In 1989 the archdiocesan diaconate program was revamped. It now required candidates to complete a two-year certificate or master's degree program in lay pastoral ministry at the Athenaeum of Ohio, in addition to a two-year diaconate formation program. By this time there were more than one hundred deacons who served in the archdiocese. The diaconate reflected a change in the use of the word "ministry."[16]

In the fall of 1975 the archdiocese also launched the Lay Pastoral Ministry Program (LPMP). Under the direction of Ellen Frankenberg, an Ursuline Sister, the program was designed to train lay pastoral ministers for service in the local church. Its program of studies, which could be completed in two to three years, was an outgrowth of a pilot lay ministry program begun through the interest of Father Robert J. Hater, director of religious education. In the fall of 1978 the archdiocese commissioned six women as its first official lay ministers. Sensing that lay ministry was "the way of the future," Hater called the occasion "a milestone" in the archdiocese. The six women, already engaged in a variety of ministries in the community, were representative of lay ministers to serve in the future. The following year seven additional lay women and one layman were commissioned. Bernardin, who regarded the LPMP as "one of the most exciting and creative programs in the archdiocese," praised the lay ministers as "partners . . . in proclaiming Jesus and His message to the world."[17]

In October 1978 the Pastoral Council supported the recommendation of the Task Force on the Future of Lay Organization that the Archdiocesan Council of the Laity, at one time considered a national model of lay activity, be discontinued. By eliminating separate lay organizational structures, the Task Force and the APC called "for increased commitment to making parish, regional and pastoral councils more effective instruments of collaborative effort within the Church." Though some people expressed reservations over the discontinuance of the ACL, by a vote of seventeen to five the APC approved it. One explanation for the decline of the ACL was the creation since the 1971 synod of new channels for lay participation in the life of the local church.[18]

In the wake of Vatican II, lay Catholics have differed only marginally from American society at large. The encyclical *Humanae Vitae* (1968), which prohibited artificial contraception, did little to change the minds of most Catholic women. Though conservative bishops at the NCCB espoused the hard line on premarital sex, abortion, homosexuality, and divorce, there were growing differences between official church teachings and the beliefs and practices of ordinary Catholics. In the 1970s the archdiocese helped the Couple to Couple League (CCL), founded in 1971 by John and Sheila Kippley, get organized on a full-time basis. The purpose of the CCL was to provide adequate instruction in natural family planning. Couples were trained to teach other couples the practice of spacing pregnancies according to the informed awareness of a woman's fertility. In 1978 the National Conference of Catholic Bishops endorsed CCL. Four years later the archdiocesan Family Life Office initiated a five-year plan to promote and implement natural family planning programs throughout the archdiocese. By the 1990s it was estimated that approximately 90 percent of the American Catholic laity rejected the church's teaching on birth control. Evidence suggested that Catholics practiced birth control pretty much like the Protestants did.[19]

A few weeks after the Supreme Court legalized abortion on January 22, 1973, the archdiocese called for an all-out, positive campaign to counteract its effects. On May 6, 1973, approximately seven thousand people jammed Cincinnati's Fountain Square for a pro-life rally sponsored by Cincinnati and Northern Kentucky Right-to-Life groups. Young and old, babies in strollers, students, parents with grade-schoolers, grandparents, priests, and women religious participated in the rally. Two years later Archbishop Bernardin and thousands of people, carrying signs and balloons, again thronged Fountain Square for the Rally for Life. Bernardin described the pro-life rallies as an effort to give "public witness to community opposition to abortion" and to demonstrate concern for "the sanctity of all human life." In the spring of 1976 Bernardin, as president of NCCB, also testified before the House subcommittee considering constitutional amendments to restrict abortion. "[I]t is not religious doctrine we wish to see enacted into law," he said, "it is respect for human dignity and human rights—specifically, the right to life itself." Though concerned for the poor and the underprivileged, he did not see abortion as the solution to their plight. "If we wish to eradicate poverty," he said, "let us destroy the causes of poverty—not destroy the life of the poor and defenseless unborn child."[20]

Both Bernardin and Pilarczyk also maintained that the church had a proper responsibility in public affairs. In the wake of Vatican II and the social unrest of the sixties the general topic of religion's role in the political process replaced the old debates over religious liberty and separation of church and state. The two local ordinaries argued that Catholics should address such issues as abortion, wars, and equity in the economy. In May 1976 Bernardin distributed guidelines, drawn up by the executive committee of the APC, to parishes. Not wanting to form a religious voting bloc nor direct persons on how they should vote, the guidelines urged parishioners to participate in the political process and to examine the positions of the candidates on the full range of issues. The guidelines also emphasized that the church had not only a right but also an obligation to speak to the moral dimension of political issues.[21]

When Ohio Attorney General Anthony Celebrezze, a Catholic candidate for governor in 1990, backed pro-abortion supporters, Pilarczyk, the new president of the NCCB, joined the other Ohio bishops in issuing a statement criticizing Celebrezze. The statement questioned the integrity and sincerity of individuals who claimed to accept Catholic Church teaching but refused to endorse the church's position against abortion. Pilarczyk denied the allegation that he and his episcopal colleagues were trying to tell politicians what to do. "What we're saying," he said, "is that there are Catholic teachings that have social consequences. If you say you accept the teaching then it seems to us you have to accept the social consequences as well."[22]

During the past twenty years pro-life vigils and Operation Rescues affirmed the strength of the antiabortion stand in the archdiocese. By the mid-1980s Birthright had helped more than ten thousand women confronted with unwanted pregnancies. At a rally at the Montgomery County Courthouse Square in January 1987, Pilarczyk warned the crowd that society was on a "slippery slope" of disregard for human dignity. That year the archbishop also joined the other Ohio bishops in condemning capital punishment. No "human life, no matter how wretched or how miserable, no matter how sinful or how lacking in love," Pilarczyk said, "is without value." In vain, the Ohio bishops asked the governor to use his authority to commute death sentences. Three years later Pilarczyk accompanied area pro-life advocates to the April Rally for Life '90 in Washington, D.C. Though archdiocesan officials endorsed pro-life processions and rallies, they disapproved of any illegal activities. When arsonists in 1985 set fire to two Cincinnati abortion clinics, Pilarczyk and his staff condemned the use of violence. They also disapproved of the tactics of Operation Rescue when they blocked entrances of local abortion clinics in order to prevent patients from going inside.[23]

As Catholics embraced America's central values of individualism, materialism, and pluralism, they became more actively involved in the mainstream of society. They appropriated values of the American culture and "Catholicized" them in the process. On most political issues that divided American liberals and conservatives, namely welfare, aid to the homeless, gun control, and equal rights for women, minorities, and homosexuals, rank-and-file Catholics were more liberal than Protestants. In comparison to non-Catholics more recent data also showed that Catholics had slightly fewer children, divorced at slightly lower rates, and were less likely to remarry after divorce. Until the middle of the twentieth century, Catholics in the archdiocese had been predominantly a low-status, working-class population. Though by 1900 Irish and German Catholics had begun to move into higher-status occupations, the depression slowed down upward mobility. The prosperity of the post–World War II period helped Catholics move up in their socioeconomic status.[24]

As Catholics became more a part of mainstream America, there was also a more positive attitude between Catholics and Protestants. In March 1970 the Ohio Catholic dioceses of Cincinnati, Columbus, Toledo, and Youngstown joined the Ohio Council of Churches, which up to then had included only Protestant groups. Two months later Leibold and Monsignor Robert J. Sherry, chairman of the Archdiocesan Ecumenical Commission, headed a delegation of priests, religious, and lay people from the archdiocese at the Ohio Festival of Ecumenical Witness in Columbus. In the 1970s the local church also participated in the Metropolitan Area Religious Coalition of Cincinnati (MARCC) and in the Dayton Metropolitan Churches United. During his administration Bernardin spoke at several interfaith services in the Cincinnati area. He often emphasized the need to make "the scandal of separation, mistrust and conflict" among denominational churches yield to "mutual love, trust and cooperation." On January 21, 1973, Bernardin joined Dr. Billy Graham, Protestant evangelist, and Rabbi Edgar F. Magnin from Los Angeles in an ecumenical prayer service at the White House as part of President Nixon's inaugural program. In the spring of 1975 the Archdiocesan Pastoral Council endorsed and promoted pulpit exchange activities. Parishioners witnessed the exchange of pulpits for the reading of scripture or preaching of a homily between a Roman Catholic minister and a minister of another Christian tradition or of the Jewish faith during the liturgical service of the respective churches. In 1980 Catholics and Lutherans joined hands in the spirit of reconciliation and unity at the Lutheran-Roman Catholic convocation at St. Peter in Chains Cathedral. Eight years later the archdiocese participated in the city's two hundredth birthday with an ecumenical service at St. Peter in Chains Cathedral. These interfaith events led to greater appreciation for each church's distinctive forms of worship. This attitude "brought an end," as one contemporary historian aptly put it, "to the long cold war of hostility and suspicion."[25]

In the post–Vatican II period archdiocesan authorities also affirmed the church's position on homosexuality. Arguing that a homosexual orientation was usually not the fault of the individual, Bernardin thought that such an orientation in itself was not sinful. But homosexual acts "are in themselves seriously wrong," he wrote, "for they are not in accord with the purposes of human sexuality, and are consequently contrary to the will of God." Though critical of homosexual acts, Bernardin urged Catholics to show compassion for the homosexual, just as the church attempted to show pastoral concern for everyone else. In the summer of 1987 Pilarczyk informed Cincinnati's Dignity chapter, one of two chapters of homosexual Catholics in the archdiocese, that it could no longer meet on Catholic church property if it opposed church teaching on homosexuality. Pilarczyk's action was in keeping with the 1986 Vatican statement that called homosexuality "a disordered sexual inclination." Rome urged bishops not to support organizations that did not clearly support church teaching on the matter. When the Cincinnati City Council considered passing gay rights legislation in 1992, however, Pilarczyk made it clear that the archdiocese strongly affirmed "the rights of and dignity of every human person and the obligation of everyone to respect and protect these rights." Like most of his episcopal colleagues, Pilarczyk distinguished between homosexual orientations and homosexual activities.[26]

Since the 1960s hundreds of priests nationally were identified as child sexual abusers. In the spring of 1991 Father George Cooley, a priest of the archdiocese, pleaded guilty to charges of sexually abusing two children while serving as associate pastor of Guardian Angels parish. He was sentenced to ninety days in jail, fined $4,000, and ordered to perform four hundred hours of community service. That summer Pilarczyk went to the parishioners of Guardian Angels to apologize and pray with them. "I am sorry and ashamed that this has happened in our local church," he said. In the fall of 1992 the archdiocese came out with a forty-five-page "Decree On Child Abuse," laying out its policies and procedures to prevent and react to all forms of child abuse committed by clergy and lay employees or volunteers of the local church. The church's pedophilia scandal came to a head in November 1993 when a former seminarian accused Chicago's Cardinal Joseph Bernardin, and Cincinnati's former archbishop, of sexually abusing him decades before at St. Gregory Seminary. The following March the plaintiff admitted he had been confused and mistaken about Bernardin's involvement and dropped the lawsuit against him. Cleared of the charge, Bernardin then forgave and befriended his accuser publicly. This act of forgiveness received much national attention. Nevertheless, because of the pedophilia scandals the image of the clergy had suffered as a consequence of the shameful acts of a few. Catholics may be well advised to remember Archbishop Elder's admonition to his flock a century earlier to worry less "at the bad examples of some few unworthy priests" and be grateful "at the sight of the great army of faithful and hard-working priests."[27]

PARISHES

Shortly after his installation Archbishop Pilarczyk gave top priority to local parishes. In February 1983 he embarked on the first leg of what he called his "little project," a four-year journey in which he visited more than 250 parishes in the archdiocese. The parish visitation program, which began at St. Aloysius parish in Bridgetown, west of Cincinnati, and concluded in December 1986 at St. Matthias's in Forest Park, northwest of the city, was an opportunity for the archbishop to learn about the parish and what went on in the parishioners' "faith life." In the process parishioners shared with him

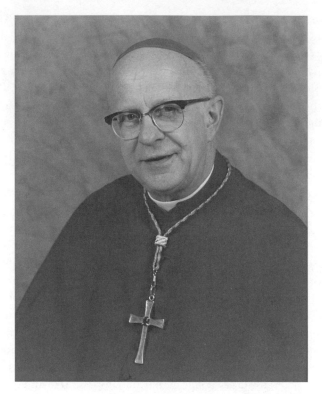

FIG 18. Archbishop Daniel Pilarczyk, 1982–

their thoughts, hopes, and dreams for their parishes. In his visits Pilarczyk met with the pastors and their staffs, school personnel, religious educators, students, and parish councils. Upon completion of the parish visitation program in 1987, the archbishop for the next four years visited the schools and institutions not included in his earlier rounds of travel. He had private pastoral meetings with each archdiocesan priest either at his office in Cincinnati or at the rectories of Immaculate Conception parish in Dayton or Holy Angels parish in Sidney. Reminiscent of the pioneer visitation tours of Cincinnati's first two ordinaries, Edward Dominic Fenwick and John Baptist Purcell, Pilarczyk by 1990 had traveled approximately 100,000 miles in his car to meet face-to-face with his people.[28]

The one pervasive element among the parishes of the post–Vatican II archdiocese was diversity in size and scope. The size of the parishes varied from Sunday Mass attendance of several thousand to fewer than one hundred. Whereas many of the parishes had just one priest as well as a limited range of services, some were staffed by a sizable group of professional ministers and had extensive and highly organized social and recreational programs. The diverse and myriad parish activities clearly revealed that much of the life of the local church was not focused in the central office in downtown Cincinnati, but rather in the parishes. "The parish is," Pilarczyk wrote in 1983, "the main delivery system of the Church's product." It was where the Christian community expressed itself most clearly, where the people worshipped together and received the sacraments.[29]

Parish councils, which had become the parishes' central administrative unit, helped make collegiality real in the parishes. Pilarczyk noted in his account of his visits that "practically everywhere there was a sense of ownership, a sense of real participation in the direction of the parish." Some parishioners felt, as one woman put it, that they were "not just in the audience any more." Bottom up approaches with much lay participation began relaxing the centralized administrative style of the early 1960s. There were more informal discussions among clergy and laity, more participation in jointly planned ecumenical services, and greater collaboration in community service. As lay ministries increased, lay persons played important roles in nearly all areas of church life. Worship, evangelization, protection of the unborn, care for the elderly, and help for the faithful in time of illness, job loss, and marital difficulty, among others, received added attention by voluntary parish groups. Parish renewal programs, like RENEW, also helped develop the spiritual life of Catholics at the local level.[30]

At the same time that the local church placed a great deal of emphasis on parish activities, Pilarczyk reminded the faithful in the 1990s that the basic unit of Catholicity was not the parish but the local church as a whole. "In the past," he wrote, "we looked on parishes as a planetary system, each parish in its own orbit with hardly any contact with the neighboring planets. Now we are beginning to see that if we maintain that approach much longer, we are going to be in big trouble because the individual, distinct planets simply do not have enough resources to survive on their own." Most parishes lacked the necessary financial and academic means to produce books and programs for liturgy or catechetics as well as provide for the training of religion teachers and other lay ministers that they needed in the post–Vatican II church. The diocese could more readily accommodate the fullness of church life. Through the local bishop, priests and deacons were ordained, and the diocese officially certified church teaching. From the earliest days of the local church there had been a kind of ongoing tension between parishes and the diocese. "This tension," Pilarczyk argued, "manifests itself in the natural tendency of Catholics to look out for the needs of their parish first and to think of the needs of the diocese second." But "the bishop," he insisted, "must look first to the well-being of the whole local church even if this means that he must make demands on the parishes which are not always appreciated by everybody in the parish."[31]

A year after Pilarczyk began his parish visitation program he established the "For the Harvest" Task Force to help prepare for the shortage of priests in the future. Seeing no signs of an imminent reversal in the decline of priests, the archdiocese saw the need for more trained and professional lay ministers and for more collaboration among parishes to manage in the absence of a pastor. The "For the Harvest" program, its title taken from scripture, was a massive effort to involve members of individual parishes throughout the archdiocese. Father Robert Schmitz, archdiocesan director of research and planning, coordinated the project. Lay leaders reviewed staffing and liturgical scheduling, speculated on the resources and church personnel that would be available in 2000, and established committees for interparish cooperation. By the spring of 1986 approximately 86 percent of all parishes in the archdiocese had "harvested" information about the future of Catholic ministries at the parish level. Each deanery eventually issued a report as part of the process. At the same time that it attempted to deal with the problem of the shortage of priests, "For the Harvest" also looked at ministry as a whole in parishes. It eventually called for small parishes to share pastors.[32]

Though there was in the 1980s an encouraging, but slight, increase in the number of ordinations and seminarians, the annual decline in the number of priests in the archdiocese nevertheless continued. In June 1980 the four-year college seminary of the archdiocese closed. St. Gregory's in Mount Washington was one of 241 seminaries nationally that closed their doors between 1964 and 1984. During that time the number of seminarians in the country preparing for the priesthood dropped from 47,500 to about 20,000. Declining enrollments and rising costs were the primary factors that contributed to the closing of St. Gregory's. In its heyday total enrollment was approximately six times what it was in 1980. In 1978 there were sixty-five students as compared with 175 in 1970 and 370 before Vatican II.[33]

In September 1981 the Athenaeum of Ohio, made up of Mount St. Mary's of the West Seminary and the Lay Pastoral Ministry Program, moved from Norwood to Beechmont Avenue in Mount Washington and occupied the former site of St. Gregory Seminary. In addition to preparing candidates for the priesthood, it became necessary to use the seminary facilities and resources to prepare others for the diverse ministries in the archdiocese. The new theologate provided the basic academic program for the formation of the permanent deacons. In the spring of 1980 St. Francis Seminary, operated by the Franciscans since 1858 for high school boys preparing to join the order, also closed. When the seminary observed its centennial in 1958 there were 144 boys enrolled; in 1980 there were 69. The following year St.

Leonard College in Dayton, which had served the Franciscan friars as their school of theology for priesthood candidates since 1958, also closed.[34]

By 1990 the number of full-time priests in the archdiocese had dropped to 287, down from 339 in 1985 and 435 in 1968. In its 1991 report on "Plunge to Scarcity" the archdiocesan office of planning and research projected a decrease in archdiocesan priests of nearly 50 percent by 2005. As in the formative years of the diocese, when there was scarcely one priest for every two thousand Catholics in Cincinnati in 1843, there was a pressing need for priests. The new archdiocesan report expected to see the average number of Catholics served by each archdiocesan priest to double. The average number of Catholics per priest was projected to increase from 1,650 in 1990 to 3,310 in 2005. Whereas at midcentury there had been one priest for every eight hundred Catholics, in some parishes in the 1990s the ratio was as high as three to four thousand people to a priest and in a few the ratio was as low as two to three hundred per priest. The 1991 report also predicted that by the end of 2005 there would be 145 active diocesan priests, down forty-eight percent from the 279 serving at the end of 1990. "Of course there is a priest shortage if we look on the '50s and '60s as the norm," Pilarczyk wrote. "But if we look on those years . . . as an atypical abundance of ordained ministers, then we are simply reverting to a more normal proportion of priests to lay people. . . . God's grace," he continued, "never left us. I'm not sure what we've been experiencing is a decline, but rather a going back to the proportions we once had in this country."[35]

In 1980 the *Official Catholic Directory* listed 398 active priests, 1,890 religious sisters, 272 religious brothers, 256 parishes, and 149 schools to serve 505,666 Catholics in the archdiocese. When the archdiocese celebrated its 175th anniversary in 1996, there were 242 active priests, 1,471 sisters, 179 brothers, 237 parishes, and 140 schools to serve the 545,300 Catholics. The archdiocese was now one of six dioceses in Ohio, in contrast to when it originally encompassed the entire state. Moreover, the Catholic population in the archdiocese in 1996 was two and a half times greater than what it had been in the whole United States at the time of Bishop Edward Fenwick's installation in 1821. Vocations, which had continued to decline in the 1980s, did not keep pace with the numbers who retired, died, or resigned from the active ministry. In the post–Vatican II period more than eighty men in the Cincinnati archdiocese left the priesthood. For the first time in its history the local church, like the national church, suffered a substantial loss of religious membership. The need for vocations to the priesthood and religious orders remained acute.[36]

As the active religious ministry declined, church-closings, mergers, and the scaled down use of some church buildings in the archdiocese became more frequent. The number of consolidations since Alter's administration included five closings in the 1950s, ten in the 1960s, ten in the 1970s, and six along with more than a dozen mergers in the 1980s through the mid-1990s. Among the many reasons for the consolidations were a shortage of clergy, a parish's inability—because of insufficient resources—to minister adequately, and population shifts. In late August 1969 St. John the Baptist Church, a landmark of Cincinnati's Over-the-Rhine area since 1845, closed its doors. The closing coincided almost to the day with the anniversary of the founding of the parish 125 years earlier. For many years St. John's was the largest parish in the archdiocese, but the movement of people to the suburbs since the end of the Second World War had left it with only small numbers of regular parishioners. These parishioners became part of St. Francis Seraph parish, one block south of St. John's. The following year Sacred Italian parish on Broadway in downtown Cincinnati merged with Sacred Heart parish in Camp Washington. In 1968 the Broadway parish had celebrated the 75th anniversary of the building of the church. Having but a few remaining parishioners within its boundaries, the parish served as the spiritual and social center of Catholics of Italian origin in the archdiocese. By the 1990s two national parishes remained in the archdiocese: St. Adalbert's for the Polish congregation and Holy Cross parish for the Lithuanian congregation, both in Dayton. Community of Christian Service (1970) in Dayton and Community of Hope (1971) in Cincinnati, nonterritorial parishes founded by hundreds of people generally frustrated with the style of worship then available, also closed in 1977 and 1989, respectively.[37]

In some instances the archdiocese took over churches previously run by religious orders. Because of the small number of Camboni missionaries in 1992 St. Michael Church in lower Price Hill in Cincinnati was once again turned over to the archdiocese. It shared a pastor with Holy Family parish. Once a thriving parish of German immigrants in the nineteenth century, St. Michael's had become a small and poor inner-city parish in an urban Appalachian neighborhood. From the merger of Cincinnati's St. Monica and St. George parishes the St. Monica–St. George Parish Newman Center in Clifton Heights was established in 1993. The following year St. Elizabeth, St. Matthew, and Sts. Peter and Paul parishes in Norwood merged into Holy Trinity parish. Two years before the formation of Holy Trinity, the archdiocese's newest parish in its 175-year-history, St. Mary's of 13th and Clay Streets in Cincinnati, the oldest Catholic church building in the archdiocese, observed its 150th anniversary. In June 1996 the 125-year-long Passionist presence in Mount Adams ended when the congregation returned pastoral care of the Holy Cross-Immaculata parish to the archdiocese.[38]

The closings and mergers were not, Pilarczyk wrote, "without pain and frustration." At times it met considerable resistance. In November 1987 St.

Joseph parish in the Hamilton Deanery rejected plans to merge with the three larger Hamilton parishes, St. Veronica's, St. Stephen's, and St. Mary's. In the fall of 1986 665 Catholics were registered in St. Joseph parish. The others had between 1,200 and 1,600 parishioners each. Archdiocesan guidelines stipulated that parishes had to remain financially solvent and ministerially complete, and they had to have seven hundred registered Catholics or a weekend Mass attendance of 350 in order to retain a full-time pastor. The chancery was prepared to go ahead with the merger without St. Joseph's, whose parish council had begun making plans to be a priestless parish. The parish was to be served by a noncleric pastoral administrator, who would perform all the duties currently done by a priest except for the sacraments. Money was not an issue in the merger, as all four parishes were financially stable; the concern was of maintaining a quality ministry. "We can't deny realities," Pilarczyk said, "and the realities are that in 1965 we had over four hundred active priests in our archdiocese."[39]

A year later a bitter dispute broke out between the three Hamilton parishes—St. Mary's, St. Stephen's, and St. Veronica's—and the chancery. More than 1,400 petitioners asked authorities in Rome to stop the merger of the three parishes and the planned renovation of the 135-year-old St. Stephen Church. They rallied in a futile effort. The three parishes were directed by the chancery to combine under the name of St. Julie Billiart and use the larger St. Stephen Church. "Consolidations," the archbishop argued, "are a way of strengthening our parishes. It's not a sign of disease or weakness." In February 1989 Vatican officials upheld Pilarczyk's decision to renovate St. Stephen Church as part of the merger of the three parishes.[40]

In 1987 the archdiocese suggested that St. Bonaventure and San Antonio Di Padova parishes in South Fairmount merge because there were not enough priests to staff both Franciscan-run parishes. Located less than a mile from each other, the parishes could no longer support full-time pastors. After over a year's deliberations the two parish councils were still deadlocked on which church to close. Finally in 1989 San Antonio Church on Queen City Avenue became a chapel of St. Bonaventure Church. Though closings and mergers became more frequent, by 1996 the archdiocese had also seen over a twenty-five year period nine new parishes established.[41]

In 1990 preparation for the archdiocesan Ministry 2000 program began. Developed by the office of planning and research in collaboration with the respective deaneries of the archdiocese, the program developed a plan to carry out the ministry of the local church in the year 2000 and beyond. Each deanery's task force considered the declining number of priests, parish finances, resources, the underutilization of church facilities, and various parish needs. By the year 1996 a lay pastoral administrator or associate assisted the pastor in

76 of the 237 parishes in the archdiocese. Close to a third of the parishes now shared pastors or had only part-time pastors. One-priest parishes were the norm and only a handful of the larger parishes had two priests. A growing concern among some Catholics was whether priestless parishes would become a fact of life in the local church.[42]

Though the pre–Vatican II parish was a vital center of Catholic life, in the post–Vatican II period it became more and more removed from the immigrant experience and took on new functions. The Second Vatican Council had called for a revitalization of people's commitment to God and to the church. "Before Vatican II," Pilarczyk observed, "we had a church of rules and regulations. But Vatican II shook many people up concerning their whole commitment to the church; being a Catholic was a lot more demanding than we had thought before." In his judgment, Vatican II had opened doors and "made the church alive. It changed ideas about the church, the world, revelation. It jarred us out of our complacency. And that's all good." The parish was no longer just a geographic gathering of people, where weddings, funerals, or baptisms were performed. Parishes were expected to provide a wide range of services, "and a tiny little parish," Pilarczyk said, "can't do that." The archbishop saw the need for greater cooperation and clustering and the sharing of priests, ministries, and resources among parishes. "We have to accustom ourselves to new levels of collaboration," he wrote, "simply because that seems to be the way in which the Lord wants the church to work."[43]

By the 1990s the so-called "people in the pew" performed a myriad of tasks in the parish. A new style of collegial governance emerged. The laity were deeply involved in practically all aspects of church life. In the wake of the shrinking numbers of priests and religious there developed more opportunities for collaboration in ministry and more lay people took on leadership roles in the local church. Even though there were fewer priests, people were "better ministered to," Pilarczyk thought, "than they were" in the 1960s. The lack of vocations contributed to a greater use of lay men and women in schools and institutions. In his 1987 report on Vocations to the pope Pilarczyk had written that what Catholics "are experiencing is a broadening of the concept of church vocation and church ministry, a concept which formerly included only priests and Religious, but which now includes lay persons in an ever increasing number of capacities different from those in which they served previously."[44]

Lay persons served the church as business managers, pastoral ministers, youth ministers, liturgy planners, musicians, religious education directors, teachers, and school principals. The lay minister could be found behind the lectern reading the Scriptures, distributing communion at the altar, and in the rectory balancing the parish's books. Lay persons, moreover, worked on finance and school committees, mentored engaged couples, organized youth ministries, prepared liturgies, headed capital fund drives, staffed parish offices, provided pre-sacramental instructions, ran prayer groups, drove the elderly to medical appointments, and attended to the bereaved, converts, and the sick in their parishes. Moreover, they helped oversee religious education, ran parish music programs, organized CCD classes, became engaged in social justice activities, provided support to single parents and widowed persons, and coached parish sports teams. In a number of parishes the Legion of Mary members made welcome, new baby, and friendship calls, visited the sick at hospitals and rest homes, took the parish census, and promoted membership in the Apostleship of Prayer.[45]

Overall, there appeared to be a deeper spirituality on the part of priests and laity through parish renewal and prayer. With the increasing collaboration in the local church's ministry, priests no longer had to attend personally to every single task in their parishes. They "are freer," Pilarczyk said, "to focus their energies on specifically priestly activities such as preaching, liturgical celebration and leadership of the Christian community." Notwithstanding this able lay assistance, data showed that priests generally still worked long hours and had stressful jobs. In some cases the increased number of parish meetings increased the workload of the parish priests. In the summer of 1982 the Senate of Priests approved a policy that provided sabbatical opportunities for eight priests each year. The recipient was given an extended period of time, not to exceed three months, to engage in an activity for his own renewal. Men who had been priests for more than seven years were eligible for sabbaticals.[46]

To assist the priests in their ministry, the archdiocese during Pilarczyk's administration sponsored four priests' convocations. In June 1984 more than 350 active priests and a few retired priests met at a resort at French Lick, Indiana, for a four-day session. They convened again at the same site six years later. They met to reflect on the meaning of priesthood in the recent church and in their lives and to discuss their hopes and concerns for the future. It marked the first time the entire archdiocesan presbyterate convened in nearly 150 years. The first recorded meeting of all the priests of the diocese was when Purcell had convened a three-day meeting in 1837. For almost 100 years, 1870 to 1965, there was virtually no change in the priesthood. According to Pilarczyk as a "servant of the people" the post–Vatican II priest was now seen as living and acting more in the midst of the people, rather than the "cultic figure" of old. Shortly after the 1984 French Lick meeting Pilarczyk established an archdiocesan priests' task force. After more than two years of study and discussion, the task force recommended higher pay and greater liberty for the clergy. Priests' salaries at the time were the

lowest of the six dioceses in Ohio. By the 1990s there was also greater tolerance with regard to priestly dress, residence outside rectories, and to the
kinds of work that the priests might do. They generally had more to say
about their assignments. In 1992 the archdiocese sold a one-hundred-acre
portion of Gate of Heaven Cemetery for $10,850,000. Proceeds went to the
archdiocesan fund for infirm and retired priests. In October 1994 the priests
of the archdiocese convened for the fourth time at Incarnation parish in Dayton to discuss their concerns for the future of their vocation.[47]

Before Vatican II the parish staff almost always consisted of the pastor,
who held the job for most of his lifetime, his housekeeper, a groundskeeper,
and perhaps a secretary. The workers were usually volunteers who were in
their retirement years. In the post–Vatican II archdiocese of Cincinnati local
pastor assignments were for six years, often renewable for one more term.
Though by the summer of 1982 retirement from administrative duties at the
age of seventy was no longer mandatory for priests of the archdiocese, any
priest who wished to retire from administrative responsibilities at that age
was permitted to do so. With the increasing shortage of clergy and religious,
educated lay professionals ran the school, catechumate, CCD, and adult religious education. A manager with business expertise oversaw the finances of
the parish. The secretary was generally computer literate. By the 1990s more
than ninety percent of the individuals working in the central offices of the
archdiocese were lay; about half a century earlier there were three lay
employees.[48]

EDUCATION

The twentieth-century emphasis on organization and specialization helped
strengthen the move toward the centralization of schools in the archdiocese.
In accordance with the recommendations of the Second Vatican Council, in
August 1970 Leibold created the new position of Vicar for Catholic Educa-
tion and appointed Monsignor William J. Franer, who had been for twenty-
three years an assistant superintendent of schools, to the post. About two
years after Bernardin's installation in 1972, Daniel Pilarczyk, rector of St.
Gregory Seminary, became vicar for education. In February 1977 a new
Archdiocesan Commission on Education was activated at a meeting in Holy
Trinity school in Dayton, replacing the archdiocesan Board of Education.
The reorganization, which helped implement the plan of the Post-Synodal
Task Force on Education, provided the means for maximum participation
and a broader sharing of responsibility in the educational mission of the local
church. The archdiocesan commission now had fourteen voting members,
including eight lay persons.[49]

By the 1960s Catholic education began facing serious problems. Mounting costs and population shifts posed new problems for parish schools. After more than a hundred years of sustained growth in the diocese, attendance at Catholic elementary schools began to decline. It was caused in part by the declining birthrate. Furthermore, the continued droughts in religious vocations and the fact that many religious were leaving education for other ministries intensified the problem. The schools faced rising payroll costs as lay teachers replaced sisters and other religious in the classroom. As a consequence, a number of parochial schools and institutions across the country were forced to close or merge. Though in the face of the new problems some people began to question the value of a parochial school education, church authorities remained committed to Catholic education. Throughout the history of the archdiocese Cincinnati ordinaries, clergy, religious, and laity have been ardent champions of Catholic schools, always emphasizing the right to establish schools that provided the religious instruction they deemed essential to the children's formation.

Shortly after his installation, Pilarczyk renewed the archdiocese's commitment to Catholic education. He took issue with the argument that Catholics should forget about Catholic schools and teach their children some other way. "[W]e have not found," he wrote, "any more effective way in which to foster and strengthen the faith and Church commitment of young people than the Catholic school. To the extent that we can measure religious attitudes, we know that Catholic schools are effective educational instruments. They cannot be written off or disregarded because of the difficulties they entail." Sister of Charity Kathryn Ann Connelly, director of educational services and the first woman to serve as superintendent of schools in the archdiocese, reminded the faithful in the 1990s that the "future of our church . . . and our communities is in the heads and hearts and hand of our young people." Connelly was appointed superintendent in 1983. Though in the past few decades the schools were staffed for the most part by lay persons, they were "still Catholic schools," Pilarczyk wrote, ". . . [a]nd they are still operating." Local Catholics had come to accept and believe, as did Monsignor Carl Ryan in 1954 in anticipation of the need for more lay teachers, that the "chief mark of a Catholic school is not the religious garb of its teachers but the Christian spirit that permeates the entire program."[50]

The decline of clergy and religious, increased costs, lower birthrates, and geographical mobility contributed to the decline of Catholic primary and secondary schools. The enrollment dropped from 90,492 in 177 Catholic schools in 1969 to 51,408 in 136 schools in 1989, a decrease of 56 percent. What helped prevent steeper decline in enrollment in the elementary schools was the fact that many parish schools had restored grade one in their programs. Though the first grade had been dropped in virtually all parish schools in 1964, in 1970 the archdiocesan Board of Education adopted a policy of allowing parish schools to reestablish grade one if conditions warranted it and to charge tuition if necessary. In the fall of that year forty schools enrolled pupils in the first grade, four charging tuition. Two years later fifteen more first grades were restored.[51]

Largely because of the academic success, religious curriculum, and discipline in the parochial schools, by the late-1980s enrollment in Catholic elementary and secondary schools in the archdiocese began a modest and gradual upward trend that continued through the mid-1990s. This was consistent with the national trend. Total enrollment in the 136 Catholic schools in the archdiocese in 1996 was 55,352 compared to 51,408 in 1989, an increase of 0.77 percent. Cincinnati had the tenth largest system of Catholic schools in the United States. As a result of consolidations and closings, the number of Catholic elementary and secondary schools in the archdiocese dropped from 146 and 31 in 1969 to 114 and 22, respectively, in 1996. In the 1990s an estimated 43.4 percent of Catholic children in grades one through twelve attended Catholic schools. Whereas approximately 70,000 students attended Catholic schools in the early 1970s as compared to 55,000 in the 1990s, there were now fewer children than there used to be. Using baptismal records, the chancery estimated in 1990 that the Catholic schools served 43.7 percent of Catholic students available in 1990 compared with approximately 40.5 percent in the early 1970s. In the 1992–1993 school year, 45.4 percent of the potential population of Catholic children were in Catholic schools with 31.2 percent in religious education programs. In contrast, in the 1974–1975 school year, when these statistics first were recorded, 40.5 percent of the children were in Catholic schools and 21.6 percent in religious education classes. In spite of the overall decrease in Ohio's school-aged population, Catholic schools educated nearly 10 percent of the state's children in 1989–1990, the same percentage as in 1980.[52]

Throughout this period Catholic schools in the United States continued to face financial problems. The cost of educating a child in the Catholic school system rose. The Supreme Court ruling in 1977 that states could pay for certain textbooks and such auxiliary services as standardized testing, diagnostic testing, and therapeutic and remedial services for nonpublic school students was of some help. Elementary tuition statewide increased from an average of $242 in 1980 to $667 in 1990, a hike of 175 percent. In the high schools, the average increase was 120 percent, from $873 to $1,922. In 1992 the Archdiocesan Pastoral Council approved the concept of need-based tuition aid for Catholic parish schools instead of the cost-based tuition or parish subsidies. The goal was to reduce significantly the parish tuition aid. The increased need for lay teachers and higher salaries had put a strain on parish finances. The archdiocesan school office often urged parishes to bring teachers' salaries up to within 15 percent of local public school lay teachers. More and more tuition aid based on need was awarded to families. To facilitate the need-based tuition policy, Pilarczyk had issued a decree in December 1991 allowing endowments for educational purposes to be established in parishes. Two months earlier the archdiocese had also initiated a mandatory Steward-ship Sunday to help increase the amount of money Catholics donated to their parishes. The additional revenue would help pay for increasing costs in the parishes and for those incurred by the archdiocese. Archdiocesan income came from three sources—parish assessments; bequests, investments, and interest; and the annual archbishop's fund drive. In the face of an operating deficit of more than $500,000 in 1991, the archdiocese that year increased the parish assessment rate of 4.2 percent of total adjusted gross income, which was the lowest among the Ohio dioceses and one of the lowest in the nation, to 5.7 percent.[53]

As it dealt with recurring financial problems, the archdiocese also addressed racial and districting issues. In January 1975 the Archdiocesan Board of Education called on parish boards of education, school principals, and pastors to "refuse admission" to students applying to enter Catholic schools for the purpose of avoiding desegregation either in a public school district or in another Catholic school. In response to the federal court man-date for Dayton to desegregate its public schools, in June 1976 nearly one hundred parishes, denominational organizations, and communities in Day-ton signed an "Interfaith Affirmation" to help assure the peaceful desegre-gation of Dayton Catholic schools. Several Catholic groups and local priests pledged their assistance to the various boards of education "in removing eco-nomic segregation in the school and community." In his homily in Holy Trinity Church in Dayton in 1976, Bishop Pilarczyk, then vicar for educa-tion, offered the faithful what he called "a brief theology of the hot potato. Every once in a while God throws us a hot potato," he said. "We don't always know what kind of potato it will be. We don't always know when it's com-ing. We don't always know whether it's going to be a really hot potato or a not-so-hot potato. But we do know that if we handle it with the strength and peace that Christ has given us, nobody's going to get burned." As busing for the purpose of desegregating Dayton's public schools began that fall, Arch-bishop Bernardin asked for prayer and a positive outlook. A year later the local church, under the guidance of such individuals as Father Egbert Figaro, a black priest and pastor of Dayton's St. James parish, also urged Catholics in Springfield to respond positively to the desegregation of the city's public schools.[54]

In the summer of 1978 the archdiocese faced a desegregation suit. The Cincinnati Board of Education took the question of funding auxiliary services at St. Mary School in Hyde Park into federal court. Two years earlier the public school board had voted to stop channeling state aid to St. Mary's pupils on the grounds that the board's defense in an upcoming desegregation suit might be jeopardized. The suit stemmed from the 1976 closing of Holy Cross Parish School in Mount Adams. Fifty-two of its pupils enrolled in St. Mary's. Because they chose the Hyde Park school, which was predominantly white, over the closer but predominantly black St. Francis de Sales parish school in Walnut Hills, they were accused of segregation. Subsequent examination by the State Department of Education, Franklin County Court of Appeals, and the Ohio Supreme Court showed that the parents of the children of St. Mary's had no segregation intent. In 1979 the U.S. District Court ruled that the Cincinnati Board of Education acted unconstitutionally in cutting off state funds.[55]

In January 1979 the archdiocesan Social Action Commission issued a working paper on Catholic school desegregation, urging that steps be taken "to eradicate any semblance of racism, tokenism or patronism" in the schools. It charged that Catholic schools in the archdiocese were "'de facto' segregated because of housing patterns and official and unofficial action that have resulted in further segregation rather than integration." Though progress had been made to admit more black students and teachers into the schools, the archdiocesan Commission on Education admitted that much more had to be done. Since the early 1970s there also had been more archdiocesan funding for black students in the inner-city schools. A subsidy of $400,000, called TA-132 funds, named for the paragraph in the synod 1971 document on temporal affairs, was established for the core area schools in Cincinnati. By the end of the decade there was more integration in the schools and a new annual scholarship fund for needy high school students was established in the archdiocese. During Pilarczyk's administration the archdiocese joined other dioceses in Ohio in providing greater support to Catholic schools that served the poor and blacks in disadvantaged urban and rural areas.[56]

An issue that also caused some commotion in parts of the archdiocese had to do with high school districting. In the aftermath of Vatican II, the local, territorial nature of the parish, developed a half-century earlier during Moeller's tenure, was less rigidly observed. The synod of 1971 gave Catholics in Cincinnati the ability to register at the parish of their choosing no matter where they resided, provided that the pastor of the parish they wished to join was willing to accept their membership. Though the option was intended chiefly for liturgical reasons, there were parents who registered at a parish for other reasons, such as sending their children to a parish's designated high school. As a consequence, high school districting became a persistent headache for archdiocesan officials. It often placed the pastors in the middle between parents, who registered at a tributary parish of the high school that they wanted their children to attend, and the archdiocese. In the late 1970s and 1980s there were several requests from parishes to alter their high school assignments. Racial and socioeconomic class prejudice or affiliation with a strong high school sports program was often seen as the "real" reason behind the arguments.[57]

The controversy resulted in the creation of a special task force in 1982 to streamline policies and possibly redraw district lines that determined the tributary parishes for high schools. Since the early years of McNicholas's administration, when he had set up the system of high schools in Cincinnati and Dayton, sanctions had existed for crossing district lines to attend high school. Over the years those sanctions changed. The rules drawn up in 1951 still applied in the 1980s. Parishes were obligated to contribute $100 per student attending a Catholic secondary school, parochial or private, to the archdiocesan Equalization Fund. Though the pastor could withhold the parish contribution when a student opted to attend a school in another district, the choice was rarely exercised. Parents of the child were expected to pay the difference in tuition, and the student could not participate in interscholastic sports as long as the child attended the school. In 1986 the Commission on Education passed a new policy. It declared that students who wished to play sports for Catholic high schools in the archdiocese would have to live within the school's district regardless of their parish affiliations. Unaffected were open enrollment policies for minority students in the Dayton area. Those policies allowed black students to enroll in any school in Dayton. Opponents of high school districting often cited open enrollment policies in such dioceses as Cleveland, Detroit, and Chicago as a way to solve boundary problems. Students in those communities could attend any high school within their diocese.[58]

SOCIAL ISSUES

Throughout the history of the archdiocese clergy, religious, and lay persons responded to the needs of the changing church and society. For 175 years thousands of clergy and religious devoted their lives to the service of others. They conducted schools, orphanages, and hospitals and worked with immigrants, the poor, and handicapped. In 1996 women religious from forty-one orders and men religious from twelve orders continued the tradition and made ample contributions to the religious life of the archdiocese. They were engaged in parish ministry, elementary, secondary, adult and university-level education, health-care administration, spiritual direction, counseling, retreat work, and ministry to the young, the elderly, and the sick. There were eleven

Catholic hospitals, thirteen homes for the aged and infirm, four residential treatment facilities for children or young adults, and two residential homes for disabled persons in the archdiocese.

A new era of service to the Cincinnati area by the Franciscan Sisters of the Poor began on May 1, 1970, with the opening of Providence Hospital. Built on the former Powel Crosley Jr. Estate on Kipling Road, it succeeded the old St. Mary Hospital in the west end. In the 1980s the Franciscan Sisters of the Poor continued their work in health care and social services under the auspices of the Franciscan Health System of Cincinnati. In addition to several health-care facilities and programs, the system oversaw St. Francis–St. George and Providence Hospitals. On July 26, 1975, the Little Sisters of the Poor moved from their eighty-year-old St. Peter Home on Riddle Road to Archbishop Leibold Home for the Aged. Leibold had supported and encouraged the construction of the new home. The new seven-story facility replaced both St. Peter's and the old St. Joseph Home on Florence Avenue, which had closed in 1973 after 105 years of service.[59]

Among the larger orders, the Sisters of Charity continued their work of education, social service, pastoral ministry, elder care, and health care in the archdiocese. In addition to operating Seton High School, College of Mount St. Joseph, and adult lay programs and centers, they continued to operate St. Joseph Home, Good Samaritan Hospitals in Cincinnati and Dayton, and Maria-Joseph Living Care Center in Dayton. The ministries of the Sisters of the Precious Blood included Regina High School, St. Theresa's Home for the Aged, St. Joseph Orphanage and Maria Joseph Home for the Aged, and Maria Stein Shrine and Retreat Center. The religious men of the order had the pastoral care of twenty-three parishes, among which were the churches of St. Mark in Cincinnati, Precious Blood and St. Joseph in Dayton, St. John in Maria Stein, and St. Augustine in Minster. The Sisters of Mercy continued their educational work at twelve schools and provided health care through six hospitals in the archdiocese. In 1989 their 116-year-old St. Joseph Infant and Maternity Home changed its purpose. Despite rising teenage pregnancies, enrollment in the home had been dwindling throughout the 1980s. The young pregnant women were choosing other kinds of services instead of the more institutional, live-in program at St. Joseph's. At its peak in the mid-1970s the home accommodated approximately 160 women a year. In its new role in the 1990s, St. Joseph Home now attended to multihandicapped, nonambulatory children and young adults. Sisters of Notre Dame de Namur continued their work in education at several schools in Cincinnati and Dayton. In the summer of 1986 the Dominican Sisters of Columbus, Sisters of Charity, Sisters of Mercy, and Franciscan Sisters of the Poor joined hands with the chancery and established the program Healthy Moms and Babes. They

hoped to reduce the city's high infant mortality rate. Among the secular clergy the Franciscans staffed several parishes, including St. Francis Seraph, and
continued to publish *St. Anthony Messenger*. In addition to continuing their
ministry in education at St. Xavier High School and Xavier University, the
Jesuits conducted retreat work at the Milford Spiritual Center, operated St.
Xavier Church in downtown Cincinnati, and provided assistance to several
parishes in need of priests. In addition to the University of Dayton, the Marianists conducted Moeller, Purcell Marian, and Chaminade-Julienne High
Schools as well as maintained pastoral responsibility over three parishes.[60]

Since the mid-1960s the archdiocese had taken a broader and more ecumenical role in social programs. The local church assisted the poor and
minority people through outreach programs and neighborhood centers. One
of the characteristics of post–Vatican II Catholics was a commitment to social
justice. In 1971 the archdiocese established the Department of Social Action
with the layman William Schumacher as director. The office, which integrated the Catholic Commission on Human Relations and the Central Planning and Budget Commission, coordinated existing social action programs.
On Pentecost Sunday, June 7, 1981, Mother Teresa came to Cincinnati to
spread her message to minister to "the poorest of the poor." More than 1,500
assembled at St. Francis Seminary in Mount Healthy for an outdoor Mass on
the seminary grounds. Local Franciscans had invited Mother Teresa to help
celebrate the 800th anniversary of the birth of St. Francis.[61]

In the fall of 1973 the archdiocese established a twelve-member Commission for World Justice and Peace. As head of NCCB Archbishop Bernardin
was very sensitive to war and peace issues. On New Year's Day 1975 close to
five hundred persons gathered at St. Peter in Chains Cathedral to celebrate
World Peace Day at a Mass concelebrated by Bernardin and two visiting
priests from Uganda. The following summer Bernardin asked the American
bishops to encourage their dioceses to accept Vietnam refugee families. By
the end of the year close to four hundred refugees were welcomed into
homes in the Cincinnati archdiocese. In 1992 the archdiocesan offices of
Social Action and World Peace, which for twenty years had been split into
two parts, Cincinnati and Dayton, merged into one. The commission's three
main priorities were peace, economic justice, and the parish.[62]

In the early 1970s Catholic Charities had social service offices in Cincinnati, Dayton, Hamilton, and Springfield. In December 1976 representatives
of the various social agencies in the archdiocese decided to federate as well
as extend services to twelve more counties, which included 85,000 Catholics
living primarily in rural areas. They adopted a new structure and gave
Catholic Charities a new name, the Federation of Catholic Community
Charities. As a result of the move, the four Catholic Charities offices

changed their respective names to Catholic Social Services. Father James Garland, a native of Wilmington, Ohio, and director of Dayton Catholic Charities, became the archdiocesan director. In 1984 he was named bishop and vicar general of Cincinnati. Catholic Social Services included child care institutions, residence institutions, neighborhood service centers, and such volunteer organizations as Catholic Big Brothers, Ladies of Charity, and St. Vincent de Paul Society. In the 1990s social services in the archdiocese consisted of Catholic Social Services of Southwestern Ohio, of Butler and Warren Counties, of Springfield, and of Miami Valley. Though these agencies received funds from the archbishop's annual fund drive, the majority of their funding came from the local Community Chest and from local, state, and federal grants.[63]

Throughout this period Catholics attended to the needs of various groups of people. In 1978 the Brothers of Christian Service had established Villa Maria, a group home for men who were mentally handicapped. Two years later the Catholic Federation for the Mentally Retarded sponsored the Connelly Home for mentally disabled women. In 1992 the two homes merged and formed a new corporate entity, Catholic Residential Services of the Archdiocese of Cincinnati. Each year the St. Vincent de Paul Society and the agencies in Catholics United for the Poor (CUP) fed, sheltered, and clothed thousands of needy people. By 1981 St. Vincent de Paul also began taking in women in its efforts to address the dire material needs of families and persons in the community. CUP agencies included Tender Mercies, which provided Over-the-Rhine residences for men and women with a history of mental illness; Bethany House of Hospitality, a Mount Auburn temporary shelter for homeless women and children; Our Daily Bread, a breakfast kitchen in Over-the-Rhine; and Over-the-Rhine Kitchen, a hot-lunch cafeteria. These agencies provided shelter to more than five hundred homeless families, supplied space for six thousand nights' rest for street people, and served more than thirty thousand breakfasts and hot lunches. In 1987 lay and religious representatives of the archdiocese successfully joined in a drive to start a home in Cincinnati for persons suffering from AIDS. Three years later the Home Builders Association, with about $300,000 in donated supplies and labor, built a two-story, sixteen-unit shelter, called Pleasant House, for the homeless in Over-the-Rhine. Pleasant House was operated and owned by Tender Mercies. By the 1990s Catholic health facilities expanded their services at outreach clinics and social agencies emphasized transitional housing and employment for the homeless.[64]

By the early 1970s the archdiocese began supporting mission work among the Spanish-speaking. Bernardin celebrated a field Mass in Spanish in Darke County each year during the tomato harvest season for migrant agricultural workers and Hispanic American families. As early as the 1950s, when thousands of migrant workers began coming to the region, local organizations sponsored programs for migrants and the Springfield Deanery Council of Catholic Men visited the camps. A Sister of Charity, Pauline Apodaca, worked among the resident and transient Hispanic people. In 1977 the archdiocese opened a center for the Spanish-Speaking Apostolate at Cranberry Prairie in southern Mercer County. It served all the Spanish-speaking in the archdiocese but especially the more than 1,700 Hispanic people living in Mercer and Darke Counties. In the 1990s the archdiocesan Catholic Hispanic Community of Greater Cincinnati attended to the more than 10,000 Hispanic Catholics. Other lay communities and related organizations in the archdiocese in 1996 were the Caritas Christi Secular Institute, Marianist Voluntary Service Communities, New Jerusalen Community, St. Andrew Kim Korean Catholic Society, St. Leonard Faith Community, Secular Franciscans, and the Vietnamese Catholic Community.[65]

During Leibold's tenure black Catholics called for more participation in decision making. In 1970 the Black Lay Catholic Caucus of the archdiocese, awarded a grant of $14,000 by the Department of Social Action, was formed. To help provide more opportunities for blacks, the archdiocese opened the office of the Black Secretariat in 1977. As blacks acquired a larger voice in the local church, evangelical-style revivals became a more popular form of evangelization in black Catholic parishes. Under the guidance of Father Clarence J. Rivers, the first black diocesan priest in Cincinnati, the sound of African drums, a one hundred-voice choir, and applause filled St. Peter in Chains Cathedral on May 22, 1977, at the "Soulful Worship" program of music, liturgy, and black culture. The mood was one of celebration and worship as more than 850 Catholics, black and white, gathered at the special liturgy. By the 1980s there was more recognition of African American culture, gospel music, and African American Catholic style liturgies.[66]

As efforts were made to address some of the concerns and interests of black Catholics, there were recurrent allegations of racism in the local church. In the summer of 1981 seventy-five pastors and parish leaders from the Cincinnati area met with Bernardin in the undercroft of St. Peter in Chains Cathedral to voice their concerns. Some angrily charged that the Catholic Church was a predominantly white institution that was insensitive to the needs of poor blacks and other minorities and treated them as "second class citizens." Arguing that local racist parishioners did not realize how much their racism was contrary to the teachings of the church, they urged Bernardin to say more on the issues of poverty and racism in the community. "We want to walk together with you so we can be proud we are working with the poor," a sister in pastoral ministry said. That was a sad evening for

Bernardin, as some of the unjustified attacks zeroed in on him personally. In February 1982 Bernardin's essay on "The Heresy of Racism," published in the *Catholic Telegraph,* cogently argued that racism was "in fundamental contradiction to some of the most basic doctrines of Christianity."[67]

In the mid-1980s the archdiocese formed a committee to supplement its long-range planning project, "For the Harvest," to help identify the specific concerns of the eight thousand or so black Catholics in the archdiocese. After months of planning and hearings, black Catholics in the fall of 1987 adopted a pastoral plan, called "Heritage, Unity and Responsibility." Its goals were to increase black leadership at the parish level, support the role of the black ministry, develop liturgy relevant to black culture, and increase evangelization efforts in the black community. Local black Catholics also helped establish an office of African American Catholic Ministries that replaced the Black Secretariat. In 1988 Pilarczyk appointed Eugene Cash as its first director.[68]

The following year a conflict erupted over the African American Catholic Ministries. Eugene Cash, head of the organization, died suddenly and Joyce Smith, who had replaced him in late spring, resigned in August because of conflicts with her supervisor in the office of Community Services. A group of black lay people, religious, and fifteen parish pastors from integrated and predominantly black parishes urged Pilarczyk to reinstate the former director. They also recommended that he implement the pastoral plan and place the African American Catholic Ministries under the Pastoral Services Department, the same office that oversaw Hispanic ministry, interfaith relations, and evangelization, among other ministries. In late August about thirty people picketed at the archdiocesan headquarters, demanding the reinstatement of Joyce Smith. The picketing continued for several weeks. On September 13 there were also prayer vigils in Cincinnati and Dayton. For some time Pilarczyk, his staff, and members of the Archdiocesan Pastoral Council had been of the opinion that the appointment of officers and departments' needs needed to be reviewed. In December George C. Findley, a parishioner at Dayton's Assumption parish and member of the archdiocesan Black Catholic Advisory Board, was named director of the Office of African American Catholic Ministries. The office was also moved to the Pastoral Services Department.[69]

In the spring of 1990 the APC and Pilarczyk established a task force to explore further means to counter racism in the archdiocese. They were hopeful that the task force would help broaden the focus of the archdiocesan pastoral plan of "Heritage, Unity and Responsibility." "Racism is a sin and we know that," Pilarczyk said. Father George Jacquemin, pastor of St. Anthony, an integrated parish in the Madisonville area in eastern Cincinnati and chairman of the Priests Council's peace and justice committee, informed the APC that there was considerable racism in the archdiocese. "We feel it's important," he said, "to look at the issue straight in the eye." Three years later the archdiocese launched a new antiracism program. "In One Body, the Archdiocesan Program to Dismantle Racism," with Ruth Richmond as project director, was developed to help local Catholics grow in awareness and understanding of themselves and of other cultures and ethnic groups. By promoting dialogue among the races archdiocesan officials hoped to challenge and help change attitudes that perpetuated racism. "It is important for us to start this venture at this time," Father William Cross, pastor of St. Andrew Church in Avondale and the first black diocesan pastor in the history of the archdiocese, said, in order "to make the church authentically Catholic. We have to be constantly working." The first phase of the "In One Body" Program involved central office directors, parish leaders, school administrators, and priests. Phase Two took the project to the parish level. By the end of 1994 ninety-six parishes had participated in the two-year program.[70]

In April 1994 Bishop Carl K. Moeddel of Cincinnati was named chairperson of a task force to deal with the problems of racism in the city. The previous June, Moeddel, a native of Cincinnati and pastor of St. James of the Valley Church at Wyoming, had been named auxiliary bishop for Cincinnati. He succeeded James Garland who, in 1992, had been appointed bishop of Marquette, Michigan. Moeddel became the ninth ordinary to serve the Cincinnati archdiocese as an auxiliary. In 1995 the local church, through the Office of African American Catholic Ministries, established the program, African American Ministry Empowered and Nurtured (AMEN). The pilot project involved a curriculum to integrate the contributions and needs of the African American experience within the context of the larger church. To help foster spiritual growth, the program included courses in discipleship, Old Testament, pastoral communications, church, liturgy, and prayer. In June local church leaders representing various faiths, including Moeddel, sponsored the Racial Harmony Conference at the Alfred E. Sabin Convention Center.[71]

CONCLUSION

The history of the archdiocese of Cincinnati is a success story. It successfully built and maintained parishes and churches, established a network of schools from kindergarten through college, and founded a system of charitable agencies and institutions. Its history over 175 years, including the relationship of Catholics to society, has been one of constant change and adaptation. Moreover, the role of the laity within the church and the community changed from time to time as did the amount of authority and influence wielded by the religious, parish pastors, and church ordinaries.

In its first sixty years the diocese, led by its ordinaries, Fenwick and Purcell, grew at an astonishing rate, becoming a significant force in the community's religious life. It developed from a scattered missionary diocese into an influential archdiocese. As it evangelized the non-Catholics and Native Americans and converted people to Catholicism, it integrated the massive influx of Catholic immigrants. As it dealt with a dominant Protestant culture, it also developed a unique Catholic identity. Though sensitive to American culture and always supportive of the republican ideas of freedom, equality, separation of church and state, and religious liberty, the archdiocese of Cincinnati remained true to its Catholic origins. Catholic schools and other organizations, though mindful of their relationship with society, separated themselves from the public schools and non-Catholic institutions. Committed to transmitting the faith to succeeding generations, Catholics chose to develop their own specific structures and policies. Furthermore, at the same time that there was a gradual strengthening of the papacy in the second half of the nineteenth century, episcopal and clerical authority also grew. Though in its early years, especially because of the shortage of clergy, the diocese was dependent upon lay leadership, gradually the role of the laity in the management and administration of church affairs waned. As it sought more uniformity the ordinary's authority in religion, finances, and education increased and the priests became more involved in the operation of the parishes.

During its bureaucratizing phase at the end of the nineteenth and first quarter of the twentieth centuries, the archdiocese of Cincinnati, under the leadership of Archbishops Elder and Moeller, became more centralized. Developing more formal channels of episcopal administration, it systematized its inner workings. As the church leaders tightened their authority and more and more power shifted from the parish to the chancery, parishes and charities were brought more directly under the archbishop's supervision. By the end of Moeller's term in 1925, Catholics in the archdiocese accepted the hierarchical concept of the church. There was also increasing influence by officials in Rome. In the wake of the first Vatican Council's declaration on the authority of the church, Elder and Moeller sought to balance diocesan rule and authority from Rome. Skeptical and resentful of too much papal interference, they felt that the future of the American church rested upon being granted more autonomy. Advocating more home rule, the Cincinnati ordinaries argued that American Catholics should embrace the principles of the new culture and bring the Catholic faith to its fullest realization in the archdiocese. In the process they promoted more mainlining of Catholics, especially immigrants, into American society. Moreover, as the archdiocese became more theologically conservative and implemented church teachings in the archdiocese, it became increasingly more responsive to American labor and social problems.

From the mid-1920s to the 1960s Cincinnati Catholics became even more assertive on social issues and confident of their own Americanism. Since the administration of Purcell the archdiocese had sustained a separate Catholic subculture. But that subculture gradually broke down, as more and more Catholics moved into the middle class and beyond and became more a part of American culture. As it defined and solidified its place in society, the archdiocese, under the supervision of Archbishops McNicholas and Alter, saw a significant increase in the number of churches, schools, hospitals, and charitable agencies. Both ordinaries were builders. In addition, the archdiocese remained theologically conservative and took public positions on a variety of ethical, social, political, and economic issues. Through their church leaders, who continually valued religion, education, family, and human rights, Cincinnati Catholics developed a specific and distinctive Catholic culture.

During the administrations of Leibold, Bernardin, and Pilarczyk, the archdiocese of Cincinnati responded to the social and political unrest of the 1960s and the Second Vatican Council. Since the 1880s the archdiocese, wedded to a traditional theology, had appeared uniform and disciplined. What had helped hold it together was its hierarchical structure and centralized teaching authority. But the social and cultural changes of the sixties and the liberalization of the church in the post–Vatican II era brought about a new model of church and authority and new forms of worship and parish activity. The authoritarian and clerical concept of church and authority was replaced with one that emphasized greater community and shared responsibility. In the process, lay people, clergy, and religious became more identified with various social issues. Because of these changes the archdiocese was very different from what it was prior to 1960. The priesthood no longer symbolized the high status conferred by the old subculture, and most lay people no longer took the priest's word as law. Catholics now witnessed the crowding of lay Eucharistic ministers around the altar before communion, and lay people alongside some clergy now typically placed the host in the communicant's hands.

As the archdiocese was about to enter the new millennium, many Catholics wondered how they would meet the spiritual needs of more educated Catholics with fewer priests and churches. Challenges facing it, as it continued to adapt to changing times, consisted of carrying on the tradition of the church, dealing with the smaller number of priests and religious, and fostering the development of ministry and leadership among the laity. The spirit and faith in parish life and the competence and creativity of lay people and ministers were a source of encouragement to the archdiocese. There was now a stabilized Mass attendance, greater participation in prayer meetings, and increasing shared clerical, religious, and lay involvement in church life at parish and diocesan levels. To many clergy, religious, and laity the future of the archdiocese appeared challenging.

APPENDIX

List of Parishes According to Year of Founding

(Source: *Clerus Cincinnatensis, A History of Clergy and Parishes of the Archdiocese of Cincinnati 1821 to 1996* [Cincinnati: Archdiocese of Cincinnati, 1996], 27–35, 87–89, 105–11.)

CINCINNATI AND HAMILTON COUNTY

1818	Christ Church (or St. Patrick), Liberty and Vine Streets. Renamed St. Peter in Chains in 1822.
1834	Holy Trinity, West End. Closed in 1958.
1840	St. Mary, Over-the-Rhine. St. James, White Oak.
1842	Our Lady of Victory, Delhi. Originally called St. Stephen. The name was changed in 1853.
1844	St. John the Baptist, Green Street. Closed in 1969. St. Peter, Lick Run (now Queen City Avenue). Called St. Bonaventure in 1868 or 1869.
1845	All Saints, Fulton. Originally called Christ Church. Closed in 1936. St. Francis Xavier, Sycamore Street.
1846	St. Philomena, Third Street. Closed in 1954. St. Joseph, Linn Street, West End.
1847	St. Michael, Lower Price Hill.
1848	St. Paul, Over-the-Rhine. Closed in 1974.
1849	St. Francis de Sales, Walnut Hills.
1850	St. Patrick, Third and Mill Streets. Closed in 1918. St. Clement, St. Bernard. Sts. Peter and Paul, Reading. Originally called Church of the 14 Holy Martyrs. After the church was destroyed in 1860, the new building was named Sts. Peter and Paul.
1851	St. John the Baptist, Harrison.
1852	St. Willibord, Liberty and Walnut Streets. Closed in 1860. St. Augustine, West End. Closed in 1978.

1853 St. Patrick, Northside. Originally called St. Aloysius.
    United with St. Boniface in 1942.
  St. Thomas, Sycamore Street. Closed in 1918.
  St. Jerome, California.

1854 Assumption, Mt. Healthy.

1857 St. Gabriel, Glendale.

1858 St. Anthony, Madisonville. Originally called St. Michael.
  St. Francis Seraph, Over-the-Rhine.

1859 Immaculata, Mt. Adams. United with Holy Cross in 1970.
  Holy Angels, O'Bryonville. Closed in 1996.

1860 St. Anthony, Budd Street. Closed in 1962.
  St. John the Baptist, Dry Ridge.
  St. Joseph, North Bend.

1861 St. Vincent de Paul, River Road.

1862 St. Boniface, Northside.

1864 St. Edward, West End. United with St. Ann in 1938. Closed in 1965.

1866 St. Aloysius Gonzaga, Bridgetown.
  St. Ann, West End. United with St. Edward in 1938. Closed in 1965.

1867 St. Bernard, Taylors Creek.
  St. Rose of Lima, East End.
  St. Stephen, Columbia-Tusculum.

1868 St. Aloysius, Delhi (now called St. Aloysius On-the-Ohio).
  St. George, Corryville. United with the University of Cincinnati Newman Center
    in 1980. In 1985, merged into St. Monica.
  St. Lawrence, Price Hill.

1869 St. Charles Borromeo, Carthage.
  St. Bonaventure, South Fairmount. Originally called St. Peter.

1870 Sacred Heart of Jesus, Camp Washington. United with Sacred Heart (Italian).
    St. Louis, Downtown.
  Atonement, West Third Street. Began as a chapel for the Sisters of Mercy. About
    1872 it became a parish church.

1872 Assumption, Walnut Hills. Originally called Presentation of the Blessed Virgin
    Mary.

1873 Holy Cross, Mt. Adams. United with Immaculata in 1970.
  St. Henry, West End. Closed in 1978.
  St. Stanislaus, Liberty and Cutter Streets. Closed in 1935.

1874 St. Andrew, Avondale.
  Blessed Sacrament, Price Hill. Closed in 1974.
  Our Lady of the Sacred Heart, Reading.

1878 Our Lady of Perpetual Help, Sedamsville. United with Holy Family and
  Our Lady of Grace in 1989.

1883 Holy Family, Price Hill. United with Our Lady of Grace and Our Lady of
    Perpetual Help in 1989.

1884 St. Elizabeth, Norwood. United with St. Matthew and Sts. Peter and Paul to form
    Holy Trinity in 1994.

1886 St. Leo, North Fairmount.

1887	St. Aloysius, Elmwood.
	St. James, Wyoming. Now called St. James in the Valley.
1890	Sacred Heart, Broadway. Closed in 1970.
1891	St. John the Evangelist, Deer Park.
1892	St. Agnes, Bond Hill.
	Guardian Angels, Mt. Washington.
1898	St. Mary, Hyde Park.
1903	St. Catharine, Westwood.
	Our Lady of Loretto, Linwood. United with St. Margaret of Cortona in 1995.
1904	Holy Name, Mt. Auburn.
1905	St. Mark, Evanston.
1906	St. Matthew, Norwood. United with St. Elizabeth and Sts. Peter and Paul to form Holy Trinity in 1994.
	Sts. Peter and Paul, Norwood. In 1994, united with St. Elizabeth and St. Matthew to form Holy Trinity.
1908	St. Cecilia, Oakley.
1909	St. Clare, College Hill.
	St. William, Price Hill.
1910	Annunciation, Clifton.
	St. Monica, Clifton Heights. (Cathedral, 1938–1957). United with St. George Parish Newman Center with the new name St. Monica–St. George Parish Newman Center of the University of Cincinnati in 1995.
	St. Pius, Cumminsville.
	St. Anthony of Padua for the Maronite congregation. First used Sacred Heart Italian Church, St. Thomas on Sycamore, then the Church of the Atonement. Although located in the archdiocese, the parish belongs to the Maronite Diocese of Los Angeles.
1911	St. Martin of Tours, Cheviot.
1914	St. Joseph of Nazareth for the Hungarian congregation. First used St. Stanislaus on Baum Street and finally St. Joseph of Nazareth. Closed in 1963.
1916	St. Teresa of Avila, Price Hill.
1917	Nativity, Pleasant Ridge.
1918	Holy Spirit Chapel, Downtown. Closed in 1982.
1919	St. Bernard, Winton Place.
	St. Michael, Sharonville.
	Resurrection, Price Hill.
1920	St. Margaret Mary, North College Hill.
1921	St. Margaret of Cortona, Madisonville.
1922	San Antonio Di Padova for the Italian. United with St. Bonaventure in 1989.
1923	St. Gertrude, Madeira.
1924	Our Lady of Mt. Carmel for the Italian congregation. Closed in 1975.
1926	Our Lord Christ the King, Mt. Lookout.
	St. Thérese, the Little Flower, Mt. Airy.
1927	St. Robert Bellarmine, Xavier University.
	St. Thomas Aquinas, North Avondale. United with St. Clement in 1988.

Our Lady of Lourdes, Westwood.

1929   Our Lady of Grace, Price Hill. United with Holy Family and Our Lady of Perpetual Help in 1989.

1933   St. Dominic, Delhi.

1935   St. Martin de Porres, Lincoln Heights. Originally called St. Christina.

1938   Mother of God, Walnut Hills. Closed in 1961.
       Our Lady of the Rosary, Greenhills.

1941   Our Mother of Sorrows, Roselawn.

1943   Our Lady of Presentation of the Blessed Virgin Mary, English Woods. Closed in 1985.
       St. Vivian, Finneytown.

1944   St. Antoninus, Western Hills.
       Immaculate Heart of Mary, Forestville.

1945   St. Richard of Chichester, College Hill.
       St. Vincent Ferrer, Kenwood.

1946   St. Ignatius, Montfort Heights.
       Mother of Christ Pastoral Center, Winton Terrace.

1947   St. John Fisher, Newtown.
       Our Lady of the Visitation, Mack.
       St. Saviour, Rossmoyne.

1949   All Saints, Montgomery.
       St. John Vianney, Madison Place.

1954   St. Ann, Groesbeck.

1956   St. Jude, Bridgetown.

1958   Corpus Christi, New Burlington.

1961   St. Bartholomew, Finneytown.

1966   St. Simon, Delhi Township.

1967   St. Matthias, Forest Park.
       Bea Community, nonterritorial experimental parish. Closed in 1972.

1971   Community of Hope, nonterritorial experimental parish. Closed in 1989.

1973   Good Shepherd, Montgomery.

1978   St. John Neumann, Colerain Township.

1993   St. Monica–St. George Newman Center. Formed by the merger of St. Monica and St. George parishes.

1994   Holy Trinity, Norwood. Formed by the merger of St. Elizabeth, St. Matthew, and Sts. Peter and Paul parishes.

DAYTON AND MONTGOMERY COUNTY

1837   Emmanuel.

1847   St. Joseph.

1852   Our Lady of Good Hope, Miamisburg. Originally called St. Michael. New name given in 1881.

1859   Holy Trinity.
       St. Mary.

1883	Sacred Heart. Closed in 1996.
1887	Our Lady of the Rosary.
1893	St. John the Baptist. Closed in 1963.
1901	Holy Angels.
1903	St. Adalbert for the Polish congregation.
1905	Holy Family.
1906	Holy Name for the Hungarian congregation. United with St. Stephen in 1974. St. Stephen for the Hungarian congregation.
1911	Corpus Christi.
1913	St. Anthony.
1914	Holy Cross for the Lithuanian congregation.
1915	St. Agnes.
1916	St. Gabriel for the Romanian congregation. Closed in 1918.
1919	St. James.
1920	Resurrection of Our Lord.
1922	St. Rita, Shiloh.
1928	Our Lady of Mercy.
1938	Our Lady of the Immaculate Conception.
1939	St. Albert the Great, Kettering.
1941	St. Augustine, Germantown.
1948	Precious Blood. Queen of Martyrs.
1949	Assumption.
1950	Incarnation, Centerville.
1953	St. Helen.
1955	Ascension, Kettering.
1957	St. Christopher, Vandalia.
1960	St. Peter, Huber Heights. St. Henry.
1962	St. Charles Borromeo, Kettering.
1969	St. Francis of Assisi
1970	Community of Christian Service, nonterritorial experimental parish. Closed in 1977.
1972	St. Paul, Englewood.
1973	Queen of Apostles, nonterritorial parish.
1975	St. Barbara. Although located in the archdiocese, the parish belongs to the Byzantine Eparchy of Parma.

OTHER CITIES AND TOWNS

1830	St. Martin, St. Martin.
1832	St. Stephen, Hamilton. Closed in 1989.
1834	St. Augustine, Minster.
1836	Sts. Peter and Paul, Petersburg. Closed in 1849 or 1860.

St. John, Maria Stein.

1837   St. Mary, Arnheim. Originally called St. Wendelin.
St. Patrick, Fayetteville.

1838   St. Michael, Fort Loramie.

1839   St. Henry, St. Henry.
St. Joseph, St. Joseph.
St. Joseph, Wapakoneta.
St. Philomena, Stonelick.
St. Denis, Versailles. Originally St. Valbert, three miles northeast of Versailles. Site and name changed in 1864.

1840   St. Michael, Ripley. Originally called St. John the Baptist.

1843   St. Mary, Piqua.

1844   St. Rose, St. Rose.

1846   Holy Family, Frenchtown.
St. Remy, Russia.

1847   Nativity of the Blessed Virgin Mary, Cassella.

1848   Holy Angels, Sidney.
St. Mary, Hamilton. Closed in 1989.

1849   St. Brigid, Xenia.
St. Raphael, Springfield.

1850   St. John, Fryburg.
St. Peter, New Richmond.

1851   St. Patrick, Bellefontaine.

1852   Holy Trinity, Middletown.
St. Anthony, St. Anthony.
St. Joseph, Egypt.
St. Mary, Hillsboro.
St. Mary, Urbana.
Holy Rosary, St. Marys.
St. Sebastian, St. Sebastian.

1853   St. Mary, Oxford.
St. Mary, Philothea.
St. Mary, Greenville.
Visitation, Eaton.

1854   St. Malachy, Morrow. Closed in 1964.
St. Andrew, Milford.

1855   St. Boniface, Piqua.

1856   St. Benignus, Greenfield.
St. Louis, Owensville.
St. Lawrence, Rhine.
St. Peter, St. Peter.
Sts. Peter and Paul, Newport.
St. Paul, Yellow Springs. Originally called Assumption.
St. Wendelin, St. Wendelin.

1857   St. Patrick, Glynwood. Originally called St. Thomas.
St. Patrick, Troy.

1858	St. Francis, Cranberry Prairie.
	Holy Ghost, Vera Cruz. Closed in 1990.
	St. John, Tipp City.
1859	St. Columban, Loveland.
1860	St. Bernard, Springfield.
1862	St. Patrick, St. Patrick.
	Mary Help of Christians, Fairborn (originally Osborne).
1864	Immaculate Conception, Celina.
1865	St. Aloysius, Carthagena.
	Immaculate Conception, Botkins.
	Holy Name, Blanchester.
	St. Michael, Mechanicsburg.
1866	St. Charles, South Charleston.
	St. Columbkille, Wilmington.
1867	Holy Trinity, Coldwater.
	St. Joseph, Hamilton.
	St. Mary, Franklin.
1868	St. Aloysius, Shandon.
	St. John the Baptist, West Liberty. Closed in 1870 or 1873.
	St. Paul, Sharpsburg.
	Sacred Heart, St. Paris.
1869	Immaculate Conception, North Lewisburg.
1870	St. Augustine, Jamestown.
	St. John, New Paris.
1871	Holy Name, Trenton.
1872	St. John, Middletown. Originally called St. Boniface.
1874	St. Bernard, Burkettsville.
	St. Michael, New Vienna.
1875	Immaculate Conception, Bradford.
1876	St. Augustine, Waynesville.
1878	St. Mary, Manchester.
1880	St. John, West Chester.
	Mary Help of Christians, Fort Recovery.
1882	St. Joseph, Springfield.
	Sacred Heart, McCartyville.
1883	St. Francis de Sales, Lebanon.
	St. John the Evangelist, Foster. Closed in 1964.
1887	Our Lady of Sorrows, Monroe. Originally called Seven Dolors. Name changed in 1984.
1892	St. Louis, North Star.
1893	St. Peter in Chains, Hamilton.
1894	St. Veronica, Hamilton. Closed in 1989.
1902	St. George, Georgetown. Originally called St. Mary.
1903	Our Lady of Guadalupe, Montezuma.
	Precious Blood, Chickasaw.

1906	Holy Trinity, Batavia. St. Nicholas, Osgood.
1909	St. Ann, Hamilton.
1921	St. Mary, Springfield.
1925	St. Mary of the Woods, Russells Point.
1931	St. Teresa, Little Flower of Jesus, Springfield.
1936	St. Teresa of the Infant Jesus, Rockford.
1938	St. Susanna, Mason.
1939	St. Lawrence, New Miami. Closed in 1987.
1940	St. Thomas More, Withamsville.
1941	St. Mary, Bethel. Queen of Angels, Hamilton. Closed in 1956. Queen of Peace, Millville.
1942	St. Mary, Camden.
1943	St. Martin, Springfield. Closed in 1952.
1944	St. Bernadette, Amelia. St. Michael, Mt. Orab.
1945	Mother of Good Counsel, Felicity.
1946	St. Mary, Middletown. Closed in 1991.
1947	St. Mary, Williamsburg.
1948	Holy Redeemer, New Bremen. St. Peter Claver, Middletown. Closed in 1969.
1949	St. Veronica, Mt. Carmel.
1950	St. Teresa of the Infant Jesus, Covington. Sacred Heart, New Carlisle. Transfiguration, West Milton. Holy Trinity, West Union.
1955	St. Luke, Beavercreek.
1956	St. Bernard, Winchester. Closed in 1960s. St. Elizabeth, Sardinia. St. Joseph Pastoral Center, Blue Creek. Closed in 1992. St. Mary Queen of Heaven, Peebles.
1957	Sacred Heart of Jesus, Fairfield.
1965	St. Philip, Morrow (Zoar).
1976	St. Elizabeth Seton, Mt. Repose.
1984	St. Margaret of York, Twenty Mile Stand.
1989	St. Julie Billiart, Hamilton. St. Maximilian Kolbe, West Chester (sometimes referred to as Princeton).
1991	Holy Family, Middletown.

NOTES

ABBREVIATIONS

AAB	Archives of the Archdiocese of Baltimore
AABo	Archives of the Archdiocese of Boston
AAC	Archives of the Archdiocese of Cincinnati
APF	Archives of the Propaganda Fide, Scritture riferite America Centrale
AUND	Archives of the University of Notre Dame

INTRODUCTION

1. *Catholic Telegraph,* July 5, 1957.

PART 1

Introduction

1. Leslie Woodcock Tentler, *Seasons of Grace: A History of the Catholic Archdiocese of Detroit* (Detroit, Mich., 1990), 17.
2. *Catholic Directory,* 1883 (New York, 1883).
3. Ibid.
4. William L. Portier, "Church Unity and National Traditions: The Challenge to the Modern Papacy, 1682–1870," in *The Papacy and the Church in the United States,* ed. Bernard Cooke (New York, 1989), 37–38.

Chapter 1

1. Robert Frederick Trisco, *The Holy See and the Nascent Church in the Middle Western United States, 1826–1850* (Rome, 1962), 20–21. Before the American Revolution the Catholic Midwest fell under the vast ecclesiastical jurisdiction of the diocese of Quebec. Following the war in 1783, it became part of the Prefecture Apostolic of the United States. Six years later the territory was under the jurisdiction of Baltimore, the premier see.
2. Ibid., 1–2, 25.
3. Flaget to Cardinal Litta, Prefect of Propaganda, October 18, 1819, APF, fols. 538 r to 545 v (Kenneally, I, 372); Trisco, *The Holy See and the Nascent Church in the Middle Western United States, 1826–1850,* 26–28. Bishops Flaget and Dubourg also proposed that a separate diocese be established in Detroit for the territory of Michigan.
4. Martin J. Spalding, *Sketches of the Life, Times and Character of the Rt. Rev. Benedict Joseph Flaget, First Bishop of Louisville* (Louisville, 1852), 216; Flaget to Maréchal, March 16, 1820, AUND, CCOP 7.

5. Flaget to Cardinal-Prefect of Propaganda, November 5, 1820, APF, fols. 617 rv and 618 rv (Kenneally, I, 386); Maréchal to Cardinal-Prefect of Propaganda, April 4, 1820, APF, fols. 613 rv and 638 r (Kenneally, 1, 394); Flaget, David, and Dubourg to Propaganda Fide, May 23, 1820, APF, vol. 927, fols. 434 rv and 435 rv (Kenneally, 5, 1703); Victor Francis O'Daniel, *The Right Rev. Edward Dominic Fenwick, O.P., Founder of the Dominicans in the United States, Pioneer Missionary in Kentucky, Apostle of Ohio, First Bishop of Cincinnati* (Washington, D.C., [c1920]), 241–242; W. A. Jurgens in *A History of the Diocese of Cleveland* (Youngstown, Ohio, 1980), 1: 71, writes that misspellings of Fenwick's name in letters addressed to him suggest that some of his contemporaries probably pronounced his name *Finnik*.

6. Quoted in Reginald M. Coffey, O.P., *The American Dominicans: A History of Saint Joseph's Province* (New York, 1970), 10–11; copy of Fenwick's appeal, August 21, 1804, APF, vol. 912, fol. 120 rv (Kenneally, 5, 1507); Propaganda Fide to Bishop Carroll, December 22, 1804, APF, vol. 87, fols. 558 rv and 559 r (Kenneally, 3, 1357); L. Concanen to Propaganda Fide, February 9, 1805, vol. 18, fol. 291 rv (Kenneally, 3, 1141) General Congregation, March 11, 1805, APF, vol. 172, fols. 2 rv and 31 rv (Kenneally, 5, 1465); *Catholic Telegraph*, July 9, 1931. Edward Fenwick was a descendant of Cuthbert Fenwick, who was among the first Catholics who colonized Maryland in the seventeenth century.

7. Loretta Petit, O.P., *Friar in the Wilderness: Edward Dominic Fenwick, O.P.* (Chicago, 1994), 13–14; O'Daniel, *The Right Rev. Edward Dominic Fenwick*, 194–96.

8. Joseph M. White, "Religion and Community: Cincinnati Germans 1814–1870" (Ph.D. diss., University of Notre Dame, 1980), 261–262. Throughout the text I use the same terminology adopted by W. A. Jurgens in *A History of the Diocese of Cleveland*, 91, 102. A parish was a place with a church building and a resident pastor. A mission had a church building and no resident pastor but was attended regularly by a visiting priest. A station had neither church building nor resident pastor but was regularly attended by a priest who went there to offer Mass in a private home or in some other building.

9. Jay P. Dolan, *The American Catholic Experience: A History from Colonial Times to the Present* (New York, 1985), 109–10, 114; Patrick W. Carey, *The Roman Catholics* (Westport, Conn., 1993), 29–30. Lay trusteeship was consistent with the ancient Catholic practice of lay patronage in order to purchase property, build churches, and organize religious communities.

10. Dolan, *The American Catholic Experience*, 113, 116, 120; James L. Heft, S.M., "From the Pope to the Bishops: Episcopal Authority from Vatican I to Vatican II," in *The Papacy and the Church in the United States*, ed. Bernard Cooke (New York, 1989), 66.

11. Fenwick to a Catholic Gentleman of London, November 8, 1818, translated from Diario di Roma, January 23, 1819, in *Catholic Historical Review* 4, 24–25; the census figure for 1820 given by Henry Howe in his *Historical Collections of Ohio*, vol. 1, 1896, 54, is 581,295; Jurgens, *A History of the Diocese of Cleveland*, 86; O'Daniel, *The Right Rev. Edward Dominic Fenwick*, 194–96.

12. *Western Spy*, September 5, 1817. A similar notice appeared in the *Ohio Watchman* of Dayton; Benedict Ashley, *The Dominicans* (Collegeville, Minn., 1990), 207; Richard C. Wade, *The Urban Frontier: The Rise of Western Cities, 1790–1830* (Cambridge, 1959), 243; Kenneth T. Jackson, *Crabgrass Frontier: The Suburbanization of the United States* (New York, 1985), 25–30; *Catholic Telegraph*, November 13, 1858; February 26, March 26, 1891; October 28, 1926. Excerpts of Flaget's journal printed in the February 26, 1891, issue of *Catholic Telegraph*.

13. The confusion over the name Christ Church stems from the fact that the congregation at Cincinnati was incorporated under the name Christ Church Congregation. It is clear in Fenwick's letter to John Hill, June 1, 1820, that the church at Cincinnati was under the patronage of St. Patrick, Fenwick to Hill, *America Centrale*, section 4, fol. 643 rv (Kenneally, 1, 1, 396); Michael O'Meara to Archbishop John T. McNicholas, November 4, 1928,

AAC; among the pioneer Catholics who joined Michael Scott were Patrick Reilly, Edward Lynch, Patrick Gohegan, John McMahon, John White, and Patrick Walsh. An old story would have it that the church was built at Northern Liberties, outside the corporate limits of Cincinnati because the civil authorities had been opposed to the establishment of a Catholic Church among them. John H. Lamott in his *History of the Archdiocese of Cincinnati, 1821–1921* (Cincinnati, 1921) found no evidence to corroborate the story. In 1818 Fenwick and Young had opened a log church, St. Joseph's at Somerset, the first Catholic church in the state. Jacob Dittoe gave the Dominicans 320 acres of land on the condition that Fenwick would build on it an institution similar to the one at St. Rose. St. Joseph Church was dedicated on December 6, 1818. The original parish consisted of ten German families. When their numbers increased, a brick church was erected. As more German Catholics moved into the area, a second log church, Saint Mary of the Assumption Church at Lancaster, was built shortly thereafter. *The Centenary of Saint Joseph's Parish, Somerset, Ohio* (Somerset, Ohio, 1918), 14–15; Anon., "The Catholic Church in Ohio," *The United States Catholic Magazine and Monthly Review* 6 (1847): 24; an alleged Indian chapel may have existed at Sandusky in 1751, Jurgens, *A History of the Diocese of Cleveland,* 40–41, 83.

14. Quoted in Petit, *Friar in the Wilderness,* 16–17; Fenwick to Hill, June 1, 1820, APF, fol. 643 rv (Kenneally, 1, 396); Flaget to Propaganda Fide, January 4, 1822, APF, fols. 728 r to 731 r (Kenneally, 1, 765). Other evidences of his unwillingness to accept the office are to be found in letter of J. A. Hill to Olivieri, January 27, 1822, APF, vol. 929, fols. 446 r to 449 v (Kenneally, 5, 1747); Fenwick to Propaganda Fide, April 16, 1823, APF, fols. 100 rv and 101 rv (Kenneally, 1, 839); Fenwick to Cardinal-Prefect of Propaganda, September 10, 1823, APF, fols. 113 rv and 114 r (Kenneally, 1, 844).

15. *Liberty Hall and Cincinnati Gazette,* March 30, 1822; *U.S. Catholic Miscellany* 6: 246; Fenwick to Stephen Badin, August 6, 1823, cited in *The United States Catholic Magazine and Monthly Review* 6 (1847): 29; *Catholic Telegraph,* March 26, 1891; Petit, *Friar in the Wilderness,* 17–18.

16. Fenwick to Propaganda, 1823, APF, fols. 93 rv and 96 r (Kenneally, 1, 837); Fenwick to P. M. Viviani, October 11, 1823, APF, fols. 125 v to 130 v (Kenneally, 1, 847); Hill to Olivieri, January 27, 1822, APF, vol. 929, fols. 446 r to 449 v (Kenneally, 5, 1747).

17. Fenwick to Secretary of Association of Propagation of Faith, Lyons, ut supra Note 40; Rese to M. Roimondo, Rector of Propaganda College, May 5, 1825, APF, (Kenneally, 1, 910); Cincinnati on the Ohio to ___, December 5, 1822, *London Catholic Miscellany* 2 (March 1823): 141; letter, Michael Mulvihill, pastor of St. Peter Cathedral (n.d.), AAC; O'Daniel, *The Right Rev. Edward Dominic Fenwick,* 247–48; *Catholic Telegraph,* March 26, 1891.

18. *Catholic Telegraph,* March 26, 1891; Alfred G. Stritch, "Trusteeism in the Old Northwest," *The Catholic Historical Review* 30 (July 1944): 162; Thomas W. Spalding, *The Premier See: A History of the Archdiocese of Baltimore, 1789–1989* (Baltimore, Md., 1989), 10.

19. Quoted in Petit, *Friar in the Wilderness,* 14, 25–26; Fenwick to John Hill, June 1, 1820, APF IV, 610r–11r; Fenwick to Propaganda Fide, February 22, 1823, APF, vol. 938, fols. 307 rv and 308 v (Kenneally, 5, 1891); Fenwick to Marechal, February 9, 1823, AAB; Fenwick to Prefect of Propaganda, April 16, 1823, AUND; Anthony Deye, "Archbishop John Baptist Purcell, Pre–Civil War Years" (Ph.D. diss., University of Notre Dame, 1959), 81; O'Daniel, *The Right Rev. Edward Dominic Fenwick,* 247–48, 250–53, 273, 278. In 1793 Francis Badin's older brother, Stephen, had become the first priest ordained in the United States.

20. Fenwick to Maréchal, June 3, 1823, AAB; Fenwick to Badin, August 8, 1823, as printed in *Catholic Telegraph,* August 15, 1891; Dubourg to Cardinal Consalvi, New Orleans, April 26, 1823, AUND; Fenwick to Propaganda Fide, February 22, 1823, APF, vol. 938, fols. 307 rv and 308 v (Kenneally, 5, 1891); Petit, *Friar in the Wilderness,* 19.

21. Fenwick to Propaganda Fide, September 10, 1823, APF, fols. 113 rv and 114 r (Kenneally, 1, 844); Fenwick to Cardinal-Prefect of Propaganda, January 21, 1824, APF, vol. 938, fols. 303 rv and 309 r (Kenneally, 1, 1889); Fenwick to Propaganda Fide, May 12, 1824, APF, fols. 285 rv and 286 r (Kenneally, 1, 869); Badin to Fenwick, December 9, 1823; Badin to Fenwick, June 18, 1825, AUND; *Catholic Miscellany* 4 (1824): 201; O'Daniel, *The Right Rev. Edward Dominic Fenwick,* 256–57; Petit, *Friar in the Wilderness,* 15–16, 19. While in Paris, Fenwick first met and became acquainted with a student at Saint Sulpice named John Baptist Purcell, who would in 1833 succeed him as bishop of Cincinnati.

22. Propaganda Fide to Fenwick, June 26, 1824, APF, vol. 305, fols. 409V and 410 rv (Kenneally, 3, 1800); A. Perier to Cardinal Caprano, August 12, 28, 1824, APF, fol. 326 rv, fol. 328 rv (Kenneally, 1, 879 and 880); Poynter to Fenwick, December 14, 1824; Badin to Fenwick, August 12, 1825, AUND; Trisco, *The Holy See and the Nascent Church in the Middle Western United States, 1826–1850,* 251.

23. Fenwick to Badin, August 8, 1823, printed in *Catholic Telegraph,* August 15, 1891; Petit, *Friar in the Wilderness,* 26.

24. Fenwick to Caprano, Propaganda Fide, undated, but probably 1823, APF, fols. 69 r to 71 r (Kenneally, 1, 1019); Fenwick to Propaganda Fide, undated, but probably 1823 or 1824, fols. 112 rv and 113 r (Kenneally, 1, 1031); Badin to Fenwick, April 7, 1825; Cardinal Somaglia to Fenwick, January 24, 1824; Rese to Fenwick, June 30, 1827, AUND; Petit, *Friar in the Wilderness,* 20, 23, 26; O'Daniel, *The Right Rev. Edward Dominic Fenwick,* 258–63, 266–68. A Spanish Dominican, Raphael Munos, also joined Fenwick's staff in 1824.

25. Propaganda Fide to Maréchal, July 1, 1826, APF, vol. 307, fols. 412 v to 414 v (Kenneally, 3, 1936); Trisco, *The Holy See and the Nascent Church in the Middle Western United States, 1826–1850,* 26, 29, 33; While in Rome Fenwick's meeting with the Dominican authorities went well. Persuaded by his plea, they sent a letter to Samuel Wilson, the Dominican Provincial in Kentucky, urging him to send more priests to Cincinnati. To help prevent future difficulties between the dioceses of Bardstown and Cincinnati, Fenwick's request for a separate Dominican province near Somerset, Ohio, was also approved. The Dominican Master General agreed to divide the Dominicans in Kentucky and Ohio into two separate provinces. But as the pope stipulated that the division had to be confirmed by the majority of the Dominicans in Kentucky, the division never materialized. Rome annulled the proposed division three years later.

26. Badin to Fenwick, June 18, August 12, 1825, AUND; Fenwick to Badin, December 5, 1824, *London Catholic Miscellany* 4 (May1825): 201; *U.S. Catholic Miscellany* 3: 398 ff.; Rese to Alumni of Propaganda, May 5, 1825, APF, fol. 434 rv (Kenneally, 1, 910); Badin to Fenwick, August 12, 1825, AUND; O'Daniel, *The Right Rev. Edward Dominic Fenwick,* 269–271; Jurgens, *A History of the Diocese of Cleveland,* 64. After a rough voyage of forty days, Fenwick arrived in New York City in early December. From there he traveled to Philadelphia and then to Baltimore, where he stayed more than two months, often conferring with Archbishop Maréchal. In March his nephew, Father Nicholas Young, and the lay Catholic John S. Dugan of Zanesville, Ohio, arrived in Baltimore to escort the bishop back to Cincinnati. On their journey in Dugan's stagecoach, they stopped in Washington, D.C. There they were joined by Gabriel Richard, a priest and member of Congress whom Fenwick had recommended for the proposed bishopric of Detroit. Until the second half of the twentieth century Richard was the only priest ever to have been elected to Congress. As they continued their journey, the coach overturned near Cumberland, Maryland, throwing the occupants to the ground. The three priests escaped with a few slight bruises, but Dugan suffered serious injuries. He died a few hours later in Fenwick's arms.

27. Flaget to Fenwick, May 15, 1825; Badin to Fenwick, June 18, 1825, AUND; Hill to Fenwick, Spring, 1824, published in *An Account of the Progress of the Catholic Church in the*

Western States of North America (London, 1824); Fenwick to Badin, December 24, 1824, *London Catholic Miscellany* 4 (May 1825): 201; *Catholic Telegraph,* April 2, 1891; O'Daniel, *The Right Rev. Edward Dominic Fenwick,* 272, 284–85.

28. Fenwick's letter quoted in O'Daniel, *The Right Rev. Edward Dominic Fenwick,* 312; Rese to Alumni of Propaganda, May 5, 1825, APF, fol. 434 rv (Kenneally, 1, 910); Rese to Fenwick, September 5, 1824; Fenwick to Madame la Superieure, Cincinnati, July 8, 1825, AUND; Petit, *Friar in the Wilderness,* 26.

29. Fenwick to P. Pallavicini, March 29, 1825, as printed in *Catholic Telegraph,* April 2, 1891.

30. Quoted in O'Daniel, *The Right Rev. Edward Dominic Fenwick,* 309, 315–16. Rese's letter is undated in the *Annales.* Neither is the name of the addressee given; but it was likely written to the editor and evidently belongs to 1826.

31. Badin to Fenwick, June 18, August 12, 1825, AUND, II-4-d; O'Daniel, *The Right Rev. Edward Dominic Fenwick,* 296.

32. Rese to Secretary of Association of Propagation of the Faith, February 24, 1826, *Annales* 2: 109; Fenwick's letter quoted in O'Daniel, *The Right Rev. Edward Dominic Fenwick,* 305–8; *U.S. Catholic Miscellany* 6: 246; 7, 342–43; White, "Religion and Community," 158.

33. Quoted in O'Daniel, *The Right Rev. Edward Dominic Fenwick,* 333; *U.S. Catholic Miscellany* 7: 343; *Catholic Telegraph,* April 2, 1891.

Chapter 2

1. *London Catholic Miscellany* 3 (February 1824): 93, article, AMERICA: Extract from a letter received from a Catholic missionary at Cincinnati; Victor Francis O'Daniel, *The Right Rev. Edward Dominic Fenwick, O.P., Founder of the Dominicans in the United States, Pioneer Missionary in Kentucky, Apostle of Ohio, First Bishop of Cincinnati* (Washington, D.C., [1920]), 294–95;

2. *The Story of St. Philomena Church* (Stonelick, Ohio, n.d.), AAC; *London Catholic Miscellany* 3 (February 1824): 93, article, AMERICA: Extract from a letter received from a Catholic Missionary at Cincinnati; O'Daniel, *The Right Rev. Edward Dominic Fenwick,* 215.

3. Fenwick's letter quoted in O'Daniel, *The Right Rev. Edward Dominic Fenwick,* 312–13; Montgomery to Fenwick, June 2, 1825, AUND, II-4-d; *Catholic Telegraph,* April 9, 1891.

4. Quoted in O'Daniel, *The Right Rev. Edward Dominic Fenwick,* 297–98.

5. An account of the Jubilee was published in *U.S. Catholic Miscellany* 6, 390; 7, 86–87, 342–43; N. D. Young to Fenwick, April 16, 1825, AUND; Joseph M. White, "Religion and Community: Cincinnati Germans 1814–1870" (Ph.D. diss., University of Notre Dame, 1980), 158; O'Daniel, *The Right Rev. Edward Dominic Fenwick,* 349, points out that services were rendered at 9 A.M. for the German-speaking members of the congregation and at 11 A.M. for the English-speaking Catholics.

6. *U.S. Catholic Miscellany* 6: 390; 7: 86–87, 342–43.

7. *U.S. Catholic Miscellany* 6: 246, 390; Edward Fenwick, "An Early Pastoral Letter" *Catholic Historical Review* 1, (1915–16): 65ff; Loretta Petit, O.P., *Friar in the Wilderness: Edward Dominic Fenwick, O.P.* (Chicago, 1994), 31; Jay P. Dolan, *The American Catholic Experience: A History from Colonial Times to the Present* (New York, 1985), 109.

8. *U.S. Catholic Miscellany* 6: 246; O'Daniel, *The Right Rev. Edward Dominic Fenwick,* 273–74; Robert Frederick Trisco, *The Holy See and the Nascent Church in the Middle Western United States, 1826–1850* (Rome, 1962), 225.

9. Fenwick to the prefect of the Propaganda, April 8, 1829, AUND.

10. Quoted in Petit, *Friar in the Wilderness,* 18; *U.S. Catholic Miscellany* 3: 431; Trisco, *The Holy See and the Nascent Church in the Middle Western United States, 1826–1850,* 168.

11. Mazzuchelli's quote in Petit, *Friar in the Wilderness,* 34; *U.S. Catholic Miscellany* 3: 382.

12. *U.S. Catholic Miscellany* 8: 382; 9: 62–63; Dejean to Badin, May 9, 1829, AUND; George C.

Stewart, Jr., *Marvels of Charity: History of American Sisters and Nuns* (Huntington, Ind., 1994), 100; *Catholic Telegraph,* October 22, 1831; Petit, *Friar in the Wilderness,* 27–28.

13. Gregory XVI to Fenwick, April 14, 1832; Pedicini to Fenwick, July 8, 1832, AUND; Propaganda Fide to Fenwick, July 28, 1832, APF, vol. 313, fols. 674 v and 675 r (Kenneally, 3, 2369); *Catholic Telegraph,* May 28, 1891; Trisco, *The Holy See and the Nascent Church in the Middle Western United States, 1826–1850,* 205, 212–14. Regrettably Maccodabinasse, son of the first chief of the Ottawa tribe, died unexpectedly in 1833. A few months later Hamelin's health also deteriorated. The Propaganda sent him back home. He never finished his training. Upon his return, Hamelin recovered his strength and became a leader of his tribe.

14. *Catholic Telegraph,* October 22, 1831.

15. Quoted in O'Daniel, *The Right Rev. Edward Dominic Fenwick,* 389, 401–2, 421.

16. Quoted in ibid., 334. The missions in the northwest were attended by Gabriel Richard, Francis Badin, John Bellamy, and Peter J. Dejean. In Ohio the priests were Frederic Rese, one of the vicars general, and James Mullon, and the Dominicans John A. Hill, also vicar general, Nicholas Young, Stephen Montgomery, Thomas H. Martin, John B. V. De Raymaecker, Daniel J. O'Leary, and Raphael Munos; Badin to Fenwick, April 19, August 2, 1826, AUND; *U.S. Catholic Miscellany* 6: 39; *Catholic Telegraph,* March 22, 1883.

17. Badin to Fenwick, April 19, August 2, September 25, 1826, AUND; *U.S. Catholic Miscellany* 6: 246; Stewart, Jr., *Marvels of Charity,* 71; *Catholic Telegraph,* March 22, 1883.

18. Quoted in O'Daniel, *The Right Rev. Edward Dominic Fenwick,* Rese to Fenwick, September 29, 1827, AUND.

19. C. B. McGuire to Fenwick, April 28, 1828, AAC; Rese to Fenwick, May 22, 1828; Flaget to Fenwick, July 28, 1828; Sister M. Francoise Vindevoghel to Fenwick, April 28, 1828, AUND. It was unfortunate that the Poor Clare Sisters community broke up when it did, for in June of that year two Flemish Sisters arrived in Cincinnati with the intention of joining the sisters in their enterprise. Disappointed that the Poor Clare Sisters had moved, they left Cincinnati soon after their arrival.

20. Fenwick to Flaget, September 22, 1824; Dubourg to Fenwick, April 22, 1825, AUND, II-4-d; Fenwick to Cardinal-Prefect of Propaganda, July 27, 1824, APF, fol. 320 rv (Kenneally, 1, 877); Thomas W. Spalding, *The Premier See: A History of the Archdiocese of Baltimore, 1789–1989* (Baltimore, Md., 1989), 89–91.

21. Kenrick to Rese, December 6, 1825, AUND, III-2-f.

22. Fenwick to Maréchal, May 26, 1826, AAB; Propaganda Fide to Maréchal, December 9, 1826, APF, vol. 307, fols. 791 v and 792 rv (Kenneally, 3, 1969); O'Daniel, *The Right Rev. Edward Dominic Fenwick,* 314.

23. Fenwick to Maréchal, May 26, 1826, AAB.

24. Fenwick to Propaganda, January 12, 1827, APF, fols. 191 rv and 192 rv (Kenneally, 1, 1046); Hill to Vicar General of the Dominicans, January 12, 1827, APF, fols. 189 rv and 190 r (Kenneally, 1, 1945); Badin to Propaganda Fide, May 24, 1827, APF, fols. 261 rv and 262 rv (Kenneally, 1, 1070); O'Daniel, *The Right Rev. Edward Dominic Fenwick,* 318, 328; Fenwick to Rese, 1827, AUND. Because of the distressing state of the diocese in 1827, Fenwick once again had resignation in mind.

25. Fenwick to Propaganda, January 12, 1827, APF, fols. 191 rv and 192 rv (Kenneally, 1, 1046); Hill to Vicar General of the Dominicans, January 12, 1827, APF, fols. 189 rv and 190 r (Kenneally, 1, 1945); Badin to Propaganda Fide, May 24, 1827, APF, fols. 261 rv and 262 rv (Kenneally, 1, 1070); Fenwick to Rese, 1827, AUND; O'Daniel, *The Right Rev. Edward Dominic Fenwick,* 318; John H. Lamott, *History of the Archdiocese of Cincinnati, 1821–1921* (Cincinnati, 1921), 177–78.

26. Agreement between Propaganda and Very Rev. Joseph M. Velzi, Vicar General of the

Dominicans, April 18, 1828, APF, fol. 626 rv (Kenneally, 1, 1151); Fenwick to Propaganda Fide, September 11, 1828, APF, fol. 698 r (Kenneally, 1, 1171); Rese to Fenwick, May 22, July 26, 1828, AUND.

27. O'Daniel suggests that Fenwick did not protest the agreement perhaps because of his lack of success in persuading the Propaganda with his earlier correspondence and the hope that the mistake might be corrected by his successor, whom he hoped would be a Dominican, O'Daniel, *The Right Rev. Edward Dominic Fenwick*, 343; Petit, *Friar in the Wilderness*, 23.

28. Rese to Fenwick, December 10, 1828, AUND, II-4-d; Trisco, *The Holy See and the Nascent Church in the Middle Western United States, 1826–1850*, 262–64. The Austrian Society was named for the emperor's recently deceased daughter, Leopoldine.

29. *U.S. Catholic Miscellany* 8: 198, 222; quoted in O'Daniel, *The Right Rev. Edward Dominic Fenwick*, 352–54; Leslie Woodcock Tentler, *Seasons of Grace: A History of the Catholic Archdiocese of Detroit* (Detroit, Mich., 1990), 51.

30. Clicteur's letter quoted in O'Daniel, *The Right Rev. Edward Dominic Fenwick*, 354–56; Fenwick to Propagation of the Faith, June 26, 1829, printed in *Catholic Telegraph*, November 19, 1891.

31. Fenwick to Kundig, October 29, 1829; Frederic Baraga to Amalia Gressel, January 21, 1831, in *Baraga Bulletin 11, no. 5*, March 1957, AAC; Fenwick to Propagation of the Faith, June 26, 1829, as printed in *Catholic Telegraph*, November 19, 1891; *U.S. Catholic Miscellany* 8: 382; W. A. Jurgens, *A History of the Diocese of Cleveland* (Youngstown, Ohio, 1980) 1: 110; M. Edmund Hussey, *A History of the Seminaries of the Archdiocese of Cincinnati, 1829–1979*, Norwood, Ohio (1979), 8.

32. *U.S. Catholic Miscellany* 9: 214–15; Spalding, *The Premier See*, 103; Edward A. Connaughton, *A History of Educational Legislation and Administration in the Archdiocese of Cincinnati* (Washington, D.C., 1946), 12; Fenwick's quote in Petit, *Friar in the Wilderness*, 24–25; Joseph P. Chinnici, O.F.M., "Organization of the Spiritual Life: American Catholic Devotional Works, 1791–1866," *Theological Studies* 40 (1979): 229, 231, 234.

33. F. Michael Perko, *A Time to Favor Zion: The Ecology of Religion and School Development on the Urban Frontier, Cincinnati, 1830–1870* (DeKalb, 1988), 60–62; David O'Brien, *Public Catholicism* (New York, 1989), 44.

34. Dubois to Fenwick, December 30, 1825, AUND; Judith Metz, S.C., "The Sisters of Charity in Cincinnati 1829–1852," *Vincentian Heritage* 17 (1996): 206; Mary J. Oates, *The Catholic Philanthropic Tradition in America* (Bloomington, Ind., 1995), 15; Eileen Mary Brewer, *Nuns and the Education of American Catholic Women, 1860–1920* (Chicago, 1987), 13. Between 1790 and 1920 thirty-eight American orders of women religious were founded.

35. Quoted in Metz, "Sisters of Charity," 206; Carol K. Coburn and Martha Smith, *Spirited Lives: How Nuns Shaped Catholic Culture and American Life, 1836–1920* (Chapel Hill, N.C., 1999), 7.

36. Fenwick to Rigagnon, February 25, 1830, *Annales* 4 (1830): 533; Sister Mary Agnes McCann, *The History of Mother Seton's Daughters* (New York, 1917), 1: 162; Coburn and Smith, *Spirited Lives*, 205; Oates, *The Catholic Philanthropic Tradition in America*, 7–8, 21; *Catholic Telegraph*, February 8, 1894; Judith Metz, "Sisters of Charity," 208; "150 Years of Caring: The Sisters of Charity in Cincinnati," *The Cincinnati Historical Society Bulletin* 37 (Cincinnati, 1979): 151. St. Peter Academy and Orphan Asylum later became St. John Hospital.

37. Sister Jordan's letter quoted in Metz, "Sisters of Charity," 209–213; *Catholic Telegraph*, October 22, 1831; July 28, 1832; O'Daniel, *The Right Rev. Edward Dominic Fenwick*, 370–71.

38. Prospectus in *Catholic Telegraph*, March 3, 1832; George A. Wilson to Purcell, February 17, 1847, AAC; O'Daniel, *The Right Rev. Edward Dominic Fenwick*, 371; Petit, *Friar in the Wilderness*, 24; Stewart, Jr., *Marvels of Charity*, 65.

39. Fenwick to Propagation of the Faith, June 1829, as printed in *Catholic Telegraph,* November 19, 1891; O'Daniel, *The Right Rev. Edward Dominic Fenwick,* 368. Father Baraga, who arrived in Cincinnati in 1831, mentions two instances when blacks were assisted by Catholic priests in Cincinnati.

40. Roman Catholic Committee of Cincinnati to Maréchal, September 25, 1820, printed in *Catholic Historical Review* 4: 30–31; *London Catholic Miscellany* 1: 475; *Catholic Telegraph,* October 29, 1831; Jurgens, *A History of the Diocese of Cleveland,* 82; J. B. Clicteur, to Central Council of Lyons, February 17, 1829, *Annales* 4: 510; *U.S. Catholic Miscellany* 8 (February 1830): 270. The English-speaking Catholics worshipped with their German brethren in St. Stephen Church, which was completed in 1833. As the Catholic population grew in the community, a new gothic and larger St. Stephen Church was built in 1855. St. Stephen's became the mother church of the churches in the counties of Butler, Preble, Miami, and parts of Shelby.

41. Frances Trollope, *Domestic Manners of the Americans* (New York, 1949), 109; Samuel Mazzuchelli, *Memoirs* (Chicago, 1967), 68; Frederic Baraga to Amalia Gressel, January 21, 1831, printed in *Baraga Bulletin* 11, no. 5 (March 1957), AAC.

42. *Catholic Telegraph,* October 29, 1831; November 19, 1891; Trisco, *The Holy See and the Nascent Church in the Middle Western United States, 1826–1850,* 15. According to Dolan in *The American Catholic Experience,* 116, cordial relations of Catholics with Protestants in the United States "remained normative through the 1820s."

43. Fenwick to P. Pallovicini, March 29, 1825, printed in *Catholic Telegraph,* April 2, 1891.

44. Articles from *The Chronicle,* August 14, September 4, 1830, printed in *Catholic Telegraph,* October 28, 1926; *Catholic Telegraph,* October 29, 1831; July 28, 1832; Iola Silberstein, *Cincinnati Then and Now* (Cincinnati, 1982), 93; *Cincinnati Chronicle and Literary Gazette,* August 14, 1830; Metz, "Sisters of Charity," 208–9; Mary Ewens, *The Role of the Nun in Nineteenth Century America* (New York, 1978), 162.

45. Fenwick to Montgomery, March 14, 1830 ("will do"); Badin to Fenwick, June 18, 1825, AUND, II-4-d; Rese to Cardinal-Prefect of Propaganda, January 20, 1830, APF, fols. 307 rv and 308 rv (Kenneally, 1, 1275); Hussey, *A History of the Seminaries of the Archdiocese of Cincinnati, 1829–1979,* 9; Spalding, *The Premier See,* 162; Anthony J. Lisska, "Dominican Ideals in Early America: The Example of Edward Dominic Fenwick," *New Blackfriars* (September 1993): 385. When Fenwick considered building a college in the diocese he probably remembered Badin's advice, when Badin tried to dissuade him from building the cathedral, that the "best speculations are made in our backwoods by the timely procuring of large house-lots in the towns likely to improve and where there is a probability of erecting churches or chapels. Your residence and the establishment of a college, . . . in the most populous in-land town in the U.S.," he argued, "would certainly give great additional value to the adjacent grounds."

46. Quoted in Petit, *Friar in the Wilderness,* 33; *Catholic Telegraph,* October 22, 1831; Hussey, *A History of the Seminaries of the Archdiocese of Cincinnati, 1829–1979,* 9–10; Lee J. Bennish, S.J., *Continuity and Change, Xavier University 1831–1981* (Chicago, 1981), 16–18.

47. Bennish, *Continuity and Change, Xavier University 1831–1981,* 18; prospectus of the Athenaeum, as printed in *Catholic Telegraph,* December 19, 1891; Hussey, *A History of the Seminaries of the Archdiocese of Cincinnati, 1829–1979,* 9–10. The Italian and German courses in the Athenaeum cost $25 extra.

48. *Catholic Telegraph,* October 22, 1831; October 26, 1833; July 30, 1885; August 30, 1906; Mullon to J. Timon, Cincinnati, August 13, 1830, AUND. The *Catholic Telegraph,* published every Saturday for $3.00 per year, $2.50 if paid in advance, has appeared weekly from the time of its founding with the exception of three weeks. A cholera plague caused the suspension of two issues in October 1832, and no paper was issued the last week of

December 1837 when the staff took a long break over Christmas. The existence of the *Catholic Telegraph* is almost synonymous with the growth of the archdiocese of Cincinnati, participating in virtually all the vicissitudes that have marked the growth of the Cincinnati Church. It is the oldest surviving Catholic periodical in the United States. From 1849 to 1862 the words *"and Advocate"* were added to *The Catholic Telegraph* following merger with a Louisville paper.

49. *Catholic Telegraph,* July 30, 1885; August 30, 1906; Fenwick to Propagation of the Faith at Lyons, June 1829, printed in *Catholic Telegraph,* November 19, 1891.

50. Rese to Fenwick, September 29, 1827; Rese to Fenwick, December 10, 1828, AUND, II-4-d; O'Daniel, *The Right Rev. Edward Dominic Fenwick,* 278, 303–4.

51. Rev. John Ryan, to Fenwick, Cincinnati, May 24, 1825, AAC; Fenwick to Maréchal, February 24, May 12, September 29, 1826, AAB; Fenwick to Propaganda Fide, February 1, 1826, APF, vol. 938, fols. 439 rv, 440 r, 445 rv and 446 r (Kenneally, 5, 1905); Fenwick to Propaganda Fide, December 15, 1827, APF, fol. 636 r (Kenneally, 1, 622); Maréchal to Propaganda Fide, May 13, 1826, APF, fols. 617 rv and 618 r (Kenneally, 1, 969); Fenwick to Cardinal-Prefect of Propaganda, June 16, 1826, APF, fol. 629 rv (Kenneally, 1, 975); Flaget to Propaganda Fide, February 26, 1827, APF, fols. 212 rv and 213 rv (Kenneally, 1, 1053); Badin to Propaganda Fide, November 28, 1827, APF, fol. 377 rv (Kenneally, 1, 1103); Cardinal Somalia to Fenwick, July 15, 1826; Rese to Fenwick, June 30, 1827, AUND, II-4-d; O'Daniel, *The Right Rev. Edward Dominic Fenwick,* 304, 342, 348–49; Trisco, *The Holy See and the Nascent Church in the Middle Western United States, 1826–1850,* 77, 99–102.

52. *Catholic Telegraph,* October 29, 1831 (rapid progress quote); Fenwick's December 1, 1831, letter to Rev. P. Potier was printed as found in *Catholic Telegraph,* October 28, 1926.

53. Fenwick to Rese, July 18, 1832; Flaget to Rese, November 9, 1832, AUND; Rese, Historical Notice on Fenwick, in *Annales* 6 (1833): 138; Mazzuchelli, *Memoirs,* 67–68; *Catholic Telegraph,* August 25, September 22, 1832; Reuben G. Thwaites, ed., *Early Western Travels, 1748–1846* (Cleveland, 1904–7), 22: 155; Robert G. Paterson, "The Decline of Epidemics in Ohio," *Ohio State Archaeological and Historical Quarterly* LV (1946): 320.

54. Fenwick to Rese, July 18, 1832, AUND; *Catholic Telegraph,* August 25, September 22, 1832; Fenwick to Whitfield, August 22, 1832, AAB; Mazzuchelli, *Memoirs,* 67; Fenwick's letter to the pope, quoted in Petit, *Friar in the Wilderness,* 34; Anthony J. Lisska, "Bishop Fenwick's Apostolate to the Native Americans," *Bulletin of the Catholic Record Society* 17, no. 12 (December 1992): 191.

55. *Catholic Telegraph,* April 4, 1832; also Powell to Rese, September 26, 1832, printed in *Catholic Telegraph,* October 6, 1832.

56. Henni to Rese, Cincinnati, September 27, October 2, 1832; N. D. Young to Rese, December 19, 1832; January 23, 1833, AUND; *Catholic Telegraph,* March 16, 1848; March 30, 1916; Powell to Rese, September 26, 1832, printed in *Catholic Telegraph,* October 6, 1832.

Chapter 3

1. England to Mullon, May 14, 1833; Kenrick to Purcell, January 20, 1834, AUND; Fenwick to Whitfield, August 22, 1832, AAB, Case 23, H 6; Fenwick to Pope Gregory XVI, August 18, 1832, APF, vol. 948, fol. 153 rv (Kenneally, 6, 91); Robert F. Trisco, *The Holy See and the Nascent Church in the Middle Western United States, 1826–1850* (Rome, 1962), 129–31.

2. Quoted in Thomas W. Spalding, *The Premier See: A History of the Archdiocese of Baltimore, 1789–1989* (Baltimore, Md., 1989), 119; England to Whitfield, May 14, 1833, AAB; England to Mullon, May 14, 1833; England to Purcell, July 1, 1837; Mullon to Purcell, July 28, 1833, AUND; quoted in Richard Shaw, *Dagger John: The Unquiet Life and Times of John Hughes of New York* (New York, 1977), 91–92.

3. Anthony H. Deye, "Archbishop John Baptist Purcell, Pre–Civil War Years" (Ph.D. diss.,

University of Notre Dame, 1959), 22–23; M. Edmund Hussey, "John Baptist Purcell: First Archbishop of Cincinnati" in Gerald P. Fogarty, S.J., *Patterns of Episcopal Leadership* (New York, 1989), 89.

4. England to Mullon, May 14, 1833; Mullon to Purcell, July 28, 1833, AUND. Not all letters to Purcell were critical of Rese. Simon Gabriel Bruté of Mount St. Mary's at Emmitsburg was sorry that Rese, because of his great knowledge of the diocese, had been removed from Cincinnati, Bruté to Purcell, April 29, 1833, AUND; Purcell to Whitfield, June 19, 1833, AAB.

5. *Catholic Telegraph,* October 26, November 29, 1833; Mary Agnes McCann, "Archbishop Purcell and the Archdiocese of Cincinnati" (Ph.D. diss., Catholic University of America, 1918), 14.

6. Rese to Purcell, Detroit, July 3, 1835, AUND; Deye, "Archbishop John Baptist Purcell," 104, 118; Deye points out that between August 30, 1834 and May 12, 1835, Purcell estimated the number of German Catholics in Cincinnati to be between three and five thousand. In April of 1834 Father Vogeler estimated their number to be five thousand or more, Vogeler to Purcell, April 5, 1834, AAC.

7. Quoted in Deye, "Archbishop John Baptist Purcell," 96; John B. Purcell, "Journal 1833–1836," *The Catholic Historical Review* 5 (July–October, 1919): 241.

8. Rese to Purcell, November 16, 1833; Purcell to Rese, January 15, 1835; Rese to Purcell, July 3, 1835; N. D. Young to Purcell, January 16, 1835, AUND; Purcell, "Journal," 240; copy of Will of Bishop Fenwick, probated October 1, 1832, Hamilton County, AAC.

9. *Souvenir Book Commemorating One Hundred Years, St. Mary Church, 1848–1948* (Hamilton, 1948), AAC; Purcell, "Journal," 242, 243, 246; John F. Byrne, C.SS.R., *The Redemptorist Centenaries* (Philadelphia, 1932), 41–51; *Catholic Almanac,* 1833, 50–51; *Catholic Almanac* (1834): 56–57; Purcell to Hughes, November 20, 1833, AANY.

10. Purcell, "Journal," 245, 255. On April 10 the bishop made his last entry in his journal, which he had started shortly after his consecration. In it he noted his need for more priests.

11. *Catholic Almanac* (1834): 130–31; *Catholic Almanac* (1837), 170; quoted in Deye, "Archbishop John Baptist Purcell," 204–6.

12. *Catholic Telegraph,* September 11, 1841, October 8, 15, 29, December 3, 1842; Deye, "Archbishop John Baptist Purcell," 236–38; Timon to Purcell, July 29, 1842, AUND.

13. *Catholic Telegraph,* May 16, 23, June 13, 27, July 18, August 1, 1834; Sister Mary Gilbert Kelly, O.P., *Catholic Immigrant Colonization Projects in the United States, 1815–1860* (New York, 1939), Monograph Series 17 of the *United States Catholic Historical Society,* 48–63.

14. *Emmanuel Catholic Church Sesquicentennial History, 1837–1987* (Dayton, 1987), AAC; *Catholic Telegraph,* August 1, 1834; April 24, July 24, September 4, 1835; November 30, 1837; March 23, 1844; S. H. Montgomery to Purcell, June 1, AUND. Emanuel Thienpont spelled his first name with one "m," unlike the spelling of Emmanuel Church. At the dedication of Emmanuel Church Purcell was assisted by Fathers Stephen Badin, John Henni, and Peter Czakert.

15. *Catholic Telegraph,* May 16, June 13, 1834.

16. Ibid., May 16, 1834; April 24, 1835; July 7, 21, 28; August 4, 18, 1836.

17. Ibid., August 18, 1836.

18. Montgomery to Purcell, June 1, 1834, AUND; quoted in Deye, "Archbishop John Baptist Purcell," 140.

19. Quoted in Deye, "Archbishop John Baptist Purcell," 141; *Catholic Telegraph,* October 3, 1834.

20. *Catholic Telegraph,* March 25, May 27, June 24, 1847; John Tracy Ellis, ed., *Documents of American Catholic History* (Chicago, 1987) 1: 278; U.S. Department of Interior, *Report on the Social Statistics of Cities, Part II, The Southern and Western States* (Washington, 1887), 358.

21. *Catholic Telegraph,* February 15, 1840; December 17, 1842; December 11, 1845; Daniel Hurley, *Cincinnati, the Queen City* (Cincinnati, 1982), 57.

22. Purcell to Rappe, 1840, AUND; Purcell to the Society for the Propagation of the Faith, Paris, September 12, 1840; April 8, 1842; February 10, 1843, SPFA; Purcell to the Society of the Faith, Lyons, February 14, 1843, SPFA; Deye, "Archbishop John Baptist Purcell," 231.

23. Purcell to Rappe, 1840, AUND; *Catholic Telegraph,* May 16, October 31, 1840; December 11, 1841; June 25, 1842; January 6, 1844; Purcell to the Society for the Propagation of the Faith, Paris, September 12, 1840; April 8, 1842, SPFA; Purcell to the Society for the Propagation of the Faith, Lyons, February 14, 1843, SPFA; Deye, "Archbishop John Baptist Purcell," 231. By the early 1840s Purcell had seen the completion of churches at Minster, St. Joseph, St. Henry, Victoria, Cleveland, Elyria, McCutchenville, Marietta, Columbus, Lancaster, East Liverpool, Sandusky, Portland, Danville, Mount Vernon, Newark, Jackson, Stonelick, Ripley, and Fayetteville.

24. Purcell, "Journal," 243–44, 249, 251, 253; *Catholic Telegraph,* January 26, 1833; January 10, 1834; January 12, 1888; July 9, 1931; Judith Metz, S.C., "150 Years of Caring: The Sisters of Charity in Cincinnati," *The Cincinnati Historical Society Bulletin* 37 (1979): 154.

25. *Catholic Telegraph,* January 26, December 20, 1833; January 10, 1834; January 12, 1888; July 9, 1931; Montgomery to Purcell, June 1, 1834, AUND; Mary J. Oates, *The Catholic Philanthropic Tradition in America* (Bloomington, Ind., 1995), 9, 12; Judith Metz, "The Sisters of Charity in Cincinnati 1829–1852," *Vincentian Heritage* 17 (1996): 214–16.

26. Metz, "The Sisters of Charity in Cincinnati 1829–1852," 24–25, 28; Oates, *Philanthropic Tradition,* 8, 12; *Catholic Telegraph,* January 8, 1842; August 28, 1842.

27. Quoted in Deye, "Archbishop John Baptist Purcell," 202–3, 208; Badin to Purcell, August 25, 1836, AUND; *Catholic Telegraph,* July 29, 1843; John Hassard, *Life of John Hughes, First Archbishop of New York* (New York, 1969), 270.

28. Deye, "Archbishop John Baptist Purcell," 152–53, 367; *Catholic Telegraph,* May 25, 1837; March 22, 1838; July 5, 1849; reference to Edward Purcell's authorization in Supreme Court of Ohio, I. J. Miller and G. Tafel, Trustees vs. William Henry Elder found in M. Edmund Hussey, "The 1978 Financial Failure of Archbishop Purcell," *The Cincinnati Historical Society Bulletin* 36 (1978): 8; the *Catholic Telegraph,* January 4, 1840, was the first issue on which Edward Purcell's name appeared as editor. For a discussion of the close relationship of the Purcell brothers see Deye, "Archbishop John Baptist Purcell," 348–60.

29. Quoted in Deye, "Archbishop John Baptist Purcell," 160, 209–11; *Catholic Telegraph,* October 11, 1838.

30. Deye, "Archbishop John Baptist Purcell," 211; a list of the annual donations from the Association of the Propagation of the Faith is found in John H. Lamott, *History of the Archdiocese of Cincinnati, 1821–1921* (Cincinnati, 1921), 174; Jeanjean to Blanc, December 14, 1838, AUND; Louise Callan, R.S.C.J., *The Society of the Sacred Heart in North America* (London, New York, Toronto, 1937), 591; Eileen Mary Brewer, *Nuns and the Education of American Catholic Women, 1860–1920* (Chicago, 1987), 13. Between 1790 and 1820, 119 European orders of sisters established foundations in the United States.

31. LeClerc to Purcell, December 18, 1838; Purcell to Blanc, February 12, 1839; Muller to Purcell, Rome, June 8, 1839, AUND; John B. Wuest, O.F.M., "Father Francis Louis Huber, The First Franciscan in Cincinnati," *The Provincial Chronicle* 12 (1939–1940): 3–16, 130–35; Deye, "Archbishop John Baptist Purcell," 213–14.

32. Fransoni to Purcell, January 13, 1838; N. D. Young to Purcell, April 10, 1838; Purcell to Blanc, Rome, February 12, 1839, AUND; Deye, "Archbishop John Baptist Purcell," 212–13; Victor Francis O'Daniel, *The Right Rev. Edward Dominic Fenwick, O.P., Founder of the Dominicans in the United States, Pioneer Missionary in Kentucky, Apostle of Ohio, First Bishop of Cincinnati* (Washington, D.C., [1920]), 340–44.

33. Oates, *The Catholic Philanthropic Tradition in America,* 4; *Catholic Telegraph,* October 10, 1839.

34. Purcell to Verhaegen, August 17, 1840, Xavier University Archives; Deye, "Archbishop John Baptist Purcell," 222–23; *Catholic Telegraph,* June 12, 1890.

35. *Catholic Telegraph,* September 26, October 24, 1840; June 12, 1890; quoted in Deye, "Archbishop John Baptist Purcell," 224–25.

36. Gilbert J. Garraghan, *The Jesuits of the Middle United States* (New York, 1938), 3: 171, 185–88; Raymond Payne, "Annals of the Leopoldine Association," *The Catholic Historical Review* 1 (1915): 60; *Catholic Telegraph,* September 12, 26, 1840; June 12, 1890; July 9, 1931; December 6, 1940; *Catholic Almanac,* 1842; Lee J. Bennish, S.J., *Continuity and Change, Xavier University 1831–1981* (Chicago, 1981), 29, 39.

37. Copy of extract from Purcell's pastoral, 1841, AAC; Deye, "Archbishop John Baptist Purcell," 225–26, 299; Purcell to Blanc, October 29, 1840, AUND; *Catholic Telegraph,* September 12, 1840; April 3, May 22, June 5, 1841; Lamott, *History of the Archdiocese of Cincinnati, 1821–1921,* 127–28.

38. Copy of extract from Purcell's pastoral, 1841, AAC; *Catholic Telegraph,* June 5, 12, December 11, 1841; January 15, 1842; *The Cincinnnati Enquirer,* March 2, 1879; Deye, "Archbishop John Baptist Purcell," 234; Hussey, "The 1978 Financial Failure of Archbishop Purcell," 10.

39. *Catholic Telegraph,* October 16, 23, November 6, 1845; [Donald A. Tenoever], *The Cathedral of St. Peter in Chains* (souvenir booklet, n.d., n.p.; Cincinnati), AAC. Christ parish was changed to All Saints' in the 1860s.

40. Charles Cist, *Cincinnati in 1841* (Cincinnati, 1841), 326–27; *Catholic Telegraph,* April 5, 1849; Talbot Hamelin, *Greek Revival Architecture in America* (New York, 1944), 285; Jay P. Dolan, *The American Catholic Experience: A History from Colonial Times to the Present* (New York, 1985), 211.

41. Purcell to Blanc, February 27, 1840, AUND; *Catholic Telegraph,* March 7, 1840; Hurley, *Cincinnati,* 34–42, 56.

42. Purcell to Blanc, November 7, 1848; February 9, 1849, AUND; Trisco, *The Holy See and the Nascent Church in the Middle Western United States, 1826–1850,* 50; James L. Heft, S.M., "From the Pope to the Bishops: Episcopal Authority from Vatican I to Vatican II" in *The Papacy and the Church in the United States,* ed. Bernard Cooke (New York, 1989), 68–69.

43. Purcell to Blanc, November 7, 1848; February 9, 1849; June 14, October 30, 1850; Spalding to Purcell, December 16, 1848; Franzoni to Purcell, August 6, 1850, AUND; *Catholic Telegraph,* October 12, 1850; Trisco, *The Holy See and the Nascent Church in the Middle Western United States, 1826–1850,* 50. Until the late 1840s, when Rome established other archdioceses, all the dioceses in the United States were within the jurisdiction of Baltimore. The first seven bishops' meetings (1829, 1833, 1837, 1840, 1843, 1846, 1849) in Baltimore were called provincial councils. The meetings later held in 1852, 1866, and 1884 were called plenary councils. These meetings included archbishops as well as bishops.

44. Deye, "Archbishop John Baptist Purcell," 320; Eccleston to Purcell, January 1846; August 25, 1847; Rappe to Purcell, September 10, 25, 1847, AUND; *Catholic Telegraph,* October 14, 1847; January 11, 1849; statistics taken from the respective issues of the *Catholic Directory.* In 1837 a territorial dispute arose between Purcell and Rese of Detroit over a small strip of land on the common border of their respective dioceses. Since the Catholic population was increasing in the area, Purcell wanted the dispute settled. Though the matter was never officially resolved ecclesiastically by Rome, the disputed land was considered part of Ohio and therefore a part of the civil boundary of the diocese of Cincinnati. See Trisco, *The Holy See and the Nascent Church in the Middle Western United States, 1826–1850,* 48, 69–71.

45. McElroy to Purcell, January 14, 1848, AUND; *Catholic Telegraph,* January 12, 1850.

46. Quoted in Deye, "Archbishop John Baptist Purcell," 307; *Catholic Telegraph,* December 16, 1847.

47. Quoted in Lamott, *History of the Archdiocese of Cincinnati, 1821–1921,* 169; *Catholic Almanac,* 1857.

48. *Catholic Telegraph,* December 7, 1850; May 8, 15, 1852; Edward A. Connaughton, *A History of Educational Legislation and Administration in the Archdiocese of Cincinnati* (Washington, D.C., 1946), 26; Trisco, *The Holy See and the Nascent Church in the Middle Western United States, 1826–1850,* 22; McCann, "Archbishop Purcell and the Archdiocese of Cincinnati," 75; Ann Taves, *The Household of Faith: Roman Catholic Devotions in Mid-Nineteenth-Century America* (Notre Dame, Ind., 1986), 129; *Catholic Almanac,* 1850.

49. *Catholic Telegraph,* June 17, 1847; Spalding to Purcell, December 16, 1848, AUND.

50. Purcell to Blanc, June 14, October, 30, 1850; November 6, 1851; Purcell to Fransoni, April 1, 1851; F. P. Kenrick to Purcell, June 30, 1851, AUND; Deye, "Archbishop John Baptist Purcell," 337–40; *Catholic Telegraph,* November 23, December 28, 1850. In the mid-1860s the diocese also had twenty-three chapels and stations.

51. *Catholic Telegraph,* July 22, 1868; Rosecrans to Purcell, May 7, 1868, AUND; *Catholic Directory,* 1867, 1868.

52. Leslie Woodcock Tentler, *Seasons of Grace: A History of the Catholic Archdiocese of Detroit* (Detroit, Mich., 1990), 58.

53. *Centenary Jubilee St. James Parish, 1843–1943* (Cincinnati, Ohio), 1943; *A Century of Catholicism, St. Benignus, 1858–1958* (Greenfield, Ohio, 1958), AAC.

54. *St. Stephen Church, 1834–1959* (Hamilton, Ohio), 1959; *Diamond Jubilee Holy Name Church, 1871–1946* (Trenton, Ohio, 1946).

55. Louis A., Rita M., and David A. Hoying, *Pilgrims All: A History of Saint Augustine Parish, Minster, Ohio, 1832–1982* (Minster, Ohio, 1982), 65–66; *St. John the Baptist Catholic Church, 1851–1978* (Harrison, Ohio, 1978); *Centenary Jubilee St. James Parish, 1843–1943* (Cincinnati, 1943); *Golden Jubilee St. Gabriel Church, 1859–1909* (Cincinnati, 1909); *25th Anniversary St. Paul Catholic Church, 1856–1981* (Yellow Springs, Ohio, 1981); *St. Boniface Parish, 1863–1963: The End of a Century . . . The Beginning of a New* (Cincinnati, 1963), AAC.

56. *100 Golden Years, St. Aloysius Gonzaga, 1866–1966* (Cincinnati, 1966); *St. Bernard Church, 1867–1967* (Taylor's Creek, Ohio, 1967); *Souvenir Golden Jubilee of Holy Trinity Congregation, 1868–1918* (Coldwater, Ohio, 1918), AAC.

57. *St. Joseph Parish, 1839–1989* (Ft. Recovery, Ohio, 1989); *Centenary Jubilee St. James Parish, 1843–1943* (Cincinnati, Ohio, 1943); *St. John the Baptist Catholic Church, 1851–1978* (Harrison, Ohio, 1978); *Diamond Jubilee Holy Name Church, 1871–1946* (Trenton, Ohio, 1946), AAC.

58. *Annals of St. Michael's Parish in Loramie, 1838–1903* (Sidney, Ohio, 1907), AAC; *Catholic Telegraph,* March 19, 1846.

59. *Catholic Telegraph,* April 22, 1847; Taves, *Household of Faith,* 11; Tentler, *Seasons of Grace,* 41. The Second Provincial Council of Cincinnati was the first episcopal assembly in the country to give official support to the parish mission.

60. Joseph M. White, "Religion and Community: Cincinnati Germans 1814–1870" (Ph.D. diss., University of Notre Dame, 1980), 274–83.

61. *Golden Jubilee St. Patrick's Congregation, 1850–1900* (Cincinnati, 1900); *Annals of St. Michael's Parish in Loramie, 1838–1903* (Sidney, Ohio, 1903); *Commemorating the Centenary of St. Clement Parish 1850–1950* (Cincinnati, 1951), AAC; *Catholic Telegraph,* May 16, June 13, July 18, 1834; April 24, July 24, August 14, September 4, 11, 1835; July 7, 21, 28; August 4, 18; September 8, 15, 1836; Patrick W. Carey, *The Roman Catholics* (Westport, Conn., 1993), 40; Taves, *Household of Faith,* 11, 30, 115.

62. Tentler, *Seasons of Grace,* 38, 57, 64–65; Taves, *Household of Faith,* 14, 18.

63. *Diamond Jubilee Holy Trinity Church, 1861–1936* (Dayton, 1936); *Our Lady of Victory Parish: A Century of Activities, 1843–1943* (Cincinnati, 1943); *Annals of St. Michael's Parish in Loramie, 1838–1903* (Sidney, Ohio, 1907); *St. Anthony Parish 125th Anniversary, 1859–1984* (Cincinnati, 1984); *History of St. Anthony's Parish* ([n.d.]); *The History of St. Mary Church* (Oxford, Ohio, [n.d.]); *Jubilee Souvenir of St. Lawrence Parish, 1869–1920* (Cincinnati, 1920); *Souvenir Diamond Jubilee of Sacred Heart Parish, 1870–1945* (Cincinnati, 1945); *Souvenir Golden Jubilee St. Charles Borromeo Church, 1869–1919* (Cincinnati, 1919); *Our Lady of Victory Parish: A Century of Activities, 1843–1943* (Cincinnati, 1943), AAC.

64. John B. Wuest, O.F.M., *St. Francis Seraph Church and Parish, Commemorating the Seventy-Fifth Anniversary of the Consecration of the Church and the Diamond Jubilee of the Parish, 1859–1934* (Cincinnati, 1934), AAC.

65. *Golden Jubilee St. Patrick's Congregation, 1850–1900* (Cincinnati, 1900); *Celebrating 125 Years: St. Stephen Church* (Cincinnati, 1992), AAC. In St. Louis parish at North Star in the early 1900s those pews closest to the altar were the least expensive. The four pews in the front were reserved for the children and were not auctioned. *100th Anniversary St. Louis Church, 1892–1992* (North Star, Ohio, 1992), AAC. The parish records of St. Stephen Church at Columbia in Cincinnati show that in 1882 pew rent generated $448.64, Sunday collections $468.97, societies $163.50, and social events $2,023.24.

Chapter 4

1. Patrick W. Carey, *The Roman Catholics* (Westport, Conn., 1993), 31, 35; Jay P. Dolan, *The American Catholic Experience: A History from Colonial Times to the Present* (New York, 1985), 127, 161.

2. *One Hundredth Anniversary of St. Mary Church, 1842–1942,* Cincinnati, 1942, AAC; *Catholic Telegraph,* October 10, 1840; Charles Cist, *Cincinnati in 1841* (Cincinnati, 1841), 37–38, 270; Gilbert J. Garraghan, *The Jesuits of the Middle United States* (New York, 1938), 3: 171; Joseph M. White, "Religion and Community: Cincinnati Germans 1814–1870" (Ph.D. diss., University of Notre Dame, 1980), 169.

3. Quoted in White, "Religion and Community," 159–60.

4. Dolan, *The American Catholic Experience,* 294; Christopher J. Kauffman, *Education and Transformation: Marianist Ministries in America Since 1849* (New York, 1999), 54.

5. "Regulations for the administration of the temporal affairs of German Roman Catholic Churches of Cincinnati," 1851, AAC; *Catholic Telegraph,* September 4, 1835; Dolan, *The American Catholic Experience,* 162; Zane L. Miller and Bruce Tucker, *Changing Plans for America's Inner Cities: Cincinnati's Over-the-Rhine and Twentieth-Century Urbanism* (Columbus, 1998), 1; White, "Religion and Community," 38–39, 178–80, 212–15. See White's dissertation for a fuller elaboration on the trustee system, or its lack thereof, in Cincinnati parishes.

6. *Catholic Telegraph,* September 4, 1835.

7. *St. Joseph Parish, 1839–1989* (Ft. Recovery, Ohio, 1989), AAC; *Catholic Telegraph,* December 19, 1844; White, "Religion and Community," 183, 262–66, 269–70.

8. Cist, *Cincinnati,* 35, 37; quoted in John B. Wuest, *St. Francis Seraph Church and Parish* (Cincinnati, 1934), 18–20.

9. *Catholic Telegraph,* April 18, October 3, 10, 1834; John B. Purcell, "Journal 1833–1836," *The Catholic Historical Review* 5 (July, 1919): 251–54; David O'Brien, *Public Catholicism* (New York, 1989), 40; White, "Religion and Community," 162. Holy Trinity parish operated with twelve trustees, six appointed by Purcell and six elected by the congregation.

10. Purcell to Rese, January 15, 1835, AUND; *Catholic Telegraph,* May 17, 1838; January 2, 1841; Purcell, "Journal," 251–54; White, "Religion and Community," 162–63, 291.

11. *Centenary Jubilee Souvenir, St. Aloysius Orphan Society* (Cincinnati, 1937), 10–12, AAC; *Catholic Telegraph,* February 23, April 20, August 3, 1837; October 8, 1891; July 9, 1931; October 11, 1934.

12. *Centenary Jubilee Souvenir, St. Aloysius Orphan Society* (Cincinnati, 1937), 10–12, AAC; *Catholic Telegraph,* February 23, April 20, August 3, 1837; October 8, 1891; July 9, 1931; October 11, 1934; White, "Religion and Community," 7. The *Wahrheitsfreund* was published by the orphan society until 1843 when it was purchased by Herman Lehman of Toledo.

13. Quoted in Judith Metz, S.C., "The Sisters of Charity in Cincinnati 1829–1852," *Vincentian Heritage* 17 (1996): 223–24; Anthony H. Deye, "Archbishop John Baptist Purcell, Pre–Civil War Years" (Ph.D. diss., University of Notre Dame, 1959), 266–67; *Catholic Telegraph,* July 4, 1839.

14. *Catholic Telegraph,* June 28, 1849; October 18, 25, 1851; October 8, 1891; July 9, 1931; Metz, "Sisters of Charity," 224–25; Judith Metz, S.C., and Virginia Wiltse, *Sister Margaret Cecilia George, A Biography* (Mount St. Joseph, Ohio, 1989), 55–56; John Hassard, *Life of John Hughes, First Archbishop of New York* (New York, 1969), 289–302; Mary Ewens, *The Role of the Nun in Nineteenth Century America* (New York, 1978), 124–27.

15. *Catholic Telegraph,* August 8, 1840; June 5, 1841; October 7, 1843; March 27, 1845; August 7, 1890; Deye, "Archbishop John Baptist Purcell," 268. At St. Mary's dedication, the bishop performed the first solemn consecration in the diocese. This meant that the church could never be used subsequently for any other purpose than divine worship.

16. *One Hundredth Anniversary of St. Mary Church, 1842–1942* (Cincinnati, 1942), AAC; *Catholic Telegraph,* July 9, 1842; October 2, 1942; Deye, "Archbishop John Baptist Purcell," 268; White, "Religion and Community," 175.

17. *Catholic Telegraph,* January 6, 17, March 23, September 21, 1844; June 26, 1845; July 17, August 7, 1890; July 9, 1931; September 29, 1892; Joseph Ferneding's consecration was the first in the new and present St. Peter in Chains Cathedral, which was in the process of being built. *Diamond Jubilee Souvenir, St. Mary Church (Cincinnati, 1917),* AAC. The brothers of the Society of Mary continued to teach the boys until 1939, when the decision was made, due to declining attendance, to combine the two schools and place them in the charge of the Sisters of Notre Dame.

18. *Catholic Telegraph,* April 3, May 22, 1841; July 9, 1842; March 27, April 3, 1845; March 25, August 27, 1846; June 29, 1848; November 29, 1849; January 26, May 18, November 9, 1850; October 6, 1892; October 31, 1895; October 13, 1944; *Diamond Jubilee Souvenir, St. Mary Church* (Cincinnati, 1917); John B. Wuest, O.F.M., *St. Francis Seraph Church and Parish, Commemorating the Seventy-Fifth Anniversary of the Consecration of the Church and the Diamond Jubilee of the Parish* (Cincinnati, 1934), AAC; White, "Religion and Community," 208.

19. Quoted in Deye, "Archbishop John Baptist Purcell," 275–76; Collins to Purcell, April 2, 1834; Peter Kenrick to Purcell, February 2, 1842, AUND; John B. Wuest, O.F.M., "Archbishop James F. Wood of Philadelphia and the Bavarian Preface to the History of Our Province," *Provincial Chronicle* 6 (1934): 108–15; and "Father Francis Louis Huber The First Franciscan in Cincinnati," *Provincial Chronicle* 12 (1939–40): 3–16, 130–35; *Catholic Telegraph,* December 11, 1841; January 29, 1842; September 28, 1848.

20. *Catholic Telegraph,* July 27, 1848; October 4, 1890; October 6, 1892; October 28, 1926; July 9, 1931.

21. Rev. Francis Fritsch to Purcell, October 7, 1848, AUND; *Catholic Telegraph,* March 22, 1850; Deye, "Archbishop John Baptist Purcell," 294–95; White, "Religion and Community," 216–18.

22. *Souvenir Golden Jubilee, St. George's Church* (Cincinnati, 1918); *Souvenir Golden Jubilee, St. Charles Borromeo Church* (Carthage, 1919); *The First One Hundred Years: Our Lady of the*

Sacred Heart Parish, 1874–1974 (Cincinnati, 1974); *Saint Paul Parish During Seventy-Five Years, 1850–1925* (Cincinnati, 1925); *St. Anthony Parish 125th Anniversary, 1859–1914* (Cincinnati, 1914), AAC; *Catholic Telegraph,* June 10, 1847; January 4, 1849; June 29, 1850; May 31, November 29, 1851; June 3, 1868; December 22, 1892; June 12, 1894; November 17, 1898; August 24, 1899; October 4, 1900; April 14, 1910; June 9, 1972; James H. Campbell, "New Parochialism: Change and Conflict in the Archdiocese of Cincinnati, 1878–1925" (Ph.D. diss., University of Cincinnati, 1981), 29–32. In the late 1840s five other Tyrolese Franciscans joined Unterthiner in Cincinnati. Under the supervision of the Franciscan Jacob Menchen, the German-speaking St. Bonaventure Church was dedicated in the western section of the city in 1869. It replaced a small church of stone structure that had been in the vicinity since the mid-1840s. In 1852 the Church of the Fourteen Martyrs was destroyed by a cyclone. A new church was built and named after the Apostles, Peter and Paul. By the 1870s a number of Irish families, who had for many years attended SS. Peter and Paul Church, expressed a desire to have a church of their own. Four years later Our Lady of the Sacred Heart parish was formed. By August they laid the cornerstone for the church. As more and more German Catholics moved to the northern hilltop of Cincinnati in the 1860s, those at Corryville, which overlooked Vine Street, petitioned for their own parish. In 1868 Purcell granted their request, and St. George Church, a combination church and school, was completed by the fall of that year. As the population grew in the outlying areas of St. Bernard and Reading, Catholic families in Carthage helped organize the parish of St. Charles Borromeo in 1869. Under the guidance of Father John Albrinck they began construction of a combination church, school, and residence. It was dedicated in July 1870. In 1873 a new church of St. Clement was built in St. Bernard, as large quarters were needed to accommodate the growth of the parish.

23. *Catholic Telegraph,* November 13, 1845; March 25, 1846; June 8, December 14, 1848; November 16, 1850; June 17, 1863; June 3, 1868; March 17, 1870; January 31, May 19, 1878; March 17, 1892; March 14, 1895; quoted in *Diamond Jubilee, St. Augustine Parish* (Cincinnati, 1932); *Souvenir Seventy-Fifth Anniversary, Our Lady of Victory* (Delhi, Ohio, 1918); *Souvenir Golden Jubilee, St. Lawrence Parish* (Cincinnati, 1920); *Souvenir Golden Jubilee, St. Rose Church* (Cincinnati, 1919); *Our Lady of Perpetual Help Church, 1878–1978* (Cincinnati, 1978), AAC; White, "Religion and Community," 172–73. When the German Catholics at St. Stephen Church on Rapid Run Road in Delhi Township, the third Catholic church in Hamilton County, accepted three acres of land donated to the parish, which had changed its name to Our Lady of Victory in 1842, the name of the church and site were changed in 1853 when Our Lady of Victory Church was built. For many years this church ministered to the needs of Catholics in Price Hill, Sedamsville, Bridgetown, Lower Delhi, and North Bend. In 1866 Catholics in Bridgetown established St. Aloysius Gonzaga parish. Two years later lower Delhi Catholics formed their own parish, built their own school, and dedicated it to St. Aloysius, which was later named St. Aloysius On-the-Ohio. Although the first settlers of the Miami Valley landed at the mouth of the Little Miami River in the latter part of the eighteenth century, it was not until 1867 that the few Catholics scattered over the Miami Valley erected St. Stephen Church at Eastern and Donham Avenues. Up to that time the Catholics were forced to worship either in St. Philomena Church in East Walnut Hills or at some of the neighboring churches. In 1861 the archdiocese built St. Vincent de Paul Church in Sedamsville. Seventeen years later a division occurred in the parish when sixty-five German Catholic families wanted their own school and, with the assistance of Otto Jair, organized the parish of Our Lady of Perpetual Help. They used the upper part of an old stone schoolhouse they had acquired for church services and the lower level as a school.

24. Quoted in Mary Agnes McCann, "Archbishop Purcell and the Archdiocese of Cincinnati" (Ph.D. diss., Catholic University of America, 1918), 76; *Diamond Jubilee of the Passionist*

Fathers at Holy Cross Monastery, 1873–1948 (Cincinnati, 1948), AAC; *Catholic Telegraph,* August 27, 1859.

25. *Catholic Telegraph,* February 29, April 11, 1872; June 26, 1873; July 9, 1931. For a history of the Passionists see *Catholic Telegraph,* October 11, 1888; August 25, 1895. Holy Cross and Immaculata merged in 1970.

26. *Catholic Telegraph,* July 27, 1848; January 24, 1857; October 4, 1890; October 28, 1926; July 9, 1931; Diomede Pohlkamp, O.F.M., "Life and Times of Father William Unterthiner, O.F.M.," *Provincial Chronicle* 15 (1942): 3–15; John B. Wuest, O.F.M., "Four Friars for Cincinnati in 1849," *Provincial Chronicle* 15 (1942): 46–51; Cardinal Franzoni to Purcell, March 3, 1851; *Souvenir Golden Jubilee, St. Francis Seraph Parish* (Cincinnati, 1909), AAC; John Capistrano Sojer to Purcell, October 9, 1857; Spalding to Purcell, October 24, 1857, AUND; White, "Religion and Community," 237.

27. *Catholic Telegraph,* September 18, 1867; June 12, September 2, December 18, 1873; March 18, 1875; August 25, September 1, 15, 1892; October 26, 1899; October 7, 1909; October 11, 1917; letter on St. Stanislaus Parish, Cincinnati [n.d., before 1920], AAC. By the end of Purcell's episcopate in 1883 the Franciscans had charge in Cincinnati of St. John Baptist Church, St. Bonaventure Church, St. Francis gymnasium and college, which was later renamed St. Francis seminary, St. Francis Church and monastery, St. George Church, Mt. Alverno protectory near Cincinnati, St. Clement Church and monastery in St. Bernard, and St. Stephen Church in Hamilton, Ohio. German Catholics of the west end, under the supervision of Otto Jair, also constructed St. Henry Church in 1873. They built a combination church, school, and parsonage. Because of the German influx to Middletown the Franciscans helped build St. Boniface Church in 1872. Ten years later the invocation was changed to St. John the Baptist. With the growth of the German population in the southern and southwestern part of Hamilton, the German Catholic families in the community began planning for their own church closer to their residence. The Franciscan Nicholas Waechter, pastor of St. Stephen's, helped direct the effort. The Franciscans established St. Joseph parish, the second German-speaking congregation in Hamilton, out of St. Stephen's in 1867.

28. John Doherty to Purcell, April 8, 1844, AAC; White, "Religion and Community," 235, 285.

29. Blanc's quote in Deye, "Archbishop John Baptist Purcell," 283; *Catholic Telegraph,* July 4, October 10, November 21, 28, December 12, 19, 1840; October 9, 16, November 6, December 11, 1841; January 13, February 17, 1844; October 16, 1858; April 14, 1867; White, "Religion and Community," 235, 285; "Commemorating a Century of Nocturnal Adoration and the Work of the Sisters of the Precious Blood in America, 1844–1944" (1944); *Souvenir Golden Jubilee, Holy Trinity Congregation* (Coldwater, Ohio, 1918); *Centenary Celebration: St. Charles Seminary Motherhouse and Major Seminary of the American Province, 1861–1961* (Cincinnati, 1961), AAC; *Clerus Cincinnatensis, A History of Clergy and Parishes of the Archdiocese of Cincinnati 1821–1996* (Cincinnati, 1996), 105–8.

30. *Catholic Telegraph,* June 1, 22, August 10, 24, 31, September 7, 1848.

31. O'Connor to Purcell, September 17, 1845, AUND; *Catholic Telegraph,* January 6, 1844; January 7, March 4, 11, 25, April 8, 1847; August 10, 24, 31, September 7, December 21, 1848; February 23, 1850; May 22, 1852; January 15, 1853.

32. *Souvenir Golden Jubilee, St. Patrick's* (Cincinnati, 1900); *Souvenir Ruby Jubilee, Blessed Sacrament Parish* (Cincinnati, 1914), AAC; *Catholic Telegraph,* May 4, June 29, November 30, 1850; September 8, 1870; July 3, 1873; May 14, August 7, 1874; July 4, 1918; White, "Religion and Community," 38. In 1881 St. Patrick Church was demolished. The encroachment of the railroads had made the further maintenance of the parish impossible.

33. Dolan, *The American Catholic Experience* 164–69, 172; as quoted in White, "Religion and Community," 214–15.

34. *Catholic Telegraph,* October 22, 1853; April 8, 1854; February 24, 1855; June 12, 1890; March 24, 1910; Mary Ellen Evans, *The Spirit is Mercy: The Sisters of Mercy in the Archdiocese of Cincinnati, 1858–1958* (Westminster, Md., 1959), 79; White, "Religion and Community," 174. By the mid-1850s the German-speaking Ursuline Sisters conducted free and pay schools in the basement of St. Augustine Church.

35. Quoted in *Character Glimpses of Most Reverend William Henry Elder, D.D.* (Ratisbon, Germany, 1911), 107–8; *Catholic Telegraph,* March 22, 1883; June 12, 1890.

36. *Souvenir Golden Jubilee, Holy Angels' Parish* (Cincinnati, 1909), AAC; *Catholic Telegraph,* July 17, November 27, 1852; March 5, April 16, May 7, 1859; August 25, 1860; May 11, November 23, 1861; June 3, 1868; January 31, May 19, 1878; March 17, 1892.

37. *Catholic Telegraph,* July 4, October 10, November 21, 28, December 12, 19, 1840; June 5, July 17, 31, October 9, 16, November 6, December 11, 1841, June 11, 1842; for Purcell's reports on these diocesan visitations see *Catholic Telegraph,* May 4, June 1, 15, 22, 29, July 13, 20, 27, August 10, 31, September 14, October 26, November 30, 1844; May 14, June 18, July 2, 16, 30, August 6, September 24, October 29, November 12, 1846; August 3, 24, September 14, 21, 28, October 5, 1848; June 29, August 3, September 28, October 19, 1850; Deye, "Archbishop John Baptist Purcell," 235–36, 429.

38. *Catholic Telegraph,* October 31, December 19, 1840; Deye, "Archbishop John Baptist Purcell," 219–20. Jean Baptist Lamy worked at Sapp's Settlement (near Danville) and Joseph Machebeuf at Tiffin.

39. Navarron to Purcell, November 27, 1839; February 8, 1850; J. N. Thisse to Purcell, February 6, June 26, 1863; *Annals of St. Michael's Parish in Loramie, 1838–1903* (Sidney, Ohio, 1903); *100th Anniversary St. Louis Church, 1892–1992* (North Star, Ohio, 1992); Oscar H. Seger, *History of St. Denis Parish Versailles, Ohio, 1839–1989* (Versailles, Ohio, 1989), 12, AAC; *Catholic Telegraph,* July 17, 1841; *Clerus Cincinnatensis,* 105–8.

40. Thomas Blake to Purcell, December 19, 1852; *Souvenir Golden Jubilee, St. Raphael Church* (Springfield, 1899); *History of the Parish, St. Joseph Church* (Dayton, 1965); *Centennial St. Joseph Church, 1883–1983* (Springfield, Ohio, 1983); *Souvenir, St. Mary's Church* (Marion, 1898); *Saint Mary Church* (Urbana, Ohio, [date?]), AAC; *Clerus Cincinnatensis,* 106–7; *Catholic Telegraph,* July 22, 1847; January 18, 1849; December 14, 1850; November 6, 1852; June 4, 1853; June 7, August 30, 1856; April 10, October 2, 1858; April 30, 1859; October 6, 1860; August 24, 1861; October 1, 1862; October 30, 1867; October 26, 1909. From Emmanuel Church Henry D. Juncker visited the increasing German population at Springfield in Clark County. In 1848 land was purchased for a church, and in the following year St. Raphael parish was organized. To accommodate the increasing German population in the eastern portion of Dayton, St. Mary parish, the second German-speaking congregation in the area, was organized in 1859 and immediately a combination church, school, and parsonage was started. That same year another German-speaking parish, Holy Trinity's, was organized in the eastern section of the city. In the 1850s, under the direction of Father Grogan, St. Mary Church was built at Urbana in Champaign County to accommodate the many Irish immigrants living there who worked in the construction of the railroads.

41. Hallinan to Purcell, May 31, 1847, AUND; J. P. Cahill to Purcell, January 22, 1846; *St. Columbkille Church, Faith Journey, 1866–1991* (Wilmington, Ohio, 1991); *Diamond Jubilee Holy Trinity Church, 1861–1936* (Dayton, 1936), AAC; *U.S. Catholic Miscellany* 5, 231; *Clerus Cincinnatensis,* 105–8; *Catholic Telegraph,* April 3, 1845; March 19, 1846; July 27, 1848; December 6, 1849; November 16, 1850; December 10, 1853; May 26, 1869; September 27, 1894; August 8, 1918; July 22, 1955; November 11, 1960. In 1865 St. Peter's was changed to St. Michael's, *Catholic Telegraph,* January 18, 1865. With the growth of Catholicity in Hamilton, Ohio, the English-speaking members of the St. Stephen Church saw the need for a second parish. They sold St. Stephen's to the German Catholics and

purchased the St. Matthew Episcopal Church on Front and Court Streets, renaming it St. Mary Church. Dedicated in July 1848, St. Mary's became the second oldest parish in Hamilton. The parish included Catholics of German, French, and Irish extraction.

42. *Catholic Telegraph,* February 20, 1858.

43. *St. Brigid Parish Sesquicentennial, 1849–1999* (Xenia, Ohio, 1999), AAC; *Catholic Telegraph,* December 19, 1840; October 4, 1849; Deye, "Archbishop John Baptist Purcell," 260–64.

44. *Catholic Telegraph,* December 19, 1840; October 4, 1849; September 6, 1856; July 11, 1857; February 20, 1858; Deye, "Archbishop John Baptist Purcell," 260–64, 419; White, "Religion and Community," 187.

45. Deye, "Archbishop John Baptist Purcell," 378–79; quoted in Dolan, *The American Catholic Experience,* 296; for an analysis of this dispute see Arthur M. Schlesinger, Jr., *Orestes A. Brownson* (New York, 1939), 208–18.

46. Purcell to Blanc, July 13, 1854; August 20, 1854, AUND, VI-1-h; *Catholic Telegraph,* July 15, 22, 29, August 12, 19, September 2, 1854; January 10, 1857; Deye, "Archbishop John Baptist Purcell," 379–80.

47. *Catholic Telegraph,* August 20, 1853; August 11, 19, 1854; March 20, 1858; Deye, "Archbishop John Baptist Purcell," 386–87; O'Brien, *Public Catholicism,* 42.

48. *Catholic Telegraph,* July 17, August 21, October 2, 1852; October 14, 21, 1854.

49. Quoted in Deye, "Archbishop John Baptist Purcell," 384–85; F. P. Kenrick to Purcell, December 18, 1852; Rappe to Purcell, January 3, 1853; St. Palais to Purcell, January 4, 1853, AUND.

50. Purcell, "Journal," 253; *Catholic Telegraph,* October 10, 1840; White, "Religion and Community," 210–15; Patrick Carey, "The Laity's Understanding of the Trustee System, 1785–1855," *Catholic Historical Review* 64 (July 1978): 357; Alfred G. Stritch, "Trusteeism in the Old Northwest," *The Catholic Historical Review* 30 (July 1944): 157; Dolan, *The American Catholic Experience,* 189.

51. *Catholic Telegraph,* February 3, 1844; October 6, 1892; John H. Lamott, *History of the Archdiocese of Cincinnati, 1821–1921* (Cincinnati, 1921), 315; White, "Religion and Community," 211.

52. *Catholic Telegraph,* February 3, 1844; October 6, 1892; *Wahrheitsfreund,* February 1, 1844; quoted in White, "Religion and Community," 218–21; Stritch, "Trusteeism in the Old Northwest," 158.

53. *Catholic Telegraph,* July 6, 1844; Deye, "Archbishop John Baptist Purcell," 285; White, "Religion and Community," 220–21. As a consequence of the controversy over church property, the German Catholic Congregation of Cincinnati went back to its former name of German Catholic Cemetery Association. In January 1845 it was changed again to St. Peter's Cemetery Association.

54. Quoted in Deye, "Archbishop John Baptist Purcell," 233–34.

55. Quoted in ibid., 289, 291.

56. Purcell to Blanc, February 19, 1850; Borgess to Purcell, March 26, 1850, AUND, V-5-m; *Catholic Telegraph,* February 9, 1850; White, "Religion and Community," 177, 223–24.

57. White, "Religion and Community," 223–24. In 1849 German Catholics bought land in St. Bernard in the hills north of the city, and formed St. John Cemetery. It was estimated that between 6,000 and 10,000 Germans were at the dedication. In 1873 they also purchased land, originally used as a dairy farm, on Ross Avenue for St. Mary Cemetery in St. Bernard. About this time St. Francis de Sales parish opened Calvary Cemetery on Duck Creek road as its parochial cemetery.

Chapter 5

1. *Catholic Telegraph,* February 27, 1835.

2. John B. Purcell, "Journal 1833–1836," *The Catholic Historical Review* 5 (July, 1919): 243–51; *Catholic Telegraph,* August 8, 15, 1834; July 30, 1885; January 6, 1898.

3. Quoted in James Hennesey, *American Catholics: A History of the Roman Catholic Community in the United States* (New York, 1981), 119–21; Samuel F. B. Morse, *Foreign Conspiracy* (New York, 1841); Lyman Beecher, *Plea for the West* (Cincinnati, 1835); *Cincinnati Gazette,* April 13, 1835; Philip Gleason, *Keeping the Faith: American Catholicism Past and Present* (Notre Dame, Ind., 1987), 157–61; Mary J. Oates, *The Catholic Philanthropic Tradition in America* (Bloomington, Ind., 1995), 4.

4. *Catholic Telegraph,* February 25, September 15, 1836; *Cincinnati Gazette,* April 13, 1835; Beecher's quote in Hennesey, *American Catholics,* 119–21; Alfred G. Stritch, "Political Nativism in Cincinnati, 1830–60," *Records* of American Catholic Historical Society 48 (September 1937): 247; Purcell's quote in Anthony H. Deye, "Archbishop John Baptist Purcell, Pre–Civil War Years" (Ph.D. diss., University of Notre Dame, 1959), 142, 157–58.

5. *Catholic Telegraph,* October 20, December 22, 1836; *Cincinnati Gazette,* October 8, 17, 1836.

6. *Catholic Telegraph,* December 22, 1836; Alexander Campbell and Rt. Rev. John B. Purcell, *A Debate on the Roman Catholic Religion* (Cincinnati, 1883), 19, 32, 189, 193, 235, 243, 284. In 1852 the Baptist Church became St. Thomas Catholic Church.

7. *Cincinnati Philanthropist,* February 3, 1837.

8. Campbell and Purcell, *A Debate on the Roman Catholic Religion,* 23, 171, 181, 186, 338, 341–44; the seven "Points at Issue" are listed in Campbell and Purcell, *Debate,* v–viii.

9. *Catholic Telegraph,* March 2, 1837; August 13, 1885; Sacred Congregation to Purcell, August 8, 1837, AUND.

10. England to Purcell, July 1, 1837, AUND, II-4-f; *Catholic Telegraph,* March 2, 1837.

11. *Annals of St. Michael's Parish in Loramie, 1838–1903* (Sidney, Ohio, 1903), AAC; Deye, "Archbishop John Baptist Purcell," 200, 305.

12. Deye, "Archbishop John Baptist Purcell," 200.

13. Purcell to Ramsay, November 5, 1836, AAC; *Catholic Telegraph,* June 26, July 3, 1835.

14. *Catholic Telegraph,* June 26, 1845; August 2, 1849; August 31, 1850; July 1, 1854; Ray Allen Billington, *The Protestant Crusade* (New York, 1938), 262–321; Robert Frederick Trisco, *The Holy See and the Nascent Church in the Middle Western United States, 1826–1850* (Rome, 1962), 18.

15. *Dedication St. James Church* (Cincinnati, 1940), AAC; *Catholic Telegraph,* September 2, 1847; August 25, 1855; April 2, 1891; May 5, 1892; Trisco, *The Holy See and the Nascent Church in the Middle Western United States, 1826–1850,* 18–19.

16. *Catholic Telegraph,* November 26, 1853; Hugh J. Nolan, *The Most Reverend Francis Kenrick, Third Bishop of Philadelphia, 1830–1851* (Washington, D.C., 1948), 288–342.

17. Billington, *The Protestant Crusade,* 300–303; quoted in James F. Connelly, *The Visit of Archbishop Gaetano Bedini to the United States, June, 1853–February, 1854* (Rome, 1960), 12–13.

18. Purcell to Blanc, December 30, 1853, AUND; *Catholic Telegraph,* December 31, 1853; Joseph M. White, "Religion and Community: Cincinnati Germans 1814–1870" (Ph.D. diss., University of Notre Dame, 1980), 346–47; Connelly, *The Visit of Archbishop Gaetano Bedini to the United States,* 98–101.

19. White, "Religion and Community," 345–48; Connelly, *The Visit of Archbishop Gaetano Bedini to the United States,* 101–2.

20. Quoted in Deye, "Archbishop John Baptist Purcell," 374; Purcell to Blanc, December 30, 1853; August 20, 1854, AUND; *Catholic Telegraph,* January 7, 1854.

21. Purcell to Blanc, January 21, March 20, 1854, AUND, VI-1-g; *Catholic Telegraph,* January 21, 28, 1854.

22. Quoted in Deye, "Archbishop John Baptist Purcell," 189, 191–92; Hughes to Purcell, June 27, 1837, AUND; James W. Sanders, *The Education of an Urban Minority: Catholics in Chicago, 1833–1965* (New York, 1977), 18–19.

23. Quoted in Deye, "Archbishop John Baptist Purcell," 193–98.

24. Quoted in ibid., 197–98, 239–40; Purcell to Blanc, October 8, 1839, AUND; *Catholic Telegraph,* January 4, 1840. The latter was the first issue that Edward Purcell's name appeared as editor. Reports on the bishop's lectures were printed in the *Catholic Telegraph,* January 18, 25, February 1, 8, 15, 22, 29, March 7, 14, 28, April 4, 11, 18, May 2, July 18, September 19, 26, October 3, 10, 17, 24, 31, 1840; F. Michael Perko, *A Time to Favor Zion: The Ecology of Religion and School Development on the Urban Frontier, Cincinnati, 1830–1870* (Chicago, 1988), 124.

25. *Catholic Telegraph,* September 5, December 12, 1840; May 4, 1844; quoted in Deye, "Archbishop John Baptist Purcell," 243–46, 442; Louis A., Rita M., and David A. Hoying, *Pilgrims All: A History of Saint Augustine Parish, Minster, Ohio, 1832–1982* (Minster, Ohio, 1982), 67–68, 92–93; Dolan, *The American Catholic Experience,* 264; Timothy Walch, *Parish School: American Catholic Parochial Education from Colonial Times to the Present* (New York, 1996), 34.

26. *Catholic Telegraph,* April 15, 1847; "Notes of the Synod of the Diocese of Cincinnati December 7th, 8th, & 9th, 1848," AAC; Perko, *A Time to Favor Zion,* 127.

27. Perko, *A Time to Favor Zion,* 127; Robert S. Michaelsen, *Piety in the Public School* (New York, 1970), 91.

28. *Catholic Telegraph,* February 4, September 23, 1843; May 4, 1844; September 30, November 11, 1847; December 21, 1850; February 8, November 11, 1851; December 4, 1852; November 26, 1853; July 9, 1858; September 10, 1859; July 9, 1862; Edward A. Connaughton, *A History of Educational Legislation and Administration in the Archdiocese of Cincinnati* (Washington D.C., 1946), 39–40; Perko, *A Time to Favor Zion,* 125–26, 139–40.

29. *Catholic Telegraph,* November 13, 1852; Perko, *A Time to Favor Zion,* 129–36;

30. Pastoral Letter of the First Provincial Council of Cincinnati to the Clergy and Laity, 1855, AAC; Dolan, *The American Catholic Experience,* 264–65, 282; White, "Religion and Community," 298; O'Brien, *Public Catholicism,* 49, 103; Walch, *Parish School,* 50; Carol K. Coburn and Martha Smith, *Spirited Lives: How Nuns Shaped Catholic Culture and American Life, 1836–1920* (Chapel Hill, N.C., 1999), 136.

31. *Catholic Telegraph,* September 28, 1848; February 16, 1856; December 3, 1861; August 24, 1871; Dolan, *The American Catholic Experience,* 264, 282; White, "Religion and Community," 292–93; Charles Cist, *Cincinnati in 1841* (Cincinnati, 1851), 58–59; Connaughton, *A History of Educational Legislation and Administration in the Archdiocese of Cincinnati,* 27; Michaelsen, *Piety in the Public School,* 93.

32. Purcell to Blanc, March 10, 22, 1853, AUND, VI-1-e; *Catholic Telegraph,* January 22, 29, February 19, 26, March 5, 12, 1853; Perko, *A Time to Favor Zion,* 141; White, "Religion and Community," 352–53.

33. *Catholic Telegraph,* June 22, 1850; February 5, 19, 26, 1853; Perko, *A Time to Favor Zion,* 140–41; Gleason, *Keeping the Faith,* 122; Leslie Woodcock Tentler, *Seasons of Grace: A History of the Catholic Archdiocese of Detroit* (Detroit, Mich., 1990), 87–88.

34. *Catholic Telegraph,* March 26, 1853; Connaughton, *A History of Educational Legislation and Administration in the Archdiocese of Cincinnati,* 41.

35. Tentler, *Seasons of Grace,* 88–89; *Catholic Telegraph,* March 26, 1853.

36. Perko, *A Time to Favor Zion,* 142–43, 147; *Catholic Telegraph,* April 9, 30, 1853; Perko writes: "Purcell had clearly misread the situation, overstepped his limits, and unwittingly set the ideological conflict ablaze."

37. Perko, *A Time to Favor Zion,* 147–49; *Western Christian Advocate,* April 13, July 6, 1853; *Catholic Telegraph,* April 9, 1853; September 29, 1855.

38. Quoted in Deye, "Archbishop John Baptist Purcell," 367, 375.

39. *Catholic Telegraph,* September 29, 1855; October 15, 1859; October 28, 1863; Daniel Hurley, *Cincinnati, the Queen City* (Cincinnati, 1982), 46.

40. *Catholic Telegraph,* April 14, May 19, 1855; April 13, 1861; Connaughton, *A History of Educational Legislation and Administration in the Archdiocese of Cincinnati,* 46, 77; Joseph M. White, *The Diocesan Seminary in the United States: A History from the 1780s to the Present* (Notre Dame, Indiana, 1989), 68; Michaelsen, *Piety in the Public School,* 91.

41. *Catholic Telegraph,* July 2, 1853; May 26, 1855; September 5, 1857; June 5, 1858; March 12, 29, 1859; April 24, May 8, 1858; August 16, 1865; May 23, 1889; Connaughton, *A History of Educational Legislation and Administration in the Archdiocese of Cincinnati,* 56, 64; Dolan, *The American Catholic Experience,* 268–69; White, "Religion and Community," 295–98.

42. Dolan, *The American Catholic Experience,* 268–69; Thomas W. Spalding, *The Premier See: A History of the Archdiocese of Baltimore, 1789–1994* (Baltimore, Md., 1989), 191; White, "Religion and Community," 295–98.

43. *Catholic Telegraph,* June 5, 1858; March 12, September 17, 1859; April 13, 27, May 4, 11, 1861; May 23, 1889.

44. *Annals of St. Michael's Parish in Loramie, 1838–1903* (Sidney, Ohio, 1903), AAC; Coveney to Purcell, September 22, 1868, AUND; *Catholic Telegraph,* February 1, 1872; Connaughton, *A History of Educational Legislation and Administration in the Archdiocese of Cincinnati,* 91; Dolan, *The American Catholic Experience,* 270.

45. *Catholic Telegraph,* November 23, 1837; May 22, March 12, 1859; October 20, 1860; Connaughton, *A History of Educational Legislation and Administration in the Archdiocese of Cincinnati,* 63, 80–87; White, "Religion and Community," 318, 325.

46. *Catholic Telegraph,* May 27, June 27, July 22, August 12, 1863; Connaughton, *A History of Educational Legislation and Administration in the Archdiocese of Cincinnati,* 80–87; Tentler, *Seasons of Grace,* 92; White, "Religion and Community," 318, 325. The first informal synod was held in Cincinnati in November 1837.

47. Connaughton, *A History of Educational Legislation and Administration in the Archdiocese of Cincinnati,* 62–63.

48. *Catholic Telegraph,* July 2, 1859; quoted in White, "Religion and Community," 309–14.

49. *Catholic Telegraph,* December 21, 1864; May 15, 1867; White, "Religion and Community," 315–17.

50. White, "Religion and Community," 325–27.

51. *Catholic Telegraph,* September 1, 14, 1869; White, "Religion and Community," 328–29; Perko, *A Time to Favor Zion,* 165–70.

52. Michaelsen, *Piety in the Public School,* 89–97; Perko, *A Time to Favor Zion,* 154–91.

53. *Catholic Telegraph,* January 12, 1871; Lamott, *Archdiocese,* 279–280.

54. *Catholic Telegraph,* June 9, August 25, 1870; James Hennesey, S.J., *The First Council of the Vatican: The American Experience* (New York, 1963), 100, 299, 303; Deye, "Archbishop John Baptist Purcell," 378–80, 432–33; James L. Heft, "From the Pope to the Bishops: Episcopal Authority from Vatican I to Vatican II" in *The Papacy and the Church in the United States,* ed. Bernard Cooke (New York, 1989), 59. In the 1860s Purcell went to Europe in 1861, 1862, 1867, and 1869.

55. Quoted in Mary Agnes McCann, "Archbishop Purcell and the Archdiocese of Cincinnati" (Ph.D. diss., Catholic University of America, 1918), 94; Goold's quote in Hennesey, *The First Council of the Vatican,* 239.

56. Quoted in Hennesey, *The First Council of the Vatican,* 239–41.

57. New York *Herald,* August 11, 1870; Hennesey, *The First Council of the Vatican,* 300–302; quoted in William L. Portier, "Church Unity and National Traditions: The Challenge of the Modern Papacy, 1682–1870" in *Papacy and the Church,* ed. Cooke, 42.

58. *Catholic Telegraph,* August 18, 25, September 1, 1870.

59. Ibid., August 25, 1870; Hennesey, *The First Council of the Vatican,* 308.

60. *Catholic Telegraph,* February 16, 1871; Barnabò to Purcell, November 11, 1870; Pius IX to Purcell, Rome, January 11, 1871, AUND.

Chapter 6

1. Mary J. Oates, *The Catholic Philanthropic Tradition in America* (Bloomington, Ind., 1995), 39.

2. Sister Mary Denis Maher, *To Bind Up the Wounds: Catholic Sister Nurses in the U.S. Civil War* (Baton Rouge, La., 1999), 19; *Catholic Telegraph,* March 17, 1855.

3. Oates, *The Catholic Philanthropic Tradition in America,* 12, 20; *Catholic Telegraph,* March 17, 1855.

4. "A Short History of the Sisters of Notre Dame de Namur in the Archdiocese of Cincinnati," n.d., AAC.

5. *Annals of St. Michael's Parish in Loramie, 1838–1903* (Sidney, Ohio, 1903), AAC.

6. Purcell's 1874 address quoted in Joan Bland, *Hibernian Crusade: The Story of the Catholic Total Abstinence Union of America* (Washington, D.C., 1951), 90; Purcell to Verhaegen, August 17, 1840, Xavier University Archives; *Catholic Telegraph,* April 18, August 8, 1840; February 27, 1841; March 20, July 3, 1852; March 17, 1855; Anthony H. Deye, "Archbishop John Baptist Purcell, Pre–Civil War Years" (Ph.D. diss., University of Notre Dame, 1959), 249; Hugh J. Nolan, *The Most Reverend Francis Kenrick, Third Bishop of Philadelphia, 1830–1851* (Washington, D.C., 1948), 210; Jay P. Dolan, *The American Catholic Experience: A History from Colonial Times to the Present* (New York, 1985), 326.

7. Quoted in Deye, "Archbishop John Baptist Purcell," 250–53; Nolan, *The Most Reverend Francis Kenrick,* 410–14; *Catholic Telegraph,* December 19, 1840; July 31, September 11, 1841; September 23, 1847.

8. *Emmanuel Catholic Church Sesquicentennial History, 1837–1987* (Dayton, 1987), AAC; Machebeuf to Purcell, June 3, 1842, AUND.

9. Christopher J. Kauffman, *Ministry and Meaning: A Religious History of Catholic Health Care in the United States* (New York, 1995), 61; *Catholic Telegraph,* June 14, 28, July 5, 12, 1849.

10. *Catholic Telegraph,* July 5, 1849; Rappe to Purcell, July 6, 1849, AUND; Judith Metz, S.C., "The Sisters of Charity in Cincinnati 1829–1852," *Vincentian Heritage* 17 (1996): 216–17.

11. Kauffman, *Ministry and Meaning,* 61–62; *Catholic Telegraph,* July 5, 1849.

12. *Catholic Telegraph,* May 11, 1848.

13. Ibid., January 17, November 21, 1857.

14. Maher, *To Bind Up the Wounds,* 19; quoted in Mary Ewens, *The Role of the Nun in Nineteenth Century America* (New York, 1978), 141–42, 199. "Evidence indicates," Ewens writes, that "all fair-minded people" in the nineteenth century "who came into intimate contact with sisters and their works praised them."

15. Metz, "Sisters of Charity," 231–41; Ewens, *The Role of the Nun in Nineteenth Century America,* 105.

16. Quoted in Judith Metz, S.C., "150 Years of Caring: The Sisters of Charity in Cincinnati," *The Cincinnati Historical Society Bulletin* 37 (Cincinnati, 1979): 157–58, 163; Metz, "Sisters of Charity," 231–41; Ewens, *The Role of the Nun in Nineteenth Century America,* 128–30, 140; *Catholic Telegraph,* October 31, 1857; February 8, 1894; July 15, 1909.

17. Metz, "150 Years of Caring," 158–61.

18. Ibid.; Dolan, *The American Catholic Experience,* 250; Frederick Rudolph, *The American College and University: A History* (New York, 1965), 310.

19. Articles of Constitution in *Catholic Telegraph,* March 20, 1852; July 9, 1931; Metz, "150 Years of Caring," 158.

20. Judith Metz, S.C. and Virginia Wiltse, *Sister Margaret Cecilia George: A Biography* (Mount St. Joseph, Ohio, 1989), 84–85; Ewens, *The Role of the Nun in Nineteenth Century America,* 98, 120, 123–24, 134.

21. *Catholic Telegraph,* June 8, 1861; December 16, 1897; December 16, 1909; Metz, "150 Years of Caring," 159–61, 163; Ewens, *The Role of the Nun in Nineteenth Century America,* 103, 274; Oates, *The Catholic Philanthropic Tradition in America,* 15.

22. Metz, "150 Years of Caring," 88–90; *The Sisters of Charity in Ohio: In Commemoration of the Sesquicentennial of Ohio's Statehood, 1803–1953* (Cincinnati, 1953), 6; *Catholic Telegraph,* July 15, 1909.

23. Brassac to Purcell, February 22, March 10 and July 12, 1840, AAC; Nicholas Joseph, Bishop of Namur, to Vicar-General of Cincinnati, April 24, 1840, AUND; *Catholic Almanac* (1840): 95, 98.

24. *Catholic Telegraph,* January 16, 1841; Dehesselle to Purcell, August 24, 1840; Rappe to Purcell, February 27, 1840, AUND; Edward A Connaughton, "A History of Educational Legislation and Administration in the Archdiocese of Cincinnati" (Ph.D. diss., Catholic University of America, 1946), 22; Eileen Mary Brewer, *Nuns and the Education of American Catholic Women, 1860–1920* (Chicago, 1987), 43; Ewens, *The Role of the Nun in Nineteenth Century America,* 98, 120, 123–24, 134.

25. *Catholic Telegraph,* January 16, 1841; December 9, 1886; October 23, 1890; June 7, July 5, 1894; July 5, 1894; July 9, 1931; Dehesselle to Purcell, August 24, 1840; Rappe to Purcell, February 27, 1840, AUND; Connaughton, "A History of Educational Legislation and Administration in the Archdiocese of Cincinnati," 22; Joseph M. White, "Religion and Community: Cincinnati Germans 1814–1870" (Ph.D. diss., University of Notre Dame, 1980), 302.

26. *Catholic Telegraph,* November 1, 1900.

27. Machebeuf to Purcell, September 5, 1844; Machebeuf to Purcell, April 29, 1845, AUND; George C. Stewart, Jr., *Marvels of Charity: History of American Sisters and Nuns* (Huntington, Ind., 1994), 143; *Catholic Telegraph,* May 23, 1895; July 9, 1931.

28. *Catholic Telegraph,* August 31, 1837; October 9, 1841; December 14, 1848; November 13, 1852; July 30, 1853; January 1, 1859; May 23, 1895; Machebeuf to Purcell, June 3, 1845, AUND; *Illustrated History of St. Mary's Church, Hillsboro* (Ohio, 1898); *Fifty Years in Brown County Convent* (Cincinnati, 1895), AAC. By 1837 the parishes of St. Patrick and St. Mary out of St. Martin's had been established at Fayetteville and Arnheim respectively. St. Martin's became the mother parish of the parishes in Clermont, Brown, Highland, and Warren Counties. When anti-Catholic bigots destroyed the Ursuline Convent at Charleston, South Carolina, in 1847 ten members of the community came to Cincinnati and operated a school on Bank Street until 1855 when the school closed. A few of the sisters then joined the Ursulines of Brown County.

29. *Catholic Telegraph,* August 16, 1849; July 13, 27, 1850.

30. Ibid., September 4, 1835; August 21, 1845; June 8, 1848; August 16, 1849; July 13, 27, 1850.

31. Ibid., July 19, 1849; Benjamin J. Blied, *Catholics and the Civil War* (Milwaukee, 1945), 126; Christopher J. Kauffman, *Education and Transformation: Marianist Ministries in America since 1849* (New York, 1999), 53.

32. *A Hundred Years of Educational Foundations by the Brothers of Mary in America, 1849–1959* (Dayton, 1959); *Emmanuel Catholic Church Sesquicentennial History, 1837–1987* (Dayton, 1987), AAC; *Catholic Telegraph,* June 10, 1909; Deye, "Archbishop John Baptist Purcell," 407; Meyers to Purcell, March 23, 1869, AUND; Kauffman, *Education and Transformation,* 56–58, 63. In the fall of 1920 St. Mary's college became known as the University of Dayton.

33. *A Hundred Years . . . by the Brothers of Mary,* AAC; Kauffman, *Education and Transformation,* 65; *Catholic Telegraph,* July 9, 1931.

34. *Mount Alverno Centennial, 1870–1970,* Cincinnati, 1970, AAC; *Catholic Telegraph,* October 28, 1926; July 9, 1931.

35. "The Sisters of the Good Shepherd Come to the United States," [n.d.], AAC; *Catholic Telegraph,* March 7, 1889; April 9, 1891; July 9, 1931; Margaret R. King, *Memoirs of the Life of Mrs. Sarah Peter* (Cincinnati, 1889), 2: 344–46; *Souvenir Album of American Cities: Catholic Churches of Cincinnati and Hamilton County Edition* (Cincinnati, 1896); M. J. Spalding, *Sketches of the Life, Times and Character of the Rt. Rev. Benedict Joseph Flaget, First Bishop of Louisville* (Louisville, 1852), 336–39; Leslie Woodcock Tentler, *Seasons of Grace: A History of the Catholic Archdiocese of Detroit* (Detroit, Mich., 1990), 108.

36. Quoted in Deye, "Archbishop John Baptist Purcell," 414–15; *Catholic Telegraph,* August 28, November 20, 1858; January 8, 1859; October 21, 1909; October 11, 1934; Mary Ellen Evans, *The Spirit Is Mercy* (Westminster, Maryland, 1959), 60, 65, 70, 79–81; Ewens, *The Role of the Nun in Nineteenth Century America,* 102; Brewer, *Nuns and Education of Catholic Women,* 27.

37. Evans, *Sisters of Mercy,* 82.

38. Ibid., 82, 101–2; Brewer, *Nuns and Education of Catholic Women,* 27.

39. *Activities of a Century in the United States: The Sisters of the Poor of St. Francis, 1858–1958* (Cincinnati, 1958, AAC); Stewart, Jr., *Marvels of Charity,* 159; *Catholic Telegraph,* September 11, 1858; October 5, 1911; October 28, 1926; October 11, 1934; June 30, 1950. While on West Fourth Street the sisters attended to patients in their ten-bed building.

40. Ewens, *The Role of the Nun in Nineteenth Century America,* 274; *Catholic Telegraph,* August 10, 1905; July 9, 1931.

41. *Catholic Telegraph,* August 10, 1905; October 28, 1926; July 9, 1931; February 16, 1951. In 1876 the Sisters of the Sacred Heart bought the Neff mansion in Clifton that became their home in Cincinnati.

42. Carol K. Coburn and Martha Smith, *Spirited Lives: How Nuns Shaped Catholic Culture and American Life, 1836–1920* (Chapel Hill, N.C., 1999), 9, 11, 129–30; Maher, *To Bind Up the Wounds,* 19; *Catholic Telegraph,* August 12, 1863.

43. Quoted in Deye, "Archbishop John Baptist Purcell," 416; *Catholic Telegraph,* August 12, 1863; Joseph H. Lackner, S.M., "The Foundation of St. Ann's Parish, 1866–1870: The African American Experience in Cincinnati," *U.S. Catholic Historian* 14 (Spring 1996): 17.

44. *Catholic Telegraph,* March 7, 14, 1840; April 8, 1863; Deye, "Archbishop John Baptist Purcell," 210, 254; Lackner, "The Foundation of St. Ann's Parish," 17.

45. *Catholic Telegraph,* September 11, 1841; January 28, 1836; December 17, 1842; Purcell to Blanc, April 2, 1841; September 9, 1841; Wood to Purcell, November 2, 1841; Purcell referred to Blanc as his "best friend." He pointed out to him that he had "had benefactors, fond relatives—kind, perhaps esteeming acquaintances,—but never, that I know of—a friend." Purcell's letter to Eccleston quoted in Deye, "Archbishop John Baptist Purcell," 256. Writing to Archbishop Eccleston in 1842 Purcell posed the question: "Can anything be done more effectually [*sic*] to provide for the religious instruction and general amelioration of the condition of the colored population of the U[nited] States?"

46. Purcell to Blanc, July 7, 1856; Kenrick to Purcell, November 21, 1862; Spalding to Purcell, September 27, 1861, AUND, II-5-b; *Catholic Telegraph,* December 1, 1860; January 10, 26, March 30, April 20, 1861; March 12, 1862; Clyde F. Crews, *An American Holy Land: A History of the Archdiocese of Louisville* (Wilmington, Del., 1987), 149; Stewart, Jr., *Marvels of Charity,* 144.

47. Martin Spalding to Purcell, April 21, 1861; John McCaffrey to Purcell, September 26, 1861, AUND; Blied, *Catholics and the Civil War,* 12, 18, 36, 41–43, 75, 130. Sylvester Rosecrans was named Titular Bishop of Pompeiopolis. There can be but one archbishop or bishop of a diocese. If there is an auxiliary or coadjutor bishop, he is given title to a see that once flourished, but where there are no longer any or few Catholics.

48. Rosecrans to Purcell, August 10, 1862, AUND, II-5-b; *Catholic Telegraph,* November 9, 1861; March 12, August 20, 1862; July 22, 1863.

49. Blied, *Catholics and the Civil War,* 34; *Catholic Telegraph,* October 11, 1838; on October 1, 1862, the diocesan paper criticized Lincoln for using sentences in the Emancipation Proclamation that were not "grammatically correct;" John McCaffrey to Purcell, September 26, 1861, AUND.

50. Blied, *Catholics and the Civil War,* 34; *Catholic Telegraph,* July 6, 1864; John Tracy Ellis, ed., *Documents of American Catholic History* (Wilmington, Del., 1987), 1: 378–79. On Purcell's impulsiveness see *Cincinnati Penny Post,* July extra, 1883; Rev. Richard Gilmour, "Funeral Oration on the Most Rev. John B. Purcell," 1883, AAC; Deye, "Archbishop John Baptist Purcell," 334.

51. Elder to Purcell, February 18, April 5, June 15, July 19, 1864, AUND, II-5-b; *Catholic Telegraph,* August 5, 1863; Blied, *Catholics and the Civil War,* 55–59.

52. Purcell to Odin, November 6, 1863, AUND, VI-2-g.

53. Purcell to Lincoln, October 18, 1864, AUND; *Catholic Telegraph,* September 17, 1862; quote on "Kitty Todd" cited in *Catholic Telegraph,* February 9, 1951; Blied, *Catholics and the Civil War,* 116–17;

54. Ewens, *The Role of the Nun in Nineteenth Century America,* 201, 221–22, 231, 236; Kauffman, *Ministry and Meaning,* 6; Maher, *To Bind Up the Wounds,* 2, 69–70, 72, 74, 101–3; *Catholic Telegraph,* June 8, 1861; July 15, 1909; October 11, 1934.

55. Evans, *Sisters of Mercy,* 86–87, 90–92, 99; Maher, *To Bind Up the Wounds,* 83.

56. Sr. Sophia to Purcell, March 2, 1862, AUND; . . . *The Sisters of the Poor of St. Francis, 1858–1958,* AAC; Maher, *Bind Up the Wounds,* 69–70, 81; *Catholic Telegraph,* October 11, 1934.

57. Ewens, *The Role of the Nun in Nineteenth Century America,* 201, 221–22, 231, 236; Coburn and Smith, *Spirited Lives,* 63; Maher, *To Bind Up the Wounds,* 100, 120, 148–49.

58. *Catholic Telegraph,* April 11, 18, November 14, 1866; April 9, 1891; August 30, 1906; Joseph H. Lackner, S.M., "St. Ann's Colored Church and School, Cincinnati, the Indian and Negro Collection for the United States, and Reverend Francis Xavier Weninger, S.J.," *U.S. Catholic Historian* 7 (1988): 145, 147–48; Oates, *The Catholic Philanthropic Tradition in America,* 60. In 1873 St. Ann Church moved to New Street, then to John Street in 1908.

59. Joseph M. White, *The Diocesan Seminary in the United States: A History from the 1870s to the Present* (Notre Dame, Ind., 1989), 25, 66.

60. Purcell to Timon, January 31, 1842; Timon to Purcell, February 16, July 29, August 29, 1842; Kenrick to Purcell, St. Louis, September 1, 1842, AUND; *Catholic Telegraph,* January 25, April 19, 1849; White, *The Diocesan Seminary in the United States,* 56, 67, 111; M. Edmund Hussey, *A History of the Seminaries of the Archdiocese of Cincinnati 1829–1979* (Norwood, Ohio, 1979), 15.

61. Francis Joseph Miller, "A History of the Athenaeum of Ohio 1829–1960," (Ed.D. diss., University of Cincinnati, 1964), 103; *Catholic Telegraph,* July 27, 1848; November 1, 1851; January 31, 1852; May 22, 1890; December 5, 1929; July 9, 1931; Hussey, *A History of the Seminaries of the Archdiocese of Cincinnati,* 15–16.

62. *Catholic Telegraph,* January 31, 1852; June 2, 1855; February 23, 1856; May 12, 1860; October 25, 1923; Spalding to Purcell, November 21, November 27, 1851; F. P. Kenrick to Peter Kenrick, November 24, 1851, AUND; Deye, "Archbishop John Baptist Purcell," 345–48, 397; Hussey, *A History of the Seminaries of the Archdiocese of Cincinnati,* 18.

63. Quoted in Deye, "Archbishop John Baptist Purcell," 395–98; *Catholic Telegraph,* May 26, 1855; Robert F. McNamara, *The American College in Rome, 1855–1955* (Rochester, N.Y., 1956), 3–40; James L. Heft, S.M., "From the Pope to the Bishops: Episcopal Authority from Vatican I to Vatican II" in *The Papacy and the Church in the United States,* ed. Bernard Cooke (New York, 1989), 69; Gerald P. Fogarty, *The Vatican and the American Hierarchy From 1870 to 1965* (Wilmington, Del., 1985), 26.

64. Purcell to Blanc, February 26, 1856, AUND, VI-1-j; *Catholic Telegraph,* February 23, 1856.
65. *Catholic Telegraph,* October 8, 1859; December 9, 1868; Purcell to Blanc, April 6, 1857; Pius IX to Purcell, Rome, June 14, 1858; October 19, 1859; Purcell to Lydia Potter, January 10, 1871, AUND; Deye, "Archbishop John Baptist Purcell," 400–402; McNamara, *The American College in Rome,* 836; White, *The Diocesan Seminary in the United States,* 101.
66. *Catholic Telegraph,* January 27, 1864.
67. Ibid., May 13, 1893; October 25, 1923; *Catholic Almanac* (1856): 306–7; White, *The Diocesan Seminary in the United States,* 71; Hussey, *A History of the Seminaries of the Archdiocese of Cincinnati,* 19–20; Hussey points out that the establishment of St. Mary's College remains "somewhat of a puzzle." A year earlier Purcell and his suffragan bishops had agreed to accept St. Thomas College at Bardstown as the minor seminary.
68. Quoted in Deye, "Archbishop John Baptist Purcell," 327–29; Hussey, *A History of the Seminaries of the Archdiocese of Cincinnati,* 12.
69. Quoted in Deye, "Archbishop John Baptist Purcell," 329–30; *Catholic Telegraph,* Sept. 21, 1848.
70. Deye, "Archbishop John Baptist Purcell," 331–33; Joseph A. Kehoe, "St. Joseph's College, 1871–1921," unpublished paper, 1988, 1, 31–32, AAC.
71. Mary Agnes McCann, "Archbishop Purcell and the Archdiocese of Cincinnati" (Ph.D. diss., Catholic University of America, 1918), 100–101.
72. *Catholic Telegraph,* September 15, 1855; February 20, April 25, 1858; Purcell to Blanc, February 4, 1859, AUND; Deye, "Archbishop John Baptist Purcell," 402–5.
73. Letter to Kenrick quoted in Deye, "Archbishop John Baptist Purcell," 405–6; Purcell to Blanc, December 5, 1857, AUND, VI-1-m; M. Edmund Hussey, "The 1878 Financial Failure of Archbishop Purcell," *The Cincinnati Historical Society Bulletin* 36 (Spring 1978): 13–14. The author provides the most definitive study of the 1878 financial debacle.
74. Purcell to Odin, October 16, 1863, AUND, VI-2-g; *Cincinnati Daily Enquirer,* March 2, 1879; Hussey, "The 1878 Financial Failure of Archbishop Purcell," 8–14.
75. Edward Purcell to Mother Superior, November 3, 17, 1878; Purcell to Sister Baptista, November 17, 1878, ("dull"), AAC; James H. Campbell, "New Parochialism: Change and Conflict in the Archdiocese of Cincinnati, 1878–1925 (Ph.D. diss., University of Cincinnati, 1981), 54–55; Hussey, "The 1878 Financial Failure of Archbishop Purcell," 14.
76. Quoted in Hussey, "The 1878 Financial Failure of Archbishop Purcell," 16; *Catholic Telegraph,* December 26, 1878.
77. *Catholic Telegraph,* December 26, 1878; *Cincinnati Daily Enquirer,* December 22, 27, 1878.
78. Gibbons to Purcell, December 31, 1878; Dwenger to Purcell, January 23, 1879, AAC; *Cincinnati Daily Enquirer,* December 24, 29, 1878; *Catholic Telegraph,* December 26, 1878.
79. Hussey, "The 1878 Financial Failure of Archbishop Purcell," 17–19.
80. Campbell, "New Parochialism," 58; Hussey, "The 1878 Financial Failure of Archbishop Purcell," 17–19.
81. Quoted in Hussey, "The 1878 Financial Failure of Archbishop Purcell," 19–20; *Cincinnati Daily Enquirer,* March 2, 1879; December 31, 1878; February 3, 26, 1879; May 24, 1879; May 12, 1880; Campbell, "New Parochialism," 60–61.
82. *Catholic Telegraph,* February 26, 1879; May 13, 1880.
83. Ibid., March 13, May 29, 1879; November 30, 1882; *Cincinnati Daily Enquirer,* September 11, 1879; Campbell, "New Parochialism," 62–64.
84. *Annals of St. Michael's Parish in Loramie, 1838 to 1903* (Sidney, Ohio, 1903), AAC; Purcell to Daniel Hudson, C.S.C., May 29, 1877, AUND; Hussey, "The 1878 Financial Failure of Archbishop Purcell," 24.
85. Sister M. Baptista, Notes of Archbishop Purcell's Life in Brown County, 1879, AAC; Gibbons' letter quoted in John Tracy Ellis, *The Life of James Cardinal Gibbons, Archbishop of*

Baltimore, 1834–1921 (Milwaukee, 1952), 1: 190; Hussey, "The 1878 Financial Failure of Archbishop Purcell," 24; Fogarty in *The Vatican and the American Hierarchy,* 21, points out that the bishops of the Province of Cincinnati had also submitted the *terna* of Bishops of Edward Fitzgerald of Little Rock, Bernard McQuaid of Rochester, and William G. McCloskey of Louisville.

86. *Catholic Telegraph,* January 29, 1880; Campbell, "New Parochialism," 64–67; Hussey, "The 1878 Financial Failure of Archbishop Purcell," 21.

87. Oates, *The Catholic Philanthropic Tradition in America,* 21–23, 87; Tentler, *Seasons of Grace,* 230.

PART II

Introduction

1. *Catholic Telegraph,* November 8, 1906.

2. *Catholic Directory,* 1904.

3. *Catholic Directory,* 1904, 1924; *Catholic Telegraph,* January 8, 1925. James H. Campbell, "New Parochialism: Change and Conflict in the Archdiocese of Cincinnati, 1878–1925" (Ph.D. diss., University of Cincinnati, 1981), 13, writes that Moeller "was a 'loner' preoccupied with the internal affairs of his own domain."

4. *Catholic Telegraph,* January 8, 15, 1925. As mentioned above, the remains of Fenwick, who died at Wooster, Ohio, in 1832, had been brought to Cincinnati to lie in a vault under the old cathedral. In 1848 Purcell had the bishop's remains placed beneath the altar of the new cathedral. Purcell's body rests in the cemetery of the Brown County Ursulines; Elder's in St. Joseph Cemetery, close to the mausoleum. Moeller's body is buried not far from Fenwick's, whose casket was placed at St. Joseph's on March 23, 1916, when it was removed from the vault under the cathedral.

Chapter 7

1. Elder to Gibbons, March 27, 1896, AAB; *Catholic Telegraph,* February 12, April 22, 1880. Elder was named titular bishop of Avara and coadjutor to Purcell. On the morning of his arrival in Cincinnati he celebrated Mass at the cathedral. Later in the day Elder confirmed a class of 138 children.

2. Gilmour to Elder, May 30, 1880; Elder to Purcell, January 10, 1883, AAC; quoted in James H. Campbell, "New Parochialism: Change and Conflict in the Archdiocese of Cincinnati, 1878–1925" (Ph.D. diss., University of Cincinnati, 1981), 69.

3. *Catholic Telegraph,* May 4, 1882; March 28, 1895; June 4, 1896; November 3, 1904.

4. *Catholic Telegraph,* May 4, 1882; March 28, 1895; June 4, 1896.

5. *Cincinnati Daily Enquirer,* April 19, 21, 1880; *Catholic Telegraph,* April 22, 29, 1880.

6. Purcell to Elder, October 15, 1880, AAC; *Catholic Telegraph,* May 13, August 12, 1880; January 27, 1881; *Cincinnati Enquirer,* January 23, 1881.

7. Dwenger to Elder, April 24, 1880; Elder to Callaghan, August 7, 1881; Callaghan to Elder, August 9, 1881; Elder to Gilmour, March 9, 1889, AAC; Campbell, "New Parochialism," 75–77.

8. Campbell, "New Parochialism," 77; *Catholic Telegraph,* December 1, 1881; November 23, December 7, 1882.

9. Gibbons to Elder, February 24, 1883, AAC; *Catholic Telegraph,* January 4, May 24, August 17, 1883; October 5, 1911.

10. Gilmour to Elder, April 8, 20, 1892; Copy of Address to Elder, April 4, 1882, AAC; Campbell, "New Parochialism," 79–82; *Cincinnati Commercial,* March 13, 14, April 2, 1882; *Catholic Telegraph,* May 4, 1882.

11. Elder to Francis Dutton, July 3, 1882; Elder to J. J. Callaghan, July 3, 1882; Elder to Ursula, July 3, 1882, AAC; Campbell, "New Parochialism," 83–86; *Cincinnati Commercial,* July 2, 1882.

12. Obituary Notice by Chancellor, July 5, 1883, AAC; *Catholic Telegraph,* July 12, 1883.

13. Elder's Diary, August 11, 1883; Corrigan to Elder, March 26, 1884; Elder to Callaghan, June 21, 1884; Martin L. Murphy to Elder, November 17, 1885; Goetz to Elder, November 2, 1880; December 8, 1883; January 29, 1884; Elder to Goetz, January 3, 1884, AAC; Campbell, "New Parochialism," 92; *Catholic Telegraph,* July 12, December 13, 1883.

14. Quoted in M. Edmund Hussey, "The 1878 Financial Failure of Archbishop Purcell," *The Cincinnati Historical Society Bulletin* 36, no. 1 (Spring 1978): 21, 27.

15. Hussey, "The 1878 Financial Failure of Archbishop Purcell," 27–32.

16. Ibid., 32–34; Albrinck to Elder, December 17, 1885, AAC.

17. Elder to James F. Wood, September 10, 1882; Elder to Wood, September 10, 1882, AAC; *Catholic Telegraph,* November 8, 1906; Hussey, "The 1878 Financial Failure of Archbishop Purcell," 24.

18. Casper Borgess to Elder, December 17, 1882; Wood to Elder, September 13, 1882; Joseph Dwenger to Elder, February 17, 1882; Hussey, "The 1878 Financial Failure of Archbishop Purcell," 25. In his letter to the Cincinnati prelate Dwenger wrote that he knew "too well how little of [the creditors'] money went for Church purposes. . . . The banking debt of Edward Purcell was no church debt and the good old archbishop had no right to acknowledge it as such."

19. *Catholic Telegraph,* July 31, December 4, 1884; October 28, 1886; April 14, 1887.

20. Elder to Gibbons, February 27, 1888; Gibbons to Elder, March 5, 29, 1888; Maes to Elder, November 6, 15, 26, December 28, 1888, AAC; *Catholic Telegraph,* December 8, 1887.

21. Albrinck to Elder, December 17, 1885; Elder to Gibbons, August 9, 1892; Moeller to William List, January 7, 1905; Moeller to Margaret Delaney, June 1, 1909; Moeller to Sister Superior, Little Sisters of the Poor, September 30, 1909; Moeller to Conde B. Pallen, May 29, 1911; Moeller to Bessie McCarry, September 30, 1922; Moeller to Rev. Martin Varley, November 22, 1924, AAC; Hussey, "The 1878 Financial Failure of Archbishop Purcell," 27–32, 37–38. Moeller always felt that Purcell "was not to be blamed for the financial cloud that darkened the last days of his life."

22. *Catholic Telegraph,* February 6, March 19, April 23, 1896.

23. Quoted in *Character Glimpses of Most Reverend William Henry Elder, D.D.* (Ratisbon, Germany, 1911), 85, 131, 173; *Catholic Telegraph,* June 29, 1893.

24. Walburg to Elder, September 18, 1891; Moeller to Lamott, January 1, 1921; *History of Fifty Years: St. John the Evangelist Church* (Cincinnati, 1941), AAC; *Glimpses of Archbishop Elder,* 93–94, 99; *Catholic Telegraph,* June 11, 1896; August 30, 1906. Cardinal Gibbons, who delivered the sermon in the cathedral on the occasion of Elder's golden jubilee celebration in 1896, expressed wonderment in the wake of the Purcell bank failure "to find the number of churches, schools, hospitals, and asylums that have been added to the list during Elder's administration."

25. Moeller to Priests, November 1, 1904, AAC; *Catholic Telegraph,* November 3, 10, 1904; October 25, 1923.

26. *Catholic Telegraph,* February 16, 1905; October 25, 1923; January 8, 1925; Patrick W. Carey, *The Roman Catholics* (Westport, Conn., 1993), 67. Archbishop Moeller's brother Bernard became diocesan chancellor in Cincinnati from 1908 to 1925; his brother Ferdinand a Jesuit at St. Ignatius College in Chicago; and his sister Anna, who became Sister Henry Maria, a Sister of Charity in Cincinnati.

27. *Catholic Telegraph,* January 8, 1925; John Tracey Ellis, *The Life of James Cardinal Gibbons, Archbishop of Baltimore, 1834–1921* (Milwaukee, 1952), 1: 264.

28. *Catholic Telegraph,* March 28, 1895; April 20, 1899; May 31, 1900; November 17, 1904; February 16, 1905; October 25, 1923. In the late 1890s the diocese of Columbus was in dire financial straits and on verge of dissolution. There was discussion of dividing it between the archdiocese of Cincinnati and the diocese of Cleveland. But church officials decided to give the diocese another try. Moeller, who had helped organize the administrative branch of the archdiocese, was named bishop, succeeding the late John Ambrose Watterson.

29. Elder to Moeller, February 12, 1903; Elder to Eugene Elder, March 7, 1904; *Annals of St. Michael's Parish in Loramie, 1838–1903* (Loramie, Ohio, 1907), AAC; Williams Papers, Elder to Archbishop John Joseph Williams of Boston, January 27, 1903, AABo; *Catholic Telegraph,* January 22, 1903; January 8, 1925.

30. Elder to Moeller, May 4, 1903, AAC; *Catholic Telegraph,* April 9, May 28, June 18, 1903. Moeller was named archbishop of Areopolis and coadjutor to Elder.

31. Jay P. Dolan, *The American Catholic Experience: A History from Colonial Times to the Present* (New York, 1985), 170–71, 225; Leslie Woodcock Tentler, *Seasons of Grace: A History of the Catholic Archdiocese of Detroit* (Detroit, Mich., 1990), 72.

32. Moeller to Diomede Falconio, July 6, August 28, September 4, 1908; December 27, 1909; Moeller to James Nolan, November 4, 1910, AAC; *Catholic Telegraph,* June 30, 1881; May 19, 1910.

33. *75th Jubilee St. Adalbert Church, 1903–1978* (Dayton, 1978); *Golden Jubilee Holy Cross Parish, 1914–1964* (Dayton, 1964), AAC; *Catholic Telegraph,* June 10, 1909; October 28, 1926; April 3, 1930.

34. *Catholic Telegraph,* February 25, March 10, 1892; *Official Catholic Directory,* 1920.

35. Maes to Elder, November 12, 1897, AAC; *Catholic Telegraph,* January 3, 1895; November 5, 1896; November 7, 1941.

36. McNicholas to Pastors, January 18, 1937, AAC; *Catholic Telegraph,* January 3, 1895; November 5, 1896; August 30, 1906.

37. Elder to Owen Smith, July 27, 29, 1889; Smith to Elder, July 29, 1889; Thomas Hart to Elder, August 29, September 6, 1899, AAC; *Catholic Telegraph,* June 29, 1893.

38. Moeller to Hart, November 15, 1918; August 30, December 29, 1919, AAC; *Catholic Telegraph,* May 27, 1920; March 20, 1924.

39. Quoted in Campbell, "New Parochialism," 115–16, 121; Elder to John Cotter, September 24, 1901, AAC; Tentler, *Seasons of Grace,* 28.

40. Gibbons to Elder, February 1, 1882, AAC; Dolan, *The American Catholic Experience,* 355; Gerald P. Fogarty, *The Vatican and the American Hierarchy From 1870 to 1965* (Wilmington, Del., 1985), 27.

41. Elder to Gilmour, November 5, 1882, March 16, 1890; Elder to Dwenger, May 6, 1885; Elder to Gilmour, August 12, 1885; Gibbons to Elder, April 22, 1885; Gibbons to Elder, March 21, 1889, AAC; Carey, *The Roman Catholics,* 66; James L. Heft, S.M., "From the Pope to the Bishops: Episcopal Authority from Vatican I to Vatican II" in *The Papacy and the Church in the United States,* ed. Bernard Cooke (New York, 1989), 69; Tentler, *Seasons of Grace,* 120.

42. Philip Gleason, *Keeping the Faith: American Catholicism Past and Present* (Notre Dame, Ind., 1987), 160–63; Fogarty, *The Vatican and the American Hierarchy,* 13; Timothy Walch, *Parish School: American Catholic Parochial Education from Colonal Times to the Present* (New York, 1996), 85.

43. Carey, *The Roman Catholics,* 52–53.

44. McCloskey to Elder, January 27, 1887, AAC; Carey, *The Roman Catholics,* 66; Fogarty, *The Vatican and the American Hierarchy,* 84–85, 115, 190; Joseph M. White, *The Diocesan Seminary in the United States: A History from the 1780s to the Present* (Notre Dame, Ind., 1989), 265.

45. Quoted in Carey, *The Roman Catholics,* 56; Robert Emmett Curran, *Michael Augustine Corrigan and the Shaping of Conservative Catholicism in America, 1878–1902* (New York,

1978), 128; Joan Bland, *Hibernian Crusade: The Story of the Catholic Total Abstinence Union of America* (Washington, D.C., 1951), 162; Fogarty, *The Vatican and the American Hierarchy,* 83; Walch, *Parish School,* 88–89; Tentler, *Seasons of Grace,* 123.

46. Elder to William G. McCloskey, October 10, 1883; Elder to Gilmour, September 13, October 1, 1887; Elder to B. A. Benedict, November 29, 1895; Moeller to Falconio, January 12, August 18, 1905; Moeller to Messmer, April 12, 1905, AAC; *Catholic Telegraph,* September 21, 1905.

47. Moeller to Sister Josephine, April 11, 1908; Moeller to Mother Margaret Mary, April 11, 24, 1908; Moeller to Mother Gabriel, April 11, 1908; Moeller to Falconio, November 6, 1908, AAC; Tentler, *Seasons of Grace,* 120.

48. Moeller to Sister Margaret Mary, December 4, 1908; Moeller to Falconio, November 6, December 11,1908; March 4, April 8, 1910; Moeller to Mother Angela, March 25, 1912, AAC. This was not the first time that the apostolic delegate had refused to back the archbishop. At the beginning of Moeller's episcopate he had refused to support Moeller's decision to uphold the expulsion of a sister by the superior of the Ursuline Order.

49. Elder to Gilmour, August 12, 1885; Gibbons to Elder, April 22, 1885; McCloskey to Elder, January 27, 1887, AAC; Campbell, "New Parochialism," 117–18; Robert F. Trisco, *Bishops and their Priests in the United States* (New York, 1988), 202–10, 237.

50. Elder to Gibbons, January 27, 1882; Elder to Gilmour, November 5, 1882, August 12, 1885; March 24, 1887; Elder to Borgess, March 28, 1887, AAC; *Catholic Telegraph,* July 25, 1889; Campbell, "New Parochialism," 132–33.

51. *Catholic Telegraph,* March 9, 16, 23, 30, 1882; October 28, 1886; December 21, 1887. The nine irremovable parishes in 1886 were Holy Trinity, St. Joseph, St. Patrick, St. Mary, and St. Paul in Cincinnati; Emmanuel and St. Joseph in Dayton; St. Raphael in Springfield; and St. Mary in Urbana. Twelve years later the parishes of St. Francis de Sales in Cincinnati and Holy Trinity in Dayton were added to the list. The first deanery took in Hamilton County; the second, the counties of Brown, Clermont, Adams, Highland, Butler, Warren, Clinton, Preble, and the western sections of the counties of Ross, Scioto, and Pike; the third, the counties of Montgomery, Fayette, Greene, Madison, Darke, Shelby, and Mercer; and the fourth, the counties of Miami, Champaign, Logan, Union, Marion, Auglaize, and Hardin.

52. *Catholic Telegraph,* July 25, 1889; March 20, 1902; February 21, 1907; Carey, *The Roman Catholics,* 67. At Cincinnati's third synod in 1898 the number of synodal examiners was increased by two to twelve while the number of deans was reduced by one to three.

53. Elder to Clergy, October 4, 1896; Moeller to Clergy, July 27, 1897; Decree to Pastors and Parishioners of Assumption, St. Francis de Sales, St. Elizabeth, St. Mary's Hyde Park, and St. Marks, August 22, 1905; Moeller to Martin Neville, October 29, 1920; *Souvenir Holy Family Church, 1905–1915* (Dayton, 1916), AAC; *Catholic Telegraph,* August 29, 1891; October 15, 1896; Campbell, "New Parochialism," 133–34. In 1891 the Cincinnati parishes of St. John and St. Francis were confined to strictly defined districts. Printed circulars, showing the boundary lines of the two parishes, were distributed to the parishioners. The children were to be christened as well as participate in marriage and funeral ceremonies in the parish in which the parents lived. Moreover, in 1898 Cincinnati's third synod intensified the local church's stand against parish raiding. In clear, unmistakable language it decreed that all priests were forbidden, under grave sin, to rent seats or to admit into their churches the faithful of a neighboring parish for the purpose of receiving the sacraments, except Holy Eucharist and Penance.

54. Moore to Moeller, January 22, 1910; Moeller to Falconio, March 10, 1910; Moeller to Charles M. Diener, December 9, 1910; Moeller to John Bonzano, May 22, 1919; Moeller to Neville, October 29, 1920, AAC; Campbell, "New Parochialism," 139–145.

55. Moeller to A. J. Roth, November 14, December 4, 1911; July 7, 1913, AAC.

56. Moeller to Kemper, March 10, 1913, AAC.

57. Moeller to William J. Halley, September 16, 1884; Moeller to A. J. Fischer, March 27, 1906; Moeller to Falconio, March 10, 1910; Moeller to Bernard Vollmers, October 24, 1911; *Celebrating 125 Years: St. Stephen Church* (Cincinnati, 1992), AAC; *Catholic Telegraph,* February 27, 1902.

58. Moeller to A. J. Fischer, March 27, 1906; Moeller to Bonzano, May 22, 1919; Moeller to Falconio, March 10, 1910; Moeller to Vollmers, October 24, 1911, AAC; Carey, *The Roman Catholics,* 54; quoted in John Tracey Ellis, *The Life of James Cardinal Gibbons, Archbishop of Baltimore, 1834–1921* (Milwaukee, 1952), 1: 355, 358; Fogarty, *The Vatican and the American Hierarchy,* 46–47. When an increasing number of English-speaking Catholics joined the German parish of St. Stephen at Columbia in the late 1870s, it became necessary to read the gospel in English as well as German. By 1880 the church gave as many English sermons as German. Four years later the English catechism was introduced at the request of the parents because most of the children no longer understood German.

59. Campbell, "New Parochialism," 163–64; Dolan, *The American Catholic Experience,* 297; Zane L. Miller, *Boss Cox's Cincinnati: Urban Politics in the Progressive Era* (New York, 1968), 135. At this time most patriots defined nationalism in cultural terms as a total way of life, a usage that deepened the long-standing division of the church into German and Irish elements.

60. Elder to Gibbons, December 16, 1886; Moeller to Mrs. Theod. Granzeier, February 24, 1906; *Diamond Jubilee of St. Augustine Parish* (Cincinnati, 1932), AAC; *Catholic Telegraph,* June 27, 1907; Campbell, "New Parochialism," 163–64; Dolan, *The American Catholic Experience,* 297; Miller, *Boss Cox's Cincinnati,* 135.

61. Gilmour to Elder, December 22, 1886; Moeller to Charles Ward, November 23, 1911; Moeller to John Timmer, June 3, 1921, AAC; *Catholic Telegraph,* March 5, 12, 1885; April 1, 1889; June 27, 1907; Campbell, "New Parochialism," 163–64; Walch, *Parish School,* 82.

62. Moeller to Rev. Hilary, O.F.M., March 9, 1905; Moeller to J. W. Freund, July 27, 1906; Moeller to Marie Anderson, April 12, 1916; Moeller to George Schrand, December 30, 1916; Moeller to Mary M. Fealy, October 2, 1918; Moeller to Rev. Francis Howard, March 31, 1919; *Diamond Jubilee St. Catharine of Siena Parish, 1903–1978* (Cincinnati, 1978), AAC.

63. Moeller to Neville, October 29, 1920; Moeller to Bonzano, May 22, 1919; Moeller to Msgr. Nicola, December 30, 1919, AAC.

64. Moeller to Rev. John Hickey, November 23, 1916; Moeller to Rev. Jordanus Karl, February 9, 1921; Moeller to T. S. Byrne, August 12, 1921; Moeller to D. A. Buckley, November 24, 1922, AAC.

65. Campbell, "New Parochialism," 176–77, 180.

66. Dominic Shunk to Moeller, April 16, 1898; Shunk to Elder, April 12, 1898, AAC; for a good analysis of the relationship between Elder and the Precious Blood priests, see Campbell, "New Parochialism," 174–98, 215–21.

67. Elder's Diary, January 24, 1884; April 14, 1885, A.A.C.

68. *Catholic Telegraph,* July 9, 1931.

69. Moeller to William Scholl, January 21, 1922; Moeller to Mother Mary, December 27, 1921, AAC.

70. Moeller to Russ, July 10, 1904; Moeller to Mark Hamburger, September 12, 1907; Minutes of the Archdiocesan Consultors, March 12, 1906; *Souvenir of Dedication, St. Mark Church* (Cincinnati, 1916); Moeller to William T. Russell, February 1, 1921, AAC; *Catholic Telegraph,* November 1, 1906.

71. Moeller to Russ, December 6, 1911; Moeller to the Trustees of St. Joseph's Orphanage, December 15, 1911; Russ to Moeller, January 8, 14, 1912; Moeller to Russ, January 16, 1912, AAC.

72. Moeller to Hindelang, May 28, 1920, AAC.

73. Moeller to Falconio, November 28, 1904; January 12, 1905; Moeller to Rev. A. Adelmann, December 2, 1912; Moeller to Buttermann, July 21, 1913; *Souvenir Silver Jubilee Celebration: St. Monica Church* (Cincinnati, 1936), AAC; Campbell, "New Parochialism," 221–35.

74. Moeller to Buttermann, July 21, 1913; Moeller to Rev. P. J. Ryan, October 24, 1918, AAC; *Catholic Telegraph,* September 2, 16, 1915.

75. Bonner to Moeller, April 6, 1918; Moeller to Bonner, March 24, 1919; April 4, 15, 1919; Dempsey to Ryan, March 18, 1918, AAC; *Catholic Telegraph,* December 17, 1914; September 16, 1915; August 29, 1918; March 27, May 15, September 11, 1919; Campbell, "New Parochialism," 235–39, 311–12.

76. Moeller to Meyer, November 8, 1919; Bernard Moeller to Mowbray, November 6, 1920; Moeller to De Lai, May 30, 1920; Chancellor to Helen Mowbray, November 6, 1920; Moeller to Your Excellency, August 23, 1922, AAC.; Campbell, "New Parochialism," 313–18; *Catholic Telegraph,* August 29, 1918.

77. Bonzano to Moeller, November 4, 1918; Moeller to Bonzano, November 7, 1918; Moeller to Brockhuis, December 30, 1919; Moeller to Bonner, April 15, June 14, 1919, AAC; Campbell, "New Parochialism," 240–42.

78. Moeller to Sele, January 17, 1907, AAC; Campbell, "New Parochialism," 244–47.

79. Moeller to Rev. James Henry, January 3, 1906; Moeller to Drexel, March 31, 1909; Moeller to R. Meyer, April 2, 1909; Moeller to Francis Heiermann, S.J., December 5, 1912; January 7, 1913, AAC; Campbell, "New Parochialism," 256; Bennish, *Xavier University,* 109–13; *Catholic Telegraph,* April 8, 1915.

Chapter 8

1. *Catholic Telegraph,* February 16, 23, March 9, 16, 23, 30, 1882.

2. *Catholic Telegraph,* March 23, 30, 1882; Philip Gleason, *Keeping the Faith: American Catholicism Past and Present* (Notre Dame, Ind., 1987), 125; Mary Ewens, *The Role of the Nun in Nineteenth Century America* (New York, 1978), 259; Gerald P. Fogarty, *The Vatican and the American Hierarchy From 1870 to 1965* (Wilmington, Del., 1985), 14, 27; Timothy Walch, *Parish School: American Catholic Parochial Education from Colonial Times to the Present* (New York, 1996), 58–59.

3. Gleason, *Keeping the Faith,* 125; Ewens, *The Role of the Nun in Nineteenth Century America,* 253.

4. *Catholic Telegraph,* March 23, 30, August 31, 1882; September 9, 1886; September 8, 1887; August 3, 1893; March 3, 1898; December 24, 1908; June 17, 1915; August 10, 1916; June 5, 1924.

5. Moeller to Anna Laws, September 4, 1912; Moeller to Mary Frances Dillon, April 5, 1911, AAC; *Catholic Telegraph,* March 23, 30, August 31, 1882; September 9, 1886; September 8, 1887; August 3, 1893; March 3, 1898; December 24, 1908; June 17, 1915; August 10, 1916; June 5, 1924; Patrick W. Carey, *The Roman Catholics* (Westport, Conn., 1993), 51–52.

6. Elder to McCloskey, November 25, 1892; Copy of Meeting of Cincinnati Province, August 31, 1892; Report on Parochial Schools [1892]; copy of Meeting of the Archbishops in New York, November 16, 1892; Moeller to John M. Lyons, S.J., April 28, 1921; Moeller to Pastors, September 20, 1923, AAC; Leslie Woodcock Tentler, *Seasons of Grace: A History of the Catholic Archdiocese of Detroit* (Detroit, Mich., 1990), 38; *Catholic Telegraph,* January 1, 1885; February 6, 1890; December 1, 1892; August 10, 1893.

7. Gibbons to Elder, September 19, 1884; Moeller to John Hickey, July 10, 1904; Moeller to Rev. J. Cotter, August 14, 1880, AAC; *Catholic Telegraph,* September 10, 1903; July 28, August 25, September 5, 1904; August 29, 1907; January 8, 1925; Mary J. Oates, "Organized Voluntarism: The Catholic Sisters in Massachusetts, 1870–1940," in *Women in American Religion,* ed. Janet Wilson James (Philadelphia, 1978), 160; Fogarty, *The Vatican and*

the American Hierarchy, 14; Walch, *Parish School,* 62, 100, 137; Carol K. Coburn and Martha Smith, *Spirited Lives: How Nuns Shaped Catholic Culture and American Life, 1836–1920* (Chapel Hill, N.C., 1999), 9, 151–52. To compensate for the lack of professional training and formal education some younger sisters received the counsel of more experienced sisters in the community.

8. *First Annual Report of Superintendent of Parish Schools of the Archdiocese of Cincinnati, 1907–08,* AAC; *Catholic Directory,* 1920; Edward A. Connaughton, *A History of Educational Legislation and Administration in the Archdiocese of Cincinnati* (Washington, D.C., 1946), 110; Jay P. Dolan, *The American Catholic Experience: A History from Colonial Times to the Present* (New York, 1985), 29; Walch, *Parish School,* 100–101. The school board established in 1906 did not function effectively and was reorganized in 1918.

9. Moeller's Secretary to W. C. Culkins, December 29, 1914, AAC; *Catholic Telegraph,* August 29, 1907; August 27, 1908; June 10, 1909; March 3, 1910; January 4, 1912; July 9, 1914; August 12, 1915; August 1, 1918; *Catholic Directory,* 1920; Hugh J. Nolan, ed., *Pastoral Letters of the American Hierarchy, 1796–1970* (Huntington, Ind., 1971), 227; Dolan, *The American Catholic Experience,* 289.

10. *First Annual Report of Superintendent of Parish Schools of the Archdiocese of Cincinnati, 1907–08; Second Report of Superintendent of Parish Schools of the Archdiocese of Cincinnati, 1908–09,* AAC.

11. Moeller to Rev. J. Cotter, August 14, 1908; *Diamond Jubilee Centennial of Sts. Peter and Paul Dramatic Club* (Cincinnati, 1927), AAC; *Catholic Telegraph,* September 3, September 10, 1908; July 9, 1931.

12. *Catholic Telegraph,* March 24, 1898.

13. Gilmour to Elder, March 21, 26, 1885; Moeller to R. W. Rives, January 29, 1910, AAC; *Catholic Telegraph,* March 30, 1882; November 27, 1884; February 5, 12, October 1, 1885; February 17, 1887; February 4, 1892; April 6, August 3, 1899; June 14, 1900; December 24, 1908; August 1, 1918.

14. Moeller to R. W. Rives, January 29, 1910; *Catholic Telegraph,* August 3, 1899.

15. Moeller to Bishop John Farrelly of Cleveland, April 1, 1915; Moeller to Henry Ott, March 15, 1915; Moeller to William R. Collins, April 28, 1915, AAC; *Catholic Telegraph,* April 8, 30, May 7, 1925; January 30, March 6, 1919; John Tracey Ellis, *The Life of James Cardinal Gibbons, Archbishop of Baltimore, 1834–1921* (Milwaukee, 1952), 2: 543–44.

16. Connaughton, *A History of Educational Legislation and Administration in the Archdiocese of Cincinnati,* 129–30; Tentler, *Seasons of Grace,* 94.

17. Moeller to Rev. G. Meyer, August 3, 1909, AAC; Connaughton, *A History of Educational Legislation and Administration in the Archdiocese of Cincinnati,* 133–34; Tentler, *Seasons of Grace,* 250.

18. Moeller to Rev. J. H. Schengber, December 21, 1921, AAC; *Catholic Telegraph,* October 25, 1923, August 28, 1942; Connaughton, *A History of Educational Legislation and Administration in the Archdiocese of Cincinnati,* 126, 135–36.

19. Moeller to Rev. William P. O'Connor, December 30, 1921; Moeller to Rev. D. A. Buckley, September 2, 1923; Moeller to Rev. George J. Mayerhoefer, January 6, 1924; Moeller to Rev. P. J. Hunes, July 10, 1924; Moeller to Rev. Henry Brinkmeyer, December 26, 1924, AAC; *Catholic Telegraph,* July 17, November 20, 1924; Connaughton, *A History of Educational Legislation and Administration in the Archdiocese of Cincinnati,* 138. In 1924 a committee of five priests and three laymen purchased ten acres in Dayton for a central high school.

20. Moeller to Joseph Berning, May 22, 1913, AAC; *Catholic Telegraph,* March 21, 1895; November 7, 1912; March 3, 1899; September 12, 1907; James H. Campbell, "New Parochialism: Change and Conflict in the Archdiocese of Cincinnati, 1878–1925" (Ph.D. diss., University of Cincinnati, 1981), 320–21; Tentler, *Seasons of Grace,* 257.

21. Moeller to Charles W. Dabney, May 16, 1908; Moeller to Rev. P. J. Stryeker, September 13, 1919; Moeller to A. M. Doex, January 2, 1923; Moeller to Ignatius Ahmann, January 2, 1923; Moeller to Rev. Frank Kelly, March 12, 1924, AAC.

22. Purcell to Archbishop Blanc, October 7, 1853, AUND; Engbers to Purcell, January 16, 1873, AAC; Joseph M. White, *The Diocesan Seminary in the United States: A History from the 1780s to the Present* (Notre Dame, Ind., 1989), 155–56.

23. Quoted in C. Joseph Nuesse, *The Catholic University of America: A Centennial History* (Washington, D.C., 1990), 16; Albrinck to Elder, November 10, 1885, AAC; *Catholic Telegraph,* May 14, 1885; May 26, 1887; May 17, 1888; May 13, 1893; April 25, 1895; October 17, 1901. For a while Elder considered placing the seminary into the hands of the Sulpicians; White, *The Diocesan Seminary in the United States,* 149, 185.

24. Elder to Albrinck, February 21, 1890, AAC; White, *The Diocesan Seminary in the United States,* 155–156; *Catholic Telegraph,* June 6, 1889; April 17, May 8, 15, July 24, August 21, 1890; August 13, 1891; April 23, May 14 , September 24, October 22, 1891; July 7, November 10, 1892; May 13, 1893; February 27, 1902.

25. Albrinck to Elder, October 2, 1891; Auditing Committee of Archdiocese to Elder, March 20, 1901; Elder to Bishops of Cincinnati Province, January 9, 1904; St. Gregory Faculty to Elder, March 28, 1904; Otto B. Auer to Elder, March 27, 1904; H. J. Pohlschneider to Elder, March 28, 1904; Dutton to Elder, March 28, 1904; Moeller to Monsignor D. J. O'Connell, March 30, 1904, AAC; *Catholic Telegraph,* February 2, 1893; December 6, 1894; April 25, 1895.

26. Moeller to Brinkmeyer, June 4, 1907; Moeller to Rev. William Scholl, August 16, 1916; Moeller to Rev. George Hickey, August 28, 1916, AAC; M. Edmund Hussey, *A History of the Seminaries of the Archdiocese of Cincinnati 1829–1979* (Norwood, Ohio, 1979), 48–51; *Catholic Telegraph,* February 2, 1893; December 6, 1894; April 25, 1895; August 18, 1904; April 13, 1905; August 30, 1906; February 21, June 27, August 29,1907; April 30, 1908; April 23, 1914; July 9, 1931.

27. Elder to Gibbon, February 23, 1898; Moeller to I. F. Horstmann, August 21, 1907; Annual Reports, 1881, 1901, for the number of parishioners in the cathedral congregation, AAC; *Catholic Telegraph,* August 29, 1907; Campbell, "New Parochialism," 341–42.

28. Moeller to O'Dell, August 9, 1906; Moeller to N. J. Walsh, August 15, 1906; Minutes of the Meeting of Consultors, March 12, 1906, AAC; *Catholic Telegraph,* August 2, 9, 1906; August 29, 1907; August 27, 1908; Tenoever, "A Monument," in *Catholic Telegraph* Supplement, June 14, 1996.

29. Moeller to O'Dell, August 9, 1906; Moeller to N. J. Walsh, August 15, 1906; Moeller to William J. Anthony, December 2, 1922, AAC; *Catholic Telegraph,* August 2, 9, 1906; August 29, 1907; August 27, 1908.

30. Moeller to Samuel Hannaford, July 17, 1911, AAC; *Catholic Telegraph,* August 29, 1907; October 1, 1908; December 15, 1910; June 28, 1923; Campbell, "New Parochialism," 342–43, 349, cites William J. Egan, *A Loving and Deserved Tribute to the Revered Memory of the Most Reverend Henry Moeller, D.D.* (Norwood, n.d.), 10.

31. Moeller to Mrs. William J. O'Dell, January 25, 1910; Moeller to Dempsey, August, 1911; July 14, 1913, August 1, 1913; Moeller to Dempsey, April 30, 1915; Moeller to A. Worth, September 8, 1916, AAC; *Catholic Telegraph,* August 29, 1907.

32. Moeller to Rev. Francis J. Walsh, October 20, 1913, AAC; *Catholic Telegraph,* September 7, 1916; March 23, April 20, 1922; June 28, July 26, October 25, 1823; July 9, 1931; Hussey, *A History of the Seminaries of the Archdiocese of Cincinnati,* 39. At the time of the building of the new seminary, some religious orders were conducting seminaries in the archdiocese. The Franciscans conducted the St. Francis Preparatory Seminary in Cincinnati and a novitiate at St. Anthony Convent in Mt. Airy; the Precious Blood Fathers a preparatory

seminary and novitiate in Burkettsville and the St. Charles Borromeo Theological Seminary in Carthagena; the Passionists the theological seminary of the western province on Mt. Adams; and the Brothers of Mary a novitiate at Mount St. John in Dayton.

33. Moeller to Rev. Lawrence Denning, June 26, 1916; Moeller to Rev. Charles Diener, July 22, 1916; Moeller to Rev. V. P. O'Daniel, February 14, 1921, AAC; *Catholic Telegraph,* June 1, 1916; August 30, October 18, 25, 1923. For the occasion of the one hundredth anniversary of the founding of the diocese, Pius XI conferred honors upon Moeller, making him an assistant at the Pontifical Throne and raising him to the rank of Papal Count.

34. Ferdinand Brossart to Moeller, September 2, 1921; Moeller to Brossart, August 31, 1921, September 4, 1921; May 2, 1922, AAC; Campbell, "New Parochialism," 349–51.

35. David O'Brien, *Public Catholicism* (New York, 1989), 32–33, 212; Dorothy M. Brown and Elizabeth McKeown, *The Poor Belong to Us: Catholic Charities and American Welfare* (Cambridge, 1997), 1–3; Christopher J. Kauffman, *Ministry and Meaning: A Religious History of Catholic Healthy Care in the United States* (New York, 1995), 64, 129; Ewens, *The Role of the Nun in Nineteenth Century America,* 252; Mary J. Oates, *The Catholic Philanthropic Tradition in America* (Bloomington, Ind., 1995), 71; Eileen Mary Brewer, *Nuns and the Education of American Catholic Women, 1860–1920* (Chicago, 1987), 43.

36. *Catholic Telegraph,* March 23, 1882; June 12, 1890; August 30, 1906; October 28, 1926; Karen Kennelly, ed., *American Catholic Women: A Historical Exploration* (New York, 1989), vii–xviii.

37. Moeller to Joseph Berning, April 5, 1924; Chancellor to Mary T. Manning, September 3, 1919, AAC; *Catholic Telegraph,* January 4, 1912; July 9, 1931.

38. McCabe to Elder, March 9, July 30, 1887, AAC; *Catholic Telegraph,* September 14, 1882.

39. McCabe to Elder, July 30, 1887; Elder to Janssens, March 18, 1893; Elder to Mother Colette, March 20, 1893, AAC; *Catholic Telegraph,* October 28, 1926; October 11, 1934.

40. *Souvenir History of the Dedication of Guardian Angels Church-Auditorium* (Cincinnati, 1949), AAC; *Catholic Telegraph,* September 14, 1882; November 17, 1892; October 28, 1896; October 5, 1911; March 15, 1917; July 9, 1931. By this time in Cincinnati the Sisters of Mercy had organized two academies; the first was established on Central Avenue, later moved to Freeman Avenue in 1860, and the second in 1915 in Westwood. The Ladies of the Sacred Heart had opened their academy in Clifton in 1869. The Ursuline Sisters of Brown County opened one at Oak Street and Reading Road in 1869. St. Ursula Academy on McMillan Street had been organized by the Ursuline Sisters in 1910. The Sisters of Charity continued to run Mount St. Vincent Academy in Price Hill and founded Mount St. Joseph Academy in Delhi in 1906.

41. Moeller to the Sisters of St. Catherine de Ricci, January 8, 1912; Moeller to Sister S. Aimie, November 9, 1912; Moeller to Mother Mary Florence, August 4, 1911; Moeller to Rev. Charles Charles Kemper, May 26, 1911; Moeller to Bishop John O'Connor, April 29, 1915, AAC; Moeller had preferred putting the Sisters of Charity in charge in Dayton, but Schwind preferred the Dominican Sisters. She felt they had more experience in this work. *Catholic Telegraph,* December 14, 1916; March 1, 1917; October 11, 1934.

42. Margaret McCabe, "Pamphlet," 1902, AAC; *Catholic Telegraph,* March 25, November 25, 1886; January 14, 1892; October 5, 1911; August 10, 1916; March 15, 1917.

43. *Catholic Telegraph,* March 4, April 22, 1915; August 10, 1916; April 25, 1918.

44. *Catholic Telegraph,* August 10, 1916; February 15, 1917; February 21, April 25, May 2, 1918; July 9, 1931.

45. Rev. J. D. Kress to Moeller, September 3, 1896; *Saint Rita School for the Deaf, 1915–1965* (Cincinnati, 1965), AAC; *Catholic Telegraph,* July 15, 1909; July 9, 1931. The Springer Institute was made possible by a generous donation from Reuben Springer.

46. Edward Cleary to Elder, June 26, 1889, AAC; *Catholic Telegraph,* July 5, 1894; May 9, 1895;

August 20, 1896; January 7, 1897; July 9, 1931.

47. Moeller to Ferdinand Moeller, S.J., June 27, 1906; Moeller to Rev. H. Buse, August 23, 1907; Moeller to Ann Hunciker, August 19, 1908, AAC; *Catholic Telegraph,* February 10, 1910.

48. Moeller to Henry Waldhaus, August 11, 1917; September 20, 1919; *Saint Rita School for the Deaf, 1915–1965* (Cincinnati, 1965), AAC; *Catholic Telegraph,* August 31, 1911; September 17, 1914; March 18, 1915; July 29, 1915; August 17, 1916; August 14, September 4, 1924; July 9, 1931.

49. *Catholic Telegraph,* December 9, 1886; October 23, 1890; July 9, 1931.

50. *Catholic Telegraph,* March 12, 1891; January 4, 1894; February 11, 1897; October 5, 1911. A bequest of $20,000 from Reuben Springer helped finance part of the construction of St. Francis Hospital. In the 1840s St. Peter's Cemetery Association had used the grounds for a cemetery, long known as St. Peter of Lick Run cemetery.

51. *Catholic Telegraph,* July 23, 1885; January 4, February 8, 1894; July 15, 1909; Judith Metz, "150 Years of Caring: The Sisters of Charity in Cincinnati," *The Cincinnati Historical Society Bulletin* 37 (Cincinnati, 1979): 163–65. The 1890 addition to Good Samaritan Hospital was made possible by the generous donation of $30,000 by Reuben Springer.

52. Moeller to Bonzano, [n.d.]; Moeller to Mother M. Blanche, February 27, 1911, AAC; Metz, "150 Years of Caring," 166; *Catholic Telegraph,* January 4, 1894; April 20, 1911; October 11, 1934; June 16, 1950.

53. Frank H. Rowe, M.D. to Elder, October 1, 1894; John F. Hickey to Elder, July 14, 1897; Moeller to Rev. John Seiffert, August 25, 1898; St. Joseph Orphan Asylum to Elder, June 9, 1891; Michael Ryan to Elder, May 4, 1901, AAC; *Catholic Telegraph,* September 29, 1887; February 27, March 12, 1896; October 8, 1891; June 10, 1909.

54. Moeller to Whom It May Concern, July 24, 1905; Moeller to Whom it May Concern, April 24, 1906; *Mount Alverno Centennial, 1870–1970* (Cincinnati, 1970), AAC; *Catholic Telegraph,* December 29, 1904; July 9, 1931; January 12, March 1, May 12, 1917; September 22, 1927; October 11, 1934. Experiencing financial difficulties during the economic depression St. Vincent Home sold its property to the city of Cincinnati in 1934. During its twenty-eight years of operation the home cared for more than two thousand boys.

55. *Catholic Telegraph,* February 22, 1917; DuBrul's quote in Zane L. Miller, *Boss Cox's Cincinnati: Urban Politics in the Progressive Era* (New York, 1968), 139.

56. David E. Dunham to Moeller, December 2, 1914, AAC; Campbell, "New Parochialism," 168.

57. Moeller to Rev. Adolph Beckman, June 22, 1917; Moeller to Gressle, February 1, 1921, AAC; *Catholic Telegraph,* February 17, March 9, December 14, 1916; February 1, 1917; Zane L. Miller, *Boss Cox's Cincinnati,* 139; Brown and McKeown, *The Poor Belong to Us,* 7; Oates, *The Catholic Philanthropic Tradition in America,* 57–58.

58. Ibid., 26–27; Tentler, *Seasons of Grace,* 228; *Catholic Telegraph,* October 26, 1893; February 7, 1895; February 28, 1901; June 1, 1905; October 5, 1911.

59. Moeller to Fred Tuke, June 28, 1917, AAC; *Catholic Telegraph,* March 14, 1918; October 11, 1934; R. Marcellus Wagner, "History of the Bureau of Catholic Charities and Social Service of the Archdiocese of Cincinnati, Ohio" (Ph.D. diss., Catholic University of America, 1922), 9, 22; Campbell, "New Parochialism," 169–70.

60. Oates, *The Catholic Philanthropic Tradition in America,* 42, 75; *Catholic Telegraph,* March 25, 1920; April 27, 1922; Miller, *Boss Cox's Cincinnati,* 140.

61. Moeller to Bishop John P. Farrelly of Cleveland, May 2, 1917; Moeller to James A. Flaherty, July 7, 1917; Moeller to E. D. Leach, January 24, 1918; Moeller to P. H. Callahan, February 16, 1918; Moeller to Rev. John A. Gnau, May 14, 1918; Moeller to Central Liberty Loan Committee, August 31, 1918; Moeller to John Monahan, August 31, 1918; Moeller to Herbert Hoover, October 17, 1918; Moeller to Bonzano, April 5, 1919; *Golden*

Anniversary St. Patrick Council Knights of Columbus, 1914–1964 (Cincinnati, 1964), AAC; Tentler, *Seasons of Grace,* 280; *Catholic Telegraph,* April 28, 1898; April 26, June 14, September 13, October 25, 1917; January 17, April 4, 18, May 30, September 12, 1918; April 24, October 30, November 6, 1919; January 8, 22, 1920; February 1, 1923; Christopher J. Kauffman, *Faith and Fraternalism: The History of the Knights of Columbus* (New York, 1992), 204–5. During the Spanish-American War in 1898 Elder wrote that Catholics "have been taught from childhood that the service of their country is a part of their service of God." Cincinnati's St. Patrick's Knights of Columbus Council alone contributed $262 toward World War I's War Fund.

62. *Catholic Telegraph,* December 5, 1918; April 24, 1919.

Chapter 9

1. Goetz to Elder, July 28, 1880; Moeller to Rev. Christopher, Church of Immaculata, April 16, 1898, AAC; Leslie Woodcock Tentler, *Seasons of Grace: A History of the Catholic Archdiocese of Detroit* (Detroit, Michigan, 1990), 25, 76; *Catholic Telegraph,* December 1, 1880; February 9, 1882; June 26; August 21, 1884.
2. Moeller to Jane Matthews, January 25, 1905; Moeller to J. O. Cotter, February 8, 1905; Moeller to Rev. William Anthony, April 13, 1921; Moeller to Francis James Finn, S.J., June 27, 1906; Moeller to U. F. Miller, C.S., July 7, 1906; Moeller to Rev. A. Overmann, March 26, 1908; Moeller to Bishops, November 4, 1911; Moeller to Wald, January 4, 1912; Moeller to Friends . . . of the Orphans, June 10, 1913; Moeller to Rev. Joseph Denning, December 19, 1913; Moeller to Edward Burns, May 1, 1918, AAC; *Catholic Telegraph,* January 12, 1905; May 25, 1905; May 31, 1906; March 7, 1912.
3. Moeller to Jane Matthews, January 25, 1905; Moeller to J. O. Cotter, February 8, 1905, AAC. Some parishes retained the pew-rental system well into the 1950s. St. Louis Church at North Star abolished it in the late 1950s. *100th Anniversary St. Louis Church, 1892–1992* (North Star, Ohio), 1992, AAC.
4. Tentler, *Seasons of Grace,* 261; *Catholic Telegraph,* March 4, 1915; March 8, 22, April 5, 1917; March 27, 1919; February 12, 1920; January 8, 1925.
5. Tentler, *Seasons of Grace,* 261; *Catholic Telegraph,* March 4, 1915; March 8, 22, April 5, 1917; March 27, 1919; February 12, 1920; January 8, 1925.
6. *Catholic Telegraph,* November 16, 23, 1922; January 8, 1925.
7. H. D. Patterson of the Society for the Suppression of Vice to Elder, April 22, 1893; William Riley to Elder, January 25, February 4, 1898; Elder to Riley, January 29, February 5, 1898, AAC; *Catholic Telegraph,* March 3, 1898; Zane L. Miller, *Boss Cox's Cincinnati: Urban Politics in the Progressive Era* (New York, 1968), 137.
8. *Catholic Telegraph,* February 9, 1882; January 25, 1883; September 9, October 28, 1886; July 8, 1897; January 10, 1895; September 7, 1945.
9. Isaac Hocter to Elder, March 12, 1892; Rev. Martin L. Dentinger to Elder, July 28, August 2, 1897; June 9, 1898; *Centennial St. Joseph Church, 1883–1983* (Springfield, Ohio, 1983); *St. Brigid Parish Sesquicentennial, 1849–1999* (Xenia, Ohio, 1999), AAC; *Catholic Telegraph,* February 9, 1882; January 3, 1884; October 1, 1885; July 11, 1889; June 9, 1892; September 13, 1894; January 10, 1895; August 11, 1896; Joan Bland, *Hibernian Crusade: The Story of the Catholic Total Abstinence Union of America* (Washington, D.C., 1951), 207, 231.
10. Moeller to Frank L. Laengle, January 24, 1905; Moeller to Ed J. Frysinger, January 3, 1915; Moeller to Rev. M. J. Loney, March 23, 1909; Moeller to Bishop Regis Canevin of Pittsburgh, August 14, 1915; Moeller to H. R. Probasco, October 15, 1915; Moeller to Rev. John Cogan, October 9, 1917; Moeller to Frances Frisbie O'Donnell, February 19, 1917, AAC; *Catholic Telegraph,* October 28, 1915; Patrick W. Carey, *The Roman Catholics* (Westport, Conn., 1993), 72.

11. Gibbons to Elder, June 12, 1889, AAC; *Catholic Telegraph,* August 8, December 12, 1901.

12. Moeller to Joseph Berning, May 28, 1913; Moeller to Rev. Peter Robertson, August 7, 1913, AAC; Alfred J. Ede, *The Lay Crusade for a Christian America: A Study of the American Federation of Catholic Societies, 1900–1919* (New York, 1988), 59–60, 82, 369–70; *Catholic Telegraph,* January 25, 1883; February 26, 1885; January 21, 1886; May 31, 1888; April 5, 1900; February 22, 1917.

13. Moeller to Mrs. Knowlton Meyer, November 29, 1916, AAC; *Catholic Telegraph,* January 20, 1910; February 15, 1912; February 6, September 25, 1913; February 25, 1915; February 22, 1917; Ede, *The Lay Crusade for a Christian America,* 244–48, 372.

14. *Catholic Telegraph,* August 7, 1913; February 22, 1917.

15. Moeller to Rev. Francis Beckmann, June 15, 1920, AAC; *Catholic Telegraph,* October 14, December 2, 1920; April 27, 1922; January 6, 1927; August 16, 1923; July 9, 1931; Angelyn Dries, O.S.F., *The Missionary Movement in American Catholic History* (Maryknoll, N.Y., 1998), 92–93, 106; Douglas J. Slawson, *The Foundation and First Decade of the National Catholic Welfare Council* (Washington, D.C., 1992), 66, 92. The American Board of Catholic Missions was an agency of the newly formed National Catholic Welfare Council.

16. A.P.A. to Elder, September 6, 1900; Moeller to A. M. Boex, August 23, 1922; January 26, 1923, AAC; *Catholic Telegraph,* February 23, 1893; October 28, 1926; Jay P. Dolan, *The American Catholic Experience: A History from Colonial Times to the Present* (New York, 1985), 257–58; Tentler, *Seasons of Grace,* 267.

17. *Catholic Telegraph,* March 26, April 2, 1903.

18. *Catholic Telegraph,* November 16, 1905.

19. Moeller to Editor, "The Republican," August 3, 1906; Moeller to F. V. Faulhaber, November 5, 1913; Moeller to Timothy S. Hogan, October 30, 1914; Moeller to Rev. Peter Robertson, November 9, 1914, AAC; *Catholic Telegraph,* November 16, 1905; August 9, 1906; September 19, 1907; February 22, 1917.

20. Moeller to Bishop John P. Farrelly of Cleveland, May 2, 1917; Moeller to Ron Mulford, Jr., May 13, 1918, AAC.

21. Moeller to Judge W. A. Geoghegan, February 21, 1921; Moeller to Rev. F. M. Lamping, February 28, 1921; Moeller to Rev. Anthony J. Montink, February 5, 1921; Moeller to A. M. Boex, August 23, 1922; January 26, February 3, 1923; Moeller to Rev. F. X. Cotter, December 6, 1924, AAC; Slawson, *National Catholic Welfare Council,* 80–81, 96–99; *Catholic Telegraph,* May 13, 1920; February 1, September 20, October 11, 18, 1923.

22. Joseph M. White, *The Diocesan Seminary in the United States: A History from the 1780s to the Present* (Notre Dame, Ind., 1989), 267–68.

23. *Seventy-Fifth Anniversary, Saint Clare Parish* (Cincinnati, 1984); *Golden Jubilee St. Monica Church, 1911–1961* (Cincinnati, 1961); *50th Anniversary [St. Mark], 1905–1955* (Cincinnati, 1955); *125th Year Anniversary St. Aloysius Church* (Shandon, Ohio, 1993); *100th Anniversary St. Louis Church, 1882–1992* (North Star, Ohio, 1992), AAC; Dolan, *The American Catholic Experience,* 212–13, 229–30.

24. Moeller to Rev. J. B. Murray, March 30, 1910, AAC; *Catholic Telegraph,* March 31, August 25, 1910; February 23, 1911; Tentler, *Seasons of Grace,* 171.

25. *Catholic Telegraph,* January 25, 1900; July 27, August 3, 10, 1916; June 28, July 5, 1917; *Character Glimpses of Most Reverend William Henry Elder, D.D.* (Ratisbon, Germany, 1911), 158.

26. Rev. F. X. LaSance to Elder, October 16, 1892; Brinkmeyer to Elder, April 5, 1897; *St. Joseph Parish, 1839–1989* (Fort Recovery, Ohio, 1989), AAC; *Character Glimpses of Most Reverend William Henry Elder, D.D.,* 103; White, *The Diocesan Seminary in the United States,* 225–26; Joseph P. Chinnici, O.F.M., *Living Stones: The History and Structure of Catholic Spiritual Life in the United States* (New York, 1989), 146–48, 153; *Catholic Telegraph,* February 11, May 13, 1897; April 16, 1903; December 8, 1904; August 31, September 7, 28,

October 5, 1911; June 28, 1923; January 8, 1925; July 9, 1931. In the 1890s the Tabernacle Society introduced the devotion of the Forty Hours in the archdiocese.

27. Moeller to Rev. Eugene Buttermann, O.F.M., October 30, 1911; Moeller to Rev. Louis J. Nau, September 15, 1920, AAC; *Catholic Telegraph,* May 12, September 15, 1910; October 12, 1911; October 24, 1935.

28. Moeller to Rev. Bernard O'Reilly, S.M., May 24, 1912, AAC; Tentler, *Seasons of Grace,* 179; *Catholic Telegraph,* May 12, October 13, 1910; September 14, 1911; November 2, 1911; January 4, 1912; October 16, 1913; October 14, 1915; October 19, 26, 1916; October 2, 1970.

29. *Catholic Telegraph,* October 19, 1916; October 16, 1919; October 12, 1922; October 18, 25, 1923; October 16, 1924.

30. *Catholic Telegraph,* January 26, 1888; Dolan, *The American Catholic Experience,* 174. Tombstones in the old St. Joseph Cemetery apparently reveal that Italians arrived in Cincinnati before 1800, *Diamond Jubilee Sacred Heart Italian Church, 1893–1968* (Cincinnati, 1968), AAC; Mary Elizabeth Brown, *The Scalabrinians in North America, 1887–1934* (New York, 1996), 48. In 1860 Italian Catholics formed the Italian Congregation of the Sacred Heart Society, hoping that the organization would help solidify their community and provide a means of raising money for the building of an Italian church. Even though the Society was short-lived and that Purcell was unsuccessful in obtaining Italian-speaking priests to care for the spiritual needs of the Italians, the interest in building a church remained strong.

31. *Diamond Jubilee Sacred Heart Italian Church, 1893–1968* (Cincinnati, 1968), AAC; Rev. A. Kirner, S.M., to Purcell, February 24, 1868; McCabe to Elder, November 26, 1890, AAC; Brown, *The Scalabrinians in North America,* 48; *Catholic Telegraph,* January 1, 1868; September 11, 1890; October 6, 1892; August 31, 1893; March 15, 1917; July 11, 1918.

32. *Catholic Telegraph,* March 31, August 25, 1898; February 7, June 25, 1901.

33. Quoted in M. Christine Anderson, "Catholic Nuns and the Invention of Social Work: The Sisters of the Santa Maria Institute of Cincinnati, Ohio, 1897 through the 1920s," *Journal of Women's History* 12 (Spring 2000): 60–61; Mary Ewens, *The Role of the Nun in Nineteenth Century America* (New York, 1978), 274; *Catholic Telegraph,* March 31, August 25, 1898; February 7, June 25, 1901.

34. Moeller to Joseph Podesta, February 1, 1923; Moeller to Rev. Carlo Jachini, May 23, 1924; *Golden Jubilee San Antonio Church, 1922–1977* (Cincinnati, 1977), AAC; *Catholic Telegraph,* June 25, 1901; February 2, 1911.

35. Moeller to Rev. Vincent Migliore, May 20, 1904, AAC; *Catholic Telegraph,* February 7, 1901; December 3, 1908; February 10, 1910; February 2, 1911; October 9, 1913; August 6, 1914; March 18, 1915; September 22, 1927.

36. Moeller to Rev. Arath Astufan, December 29, 1905; Moeller to Kayata, May 23, 1908, AAC; *Catholic Telegraph,* February 17, December 15, 1910; August 3, 1911; September 14, 1916.

37. Moeller to Rev. Francis Wakim, January 6, 20, 1911; Moeller to Rev. Tobias Dahdah, August 29, 1911, AAC; *Catholic Telegraph,* September 14, 1916.

38. Purcell's Circular Letter, n.d., [1877]; Weninger to Elder, October 11, 1880; July 25, August 14, 1883; September 27, 1883; October 10, 1884; August 6, 1885; May 12, 1886; [Francis Xavier Weninger], "The Care of the Indian and African Races," AAC; Mary J. Oates, *The Catholic Philanthropic Tradition in America* (Bloomington, Ind., 1995), 62; James H. Campbell, "New Parochialism: Change and Conflict in the Archdiocese of Cincinnati, 1878–1925" (Ph.D. diss., University of Cincinnati, 1981), 251, cites John B. Purcell, Circular Letter to the Reverend Clergy and Faithful People of the Diocese of Cincinnati, [n.d.]; *Catholic Telegraph,* March 30, 1882; February 17, 1887; February 13, 1890; February 19, 1903; Peter Claver was canonized in 1880.

39. Weninger to Elder, May 12, 1886; Joseph Oster to Elder, September 21, 1891; Elder to E. R. Dyer, July 12, 1897, AAC.

40. Daniel Rudd to Elder, May 3, 1888, AAC; Dolan, *Catholic Experience,* 365; Oates, *The Catholic Philanthropic Tradition in America,* 67.

41. *Catholic Telegraph,* March 4, 1909.

42. Willis Kennedy to John Driessen, December 11, 1907; Moeller to Albert Heekin, May 13, 1908; Moeller to James J. Heekin, August 22, 1908; Moeller to Samuel Hannaford and Sons, November 13, 1908; Moeller to Mother Katherine Drexel, August 30, December 19,1908; January 10, March 31, 1909, AAC; Campbell, "New Parochialism," 255.

43. Moeller to James Henry, January 3, 1906; Moeller to Rev. John E. Burke, August 29, 1908; R. J. Meyer to Moeller, April 23, 1909, AAC; Campbell, "New Parochialism," 250; Lee J. Bennish, S.J., *Continuity and Change: Xavier University 1831–1981* (Chicago, 1981), 109–12.

44. Moeller to Drexel, July 30, 1909; Moeller to Rev. Edward Cleary, March 5, 1911; April 9, 1914; Annual Reports, 1909, 1913, AAC; *Catholic Telegraph,* November 24, 1910; January 26, March 30, 1911; Campbell, "New Parochialism," 258–59.

45. Moeller to Sister Borgia, S.N.D., December 20, 1913; Annual Reports, 1926, AAC; *Catholic Telegraph,* November 24, 1910; March 8, April 29, 1915; October 28, 1926; July 9, 1931.

46. Quoted in Campbell, "New Parochialism," 260–61; Dolan, *The American Catholic Experience,* 365.

47. Mother Laurence to Moeller, May 4, 1911; Sister Mary of St. Lawrence to Moeller, May 4, 1911; Financial Report, Convent of the Good Shepherd, Mt. St. Mary's, 1912, AAC; *Catholic Telegraph,* August 30, 1906; Campbell, "New Parochialism," 262–64.

48. Charles P. Taft to Moeller, April 7, 1916; Moeller to Taft, April 7, 1916, AAC; Tentler, *Seasons of Grace,* 108; *The Cincinnati Times-Star,* March 31, April 5, 1916.

49. Mother M. Stanislaus to Elder, March 9, 1881; Sister Mary of the Presentation to Elder, May 1, 1882; Sister Mary Getrude [to Elder?], May 26, 1882; Anonymous Letter to Elder, March 21, 1884; Sister M. of St. Jane to Elder, April 8, 1886; Sister Joseph David to Elder, April 17, 1888; September 19, 1889; Sister M. St. Albert to Elder, May 11, 1892; Moeller to the Magdalen Community, July 15, 1904; Moeller to Mother Stanislaus, July 15, August 7, 1904; Moeller to Mother M. of St. Laurence, March 2, 1906; Moeller to Mother Superior, November 3, 1913; Sister Mary of St. Aloysius to Moeller, 1913; Moeller to Taft, April 7, 1916; Moeller to Mother Compassion, June 25, 1918; Elder's Diary, September 29, 1885, AAC; *The Cincinnati Times-Star,* April 7, 1916. For more extensive coverage of controversy see Campbell, "New Parochialism," 269–77.

50. *Catholic Telegraph,* March 30, April 6, 1882; August 6, 1885; December 22, 1887; November 18, 1897.

51. Ibid., August 6, 1885; December 22, 1887; November 18, 1897; quoted in Henry J. Browne, *The Catholic Church and the Knights of Labor* (Washington, D.C., 1949), 24, 81, 319–21.

52. *Catholic Telegraph,* January 8, 1920; August 10, 1922.

53. Ibid., May 1, 6, 1886; March 15, July 19, 1888; October 16, 23, 1902.

54. Moeller to Pastors, May 14, 1913, AAC; *Catholic Telegraph,* October 16, 23, 1902.

55. *Catholic Telegraph,* November 18, 1897; June 30, 1898; March 6, 1902; January 23, 1913; June 13, 1918.

56. Moeller to Dietz, June 10, 1919; Moeller to James McCabe, S.J., February 9, 1920, AAC; Mary Harrita Fox, *Peter E. Dietz, Labor Priest* (Notre Dame, 1953), 177–88.

57. Moeller to Dietz, April 23, 1922; Moeller to Rev. William Scullen, September 16, 1922, AAC.

58. Moeller to Bonzano, July 20, August 23, 1922; Moeller to Daniel J. Tobin, August 3, 1922; Moeller to Linus G. Dey, January 18, 1923; Moeller to Rev. Thomas Shahan, March 17, 1923, AAC; Fox, *Peter E. Dietz,* 206, 219–21. About fourteen years after Dietz left Cincinnati he was somewhat vindicated when John T. McNicholas, then archbishop of Cincinnati, invited him to return to the archdiocese to resume his work in the community. Dietz thought that younger priests should now conduct the work.

59. *Catholic Telegraph,* May 24, 1888; July 20, 1899; October 30, 1902; James J. Kenneally, "Eve, Mary, and the Historians: American Catholicism and Women" in *Women in American Religion,* ed. Janet Wilson James (Philadelphia, 1978), 195.

60. *Catholic Telegraph,* July 20, 1899; May 5, 1904.

61. Ibid., July 17, 31, 1913.

62. Moeller to Rev. S. P. Messmer, July 29, 1913, AAC; *Catholic Telegraph,* August 28, 1913; April 9, 1914; July 9, 1931.

63. Moeller to Stanley Bowdle, April 18, 1912; Moeller to Patton Hudson, April 9, 1914, AAC; *Catholic Telegraph,* April 9, July 9, 1914; October 3, 1918; David O'Brien, *Public Catholicism* (New York, 1989), 135.

64. Moeller to Sisters, October 12, 1920, AAC; *Catholic Telegraph,* September 2, 1915; October 7, 1920; Judith Metz, S.C., "150 Years of Caring: The Sisters of Charity in Cincinnati," *The Cincinnati Historical Society Bulletin* 37 (Cincinnati, 1979): 167; Tentler, *Seasons of Grace,* 253; Carol K. Coburn and Martha Smith, *Spirited Lives: How Nuns Shaped Catholic Culture and American Life, 1836–1920* (Chapel Hill, N.C., 1999), 177, 179–80; Eileen Mary Brewer, *Nuns and the Education of American Catholic Women, 1860–1920* (Chicago, 1987), 15. Mt. St. Joseph was the second Catholic college for women in Ohio.

PART III

Introduction

1. Stritch to McNicholas, March 11, 1944, AAC.

2. *Cincinnati Times-Star,* April 24, 1950; Gerald P. Fogarty, *The Vatican and the American Hierarchy from 1870 to 1965* (Wilmington, Del., 1985), 348. As the Catholic Church in the United States became more assertive nationally, four of Cincinnati's five ordinaries from McNicholas's time to the present—McNicholas, Karl Alter, Joseph Bernardin, and Daniel Pilarczyk—headed the National Catholic Welfare Conference since its establishment in 1922.

3. Fogarty, *The Vatican and the American Hierarchy,* 348; Steven M. Avella, "John T. McNicholas in the Age of Practical Thomism, *Records of the American Catholic Historical Society of Philadelphia* 97 (March-December 1986): 16; *Cincinnati Enquirer,* May 11, 1938.

4. *The Post & Times-Star,* July 23, 1969; *Cincinnati Post,* August 24, 1977.

Chapter 10

1. *Cincinnati Enquirer,* August 12, 13, 1925; *Cincinnati Post,* April 24, 1950. McNicholas and Purcell, both from Ireland, were the only foreign-born prelates of the archdiocese of Cincinnati.

2. *Cincinnati Times Star,* April 24, 1950; *Cincinnati Enquirer,* August 12, 1925; April 23, 1950.

3. McNicholas to Rev. Thomas Conlon, January 15, 1934, AAC; Steven M. Avella, "John T. McNicholas in the Age of Practical Thomism," *Records of the American Catholic Historical Society of Philadelphia* 97 (March-December 1986): 18–19; *Catholic Telegraph,* October 24, 1935; *Cincinnati Enquirer,* April 23, 1950; *Cincinnati Post,* September 8, 1938; *Cincinnati Times Star,* April 24, 1950.

4. *St. Aloysius Church, 125th Year Anniversary* (Shandon, Ohio, 1993); *St. Joseph Church Centennial, 1883–1983* (Springfield, Ohio, 1983); *St. Brigid Parish Sesquicentennial, 1849–1999* (Xenia, Ohio, 1999), AAC; Patrick W. Carey, *The Roman Catholics* (Westport, Conn., 1993), 78.

5. Timothy Walch, *Parish School: American Catholic Parochial Education from Colonial Times to the Present* (New York, 1996), 115–16, 158; *Catholic Telegraph,* November 9, 1933.

6. McNicholas Address, Music Hall, November 18, 1928, AAC; *Catholic Telegraph,* November 22, 1928; March 28, 1929; *Cincinnati Enquirer,* August 13, 1925; *Cincinnati Times-Star,*

November 19, 1928; Carey, *The Roman Catholics,* 81. The publication in 1922 of John A. Ryan's and Moorhouse Millar's *The Church and the State,* which urged the state to make a public profession of religion, reinforced American fears of the incompatibility of Catholicism and America.

7. McNicholas to Albers, November 7, 1928, AAC; *Cincinnati Post,* March 26, 1934; *Cincinnati Enquirer,* August 12, 13,1925.

8. McNicholas, "Duty of Voting," October 1, 1929; a second leaflet was published September 1, 1939, AAC; *Catholic Telegraph,* March 22, 1928; September 8, 1939; *Cincinnati Post,* March 29, 1934.

9. *Cincinnati Times-Star,* June 3, 1959; September 16, 1980.

10. McNicholas to Dowling, September 25, 1926; McNicholas to Noll, September 13, 1929; McNicholas to William Albers, September 28, 1929, AAC; Douglas J. Slawson, *The Foundation and First Decade of the National Catholic Welfare Council* (Washington, D.C., 1992), 96–100, 228–31, 265.

11. McNicholas Address, Convention of NCCM, Fort Wayne, October 20, 1929; McNicholas to Pastors, January 15, 1931; May 20, 1947, AAC; *Catholic Telegraph,* January 12, May 24, 1928; Leslie Woodcock Tentler, *Seasons of Grace: A History of the Catholic Archdiocese of Detroit* (Detroit, Mich., 1990), 433; Joseph P. Chinnici, O.F.M., *Living Stones: The History and Structure of Catholic Spiritual Life in the United States* (New York, 1989), 166–68.

12. *Cincinnati Enquirer,* June 21, 1950; *Cincinnati Post,* June 21, 1950.

13. *Cincinnati Enquirer,* June 21, 1950; *Cincinnati Post & Times-Star,* September 26, 1960; *The Cincinnati Post,* August 24, 1977.

14. *Cincinnati Enquirer,* June 21, 1950; *Cincinnati Times-Star,* September 22, 1950; *Cincinnati Post,* April 24, 1950; *Cincinnati Post & Times-Star,* September 26, 1960. Steven Avella points out in his study that McNicholas was also seen as authoritarian in his dealings with the clergy in Duluth, Avella, "McNicholas," 20.

15. *Catholic Telegraph,* September 29, 1950; *Cincinnati Post,* September 26, 1950.

16. *Catholic Telegraph,* January 6, September 29, 1950.

17. Alter to Guisuppe Cardinal Pizzardo, December 13 1951, AAC; *Cincinnati Enquirer,* June 21, 1950.

18. *Catholic Telegraph,* November 14, 1952; May 6, 1955. In 1954 Clarence Issenmann was ordained auxiliary bishop for the archdiocese. Three years later he became the sixth bishop of Columbus.

19. *St. John Fisher, 1947–1972* (Cincinnati, 1972); *We Are His People: St. Susanna Church, 1938–1988* (Mason, Ohio, 1988); *St. Antoninus Parish* (Cincinnati, 1969); *25th Anniversary Saint Bartholomew Church, 1961–1986* (Cincinnati, 1986), AAC; *Catholic Telegraph,* August 11, 1950; September 23, 1955.

20. *Catholic Telegraph,* August 11, 1950; September 23, 1955.

21. Paul F. Hurst, "The History of Cincinnati's Old St. Mary's Parish: An Example of the Catholic Church's Response to Some Social Problems of American Cities" (unpublished paper, University of Cincinnati, 1969), 32; *Commemorating the Centenary of St. Clement Parish, 1850–1950* (Cincinnati, 1951); *Dedication St. Agnes Church* (Cincinnati, 1956); *St. Joseph Church Centennial Year* (Hamilton, Ohio, 1965), AAC.

22. McNicholas to Rev. Thomas F. Conlon, January 15, 1934; Chancellor Issenmann to Priests, October 1, 1946; McNicholas to Cardinal Mooney, October 7, 1946; *St. Antoninus Parish* (Cincinnati, 1969), AAC; *Catholic Telegraph,* October 11, 1934; October 24, 1935; October 18, 1946; December 30, 1949; October 16, 1969; October 2, 1970; Tentler, *Seasons of Grace,* 428.

23. *All Saints Church: On Occasion of the 25th Anniversary of All Saints Parish* (Cincinnati, 1974); *25th Anniversary Saint Bartholomew Church, 1961–1986* (Cincinnati, 1986); *50th Anniversary*

Our Lady of Lourdes Parish, 1927–1977 (Cincinnati, 1977); *St. Antoninus Parish* (Cincinnati, 1969), AAC.

24. *Diamond Jubilee St. William Parish, 1909–1984* (Cincinnati, 1984); *Centennial Year St. Joseph Church* (Hamilton, Ohio, 1965), AAC.

25. *We are His People: St. Susanna Church, 1938–1988* (Mason, Ohio, 1988); Chancellor to McNicholas, December 10, 1936; Chancellor to Rev. Edwin Richter, May 22, 1937; McNicholas to Pastors, January 29, 1938; Bishop Hartley to McNicholas, December 8, 1941; McNicholas to Hartley, May 24, 1943; Monsignor Freking to Pastors, October 28, 1943, AAC; *Catholic Telegraph,* August 13, 1943.

26. McNicholas, Catholic Action, 1931, AAC; *Catholic Telegraph,* January 8, 1931.

27. McNicholas Address, National Council of Catholic Women, October 9, 1932; McNicholas Address, National Convention of Catholic Women, November 17, 1935, AAC; *Catholic Telegraph,* August 26, 1926; May 2, 1935; *Cincinnati Enquirer,* March 25, 1952; March 17, 1955; *Cincinnati Post,* March 12, 1951; Jeffrey M. Burns, *Disturbing the Peace: A History of the Christian Family Movement, 1949–1974* (Notre Dame, Ind., 1999), 18–22.

28. McNicholas to Pastors, January 11, 1949; Alter to Dr. and Mrs. J. C. Willke, January 5, 1967; Alter Pastoral, July 31, 1968, AAC; *Catholic Telegraph,* February 5, 1960; June 9, 1967; November 21, 1968.

29. McNicholas, "Our Youth of Tomorrow," August 18, 1937; Peter Cardinal Fumasoni Biondi to Monsignor Edward Freking, June 15, 1938; Rev. Richard Schumacher to McNicholas, June 5, 1945; Rev. Henry J. Vogelpohl to Rev. James N. Lunn, March 19, 1949, AAC; *Catholic Telegraph,* May 15, September 4, 1970.

30. *Catholic Telegraph,* July 5, 1957.

31. Ibid., April 18, 1958; February 27, December 4, 1959.

32. McNicholas to Dowling, September 25, 1926; McNicholas to Albers, May 15, 1929, AAC; *Catholic Telegraph,* January 12, May 24, 1928; October 11, 1934; August 9, 1940; Chinnici, *Living Stones,* 157, 166–67. In the spring of 1928 more than one hundred laymen attended the first reunion of laymen who had taken part in the diocese's weekend retreats. In 1929 the retreat ministry of the Jesuits, who had built a retreat house in Milford, Ohio, became known as the "Men of Milford."

33. Chancellor Henry Vogelpohl to Miss Pauline Ling, March 3, 1965, AAC; *Catholic Telegraph,* February 9, 1951; September 10, 24, 1954; August 12, 1955; October 3, 1980; Chinnici, *Living Stones,* 159. On December 31, 1980, the Sisters of Mary Reparatrix, who had served the people of the archdiocese for three decades, closed their retreat house and convent in Clinton due to increasing costs and declining membership in the congregation.

34. McNicholas Address to Catholic Press Association, May 17, 1929, AAC; *Catholic Telegraph,* November 18, 1925.

35. McNicholas to Mooney, September 16, 1937; McNicholas to Mons. Francis Thill, May 14, 1937; McNicholas to Pastors, January 18, August 24, 1937, AAC; *Catholic Telegraph,* September 9, 16, 1937; November 7, 1941; July 17, 1942. The columns in the *The Catholic Telegraph-Register* bearing the heading "Official," and which had the signature of one of the authorities of the archdiocese, were regarded as official. Those columns entitled "Our Comments" provided opportunities for priests and, at times, laymen to contribute.

36. Rev. Lawrence C. Walter to Alter, April 1, 1958; Board Meeting of *Catholic Telegraph,* May 13, 1964; January 27, 1967. Alter to Clergy, January 20, 1965; Alter to Rev. Lawrence C. Walter, December 28, 1966; Alter to Clergy, January 11, 1961; January 27, 1962, AAC; *Catholic Telegraph,* January 27, 1967.

37. McNicholas, "The Episcopal Committee and the Problem of Evil Motion Pictures," *The Ecclesiastical Review,* August 1934; McNicholas letter to Apostolic Delegate, June 3, 1935, AAC; Frank Walsh, *Sin and Censorship: The Catholic Church and the Motion Picture Industry*

(New Haven, Conn., 1996), 86–88; Gregory Black, *The Catholic Crusade Against the Movies, 1940–1975* (Cambridge, 1998), 22; *Catholic Telegraph*, November 23, 1933; June 7, July 5, 1934.

38. McNicholas to Clergy, April 4, 1934; McNicholas to Apostolic Delegate, June 3, 1935, AAC; Walsh, *Sin and Censorship*, 92–93; *Catholic Telegraph*, March 8, April 5, 19, June 28, 1934.

39. McNicholas to Noll, April 15, 1934, AAC; Walsh, *Sin and Censorship*, 94; *Catholic Telegraph*, June 28, 1934; *Time*, July 2, 1934.

40. McNicholas, "The Episcopal Committee and the Problem of Evil Pictures," *The Ecclesiastical Review*, August 1934; Albers to Noll, August 18, 1934; McNicholas to Apostolic Delegate, June 3, 1935; October 23, 1935; McNicholas Radio Address, NBC Blue Network, September 21, 1934; Paul W. Facey, *The Legion of Decency: A Sociological Analysis of the Emergence and Development of a Social Pressure Group* (New York, 1974), 54; *Catholic Telegraph*, July 5, 26, August 23, September 13, 27, 1934; February 6, 1936; *Time*, July 2, 1934.

41. Archbishop House Memo, June 9, 1934; Noll to McNicholas, May 12, 1934; McNicholas to Apostolic Delegate, June 3, 1935; Chancellor Matthias F. Heyker to Rev. John J. McClafferty, November 6, 1941, AAC; Walsh, *Sin and Censorship*, 111; Black, *The Catholic Crusade Against the Movies*, 23; *Catholic Telegraph*, July 26, 1934; *Cincinnati Times-Star*, April 24, 1950; Facey, *The Legion of Decency*, 58.

42. McNicholas to Apostlic Delegate, June 3, 1935, AAC; Walsh, *Sin and Censorship*, 151; Black, *The Catholic Crusade Against the Movies*, 241; *Catholic Telegraph*, November 22, 1934; March 14, 1935; March 5, 26, September 17, November 19, 1936; *Cincinnati Enquirer*, August 22, 1938; *Cincinnati Post*, November 4, 1947.

43. *Catholic Telegraph*, July 26, September 27, 1934; *Cincinnati Post*, March 30, 1934; *Cincinnati Enquirer*, August 18, 1937.

44. "How To Judge the Morality of Motion Pictures," November 9, 1936, Cicognani to McNicholas, June 2, 1939, AAC; Walsh, *Sin and Censorship*, 146; Black, *The Catholic Crusade Against the Movies*, 240; *Catholic Telegraph*, December 9, 1955; *Cincinnati Enquirer*, December 12, 1964.

45. Alter to Keating, January 23, 1964, December 1, 1965, AAC; *Catholic Telegraph*, November 27, 1953; May 6, 1955; March 4, 1960.

46. McNicholas Address at Rural Life Conference, Cincinnati, October 20–21, 1926; McNicholas to Rev. Timothy Sparks, November 25, 1948, AAC; quoted in Timothy Michael Dolan, *"Some Seed Fell on Good Ground": The Life of Edwin V. O'Hara* (Washington, D.C., 1992), 93; Christopher J. Kauffman, *Mission to Rural America: The Story of W. Howard Bishop, Founder of Glenmary* (New York, 1991), 60, 65. The first Catholic Rural Life Conference was organized by Father Edwin V. O'Hara, first director of the Catholic Rural Life Bureau in the Social Action Department of the National Catholic Welfare Council.

47. McNicholas to O'Callaghan, October 26, 1925; O'Callaghan to McNicholas, December 24, 1925; McNicholas to Bishop, August 15, 1937; Announcement on Home Mission Society, August 1937; McNicholas to Apostolic Delegate, November 5, 1944; McNicholas to Mons. Luca Ermenegildo Pasetto, May 19, 1947; McNicholas to Cicognani, September 29, 1947; Mulloy to Issenmann, January 21, 1948; McNicholas to Bishop ___, November 12, 1948, AAC; *Catholic Telegraph*, August 29, 1941; February 9, 1951; quoted in Kauffman, *Mission to Rural America*, 61, 132, 135–37.

48. McNicholas to Archbishop ___, June 3, 1945; McNicholas to Cicognani, December 25, 1945, AAC; *Catholic Telegraph*, July 14, 1944.

49. McNicholas to Cicognani, December 25, 1945; Mulloy to Issenmann, January 21, 1948, AAC; *Catholic Telegraph*, February 4, May 12, July 14, 1944; January 16, 1948; Jay P. Dolan, *The American Catholic Experience: A History from Colonial Times to the Present* (New York,

1985), 414; Alden V. Brown, *The Grail Movement and American Catholicism, 1940–1975* (Notre Dame, Ind., 1989), 25, 42–44; Kauffman, *Mission to Rural America,* 192–93.

50. *25th Anniversary Queen of Peace Church* (Hamilton, Ohio, 1966), AAC; *Catholic Telegraph,* October 12, 1945; April 27, May 4, 1951.

51. *Catholic Telegraph,* April 6, May 11, 1951.

52. Alter to Joseph V. Urbain, April 2, 1955, AAC; *Catholic Telegraph,* February 8, 1952; April 15, 1955.

53. *Clerus Cincinnatensis, A Directory of Clergy and Parishes of the Archdiocese of Cincinnati, 1821 to 1996* (Cincinnati, 1996), 32–33; *Catholic Telegraph,* November 24, 1950.

54. *Catholic Telegraph,* August 26, 1926.

55. *The One Hundredth and Fiftieth Anniversary Keepsake Book, Saint Joseph Church and School* (Cincinnati, [n.d.]), AAC; *Catholic Telegraph,* November 11, 1960; November 2, 1963.

56. McNicholas to William Albers, October 15, 1929, AAC; M. Edmund Hussey, *A History of the Seminaries of the Archdiocese of Cincinnati 1829–1979* (Norwood, Ohio, 1979), 51; *Catholic Telegraph,* July 9, 1931; October 3, 1941.

57. McNicholas to Archbishop Dowling, July 24, 1928, AAC; Hussey, *A History of the Seminaries of the Archdiocese of Cincinnati,* 51–52; Carey, 77; *Catholic Telegraph,* December 5, 1929; October 3, 1941.

58. Avella, McNicholas, 15, 20–21; Philip J. Murnion, *The Catholic Priest and the Changing Structure of Pastoral Ministry New York 1920–1970* (New York, 1978), 10–14.

59. McNicholas to the Catholic Press Association, May 17, 1929, AAC; Hussey, *A History of the Seminaries of the Archdiocese of Cincinnati,* 52; Zane L. Miller and Bruce Tucker, *Changing Plans for America's Inner Cities: Cincinnati's Over-the-Rhine and Twentieth-Century Urbanism* (Columbus, Ohio, 1998), 29–40; *Catholic Telegraph,* July 11, September 26, 1952. A fire in 1956 destroyed the south wing of the older brick building at St. Gregory's. Repairing that damage increased the cost of the overall expansion.

60. *Catholic Telegraph,* October 4, 1957; Supplement, June 14, 1996; *Cincinnati Post & Times-Star,* September 28, 1960; *Cincinnati Post,* August 29, 1977.

61. Alter Pastoral, September 9, 1959, AAC.

62. Alter to Rev. Charles Murphy, July 16, 1952; Alter to Brother H. Bernard, October 24, 1960; Clergy Bulletin, November 11, 1953; Alter to Clergy, August 29, 1951; Alter to Bishop John Wright, May 8, 1962; Alter to Sister Miriam, O.S.F., September 1, 1962; Brief History of Archdiocesan Vocation Endeavor, 1962; By-Laws of Archdiocesan Vocation Endeavor, 1963, AAC; *Catholic Telegraph,* June 15, 1962; July 8, 1966.

63. Alter Synodal Letter, October 18, 1954, AAC; *Catholic Telegraph,* October 29, December 17, 1954.

64. McNicholas to Archbishop Cantwell, February 10, 1937; Cicognani to McNicholas, May 24, 1937; McNicholas to Rehring, January 22, 1942; Alter to Rev. Bernard Piening, July 5, 1966, AAC; *Catholic Telegraph,* July 9, 1931; June 3, 1937. In June 1937 the Cincinnati native Joseph H. Albers, who had served as McNicholas's chancellor since 1925 and as auxiliary bishop since 1929, became the first bishop of Lansing, Michigan. Two months later Monsignor George J. Rehring, a native of Price Hill in Cincinnati and rector of Mt. St. Mary's of the West Seminary, was named auxiliary bishop of Cincinnati. Among the new deaneries in the archdiocese was Springfield, established in 1942. The new division embraced eight counties in the northeastern part of the archdiocese. The following year the archdiocese established four new deaneries. These consisted of the Cathedral deanery and St. Francis de Sales deanery in Hamilton County, the Chillicothe deanery, and the Hamilton deanery. During Alter's episcopate the St. Lawrence and St. Margaret Mary deaneries were also established.

65. McNicholas to Cicognani, July 25, 1943; Cicognani to McNicholas, March 27, 1945; John C. Dempsey to McNicholas, November 29, 1946; McNicholas to Cicognani, October 5,

1947, AAC; *Catholic Telegraph,* July 9, 1931; June 3, August 12, 1937; October 2, 1942; January 1, November 12, 1943; November 24, 1944; January 6, 1950. The counties affected by the establishment of the Columbus diocese were Hardin, Marion, Union, Madison, Fayette, Pickaway, Ross, Pike, and Scioto.

Chapter 11

1. Fred Tuke to McNicholas, October 7, 1926, AAC; *Catholic Telegraph,* November 18, 1926; October 11, 1934; Dorothy M. Brown and Elizabeth McKeown, *The Poor Belong to Us: Catholic Charities and American Welfare* (Cambridge, 1997), 93–94, points out that in 1926 the National Conference of Catholic Charities, at McNicholas's request, reviewed the diocesan bureau of charities and institutions and recommended substantial changes.
2. *Catholic Telegraph,* November 18, 1926; July 9, 1931.
3. "An Analytical Summary of the Catholic Charities. . . ," 1939, 3–5; Chancellor to Rev. Bede Mitchell, September 28, 1937; Catholic Charities Annual Report, 1940, AAC; *Catholic Telegraph,* July 9, 1931; February 4, 1966; Judith Metz, S.C., "150 Years of Caring: The Sisters of Charity in Cincinnati," *The Cincinnati Historical Society Bulletin* 37 (1979): 158.
4. McNicholas Testimonial for Sisters of Charity, n.d., [1928], AAC; *Catholic Telegraph,* October 28, 1926.
5. *Catholic Telegraph,* June 9, 1950.
6. Ibid., July 9, 1931; January 12, 1951.
7. Ibid., July 9, 1931.
8. McNicholas Address, First General Chapter of the Sisters of Mercy, August 28, 1929, AAC; *Catholic Telegraph,* October 28, 1926; July 9, 1931; June 2, 1950.
9. McNicholas to Cicognani, April 11, September 19, 1940; January 31, 1942; McNicholas to Mother M. Hyacinth, January 29, 1938; *St. Thomas Aquinas Golden Jubilee, 1927–1977* (Cincinnati, 1977), AAC; *Catholic Telegraph,* August 29, 1941; November 24, 1950; January 26, February 16, 1951.
10. McNicholas Sermon, The National Council of Catholic Women, Cleveland, October 7, 1928, AAC; *Catholic Telegraph,* November 18, 1926; September 13, 1928; June 25, 1931.
11. *Catholic Telegraph,* July 9, 1931.
12. *Centenary Souvenir, Congregation of the Sisters of the Poor of St. Francis, 1845–1945 (Cincinnati, 1945),* 5, AAC; *Catholic Telegraph,* July 9, 1931; October 11, 1934. In the early 1930s the Franciscan Fathers, who ran the Friars Athletic Club opposite the Franciscan monastery on Vine Street in Cincinnati, erected an Athletic Club at Ohio Avenue and McMillan Street.
13. *25th Anniversary Saint Bartholomew Church, 1961–1986* (Cincinnati, 1986); Alter to Clergy, July 19, 1955, AAC; *Catholic Telegraph,* July 9, 1931; October 11, 1934.
14. McNicholas to Pastors, March 21, 1935; Rev. Bernard Sheil to McNicholas, July 24, 1939, AAC; *Catholic Telegraph,* March 21, 1935; August 4, 1950; *The Cincinnati Post & Times Star,* July 23, 1969. In the 1930s the Boy Scout movement was incorporated in the CYO. The Young Christian Student Movement (YCS) and the Lay Organizations Department in the Ohio Catholic Welfare Conference were other examples of lay involvement in the archdiocese.
15. McNicholas to Pastors, April 12, 1928; McNicholas to Hartley, March 6, 1940; Statement of Rev. Francis Culley, Director, Catholic Charities Office, Dayton, 1941; McNicholas to John Matthews, January 20, 1929; Alter to Pastors, March 1, 1955; Alter Pastoral, September 26, 1957, AAC; *Catholic Telegraph,* October 11, 1934; *Cincinnati Times-Star,* September 12, 1939.
16. Alter to Pastors, September 25, 1962, Bulletins, AAC; *Catholic Telegraph,* June 2, 9, 1950; November 4, 1960. St. Margaret Hall facility was made possible by a contribution by the Walter E. Schott family.

17. Clergy Pledge Committee Cincinnati Hospital Drive to Clergy, May 8, 1956, Bulletins; Alter Pastoral, October 11, 1965, AAC; *Catholic Telegraph,* June 16, 23, 30, 1950.

18. *Cincinnati Enquirer,* August 12, 1925; Jay P. Dolan, *The American Catholic Experience: A History from Colonial Times to the Present* (New York, 1985), 406–7.

19. McNicholas, "Justice Makes Demands," 1931; McNicholas to Boyle, May 4, 1932, AAC; quote on Community Chest is in Brown and McKeown, *Poor Belong to Us,* 157; *Catholic Telegraph,* November 13, 1930; September 17, 1931.

20. *Catholic Telegraph,* March 24, 1932; April 5, December 6, 1934; December 5, 1935.

21. *Catholic Telegraph,* October 1, 1931; March 9, 1933; *Cincinnati Post,* March 31, 1934. Even though McNicholas supported private property, because of his criticisms of certain aspects of capitalism some individuals nevertheless called him a Bolshevik.

22. McNicholas Address, Convention of American Federation of Labor, November 22, 1932, AAC; *Catholic Telegraph,* June 28, 1928; October 1, 1931; January 11, 1946.

23. McNicholas to Hartley, March 27, 1932; Auxiliary Bishop to Rev. Joseph Tetzlaff, September 17, 1932; McNicholas to Archbishop Curley, January 17, 1934; Mons. Wagner to Pastors, September 24, 1931; *100th Anniversary St. Louis Church, 1892–1992* (North Star, Ohio, 1992), AAC. In the spring of 1932 McNicholas resigned as chairman of the fundraising committee of Catholic University.

24. McNicholas Address, "The Need of a Fixed Moral Code," Regional Industrial Conference, March 26, 1935, AAC; *Catholic Telegraph,* March 28, 1935; July 15, 1937; *Cincinnati Post,* March 27, 1934.

25. *Cincinnati Post,* March 26, 27, 1934; April 24, 1950.

26. McNicholas Address, Catholic Conference on Industrial Problems, June 20–21, 1928; Lynn Bresette to McNicholas, October 19, 1928; J. D. Reilly to Rev. Louis G. Reinhold, April 24, 1934; Mooney to McNicholas, February 29, 1940, AAC; *Catholic Telegraph,* June 28, 1928; November 4, 1932; January 21, February 11, April 1, 1937; April 1, 1938; *Cincinnati Post,* March 31, 1934.

27. McNicholas Address, American Federation of Labor, October 11, 1939, AAC; *Catholic Telegraph,* March 22, 29, 1928; May 2, 1929; March 26, 1931; *Cincinnati Post,* March 21, 1934. In a letter to a Vatican official the previous year McNicholas expressed concern that President Roosevelt had "been given unprecedented powers by Congress," quoted in Gerald P. Fogarty, *The Vatican and the American Hierarchy from 1870 to 1965* (Wilmington, Del., 1985), 256.

28. Rev. Richard Schumacher to McNicholas, June 5, 1945; McNicholas to Pastors, November 3, 1945; Rev. Henry J. Vogelpohl to Rev. James N. Lunn, March 19, 1949, AAC; *Catholic Telegraph,* July 15, 1937; June 28, 1940; November 9, 1945; *Cincinnati Enquirer,* November 6, 1945.

29. McNicholas Statement on Coughlin's Address in Cincinnati, n.d. [1936]; McNicholas to Pinten, June 7, 1933, AAC; *Catholic Telegraph,* March 2, 30, 1933; quote on "fundamentals" in Fogarty, *The Vatican and the American Hierarchy,* 239.

30. McNicholas to Monsignor Egidio Vagnozzi, August 14, 1936; McNicholas to Mooney, n.d. [1936], AAC.

31. McNicholas, "The Catholic Position," Radio Address, November 4, 1945; Issenmann to H. E. Fast, December 8, 1945; William Kircher to H. E. Fast, December 6, 1945; Issenmann to Pastors, April 17, 1946, AAC; *Catholic Telegraph,* April 26, 1946; Dolan, *The American Catholic Experience,* 392–93.

32. Alter to Issenmann, March 24, 1958; Alter to Rehring, April 2, 1958; Mons. Earl L. Whalen to Pastors, September 12, 1968, AAC; *Catholic Telegraph,* May 6, 1955; September 5, 1968; *Cincinnati Post,* September 25, 1950; *Cincinnati Enquirer,* October 31, 1952; March 21, 1958.

33. *Cincinnati Enquirer,* January 5, October 21, 1929; *Cincinnati Times-Star,* December 20, 1944; Patrick Carey, *The Roman Catholics* (Westport, Conn., 1993), 87.

34. *Cincinnati Enquirer,* May 11, 1938; J. B. Moorman, *The Medievalists: A Brief History of the Cincinnati Chapter* (Cincinnati Historical Society Collection, n.d.).

35. McNicholas to Pastors, May 29, 1935, AAC; *Catholic Telegraph,* October 18, 1940; *Cincinnati Times-Star,* November 19, 1928; October 15, 1945; *Cincinnati Post,* July 7, 1938; October 31, 1941; February 19, May 26, 1949.

36. *Catholic Telegraph,* March 30, June 1, 8, 1933; March 8, 1934; September 2, October 7, 1938.

37. McNicholas to Bishop Hugh C. Boyle of Pittsburgh, May 4, 1932; McNicholas to Curley, February 15, 1937; McNicholas to Cantwell, February 15, 1937; McNicholas to Pinten, February 27, 1937; Ready to McNicholas, April 17, 1937; McNicholas, "Communism: Its Evils and Causes," 1937, AAC; *Catholic Telegraph,* November 24, 1932; February 11, 1937; October 31, 1941; May 1, 1945; *Cincinnati Post,* July 7, 1938; *Cincinnati Times-Star,* October 15, 1945; David O'Brien, *Public Catholicism* (New York, 1989), 197; Fogarty, *The Vatican and the American Hierarchy,* 272–76; 355–56. In 1941 McNicholas, at Archbishop Mooney's request, drafted a pastor letter explaining how the extension of Lend-Lease to the Soviets, in order to help defeat Nazi Germany, did not violate the papal prohibition of cooperation with Catholicism.

38. *Cincinnati Post,* March 31, 1934; March 3, April 21, 1939; *Cincinnati Enquirer,* January 22, 24, December 9, 1939; December 14, 1944; September 7, 1945, August 8, 1949; *Cincinnati Times-Star,* February 25, 1930; November 16, 1944, November 19, 1946; Robert J. Gannon, S.J., *The Cardinal Spellman Story* (Garden City, N.Y., 1962), 129; quoted in Fogarty, *The Vatican and the American Hierarchy,* 256. Fogarty also cites personal interviews with John McMahon, S.J., the librarian at the Gregorian University in Rome in the late 1930s and with Bishop Clarence Issenmann, McNicholas's secretary, who confirmed the story of McNicholas's appointment as archbishop of New York.

39. Fr. Cyprian Emmanuel to Chancellor Heyker, March 31, 1939, AAC; Fogarty, *The Vatican and the American Hierarchy,* 270–71, 273; *Catholic Telegraph,* September 15, 1939; June 14, 1940; January 3, 1941.

40. McNicholas to Cicognani, December 10, 1941; McNicholas Sermon, December 25, 1941; McNicholas to Pastors and Faithful, January 13, 1944, AAC; *Catholic Telegraph,* January 2, 1942.

41. Mooney to McNicholas, October 16, 1942; McNicholas Address to the Cincinnati Federation of the National Council of Catholic Women, July 8, 1942; Cantwell to McNicholas, November 23, 1942; Alter to McNicholas, November 5, 1943, AAC; *Catholic Telegraph,* February 13, July 17, 1942; *Cincinnati Post,* February 12, 1942; Fogarty, *The Vatican and the American Hierarchy,* 311, 348.

42. Bishops' Statements, "On International Order," November 16, 1944, and "On Organizing World Peace," April 15, 1945; Stritch to McNicholas, April 3, 1945, AAC; Leslie Woodcock Tentler, *Seasons of Grace: A History of the Catholic Archdiocese of Detroit* (Detroit, Mich., 1990), 354–55; *Catholic Telegraph,* July 17, 1942; November 5, 1943; October 13, 1944; August 3, 1945; *Cincinnati Times-Star,* July 8, 1942; *Cincinnati Post,* November 20, 1943.

43. McNicholas to President Truman, May 7, 1947; January 4, 1948; McNicholas to Cicognani, July 11, 1947, AAC.

44. McNicholas to William Albers, December 19, 1945; McNicholas Sermon, December 25, 1945, AAC; *Catholic Telegraph,* August 3, 1945; January 3, 1947; *Cincinnati Post,* April 25, October 26, 1946; *Cincinnati Enquirer,* May 29, 1946; April 3, 1948.

45. McNicholas to Cardinal Mooney, October 7, 1946; McNicholas to Cicognani, May 1, 1948; McNicholas to Pastors, January 11, 27, 1949; McNicholas to President Truman, December

29, 1948; McNicholas to Monsignor Montini, December 29, 1948, AAC; *Catholic Telegraph,* October 11, 18, 1946; January 7, February 4, 18, April 29, 1949; *Cincinnati Enquirer,* October 7, 1946; July 24, 1948; *Cincinnati Times-Star,* February 8, 1949. In 1949 the aging McNicholas was delegating many of his duties to his chancellor Paul F. Leibold, vicar general Clarence G. Issenmann, and Auxiliary Bishop George J. Rehring. Though Mindszenty was sentenced to life imprisonment he was set free during the uprising in Hungary in 1956.

46. McNicholas to Pastors, November 28, 1945; Rev. Francis D. Alwaire to Chancery, May 17, 1946; McNicholas Radio Address, March 4, 1948; *Commemorating the Centenary of St. Clement Parish, 1850–1950* (Cincinnati, 1951), AAC; *Catholic Telegraph,* July 22, 1949; *Cincinnati Post,* November 18, 1946; *Cincinnati Enquirer,* February 7, 1948; Carey, *The Roman Catholics,* 91.

47. *Catholic Telegraph,* November 24, 1950; September 28, November 27, 1953; November 21, 1958; *Cincinnati Enquirer,* September 27, October 2, 1950. As head of the NCWC Administrative Board Alter personally oversaw the National Catholic Community Service, War Relief Services, and other NCWC agencies that did not function under a separate episcopal chairperson.

48. Alter to Pastors, November 13, 1958, AAC; *Cincinnati Enquirer,* November 21, 1953; March 12, 1963.

49. Rev. Albert Von Hagel to McNicholas, August 18, 1925; McNicholas to Pastors, April 24, 1934, AAC; *Catholic Telegraph,* October 8, 1925.

50. Robert B. Fairbanks, "Cincinnati Blacks and the Irony of Low-Income Housing Reform, 1900–1950" in *Race and the City: Work, Community, and Protest in Cincinnati, 1820–1970,* ed. Henry Louis Taylor, Jr. (Urbana, 1993), 196; *Catholic Telegraph,* October 8, 1925; article by John M. Martin, *Ecclesiastical Review,* 1935, reprinted in *Catholic Telegraph,* August 29, 1935.

51. McNicholas to the Colored People of the Archdiocese of Cincinnati, [October 1925], AAC; *Catholic Telegraph,* October 8, 1925; November 29, 1934; Martin's *Ecclesiastical Review* article in *Catholic Telegraph,* August 29, 1935.

52. *Centenary Celebration: Holy Trinity Church, 1834–1934,* Cincinnati, 1934; McNicholas to Mother Katharine, February 12, 1926; McNicholas Address, Holy Trinity Church, August 15, 1926; Mother Katharine to Walsh, February 27, 1926, AAC; Martin's *Ecclesiastical Review* article in *Catholic Telegraph,* August 29, 1935.

53. *Centenary Celebration: Holy Trinity Church, 1834–1934* (Cincinnati, 1934), AAC; *Catholic Telegraph,* May 8, 1930; July 9, 1931; February 9, 1951.

54. Christopher J. Kauffman, *Ministry and Meaning: A Religious History of Catholic Health Care in the United States* (New York, 1995), 258; *Catholic Telegraph,* March 10, 1927; February 2, 1928.

55. McNicholas to [Cicognani], September 11, 1930; Chancellor to T. J. Owens, May 8, 1931; Auxiliary Bishop to Nathaniel E. Squibb, January 20, 1932, AAC; *Catholic Telegraph,* March 28, 1929; May 8, 1930. Every year in the 1930s and 1940s the archdiocese also maintained a summer camp for the black children.

56. McNicholas, "Organized Catholic Action," Address at NCIF, September 3, 1933, AAC; *Catholic Telegraph,* November 15, 1946; February 9, 16, 1951; Martin's *Ecclesiastical Review* article in *Catholic Telegraph,* August 29, 1935.

57. McNicholas, "Organized Catholic Action," Address at NCIF, September 3, 1933; Archbishop Curley to McNicholas, March 25, 1933, AAC; Fairbanks, "Cincinnati Blacks," 202; *Catholic Telegraph,* June 7, 22, 1933.

58. *Catholic Telegraph,* April 20, 1945; June 28, 1928; October 1, 1931.

59. Chancery Notes, October 22, 1928; C. M. Stegner to McNicholas, September 10, 1929, AAC; *Catholic Telegraph,* October 26, 1933; September 10, 1936; Martin's *Ecclesiastical Review* article in *Catholic Telegraph,* August 29, 1935.

60. Rev. E. Mason to McNicholas, January 20, 1940; McNicholas to Cardinal Mooney, April 7, 1949, AAC; *Catholic Telegraph,* February 2, 1946; November 24, 1950; January 26, 1951.

61. McNicholas to Rev. John T. Gillard, January 16, 1941; Chancellor Heyker to Whom it May Concern, [1941]; McNicholas to Cicognani, November 8, 1945; Rev. Charles Murphy to Chancellor Thill, July 18, 1936; McNicholas to Rev. John Cogan, December 13, 1940; January 22, 1942; *St. Joseph Church Centennial 1883–1983* (Springfield, Ohio, 1983), AAC; *Catholic Telegraph,* July 9, 1931; August 29, 1941; January 1, 1943; February 22, 1946.

62. Disgusted Catholics to Rev. Gregory Miller, November 1, 1946; McNicholas to Steiner, March 7, 1943; Steiner to McNicholas, March 26, 1943; McNicholas to Archbishop Ritter, September 30, 1947, AAC; Carey, *The Roman Catholics,* 85; Dolan, *The American Catholic Experience,* 368.

63. Msgr. August Kramer to Pastors, May 15, 1946; *The Apostolate,* Autumn 1949, AAC; *Catholic Telegraph,* April 5, 1946; February 18, 1949; January 19, 1951; *Cincinnati Times-Star,* February 19, 1949.

64. McNicholas to Pastors, February 13, 1947; Shands to Alter, September 1, 1959; Leibold to Kramer, September 4, 1959; Kramer to Leibold, September 11, 1959, AAC; *Catholic Telegraph,* February 18, 1949; January 19, 1951.

65. George Conrad to Col. P. A. Callahan, November 13, 1933; Mother Katharine to McNicholas, October 24, 1938, AAC; *Catholic Telegraph,* February 11, 1937; August 5, 1938.

66. Benjamin E. Simpson to Chancery Office, August 1953; Leibold to Simpson, August 10, 1953, AAC; Carey, *The Roman Catholics,* 106.

67. Rev. William J. Cole to Alter, May 3, 1961; Alter to Rev. Willism Schroeder, June 22, 1963; Alter Pastoral, July 16, 1963, AAC; *Catholic Telegraph,* October 6, 1961; February 1, 8, March 29, July 19, 1963.

68. Alter to Rev. Philip Hoelle, S.M., January 8, 1966, AAC; *Catholic Telegraph,* July 26, 1963; August 14, 1964; January 8, 1965; Zane L. Miller and Bruce Tucker, *Changing Plans for America's Inner Cities: Cincinnati's Over-The-Rhine and Twentieth Century Urbanism* (Columbus, Ohio, 1998), 64.

69. Alter to Rev. William Schroeder, June 22, 1963, AAC; *Catholic Telegraph,* February 1, March 29, 1963; April 23, July 16, September 3, 1965. In April 1965 McCarthy, a native of Cincinnati who had served for fourteen years as secretary to the archbishop of Cincinnati, had been named an auxiliary to Alter. Four years later he became the first bishop of the diocese of Phoenix, Arizona.

70. Alter to Donald Emerson, March 23, 1964; Rev. Edward McCarthy to Pastors, January 8, 1968; Alter to Robert Vogelpohl, July 7, 1967; July 25, 1969, AAC; *Catholic Telegraph,* September 28, November 9, 1967; January 4, February 22, April 18, 1968; *Cincinnati Enquirer,* February 23, 1968.

71. *Catholic Telegraph,* April 28, July 20, 1967. A gym at Purcell high school was built at this time for use after school.

72. Rev. McCarthy to Rev. Leibold, October 2, 1968, AAC; *Catholic Telegraph,* May 9, July 4, 1968.

73. Kramer to Leibold, September 11, 1959; Auxiliary Bishop McCarthy to Margaret Hill, May 13, 1968, AAC; *Catholic Telegraph,* September 26, 1968.

74. Alter to Faithful, September 21, 1966, AAC; *Catholic Telegraph,* July 24, 1964; October 7, 1966; February 3, 1967.

75. Alter, Function of Central Planning and Budget Commission, May 8, 1968; Rev. Edward McCarthy to Rev. Aloysius Welsh, September 5, 1968; Alter to Pastors, December 9, 1968; Rev. Ralph A. Asplan to Clergy and Religious, January 20, 1969, AAC; *Catholic Telegraph,* December 12, 1968; *The Cincinnati Enquirer,* August 24, 1977.

Chapter 12

1. Patrick W. Carey, *The Roman Catholics* (Westport, Conn., 1993), 83; Jay P. Dolan, *The*

American Catholic Experience: A History from Colonial Times to the Present (New York, 1985), 352; Philip Gleason, *Keeping the Faith: American Catholicism Past and Present* (Notre Dame, Ind., 1987), 77; Steven M. Avella, "John T. McNicolas in the Age of Practical Thomism," *Records of the American Catholic Historical Society of Philadelphia* 97 (March-December 1986): 15, 17.

2.. *Catholic Telegraph,* September 10, 1925; September 2, 1926; August 18, 1937; June 9, 1944; July 10, 1953; Gleason, *Keeping the Faith,* 168–69. Like his predecessor, Alter in July 1953 also underscored the importance of religion, moral training, and character formation in education.

3. Timothy Michael Dolan, *"Some Seed Fell on Good Ground": The Life of Edwin V. O'Hara* (Washington, D.C., 1992), 126–27, 144–45; *Catholic Telegraph,* February 21, 1941.

4. McNicholas to Archbishop Curley, January 12, 1937; Bishop Edwin O'Hara to McNicholas, August 27, 1936; Cicognani to McNicholas, June 18, 1948; McNicholas to Rev. John Forest, March 31, 1949; McNicholas to Cicognani, April 10, 1949, AAC; *Catholic Telegraph,* June 27, 1941; Dolan, *The American Catholic Experience,* 391; T. Dolan, *"Some Seed Fell on Good Ground,"* 156–62.

5. Rev. Henry Waldhaus to McNicholas, February 27, 1927; McNicholas to Archbishop Ritter of St. Louis, September 7, 1946; *Saint Rita School for the Deaf, 1915–1965* (Cincinnati, 1965), AAC; *Catholic Telegraph,* September 8, 1927; August 30, September 20, 1928; July 9, 1931; August 29, 1941.

6. McNicholas to Bishop Hartley, November 5, 1927, AAC; *Catholic Telegraph,* September 9, 1926; July 9, 1931; June 14, 1934.

7. McNicholas to Archbishop Ritter, September 7, 1946, AAC; *Catholic Telegraph,* September 29, 1927; September 20, 1928; *Cincinnati Enquirer,* April 23, 1950.

8. *Catholic Telegraph,* March 24, 1944.

9. Gerald P. Fogarty, *The Vatican and the American Hierarchy from 1870 to 1965* (Wilmington, Del., 1985), 346; *Catholic Telegraph,* August 29, 1941; March 24, 1944.

10. McNicholas to Ritter, September 7, 1946, AAC; *Catholic Telegraph,* June 16, 1950; January 19, 1951; January 13, October 5, 1956; *Cincinnati Times-Star,* April 24, 1950.

11. Alter to Clergy, September 14, 1955, AAC; *Catholic Telegraph,* October 5, 1956.

12. Confidential Report to Pastors, January 7, 1957; Alter Pastoral, April 3, 1957; Alter to Mother Helen, O.S.U., February 4, 1960, AAC; *Catholic Telegraph,* April 12, 1957; January 24, 1958; January 8, 1965; *Cincinnati Enquirer,* March 24, April 26, May 14, 1957; *Cincinnati Post,* May 10, 1957.

13. Confidential Report to Pastors, January 7, 1957; Alter Pastoral, April 3, 1957; Rehring to Alter, June 13, 1957; Alter to Mother Helen, O.S.U., February 4, 1960, AAC; *Catholic Telegraph,* January 13, October 5, 1956; April 12, 26, 1957; January 24, 1958; January 8, 1965; *Cincinnati Enquirer,* March 24, April 26, May 14, 1957; *Cincinnati Post,* May 10, 1957.

14. *Catholic Telegraph,* January 24, 1958.

15. Alter to Connaughton, December 24, 1962, AAC; *Catholic Telegraph,* April 10, May 8, 1959.

16. *Catholic Telegraph,* January 8, December 7, 1965; *Cincinnati Post & Times-Star,* September 26, 1969.

17. *Catholic Telegraph,* May 8, 1930.

18. Ibid., February 4, June 6, November 21, 1935.

19. McNicholas, "Pastoralia," 1928, AAC; *Catholic Telegraph,* March 8, 1928; June 14, 1934; May 2, August 1,1935.

20. McNicholas to Hartley, May 8, June 11, 1933; McNicholas to Hartley, May 5, 1935; Hartley to McNicholas, December 1, 1935; November 5, 1936, AAC.

21. McNicholas, "School and Tax Reform," August 31, 1937, AAC.

22. McNicholas to Cicognani, October 30, 1944; *Diamond Jubilee Holy Trinity Church, 1861–1936* (Dayton, Ohio, 1936), AAC.

23. McNicholas to Taft, June 28, 1946; Radio Broadcast on Education, July 7, 1946; McNicholas to Spellman, August 14, 1947, AAC; *Catholic Telegraph,* April 6, February 16, 1945; July 5, 1946; March 26, 1948; March 24, November 24, 1961; *Cincinnati Post,* July 6, 1946; March 8, 1948; *Cincinnati Enquirer,* July 8, 1946; July 6, 1947; Robert Wuthnow, *The Restructuring of American Religion: Society and Faith Since World War II* (Princeton, N.J., 1988), 73; Fogarty, *The Vatican and the American Hierarchy,* 368. As chairman of the administrative board of the NCWC in 1950, McNicholas continued to speak in favor of the American separation of church and state.

24. McNicholas to Ready, May 12, 1946; McNicholas Address, Archdiocesan High Schools, June 7, 1946; McNicholas to Pastors, March 22, 1948; McNicholas to S.E.R. Mons. Arborio-Mella, November 2, 1948; Rev. George Rehring to Taft, May 10, 1950, AAC.

25. McNicholas to Cicognani, September 2, 1945; McNicholas Radio Broadcast, July 7, 1946; McNicholas to President Truman, January 2, 1948; Rev. George Rehring to President Truman, May 10, 1950, AAC; *Cincinnati Enquirer,* June 8, July 8, 1946.

26. *Catholic Telegraph,* July 11, 1947; *Cincinnati Enquirer,* May 24, 1954; May 14, 1957.

27. *Catholic Telegraph,* April 13, 1956; October 5, 1958; September 26, 1958; *Cincinnati Post,* April 11, 1956; *Cincinnati Enquirer,* February 9, 1962; *Cincinnati Times-Star,* September 22, 1950; December 19, 1952; July 6, 1956.

28. Alter to Kuhn, June 5, 1964; Rev. Ralph A. Asplan to James Hollern, January 21, 1965; Citizens for Educational Freedom to Legislators, February 27, 1965; Vogelpohl to Pastors, December 12, 1964; Alter to Pastors, July 14, 1965; Alter to Issenmann, February 7, 1959, AAC; *Catholic Telegraph,* January 30, 1969.

29. *Catholic Telegraph,* June 22, 1933; August 28, 1942.

30. Minutes of Meeting on Central Normal School Problems, March 31, 1927; McNicholas to Pastors, July 30, 1928; McNicholas to Archbishop Austin Dowling, October 6, 1928; McNicholas to Hubert Brockman, S.J., July 9, 1927; NCEA Bulletin, February 1931; McNicholas to Ritter, June 27, 1947; Agreement between Archbishop Moeller and the Society of Jesus, [n.d.]; Moeller to James McCabe, S.J., June 1, 1920, AAC; Timothy Walch, *Parish School: American Catholic Parochial Education from Colonial Times to the Present* (New York, 1996), 142–45; *Catholic Telegraph,* June 17, November 18, 1920; August 2, 1928; July 9, 1931; June 13, 1947; *Catholic Enquirer,* February 21, 1947.

31. *Catholic Telegraph,* June 13, 1947.

32. Joseph M. White, *The Diocesan Seminary in the United States: A History from the 1780s to the Present* (Notre Dame, Ind., 1989), 391–92.

33. "A Decade of Progress, 1923–1933," The Newman Club, University of Cincinnati, 1933; *The History of St. Mary Church* (Oxford, Ohio, [n.d.]), AAC; *Catholic Telegraph,* April 10, 1930; Lee J. Bennish, S.J., *Continuity and Change: Xavier University 1831–1981* (Chicago, 1981), 146. In 1970 Our Lady of Cincinnati College changed its name to Edgecliff College. Ten years later Xavier University purchased Edgecliff College, incorporating some of its academic programs into the Univesity's curriculum.

34. C. Joseph Nuesse, *The Catholic University of America: A Centennial History* (Washington, D.C., 1990), 251, 270, 280–81.

35. McNicholas to Curley, November 12, 1936; October 5, 1938; McNicholas to Cantwell, December 17, 1937; McNicholas, "The Present Opportunity of Scholastic Philosophy," *Proceedings* of the American Catholic Philosophical Association, December 28–29, 1938, 92–93; McNicholas to Rev. Edward Mason, January 13, 1940; McNicholas to Pastors, October 17, November 8, 1944; January 11, 1945; Ritter to McNicholas, September 26, October 6, 1947; McNicholas to Stritch, December 22, 1947, AAC; *Catholic Telegraph,* August 7, 1930; May 16, 1935; *Cincinnati Post,* June 2, 1942.

36. *Cincinnati Times-Star,* April 24, 1950.

37. *Catholic Telegraph,* April 17, 1970.
38. Clergy Bulletin, September 9, 1958; Alter to Mother Mary Anselm, January 26, 1959; Alter Pastoral, September 9, 1959, AAC; *Catholic Telegraph,* February 21, 1958; August 14, November 13, 1959.
39. Profile 1962 - Catholic Education in the Archdiocese of Cincinnati; Alter to Ryan, December 13, 1963, AAC; *Cincinnati Enquirer,* February 9, 1962.
40. Alter to Rev. John A. Elbert, November 18, 1957; Alter to Rev. James M. Darby, May 19, 1960, AAC; *Catholic Telegraph,* July 20, 1951; May 19, 1961.
41. Clergy Bulletin, April 1, 1964, AAC; *Catholic Telegraph,* March 6, 13, December 11, 1964; March 26, 1966.
42. *Catholic Telegraph,* February 21, 1941.
43. Chancellor Leibold to Pastors, November 20, 1956; Alter Pastoral, August 19, 1964; Clergy Bulletin of the Archdiocese, August 10, 1955; Alter to Sr. Loretto Julia, Sister of Notre Dame, November 25, 1967, AAC; *Catholic Telegraph,* January 14, 1966; October 19, 1967. In the 1960s CCD's summer vacation schools enrolled more than ten thousand children and involved a teaching staff of more than six hundred.
44. Francis Mueller to Alter, April 8, 1965; Alter to Mueller, April 18, 1965, AAC; *Catholic Telegraph,* May 14, 1965; April 29, 1966.
45. *Catholic Telegraph,* December 2, 1966; January 20, February 3, October 19, 1967.
46. Ibid., October 5, 1967.
47. Ibid., September 26, 1968.
48. Ibid., January 30, February 20, March 27, 1969.
49. Ibid., April 24, May 2, 8, June 26, 1969.
50. Ibid., July 10, September 11, 1969.

PART IV

Introduction

1. Leslie Woodcock Tentler, *Seasons of Grace: A History of the Catholic Archdiocese of Detroit* (Detroit, Mich., 1990), 524; Jay P. Dolan, *The American Catholic Experience: A History from Colonial Times to the Present* (New York, 1985), 423.

Chapter 13

1. Jay P. Dolan, *The American Catholic Experience: A History from Colonial Times to the Present* (New York, 1985), 425–26.
2. *Cincinnati Enquirer,* August 24, 1977.
3. Alter to Clergy, February 8, 1952, AAC; Dolan, *Catholic Experience,* 388–89; Leslie Woodcock Tentler, *Seasons of Grace: A History of the Catholic Archdiocese of Detroit* (Detroit, Mich., 1990), 414; Timothy Kelly, "The Laity and the Decline of Devotional Catholicism," paper at the Cushwa Center Conference, University of Notre Dama, March 2000.
4. Alter's pastoral letter of January 1953 refers to the reorganization of the ACCM and ACCW, AAC; *Catholic Telegraph,* January 9, 1953; Tentler, *Seasons of Grace,* 440.
5. "Cursillo de Cristiandad . . . Celebrating the Beginning of Our Second Decade, 1962–1972," AAC.
6. Alter to Cardinal Stritch, August 27, 1957; John E. Kuhn to Pastors, February 2, 1956; Alter Pastoral, July 16, 1958, AAC; *Catholic Telegraph,* January 6, 1956.
7. *Golden Jubilee St. Mary of the Woods Church, 1927–1977* (Russells Point, Ohio, 1977), AAC; *Catholic Telegraph,* January 6, 13, May 11, 1956; March 7, 1958.
8. Alter to Cardinal Stritch, August 27, 1957; January 24, 1958; Alter to Archbishop Muench of Germany, December 12, 1957; Alter Pastoral, July 16, 1958; Mother Mary Romana,

Mother General, Sisters of Mercy, to Alter, August 23, 1958, AAC; *Catholic Telegraph,* August 23, 1957; March 7, July 18, August 15, 22, September 26, 1958.

9. *Catholic Telegraph,* May 29, 1959.

10. Alter to Clergy, December 10, 1963; Alter to Clergy and Religious, February 2, 1964; Alter to Cardinal Paul Marella, February 22, 1964, AAC; *Catholic Telegraph,* May 26, July 7, 1961; October 26, 1962; December 20, 1963; February 21, May 8, 1964; *Cincinnati Enquirer,* October 13, 1960; October 21, 1962; December 13, 1963.

11. Alter to Pastors, August 24, 1964; Leibold to Pastors, November 11, 1964; Alter to Rev. James L. Krusling, November 20, 1964, AAC.

12. Alter Pastoral, February 3, 1965; Alter Pastoral, September 3, 1965; Archdiocese Liturgical Bulletin, November 22, 1965; Alter Decree, October 20, 1967, AAC; *Catholic Telegraph,* May 8, August 7, September 4, 18, December 4, 1964; February 5, November 12, 1965. Parishioners before Vatican II also often followed the Mass in a missal, a book containing all the prayers and responses necessary for celebrating the Mass.

13. *St. John the Evangelist Catholic Church: A Centennial History, 1891–1991* (Cincinnati, 1991); *The Story of St. Philomena Church* (Stonelick, Ohio, [n.d.]), AAC; *Catholic Telegraph,* October 2, 1970. The first evening Mass in the archdiocese of Cincinnati was celebrated on December 8, 1953.

14. *St. Antoninus Parish* (Cincinnati, 1969), AAC; *Catholic Telegraph,* May 23, 1968.

15. *Catholic Telegraph,* August 30, 1963.

16. David O'Brien, *Public Catholicism* (New York, 1989), 440.

17. Alter to Clergy, Advent, 1965, AAC.

18. Decree on Pastoral Council, September 26, 1966, AAC; *Catholic Telegraph,* January 28, September 23, 1966.

19. *Catholic Telegraph,* November 18, 1966; May 5, 1967; January 30, May 8, 1969.

20. *Catholic Telegraph,* May 27, June 17, 1966.

21. Decree on Senate of Priests, June 29, 1966, AAC; *Catholic Telegraph,* August 5, October 14, 1966.

22. M. Edmund Hussey, *A History of the Seminaries of the Archdiocese of Cincinnati 1829–1979* (Norwood, Ohio, 1979), 57.

23. Vatican II Files: Folder "Liturgical Commission 1967–69," AAC.

24. *The Post & Times-Star,* September 21, 1964; September 21, 1966.

25. Alter to Members of Religious Institutes, May 11, 1965, AAC.

26. Report of Fact-Finding Committee of the University of Dayton, February 1967, AAC; Christopher J. Kauffman, *Education and Transformation: Marianist Ministries in America since 1849* (New York, 1999), 256; *Catholic Telegraph,* January 13, 27, 1967.

27. Rev. Francis Langhirt to Vogelpohl, March 30, 1966; Clergy Bulletin of the Archdiocese, August 29, 1966; Alter to Mrs. Paul Grubbs, January 21, 1967; Report of Fact-Finding Committee . . . , February, 1967; Alter to Rev. John L. Reedy, April 6, 1967, AAC; *Catholic Telegraph,* January 13, 27, 1967.

28. University of Dayton Faculty Petition Letter, January 17, 1967, AAC; *Catholic Telegraph,* February 27, 1967.

29. Report of Fact-Finding Committee . . . , February 1967, AAC; Kauffman, *Education and Transformation,* 256; *Catholic Telegraph,* February 17, 1967.

30. Alter to Rev. Paul L. O'Connor, April 12, 1966; Rev. McCarthy to L. Brent Brozell, March 28, 1967, AAC; *Catholic Telegraph,* June 16, 1967.

31. Alter to Raymond A. Dean, Sr., November 23, 1968; Alter to A. J. Long, October 19, 1968; Alter to O'Connor, September 1, 1972, AAC.

32. Chancellor Vogelpohl to ____, October 1, 1962, AAC; *Catholic Telegraph,* September 29, 1950; January 14, 1955; April 8, May 26, July 7, November 17, December 1, 1961; January 31, 1964.

33. *Catholic Telegraph,* January 14, 1955; May 1, July 24, 1959.

34. Ibid., March 27, May 8, September 4, 1964; *The Post & Times-Star,* May 6, 1964.

35. Alter to Pastors, February 14, 1966, AAC; *Catholic Telegraph,* January 14, 1966.

36. Vicar General Edward A. McCarthy to Edward Brueggeman, S.J., May 10, 1967; Rev. Ralph A. Asplan to Pastors, October 11, 1967; *St. Bonaventure Church* (Cincinnati, 1990); *Golden Jubilee St. Mary of the Woods Church, 1927–1997* (Russells Point, Ohio), 1977; Clergy Bulletin, January 15 1968, AAC; *Catholic Telegraph,* October 5, 1967; *Cincinnati Post,* August 24, 1977.

37. Vatican II, File 7, handwritten notes by Alter, to be presented to meeting of U.S. Bishops on October 21, 1963, AAC; Gerald P. Fogarty, *The Vatican and the American Hierarchy from 1870 to 1965* (Wilmington, Del., 1985), 390, 396; *Catholic Telegraph,* December 20, 1963.

38. Murray to Alter, July 15, August 23, 1964; NCWC Newsservice, September 15, 1965, AAC; *Catholic Telegraph,* October 2, 1964; Walter M. Abbott, Documents of Vatican II (New York, 1966), 672–74; Fogarty, *The Vatican and the American Hierarchy,* 313. Before his death Archbishop McNicholas, too, had come to espouse religious liberty as compatible with official Catholic doctrine.

39. *The Post & Times-Star,* July 23, 1969; *Cincinnati Post,* August 18, 1975; September 9, 1977. In 1977 the archdiocese sold the College Hill residence on Belmont Avenue. It had served as the residence for McNicholas and Alter. Joseph Bernardin, then archbishop of Cincinnati, resided in the chancery building in downtown Cincinnati.

40. *Cincinnati Post,* August 18, 1975; August 24, 1977.

Chapter 14

Note: In writing this chapter the author did not have access to any of the correspondence of the Cincinnati church prelates.

1. *Catholic Telegraph,* December 18, 1969; February 6, 20, May 1, October 2, 23, 1970; February 4, March 24, 1972.

2. Ibid., November 6, 1970; February 5, 12, April 30, October 12, 1971; July 28, 1972.

3. Ibid., November 6, 1970; January 14, June 9, 1972.

4. Ibid., November 6, 1970; January 14, June 9, 1972; June 15, 1973; May 31, 1974; August 29, 1975; March 2, 1984; January 3, 1986.

5. Ibid., August 13, 1971; March 3, 1972; April 19, 1985.

6. Ibid., November 22, 1974; September 26, 1980.

7. Ibid., December 7, 1963; May 3, June 28, 1974; June 1, 1990. The eleven deaneries were the Cathedral, St. Andrew, St. Francis de Sales, St. Lawrence, St. Margarey Mary, Dayton, Hamilton, St. Martin, St. Mary's, Sidney, and Springfield.

8. Ibid., March 29, August 30, 1974; May 2, 1975; October 22, 1976; January 27, March 3, April 21, 1978.

9. Ibid., November 15, 1974; November 5, 1982. Pilarczyk became titular bishop of Holdem, an ancient see in Dumfriesshine, Scotland.

10. Ibid., July 29, 1988; November 10, 1989; May 31, 1991.

11. Ibid., January 9, 23, 1970; May 22, 1981; March 24, 1989.

12. *Diamond Jubilee St. William Parish, 1909–1984* (Cincinnati, 1984), AAC; *Catholic Telegraph,* February 11, 1983; May 18, 1984; September 25, November 6, 1987; April 1, 1988; January 13, 1989; June 1, 1990; February 7, December 11, 1992; Charles R. Morris, *American Catholic: The Saints and Sinners Who Built America's Most Powerful Church* (New York, 1997), 308.

13. *All Saints Church, 25th Anniversary* (Cincinnati, 1974); *Immaculate Heart of Mary Parish, 1944–1994* (Cincinnati, 1994), AAC; *Catholic Telegraph,* January 30, March 5, June 4, 1976; September 23, 1979; February 11, July 22, 1983; April 1, 1988; January 13, 1989. Movements

like the Charismatic Renewal and Christ Renews His Parish tried to channel increased interest in faith as well as to help bring former Catholics back into the church fold.

14. Mary Chaves and James C. Cavendish, "More Evidence on U.S. Catholic Church Attendance," *Journal for the Scientific Study of Religion* (Fall 1994): 376–81; *Catholic Telegraph,* February 4, 1994.

15. *Catholic Telegraph,* February 27, March 27, 1970; June 10, 1977; February 16, 1979.

16. Ibid., September 20, 1974; August 3, 1979; July 21, 1989.

17. Ibid., May 5, December 1, 1978; November 30, 1979.

18. Ibid., October 27, 1978; February 23, 1979.

19. Ibid., July 4, 1978; February 5, 1982; Patrick W. Carey, *The Roman Catholics* (Westport, Conn., 1993), 134, 136; Morris, *American Catholic,* 305; Jay P. Dolan, *The American Catholic Experience: A History from Colonial Times to the Present* (New York, 1985), 435.

20. *Catholic Telegraph,* February 2, March 2, 30, May 11, 1973; April 26, 1974; October 31, 1975; April 2, 1976.

21. Ibid., February 27, May 21, 1976; Carey, *The Roman Catholics,* 138–39.

22. *Catholic Telegraph,* December 22, 1989.

23. Ibid., April 6, 1984; January 10, July 4, 1986; January 23, March 6, 1987; January 26, 1990; October 25, 1991; December 11, 1992.

24. Morris, *American Catholic,* 303–5.

25. *Catholic Telegraph,* March 20, May 15, November 13, 1970; January 19, 1973; January 25, 1974; April 25, 1975; Dolan, *The American Catholic Experience,* 434.

26. *Catholic Telegraph,* November 12, 1776; June 19, 1992. The Dignity chapter in Dayton, however, could continue to meet because its members had submitted a letter accepting church teachings on homosexuality.

27. Quoted in *Character Glimpses of Most Reverend William Henry Elder, D.D.* (Ratisbon, Germany, 1911), 103–4; *Catholic Telegraph,* January 10, 1992; Morris, *American Catholic,* 292, 294.

28. *Catholic Telegraph,* Februay 4, 1983; January 23, 1987; November 10, 1989; February 9, 1990; December 11, 1992.

29. Ibid., February 11, 1983; January 23, 1987; February 15, 1991.

30. Ibid., January 23, 1987.

31. Ibid., February 15, 1991; March 29, 1996.

32. Ibid., March 14, 1986; May 29, 1987.

33. Dolan, *The American Catholic Experience,* 437.

34. *Catholic Telegraph,* October 26, 1979; March 28, 1980; May 20, 1981; March 12, 1982.

35. Ibid., October 7, 1843; August 21, 1970; April 1, 1988; February 9, September 28, 1990; January 18, 1991.

36. Ibid., July 28, August 25, 1989; Supplement, June 14, 1996.

37. Ibid., July 3, 31, 1969; February 24, March 24, June 23, 1989; May 18, 1990; March 15, 22, June 7, July 19, 1991; *Clerus Cincinnatensis: A History of Clergy and Parishes of the Archdiocese of Cincinnati 1821 to 1996* (Cincinnati, 1996), 33, 87–88.

38. *Catholic Telegraph,* September 18, 1992; September 24, 1993; April 4, 1995; June 7, 1996.

39. Ibid., December 4, 1987.

40. Ibid., December 9, 1988; February 24, March 3, 1989.

41. Ibid., July 10, 1987; December 9, 1988; April 21, 1989; *Clerus Cincinnatensis,* 33, 89, 110. The new parishes were St. Paul in Englewood in 1972; Queen of Apostles, a nonterritorial parish in Dayton, in 1973; Good Shepherd in Montgomery in 1973; St. Barbara (Byzantine) in Centerville in 1974; St. Elizabeth Ann Seton in Milford in 1976; St. John Neumann in Springfield Township in Fairfield in 1978; St. Margaret of York in Landen in 1984; St. Maximilian Kolbe in West Chester in 1989; and Holy Family in Middletown in 1991.

42. *Catholic Telegraph,* January 14, May 6, 1994; March 29, 1996; *Official Catholic Directory,* 1996.

43. *Catholic Telegraph,* November 5, 1982; December 3, 1993.

44. Ibid., May 23, 1986; September 25, 1987.

45. *Immaculate Heart of Mary Parish, 1944–1994* (Cincinnati, 1994); *St. Antoninus Parish* (Cincinnati, 1969), AAC.

46. *Catholic Telegraph,* June 18, 1982; September 25, 1987; Morris, *American Catholic,* 377.

47. *Catholic Telegraph,* February 24, June 22, 1984; August 15, 1986; June 22, 1990; May 29, 1992; November 4, 1994.

48. Ibid., November 19, 1971; July 9, 1982; May 25, 1990; September 20, 1991.

49. Ibid., August 21, 1970; May 24, July 19, 1974; February 11, 1977.

50. Timothy Walch, *Parish School: American Catholic Parochial Education from Colonial Times to the Present* (New York, 1996), 176, 180; *Catholic Telegraph,* February 11, 1983; September 29, 1995; Supplement, June 14, 1996.

51. *Catholic Telegraph,* February 20, August 7, 1970; June 23, 1972; February 16, 1973; August 23, 1974; *Official Catholic Directory,* 1996.

52. *Catholic Telegraph,* September 27, 1985; January 29, 1988; September 14, 1990; July 5, 1991; January 15, 1993; September 29, 1995.

53. *Diamond Jubilee St. William Parish, 1909–1984* (Cincinnati, 1984), AAC; *Catholic Telegraph,* January 5, June 29, 1973; July 1, 1977; September 28, 1990; February 8, March 22, 1991; March 27, 1992; March 18, 1994.

54. *Catholic Telegraph,* February 25, 1972; January 17, 1975; June 18, August 20, September 3, 1976; May 27, 1977.

55. Ibid., July 7, 1978; July 6, 27, 1979.

56. Ibid., November 1, 1974; January 19, March 31, 1978; February 1, 1980; September 21, 1990.

57. Ibid., April 22, 1983.

58. Ibid., April 15, 1983; February 21, July 4, 1986.

59. Ibid., April 30, 1971; June 23, 1972; August 1, 1975.

60. Ibid., August 22, 1986; August 4, 1989; January 10, 1992.

61. Ibid., June 18, November 5, 1971; June 12, 1981.

62. Ibid., November 30, 1973; January 10, 1975; February 6, 1981; April 15, 1994; June 13, November 14, 1975.

63. Ibid., December 17, 1976; June 8, 1984; April 14, 1989.

64. Ibid., February 3, 1978; June 20, 1986; January 16, 1987; April 6, 1990.

65. Ibid., July 27, 1973; September 9, 1977; September 5, 1980.

66. Ibid., May 27, 1977. Shortly after the formation of the Black Secretariat the Black Lay Catholic Caucus was dissolved.

67. Ibid., June 26, 1981; February 19, 1982. In a letter to author, dated August 9, 1999, James Shappelle, pastor of St. Bernard Church in Cincinnati, pointed out that some of the attacks on Bernardin were unjustified. "That was," he wrote, "a sad evening for Archbishop Bernardin."

68. *Catholic Telegraph,* October 15, 1976; February 21, July 24, 1986; July 22, August 12, 1988; August 18, 1989.

69. Ibid., August 18, 25, September 1, 22, December 8, 1989.

70. Ibid., July 22, 1988; August 18, 1989; March 23, June 1, 1990; February 12, June 18, 1993; January 21, December 9, 1994. Before Cross's appointment as pastor, other black pastors who had served in the archdiocese were religious order clergy.

71. Ibid., June 8, 1984; June 18, 1993; March 3, June 9, 1995.

BIBLIOGRAPHY

PRIMARY SOURCES

Archives and Manuscript Collections

Archives of the Archdiocese of Baltimore
Archives of the Archdiocese of Boston
Archives of the Archdiocese of Cincinnati
Archives of the Propaganda Fide
Archives of the University of Notre Dame
Archives of Xavier University of Cincinnati

Printed Sources

Beecher, Lyman. *Plea For the West.* Cincinnati: Truman & Smith, 1835.

Campbell, Alexander, and Rt. Rev. John B. Purcell. *A Debate on the Roman Catholic Religion.* Cincinnati: 1883.

Cist, Charles. *Cincinnati in 1841.* Cincinnati: 1841.

Ellis, John Tracy, ed. *Documents of American Catholic History.* 3 vols. Chicago: M. Glazier, 1987.

Fenwick, Edward, "An Early Pastoral Letter," 1827. *Catholic Historical Review* 1 (1915–16).

Mazzuchelli, Samuel. *Memoirs.* Chicago: Priory Press, 1967.

McNicholas, John T. "The Episcopal Committee and the Problem of Evil Motion Pictures." *The Ecclesiastical Review* (August 1934).

Morse, Samuel F. B. *Foreign Conspiracy.* New York: Leavitt, Lord, 1841.

Nolan, Hugh J., ed. *Pastoral Letters of the American Hierarchy, 1796–1970.* Huntington, Ind.: Our Sunday Visitor, Inc., 1971.

Purcell, John B. "Journal 1833–1836." *The Catholic Historical Review* 5 (July–October, 1919).

Thwaites, Reuben G., ed. *Early Western Travels, 1748–1846.* 32 vols. Cleveland: A. H. Clark, 1904–7.

Trollope, Frances. *Domestic Manners of the Americans.* New York: Knopf, 1949.

SECONDARY WORKS

Books

Character Glimpses of Most Reverend William Henry Elder, D.D. Ratisbon, Germany: Frederick Pustet & Co., 1911.

Clerus Cincinnatensis: A Directory of Clergy and Parishes of the Archdiocese of Cincinnati 1821–1996. Cincinnati: Archdiocese of Cincinnati, 1996.

The Sisters of Charity in Ohio: In Commemoration of the Sesquicentennial of Ohio's Statehood, 1803–1953. Cincinnati: College of Mount St. Joseph on the Ohio, 1953.

Ashley, Benedict. *The Dominicans.* Collegeville, Minn.: Liturgical Press, 1990.

Bennish, Lee J., S.J. *Continuity and Change, Xavier University 1831–1981.* Chicago: Loyola University Press, 1981.

Billington, Ray Allen. *The Protestant Crusade.* New York: The Macmillan Company, 1938.

Black, Gregory. *The Catholic Crusade Against the Movies, 1940–1975.* Cambridge, U.K.: Cambridge University Press, 1998.

Bland, Joan. *Hibernian Crusade: The Story of the Catholic Total Abstinence Union of America.* Washington, D.C.: Catholic University of America Press, 1951.

Blied, Benjamin J. *Catholics and the Civil War.* Milwaukee, Wisc.: 1945.

Brewer, Eileen Mary. *Nuns and the Education of American Catholic Women, 1860–1920.* Chicago: Loyola University Press, 1987.

Brown, Alden V. *The Grail Movement and American Catholicism, 1940–1975.* Notre Dame, Ind.: University of Notre Dame Press, 1989.

Brown, Dorothy M., and Elizabeth McKeown. *The Poor Belong to Us: Catholic Charities and American Welfare.* Cambridge, Mass.: Harvard University Press, 1997.

Brown, Mary Elizabeth. *The Scalabrinians in North America, 1887–1934.* New York: Center for Migration Studies, 1996.

Browne, Henry J. *The Catholic Church and the Knights of Labor.* Washington, D.C.: Catholic University of America Press, 1949.

Burns, Jeffrey M. *Disturbing the Peace: A History of the Christian Family Movement, 1949–1974.* Notre Dame, Ind.: University of Notre Dame Press, 1999.

Byrne, John F., C.SS.R. *The Redemptorist Centenaries.* Philadelphia: Dolphin Press, 1932.

Callan, Louise, R.S.C.J. *The Society of the Sacred Heart in North America.* London: Longmans, Green and Co., 1937.

Carey, Patrick W. *The Roman Catholics.* Westport, Conn.: Greenwood Press, 1993.

Chinnici, Joseph P., O. F. M. *Living Stones: The History and Structure of Catholic Spiritual Life in the United States.* New York: Macmillan, 1988.

Coburn Carol K., and Martha Smith. *Spirited Lives: How Nuns Shaped Catholic Culture and American Life, 1836–1920.* Chapel Hill: University North Carolina Press, 1999.

Coffey, Reginald M. O.P. *The American Dominicans: A History of Saint Joseph's Province.* New York: Saint Martin de Porres Guild, 1970.

Connaughton, Edward A. *A History of Educational Legislation and Administration in the Archdiocese of Cincinnati.* Washington, D.C.: The Catholic University of America Press, 1946.

Connelly, James F. *The Visit of Archbishop Gaetano Bedini to the United States, June, 1853–February, 1854.* Rome: Gregorian University, 1960.

Cooke, Bernard, ed. *The Papacy and the Church in the United States.* New York: Paulist Press, 1989.

Crews, Clyde F. *An American Holy Land: A History of the Archdiocese of Louisville.* Wilmington, Del.: M. Glazier, 1987.

Curran, Robert Emmett. *Michael Augustine Corrigan and the Shaping of Conservative Catholicism in America, 1878–1902.* New York: Arno Press, 1978.

Dolan, Jay P. *The American Catholic Experience: A History from Colonial Times to the Present.* New York: Doubleday, 1985.

Dolan, Timothy Michael. *"Some Seed Fell on Good Ground": The Life of Edwin V. O'Hara.* Washington, D.C.: Catholic University of America Press, 1992.

Dries, Angelyn, O.S.F. *The Missionary Movement in American Catholic History.* Maryknoll, N.Y.: Orbis Books, 1998.

Ede, Alfred J. *The Lay Crusade for a Christian America: A Study of the American Federation of Catholic Societies, 1900–1919.* New York: Garland, 1988.

Egan, William J. *A Loving and Deserved Tribute to the Revered Memory of the Most Reverend Henry Moeller, D.D.* Norwood, Ohio: Mt. St. Mary's Seminary of the West, n.d.

Ellis, John Tracy. *The Life of James Cardinal Gibbons, Archbishop of Baltimore, 1834–1921.* 2 vols. Milwaukee, Wisc.: Bruce Pub. Co., 1952.

Evans, Mary Ellen. *The Spirit is Mercy: The Sisters of Mercy in the Archdiocese of Cincinnati, 1858–1958.* Westminster, Md.: Newman Press, 1959.

Ewens, Mary. *The Role of the Nun in Nineteenth Century America.* New York: Arno Press, 1978.

Facey, Paul W. *The Legion of Decency: A Sociological Analysis of the Emergence and Development of a Social Pressure Group.* New York: Arno Press, 1974.

Fogarty, Gerald P, ed. Patterns of Episcopal Leadership. New York: Macmillan, 1989.

Fogarty, Gerald P. *The Vatican and the American Hierarchy From 1870 to 1965.* Wilmington, Del.: Michael Glazier, 1985.

Fox, Mary Harrita. *Peter E. Dietz, Labor Priest.* Notre Dame, Ind.: University of Notre Dame Press, 1953.

Gannon, Robert J. S.J., *The Cardinal Spellman Story.* Garden City, N.Y.: Doubleday, 1962.

Garraghan, Gilbert J. *The Jesuits of the Middle United States.* 3 vols. New York: America Press, 1938.

Gleason, Philip. *Keeping the Faith: American Catholicism Past and Present.* Notre Dame, Ind.: University of Notre Dame Press, 1987.

Hamelin, Talbot. *Greek Revival Architecture in America.* New York: Oxford University Press, 1944.

Hassard, John. *Life of John Hughes, First Archbishop of New York.* New York: Arno Press, 1969.

Hennesey, James S.J. *American Catholics: A History of the Roman Catholic Community in the United States.* New York: Oxford University Press, 1981.

————. *The First Council of the Vatican: The American Experience.* New York: Herder and Herder, 1963.

Hurley, Daniel. *Cincinnati, the Queen City.* Cincinnati: Cincinnati Historical Society, 1982.

Hussey, M. Edmund. *A History of the Seminaries of the Archdiocese of Cincinnati 1829–1979.* Norwood, Ohio: Mt. St. Mary's Seminary of the West, 1979.

Jackson, Kenneth T. *Crabgrass Frontier: The Suburbanization of the United States.* New York: Oxford University Press, 1985.

James, Janet Wilson, ed. *Women in American Religion.* Philadelphia: University of Pennsylvania Press, 1978.

Jurgens, W. A. *A History of the Diocese of Cleveland.* 2 vols. Cleveland, Ohio: Catholic Diocese of Cleveland, 1980.

Kauffman, Christopher J. *Education and Transformation: Marianist Ministries in America since 1849.* New York: Crossroad Pub. Co., 1999.

————. *Faith and Fraternalism: The History of the Knights of Columbus.* New York: Simon & Schuster, 1992.

————. *Ministry and Meaning: A Religious History of Catholic Health Care in the United States.* New York: Crossroad, 1995.

————. *Mission to Rural America: The Story of W. Howard Bishop, Founder of Glenmary.* New York: Paulist Press, 1991.

Kelly, Mary Gilbert, O.P. *Catholic Immigrant Colonization Projects in the United States, 1815–1860.* New York: United States Catholic Historical Society, 1939.

Kennelly, Karen, ed. *American Catholic Women: A Historical Exploration.* New York: Macmillan, 1989.

King, Margaret R. *Memoirs of the Life of Mrs. Sarah Peter.* 2 vols. Cincinnati: R. Clarke & Co., 1889.

Lamott, John H. *History of the Archdiocese of Cincinnati, 1821–1921.* Cincinnati: Frederick Pustet Company Inc., 1921.

Maher, Sister Mary Denis. *To Bind Up the Wounds: Catholic Sister Nurses in the U.S. Civil War.* Baton Rouge: Louisiana State University Press, 1999.

McCann, Sister Mary Agnes. *The History of Mother Seton's Daughters.* 3 vols. New York: Longmans, Green, 1917.

McNamara, Robert F. *The American College in Rome, 1855–1955.* Rochester, N.Y.: Christopher Press, 1956.

Metz, Judith, S.C., and Virginia Wiltse. *Sister Margaret Cecilia George, A Biography.* Mount St. Joseph, Ohio: College of Mount St. Joseph on the Ohio, 1989.

Michaelsen, Robert S. *Piety in the Public School.* New York: Macmillan Co., 1970.

Miller, Zane L. *Boss Cox's Cincinnati: Urban Politics in the Progressive Era.* New York: Oxford University Press, 1968.

Miller Zane L., and Bruce Tucker. *Changing Plans for America's Inner Cities: Cincinnati's Over-the-Rhine and Twentieth-Century Urbanism.* Columbus: Ohio State University Press, 1998.

Morris, Charles R. *American Catholic: The Saints and Sinners Who Built America's Most Powerful Church.* New York: Times Books, 1997.

Murnion, Philip J. *The Catholic Priest and the Changing Structure of Pastoral Ministry New York 1920–1970.* New York: Arno Press, 1978.

Nolan, Hugh J. *The Most Reverend Francis Kenrick, Third Bishop of Philadelphia, 1830–1851.* Washington, D.C.: Catholic University of America Press, 1948.

Nuesse, C. Joseph. *The Catholic University of America: A Centennial History.* Washington, D.C.: Catholic University of America Press, 1990.

Oates, Mary J. *The Catholic Philanthropic Tradition in America.* Bloomington: Indiana University Press, 1995.

O'Brien, David. *Public Catholicism.* New York: Macmillan, 1989.

O'Daniel, Victor Francis. *The Right Rev. Edward Dominic Fenwick, O.P., Founder of the Dominicans in the United States, Pioneer Missionary in Kentucky, Apostle of Ohio, First Bishop of Cincinnati.* Washington, D.C.: The Dominicana, [c. 1920].

Perko, F. Michael. *A Time to Favor Zion: The Ecology of Religion and School Development on the Urban Frontier, Cincinnati, 1830–1870.* DeKalb, Ill.: Educational Studies Press, Northern Illinois University, 1988.

Petit, Loretta, O.P. *Friar in the Wilderness: Edward Dominic Fenwick, O.P.* Chicago: Project OPUS, 1994.

Rudolph, Frederick. *The American College and University: A History.* New York: Vintage Books, 1965.

Sanders, James W. *The Education of an Urban Minority: Catholics in Chicago, 1833–1965.* New York: Oxford University Press, 1977.

Schlesinger, Jr., Arthur M. *Orestes A. Brownson.* New York: Octagon Books, 1939.

Shaw, Richard. *Dagger John: The Unquiet Life and Times of John Hughes of New York.* New York: Paulist Press, 1977.

Silberstein, Iola. *Cincinnati Then and Now.* Cincinnati: Voters Service Education Fund of the League of Women Voters of the Cincinnati Area, 1982.

Slawson, Douglas J. *The Foundation and First Decade of the National Catholic Welfare Council.* Washington, D.C.: Catholic University of America Press, 1992.

Spalding, Martin J. *Sketches of the Life, Times and Character of the Rt. Rev. Benedict Joseph Flaget, First Bishop of Louisville.* Louisville: Webb & Levering, 1852.

Spalding, Thomas W. *The Premier See: A History of the Archdiocese of Baltimore, 1789–1989.* Baltimore, Md.: Johns Hopkins University Press, 1989.

Stewart, George C. Jr. *Marvels of Charity: History of American Sisters and Nuns.* Huntington, Ind.: Our Sunday Visitor, 1994.

Taves, Ann. *The Household of Faith: Roman Catholic Devotions in Mid-Nineteenth-Century America*. Notre Dame, Ind.: University of Notre Dame Press, 1986.

Taylor, Jr., Henry Louis. *Race and the City: Work, Community, and Protest in Cincinnati, 1820–1970*. Urbana: University of Illinois Press, 1993.

Tentler, Leslie Woodcock. *Seasons of Grace: A History of the Catholic Archdiocese of Detroit*. Detroit, Mich.: Wayne State University Press, 1990.

Trisco, Robert F. *Bishops and Their Priests in the United States*. New York: Garland Pub., 1988.

———. *The Holy See and the Nascent Church in the Middle Western United States, 1826–1850*. Rome: Gregorian University, 1962.

Wade, Richard C. *The Urban Frontier: The Rise of Western Cities, 1790–1830*. Cambridge, Mass.: Harvard University Press, 1959.

Walch, Timothy. *Parish School: American Catholic Parochial Education from Colonial Times to the Present*. New York: Crossroad Pub. Co., 1996.

Walsh, Frank. *Sin and Censorship: The Catholic Church and the Motion Picture Industry*. New Haven, Conn.: Yale University Press, 1996.

White, Joseph M. *The Diocesan Seminary in the United States: A History from the 1780s to the Present*. Notre Dame, Ind.: University of Notre Dame Press, 1989.

Wuthnow, Robert. *The Restructuring of American Religion: Society and Faith Since World War II*. Princeton, N.J.: Princeton University Press, 1988.

ARTICLES AND PAPERS

Anderson, M. Christine. "Catholic Nuns and the Invention of Social Work: The Sisters of the Santa Maria Institute of Cincinnati, Ohio, 1897 through the 1920s." *Journal of Women's History* 12 (Spring 2000).

Avella, Steven M. "John T. McNicholas in the Age of Practical Thomism." *Records of the American Catholic Historical Society of Philadelphia* 97 (March–December 1986).

Carey, Patrick. "The Laity's Understanding of the Trustee System, 1785–1855." *Catholic Historical Review* 64 (July 1978).

Chaves Mary, and James C. Cavendish. "More Evidence on U.S. Catholic Church Attendance." *Journal for the Scientific Study of Religion* (Fall 1994).

Chinnici, Joseph P., O.F.M. "Organization of the Spiritual Life: American Catholic Devotional Works, 1791–1866." *Theological Studies* 40 (1979).

Hussey, M. Edmund. "The 1878 Financial Failure of Archbishop Purcell." *The Cincinnati Historical Society Bulletin* 36 (Spring 1978).

Kelly, Timothy. "The Laity and the Decline of Devotional Catholicism." Paper at the Cushwa Center Conference, University of Notre Dame, March 2000.

Lackner, Joseph H., S.M. "St. Ann's Colored Church and School, Cincinnati, the Indian and Negro Collection for the United States, and Reverend Francis Xavier Weninger, S.J." *U.S. Catholic Historian* 7 (1988).

———. "The Foundation of St. Ann's Parish, 1866–1870: The African American Experience in Cincinnati." *U.S. Catholic Historian* 14 (Spring 1996).

Lisska, Anthony J. "Bishop Fenwick's Apostolate to the Native Americans." *Bulletin of the Catholic Record Society* 17 (December 1992).

———. "Dominican Ideals in Early America: The Example of Edward Dominic Fenwick." *New Blackfriars* (September 1993).

Metz, Judith, S.C. "150 Years of Caring: The Sisters of Charity in Cincinnati." *The Cincinnati Historical Society Bulletin* 37 (Cincinnati 1979).

———. "The Sisters of Charity in Cincinnati 1829–1852." *Vincentian Heritage* 17 (1996).

Moorman, J. B. *The Medievalists: A Brief History of the Cincinnati Chapter.* Cincinnati Historical

Society Collection, n.d., n.p.

Paterson, Robert G. "The Decline of Epidemics in Ohio." *Ohio State Archaeological and Historical Quarterly* LV (1946).

Payne, Raymond. "Annals of the Leopoldine Association." *The Catholic Historical Review* 1 (1915).

Pohlkamp, Diomede, O.F.M. "Life and Times of Father William Unterthiner, O.F.M." *Provincial Chronicle* 15 (1942).

Stritch, Alfred G. "Political Nativism in Cincinnati, 1830–60." *Records* of American Catholic Historical Society 48 (September 1937).

———. "Trusteeism in the Old Northwest." *The Catholic Historical Review* 30 (July 1944).

Wuest, John B., O.F.M. "Archbishop James F. Wood of Philadelphia and the Bavarian Preface to the History of Our Province." *Provincial Chronicle* 6 (1934).

———. "Father Francis Louis Huber, The First Franciscan in Cincinnati." *Provincial Chronicle* 12 (1939–40).

———. "Four Friars for Cincinnati in 1849." *Provincial Chronicle* 15 (1942).

Unpublished Manuscripts

Campbell, James H. "New Parochialism: Change and Conflict in the Archdiocese of Cincinnati, 1878–1925." Ph.D. diss., University of Cincinnati, 1981.

Deye, Anthony H. "Archbishop John Baptist Purcell, Pre–Civil War Years." Ph.D. diss., University of Notre Dame, 1959.

Hurst, Paul F. "The History of Cincinnati's Old St. Mary's Parish: An Example of the Catholic Church's Response to Some Social Problems of American Cities." Unpublished paper, University of Cincinnati, 1969.

McCann, Mary Agnes. "Archbishop Purcell and the Archdiocese of Cincinnati." Ph.D. diss., Catholic University of America, 1918.

Miller, Francis Joseph. "A History of the Athenaeum of Ohio 1829–1960." Ed.D. diss., University of Cincinnati, 1964.

Wagner, R. Marcellus. "History of the Bureau of Catholic Charities and Social Service of the Archdiocese of Cincinnati, Ohio." Ph.D. diss., Catholic University of America, 1922.

White, Joseph M. "Religion and Community: Cincinnati Germans 1814–1870." Ph.D. diss., University of Notre Dame, 1980.

Parish Histories and Local Studies

A Century of Catholicism, St. Benignus, 1858–1958 (Greenfield, Ohio, 1958).

A Hundred Years of Educational Foundations by the Brothers of Mary in America, 1849–1959 (Dayton, Ohio, 1959).

All Saints Church: On Occasion of the 25th Anniversary of All Saints Parish (Cincinnati, 1974).

Annals of St. Michael's Parish in Loramie, 1838–1903 (Sidney, Ohio, 1903).

Celebrating 125 Years: St. Stephen Church (Cincinnati, 1992).

Centenary Celebration: Holy Trinity Church, 1834–1934 (Cincinnati, 1934).

Centenary Celebration: St. Charles Seminary Motherhouse and Major Seminary of the American Province, 1861–1961 (Cincinnati, 1961).

Centenary Jubilee St. James Parish, 1843–1943 (Cincinnati, Ohio, 1943).

Centenary Jubilee Souvenir, St. Aloysius Orphan Society (Cincinnati, 1937).

The Centenary of Saint Joseph's Parish, Somerset, Ohio (Somerset, Ohio, 1918).

Centenary Souvenir, Congregation of the Sisters of the Poor of St. Francis, 1845–1945 (Cincinnati, 1945).

Centennial St. Joseph Church, 1883–1983 (Springfield, Ohio, 1983).

Centennial Year St. Joseph Church (Hamilton, Ohio, 1965).

Commemorating the Centenary of St. Clement Parish 1850–1950 (Cincinnati, 1951).
Dedication St. Agnes Church (Cincinnati, 1956).
Dedication St. James Church (Cincinnati, 1940).
Diamond Jubilee Centennial of Sts. Peter and Paul Dramatic Club (Cincinnati, 1927).
Diamond Jubilee Holy Name Church, 1871–1946 (Trenton, Ohio, 1946).
Diamond Jubilee Holy Trinity Church, 1861–1936 (Dayton, Ohio, 1936).
Diamond Jubilee of St. Augustine Parish (Cincinnati, 1932).
Diamond Jubilee of the Passionist Fathers at Holy Cross Monastery, 1873–1948 (Cincinnati, 1948).
Diamond Jubilee Sacred Heart Italian Church, 1893–1968 (Cincinnati, 1968).
Diamond Jubilee St. Catharine of Siena Parish, 1903–1978 (Cincinnati, 1978).
Diamond Jubilee St. William Parish, 1909–1984 (Cincinnati, 1984).
Diamond Jubilee Souvenir, St. Mary Church (Cincinnati, 1917).
Emmanuel Catholic Church Sesquicentennial History, 1837–1987 (Dayton, Ohio, 1987).
50th Anniversary Our Lady of Lourdes Parish, 1927–1977 (Cincinnati, 1977).
50th Anniversary [St. Mark], 1905–1955 (Cincinnati, 1955).
Fifty Years in Brown County Convent (Cincinnati, 1895).
The First One Hundred Years: Our Lady of the Sacred Heart Parish, 1874–1974 (Cincinnati, 1974).
Golden Anniversary St. Patrick Council Knights of Columbus, 1914–1964 (Cincinnati, 1964).
Golden Jubilee Holy Cross Parish, 1914–1964 (Dayton, Ohio, 1964).
Golden Jubilee St. Gabriel Church, 1859–1909 (Cincinnati, Ohio, 1909).
Golden Jubilee St. Mary of the Woods Church, 1927–1997 (Russells Point, Ohio, 1977).
Golden Jubilee St. Monica Church, 1911–1961 (Cincinnati, 1961).
Golden Jubilee St. Patrick's Congregation, 1850–1900 (Cincinnati, 1900).
Golden Jubilee San Antonio Church, 1922–1977 (Cincinnati, 1977).
History of Fifty Years: St. John the Evangelist Church (Cincinnati, 1941).
History of St. Anthony's Parish (n.d.).
History of the Parish, St. Joseph Church (Dayton, Ohio, 1965).
The History of St. Mary Church (Oxford, Ohio [n.d.]).
Hoying, Louis A., Rita M., and David A. *Pilgrims All: A History of Saint Augustine Parish, Minster, Ohio, 1832–1982* (Minster, Ohio, 1982).
Illustrated History of St. Mary's Church (Hillsboro, Ohio, 1898).
Immaculate Heart of Mary Parish, 1944–1994 (Cincinnati, 1994).
Jubilee Souvenir of St. Lawrence Parish, 1869–1920 (Cincinnati, 1920).
Mount Alverno Centennial, 1870–1970 (Cincinnati, 1970).
100 Golden Years, St. Aloysius Gonzaga, 1866–1966 (Cincinnati, 1966).
One Hundredth Anniversary of St. Mary Church, 1842–1942 (Cincinnati, 1942).
100th Anniversary St. Louis Church, 1882–1992 (North Star, Ohio, 1992).
125th Year Anniversary St. Aloysius Church (Shandon, Ohio, 1993).
The One Hundredth and Fiftieth Anniversary Keepsake Book, Saint Joseph Church and School (Cincinnati, [n.d.]).
Our Lady of Perpetual Help Church, 1878–1978 (Cincinnati, 1978).
Our Lady of Victory Parish: A Century of Activities, 1843–1943 (Cincinnati, 1943).
Saint Mary Church (Urbana, Ohio, [n.d.]).
Saint Paul Parish During Seventy-Five Years, 1850–1925 (Cincinnati, 1925).
Saint Rita School for the Deaf, 1915–1965 (Cincinnati, 1965).
St. Anthony Parish 125th Anniversary, 1859–1984 (Cincinnati, 1984).
St. Antoninus Parish (Cincinnati, 1969).
St. Bernard Church, 1867–1967 (Taylor's Creek, Ohio, 1967).
St. Bonaventure Church (Cincinnati, 1990).
St. Boniface Parish, 1863–1963: The End of a Century . . . The Beginning of a New (Cincinnati, 1963).

St. Brigid Parish Sesquicentennial, 1849–1999 (Xenia, Ohio, 1999).

St. Columbkille Church, Faith Journey, 1866–1991 (Wilmington, Ohio, 1991).

St. John Fisher, 1947–1972 (Cincinnati, 1972).

St. John the Baptist Catholic Church, 1851–1978 (Harrison, Ohio, 1978).

St. John the Evangelist Catholic Church: A Centennial History, 1891–1991 (Cincinnati, 1991).

St. Joseph Church Centennial, 1883–1983 (Springfield, Ohio, 1983).

St. Joseph Church Centennial Year (Hamilton, Ohio, 1965).

St. Joseph Parish, 1839–1989 (Fort Recovery, Ohio, 1989).

St. Stephen Church, 1834–1959 (Hamilton, Ohio, 1959).

St. Thomas Aquinas Golden Jubilee, 1927–1977 (Cincinnati, 1977).

Seger, Oscar H. *History of St. Denis Parish Versailles, Ohio, 1839–1989* (Versailles, Ohio, 1989).

Seventy-Fifth Anniversary, Saint Clare Parish (Cincinnati, 1984).

75th Jubilee St. Adalbert Church, 1903–1978 (Dayton, Ohio, 1978).

Souvenir Album of American Cities: Catholic Churches of Cincinnati and Hamilton County Edition (Cincinnati, 1896).

Souvenir Book Commemorating One Hundred Years, St. Mary Church, 1848–1948 (Hamilton, Ohio, 1948).

Souvenir Diamond Jubilee of Sacred Heart Parish, 1870–1945 (Cincinnati, 1945).

Souvenir Golden Jubilee, Holy Angels' Parish (Cincinnati, 1909).

Souvenir Golden Jubilee, Holy Trinity Congregation (Coldwater, Ohio, 1918).

Souvenir Golden Jubilee, St. Charles Borromeo Church (Carthage, Ohio, 1919).

Souvenir Golden Jubilee St. Charles Borromeo Church, 1869–1919 (Cincinnati, 1919).

Souvenir Golden Jubilee, St. Francis Seraph Parish (Cincinnati, 1909).

Souvenir Golden Jubilee, St. George's Church (Cincinnati, 1918).

Souvenir Golden Jubilee, St. Lawrence Parish (Cincinnati, 1920).

Souvenir Golden Jubilee, St. Patrick's (Cincinnati, 1900).

Souvenir Golden Jubilee, St. Raphael Church (Springfield, Ohio, 1899).

Souvenir Golden Jubilee, St. Rose Church (Cincinnati, 1919).

Souvenir History of the Dedication of Guardian Angels Church-Auditorium (Cincinnati, 1949).

Souvenir Holy Family Church, 1905–1915 (Dayton, Ohio, 1916).

Souvenir of Dedication, St. Mark Church (Cincinnati, 1916).

Souvenir of the Golden Jubilee of Holy Trinity Congregation, 1868–1918 (Coldwater, Ohio, 1918).

Souvenir Ruby Jubilee, Blessed Sacrament Parish (Cincinnati, 1914).

Souvenir, St. Mary's Church (Marion, Ohio, 1898).

Souvenir Seventy-Fifth Anniversary, Our Lady of Victory (Delhi, Ohio, 1918).

Souvenir Silver Jubilee Celebration: St. Monica Church (Cincinnati, 1936).

The Story of St. Philomena Church (Stonelick, Ohio [n.d.]).

[Tenoever, Donald A.]. *The Cathedral of St. Peter in Chains* (souvenir booklet, n.d., n.p.; Cincinnati).

25th Anniversary Queen of Peace Church (Hamilton, Ohio, 1966).

25th Anniversary Saint Bartholomew Church, 1961–1986 (Cincinnati, 1986).

25th Anniversary St. Paul Catholic Church, 1856–1981 (Yellow Springs, Ohio, 1981).

We Are His People: St. Susanna Church, 1938–1988 (Mason, Ohio, 1988).

Wuest, John B., O.F.M. *St. Francis Seraph Church and Parish, Commemorating the Seventy-Fifth Anniversary of the Consecration of the Church and the Diamond Jubilee of the Parish, 1859–1934* (Cincinnati, 1934).

INDEX

Abbelen, Peter, 186
abortion, 270, 368, 369
abstinence, 348
academic freedom, 351–53
Acheson, Dean, 304
Acton, Lord John, 123
Adams County, 278
Aeterni Patris, 317
African American Catholic Ministries, 390, 391
African American Ministry Empowered and Nurtured (AMEN), 391
African Americans: in Catholic schools, 384; churches of, 145–46; participation in decision making, 389–91; services for, 145–46, 160, 223, 239–45, 285, 305–16; sisters, 140; and slavery, 141
aged, homes for, 139, 210–11, 291, 386
Albers, Joseph H., 325, 448n. 64
Albers, William, 271, 281–82
Albrecht, Fidelis, 344
Albrinck, John C., 151, 185, 204–205, 237
Alemany, Joseph S., 162
All Saints Church (Kenwood in Cincinnati), 268
All Saints parish school, 182
Alter, Karl, 303 fig. 15; accomplishments of, 256; administrative changes under, 257; and African Americans, 305–16; appointment to archbishop, 264, 333; on Catholic Rural Youth Organization, 280; and *Catholic Telegraph,* 273; celebration of Marian Year, 267; on communism, 304–305; early career of, 263; on ecumenism, 353–56; on education, 322–25, 328–29, 333–38, 343; on family life, 269–70; on hospitals, 292; on Institutum Divi Thomae, 333; on labor issues, 297; on laity, 263, 265, 270–72, 343–46, 348–49; on morality, 277; on politics, 261–62, 329, 355–56; on priest shortage,

283; on recodification of statutes, 284; renovation of St. Peter in Chains, 282–83; resignation and death, 357; and sisters, 347–48; on Soviet Union, 302; on University of Dayton controversy, 352–53; and Vatican Council II, 345–46, 350–51
American Academy of Christian Democracy, 247
American Association of University Professors, 352
American Board of Catholic Missions (ABCM), 160, 229
American Catholic Philosophical Association, 332
American Catholic Tribune, 241
American College in Rome, 172–73
American Federation of Catholic Societies (AFCS), 227–28
American Protective Association (APA), 229–30
American Protestant, 107
American Protestant Association, 107
American Revolution, 13
American Temperance Union, 127
Ancarani, Tommaso, 28
Ancient Order of Hibernians, 227
Angelico College, 259
annulment, 365
anti-Catholicism: Clancy's criticism of, 60; and cultural assimilation, 95; of Protestants, 41–42; Purcell on, 101–103, 107–110; resurgence in Midwest, 229–32; in schools, 112, 114
anti-Semitism, 297–99
Apodaca, Pauline, 389
Apostleship of Prayer, 379
Apostleship of Prayer and Devotion to the Sacred Heart Societies, 75
Apostolate of the Negro, 311
apostolic delegates, 179–82
Appalachian white community, 316